THE HERITAGE OF SUFISM

VOLUME III

D0872580

The Heritage of Sufism

Volume I, *Classical Persian Sufism from its Origins to Rumi (700–1300)*, ISBN 1–85168–188–4
Volume II, *The Legacy of Medieval Persian Sufism (1150–1500)*, ISBN 1–85168–189–2
Volume III, *Late Classical Persianate Sufism (1501–1750)*, ISBN 1–85168–193–0

Related Titles Published by Oneworld:

City of Wrong: A Friday in Jerusalem, M. Kamel Hussein (trans. Kenneth Cragg), ISBN 1–85168–072–1
Common Prayer: A Muslim–Christian Spiritual Anthology, Cragg (ed.), ISBN 1–85168–181–7
Companion to the Qur'an, Watt, ISBN 1–85168–036–5
Defenders of Reason in Islam: Mu'tazilism from Medieval School to Modern Symbol, Martin, Woodward and Atmaja, ISBN 1–85168–147–7
The Event of the Qur'an: Islam in its Scripture, Cragg, ISBN 1–85168–067–5
The Faith and Practice of Al-Ghazálí, Watt, ISBN 1–85168–062–4
The Formative Period of Islamic Thought, Watt, ISBN 1–85168–152–3
Islam: A Short History, Watt, ISBN 1–85168–152–3
Islam: A Short Introduction, Tayob, ISBN 1–85168–192–2
Islam and the West, Daniel, ISBN 1–85168–129–9
Jesus and the Muslim, Cragg, ISBN 1–85168–180–9
Jesus in the Qur'an, Parrinder, ISBN 1–85168–094–2
Muhammad: A Short Biography, Forward, ISBN 1–85168–131–0
Muhammad and the Christian, Cragg, ISBN 1–85168–179–5
Muslims and Christians Face to Face, Zebiri, ISBN 1–85168–133–7
Muslim Devotions, Padwick, ISBN 1–85168–115–9
On Being a Muslim, Esack, ISBN 1–85168–146–9
The Qur'an and its Exegesis, Gätje, ISBN 1–85168–118–3
Qur'an, Liberation and Pluralism, Esack, ISBN 1–85168–121–3
Rabi'a, Smith, ISBN 1–85168–085–3
Revival and Reform in Islam: A Study of Islamic Fundamentalism, Rahman, ISBN 1–85168–204–X
Rumi: Past and Present, East and West, Lewis, ISBN 1–85168–167–1
Rumi: Poet and Mystic, Nicholson, ISBN 1–85168–096–9
A Short Introduction to Islamic Philosophy, Theology and Mysticism, Fakhry, ISBN 1–85168–134–5
Tales of Mystic Meaning, Nicholson, ISBN 1–85168–097–7
What Muslims Believe, Bowker, ISBN 1–85168–169–8

BP
188.6
H47
1999
V.3

49574

THE HERITAGE OF SUFISM

VOLUME III

Late Classical Persianate Sufism (1501–1750)
The Safavid & Mughal Period

EDITED BY LEONARD LEWISOHN & DAVID MORGAN

ONEWORLD
OXFORD

Université de Sudbury | University of Sudbury

THE HERITAGE OF SUFISM
VOLUME III

Oneworld Publications
(Sales and Editorial)
185 Banbury Road
Oxford OX2 7AR
England
http://www.oneworld-publications.com

Oneworld Publications
(US Marketing Office)
160 N. Washington St.
4th floor, Boston
MA 02114
USA

© Leonard Lewisohn and David Morgan 1999

All rights reserved
Copyright under Berne Convention
A CIP record for this title is available
from the British Library

This book has been produced in association with
the Centre of Near and Middle Eastern Studies,
SOAS, University of London.

Reproduction of the illustrations
has been made possible by a generous grant
from the British Institute of Persian Studies.

Front cover: Episode in a Mosque, by Shaykh-zāda,
from a *Dīvān* of Ḥāfiẓ. Safavid period, Tabriz, *c.* 1527.
Courtesy of the Arthur M. Sackler Museum,
Harvard University Art Museums, anonymous loan.

The calligraphic motifs on the part title pages are traditional renditions from the pen of Dr Hossein Ilahi Ghomshei, former director of the National Library of Tehran, of the famous *Mukhammas* (a five-lined poem of seven stanzas) by the Safavid sage Shaykh Bahā'ī (d.1621). Translated by Leonard Lewisohn.

ISBN 1-85168-193-0

Cover design by Design Deluxe
Typeset by LaserScript Limited, Mitcham, Surrey
Printed and bound in England by Clays Ltd, St Ives plc

Contents

IV. SUFISM & ISHRAQĪ & AKBARIAN PHILOSOPHY

V. ESOTERIC MOVEMENTS & CONTEMPLATIVE DISCIPLINES

VI. PERSIANATE SUFISM IN INDIA, CENTRAL ASIA & CHINA

VII. PERSIANATE SUFI POETRY IN IRAN & INDIA

Illustrations

PLATES

FIGURES AND CHARTS

TABLES

Contributors

SERGEI ANDREYEV did his doctoral dissertation on the Rawshaniyya Movement at the University of Oxford. He is currently a research fellow at the Department of Academic Research and Publications at the Institute of Ismaili Studies, London.

WILLIAM C. CHITTICK is Professor of Religious Studies, State University of New York, Stony Brook, New York.

FARHAD DAFTARY is currently the head of the Department of Academic Research and Publications at the Institute of Ismaili Studies, London.

DEVIN DeWEESE is Assistant Professor in the Department of Central Eurasian Studies and Director of the Research Institute for Inner Asian Studies at Indiana University.

CARL W. ERNST is former Associate Professor and Chair of Religion at Pomona College, California and is presently Professor and Chair of the Department of Religious Studies at the University of North Carolina, Chapel Hill.

HEIDEH GHOMI, former Honorary Research Fellow at the University of Manchester, currently holds a research fellowship for postdoctoral research on Persian literature at the Institute of Oriental Culture of the University of Tokyo.

TERRY GRAHAM is editor and translator for Khanaqahi Nimatullahi Publications' Persian Sufi Texts and Translation Series and also assistant editor of *Sufi: A Journal of Sufism.*

MARCIA K. HERMANSEN is former Professor of Islam and Religious Studies at San Diego State University and currently Professor of Islamic Studies at the Department of Theology, Loyola University, Chicago.

FARHANG JAHANPOUR is a former professor and dean of the Faculty of Languages at the University of Iṣfahān in Iran and is currently news editor for the Middle East and North Africa at the BBC Monitoring Service in Reading, England.

MUHAMMAD REZA JUZI is an occasional lecturer in Islamic Philosophy at the University of Tehran, specializing in Shī'ite philosophical mysticism.

LEONARD LEWISOHN is currently a research associate at the Centre of Near and Middle Eastern Studies in the School of Oriental and African

Studies, University of London, and Outreach Coordinator at the Department of Academic Research and Publication at the Institute of Ismaili Studies, London, where he also teaches Persian.

DAVID MORGAN is Reader in the History of the Middle East at the School of Oriental and African Studies, University of London.

SACHIKO MURATA is Professor of Religious Studies at the State University of New York, Stony Brook.

SEYYED HOSSEIN NASR is University Professor of Islamic Studies at The George Washington University, Washington, DC.

IAN RICHARD NETTON, former lecturer in and head of the Department of Arabic and Islamic Studies, University of Exeter, is currently Professor of Arabic Studies and head of the Department of Arabic and Middle Eastern Studies in the University of Leeds.

ANDREW J. NEWMAN is Lecturer in Islamic Studies and Persian at the University of Edinburgh.

JAVAD NURBAKHSH, Professor Emeritus and former head of the Department of Psychiatry, University of Tehran, is the present Master of the Nimatullahi Sufi order.

SHOLEH A. QUINN, served as visiting Assistant Professor of History at the University of Hawaii at Hilo (1993–4) and is presently Assistant Professor of History at Ohio University in Athens, Ohio.

ANNEMARIE SCHIMMEL, Dr.Phil., Dr.h.c.mult. was for many years Professor of Indo-Muslim Culture at Harvard University and before that Professor of Islamic Studies in Ankara, Turkey, and Bonn, Germany.

CHRISTOPHER SHACKLE has been Professor of Modern Languages of South Asia in the School of Oriental and African Studies, University of London, since 1985 and is currently its Pro-director.

M.Z.A. SHAKEB taught in the Department of Indology at the School of Oriental and African Studies, University of London, and is presently a consultant in Christies' Department of Islamic Works of Art, London.

SIMON WEIGHTMAN is head of the Department for the Study of Religion and Senior Lecturer in Hindi in the South Asia Department of the School of Oriental and African Studies, University of London.

System of Transliteration

CONSONANTS

ء	’	ض	ḍ
ب	b	ط	ṭ
پ	p	ظ	ẓ
ت	t	ع	‘
ث	th	غ	gh
ج	j	ف	f
چ	ch	ق	q
ح	ḥ	ك	k
خ	kh	گ	g
د	d	ل	l
ذ	dh	م	m
ر	r	ن	n
ز	z	ه	h
ژ	zh	و	w
س	s	ی	y
ش	sh	ة	-a (-*at* in construct state)
ص	ṣ		

VOWELS

Long:	آ	ā
	أو	ū
	إي	ī
Doubled:	ـِيّ	iyy
	ـُوّ	uww
Diphthongs:	أو	aw
	أي	ay
Short:	ـَ	a
	ـُ	u
	ـِ	i

Preface

This last volume of *The Heritage of Sufism* is devoted to the examination and celebration of the artistic, literary and mystical culture and the intellectual life of Safavid Iran and Mughal India in the sixteenth and seventeenth centuries and the first half of the eighteenth century. Containing essays by some twenty-four specialists and scholars, many of international repute, it features a worldwide roster of contributors of diverse provenance, hailing from Iran, Europe and the United States.

Although during the three centuries under review here, the cultural forms associated with the Persian language, notably in poetry, culminated in the charming – if convoluted – 'Indian style', generating what has been appropriately called by Marshall Hodgson a "Persianate flowering",[1] the greatness of the epoch still remains concealed under its baroque extravagance

---

[1] "The whole age from Bihzād the painter (b. *c.*1450) through Mullā Ṣadrā the philosopher (d. 1640), in which the cultural forms associated with the Persian language culminated, ranks as something of a golden age and may usefully be called the 'Persianate flowering'," pronounced Marshall Hodgson, (*The Venture of Islam*, III: *The Gunpowder Empires and Modern Times* [Chicago: University of Chicago Press 1974], p. 49). Our use of the term 'Persianate' is partially inspired by the second volume of *The Venture of Islam* where, discussing "The Bloom of Persian Literary Culture and its Times, *c. 1111–1274*", the period from the death of Muḥammad Ghazālī to the death of Rūmī, Hodgson pointed out that the rise of the Persian language not only had literary consequences, but "served to carry a new overall cultural orientation within Islamdom. While Arabic held sway as the primary language of religious disciplines, natural science and philosophy, Persian became, in an increasingly large part of Islamdom, the language of polite culture; it even invaded the realm of scholarship with increasing effect. It was to form the chief model for the rise of still other languages to the literary level. Gradually a third 'classical' tongue emerged, Turkish, whose literature was based on the Persian tradition; it was almost as widespread in use geographically as was Persian, but in most places it was used in more limited social circles, and it never reached the level of Persian as a major cultural vehicle. Most of the more local languages of high culture that later emerged among the Muslims likewise depended upon Persian wholly or in part for their prime literary inspiration. We may call these cultural traditions, carried in Persian or reflecting Persian inspiration, 'Persianate' by extension". (*ibid.*, II, p. 293). Hodgson distinguished between an 'Arabic zone' and a 'Persianate zone' of Islamic civilization; the former being located in the Arabic-speaking lands west of Iraq, the latter in the north and the east. The central socio-cultural factor distinguishing the 'Arabic' from the 'Persianate' zone was the former's "common ignorance of the Persianate

and ornateness. However, as all the chapters below illustrate, throughout these developments, whether in the spheres of literature, politics, philosophy or art, Sufi mysticism played a central role. Although in Safavid Iran (1501–1722) most of the Sufi orders were ruthlessly suppressed, in the subcontinent the situation was quite the opposite. Here, under the Mughals (*c.*1526–1720), Islamic religious culture was largely dominated and influenced by the presence of Sufi orders of Persian origin, Persian being the dominant literary medium among the Indian Sufis.

Sufi teachings did continue to flourish, despite the suppression of the orders in Safavid Iran, in the notable form of the famous school of Illuminationists in Iṣfahān, which has been compared in certain respects with the Cambridge Platonists of England who were its contemporaries. This remarkable philosophical school, which combined Peripatetic, *kalām* theology and Illuminationist theosophy with the mystical Sufism of Ibn 'Arabī to form a kind of humanistically universal Islamic philosophy, is given ample treatment in the first three chapters of this book. In Mughal India during this period, Ibn 'Arabī's theories of the 'Unity of Being' took root, leading many mystics to seek points of correspondence between Sufi thought and the Vedanta system of Hindu philosophy.[2] Some Sufis wrote tracts on Yogic practices and many of the Sanskrit mystical classics in this field were translated into Persian (and thence into many European languages) during this period. William Chittick, Muhammad Juzi and Carl Ernst examine these themes in their contributions.

The great diplomatic and cultural unity which existed between the Ottoman, Safavid and Mughal empires during this period is reflected in our concentration on the religious and literary culture and history of Indian and Persian Sufism. "All the [three great] Muslim powers of the time formed a single far-flung diplomatic world", Marshall Hodgson points out, "though all the ruling families were Turkic, the language of diplomacy, of course, was Persian. ... This world was a diplomatic unity because it remained, despite the tendency of each empire to develop a distinctive regional culture centred on the court, a

tradition" which effectively cut it off from Islamdom's "most creative currents that were inspiring the majority of Muslim peoples." (*ibid.*, II, p. 294) The Persianate zone was characterized by the fact that Persian became the most favoured language in the literary field, and the most widely used tongue, even if Arabic maintained its own place as the standard Islamic language for theology and science (*ibid.*, II, pp. 484–6) Hodgson also outlined in bold and vigorous strokes 'the Persianate zone', maintaining that 'ṭarīqah Shī'ism', for instance (that is, Shī'ite Sufism centred around a charismatic *pīr*) was to be found only in the Persianate zone (*ibid.*, II, p. 498).

[2] See Francis Robinson, "Perso-Islamic Culture in India from the Seventeenth to the Early Twentieth Century", in *Turko-Persia in Historical Perspective*, ed. Robert Canfield (Cambridge: Cambridge University Press 1991), pp. 108–12; Annemarie Schimmel, *Mystical Dimensions of Islam* (Chapel Hill: University of North Carolina Press 1975), pp. 357ff.

cultural unity. In this unity, the Safavī empire doubtless held the central place; but India was close behind as a focus of cultural influence".[3] If the focus on Persianate Sufi literature and thought *in India and Persia* in this volume has not encompassed Ottoman culture and society in which the great international Sufi orders "set the official tone of religion",[4] it does not, thereby, necessarily exclude it. It was inevitable that some limit had to be imposed on the volume's coverage; and it can be argued that because the varieties of social intercourse and cultural exchange between Persia under Safavid and India under Mughal rule were more continuous, and the antagonism in political relations and the opposition caused by the sectarian differences between Mughal India and Safavid Iran less severe than those that obtained between zealously Shī'ite Iran and staunchly Sunni Ottoman Turkey, it was reasonable to have excluded coverage of the 'Persianate' Sufi cultural traditions which played a "dominant"[5] role in Ottoman Turkey from this volume (unlike volume II of *The Heritage of Sufism* whose chronological framework, covering very different political conditions, did embrace Ottoman Anatolia).

In this volume, a host of issues are discussed, under seven headings, ranging from the ethereal metaphystics of Ishrāqī and Akbarian theosophy and patterns of Sufi contemplative disciplines, to the heretofore unexplored relationship of Sufism to sectarian movements (such as the Ismā'īliyya and Rawshaniyya), and the strife of clerics with mystics. Most of the essays furnish extended discussions of both the philosophical/ literary and the hagiographical/ historical contexts of Sufism, embracing mundane matters such as the historiography of Sufi histories and the impact of political circumstances on dervish institutions and society in India and Persia, as well as sublime and sophisticated esoteric issues. The latter include the significance of mystical diagrams in Indian Sufism, poetic symbolism in both the 'high classical' and the 'popular vernacular' Sufi Persianate literary traditions, and the fascinating blend of Platonic theosophy with Peripatetic ontology and metaphysics, capped by the quintessentially Islamic development of a dynamic unitarian doctrine.

---

[3] Hodgson, *The Venture of Islam*, III, pp. 81–2. Likewise, Robert Canfield points out that "the Ottoman, Safavid, and Mughal empires fostered specific variants of a broadly similar Turko-Persian tradition. Across the territories of Western, Central and South Asia there was a remarkable similarity in culture, particularly among the elite classes". (*Turko-Persia in Historical Perspective*, introduction, p. 20).

[4] Hodgson, *The Venture of Islam*, III, p. 122.

[5] Hodgson, *The Venture of Islam*, III, pp. 123–4. As was pointed out by Victoria Holbrook in the second volume of *The Heritage of Sufism*, both the Ottoman and Iranian Sufi orders shared the admiration and cultivation of Persian literature, the Ottomans having patronized Persian literature for some five and a half centuries. See also Ira M. Lapidus, "Sufism and Ottoman Islamic Society", in *The Dervish Lodge: Architecture, Art, and Sufism in Ottoman Turkey*, ed. Raymond Lifchez (Berkeley: University of California Press 1992), p. 28; Canfield, *Turko-Persia in Historical Perspective*, p. 19.

In his foreword, Dr Nurbakhsh reminds us, with some fascinating quotations, of the classics and the classical period of early Sufism, which should always remain the focal concern of students of Sufism. This early classical period – to which the first volume of *The Heritage of Sufism* was devoted – is certainly always the *fons et origo* of all later manifestations of Sufism. His emphasis is thus especially appropriate in light of the fallacious tendency among many Islamicists to consider the medieval period of Islamic history, including the metahistory of its spirituality, to be an embarassing prelude to our modern 'progressive' age.

Furthermore, the sense of decline, loss and disappearance of spirituality stressed by Dr Nurbakhsh at the end of his foreword is one of the eternal topoi of Persianate Sufi spirituality dealt with by several contributors to this volume. Although the twelfth- and thirteenth-century revival of Sufism,[6] to which volume II of the present collection was devoted, no doubt constitutes the cultural zenith of Persian Sufism, the decline of Sufism has been lamented ever since its origin. A millennium ago, this sentiment was echoed by Abū'l-Ḥasan Pūshangī, who wryly quipped: "Why today it [Sufism] is but a name with no underlying reality apparent. At one time, it was a reality, but without a name."[7] "In the first century following the death of the Prophet," Abū Muḥammad Jurayrī (d. 311/ 923) observed:

> spiritual conduct (*mu'amalat*) was based on religiousness (*dīn*). When the adepts of that century passed away, religion became decadent, so in the second century they based their spiritual practice on fidelity (*wafā*). As they passed on, fidelity perished with them. In the third century, they based their spiritual practice on chivalric humaneness (*muruwwat*), but after they passed away, neither chivalry or humaneness were left! They based their spiritual conduct on pious modesty (*ḥiyā*) during the following century, but when they perished, all modest piety disappeared with them! So now, everyone must conduct themselves in utter fear (*rahbat*).[8]

The centuries pass but the same cry of regret remains – intensified perhaps. We hear Jurayrī's lament echoed in Mongol Persia by the Kubrawī Shaykh Nūr al-Dīn Isfarayīnī (639/1242–717/1317):

> Today, it is impossible to find any masters of the Way (*arbāb-i ṭarīqat*). Even if one finds, off in the suburbs, one of them, he too is worthless! Alas! A thousand times over – alas! The birds of this flock have quit the meadow; before the darkening tenebrity of their novices (*mubtadi'ān*), they have withdrawn and lowered their crowns under domes of divine jealousy. . . . Yes, this is again the same thing which my Lord and Master, Shaykh Majd al-Dīn

---

[6] See Leonard Lewisohn, "Iranian Islam and Persianate Sufism," in *The Heritage of Sufism*, II ed. L. Lewisohn (Oxford: Oneworld 1999), pp. 11–59.

[7] 'Aṭṭar, *Tadhkira al-awliyā'*, ed. M. Isti'lāmī (Tehran: Zawwār 1372 A.Hsh./1993; 3rd edn), p. 522.

[8] 'Aṭṭar, *Tadhkira*, pp. 58–81.

> Baghdādī[9] – may God bless his dear spirit, and may the dust of my flesh be offering for his spilled blood! – spoke when he said, 'Soon this group [the Sufis] will be as rare as the philosopher's stone, and they will vanish from all corners of the world, and even if off in some distant province, a master be found, he would be considered of less value than earth [in mens' eyes].' Yes, my friend, one must deplore this age, that men can live as they do. Alas! Those masters who once shielded their disciples have taken away the shield; and even if one finds among their successors, however rarely, a follower of the Path according to tradition (*sunna*), adhering to the rule of his predecessors, on retiring he finds himself confronted by a host of adversaries. However, if a beginner, whether in the past or present, takes one step in proposing some heretical innovation (*bid'at*), he immediately gains himself a thousand disciples and lovers![10]

This same lament reverberates throughout the whole Safavid threnody of Sufism. Ibn Karbalā'ī (writing in 975/1567), in the course of a description of the dilapidated condition of a certain Sufi's *khānaqāh* in Tabrīz, bemoaned the fact that "there are no dervishes there – rather, nowhere are there any dervishes to be found [today] – this age is under the aegis of the divine Name 'the Inward' (*al-bāṭin*)".[11] A dirge chanted in fortissimo tones over the decline in spiritual standards resounds during the last half of the Safavid mullocracy from within the tomes of Mullā Ṣadrā and the poems and tracts of Fayḍ Kāshānī (d. 1091/1680), key members of what S.H. Nasr describes in his introduction as the "school of Iṣfahān".[12] These Safavid theosophists vented their righteous fury at certain corrupt groups of Sufis who:

> have drunk the cup of pride from Satan's hand, and in following their sensual appetites and passions, contented themselves with a few idle cries and exclamations. Those who actually worship God among this group are few and far between. Few are those who find the path to Him, and yet – one must still irrigate a thousand thorns for the sake of a single rose.
>
> Oftentimes in beggars' rags one finds enlightened men;
> Draped in felt and sackcloth are hid the men of heart.
> Amid the dervish crowd, one man alone is meant
> But don't scorn the rest – that they're ignorant.[13]

---

[9] Isfarāyinī believed that the execution of Majd al-Dīn Baghdādī (d. 616/1219) at the hands of the Shāh of Khwārazm, Muḥammad ibn Tikish, was the true cause of the Mongol holocaust.

[10] *Kashf al-asrār*, ed. H. Landolt, as *Nuruddin Isfarayini: Le Révélateur des mystères* (Paris: Verdier 1986), p. 58.

[11] *Rawḍāt al-janān wa jannāt al-jinān*, ed. Ja'far Sulṭān al-Qurrā'ī (Tabrīz, B.T.N.K. 1344 A.H.sh./1965), II, p. 75.

[12] See also the essay by Leonard Lewisohn in this volume.

[13] *Al-Muḥākama*, in *Dah risālah-yi Muḥaqqiq-i Buzurg-i Fayḍ Kāshānī*, ed. R. Ja'fariyān (Iṣfahān: Markaz-i taḥqīqāt-i 'ilmī va dīnī Imām Amīr al-Mū'minīn 'Alī 1371 A.Hsh./1992), pp. 102–3.

And with the fall of the Safavid dynasty in 1722, the topos of the 'decline of Sufism' is commemorated in the Dhahabī master Nayrīzī's celebrated Arabic poem *Faṣl al-khiṭāb*, written *circa* 1720–30, attacking the corruption of the Safavid clerical establishment, cataloguing in detail the persecution endured by the Sufis and the destruction of their *khānaqāh*s at the hands of the mullās. "In every province of the entire country of Iran," we read in one verse, "all cloisters, all *khānaqāh*s of the dervishes (*ahl al-faqr*) lie destroyed.'[14] The decadence of the times is bemoaned right down to early modern times. Writing in the early 1840s, we hear the renowned Ni'matu'llāhī master Zayn al-'Ābidīn Shirvānī (Mast 'Alī Shāh) replicating Nayrīzī's lament in prose, in complaining that "in the whole land of Iran there is neither abode nor site where a dervish can lay his head . . . In the rest of the inhabited quarters of the world, among all its different races and peoples, hospitals for the sick and *khānaqāh*s for the dervishes are built – except in Iran, where there is neither *khānaqāh* nor hospital!"[15]

Likewise, the topos of the "decline of Sufism" is also present in both Western orientalist writings and Persianate Sufi literature composed in India during the sixteenth to eighteenth centuries.[16] In its Indian context, dealing with the spiritual and contemplative dimension of the subject, Marcia Hermansen and Carl Ernst examine this 'paradigm of decline' in their essays, while Andrew Newman and Leonard Lewisohn adumbrate this topos as it interpenetrates political, theological and literary debates in Persia.

[14] Cited by Iḥṣānu'llāh 'Alī Istakhrī, *Uṣūl-i taṣawwuf*, (Tehran: Kānūn-i Ma'rifat 1338 A.Hsh./1959), p. 435.

[15] Shīrwānī, *Ḥadā'iq al-siyāḥat*, (Tehran 1348 A.Hsh./1929), p. 258. For further discussion of the so-called 'decline of Sufism' in Persia, see Leonard Lewisohn, "An Introduction to the History of Modern Persian Sufism, Part 1: The Ni'matullāhī Order: Persecution, Revival, and Schism", BSOAS, 61/3 (1998), pp. 437–64; and esp. part 2 of the same article entitled "A Socio-Cultural Profile of Sufism, from the Dhahabī Revival to the Present-Day", *BSOAS*, 62/1 (1999), pp. 1–24.

[16] Michel Mazzaoui points out that from the fifteenth century onwards, the capital cities of the five great empires: "such as Istanbul, Bursa, and Edirne for the Ottomans; Tabriz, Qazvin, and Isfahan for the Safavids; Bukhara, Samarqand, and Herat for the Uzbeks; Agra, Lahore, and Delhi for the Mughals; as well as Cairo, Damascus, and Aleppo for the Mamluks – were great centers of Islamic culture that could hold their own compared with the great Renaissance cities of Western Europe. The architectural monuments in these great metropolitan centers have survived in all their beauty and splendor. In spite of these and other cultural achievements, both Western (orientalist) and Eastern (Islamic) writers alike continue to talk of a period of decline (*'asr al-inhitāt*) culminating in the eighteenth century. This thesis, at least at the intellectual level, is no longer defensible. A closer look at the Muslim world, including Iran and Central Asia, during the eighteenth century, (the last period of 'decline' just before the West makes its long-awaited epiphany) provides a totally different picture. It is clear that . . . the Muslim world was undergoing a process comparable, if not similar, to the period of the Enlightenment in Western Europe that produced the French Revolution', "Islamic Culture and Literature in the Early Modern Period", in Canfield, *Turko-Persia in Historical Perspective*, pp. 87–8.

In his introduction, S.H. Nasr underlines the difficulty of exploring the mysticism of the Safavid period, owing to the special political conditions of the period, and proposes that Sufi spirituality of Safavid times be partially understood as a kind of intellectual esotericism, partaking of the amorphous pre-*ṭarīqa* form of Islamic mysticism found prior to the twelfth century. His essay is devoted to the Safavid 'school of Iṣfahān' (a term he coined with Henry Corbin in the 1960s), its unique synthesis of philosophy with speculative Sufism; he places this school at the heart of the intellectual life of Iran and India.

David Morgan opens part II with what he hopes will be a provocative article rethinking the conversion of the Safavids to Shī'ism and the nature of Shāh Ismā'īl I's religious commitment. This is followed by Farhang Jahanpour's wide-ranging essay charting Western encounters with Persian Sufi literature. Jahanpour gives a compact historical overview of the subject, and a valuable account of many of the various correspondences and contacts between early Western orientalism and Persian Sufism. Examining the entire late classical period from the founding of the Sir Thomas Adams Chair of Arabic at Cambridge in 1632 through the pioneering translation works of orientalists such as Sir William Jones, the travel accounts of Jean Chardin, down to Ralph Waldo Emerson and the English Romantic poets, Jahanpour delineates the various cultural channels through which "Sufism has already made its presence felt in the spiritual and intellectual life of the West".

Part III, devoted to Sufism in Safavid Persia (1501–1722), is opened by Leonard Lewisohn's long essay on the place of Sufism in the thought of two of the foremost theosophists of the school of Iṣfahān: 'Abd al-Razzāq Lāhījī and Fayḍ-i Kāshānī. Focusing on the political underpinnings of the Safavid theocracy which arose "in the milieu of Sufism and of extremism",[17] this essay takes a fresh look at the historical conflict between legalitarian clericalism and antinominian mysticism in Islamic culture, viewing it as an archetypal struggle between Eros and Nomos, tolerance and fundamentalism, charismatic inspirationalism and religious formalism: the same battle still being fought out in the political theatres of most modern Islamic countries. The next two essays trace the Ni'matu'llāhī Order's legacy in Safavid Iran: Terry Graham provides the most substantial and comprehensive history available of this order in post-Tīmūrid Iran and India, and Sholeh Quinn furnishes not only an excellent introduction to the historiography of Safavid chronicles, but an original survey of Ni'matu'llāhī–Safavid family connections according to the primary sources.

Andrew Newman's essay, tracing the successive waves of anti-Sufi polemic in Safavid Iran and concentrating on the issue of singing (*ghinā'*) in the clerical assault on Sufi practices, concludes part III. Typical of the clerical

[17] R. Savory, *Iran Under the Safavids* (Cambridge: Cambridge University Press 1980), p. 77.

viewpoint was the ascription of extreme behaviour, aberrant behaviour – and even derogatory names – to Sufi groups. The mullās' intention in their battle with Sufism was to destroy the venues of *samā'*, thus eradicating the centres where the Sufis' passion for poetry – the supreme imaginative enterprise of the Persian psyche – was enacted, entertained and sustained. The polemics of these puritan clerics against mystical song and dance, so meticulously annotated in this contribution, demonstrate not only the depths of Shī'ite pharisaical legalism, but exhibit the passion and paranoia of the lost world of religious war and struggle which characterizes the period.

Part IV, which is devoted to 'Sufism and Ishrāqī and Akbarian philosophy', opens with Ian Netton's study of the contribution of Mīr Dāmād to the philosophy of time in Islamic thought in Safavid Persia, pointing out the many parallels between Dāmād's life and thought and that of Shihāb al-Dīn Suhrawardī. William Chittick follows with an essay on the metaphysical teachings of Maḥmūd Khwush-Dahān (d. 1026/1617), a little-known Chishtī master. "One of the major reasons for the fact that most Sufi writing of India has remained unstudied", Chittick notes, "is that modern scholars have focused on social and political history and have had little interest in the goals and intentions of the Sufi authors themselves." In regard to Khwush-Dahān, Chittick rectifies this omission by giving the first systematic exposition of the doctrines contained in his seminal text *Ma'rifat al-sulūk* (The True Knowledge of Wayfaring). Muhammad Reza Juzi concludes the chapter with an exploration of the relationship of the foremost Safavid-period philosopher Mullā Ṣadrā (d. 1050/1640) to the thought of Ibn 'Arabī, convincingly arguing that "the whole body of Mullā Sadrā's transcendental theosophy functions as the rational structure and logical articulation of Ibn 'Arabī's teaching".

Part V: "Esoteric Movements and Contemplative Disciplines", features four contributions. Farhad Daftary, in his "Sufi–Ismā'īlī Relations in Early Post-Alamūt and Safavid Persia", discusses the complex interrelationship and interaction between Shī'ism, Sufism and Ismā'īlism down to the end of the Safavid period. He points out that after 868/1463, when Mustanṣir bi'llāh, the thirty-second Ismā'īlī Imām succeeded to the imāmate, it became customary for the Nizārī Ismā'īlī Imāms to adopt Sufi names, adding terms such as Shāh and 'Alī to their names like Sufi masters, appearing as one Sufi order among others. Later on, during the Safavid period in Persia and under the Mughals in India, the Ismā'īlīs often observed *taqiyya* in the form of Twelver Shī'ism. Daftary's sectarian concerns are critically addressed in the Afghan context by Sergei Andreyev, who offers us the most comprehensive introduction available to the history and doctrine of the Rawshaniyya in his "The Rawshaniyya: A Millenarian Sufi Movement in the Mughal Tribal Periphery". This includes a comprehensive socio-biographical study of Bāyazīd Anṣārī (*c.* 927 or 931/1521 or 1552–1572 or 1575–980 or 983), the founder of this important proto-Sufi sect.

Re-examining the so-called 'decline of Sufism' debate, Marcia Hermansen, in "Contemplating Sacred History in Late Mughal Sufism: The Case of Shāh Walī Allāh", explores the various notions of the 'decline' proposed by Western scholars (Trimingham, Meier, Lapidus, etc.), noting that while "the model of decline, so facilely applied to this period after the fact and in consonance with an overriding narrative of Muslim stagnation and European rise", has been favoured by European scholars of Persianate Sufism, it was seldom in favour among Sufis themselves, who viewed their history in 'a developmentally progressive way'. Noting that the eighteenth century "is considered 'baroque' in the sense of a flowering and confluence of a number of intellectual styles, but also the last gasp before the decline into popularization and saint cults", she concludes that Sufis such as Shāh Walī Allāh understood "the development of the Sufi tradition in the light of a broader framework of 'Perfection history'," rather than decline. Following Hermansen, Carl Ernst, in "Chishtī Meditation Practices of the Late Mughal Period" criticizes what he calls the "the 'golden age' syndrome" favoured by orientalists, observing that:

> The 'classicism and decline' model has long since exercised a fascination over students of Islamic culture. It is especially odd to notice that the 'decline' of Islamic civilization has been an unquestioned axiom accepted until recently by most orientalists, secular modernists and fundamentalists, but for different reasons. In all these cases, the colonization of much of the Muslim world and the consequent loss of political power by Muslims were interpreted moralistically as the judgement of either history or God upon a civilization that had become inadequate. The notion of the decline of Muslim nations was especially attractive to the self-image of Europeans in the colonial period, since it provided a noble justification for conquest and empire on the basis of the 'civilizing mission' of the West (also known as 'the white man's burden'). If, however, we do not intend to support any of these agendas, then the notion of 'classicism and decline' is distinctly unhelpful in the study of a tradition such as Sufism.

Part VI, "Persianate Sufism in India, Central Asia and China", geographically speaking, contains the most wide-ranging contributions in the book, with essays devoted to Indian, Chinese and Central Asian Sufism. Opening the chapter, M.Z.A. Shakeb traces the political and socio-cultural history of Sufism in the Deccan from the early fifteenth to the late seventeenth century, highlighting the relations between Sunnism and Shī'ism. Despite the fact that "it was against a background of clerical intimidation and Shī'ite fanaticism that the Sufis of the Deccan had to carry on their mission," Shakeb reveals that the Sufis "generally kept aloof from the polemical debates raging in the Shī'ite literature of the period, whether it was produced in Iran or the Deccan." His essay illustrates the central role played by the Sufis in maintaining social stability in Indian society and their furtherance of the spirit of Islam together with respect for other faiths. Sachiko Murata presents the key study of Sufism in medieval China (the first such study, in fact, available in any language); pointing out that "only four Islamic books are known for certain to have been rendered into Chinese before the present century, and all are well-known Persian Sufi texts", she proceeds to examine the significance of these texts for the history of Chinese Islam.

In the final essay of Part VI Devin DeWeese examines the remarkable vitality and dynamism of Central Asian Sufism during the sixteenth and seventeenth centuries, concentrating on 'Ālim Shaykh of 'Alīyābād, the dominant figure in the Yasavī order. While the Yasavī Sufis left their most substantial literary legacy almost entirely in Persian, their order being centred in traditionally Persophone regions of Central Asia, neither the history of the order nor its literary and hagiographical legacy during this period has received much scholarly attention. His study concludes that "the lesson learned from a closer study of the Yasavī tradition during the sixteenth and seventeenth centuries is precisely the indivisible coherence of Central Asian civilization".

Annemarie Schimmel's study, "The Vernacular Tradition in Persianate Sufi Poetry", underlining the central importance of the Persianate Sufi tradition and Indian Sufi saints in Indian culture, inaugurates the final section of the book, which is devoted entirely to literary themes. She reveals the profound impact of such Sufi poets as Qaḍī Qādan (d. 1551), Sulṭān Bāhū (d. 1691), Shāh 'Abd al-Laṭīf (1689–1752) and Bullhē Shāh (d. 1754) on the development of literatures in the regional languages of India. Christopher Shackle follows her literary emphasis but with a slightly different flavour, covering the 'high literary' ground of Indo-Persianate *belles-lettres* in his essay on the *Narang-i 'ishq* (1685) of Ghanīmat Kunjāhī. Endeavouring to disentangle the relationships between Sufism and Sufi poetry and poetry which uses Sufi imagery, he concentrates on the Qādiriyya in the Punjab in Mughal times, highlighting the role of this order in the development of Sufi poetry written in Persian and successfully grappling with the Indian context of this poetry in which the distinction between 'Persian' and 'Persianate' is always worth attention. While his essay provides a good introduction to the poetic themes and theories of Ghanīmat, it also gives an excellent overview of the contribution of the Qādiriyya to Persianate Sufi literature and Punjabi poetry in the subcontinent.

Simon Weightman's essay returns to the theme of vernacular literature, while remaining very much on 'high literary' ground, as he elucidates the complex quasi-Sufi mystical theology of Manjhan, a respected teaching Shaykh of the Shaṭṭārī order, whose *Madhumālatī* best represents the genre of the Sufi *premākhyān* in Awadhi. His study reveals the predominance of Persianate Sufi motifs in this work, in which "underneath the *yogi* there is the *'āshiq* and the *sālik*, the lover and the traveller or Sufi". His startlingly original analysis of the various levels of symbolism concealed within this great Sufi romance, which proves that well-established macro-compositional principles may well underlie many other mystical works of this nature, is of ground-breaking significance for our understanding of Muslim literary history in general and Persianate Sufi poetry in particular. Heideh Ghomi's highly original essay, "The Imagery of Annihilation in Ṣā'ib Tabrīzī", one of the most capable Safavid poets of the 'Indian style', concludes the volume.

The remarkable intensity and originality of the intellectual focus brought to bear by the volume's various contributors will, we hope, be apparent to the reader of the following pages. No doubt, the chronological breadth, intellectual diversity and historical scope of the present book also attests to the cultural achievements in the history, philosophy and poetry of Sufism in Persianate culture in Iran, Central Asia and India during the Safavid and Mughal period.

However, the discovery, presentation and elaboration of these wide-ranging themes are the product of many diverse factors and are indebted to the labours of a variety of persons. Throughout the preparation of this volume, the editors, as convenors of the conference held at the School of Oriental and African Studies, University of London, 19–21 May 1997 on which it is based, have received much help, encouragement and support from various organizations and individuals. The conference was made possible by funding from the School of Oriental and African Studies, the Royal Asiatic Society of Great Britain, the British Institute of Persian Studies, the British Academy and Curzon Press. We would like to express our gratitude to these institutions for their generous grants, without which the conference would have been impossible to arrange. We also thank Dr Javad Nurbakhsh and the Ni'matullahi Research Centre for sponsoring and organizing the concert of traditional Persian Sufi music on 20 May 1997, which, by using Persian poetry of the Safavid period as its basic repertoire, served to celebrate the mystical themes of the conference in the musical dimension.

We would like to thank Dr Charles Tripp, former head of the Centre of Near and Middle Eastern Studies at SOAS, and Dr Tudor Parfitt, the present head, for their support. Our thanks go to Sara Stewart in particular and the staff of the Centre of Near and Middle Eastern Studies in general for their sustained services in the preparation and production of the printed material involved in, and expert handling of, the conference organization, as well as their subsequent secretarial assistance in preparing the contributions to this collection. We would also like to acknowledge our gratitude to Dr Hossein Ilahi Ghomshei for gracing the chapter headings of this volume with his lovely illustrations in original Persian calligraphy of the poem by Shaykh Bahā'ī (translated by Leonard Lewisohn). We would also like to thank Heather Sacco for contributing her time and energy to editing many of the articles herein. The generosity of Dr Cary Stuart Welch and the Harvard University Art Museums for granting us permission to use the splendid Shaykh-zāda miniature on the cover of this volume is also gratefully acknowledged.

In conclusion, if, as the Shaykh al-Ṭā'ifā Junayd was known to say, "The furthest reach of divine Unity (*tawḥīd*) is the denial of Unity", by extension, the ultimate degree of Sufism is the erasure of all trace of Sufism. On Junayd's maxim 'Aṭṭār reflected that "any knowledge one has of divine Unity is suspect, to be rejected in terms of its being still not yet [true] unity."[18] So, at our book's beginning, it remains to deny that 'Sufism' has been herein explained, yet to affirm that its elusive reality still remains.

D.M. & L.L.

[18] 'Aṭṭar, *Tadhkira*, pp. 442–3.

Foreword

The Evolution of Sufism

JAVAD NURBAKHSH

The school (*madhhab*) of classical Sufism originated in Khurāsān in northern Iran and from there was transmitted south-west to Baghdad. In the early days of Islam, the great representative masters of the Path in Khurāsān included the likes of Abū'l-Faḍl Qaṣṣāb Āmulī, Abū Sa'īd ibn Abī'l-Khayr (d. 440/1049), Abū'l-Ḥasan Kharaqānī (d. 426/1034) and Bāyazīd Bisṭāmi (d. 262/875).

The paradoxical sayings of Bāyazīd Bisṭamī, even in his own day, gained a wide circulation in Iraq and soon exerted a captivating influence over the minds of students in search of the spiritual path of divine Unity and seekers who aspired to understand the meaning of the 'Unity of Being'. In particular, his ideas deeply affected the thinking of Abū'l-Qāsim Junayd (d. 295/910), Abū Naṣr Sarrāj al-Ṭūsī (d. 378/988), Dhū'l-Nūn al-Miṣrī (d. 245/859) and many others, inspiring them to write extensive commentaries on his sayings.

Persian Sufism from the very beginning – even prior to Junayd – had a great effect on the Sufi masters of Baghdad, many of whom were also of Iranian descent. One may well speculate that Ḥasan al-Baṣrī (d. 110/728), for instance, who fought with the Muslim armies in battles to subdue Khurāsān in northern Iran, very likely associated with, and frequented the company of, the spiritual masters of this region during these campaigns. Amongst his sayings one finds the statement: 'The lover is in a state of intoxication, from which he awakes only during contemplation of his Beloved.'[1]

Mālik reportedly asked Ḥasan al-Baṣrī, "Wherein does this world's chastisement lie?"

"In the heart's death," replied Ḥasan.

"What is the 'heart's death'?" asked Mālik.

"Love of the world," he replied.[2]

---

[1] Sha'rānī, *Ṭabaqāt al-kubrā*, I, p. 30.

[2] Aṭṭā, *Tadhkirat al-awliyā*, ed. Muḥammad Isti'lāmī (Tehran: Zawwār 1372 A.Hsh./1993; 3rd ed.), p. 37..

A century later, some of the finer points of Sufism appear expressed by the sayings of Ma'rūf Karkhī (d. 200/815), such as: "The Sufi is but a guest here, for a guest to request anything of his host is discourtesy. A courteous guest waits with confidence, rather than pressing his petition."[3] Ma'rūf Karkhī also is known for his statement that "hroughout all being, naught but God exists."[4]

In the generation following Ma'rūf Karkhī, one finds some extraordinary sayings among the masters of the Baghdad school of Sufism. Junayd's master, Sarī Saqaṭī (d. 255/871), for instance, when asked to describe the Sufis, explained, "The food they eat is like that eaten by the sick, and their sleep is like that of the drowned."[5] Junayd reported that Sarī once said, "Love between two people is not equitable until the one says to the other, 'O me . . .!' [instead of 'O you . . .!']; that is to say, that there is no place for separate individual identity in love."[6] Sarī's lovely remarks about the 'idolatry of beards' are worth quoting in this context:

> There exist two types of idolatry in keeping a beard. Firstly, one must either comb it for the sake of people, or secondly, leave it to become matted so as to maintain an ascetic facade.
>
> If a visitor to drop by to see me, and were I stroke and comb my beard with my hand to please him, in my own eyes, I'd be an idolater.[7]

As if describing the passage of Sufism from Khurāsān to Iraq outlined above, Sarī also remarked, "As long the science of Sufism was preserved in Khurāsān, one found it (diffused) everywhere, but ever since it came to an end there, it cannot be found anywhere."[8]

However, by the time of Abū'l-Qāsim Junayd (d. 295/910; born in Nahāvand near Hamadān in western Persia), the school (*madhhab*) of classical Sufism had blossomed luxuriously and little by little acquired innumerable advocates, devoted followers and spiritual masters. As a matter of course, this excited the jealousy of the exoteric authorities. Particularly alarmed by the Sufi's popularity were those jurisprudents and judges who, in order to further their own dictatorial aims, wished to live freely off the state by collaboration with the caliphs. In an attempt to curb the rise and diffusion of Sufism, these authorities began to harass and issue *fatwās* for the death of some of the Sufis such as Ḥallāj and Ibn 'Aṭā.

---

[3] Khwāja 'Abdullāh Anṣārī, *Ṭabāqāt al-ṣufiyya*, ed. Muḥammad Sarwar Mawlāyī (Tehran: Sahāmī'ām 1362A.Hsh./1983), p. 39.

[4] Ayn al-Qūḍāt Hamadanī, *Tamhīdāt*, ed. A. Osserian (Tehran: 1962), p. 256.

[5] Bākharzī, *Awrād al-aḥbāb wa fuṣūṣ al-ādāb*, II, ed. Īrāj Afshār (Tehran 1345 A.Hsh./1966), p. 121.

[6] Qushayrī, *Tarjuma-yi Risāla-yi Qushayriyya*. Persian trans. Abū 'Alī Ḥasan ibn Aḥmad al-'Uthmānī, ed. B.Z. Furūzānfar (Tehran 1321A.Hsh./1942), p. 564.

[7] Abū Ṭālib Makkī, *Qūt al-qulūb* (Beirut: Dār Ṣādir n.d.), II, p. 144.

[8] Jāmi, *Nafaḥāt al-uns*, ed. Maḥmshad 'Abidī (Tehran: Mū'assasa-yi Iṭilā'āt 1370 A.Hsh./1991), p. 51.

One reason for their animosity was that the school of divine Unity (*tawḥīd*) and Sufism in Islam is based on the principles of freedom, chivalry, altruism, service to all humanity and advocacy of human rights, the very principles which these exoteric judges and jurisprudents discerned – quite correctly – to be directed at neutralizing their own dogmatic control of Islamic thought. By way of allusion to these oppressive social conditions, Junayd said, "For twenty years I have been discoursing only on marginal aspects of this science [of Sufism], but of what concerns its profoundest depths have not breathed a word, for tongues have been forbidden to utter that and hearts not permitted to apprehend it."[9] One may also interpret Abū Bakr Shiblī's (d. 334/945) remark, "Now is a time of silence, of seclusion in houses and putting one's trust in God, the Everlasting"[10] in the same vein.

THE SCHOOLS OF INTOXICATION AND SOBRIETY

The school of Khurāsān, which was also known as the school of intoxication (*sukr*), pertained to Bāyazīd Bisṭāmi and his followers. Since Khurāsān was beyond the reach of the caliph and the theologians on his payroll, Bāyazīd was able to express his ideas more openly, with less inhibition and greater boldness, although some of his adages took the form of ecstatic sayings couched in symbolic paradoxical allusions (*shaṭḥ*).

The school of sobriety (*ṣaḥw*) – also known as the school of Baghdad – which pertained to Junayd and his disciples, who maintained that there was a second sobriety which is higher than intoxication, was on the other hand, subjected to the powerful autocracy of state-controlled Islam, so that most of Junayd's sayings bear the influence of the oppressive political milieu in which he lived. Although 'sobriety' literally denotes the state of temperate consciousness following drunkenness, the term also contains political overtones, implying: "Put a halter on this spiritual drunkenness; be vigiliant lest the mullās declare you a heretic!"

Whereas the spiritual attitude of the school of intoxication in which the ideals of classical Persian Sufism are best represented, might be summed up by Kharaqānī's maxim: "Give bread to all those who enter the *khānaqāh*, but do not interrogate visitors about their faith;" the Baghdad school, based on temperance and sobriety, would have voiced the opposite sentiment: "Interrogate all who enter the *khānaqāh* about the probity of their faith, and only then, if acceptable, admit them."

Therefore, one can say that up until the middle of the fourth Islamic/tenth Christian century, a trace of genuine Sufism was still left, although this gradually disappeared and became forgotten. After that date, however, despite

---

[9] Aṭṭār, *Tadhkirat al-awliyā'*. p. 421.
[10] Makkī, *Qūt al-qulūb*, III, p. 93 (marginal note).

appearances and the often great popularity and widespread following of significant figures in Sufism in the lands of Iran beyond the borders of the school of Baghdad – in particular one should cite the names of Farīd al-Dīn 'Aṭṭār, 'Ayn al-Quḍāt Hamadhānī, Suhrawardī, Ghazālī, Rūzbihān, Jalāl al-Dīn Rūmī, 'Abdu'llāh Anṣārī, Najm al-Dīn Kubrā and Ibn 'Arabī (albeit in Spain) – most of these Sufis were either slain, exiled or subjected to severe pressures by the religious authorities of the state.

In a word, one may say that upon the death of Junayd in 295/910, the expanse of gnostic Sufism (*taṣawwuf-i 'ārifāna*) was folded up and came to an end, and with the death of Rūzbihān Baqlī three hundred years later in 606/1210, the flame of Sufism based divine love (*taṣawwuf-i 'āshiqāna*) was snuffed out. What is left of Sufism today can be summed up in the poet's verse:

> So togged up
> in gild and lacquer
> you'd never recognize it
> if you saw it.

I
INTRODUCTION

هو العزیز

تا کی به تمنای وصال تو یگانه

اشکم شود از هر مژه چون سیل روانه

خواهد به سر آید شب هجران تو یا نه؟

ای تیر غمت را دل عشاق نشانه

جمعی به تو مشغول و تو غایب ز میانه

How long, how long — in longing for you — will tears
Roll from each eyelash of mine and be a river
In flood towards you who are the Single One?
When lovers part, how long, I ask, how long
Will this, the parting-night of the lovers last?
Alas, your grief dart pierces lovers' hearts;
You're nowhere present yet the company's astir with you.

The Place of the School of Iṣfahān in Islamic Philosophy and Sufism

SEYYED HOSSEIN NASR

In the name of the Author
of the book of creation . . .

It is a great pleasure to contribute an introduction to this third volume of a series of books which have attempted to evaluate the entire history of Persian Sufism down to the beginning of the modern period.[1] Insofar as the present volume is devoted specifically to the Safavid and Mughal period of Sufism, I felt it appropriate (for reasons which are explained below) to confine my remarks to the place and significance of the school of Iṣfahān in Islamic philosophy and Sufism. Of course, after perusing Dr Nurbakhsh's foreword, one might well imagine that nothing remained of the living tradition of Sufism in Islam after the sixth Muslim/thirteenth Christian century, and that what did survive of the Islamic mystical tradition was merely a body without a spirit! However, looking more deeply into the matter, examining the very complicated circumstances of the Safavid period in particular, one soon finds that this – the late classical – period was characterized by an abundance of mystical and philosophical currents which criss-crossed each other, creating many profoundly original and interesting syntheses of ideas.

However, it will be of historical interest and relevance to our theme here if, first of all, we examine the history of the coinage of the expression 'School of Iṣfahān', employed for the first time by Henry Corbin in the mid-1950s in an article on Mīr Dāmād and the school of Iṣfahān entitled "L'École d'Ispahan."[2] Following long discussions held between us in Tehran, we

---

[1] See my previous introductions to Leonard Lewisohn (ed.), *The Heritage of Sufism*, I (Oxford Oneworld 1999), pp. 1–18 and *idem. The Heritage of Sufism*, II (Oxford: Oneworld 1999), pp. 1–10.

[2] *Confessions extatiques de Mīr Dāmād*, in *Mélanges Louis Massignon* (Damasins: Institut français de Damas 1956), I, pp. 331–78. This study also opens book V of Corbin's *En Islam iranien* (Paris: Gallimard 1972), IV, pp. 8ff. The whole of livre V is entitled "L'École d'Ispahan".

decided together to try to 'launch' this phrase, and specifically, to utilize it as a generic term to characterize the whole intellectual effort of the Safavid period. Gradually, over the course of several decades, our term gained popular acceptance and eventually became so prevalent that today it is used to denote the school of philosophy/theosophy which began in the city of Iṣfahān in Safavid Persia.

Albeit, I should draw attention to the fact that this school with its salient characteristics probably began in the mid-sixteenth century in Qazwīn and it was only later, after 998/1589, when Shāh 'Abbās transferred the capital of Persia from Qazwīn to Iṣfahān, that the latter city became its main centre. In any case, the school remained in Iṣfahān, persisting for almost another two hundred years, down to the early eighteenth century. However, with the invasion and destruction of the city by Maḥmūd the Afghān in 1135/1722, many of its thinkers were forced to take refuge in other cities, especially Qum, and it was only later on, in the Qājār period, that the school was resuscitated in both Iṣfahān and Tehran. Fortunately today, the school of Iṣfahān is much better known now than it was forty years ago and has been made the subject of numerous articles and books going back to the pioneering works of Corbin.[3]

In earlier periods of Islamic thought, the various fields and subject-areas of knowledge were separated into distinct water-tight compartments, and to 'mix one field of academic discussion with another field' (in Arabic: *khalṭ al-mabḥath*) was considered to be a grievous intellectual sin. Each discipline and science had its own individually distinct methodology and approach to its respective field which it considered to be its own sacroscant preserve. Hence, philosophy, theology (*kalām*), theoretical Sufism (*taṣawwuf-i naẓarī*), etc. were all strictly segregated from one another. After the passage of centuries, however, and with the advent of the Safavid period in particular, one tends to notice a synthesis taking place between various schools of thought, the most important of which are, for the present discussion, the Islamic Aristotelian philosophers (*mashsha'ī*), Illuminationist (*ishrāqī*) philosophy/theology, the Akbarian school of Ibn 'Arabī and his followers and other schools of Sufism, and *kalām*, both Sunni and Shī'ite. One aspect of the unique character of the school of Iṣfahān, which distinguishes it from philosophical developments over the previous centuries, is precisely this synthetic nature of its teachings.

[3] See especially Corbin, *ibid.*; also "The School of Isfahan", in my *The Islamic Intellectual Tradition in Persia*, ed. M.A. Razavi (London: Curzon Press 1997), pp. 239–319. (This chapter is a reprint of the essay written originally in the early 1960s for M.M. Sharif, *A History of Muslim Philosophy* (Wiesbaden: Harrassowitz 1966), pp. 904–32.

THE SCHOOL OF SHĪRĀZ

The School of Iṣfahān did not, so to speak, mushroom up out of nowhere; its historical roots can in fact be traced back some two centuries before the Safavid period to intellectual activities and currents prevalent in the city of Shīrāz, south of Iṣfahān, currents which may be said to have themselves constituted an independent philosophical 'School of Shīrāz'.[4] This school benefited from the exceptional political circumstances obtaining in the region of Fars which, following upon the wake of the Mongol invasion, thrived as a kind of oasis of relative peace and calm in Iran, which was divided into many small provinces under the Īlkhānid system of government. The result was that numerous scholars took refuge there, while those from the area were able to teach and write in an atmosphere of relative security and therefore rarely migrated elsewhere (except for those who went to India). The School of Shīrāz remains still nearly unknown, and just as only a generation ago scholars who wished to carry out research on the School of Iṣfahān were obliged first of all to write independent monographs on various members of the school, today we are almost equally benighted regarding detailed philosophical developments of this earlier School, lacking any comprehensive view of its major figures and trends. A brief review of some of its most important figures and key features on the basis of what is known is, therefore, very much in order here.

Most of the primary figures of this school hailed from Shīrāz and its surrounding towns and were members of the influential Dashtakī family, among whom may be mentioned Mīr Ṣadr al-Dīn Dashtakī (d. 903/1497), to whom Mullā Ṣadrā refers frequently in his *Asfār*. In fact, because both Mullā Ṣadrā and Dashtakī were known as 'Ṣadr al-Dīn', later scholars have often confused the two thinkers. Since Ṣadr al-Dīn Dashtakī's thought was expressed mostly in the form of glosses and commentaries on philosophical and religious works, unfortunately his writings have been almost completely overlooked by both contemporary Persian scholars and Western orientalists. The reason for this sad neglect lies partially in the short-sightedness of nineteenth-century orientalists who considered commentaries to be repetitious, boring and devoid of original ideas, and who therefore resolved to concern themselves exclusively with original texts. Owing to their prejudice and lack of interest, which has also influenced Muslim scholars, many famous commentators' new ideas and discoveries have remained buried in the dust of library shelves even into this century. Only today are we gradually beginning to recognize how

---

[4] In the same way that Henry Corbin and I launched the phrase 'School of Iṣfahān' almost half a century ago, it now may be an appropriate moment to inaugurate in English the expression 'School of Shīrāz'. Already a number of Persian scholars are using this term. See especially Qāsim Kākā'ī, "Shīrāz, mahd-i ḥikmat", *Khiradnāma-yi Ṣadrā*, 1/2 (August 1995), pp. 63–9; *idem*, "Āshnā'ī bā maktab-i Shīrāz", *ibid.*, 1/3 (March 1966), pp. 82–9; and *idem*, "Āshnā'ī bā maktab-i Shīrāz-i Amīr Ghiyāth al Dīn Manṣūr Dashtakī", *ibid.*, 2/5–6 (Autumn–Winter 1997), pp. 83–90.

significant these commentaries are. Mīr Ṣadr al-Dīn Dashtakī, for example, wrote commentaries and glosses on the famous *Tajrīd* of Naṣīr al-Dīn Ṭūsī and the Koranic commentary of Zamakhsharī, as well as composing several books of his own on philosophical theology. He also wrote several treatises on logic and the sciences, specifically agriculture and astronomy, a fact which points to one of the main characteristics of the school of Shīrāz: namely, that most of its main figures were scientists as well as philosophers. This school is therefore of importance for the history of Islamic science as well as for the history of Islamic philosophy and Sufism.

The most famous member of the school was Ṣadr al-Dīn's son Ghiyāth al-Dīn Manṣūr Dashtakī (d. 949/1542), at once an eminent physician, founder of a well-known medical school in Shīrāz, and a major philosopher renowned for his commentaries on Ibn Sīnā and Suhrawardī. His glosses on Ṭūsī's commentary on Ibn Sīnā's "Book of Directives and Remarks" (*Ishārāt*) and his commentary on the "Temples of Light" (*Hayākil al-nūr*) of Suhrawardī are particularly important; the latter work in fact constitutes the main link – alongside the works of Jalāl al-Dīn Davānī – between Mīr Dāmād, the founder of the School of Iṣfahān, and Suhrawardī himself.

Another important thinker of the Shīrāz school was Muḥammad Khafrī (d. 957/1550), a pupil of Ṣadr al-Dīn Dashtākī. Khafrī was very much interested in Sufism, in both its theoretical and practical dimensions, and was also author of a large number of works on philosophy, astronomy, the hidden sciences and Koranic exegesis. It was Khafrī who sought to bring Sufism and philosophy together in a single perspective and who for the first time coined the famous phrase 'transcendent theosophy' (*al-ḥikmat al-muta'āliyya*) in the same sense given to it by Mullā Ṣadrā some time later. These facts alone indicate how close the intellectual developments of the school of Shīrāz were to those of the school of Iṣfahān.

Another figure worthy of mention in the school of Shīrāz is an important Peripatetic thinker and a pupil of Khafrī named Shāh Ṭāhir ibn Rāḍī al-Dīn (d. 956/1549) who was a near contemporary of Mīr Dāmād and who wrote a commentary on Ibn Sīnā's *Kitāb al-shifā'* "The Book of Healing". Many are the other important figures in this school who provided the philosophical foundations for the school of Iṣfahān, but unfortunately, for reasons of space, further discussion of their works is precluded here.

THE SCHOOL OF IṢFAHĀN

The main philosophical issue confronting the thinkers of the school of Iṣfahān was how to create concord between the three great ways which lie open to man for the attainment of knowledge and spiritual guidance. These paths are respectively that of (1) the divine law (*sharī'a*) which connotes the exoteric and legal aspect of religion; (2) *kashf*, intuitive unveiling and illumination; and

Plate 1: Pavilion of the Royal Palace in Iṣfahān. From *Voyages du Chevalier Chardin, en Perse et autres lieux de l'orient*. Ed. L. Langlès. Paris 1811. Pl. 39.

finally (3) *'aql*, which may be translated as either 'intellect' or 'reason' depending on the context.[5] Almost all the great thinkers of the Safavid period were involved in the endeavour to reconcile and integrate these three distinct approaches to the problem of knowledge. Discussions often focused around the meaning of technical terms such as 'logical reasoning' (*istidlāl*) and 'intellect' (*'aql*). As an example of these discussions, one might well cite some interesting verses by the founder of the school of Iṣfahān, Mīr Dāmād (d. 1041/1631–2) whose thought is discussed at length by Ian Netton later on in this volume. To Rūmī's famous verse in the *Mathnawī*:

> Rationalists' legs are just like stilts;
> How unfixed and stolid are feet of wood![6]

Mīr Dāmād chose to take exception and, attempting to refute Rūmī, wrote the following verses in reply:

> O! You who say the legs on which
> Rationalists tread "are stilts" . . . despite these
> Remarks, Fakhr-i Rāzī[7] would be unmatched.
> But since, of course, your mind is warped and biased,
> Between Intelligence – the *nous*,
> And vain opinion, you could not see the difference.
> But don't dismiss so quick the use of proofs,
> Since I have made, by Almighty Grace,
> Those "feet of wood" ironclad in proofs of truth;
> I've cast at last in stiffest iron those "stilts"
> Of inference you mocked and scoffed.[8]

---

[5] Regarding the latter term, I might add that for some twenty-five years Dr Javad Nurbakhsh and I, on numerous occasions over lunch and dinner in Tehran, discussed the meaning of this word, yet never reached an agreement concerning either its meaning or proper translation. Dr Nurbakhsh always preferred to interpret and translate *'aql* as 'reason', that is, as mere human ratiocination, mental processes having no spiritual significance, while I have always understood it to imply the 'intellect' (in the sense of the Latin *intellectus* used by the Scholastics), connoting the transcendental and cosmic dimension of man's universal intelligence without the term being devoid of the meaning of reason as understood by later philosophers.

[6] *Mathnawī*, ed. R.A. Nicholson, 8 vols (London: Luzac & Co. 1925–40), I: 2127. Rūmī, however, distinguishes clearly between the meaning of *'aql* as intellect and the very instrument of revelation and its connotation as reason whose exclusive claim to knowledge he criticized. See Jalāl Humā'ī, *Mawlawī chah mīgūyad* (Tehran: High Council of Culture and Art 1976), 2 vols, which contains numerous references to the use of *'aql* in both its positive and negative aspects; and Kāẓim Muḥammadī, *Mawlānā wa difā' az 'aql* (Tehran: Mahdi Press 1994), devoted completely to this subject.

[7] Referring to Fakhr al-Dīn Rāzī (d. 606/1209), the famous Sunni Ash'arite theologian.

[8] Mīr Dāmād's verses are cited by Akbar Hādī, *Sharḥ-i ḥāl-i Mīr Dāmād va Mīr Findariskī* (Iṣfahān: Intishārāt-i Mītham Tamār 1363 A.Hsh./1984), p. 42. See also Jawād Muṣliḥ, *Falsafa-yi 'ālī yā ḥikmat-i Ṣadr al-muta'allihīn* (Tehran: Tehran University Press 1353 A.Hsh./1974), introduction, pp. yz–bh.

The above-cited couplet by Rūmī often formed the basis of philosophical discussions about problems of epistemology, bandied back and forth *pro et contra* among scholars who opposed philosophical discourse, denying the possibility of knowing the truth through the use of *'aql*, and those who advocated philosophy and the uses of intellection. Mīr Dāmād was not the only thinker to discuss them. At the end of the Safavid period Quṭb al-Dīn Nayrīzī Shīrāzī (d. 1173/1759–60), a leading Dhahabī Sufi master, took up his challenge and coming to Rūmī's defence, penned this powerful riposte to Mīr Dāmād's satire:

> O! You who jeer and sneer at Rūmī,
> How blind in mind you are, at loss
> To understand the *Mathnawī*! –
> A book which sets the soul aglow,
> With flashes of the Spirit's light illumines us;
> Its verses writ with mother pearl
> And set in ruby-coral! If you, alas
> Had but the scope of mind to grasp
> This *Mathnawī*, such taunts and scorn
> You'd never speak. For if in tones
> Of scorn the poet berated 'intellect',
> He meant not that Universal Intellect
> Which leads and guides us on every course
> And path; his aim was just man's *finite mind*,
> The petty reason of philosophy that disdains
> The fair looks that lit Joseph's face,
> A finite partial reason which poisons
> The mind with the gall of its delusions
> – It's just that reason all the saints berate.[9]

This example of a poetic jousting contest illustrating contrary philosophical positions and carried on over centuries is indicative of the often creative intellectual tensions prevalent in the Safavid period. As a matter of fact, when we examine the major intellectual figures of the Safavid period, all of them appear to be philosophers interested in Sufism, or at least in mysticism, in the classical meaning of the term.[10]

However, one must bear in mind that owing to the unusual political and religious circumstances of the Safavid period, the various currents of Islamic esotericism and, more specifically, Sufism, were expressed through personal transmission of initiation and spiritual instruction as well as the traditional institutional, *khānaqāh*-centred *ṭarīqa* forms. This distinction which surfaces

---

[9] Hādī, *Sharḥ-i ḥāl*, pp. 42–3.

[10] In using the word 'mysticism' here, my reference is solely to the original English sense of the term which relates to the divine mysteries, the *Mysterium*, and not to the nebulous and ambiguous meaning given to the term in some circles today.

in the Safavid period between the traditional/institutional and the individual/personal patterns of initiation into esoteric teachings is one of the most difficult and sensitive issues in the entire history of Persian Sufism. One of the best examples of the difficulty of understanding and penetrating this distinction in types of esotericism is found in the works of Mullā Ṣadrā (d. 1050/1640). For many years, I investigated his biography with a view to discovering the source of his spiritual teachings, in order to determine from whence he had received his esoteric instruction. It is certain from a purely spiritual point of view that just as mountains cannot be scaled without a guide, so it is impossible for anyone to climb the spiritual mountain without a spiritual teacher and to have the door to the higher worlds opened unto him unless instruction is vouchsafed him by someone who has the key. Who then was Mullā Ṣadrā's guide, and how did he obtain such an exalted degree of knowledge and gnosis (*'irfān/ma'rifat*)?

Unlike Ibn 'Arabī, who wrote extensively about his various spiritual teachers, describing his association with them in great detail,[11] to all appearances Mullā Ṣadrā wrote nothing of whether he belonged to any regular Sufi order (*silsila*) or followed any known master. Examining his biography from the outside, it is thus very difficult to ascertain the source – as understood in the technical Sufi sense – of his initiation and spiritual training. And yet, it is inconceivable that a mystic of his calibre had not undergone the process of initiation or obtained guidance from a living master. Finally, after many years of research and investigation on the matter, I discovered at last a facet of Islamic esotericism in Persia previously little known to scholars in either the West or the East, and which has not been studied fully until now. This facet, I believe, goes a long way towards explaining the secret initiatory sources of Mullā Ṣadrā's teachings, and also offers a commentary on the particular relationship of *'irfān* and *taṣawwuf* in Safavid Persia.

Although familiar to mystics of the Safavid period, few scholars today recognize the fact that there existed a form of esoteric transmission outside the normative, traditional *ṭarīqa* framework, the external institutional form of a *silsila*. This was a form of Sufi transmission which can be seen in the late classical and early modern history of *taṣawwuf*, and yet which was also a form very similar to that which existed in the early centuries of Sufism before the establishment of the Sufi orders and even before Abū'l-Qāsim Junayd (d. 295/910). As is well known, before Junayd, Sufism did not have any organized institutional form. Although Junayd created a well-known Sufi circle (*ḥalqa*) around himself, it was not in fact until the fifth/eleventh century, when figures such as Aḥmad Rifā'ī (d. 573/1178) and 'Abd al-Qādir Gīlānī (d. 561/1166) appeared, that the social structure and organization of the Sufi brotherhoods as

---

[11] See R.W.J. Austin, *Sufis of Andalusia: The* Rūḥ al-quds *and* al-Durrat al-fākhirah *of Ibn 'Arabī* (London: Allen & Unwin 1971).

we know them today became crystallized. Hence, it would be anachronistic to ask, for instance, to which Sufi order Junayd belonged; he belonged to none because there were none at the time. In that early classical period of Sufism, initiation into and transmission of Islamic spiritual teachings took place from master to disciple without the existence of an external organizational framework.

Parallel to the foundation and establishment of the major Sufi orders in the sixth/twelfth century and the division of Islamic mysticism into socially approved and distinct *ṭarīqa*s, however, something of the early, 'amorphous' structure of Sufism still persisted among the intellectual elite, carried on in great secrecy. One of the most important recurrent manifestations of this unexplored aspect of Islamic esotericism, not of a popular but of a highly intellectual type, is found in the figures of the mystical philosophers or *ḥakīm*s of the Safavid period among whom Mullā Ṣadrā is our prime example.[12] This, at least, is my understanding of the subject at present on the basis of research into this matter:[13] that all the great philosophical figures of the school of Iṣfahān now known to us had been vouchsafed a certain esoteric spiritual training which is virtually invisible to public scrutiny. While it is extremely hard to find any hard evidence of the esoteric affiliation of any of the figures of this school, yet, "by their fruits ye shall know them" (Matthew VII:20). It is the fruit of the tree, that is, their gnosis, which testifies that they must all have been endowed with an *initiatory* attachment to the currents of Islamic esoterism; that they were affiliated to a type of Islamic spirituality related to Sufism without actually participating in formal Sufi orders with all the political tensions, disputations and quarrels to which most of these orders (Dhahabiyya, Ni'matullāhiyya, etc.) were subjected during the Safavid period.

---

[12] See my "Oral Transmission and the Book in Islamic Education: The Spoken and the Written Word", *Journal of Islamic Studies*, 3/1 (1992), pp. 10–12, where I have developed a similar thesis in respect to the school of Iṣfahān and other mystical philosophers in Islam. It is hoped that, despite the paucity of documents, future students of Sufism will take up this idea and examine it in depth.

[13] Even in the recent history of philosophy in Persia, one finds numerous examples of this phenomenon of very high mystical attainment without any outward affiliation with a Sufi order, for instance, in figures such as (my own teachers) Sayyid Muḥammad Kāẓim 'Aṣṣār and 'Allāmah Ṭabāṭabā'ī (on the latter's biography, see 'Allāmah Ṭabāṭabā'ī, *Shi'ite Islam*, trans. S.H. Nasr; Albany: SUNY Press 1977, pp. 22–6; Hamid Dabashi, *Theology of Discontent: The Ideological Foundation of the Islamic Revolution in Iran*, New York: New York University Press 1993, pp. 273–323). Having been myself intimately acquainted with these teachers, I discovered how they had received initiation and spiritual training from masters of the Tradition who were virtually unknown outside the small circle of their intimate disciples. One such master of the esoteric tradition in contemporary Iran and Iraq, unknown until recently to the larger public, was Sayyid Hāshim Mūsawī Ḥaddād who, although unaffiliated to any Sufi order, was considered among his disciples to be a sun in the spiritual world. His teachings were based on an esoteric transmission which was traced back, exactly like a Sufi order, to the origin of Islam. See 'Allāmah Sayyid Muḥammad Ḥusayn Tihrānī, *Rūḥ-i mujarrad* (Tehran: Ḥikmat Publications 1996).

The first of these figures was Mīr Dāmād (d. 1040/1631–2), the father of the school of Iṣfahān, an author whose writings are extremely hard to fathom; his Arabic prose is convoluted and his Persian even more abstruse than his Arabic. Describing the renowned difficulty of one of his Arabic books – entitled the 'Straight Path' (*Sirāṭ al-mustaqīm*) – it was a popular adage in Persian that jested that "The 'Straight Path' has never been fathomed by a Muslim or apprehended by any infidel," (*Sirāṭ al-mustaqīm-i Mīr Dāmād: musalmān nashavad, kāfir nabīnad*)! It is evident, however, that Mīr Dāmād's resort to arcane terminology was mainly a kind of literary contrivance to disguise the esoteric nature of his teachings. Despite the fact that he was a master of rational philosophical speculation, and even composed the poem which was cited above, attacking what he perceived to be Rūmī's anti-intellectualism, he was also the author of such a remarkable treatise as the *Khalsat al-malakūt* which, composed in Qum, was dedicated to describing his spiritual visions. Indeed, if we did not know the identity of the author of this treatise, one might easily imagine that he was a bona fide Sufi of high spiritual attainment who had realized advanced stations on the mystical Path.

Another important figure in the school was Mīr Dāmād's contemporary, the enigmatic Abū al-Qāsim Findiriskī (d. 1050/1640–1) whose many works include a treatise on alchemy still awaiting publication. He is renowned for his famous poem on divine knowledge beginning with the verse:

> Heaven with these stars is clear, pleasing and beautiful
> Whatever is there above has below it a form ...[14]

Mystical tendencies pervade many of his writings; among these may be mentioned a commentary on the *Yoga Vasiṣṭha*, a treatise comparing Sufi and Hindu metaphysical and cosmological doctrines. Another great figure of the school was Bahā' al-Dīn 'Āmilī (d. 1030/1621) who was much more popular than Mīr Findiriskī, perhaps because he was more 'populist' and less 'elitist' in his approach to Sufism. He composed many *mathnawī* poems such as *Nān wa ḥalwā* modelled on the great *Mathnawī* of Jalāl al-Dīn Rūmī. 'Āmilī's esoteric dimension is revealed not only in his popular *mathnawī*s, but also in his devotion to the metaphysical aspect of mathematics and the hidden sciences. 'Āmilī was not only a Sufi poet, considered by some authorities on the history of Persian literature to be the greatest Persian poet of the eleventh/seventeenth century, but also an authority on the whole Sufi literary tradition in both Arabic and Persian. This is evident in his *al-Kashkūl* (Begging Bowl), which is justly famous in both the Persian and Arab worlds.

---

[14] For a further study of Mīr Findiriskī's thought and a translation of some of the verses of this poem, see my article: "The School of Iṣfahān", in *A History of Muslim Philosophy*, ed. M.M. Sharif, II, pp. 923–4.

Finally, we come to the greatest and central figure of the school of Iṣfahān, Ṣadr al-Dīn Shīrāzī or Mullā Ṣadrā, mentioned above, whose numerous writings are a testimony to his profound knowledge and love of God, and whose life of intense piety, asceticism and purity of devotion admirably complemented his remarkable intellectual prowess.[15] It is nearly impossible to study the works of Mullā Ṣadrā without feeling that one is in the presence of one who actually 'knows' the subject he is discussing rather than simply theorizing about it. He was first and foremost a man of gnosis, and it is significant that many of his students openly expressed their interest in Sufism even more than their master. His student 'Abd al-Razzāq Lāhījī (d. 1072/1661–2), often considered to be the chief advocate of Shī'ite philosophical theology (*kalām*) in the Safavid period, was deeply impregnated with Sufi doctrine. Muḥsin Fayḍ Kāshānī (d. 1091/1680), another student of Mullā Ṣadrā, was a practising Sufi and author of a beautiful *Dīvān* of Sufi poetry.

Qāḍī Sa'īd Qummī (d. 1103/1691–2), a student of theirs, is the last important member of the school of Iṣfahān whom space permits me to mention here. He composed a commentary on the *Kitāb al-tawḥīd* of Shaykh Saduq Ibn Bābūyah (d. 381/992) comprising the incredibly rich work in Arabic *Asrār al-'ibāda* (Mysteries of Divine Worship). This treatise is one of the best treatments of the inner significance of the devotional practices in Islam, very much in the tradition of well-known Sufi treatises on the subject by such masters as Abū Ḥāmid Muḥammad Ghazālī, Ibn 'Arabī, and more recently, Shaykh Aḥmad al-'Alawī.

CONCLUSION

By way of conclusion, I would like to present a few general observations on the contribution of the school of Iṣfahān to Islamic thought. The historical situation of the school of Iṣfahān inaugurating the last phase of the history of Islamic philosophy gives it special significance, which is reflected in the major characteristic of the school mentioned above: namely, the emphasis on the integration and reconciliation of the three paths to knowledge: revelation, unveiling and intellection (*shar'*, *kashf*, *'aql*).

Furthermore, more than any of the other former philosophical schools in Islam, the thinkers of the school of Iṣfahān were very much interested in understanding the doctrines of other religions. Their philosophical interest in religious diversity embraced, first of all, Judaism and Christianity, religions which had been examined by Muslim theologians before them, yet which had

[15] See S.H. Nasr, *The Transcendent Theosophy of Ṣadr al-Dīn Shīrāzī* (Tehran: Institute for Humanities and Cultural Studies 1997; 2nd edn), and the articles on Mullā Ṣadrā by S.H. Nasr and H. Ziai in *History of Islamic Philosophy*, ed. S.H. Nasr and O. Leaman, (London: Routledge 1996), II, pp. 635–62.

seldom been made the subject of inquiry by Islamic philosophers. Several philosophers of the Safavid period composed treatises on the Bible and a few others studied Hebrew with a view to understanding the Torah. Another religion which attracted their interest was Hinduism, so that for the first time in Islamic thought (with the possible exception of the scientist-cum-philosopher Birūnī), one finds Persian-Islamic thinkers composing studies and commentaries on Hindu texts in Persia itself as well as in India, where the school of Iṣfahān had many followers.

Another important aspect of the school of Iṣfahān was the great interest of its members in earlier Islamic philosophical texts, such that numerous commentaries on Ibn Sīnā, Suhrawardī, Ṭūsī, etc. were composed by the Safavid sages. Parallel to their absorption in early Islamic texts, an attempt was made by the Safavid philosophers, for the first time in the history of Islam, to synthesize and summarize the entire history of Muslim philosophy down to their own day. One of the best examples of this synoptic tendency is found in the *Maḥbūb al-qulūb* of Quṭb al-Dīn Ashkiwarī (*fl.* eleventh/seventeenth century), a history of philosophy from Adam to Mīr Dāmād which attempts to trace the origin of *ḥikmat*, not only back to the origin of Islam or the beginnings of Greek philosophy, but back to the very origin of humanity itself. Henry Corbin in his eloquent and beautiful French, has designated this tendency as a *speculum historiale* of "divine philosophy."[16]

During the same period there occurred a resuscitation of the Ishrāqī doctrines of Shihāb al-Dīn Yaḥyā Suhrawardī (d. 587/1191). This renewal of interest in the school of Illumination was quite widespread, and is particularly reflected in texts such as the *Anwāriyya* written in India by Muḥammad Sharīf Hirāwī, who carried out a comparative study between Ishrāqī doctrines and the Advaita Vedanta.[17] This current also affected developments in Zoroastrian religious thought as well.

In summary, the remarkable intellectual activity of the school of Iṣfahān, which only a generation ago remained virtually unknown in the West, has dominated the entire philosophical and intellectual life of Islam in its eastern lands during the past four centuries and down to the present day. Although in the Arab world beyond the borders of Iraq the intellectual activity of the Safavid thinkers has not been very influential, there is much interest in the works of both Mīr Dāmād and Mullā Ṣadrā in present-day Egypt (an interest which the lack of political relations between Iran and Egypt has unfortunately done much to stifle). As for India and Turkey, it is nearly impossible to study the development of Islamic philosophy in those lands in recent centuries

---

[16] Corbin, *En Islam iranien*, IV, p. 28. On the Safavid philosophers/theologians see also Corbin, *La Philosophie iranienne islamique aux XVII et XVIII siècles* (Paris: Buchet/Chastel 1981).

[17] See his *Anwāriyya*, ed. H. Ziai (Tehran: Amīr Kabīr 1358 A.Hsh./1979).

without taking into account the role of the school of Iṣfahān, although its role is much more manifest in the Indian world than in the Ottoman empire.

That is not to say, however, as some wrongly assert, that after Mullā Ṣadrā all philosophy in Persia was converted to his doctrines. There were, in fact, other currents of thought which were defended quite vigorously by those who opposed his teachings. The school of Iṣfahān consists, in fact, of several strands of thought and not only the school of Mullā Ṣadrā. As for this latter school, whereas in India it was the main influence in Islamic philosophical currents from the end of the seventeenth century,[18] in Persia itself it was only from the Qājār period onwards, when Sufism experienced a revival in that land, that the school of Mullā Ṣadrā once again became central. In summary, since the school of Iṣfahān has dominated much of the intellectual, philosophical and mystical life of Persia during the last four hundred years and is of great importance for the intellectual history of Islam in India, it is eminently appropriate that this last of three major volumes devoted to the entire history of Persian Sufism should begin with this brief account of the school of Iṣfahān which constituted the heart of the intellectual life of the Safavid and Mughal periods.[19]

---

[18] It is a singular lacuna in Islamic scholarship today that there exists no thorough history of Muslim philosophy in India in any European language.

[19] For further discussion of this issue, see S.H. Nasr, "Spiritual Movements, Philosophy and Theology in the Safavid Period", *The Cambridge History of Iran* (Cambridge: Cambridge University Press, 1968), V, pp. 656–97.

II

PERSIANATE SUFISM IN HISTORICAL PERSPECTIVE

هو العزیز

رفتم به در صومعهٔ عابد و زاهد

دیدم همه را پیش رخت راکع و ساجد

در میکده رهبانم و در صومعه عابد

گه معتکف دیرم و گه ساکن مسجد

یعنی که ترا می طلبم خانه به خانه

I visited the hermitage of pietists and priests;
I witnessed they all knelt in awe and reverence
Before her visage there. Since in the winecell of the monk
And in the chapel of the pietist I was
At home, it's there I dwell. At times I make residence
The mosque, at times the cell: which is to say, it's you
I seek in every place, both in the tavern and the church.

Rethinking Safavid Shīʿism

DAVID MORGAN

The religious history of the Safavid dynasty and of Persia during its rise to power and rule is punctuated by a series of curious paradoxes or contradictions. The Safavids began, in the time of Shaykh Ṣafī al-Dīn Ardabīlī, as a Sufi fraternity of impeccably Sunni credentials. In the course of the fifteenth century that fraternity moved far away from its foundations, going beyond any respectable form of Shīʿism to a complex of beliefs to which the term *ghuluww* can certainly be attached, and in which the head of the fraternity came to be regarded, and perhaps regarded himself, as in some sense divine. When that quasi-divine leader became shāh of Persia at the beginning of the sixteenth century, however, he declared a highly reputable form of Shīʿism, the Twelver variety, to be the official – indeed, the compulsory – form of Islam for his empire. And from that time on, in varying degrees at different times, the regime's attitude towards Sufis, those from whom it had itself emerged, became basically hostile. Sufi orders were persecuted and suppressed. Can any sense be made of these extraordinary shifts across the religious spectrum?

I venture into these choppy waters with a good deal of hesitation. I am not a historian of religion, let alone of Sufism. I am not even, primarily, a historian of the Safavids, though I have written four chapters about them in a general history of medieval Persia.[1] What follows, then, is not the result of any kind of original research. It is simply a series of reflections, based on the work of others, plus a little speculative thought on my own part about the problems.

There can be no doubt that the Safavid order, like most Sufi orders, was Sunni in origin. As is well known (a phrase beloved of historians who are about to refer to some particularly obscure fact), Ibn Bazzāz's biography of Shaykh Ṣafī al-Dīn Ardabīlī, the *Ṣafwat al-ṣafā'*, written during the time of Ṣafī al-Dīn's successor Ṣadr al-Dīn, made it absolutely – and from a later point of view inconveniently – clear that the order's founder was neither Shīʿī nor made any claim to descent from the Imāms. Hence the reign of Shāh Ṭahmāsp saw the revision of the text, so that Ṣafī al-Dīn could be shown to have

[1] *Medieval Persia 1040–1797* (London: Longman 1988).

professed more suitable opinions. That much is clear enough. What is by no means so clear, even now, is the point at which the Safavid order did in fact become Shīʻī. Evidently the order remained conventional enough for many years, steadily accumulating property and influence in Azerbaijan. No doubt the great change came with Junayd, but whether that can justly be called a great change in the religious orientation of the Safavid order as such is not so obvious, since the actual head of the order at Ardabīl in Junayd's day was his uncle and sworn enemy Jaʻfar.

Junayd's long years of itinerant exile in eastern Anatolia and northern Syria from 1447 to 1459 were critical: the Turcoman followers he acquired, the nucleus of the Qizilbāsh, were to be the mainstay of Safavid power from then on. Were the Qizilbāsh Shīʻī? Not, it would seem, in any even remotely mainstream sense. It is generally said that they regarded Junayd, and subsequently Ḥaydar and Ismāʻīl, as divine. No doubt it can be argued that so far as these dignitaries themselves were concerned, if they thought of themselves as divine it was probably in a quite normal Sufi sense – that they felt a personal near-identification with God – rather than that they suffered from the delusion that they *were* God. This would certainly seem to be the most natural interpretation of the poetry of Shāh Ismāʻīl, which is often taken by literal-minded historians to be evidence that the shāh regarded himself as divine, no more and no less. I am not so sure, however, about the Safavids' Turcoman followers from the time of Junayd. I strongly suspect that they were in fact simple-minded and literal in their belief in their truly divine leader. That this belief, whatever it may precisely have been, was singularly strong is shown by the fact that it does not appear to have been shaken by the deaths of both Junayd and Ḥaydar in battle (a consideration which, incidentally, might make us sceptical of the often-repeated view that Shāh Ismāʻīl's standing in the eyes of the Qizilbāsh was shattered by his defeat at Chāldirān in 1514).

What, then, are we to call the religious stance of the Qizilbāsh followers of the Safavids before 1501, if not Shīʻī? Personally, I tend to resort to the late H.R. Roemer's tempting expedient[2] of calling it 'folk Islam', though that is open to the objection that the term merely describes the problem without solving it. At least we can agree that the Qizilbāsh were not Twelver Shīʻites. What about the leadership of the Safavid order? Again, I am inclined to follow Roemer, who took the view that the first of whom we can say that he was in some fully fledged sense Shīʻī was Ismāʻīl: here the fact that he spent so much of his childhood in Gīlān, in a Shīʻī environment (which is more than can be said of his father and grandfather) is clearly significant. At the very least, Ismāʻīl was exposed to marked Shīʻī influences during his formative years.

---

[2] See his admirable chapters in *The Cambridge History of Iran*, VI: *The Timurid and Safavid Periods*, ed. P. Jackson and L. Lockhart (Cambridge: Cambridge University Press 1986).

Plate 2: A Mounted Qizilbāsh Knight. From Chardin, *Voyages*, Pl. 29.

It is not so easy to say with any certainty, however, precisely what kind of Shī'ī influences these were. As Michael Cook has reminded me, the traditional form of Shī'ism in Gīlān, including Lāhījān, where Ismā'īl stayed, was not Twelver but Zaydī Shī'ism. Zaydism in Gīlān seems, by the beginning of the sixteenth century, to have been somewhat vestigial, and early in the reign of Ismā'īl's successor, Ṭahmāsp, most of the remaining Zaydīs in the Caspian region converted to Twelverism. But the ruler of Lāhījān in the 1490s, when Ismā'īl was there, may well have been a Zaydī. Yet in the welter of conflicting evidence about Ismā'īl's religious views, there is no hint of any inclination towards Zaydism, unless it is felt that Ismā'īl's appropriation of such titles as 'the just, the perfect Imām' is to be explained by the fact that he claimed descent from the Imām Mūsā al-Kāẓim, and was leading an armed rising against illegitimate rulers: hence he might have convinced himself that he had the necessary qualifications for a Zaydī Imām (he could hardly have been a Twelver Imām unless he saw himself as the returning Mahdī). On the other hand, A.H. Morton has pointed out to me that Ismā'īl and his followers were not expected to stay for ever in Lāhījān, and that it is unlikely that they would have been under any great pressure on the part of their hosts to conform to Zaydism. It may be that the significant figure was not the ruler but Ismā'īl's tutor at that time, Shams al-Dīn Lāhījī. It would be convenient to be able to establish what his *madhhab* was in the period before he and Ismā'īl left Gīlān, but there is little to go on, except some fairly unmistakable indications that Lāhījī was not himself much of a scholar, of whatever *madhhab*. The instruction he gave his pupil appears to have been of a very elementary kind. The distinctions between Zaydism and Twelverism were no doubt clear enough to scholars then as they are to scholars today, but there may be some reason to wonder whether they were necessarily so clear to a Gīlānī schoolmaster of the 1490s, which is essentially what Lāhījī was, or to his pupil who, we should bear in mind, was only twelve years old when he left Gīlān for good in 1499. After Ismā'īl seized power in Tabriz, Lāhījī was appointed Ṣadr, head of the at least theoretically Twelver religious institution in the new kingdom. Admittedly, he did not last long in that high office, but it is perhaps unlikely that he would have been appointed to it at all had he been a firmly committed Zaydī.

Does this help to explain what happened when Ismā'īl seized power in Persia at the beginning of the sixteenth century? What then happened is certainly very odd. I do not think we can say with confidence that the Safavid order had any significant background in Twelver Shī'ism in 1501, yet it was this variety of Islam that was declared to be the religion of Persia by the new regime. It is not even the case that the old 'folk Islamic' ways were abandoned after 1501. As A.H. Morton has put it, "the behaviour of Ismā'īl and his court was highly unorthodox in any Islamic terms right up to the end of the reign." As a conspicuous example, he quotes the court's attitude towards alcohol:

"Wine was indulged in among the Qizilbāsh in the reign of Ismāʿīl, not shamefacedly and in private as an illegal vice, but openly and with enthusiasm as part of public rituals."[3]

Why, then, was Twelver Shīʿism enforced on the population at large, if it was not the religion of the elite of the new regime nor, apparently, of the shāh himself? It is worth noting that it *was* enforced, and with great brutality: conversion from Sunnism was not voluntary, and not a few of those who declined to take that step were executed. This was something of a new departure. There had been states ruled by Shīʿīs in the Islamic world before – most notably the Fatimid and Buyid empires. But no attempt had been made by such governments to compel their subjects to change their allegiance from one form of Islam to another, more favoured variety. It is perhaps this curious fact, coupled with doubts, based on the practices which prevailed at the court, of the shāh's own Twelver sincerity, which have impelled many historians to ascribe Persia's involuntary conversion to Shīʿism to reasons of state, if not simply cynical political calculation. The line of argument goes that the advantage of Shīʿism, in the eyes of Shāh Ismāʿīl and his advisers, was not that it was necessarily true, but that it served to differentiate Persia from the Ottoman Empire, to provide the new Safavid state, whose people perhaps lacked a sufficiently nineteenth-century concept of national feeling, with a sense of a distinct and coherent identity: Shīʿism = Persia.[4]

This cynical view of Safavid motivation can be carried further, to help explain another phenomenon: the religious brain drain of Twelver Shīʿī *'ulamā'* to Persia from the Arab world, especially from Jabal ʿĀmil in Lebanon. The story, it will be recalled – a rather late one – is that the dearth of Twelver books and personnel in Persia was so great that Ismāʿīl had no alternative but to import them if he was to provide his country with a new religious establishment, and that many of the Twelver scholars of south Lebanon, chafing under the Sunni Ottoman yoke, were only too pleased to swallow any theoretical reservations they may have had about the legitimacy of royal government so as to enter into a promised land of riches and preferment: if they were worried about Safavid claims to descent from the Imāms, and so forth, they kept quiet about it except sometimes when writing for each other in the obscurity of a learned tongue – Arabic.

Such is an only slightly caricatured summary of what was until recently more or less the accepted orthodoxy. It was neatly encapsulated in an article,[5] "From Jabal ʿĀmil to Persia," which I persuaded the late Albert Hourani, who

---

[3] Michele Membré, *Mission to the Lord Sophy of Persia (1539–1542)*, translated with an introduction and notes by A.H. Morton (London: SOAS Publications 1993), p. xvi.
[4] See e.g. R.M. Savory, *Studies on the History of Ṣafawid Iran* (London: Variorum 1987), p. xii.
[5] *BSOAS*, 49/1 (1986), pp. 133–40.

knew a thing or two about Lebanon, to contribute to a Festschrift for Professor A.K.S. Lambton, published in 1986. Now the whole issue is the subject of scholarly debate again, with Dr Andrew Newman arguing that the clerical migration is largely a myth,[6] and others not convinced of this. I do not have the impression that any new consensus has yet emerged, though for myself I find Newman's arguments persuasive. But from the point of view of supporting the theory of Shāh Ismā'īl as a political opportunist, the function of the clerical migration, if it occurred, would presumably be to show that he wanted to build up a new establishment that had no local loyalties in Persia and which could therefore be relied on by the regime. To quote a parallel case, such was Marco Polo's explanation of the fact that Qubilai Qa'an used foreigners, not Chinese bureaucrats, in the highest offices of the Mongol government of China in the second half of the thirteenth century.[7]

In neither case is this an obviously nonsensical argument: indeed, in the Mongol instance my own view is that it is likely to be right. So far as the Safavid case is concerned, it works, perhaps, so long as we accept the premise: that is to say a less than flattering estimation of Shāh Ismā'īl's motivation. It is tempting to do so, and to take a fairly dim view of Ismā'īl and the system he established. I quote, for example, the opening sentence of section II of my co-editor (Dr Lewisohn's) essay, where he comments: "The Safavid theocracy [and] 'totalitarian state' as Roger Savory termed it, was based on a politicalization of the Sufi master–disciple relationship, focusing upon an idolatrous cult of personality built around the ruler as both 'perfect master' (*murshid-i kāmil*) and absolute monarch." Well, there is no doubting where Dr Lewisohn stands on the Safavids, and it is refreshing to find his view expressed without all the qualifications and tortuous avoidances of value judgements that historians often feel themselves obliged to go in for. And I have to say that I doubt, myself, that most of the Safavid rulers were especially nice people: few of Persia's rulers were. Even Karīm Khān Zand, to judge from Professor John Perry's excellent study,[8] seems to have been dangerous to be near at times. No more do I much favour attempts to show that the Mongols, with whom I spend most of my research time, have been grievously misjudged. On the other hand, I greatly doubt that the Safavid state can be termed 'totalitarian' in anything like the modern sense: indeed, I do not think that such a totalitarianism was even possible at the time, or until much later. We seem to owe this conception of the Safavid state largely to the fact that Professor Roger Savory, at a

---

[6] A. Newman, "The Myth of the Clerical Migration to Safavid Iran", *Die Welt des Islams*, 33 (1993), pp. 66–112.

[7] A. Ricci (trans), *The Travels of Marco Polo* (London: George Routledge & Sons 1931), p. 127.

[8] J.R. Perry, *Karim Khan Zand: A History of Iran, 1747–1779* (Chicago–London: Chicago University Press, 1979).

formative stage in his career, came under the strong influence of that undeniably great scholar Vladimir Minorsky.[9] It is perhaps understandable that Minorsky, in the light, if such it was, of his personal experience, should have yielded to the temptation to draw dubious historical parallels with the Bolsheviks; but that is no excuse for anyone else.

When it comes to believing that Shāh Ismāʿīl enforced Shīʿism because he wanted simply to differentiate his realm from that of his principal political enemy, and that he imported Shīʿī *ʿulamāʾ* because he was unable to trust the Persians, not primarily because they professed a particular faith, I wonder if we are not in some danger of thinking anachronistically. Yes, if I had taken over Persia at the beginning of the sixteenth century, had seen that my regime was insecurely based and that it faced potentially fatal opposition at the hands of two Sunni powers, the Ottomans and the Uzbeks, I might well have acted as Ismāʿīl did, from the motives we attribute to him. But did people at that time think and act like that? Did they draw such distinctions in their minds? I rather doubt it. This is not to say that I necessarily have a better explanation. If Ismāʿīl had shown himself to be a devoted Twelver (which, as we have seen, he did not), it would have been possible to argue, unfashionably but plausibly, that he enforced Twelver Shīʿism for the simple reason that he had the power to do so, and that he believed it to be true. It is hazardous, in my view, to assume that in default of hard facts we can look behind the apparent motives and beliefs of men long dead and decide, on the basis of purely circumstantial evidence, what they must *really* have been. However, I shall not allow that to deter me from doing something very similar myself.

One way out of this impasse does occur to me. It is wholly speculative, but I offer it nevertheless. Let us assume, for the sake of argument, that – perhaps as a result of his upbringing in Gīlān – Ismāʿīl *was* in fact a fully converted and convinced – if superficial and distinctly ill-informed – Twelver, and that this is why he established that form of Shīʿism as the state religion of Persia. How do we explain his tolerance of and participation in the very dubiously Islamic practices of the Qizilbāsh throughout his reign? There is a possible answer which I propose to put forward: so far as I am aware this has not been suggested before, at any rate in print. But some years ago a graduate student of mine, Adam Jacobs, very interestingly proposed in an essay that the key might be none other than our old friend *taqiyya*, 'tactical dissimulation' as it is sometimes translated. I thought at the time, and I still think, that this idea is worth exploring. Consider: Ismāʿīl had been brought to power on the spears of Qizilbāsh warriors who held him to be something like divine. Without their support, he was nothing, and the regime could not hope to survive. What would have been their attitude had their *murshid* declared that their beliefs

---

[9] R.M. Savory, "Some Reflections on Totalitarian Tendencies in the Ṣafavid State," *Der Islam*, 53 (1976), pp. 226–41.

were un-Islamic nonsense, that their cherished rituals must cease forthwith, that he himself was no more divine than they were, and that they must become good and practising Twelvers immediately, on pain of death? There can surely be little doubt about the answer: it would have been nasty, brutish and short. Now, according to the doctrine of *taqiyya*, a good Twelver is permitted, even obliged, to conceal his true beliefs if to do otherwise involves him in serious danger. What danger could be more serious than the total collapse of the new regime, and the certain death of its founder at the hands of his disillusioned ex-disciples? What could have been more disastrous for the Twelver cause? Well, this is at least a possible scenario: for the historian, of course, the frustrating feature of *taqiyya* is that insofar as it has been practised successfully, its practice has tended to elude us.

If this way of looking at things is extended into the reign of Shāh Ṭahmāsp, Ismāʿīl's successor, it is again potentially helpful. Morton's work on the account of the Venetian envoy Membré has shown that old-style Qizilbāsh practices were very far from extinct at Ṭahmāsp's court – for example, ritual beatings with a stick, the *chūb-i ṭarīq*.[10] But the second Safavid Shāh seems to have been unhappy with such behaviour, especially after about 1533–4, when, according to his own account, inspired by dreams, he repented of sinful practices – and required everyone else to do likewise: the drinking of alcohol, the use of other stimulants, and various forms of sexual immorality were banned, and the ban enforced, where necessary, with executions. Morton believes that Ṭahmāsp's later transfer of the capital from Tabrīz to Qazvīn was more than a strategically determined move away from the Ottoman frontier: "Like the episode of the repentance from sin, the withdrawal to Qazvin was a move away from early Qizilbāsh practice."[11] What we see in the decades after the death of Ismāʿīl, then, is a gradual – by no means a hurried – abandonment of aspects of the Qizilbāsh way of doing things and, of course, an equally gradual reduction of the regime's dependence on Qizilbāsh military support. It was Ṭahmāsp who began the process, more conspicuously associated with Shāh ʿAbbās I, of incorporating non-Qizilbāsh *ghulāms* into the Safavid armed forces. And during the time of Shāh ʿAbbās and after, the process of reducing the influence both of the Safavid order and the Qizilbāsh tribesmen in the state went much further.

If we look at the other great Safavid paradox – that a regime which rose to power as a Sufi order proceeded, almost immediately, to persecute and suppress other Sufi orders – this again fits in well enough with my suggested scenario. If Shāh Ismāʿīl was a convert to Twelver Shīʿism who was obliged,

---

[10] A.H. Morton, "The *chūb-i ṭarīq* and *Qizilbāsh* Ritual in Safavid Persia", in *Etudes Safavides*, ed. J. Calmard (Paris–Tehran: Institut Français de Recherche en Iran 1993) pp. 225–45.

[11] Membré, *Mission to the Lord Sophy of Persia*, p. xxiv.

because of his military dependence on his Qizilbāsh disciples, to pretend otherwise when in their company, no such indulgence need have been extended to other Sufi groups to whom the Safavids owed no obligation. Towards them their attitude could well have been the deeply suspicious one characteristic of the Twelver *'ulamā'*. There was no need to tolerate such people. And tolerated they were not. Again, intolerance reached its height at a later stage of the dynasty, when the part played by the Safavid Order had been reduced to almost nothing and the ascendancy of *'ulamā'* like Muḥammad Bāqir Majlisī over the shāh had reached previously unprecedented heights.

Such, then, is the hypothesis I offer. I suggest that from the time of Shāh Ismā'īl I – not before – the Safavids, for all that they may still have been *murshids* of the Ṣafavī order, were in fact perfectly genuine, though perhaps somewhat idiosyncratic, converts to the faith which they enforced on the people of their empire: Twelver Shi'ism. But because of their dependence on Qizilbāsh tribesmen who were very far indeed from being Twelvers, they were obliged for a time, for fear of precipitating the regime's collapse, to practise a degree of *taqiyya*: they could not simply abandon their Sufi and *ghulāt* heritage, whatever their personal preference might have been. I concede, of course, that I have no evidence to support this hypothesis: but in the nature of the case, there would be no evidence. This is one of those instances in which, as the saying goes, absence of evidence is not necessarily evidence of absence. Adam Jacobs and I may be right, we may be wrong. If we are right, some puzzling phenomena become rather more explicable. And, I suggest, it will be extraordinarily difficult to prove that we are wrong.

Western Encounters with Persian Sufi Literature

FARHANG JAHANPOUR

I. INTRODUCTION: CHRISTIANITY, PERSIA AND ORIENTALISM

Contrary to Kipling's well-known adage that "East is East, and West is West, and never the twain shall meet," the history of civilization has proved to be a continuous meeting of East and West in all aspects of life. In the Middle East, most of these early contacts were connected with religion and spirituality. Starting from the earliest phases of Judaism there was a great deal of physical and spiritual contact between the Hebrews and the Persians, to which the many references to Iran, Iranian history and Iranian kings in the Bible bear ample witness. Fourteen books of the Old Testament either directly deal with an event that happened in Persia, or contain references to Persia.[1]

While the close connection between Christianity and Persia is generally acknowledged – the story of the three Persian Magi visiting the new-born Jesus is well known – it is not, however, generally realized that Persia also played a leading role in the spread of early Christianity. Many Christian churches were established in Persia when the Christians were still savagely persecuted by the Roman Empire. The persecution of Christians in Iran started only after Christianity was adopted as the official religion of the Roman Empire, which was at war with Persia. According to historical documents, Christianity spread to Persia towards the end of the first century AD, and Persian Christianity had organized churches and bishops.[2] Persian missionaries were the first to take Christianity to India and China. For instance, in AD 635

---

[1] See Shaul Shaked, "Two Judeo-Iranian Contributions, 1: Iranian Function in the Book of Esther," in *Irano-Judaica: Studies Relating to Jewish Contacts with Persian Culture Throughout the Ages*, ed. Shaul Shaked (Jerusalem: Ben Zvi Institute for the Study of Jewish Communities in the East 1982), pp. 292–303; cited by Hāyida Sahīm, "Khāṭirāt-i Yahūdiyān-i Īrān," *Iran Nameh*, 15/1 (Winter 1997), p. 52.

[2] *The Chronicle of Arbil* written by Mashiha Zakha early in the sixth century, provides the biographies of twenty leading bishops of the Christian church in Persia, the first of whom lived in AD 99. An Iranian bishop called Yuhanna or John represented the Persian church in the first Council of Nicaea, held in 325. From the letters written by the Christian patriarch in Persia, a man called Ishuyab, to various Christian churches in AD 650 and 651, we learn that

the Persian church sent a team of missionaries led by an Iranian monk called A-lo-pen to the Chinese capital Ch'ang-an. The names of two other Iranian missionaries, Mihrdād and Gushansāb, are given in an inscription inscribed in Hsi-an in AD 781.

Studying the early encounter between Persia and the West, we find that according to legend the first Persian to visit the British Isles was a certain bishop of the Nestorian Church named Ivon. In the sixth century, when the Nestorians were sending missionaries to India and China, Ivon is supposed to have gone in the opposite direction, to England, and to have resided there until his death. When a ploughman in the county of Huntingdon turned up his bones in the year 1001, the bishop straightaway became a saint and gave his name to the church of St Ives built on the spot.[3]

The Persians and the Persian language also played a major role in the propagation and the spread of Islam in the subcontinent, Central Asia and even as far as China and the Far East.[4] The Persian language became the second most important Islamic language and the lingua franca of Eastern Islam.[5] At its height, Perso-Islamic culture stretched from the Aegean in the west to Sinkiang and the Bay of Bengal in the east, and from the Russian steppes in the north to the Indian Ocean in the south.

Looking at the mystical dimension of Islam in Persia – the subject of this essay – we find that from the earliest days of the establishment of Islam in Iran, Sufism has been an integral part of Iranian Islam, and consequently Sufi literature and various Sufi orders have played a leading role in the spread of Islam in the subcontinent and Central Asia, as well as in the Ottoman Empire. It is interesting that today, with the collapse of communism in the post-Soviet era, it is the mystical form of Islam that is regaining popularity in many of the new Central Asian republics, as well as among the Muslims in the Russian Federation. The resurgence of Sufi orders can even be observed in Kazan, the capital of Tatarstan, which was conquered by Ivan the Terrible in the sixteenth century. The strange onion-domed Orthodox cathedrals opposite the Kremlin in Moscow's Red Square were actually built to celebrate the victory of

---

the Christian church in Persia had a patriarch, two archbishops and at least thirty-eight bishops at the time of the Arab invasion. For further information about the history of early Christian churches in Iran, see Bishop H.B. Dehqani-Tafti, *Christ and Christianity among the Iranians* [Persian title: *Masīḥ va masīḥiyyat nazd-i Īrāniyān]*, (London: Sohrab Books 1992), I, pp. 13–28.

[3] John D. Yohannan, *Persian Poetry in England and America: A 200-Year History* (New York: Caravan Books 1977), p. x.

[4] See R. Canfield (ed.) *Turko-Persia in Historical Perspective* (Cambridge: Cambridge University Press 1991).

[5] E. Yarshater, "Persian Poetry in the Timurid and Safavid Periods," in *The Cambridge History of Iran*, VI, ed. P. Jackson and L. Lockhart (Cambridge: Cambridge University Press 1986), pp. 965–94.

Christian forces over Islam in Kazan. Kazan was thoroughly Christianized and many Tatars were expelled or brutally integrated in the Russian empire. Yet, after four hundred years, Sufism is today expanding into the religious vacuum that communism left behind and Sufi orders, both the Qādiriyya and Naqshbandiyya *ṭarīqa*s, are flourishing and have considerable followings.[6]

* * *

In examining the effect of Persian Sufi literature on the West, there are several issues to be considered. First, there is the matter of important early accounts of Sufism by Western travellers who visited Iran during the Safavid and Qājār periods and the subsequent translations of Sufi texts into Western languages. Second, there is the interest shown by Western writers and poets in these works with the ensuing literary influences such translations had upon them. Lastly, there is the role played by Sufism as a bridge between Islam and Christianity: its tolerance and idealism, which often softened the initially hostile reaction of many Western thinkers and scholars towards exoteric Islam's stern legalism, while also making Muslims more open towards Christianity. In this respect, there are several interesting matters that might also be addressed – the effect of Sufi metaphysics on later Western scholastic philosophy, for instance – but as space is limited, in the present essay I shall merely attempt to review the above three themes, focusing chronologically on how Western perceptions of Persian and Indian Sufism developed during the Safavid period, and finally examining the impact of Persian Sufi mysticism on nineteenth-century English and American Romanticism.

In the West, orientalism is considered to have commenced its formal existence with the decision of the Church Council of Vienna in 1312 to establish a series of chairs in Arabic, Greek, Hebrew, and Syriac at Paris, Oxford, Bologna, Avignon, and Salamanca.[7] The suggestion was Raymond Lull's, who advocated learning Arabic as the best means for the conversion of the Arabs. Although chairs in oriental languages had been founded at the universities of Paris, Louvain, and Salamanca by the year 1311, all of them suffered from the lack of teachers and reliable source material. Nevertheless, the decision of the Church Council of Vienna showed both the beginning of an interest in the East and the desire to engage in missionary work among the Muslims.

In England, the serious study of the East did not start until the beginning of the seventeenth century. In 1632 the Sir Thomas Adams Chair of Arabic was

---

[6] See Anthony Hyman, "Letter from Kazan," *Middle East International*, 16 May 1997, p. 24.
[7] R.W. Southern, *Western Views of Islam in the Middle Ages* (Cambridge, Mass: Harvard University Press, 1962); quoted by Edward W. Said, *Orientalism* (first published by Routledge & Kegan Paul, Harmondsworth, 1978; repr: Penguin Books 1995), pp. 49–50. Also see Francis Dvornik, *The Ecumenical Councils* (New York: Hawthorn Books 1961), pp. 65–6.

established at Cambridge, and four years later, Archbishop Laud established a similar chair at Oxford. It is interesting that most of the famous holders of the Thomas Adams Chair of Arabic would turn out to be Persian experts who devoted most of their time to Persian studies: from E.G. Browne, the greatest Western scholar of Persian literature, who was also very interested in a number of religious and mystical movements, R.A. Nicholson, the great translator and interpreter of Rūmī and Persian Sufism and, Professor Storey with his erudite *Bio-Bibliographical Survey of Persian Literature*,[8] down to A.J. Arberry with his numerous works on and translations of Sufi texts by 'Aṭṭār, Rūmī, Ḥāfiẓ, 'Umar Khayyām and others.

The same story is true to some extent of Oxford University. One of the most distinguished early English orientalists was Thomas Hyde (1636–1703) of Oxford, who became Professor of Arabic and Librarian of the Bodleian Library. Although Professor of Arabic, one of his main interests was in the ancient Persian religion of Zoroaster. Around 1690 he translated into Latin, for almost the first time in Western history, some ghazals of Ḥāfiẓ (his translation was only preceded by that of Pietro della Valle whose *Viaggi* – published in Venice in 1650 – contained the first European account of Ḥāfiẓ's poetry, featuring a translation of one of his ghazals[9]). Hyde is also to be credited with the first translation of a *rubā'ī* by 'Umar Khayyām and incidentally, the first reference in Western literature to Khayyām himself, in the form of a quatrain attributed to 'Umar's ghost, who recited it in a dream to his mother, recorded by Hyde in the year 1700 in his *History of the Religion of the Ancient Persians, Parthians and Medes*.

II. THE ENCOUNTER WITH SUFISM BY WESTERN TRAVELLERS TO SAFAVID PERSIA

As a result of greater commercial and political contacts between the West and the Safavid and Mughal governments during the sixteenth and seventeenth centuries,[10] the interest of Europeans in Perso-Islamic literature and Sufi mysticism, present both in Persia and at the court of the Mughal emperors, was aroused. The works of travellers, merchants and diplomats such as Anthony Jenkinson (1562), Thomas Alcock (1564), Richard Cheney (1564), John Newbury (1580) and Ralph Fitch (1583–91), the three English brothers Sir Thomas, Sir Anthony and Robert Sherley (who stayed in Persia for a long time and even acted as Iran's ambassadors to various European courts), Thomas

---

[8] (London: Luzac & Co. 1953; repr. 1972). This survey was incomplete on Storey's death but has since been continued by François de Blois (London: Royal Asiatic Society 1992–).

[9] See Robert Rehder, "Review Article: Persian Poets and Modern Critics," *Edebiyat*, 1/1 (1977), p. 93.

[10] See Laurence Lockhart, "European Contacts with Persia, 1350–1736," in Jackson and Lockhart, *The Cambridge History of Iran*, VI, pp. 373–409.

Plate 3: Safavid State Reception of an Ambassador from Holland. From Chardin, *Voyages*, Pl. 32.

Herbert (1627–29), Jean Chardin and J.B. Tavernier from France, opened the gates of the Orient to the West and introduced Western readers to the mysteries of the East, including Persian literature and Sufism.

The Safavid dynasty had originally started out as Sufi order, but after consolidating its grip on political power, it gradually turned against Sufism and started persecuting the Sufis. It is thus somewhat ironic that Shāh ʻAbbās I ('the Great', *reg.* 1588–1629) was himself known in the West as the Great Sophy (= Sufi) as Shakespeare's two references in *Twelfth Night* indicate (II. v. 181, III. iv. 280). The serious persecution of the Sufis started during the latter part of the Safavid dynasty, as the power of the *'ulamā'* grew. By the reign of Shāh Sulṭān Ḥusayn (1694–1722), most Shīʻite clerics were hostile to Sufism, and the government, under the influence of the Mullābāshī Muḥammad Bāqir Majlisī II, began to persecute both Sufi-minded Shīʻites non-Shīʻite religious groups, effecting the forcible conversion of the Zoroastrians and the Jews.[11] As S.H. Nasr has put it: "The dynasty that had begun as the extension of a Sufi order ended by opposing all Sufism and gnosis itself."[12]

Knowledge of Sufism came to the West from various sources, both through the works of Persians writing about their country and their religion for Western audiences and from Western travellers and scholars who learned what they could about Islam and Sufism. One book that achieved a great deal of fame and exerted some influence on the works of Western writers writing about Iranian Islam was *Relaciones.*[13] In 1604, one year before the first edition of the first volume of Don Quixote was printed, the *Relaciones* of Don Juan of Persia was published at Valladolid. The author, whose real name was Ulugh Bey (or Uruch Beg), was a Persian Muslim who had converted to Spanish Roman Catholicism. He had left Iran in the year 1599, being one of the four secretaries to the Persian ambassador sent by Shāh ʻAbbās to the princes of Europe under the guidance of Sir Anthony Sherley.

During the years 1602 and 1603 in Spain, and after he had become an ardent Roman Catholic, Don Juan of Persia, as he was now called, compiled his *Relaciones.* In this book the author speaks in detail about social and political events under the Safavids, Persian laws and customs, as well as providing a good deal of information about Islam and Sufism. Speaking about Sufism, for instance, he correctly points out that the term *ṣūfī* is derived from the word *ṣūf* (wool), but that the terms 'Sufi' and 'Safavid' are etymologically unrelated. However, he stresses the Sufi origin of the Safavids and, on more

[11] Roger Savory, *Iran Under the Safavids* (Cambridge: Cambridge University Press 1980), p. 251.

[12] S.H. Nasr, "The School of Iṣfahān," in *A History of Muslim Philosophy*, ed. M.M. Sharif (Wiesbaden: Harrassowitz 1966), II, p. 931.

[13] For an English translation of the book see *Don Juan of Persia: A Shi'ah Catholic 1560–1604*, translated and edited with an introduction by G. Le Strange, ed. Sir Denison Ross and Eileen Power (The Broadway Travellers Series; London: George Routledge & Sons 1926).

than one occasion, states very emphatically that Shāh Ismā'īl I (1501–24), whom he calls the Grand Sophy, was indeed a great Sufi and dervish.

Although most of the early European travellers to Iran were interested mainly in trade and politics and did not show much interest in literary and religious issues, one of the earliest British travellers to show some interest in the cultural side of Persian life was Thomas Herbert. The youthful Herbert embarked for Persia in 1627, as a secretary in the suite of the British ambassador, Sir Dodmore Cotton. He kept careful notes of his travels in Persia between 1627 and 1629, and these provided the basis for the appearance in 1634, four years after his return to London, of a folio volume of about 250 pages, entitled *Travels in Persia: 1627–29.*[14] Herbert was a keen observer of Persian life and his book provides a great deal of information about contemporary life in Iran. Of Persians, he had a high opinion, writing: "The Persian has this character of old, *cunctorum hominum sunt mitissimi*, of all men the most civil; which disposition they reserve unto this day, being generally of a very gentle and obliging nature . . ."[15]

Although Herbert refers to the Persians' love of poetry, he seems to have gained little knowledge of Persian poetry, confusing the names of some poets with philosophers and mystics, both Iranian and Arab. He writes:

> Above all, poetry lulls them, that genius seeming properly to delight itself amongst them. Howbeit, mimographers I must call them, their common ballads resounding out the merry disports of Mars and his mistress to which saints they dedicate their amorous devotion – Abul-Casen, who lived AH 385, Elgazzuly, Ibnul-Farid, and Elfargani are their principal poets in those fancies. Nor have I read amongst the Romans, or in any other parts, poetry has been better rewarded.[16]

Elsewhere, Herbert also refers to the two greatest poets of Persia, Ḥāfiẓ and Sa'dī (although with strange spellings), and mentions the Latin translation of the *Gulistān*. Describing his visit to the city of Shīrāz, he writes: "A little out of the town is interred that learned poet and philosopher Musladini Saddi who wrote Rosarium which is lately turned into Latin by Gentius;[17] and near him his brother-poet Hodgee Haier, whose poems are of great esteem in Persia."[18]

J.B. Tavernier's *Travels through Turkey, Persia and the East Indies*[19] was also a mine of information about the East. Unlike many earlier travellers, Tavernier paid a great deal of attention to religious and social issues in the countries that he visited. One short chapter of his book is entitled "Of the

[14] Thomas Herbert, *Travels in Persia: 1627–29,* abridged and edited by Sir William Foster, with an Introduction and Notes (The Broadway Travellers Series London: George Routledge & Sons 1928).
[15] *Ibid.,* p. 247.
[16] *Ibid.*
[17] Georgius Gentius published a Latin translation of Sa'dī's *Gulistān* in 1651.
[18] Herbert, *Travels in Persia*, p. 72.
[19] J.B. Tavernier, *Travels through Turkey, Persia and the East Indies* (London: n.p. 1684).

Faquirs, or poor Mahometan Volunteers in the East Indies." He estimated that there were more than 800 000 Muslim "Faquirs," as opposed to twelve hundred thousand "Idolaters" in India. Although he did not have a high opinion of the Faquirs, calling them "Vagabonds, and lazy Drones, that dazzle the eyes of the people with a false zeal, and make them believe that whatever comes out of their mouths is an Oracle," nevertheless, he described different types of the Faquirs, their garments, their way of life and their beliefs.

Dr John Fryer, a graduate of Cambridge University and Fellow of the Royal Society, was another important English traveller to visit Iran during the Safavid period. He left four volumes of his fascinating – albeit condescending, often chauvinistic and biased – account of travels in Iran during the years 1677–8 to posterity. As a professed rationalist and follower of Descartes, Fryer cast a highly critical gaze on the alien society in which he found himself. He seldom had anything good to say about Islam, Persian society, religious customs, philosophy or practices. In his brief account of "the *dervises* professing Poverty" in Iran, he describes them as "vagrants" and "beggars" who lived in constant danger, and painted a forlorn picture of the condition to which the Sufis in late Safavid Iran had been reduced:

> They ramble up and down . . .being without Beasts of Burthen, without Wallets full of Provisions, which the others seize by force, without Attendance, without other Ensigns or Weapons more than a Staff and Horn; travelling without Company, or indeed any Safe-pass; and if they fix up their Standard, it is among the tombs; none giving them harbour, or encouraging this sort of Madness, as well for the natural Antipathy to Beggery; as for that, under this Cloak many Intrigues and ill Designs have been carried on.[20]

His depiction of the Sufis in East India is even less flattering:

> A *Fakier* is a Holy Man among the Moors; for all who Profess that strictness (for such it should be) they esteem sacred; and though before apparent Traytors, yet declaring for this kind of life, and wearing a patch'd Coat of a Saffron Colour, with a pretended careless neglect of the World, and no certain Residence, they have Immunity from all Apprehensions, and will dare the Mogul himself to his Face: Of this Order are many the most Dissolute, Licentious, and Prophane Persoans in the World, committing Sodomy, will be Drunk with *Bang*, and Curse God and *Mahomet*; depending on the Toleration the *Mogul* indulges them with . . . these People Beg up and down like our *Bedlams* with an Horn and Bowl, so that they enter an House, take what likes them, even the Woman of the House; and when they have laid their mad Pranks, away they go to repeat them elsewhere. Under this Disguise many pass as Spies up and down, and reap the best Intelligence for the benefit of the Prince that employs them.[21]

---

[20] John Fryer, *A New Account of East India and Persia, being Nine Years' Travels 1672–1681*, ed. William Crooke (London: Hakluyt Society 1909–15), III, p. 125.
[21] *Ibid.*, II, pp. 113–14.

The most celebrated Western traveller to Persia, whose voluminous books had a great deal of influence in both France and Britain, was the French jeweller Jean Chardin (1643–1713). His works were acknowledged by Montesquieu, Rousseau, Voltaire, Gibbon and Sir William Jones among others, and his information on Safavid Persia, in the words of John Emerson, "outranks that of all other Western writers in range, depth, accuracy, and judiciousness."[22] Indeed, in view of the scope and general accuracy of Chardin's observations of Safavid Persia, his work may be compared to the seminal work of his fellow countryman Alexis de Tocqueville on the United States *(De la démocratie*, 1835–40), written about a century and a half later.

In 1665 he travelled to Persia and India, and later published an account of that journey, together with the details of the coronation of the new Persian Shāh Sulaymān (*reg*. 1666–94).[23] In 1671 Chardin embarked on a second journey to Persia. After nearly two years of arduous travel through Turkey, the Crimea and the Caucasus, he finally arrived in Iṣfahān. This time his sojourn in Persia lasted four years, after which he returned to France in 1677. Several years later, however, he fled to England to avoid French persecution of the Huguenots. Appointed jeweller to the Crown, he was subsequently knighted by King Charles II.

Chardin became a great scholar of both Persian language as well as the Persian way of life. In fact, he boasts: "In a word I was so solicitous to know Persia, that I know Isfahan better than Paris (though I was Bred and Born there). The Persian language was as easie to me as French, and I could currently Read and Write it."[24] In addition to detailed accounts of court life, business and commerce in Iran, Chardin also wrote a great deal about religious issues. He speaks warmly of the high degree of religious tolerance which existed in Iran:

> The most commendable Property of the Manners of the Persians is their kindness to Strangers; the Reception and Protection they afford them, and their Universal Hospitality, and Toleration, in regard to Religion, except the Clergy of the Country, who, as in all other Places, hate to a furious Degree, all those that differ from their Opinions. The Persians are very civil, and very honest in Matters of Religion; so far that they allow those that have embraced theirs, to recant, and resume their former Opinion; whereof, the Cedre [Sadr], or Priest, give them an Authentick Certificate for Safety sake, in which he calls them by the Name of Apostat, which among them is the highest Affront.[25]

---

[22] John Emerson, "Chardin, Sir John," *Encyclopedia Iranica,* V, p. 373.

[23] *The Travels of Sir John Chardin into Persia and the East Indies, the First Volume, Containing the Author's Voyage from Paris to Ispahan to which is added the Coronation of this Present King of Persia, Solyman the Third* (London: printed for Moses Pitt in Duke Street, Westminster 1686).

[24] Sir John Chardin, *Travels in Persia 1673–1677,* with a preface by N.M. Penzer and an introduction by Sir Percy Sykes, (London: Dover Publications 1927), introduction, p. xv.

[25] *Ibid., p.* 185.

He says that the Persians believe that the prayers of other faiths are as valid as theirs, and that many Muslims even ask the followers of other religions to pray for them, adding: "I have seen it practised a thousand Times. This is not to be imputed to their Religious Principles, tho' it allows all sorts of Worship; but I impute it to the sweet Temper of that Nation, who are naturally averse to Contest and Cruelty."[26] Commenting on the death of Shāh Sulaymān, Chardin writes:

> But those who most laid to heart the mournful death of the deceased King were the Christians. That Prince had always shewed himself kind and favourable to their Religion, shewing them extraordinary Civilities ... insomuch as the *Armenians* would say one among another, that he was more a Christian than a Mahometan. Not but that he was not devoted to his own Religion, even as much as the most zealous of his predecessors; only he thought that the violence of Princes toward the Liberty of men's Consciences was a thing neither acceptable to God, nor conformable to Reason.[27]

In his description of the famous coffee houses or "Cahue Kahne" (*qahva-khāna*) of Iṣfahān, Chardin gives a delightful account of "Repeaters in Verse and Prose, which the Mollas, Derviches, or poets" take their turns to recite poetry and preach sermons to the people. He describes how "A Molla stands up in the Middle, or at one End of the Cahue Kahne, or Coffee-House, and begins to preach with a loud Voice; or else a Dervish comes in all at once, and harangues the whole Company, concerning the Vanity, Riches, and Honours of the World." The author expresses his wonder at the degree of tolerance which exists in these gatherings for both the sermons of the mullās and the preaching and poetry of the dervishes: "In short with Regard to that, there is the greatest Liberty taken in the World; the serious Man dares not say a Merry Thing; each makes his own Harangue and listens to what he likes."[28]

However, it is in chapter 11, "De la Philosophie" of the fourth volume of his celebrated *Voyages,* where Chardin provides a fifteen-page account of Sufis and Sufism – more detailed, in fact, than anything which the Western world had previously known – that the most accurate information about Persian Sufism hitherto recorded by any Western traveller of the period is provided. In view of the importance and novelty of Chardin's remarks on Sufism, and the fact that the greater part of his account of Sufism has not been translated into English, I shall give extensive excerpts of his comments on Sufism below.

Opening his discussion of Islamic philosophy, Chardin more or less accurately delineates the substance of, and differences between, Islamic philosophical theology (*'ilm al-kalām*), sapiential knowledge (*ḥikma*, which he calls "*la science par excellence*"), metaphysics (mistakenly describing Persian

---

[26] *Ibid., p.* 186.
[27] *The Travels of Sir John Chardin into Persia and the East Indies, the First Volume*, *p.* 58.
[28] *Ibid.*, p. 185.

metaphysics as exclusively of the Peripatetic school), and then briefly mentions the contribution of Avicenna and Khwāja Naṣīr al-Dīn Ṭūsī (d. 672/1274) to Islamic Peripetaticism.[29] Although he notes that both the philosophical systems of Democritus or Epicurus are unknown to the Persians, he does compare Sufism to Pythagorean thought:

> This philosophy is taught among the Muḥammadans, and particularly among the Persians, by a cabal of folk especially known by the name of *soufys*. It is an ancient and celebrated sect, but which is nevertheless little known, for those who profess it make their principal tenet not to reveal the essence other than very discretely and in hidden character – and hence they do not disturb either the religion or the philosophy of the country.[30]

The fact that the rest of this chapter on "la Philosophie" concerns *Sufism* and not Peripatetic philosophy probably indicates Chardin's own interest in, and good relations with, the local Sufis of Iṣfahān. Noting that the origin of the word 'Soufy' "est fort contestée," he then provides seven different etymologies of the term in the space of three pages (pp. 450–3). Chardin's considerations are, for his day and age, on the whole etymologically thorough and credible, and his conclusions echo similar discussions of the word in Muslim circles.

1. His first etymology, even if not completely accurate, has the advantage – as unusual among seventeenth- as among nineteenth-century orientalists – of at least recognizing the *Islamic* origin of Sufism. It also closely resembles the discussion of the term given by the earliest Persian Sufi author, Ḥujwīrī.[31] Some "learned doctors," he writes, derive the name from an Arabian tribe from which "the progenitor of this sect originated:" hence *Alsoufa* may mean "the golden race." Alternatively, if spelled *Alsaphan,* it can also mean "the pure race since this tribe had been the most devout and religious of all the others." This "tribe" had the special responsibility for taking care of the Ka'ba at Mecca:

> They have said that they have given this name to the sect of the Soufys because of the resemblance which they [the Sufis] have amongst themselves – which is as much for the austerity of their personal lives and the constancy of their cultic practise, as for their fondness for gnosis and the extraordinary purity which they assume for themselves.[32]

2. The second etymology given by Chardin derives 'Sufi' from the *ahl-i suffa,* "the People of the Veranda," the most intimate companions of the

---

[29] Chardin, *Voyages du Chevalier Chardin, en Perse et Autres Lieux de l-Orient*, ed. L. Langlès, 10 vols (Paris: Le Normant 1811), IV, pp. 445–7.

[30] *Ibid., p.* 449. Some pages later (p. 454), he again points out that the esoteric nature of Sufism, characterizing Sufis as "une cabale où est difficilement initié, et où le secret est le premier et les plus important précepte."

[31] 'Alī al-Hujwīrī, *The* Kashf al-maḥjūb: *The Oldest Persian Treatise on Sufism.* trans. R.A. Nicholson (Gibb Memorial Series, no. 17; London: Luzac & Co. 1911, rpr. 1976), p. 34.

[32] Chardin, *Voyages,* IV., p. 450.

Prophet who gathered at his mosque in Medina who, "in order to secretly serve certain devotees, had abandoned their own houses and their welfare in order to follow him [the Prophet], and who had secluded themselves there in order to better study the new religion."[33] This etymology is also defended by a number of traditional Muslim authorities.[34]

3. In his third etymology, Chardin derives *Soufy* from *Sou* "which is the name of a borough in Arabia, near Aleppo, where cheap goods were manufactured, plus *fy*, which in Arabic matches our preposition *dans* [in]; these sectarians call themselves by this name due to the simplicity of their attire, which is always made of wool."[35]

4. A fourth etymology derives the word from a certain "docteur célèbre" who flourished in the third century AH, "the author of this rigid and austere sect of Sufis." Chardin notes, however, that "the Persians do not consider this etymology suitable, pretending that the sect of which I speak was established in the second century of their epoch."[36]

5. Others derive the term *soufy* from *saf* (*sâf*), that is to say, "'order' or 'class', as if to say that this company holds a 'first-class' place among all other religious sects."

6. Still others derive it from wisdom, "the Greek *sofos,* which it to say *sagesse*, because these Soufys have been considered to be the true philosophers of true sages of Mahométisme."[37]

Concluding his etymological considerations, Chardin returns to the first and third etymologies above and draws his conclusions:

> Undoubtably, the two most common etymologies of the word *soufy* are derived from the words *safa*, meaning purity; and from *souf*, meaning wool, or rather goat's hair (since there is little darning done in wool in Arabia); one or the other of these etymologies is probably the most genuine. Those who endorse the first say that the Sufis, who claim to be in conduct more just (*réformé*) and purer than others in their doctrines and morals, have thus been given the name *Soufys*, as if to say [they are] *the most pure*; and Scaliger, among our own critical scholars in Europe, strongly supports this opinion, and ridicules those who entertain any

---

[33] Chardin, *Voyages*, IV, p. 450.

[34] See Peter Awn, "Sufism," in *The Encylopedia of Religion*, ed. M. Eliade (New York: Macmillan 1993), XIV, p. 105.

[35] Chardin, *Voyages,* IV, p. 451. This is the definition usually preferred by the Sufis themselves; see Hujwīrī, *Kashf al-maḥjūb*, ed. Zhūkūfskī, (Tehran: Ẓuhūrī 1375 A.Hsh./1996), p. 34.

[36] *Ibid.* Indeed, it is Qushayrī who traced the origin back to the second century; see R.A. Nicholson, "A Historical Enquiry Concerning the Origin and Development of Sufiism, With a List of Definitions of the terms 'Ṣūfī' and 'Taṣawwuf,' Arranged Chronologically," *Journal of the Royal Asiatic Society*, 1 (1906), pp. 303–53.

[37] Chardin, *Voyages*, IV, p. 451. This etymology is also given by Abū Rayḥān Bīrūnī; see J. Nurbakhsh, *Sufism*, I: *Meaning, Knowledge and Unity* (New York: Khaniqahi Nimatullahi Publications 1993), p. 11.

> other view. However, should this etymology which he approves be correct, one should rather call the people of this sects *Sephis,* and not *Soufys.* The common opinion of the Orientals supports the other etymology, which is to say that those who have named these folk *Soufys* did so because they renounce all type of extravagance and bodily comfort, not because they wore clothes made of goat's wool – which is anyway the ordinary material from which garments are made in Arabia, and where, as a matter of fact, they have long robes or jackets, which they call *haba* (*a'bâ*), and which are quite handsome. What makes me believe that this [latter] etymology is the more reliable than the others is the fact that the devout Mahométans, particularly men of the church and men of letters, only wear cloths made out of this type of woollen material; and that even the greatest noblemen, when they wish to say their prayers, will take off their precious robes made of golden thread or silk, and dress themselves in these same robes of goat's hair. The prophets, according to the Old Testament, and the hermits and cenobites of the first centuries of Christianity, apparently used to clothe themselves as these Soufys do.[38]

Concerning the historical origins of Sufism, Chardin, as mentioned above, correctly notes that Muslims trace it back to Persia of the second/eighth century. He asserts the originator of the Sufis was Shaykh Abū Sa'īd ibn Abī'l-Khayr (357/967–440/1049), whose date of birth, however, he mistakenly gives as AH 200. As Abū Sa'īd was certainly the first mystic to codify the regulation of conduct for Sufis in their *khānaqāhs*,[39] Chardin is hardly wrong in citing him as their founding father, although from his characterization of this master as being a "grand philosophe; homme forte austère, et qui prétendoit à une plus étroite observance de la religione mahométane, que tous les autres docteurs,"[40] it is obvious that Chardin had no familiarity with Abū Sa'īd's unconventional biography, and was completely unaware of the *malāmatī* character of this master's maturer life. Nonetheless, the citation of Abū Sa'īd is of great historical significance since it correctly situates, for the first time in European orientalism at least, the great mystic of Mayhana amongst major Islamic thinkers.

Chardin next introduces the famous Persian poem *Gulshan-i rāz* – "c'est-à-dire *Parterre de Mystères*," (without, however mentioning its author Shabistarī) – as being the central *somme thèologique* of Persian philosophy and theology. Taking Shabistarī's poem as a point of departure, he launches into a profound exposition of Sufi doctrine which, in terms of its objectivity and insight, is unrivalled by anything composed about Sufism in a European language during the seventeenth century:

---

[38] Chardin, *Voyages*, IV, pp. 451–2.

[39] See Terry Graham, "Abū Sa'īd ibn Abī'l-Khayr and the School of Khurāsān," in *The Heritage of Sufism*, I: *Classical Persian Sufism: From its Origins to Rumi*, ed. L. Lewisohn (Oxford: Oneworld 1999), pp. 83–135.

[40] Chardin, *Voyages,* IV, p. 453.

They [the Sufis] say about this [esoteric nature of their teachings] that true wisdom should have as its purpose the repose and tranquillity of society, and as for the tranquillity of the spirit, it is not necessary to create a public disturbance for its sake, which would be going against received mores. *If you have no doubt,* they say, *concerning the received opinions of your fathers, hold onto that, for it will suffice you. If you doubt, seek the truth gently, without disturbing others.* In conformity with this principle, they state furthermore, that *the beliefs of sages must be of three different types: the first is grounded in the opinions of the land, like, for example, the dominant religion and the traditional received philosophy [of the land]; the second, are those opinions which he is permitted to communicate to those who are also in doubt, and who seek the truth; the third, are those opinions which he keeps to himself, and concerning which he confides unto none except those who share the same sentiment.* They call doubt *the key to knowledge,* concerning which they have an adage: *Whoever does not doubt a point, does not examine it; whoever does not examine it, discerns nothing; whoever does not discern a matter is blind, and will remain blind.*[41]

After this fascinating, albeit somewhat theologically uninformed, description of the Muslim mystical doctrine of the relation of philosophical doubt to pious faith (which, some half a millennium before Descartes, had been brillantly espoused by Abū Ḥāmid Ghazālī[42]), Chardin passes on to an interesting summary of the Sufi metaphysics of the 'Unity of Being'.[43] Here, his exposition is of great historical significance on three counts: in the first place, it is the only exposition of this basic principle of Sufism in a European language composed during this period; second, it furnishes one of the first Western accounts of the bitter theological rivalry and dispute between the exoteric *'ulamā'* and the Persian Sufis; and third, it provides a well-informed, though not completely accurate, introduction to the spiritual practices and disciplines of the Persian Sufis. Struggling to interpret the metaphysics of the great Sufis, the French jeweller comments that their sages believe that:

Whatever you see is like a cloak covering the infinite, eternal Essence, which they call God. The devout Mohametans accuse them quite clearly of being atheists, of not believing in any of the dogmas concerning God or the resurrection; yet among themselves they cite this couplet, which they state is *the mystery of the Soufys:*

Yek Vojoud amed vely souret azar
Kesret souret ne dared ahtebar

Which means:

There is no more than one sole Essence,
But there are a thousand forms or figures.
None of these forms have any consistency or reality.

---

[41] Chardin, *Voyages,* IV, p. 454. Italics are Chardin's own.
[42] Se W.M. Watt, *The Faith and Practice of al-Ghazálí* (Oxford: Oneworld 1994), chaps. 1, 2.
[43] Concerning this doctrine, see the article by Muhammad Juzi in the present volume (Eds).

– which is as much to say that "all which appears to your eyes as being 'real' is, in fact, nothing but diverse forms of a single immutable essence." There comes to my mind a certain preacher in Isfahan who was preaching one day in a public place and spoke out ferociously against these same Soufys, saying that they were atheists who should be consigned to hellfire; that he was himself astonished how anyone could let them live, and that to kill a Soufy would be a deed quite pleasing to God, better in fact, than saving the lives of ten good men! Now, following his sermon five or six Soufys who were among his listeners threw themselves at him and flogged him terribly. Howeversomuch I strove to prevent them, they rebuked me, saying: *a man who preaches death, can he complain if he is thrashed?*

Nevertheless, they defended themselves robustly against the charge of atheism, and spoke highly, on the contrary, of communion with God, continually talking about revelations and modes of union with the Supreme Being, after the manner of enthusiasts or inspired folk. During the evening, they have gatherings for 'commemoration of God', as they say; and here is the particular manner in which they perform their devotions: they grasp each other by the hands, and turning and shaking their heads, cry out with all their might to each other, *Hou, Hou,* that is to say 'God', or 'Being' itself. They continue like this until they are foaming at the mouth and out of breath, and then they fall to the ground. When they come to themselves, they keep to where they were sitting, and then begin shaking their heads and bodies again, and continue their repetition of the name of God. They call this *putting themselves into ecstasy,* or *uniting themselves with God.* They say that they enter into rapture or ecstasy in yet another manner, which is to have their heads inclined towards the right, and to fix their gaze on the tip of their nose; meanwhile, they avail themselves even more of singing in communion, of dance and music, saying that it produces with even greater certainty their ecstasy, by which it must be meant a dizziness – the same which is spoken about those false prophets who are in the tenth chapter of the first book of Samuel, who seem to me altogether like the Soufys.

These Soufys teach that in order to realize complete detachment from earthly things, and to attain spiritual union with God, one [of necessity] raises oneself to the degree of ecstasy, [such that] one is inspired like the prophets, one knows the future and one senses, at intervals, the felicities of paradise.

Among all the different means that they propound to realize union with God, they recommend fasting, and they engage in much austerity, for which one can say that they are unrivalled, since they spend five or six days in a row eating nothing but dried fruit; while others, for twenty-four hours at a time, will eat nothing at all; and, to top it all, every year they do a fast like this which lasts for forty days. The times for doing this are not regular but each of them begins whenever he pleases; and here is the manner how they observe this fast: they confine themselves to a small room during these forty days; they refrain from sleeping as far as possible, and finally, they reduce their consumption of food so much that during the last days of the fast they eat no more than twelve almonds during a twenty-four-hour period. Their occupation, during this long term, is exclusively meditation, thinking of God, and doing works of divine love. However, after all, the fruit of this austere retreat is nothing other than to return filled with a thousand chimeras in their hollow skulls which they call visions, saying *God told us this; we asked Him this question and He replied in this way.*

I have seen those who appeared entirely extravagant to me and who, nonetheless, felt themselves to be in possession of the greatest sense. They boast of having knowledge of the future and even of knowing the very essence of other people's thoughts, but I never witnessed this myself. If one raises the objection to them that there is nothing rational or coherent about their sentiments and that their cult is filled with stupid people, they reply that we should blame our own incredulity; that their religion is better felt than understood; that it is an inner light which is ineffable though very clear; and that it is in vain that we try to approach their mysteries through our sciences, such as logic and physics, for they are all human inventions that do more to hide than to reveal the light.

They interpret the Koran in its entirety in spiritual terms, and they spiritualize all the precepts concerning ritual as well as religion in its external sense; and though they engage in physical purifications much as do other Mahometans, they do not give it any credence, saying that all that concerns devotion to God is internal; and it is from this dogma in particular that stems the hatred of them felt by the clergy. As for themselves, they claim to love the entire world and to despise no one, seeing all men as the products of a common father; and the diverse sects of men as so many slaves and servants of the same Lord. They teach that the joy of paradise lies in the intimate knowledge of God, and in the close union with Him; just as the sufferings of hell consist, on the contrary, of regret at separation from Him. They add that the senses will, nevertheless, feel their joys or their sufferings through the objects that God will create ...

A priest, who lived in Isfahan for nearly forty years, by the name of Father Raphael from Le Mans, pointed out to me on a number of occasions a certain Soufy, who was so convinced of the truth of his religion and the falsity of all others that he proposed to demonstrate which of them was taking the right path on the basis of which one of them would be least hurt upon leaping together off the top of the house. *Raphael,* he would say, *let us climb on to the terrace and throw ourselves down whilst holding hands. If I hurt myself more than you, I will convert to your religion; if not, you will convert to mine.*

It is said that the clergy detests these Soufis. Magistrates are also at war with them because their fasts and their raptures detach them exceedingly from the world and make them neglect the things one must constantly attend to in society. In view of the natural tendency of men towards carelessness and indolence, men succumb easily to ideas such as revelations, union with God, rapture – all things that run counter to applying oneself to the demands of life. That is why it is advisable not to persist blindly in following such an opinion which is so contrary to the good of society.

The sect has produced a number of celebrated authors and, among others, a certain el-Jonaid [al-Junayd],[44] who was named *the king of the Soufy sect*, not so much for his great learning as the austerity of his life and that of his disciples, to whom he principally taught disregard from the world as the shortest and most certain path to achieving that contemplation which ensures communion and familiarity with God. Enemies of his sect accuse him of casting spells and called him a blasphemer, in view of this intimate union he claimed to have with God and that anyone could also have if they pursued the same means.

---

[44] Abū'l-Qāsim Junayd, born in Nahāvand near Hamadan in western Persia and died in Baghdad in 298/910.

There are several works, in prose and in verse, that explain, elucidate and illustrate the book Gulshendras [*Gulshan-i Rāz*],[45] which is, as I said, the Soufys' sacred text. The most highly regarded of these is the *Menavi* [*Mathnawī*],[46] a huge work of mystical theology, where, on the one hand, divine love and intimate union with God is described in rapturous terms and, on the other, the vanity of the world, the dignity of virtue and the enormity of vice are vividly depicted. In this book, the inner life is described as consisting of three parts: knowledge, purgation and illumination. One sees there that there are three proofs of the existence of God in man: detachment from the world, the constant desire for God and perseverance in prayer. One encounters there these beautiful precepts: *Do not get involved in conversation with the first person that comes along, but in all your dealings with other men, keep your mind fixed on God. Never cease to have an ardent love for God or to declare His glory and His grace. In this way, you will amply possess true life in this world and the next. The soul enlightened by the rays of heaven is the mirror in which can be discovered the most hidden secrets.*

One can find in the commentary this marvellous transport: *O ardent love of God! Come to my aid, so that we can both burn endlessly; for one must so burn to convey the state of a heart inflamed by love. The source of perfect pleasures lies in the bosom of the beloved; as for myself, I strive for nothing other than to hurl myself body and soul into this abyss. O you! Who call me to the delights of paradise, it is not paradise that I seek; I seek the face of the one who creates paradise.*

As for the rest, the Persians hold that it is difficult indeed to distinguish and tell apart the Soufys from the atheists or *molhed* [*mulḥid*], as the Persians call them, for the *el taricat*,[47] who are the contemplators or the fanatics who resemble the illuminados of Spain or the molinosisters of Italy or the quietists of France. There are many indications suggesting that this mystical theology of the Soufys has travelled from the East to the West, by way of Africa, and that it infected, in this way, Spain first of all and then the rest of Europe thereafter.

I note, finally, that in Persian they distinguish between these Soufys and other Soufys, who are the guards of the king's palace and of himself. The former are called *Soufy Cherki*, that is to say *whirling Soufys*, because of the way they spin in their devotions in order to achieve rapture, as I explained; and the latter, *Sefevi Soufys*, that is to say the Soufys of the Sefy, referring to the name of the prince who founded them, which is the stock of the royal line that reigns to this day.[48]

As can be seen from the above extracts, Chardin had made a thorough study of Sufism and had gained a good grasp of some key Sufi concepts. He was familiar with the names and, to some extent, the ideas of the founding fathers of Sufism, Abū Sa'īd ibn Abī'l-Khayr and al-Junayd, and quoted from two of the seminal Persian Sufi texts, the *Mathnawī* of Jalāl al-Dīn Rūmī and the

---

[45] The great Persian Sufi poetic classic by Maḥmūd Shabistarī (d. after 737/1337): see L. Lewisohn, *Beyond Faith and Infidelity: The Sufi Poetry and Spiritual Teachings of Maḥmūd Shabistarī* (London: Curzon 1995).

[46] Composed by Jalāl al-Dīn Rūmī (d. 672/1273).

[47] Perhaps a corruption of the Arabic term *al-ṭarīqat*, meaning the Sufi spiritual 'way'.

[48] Chardin, *Voyages*, IV, pp. 459–64.

Gulshan-i rāz of Maḥmūd Shabistarī. For the first time in history Europeans were provided with a sympathetic account of Sufi beliefs. What is more, owing to the great popularity of Chardin's travel books in the West, many leading European writers and intellectuals received a favourable account of Sufi ideas and practices. Contrary to the prevailing prejudices about the dogmatism and fanaticism of contemporary Islamic societies, Chardin demonstrated that a high degree of religious tolerance existed in Safavid Iran. This, in fact, contrasted with the prevalence of religious wars and sectarian disputes in seventeenth-century Europe (Chardin himself having been the victim of religious intolerance in France), and attracted the admiration of European intellectuals who valued religious tolerance and intellectual freedom. With his inquisitive and unbiased mind, Chardin made a significant contribution both to a greater understanding between the East and the West, and to the cause of religious freedom and enlightenment in the West.

It should be noted that it was owing to the relative tolerance of the Safavids that Iṣfahān also became the Mother House for the Carmelites, not only for their missions in the East, but in a sense for the missionary work of the entire 'Reformed' order for all time. After the formation of a convent in Hormoz in 1612; of a hospice at Tatta which gradually became a permanency between 1613 and 1619; of a convent in Goa in 1620; of residences at Baṣra and Shīrāz in 1623; of another at Din, in the Gulf of Bombay, in 1630 the number of 'Religious' – clerics and lay brothers – required to man those houses grew so great that centralized control had to be provided. This was done by the establishment of the Mother House in Iṣfahān. In addition to their religious work, the Religious were required to apply themselves to the study of Persian and other oriental languages, for which a 'Praelector' was assigned by the Vicar Provincial to teach each of them daily, at fixed times. They had to take their language studies very seriously. On 10 June 1683, the Definitory General decreed "suspension from office for one year against any Prior or Vicar, who did not provide for such language masters: and Religious negligent in learning the language would be confined to the House till they had learnt enough of it in the opinion of their Superior."[49]

Lady Sheil, the wife of the British diplomat in Tehran, spent about four years in Iran, and her nineteenth-century travelogue *Glimpses of Life and Manners in Persia*,[50] provides a perceptive account of the upper-class life with which she came into contact in Iran during the Qājār period. She too speaks about the freedom of religion in Iran, despite the fact that severe persecution of religious minorities was going on at the time when she was living in Iran, some of which she describes in graphic detail. She wrote: "Freedom of speech in

[49] *A Chronicle of the Carmelites in Persia and the Papal Mission of the XVIIth and XVIIIth Centuries* (London: Eyre & Spottiswoode 1939), II, p. 751.

[50] Lady Sheil, *Glimpses of Life and Manners in Persia* (London: John Murray 1856).

Persia is on an equality with freedom of religion. It is the Persian substitute for liberty of press, and the safety-valve of popular indignation. Every one may say what he likes."[51] Lady Sheil devoted a chapter of her book to the dervishes and briefly referred to the "Ajem, Khaksar, Niamet-oolahee, Zehabee, Jellalee, Kembree, Dehree and Ali-Illahee" Sufi Orders.[52]

III. PERSIAN SUFI TEXTS IN EUROPE IN THE EIGHTEENTH AND NINETEENTH CENTURIES

As the result of the works of these early European travellers and diplomats, Western writers began to get acquainted with Eastern lands, leading to a gradual change of perception towards the East and Eastern religions and philosophies. However, the real change of attitude in the West towards the East in general, and towards Islam and Sufism in particular, came about as the result of the dedicated work of a number of distinguished scholars and orientalists.

The first person truly to introduce the Persian language and its mystical poetry to the English-speaking world was Sir William Jones (1746–94). An extraordinary personality, Jones was at once a judge, a diplomat, a great linguist and a poet and should also be acknowledged as one of the founders of both comparative religion and comparative literature. He was, in the words of Samuel Johnson, "one of the most enlightened of the sons of men." While he did a great deal in introducing some great masterpieces of Indian philosophy and literature to the West, his role as one of the first serious students of Persian studies is also very important. As R.M. Hewitt remarked in a delightful essay, "Harmonious Jones:"

> [Sir William] takes every opportunity to associate the East and the West. He compares Firdausi with Homer, Hafiz with Petrarch and Shakespeare. His treatment of Islam and Hinduism shows a similar absence of condescension.[53]

At Harrow, Jones had studied Hebrew; this in turn took him on to Arabic, and this to Persian, which made the greatest impact on his life. His biographer tells us: "His life was permanently changed by his first reading of Hafiz, which acted to him as the *Fairie Queene* on Keats, and for about six years he engaged in advocating the claims of Eastern poetry . . ."[54]. Describing the beliefs of the Sufis, Jones penned this beautiful account:

---

[51] *Ibid.*, p. 200.
[52] *Ibid.*, chap. 13, pp. 192–200.
[53] R.M. Hewitt, *Essays and Studies by Members of the English Association*, ed. R.W. Chapman (Oxford: Clarendon Press 1943), pp. 43ff.
[54] Sir William Jones, *Works,* with a Life by Lord Teignmouth (London 1807), II, p. 146.

> The tenets [of the Sufis] varied from place to place and even from Sufi to Sufi, but common to all was the belief that the individual, by his own efforts, could attain spiritual union with God, that the human soul was an emanation from the essence, and that like a reed torn from its native brook, like wax separated from its delicious honey, the soul of man bewails its disunion with melancholy music and sheds burning tears like a lighted taper, waiting passionately for the moment of its extinction, as a disengagement from its earthly trammels, and the means of returning to its only beloved.[55]

F.R. Tholuck was another scholar to write extensively on Sufism[56] which he described as a form of pantheism, comparing it to Neoplatonism. His works managed to make Sufism intelligible and respectable for Western audiences, and also influenced the works of some English poets.

Sir Gore Ouseley (1770–1844) became the first ambassador sent from England to Iran since Sir Dodmore Cotton, the ambassador of Charles I. In 1823 Sir Gore Ouseley assisted in the founding of the Royal Asiatic Society of London, and in 1842 he was appointed president of the Society for the Publication of the Oriental Texts. It was under his direction that the *Gulistān* of Sa'dī with the translation by Francis Gladwin was printed. It is interesting to note that Sir Gore's only printed work was devoted to Persian literature: *Biographical Notices of Persian Poets, with Critical and Explanatory Remarks.*[57]

Edward H. Palmer (1840–82), another remarkable figure who combined political adventure with oriental scholarship, was one of the most important pioneers in introducing Sufism to the West. Although he made a number of translations of both Persian and Arabic works for *The Eagle,* a magazine published at Cambridge, he is more important for having also published *Oriental Mysticism: A Treatise on the Sufistic and Unitarian Theosophy of the Persians*,[58] which contained a useful lexicon of Sufi terms and their allegorical meanings. In 1877 Palmer published his *Song of the Reed* which included translations from a number of Persian poets, including the introduction to the *Mathnawī* of Rūmī (Song of the Reed) and some other poems by Rūmī.

An even more important translator of Persian Sufi poetry was E.H. Whinfield (1836–1922), whose influence on the study of Persian literature in England was considerable. Whinfield was deeply interested in Sufism and in 1880 brought out an edition and translation of the *Gulshan-i Rāz* by Maḥmūd Shabistarī,[59] a remarkably accurate translation for its day and age, and one

---

[55] Sir William Jones, *Sixth Discourse on the Persians* (1799), quoted by Sir Roger Stevens, *The Land of the Great Sophy* (London: Methuen & Co. 1965), p. 45.

[56] F.R. Tholuck's major works are: *Sufismus sive Theologia Persica Pantheistica* (Berlin 1821) and *Bluthensammlung aus der Morgenlaendischen Mystik* (Berlin 1825).

[57] Published posthumously, London 1846.

[58] Cambridge: Deighton, Bell & Co. 1867.

[59] *Gulshan-i Raz: The Mystic Rose Garden of Sad ud din Mahmud Shabistari* (London: Truebner 1880).

which is still useful. This work lent greater status and dignity to Sufism and showed it to be a well-developed mystical and philosophical system.

During the nineteenth century, the most popular book in English on mysticism was Robert Vaughan's *Hours with the Mystics*, which first appeared in 1856 and had run through seven editions by 1895. In this book Vaughan provides an account of Persian Sufism based on the works of Tholuck, Sir William Jones and Sir John Malcolm. Although his account lacked originality, it had the merit of presenting a systematic account of Sufism and portraying it as more than the unintelligible and exotic form of religious enthusiasm that it had been described as in the scattered accounts of earlier authors.

IV. PERSIAN SUFI POETRY AND ENGLISH ROMANTIC ORIENTALISM

The earliest reference to Persian poetry in English appears to be in *The Arte of English Poesie*, (1589), in which George Puttenham gives four poems in translation. He mentions receiving them from a gentleman in Italy who had been to the East. The German orientalist Adam Olearius was perhaps the first Western traveller to introduce the great poets of Persia to the rest of the European West. He visited Iran in 1633 as secretary to the ambassador of Frederick III of Schleswig-Holstein. In his works he compares Persian with French literature and describes the Persians as people who are the most addicted to poetry in the world; his translation of Sa'dī's *Gulistān*, *Persianischer Rosenthal*, appeared in 1654 and 1660. Among the leading Persian poets he mentions Firdawsī, Sa'dī, Ḥāfiẓ and Niẓāmī.[60] In 1774, J. Richardson issued his *Specimen of Persian Poetry*, based on the work of Count de Rewiczki; and in 1787 J. Nott published his *Select Odes of Hafiz.* These in turn encouraged a large number of other translations of the works of Ḥāfiẓ, Sa'dī and other Persian poets into English.

The year 1858 is important in marking the publication in England of two significant books which have enjoyed enormous popularity up to the present time. Darwin's *Origin of Species* was printed in that year, as well as the first version of the *Rubā'īyāt* of 'Umar Khayyām translated by Edward Fitzgerald. Although Fitzgerald has, of course, become famous in the West for his masterly translation of the *Rubā'īyāt*, which became the most popular translation of any literary work from any language, he was also very interested in Persian Sufi literature. In addition to the *Rubā'īyāt*, Fitzgerald also translated the great mystical allegory, *Salāmān and Absāl* (1850) by Jāmī (1414–92), and a summary of the *Parliament of Birds* (*Manṭiq al-ṭayr*) by

---

[60] Adam Olearius, *The Voyages and Travels of the ambassador Sent by Frederick Duke of Holstein, to the Great Duke of Muscovy and the King of Persia . . .*, trans. J. Davies (London: Starkey & Basset 1662), p. 251.

Farīd al-Dīn 'Aṭṭār (d. *c.* 618/1221). Although both Fitzgerald's versions are very fine literary translations, none of them achieved the same fame as the *Rubā'īyāt*. He also tried his hand at Iran's greatest lyric poet Ḥāfiẓ, but in the end decided that he was untranslatable. He referred to the metaphysical *Mathnawī* of Rūmī as "the best Persian poem," urging Mrs Cowell to ask his former teacher, the Reverend E.B. Cowell (1826–1903) who had introduced him to the *Rubā'īyāt*) to translate the *Mathnawī*, adding that "surely the finest Persian poem ought to be done in English."[61]

Although Fitzgerald's teacher Reverend Cowell disapproved of the philosophy of 'Umar Khayyām (when Fitzgerald wanted to dedicate his book to Cowell, he refused, saying that in these weighty matters he "would rather turn to Nazareth than to Nishapur"), he was very sympathetic towards Sufism.[62] Cowell translated a number of poems by Ḥāfiẓ, defended Sa'dī's religion and, while praising the thoroughly unWestern and new charm of his *Gulistān*, admired the unorthodox and non-sectarian character of its ethics. Regarding Sufism, Cowell wrote:

> The Sufis . . . spring up apparently by a necessary law in the human mind . . . The inherent love of mysticism, which lies in the heart, finds in every religion the necessary warmth to quicken it. . . The Eleusinian mysteries, the Hindu Brahmanism, the Persian Sufeyism, and, in our own time, the new German philosophy, are only developments of the same deep rooted principles in the soul, under different outward circumstances of time and place.[63]

Although Persian Sufi literature had a great influence on many of the Romantic poets in Britain, this influence cannot be discussed without reference to the effect of this poetry on German literature. As this topic has been dealt with by Professor Annemarie Schimmel[64] and others elsewhere, I will only refer to the pioneering translations of Persian poetry into German which had the greatest influence on British and American writers, as well as on the German poets. The Austrian diplomat and orientalist Joseph von Hammer-Purgstall's (1774–1856) translation of the entire *Dīvān* of Ḥāfiẓ which appeared in two volumes in 1812–13, and his anthology of some two hundred Iranian poets were extremely influential. These translations not only formed the basis of the familiarity of many German writers and poets with Persian poetry, but also became a source of information for many British and American writers, including Samuel Taylor Coleridge and Ralph Waldo Emerson.

---

[61] George Cowell, *Life and Letters of Edward Byles Cowell* (London: Macmillan 1904), p. 239.

[62] For further discussion of Cowell's relation to Sufism and Persian poetry, see Peter Avery, "Fitzgerald's Persian Teacher and Hafez," *Sufi: A Journal of Sufism*, 6 (1990), pp. 10–15.

[63] Cited by Yohannan, *Persian Poetry in England and America*, pp. 63–4.

[64] See her *Mystical Dimensions of Islam,* (Chapel Hill: University of North Carolina Press 1975), pp. 6–12.

Hammer-Purgstall himself was a great admirer of Rūmī and in his *Geschichte der schonen Redekunste Persians*, the first comprehensive history of Persian literature, he refers to Rūmī's *Mathnawī* as "the handbook of all Sufis from the borders of the Ganges up to the borders of Bosphorus." His remarks about the *Dīvān-i Shams*, although flowery by modern taste, yet show his remarkable insight:

> On the wings of the greatest religious enthusiasm, which, high above all outward forms of positive religions, prays in the most perfect seclusion from all sensual and worldly things to the eternal being, the purest source of eternal light. Mawlana rises unlike other lyrical poets, and even Ḥāfiẓ, not just above suns and moons, but above time and space, above the creation and destiny, above the original contract of predestination and above the verdict of the final judgement into eternity, where he melts into one, as the eternal suitor with the eternal being, the eternal lover with his eternal love.[65]

It was due to Hammer-Purgstall that Hegel became acquainted with "the excellent Rūmī," although Hegel mistakenly regarded Rūmī as a perfect model of pantheistic thought. However, it was through Hegel's interest in Rūmī that many other European philosophers and historians of religion became interested in Persian poetry and Sufism, just as it was also through von Hammer-Purgstall that the great German poet Goethe was inspired to compose his *West-östlicher Divan* in 1819.[66]

As we turn now to the influence of Persian poetry on the English Romantic movement, it should first be pointed out that Persian Romantic poetry exalted imagination as the noblest of human faculties. The English Romantic poets – like their Persian and Oriental fellow bards – gave free vent to the imagination and saw the world through their inner eyes rather than through their senses or rational faculties. Nature is invested with personality; human moods and moral impulses are seen reflected in it. Romantics see nature through the lenses of emotion, usually coloured with melancholy as well as joy, with nostalgia as well as regret, and above all with spirituality, seeing in nature a reflection of the divine. This use of imagination to attain insight into the innermost workings of nature and the presence is evident in the poetry of Percy Bysshe Shelley, who had been inspired by Sir William Jones to study Arabic. He actually wrote some poems in imitation of the ghazals of Ḥāfiẓ as translated by Sir William Jones.

The title of Shelley's poem "From the Arabic," is somewhat misleading: it is in fact written in imitation of Jones's translation of Ḥāfiẓ, such that the combination of rhyme and refrain in its opening lines closely approximates the ghazal form:

---

[65] Cited by Annemarie Schimmel, *The Triumphal Sun* (New York: SUNY Press 1993), p. 388 (quotation translated by Connie Kerbst).

[66] For a study of Sufi influences in Germany see *ibid.*, pp. 368–96.

My faint spirit was sitting in the light
  of thy looks, my love;
It panted for thee like the hind at noon
  For the brooks, my love.

The poem even imitates Ḥāfiẓ's habit of weaving his name into the last stanza of the poem:

Less oft is peace in Shelley's mind
Than calm in waters seen.

– lines which remind one of the last two verses of a ghazal by Ḥāfiẓ:

Say not, O friend, to Ḥāfiẓ "Quiet thee now and rest!"
Calm and content, what are they? Patience and peace, O where?[67]

Courthorp in his *History of English Literature* suggests some connection between the Italian word *canzone* and the Persian and Arabic ghazal, thereby putting forward the theory that the Italian sonnets were imitations of the Persian and Arabic prototype. If this is so, then Persian literature has inspired the appearance of the beautiful sonnet to the Italian and English literature.[68] There are, of course, many similarities both in form and content between the Persian ghazal and Italian and English sonnet like the sonnet, the Persian ghazal usually has between eight and fourteen lines. Both forms deal with a single topic, focusing on lyrical, erotic or mystical subjects.

Alfred, Lord Tennyson was another important English Romantic poet who was not only familiar with Persian poets through English translations but, together with his friend Edward Fitzgerald, had started on his study of Persian and finished reading the *Dīvān* of Ḥāfiẓ with the help of Reverend Cowell. A number of his early poems show that he was strongly influenced by the example of Lord Byron (another Romantic poet who was deeply influenced by the Turkish Sufi tradition[69]), such as his pseudo-oriental poems, including "Written by an Exile of Bassorah," "The Expedition of Nadir Shah," "Babylon," "Egypt," and "Persia." In his later life he was so imbued with the influence of Persian poetry that some of his own poems read almost like translations of Ḥāfiẓ. For instance, the following lines:

Then stole I up, and trancedly,
Gazed on the Persian girl alone,
Serene with argent-lidded eyes
Amorous, and lashes like to rays

[67] Yohannan, *Persian Poetry in England and America*, p. 33.
[68] Lotfali Suratgar, "Traces of Persian Influence upon English Literature During the Fifteenth and Sixteenth Centuries," (Unpublished Ph.D. thesis, University of London, May 1939), p. 338.
[69] See Mohammad Sharafuddin, *Islam and Romantic Orientalism* (London: I.B. Tauris 1994), pp. 224–5, 234.

Université de Sudbury | University of Sudbury

Of darkness, and a brow of pearl
Tressed with redolent ebony,
In many a dark delicious curl,
Flowing beneath her rose-hued zone,
The sweetest lady of the time,
Well worthy of the golden prime
Of good Harun Alraschid.[70]

may be compared with certain lines by Ḥāfiẓ translated by John Hindley with which Tennyson must have been familiar in both their original and their translated versions:

Thy soft down and sweet mole of thy cheek,
Eyes and eyebrows and stature my senses enchain ...
On my memory thy locks have a grateful perfume,
Far more fragrant than jasmine's sweet scents.
While I gaze, not one word can I speak.

Even clearer is the resemblance between the poetry of Ḥāfiẓ and the following lines from Tennyson's *Maud*, which have a more distinctly Persian flavour:

She is coming, my own, my sweet;
Were it ever so airy a tread,
My heart would hear her and beat,
Were it earth in an earthy bed;
My dust would hear her and beat,
Had I lain for a century dead,
Would start and tremble under her feet,
And blossom in purple and red.[71]

The above lines clearly remind one of the beautiful ghazal of Ḥāfiẓ as translated by Gertrude Bell:

Where are the tidings of union? that I may arise –
Forth from the dust I will rise up to welcome thee!
When to my grave thou turnest thy blessed feet,
Wine and the lute shalt thou bring in thy hand to me,
Thy voice shall ring through the folds of my winding-sheet
And I will arise and dance to thy minstrelsy.

V. PERSIAN SUFI POETRY IN THE UNITED STATES

In the early nineteenth century, Persian Sufi poetry in translation attracted the interest of a number of eminent American writers, among whom may be mentioned Ralph Waldo Emerson, Henry David Thoreau, Henry Longfellow,

[70] Alfred Lord Tennyson, *Tennyson's Poetry*, selected and edited by Robert W. Hill Jr. (New York and London: W.W. Norton & Co. 1971), pp. 543–4.
[71] *Ibid*., Part 1, XXII, p. 238.

Nathaniel Hawthorn and Walt Whitman.[72] Emerson became familiar with Persian literature through a number of English and German translations of Persian poetry. In 1820, when he was only seventeen years old, he read *The Asiatick Miscellany*, which contained translations from Sa'dī, Ḥāfiẓ and Jāmī; Ghodzko's *Specimens of the Popular Poetry of Persia*, from which he made a number of quotations in his journals for 1846; and W.R. Alger's *The Poetry of the East* which contained some translations of Persian poetry. He had also read and absorbed nearly all the writings of Sir William Jones, which had become very popular. Persian prose literature also engaged his interest, and in addition to a number of historical documents, he read and admired James Ross's translation of the *Gulistān* of Sa'dī, and also wrote the introduction to the American edition of the *Gulistān* translated by Francis Gladwin, published in 1865 by Ticknor & Fields.

However, the chief source of Emerson's information concerning Persian poetry was von Hammer-Purgstall's voluminous anthology of Persian poetry and German translation of the *Dīvān* of Ḥāfiẓ. Emerson translated some seven hundred lines of Persian poetry from German, nearly half of them from Ḥāfiẓ, but also fifty-four lines of 'Aṭṭār, thirty-four lines of Sa'dī, thirty-four lines of Shāh Ni'matu'llāh, and smaller portions from a number of other poets, including Rūmī and Jāmī. He also had the distinction of being the first translator of 'Umar Khayyām in the United States (three quatrains), predicting that "Khayyām will grow in Western estimation." A few years later, when Fitzgerald translated his verse version of the *Rubā'īyāt*, he dedicated it to Emerson.

Emerson penned four major articles and poems on Persian poetry. One was an essay, 'Persian Poetry' in which he refers to the main qualities of Persian literature, but speaks mainly about Ḥāfiẓ.[73] He wrote a long introduction to the first American edition of Sa'dī's *Gulistān* by Francis Gladwin, in which he spoke mainly about the genius of Sa'dī.[74] Poems by Emerson dealing specifically with Persian Sufi poetry include a long poem under the title of "Saadi," which is clearly on Sa'dī,[75] a poem entitled "Fragments on the Poet and the Poetic Gift,"[76]

---

[72] On the influence of Sufism on Longfellow and Hawthorne (not discussed below), see Phillip Edmundson, "The Persians of Concord," *Sufi: A Journal of Sufism*, 3 (Spring 1989), pp. 14–18; *idem.*, "Hawthorne Turns to the East: Persian Influences in the *Blithedale Romance*," *English Language Notes*, 28/2 (1990), pp. 25–38.

[73] R.W. Emerson, *Complete Works*, (Boston: Riverside Press, centenary edition 1903–4), VIII, pp. 236–65.

[74] *The Gulistan or Rose Garden, by Musle-Huddeen Sheik Saadi*, translated from the original by Francis Gladwin with . . . a Preface by R.W. Emerson (Boston: Ticknor & Fields 1865).

[75] First published in *The Dial* (1842). Reprinted in R.W. Emerson, *Collected Poems and Translations*, ed. Harold Bloom (New York: Library of America 1994), pp. 98–103.

[76] R.W. Emerson, *Complete Works*, IX, pp. 320–4.

which mainly concerns Ḥāfiẓ,[77] and a translation of some lines from the conclusion of 'Aṭṭār's *Manṭiq al-tayr.*[78] In his essay on Persian literature, Emerson compares Ḥāfiẓ with Shakespeare, observing that "Ḥāfiẓ is the prince of Persian poets, and in his extraordinary gift adds to some of the attributes of Pindar, Anacreon, Horace and Burns the insight of a mystic, that sometimes affords a deeper glance at Nature that belongs to either of these bards."[79]

Describing Sa'dī in his introduction to Gladwin's *Gulistān* translation, Emerson wrote: "I find in him a pure theism. He asserts the universality of moral laws, and the perpetual retributions. He celebrates the omnipotence of a virtuous soul." Again, Emerson mentions Sa'dī as being among the greatest poets of the world and writes: "Through his Persian dialect he speaks to all nations, and like Homer, Shakespeare, Cervantes, and Montaigne, is perpetually modern."[80]

In addition to his translations, many of his own poems show signs of borrowing from Persian poetry and the influence of Sufi literature on his work.[81] It was in imitation of the *Saqīnāma* of Ḥāfiẓ that Emerson wrote his poem, "Bacchus." In July 1846, in a letter to Elizabeth Hoar, Emerson wrote that he had been working on some poems which he felt impatient to show her, "especially some verses called Bacchus... not, however, translated from Ḥāfiẓ."[82] He is correct to warn us that the poem is not a close translation of Ḥāfiẓ's *Saqīnāma,* but one can definitely see the influence of *Saqīnāma* in it – and it does somewhat resemble his own verse translation of that work.[83]

In contrast to traditional Western poems about wine which praise its physical intoxication, in imitation of Ḥāfiẓ, Emerson's "Bacchus" produces intellectual and spiritual intoxication. The poem starts with these lines:

> Bring me wine, but wine which never grew
> In the belly of the grape.

He then goes on to praise that wine which is

> Water and bread,
> Food which needs no transmuting,

---

[77] Some seventy-seven fragments of Emerson's verse translations from Ḥāfiẓ, including twenty full ghazals, are given in Bloom's edition of his *Collected Poems and Translations*, pp. 256–66; 465–91.

[78] *Collected Poems and Translations*, pp. 268–9.

[79] R.W. Emerson, *Complete Works*, "Persian Poetry," pp. 236–65.

[80] *The Gulistan or Rose Garden by Musle-Huddeen Sheik Saadi*, p. vii.

[81] See Marwan M. Obeidat, "Ralph Waldo Emerson and the Muslim Orient" *The Muslim World*, 78/2 (1988), pp. 132–45.

[82] R. Emerson, *Letters of Ralph Waldo Emerson*, ed. Ralph L. Rusk, 6 vols (New York: Columbia University Press 1939), III, p. 341.

[83] His poem "From the Persian of Hafiz" (*Collected Poems and Translations*, pp. 104–8) is a translation (from the German of Von Hammer) of Ḥāfiẓ's *Saqīnāma.*

Rainbow-flowering, wisdom fruiting
Wine which is already man,
Food which teach and reason can.
Wine which Music is ...
Music and wine are one,
That I, drinking this
Shall hear far Chaos talk with me;
Quickened so will I unlock
Every crypt of every rock.
Pour, Bacchus the remembering wine;
Retrieve the loss of me and mine ...
Haste to cure the old despair, –
Reason in Nature's lotus drenched,
The memory of ages quenched ...
And write my old adventures with the pen
Which on the first day drew
Upon the tablets blue
The dancing Pleiades and eternal men.[84]

Emerson's poem "Pan" reads:

Of what are heroes, prophets, men,
But pipes through which the breath of Pan doth blow
A momentary music. Being's tide
Swells hitherward, and myriads of forms
Live, robed with beauty, painted by the suns
Their dust, pervaded by the nerves of God,
Throbs with over mastering energy
Knowing and doing. Ebbs the tide, they lie
While hollow shells upon the desert shore,
But not the less eternal wave rolls on
To animate the new millions and exhale
Races and planets, its enchanted foam.

Emerson's imagery of prophets and poets as pipes through which the breath of God plays music is reminiscent of the first beautiful poem of Rūmī's *Mathnawī:*

Hear, how yon reed in sadly pleasing tales
Departed bliss and present woe bewails ...
'Tis love, that fills the reed with warmth divine,
'Tis love, that sparkles in the racy wine ...[85]

Emerson's imagery of sea, shore, wave, desert and shell finds parallels too, in another of Rūmī's poems:

Happy was I
In the pearl's heart to lie;

[84] Emerson, *Collected Poems and Translations*, pp. 95–6.
[85] A.J. Arberry, *Classical Persian Literature* (London: George, Allen & Unwin 1958), p. 223.

Till, lashed by life's hurricane,
Like a tossed wave I ran.

The secrets of the sea
I uttered thunderously;
Like a spent cloud on the shore
I slept, and stirred no more.[86]

Emerson's close friend Henry David Thoreau (1817–62), although not as well read in Persian literature as Emerson, was nevertheless very interested in Persian poetry. His famous *Walden* includes several references to Sa'dī. He quotes Sa'dī's description of the cypress tree as *āzād* or free, since it does not bow down to the wind and is not subject to the seasonal change of bloom and withering. He concludes in Sa'dī's words: "If thy hand has plenty, be liberal as the date tree; but if it affords nothing to give away, be *āzād*."[87]

Like Emerson's, Thoreau's references to Ḥāfiẓ and Sa'dī are extremely warm. The transcendental *Week* cites both Ḥāfiẓ and Sa'dī in an inspirational vein: "Yesterday at dawn God delivered me from all worldly affliction; and amidst the gloom of night presented me with the water of immortality." (Ḥāfiẓ).[88]

Thoreau's feelings about Sa'dī and himself are best summed up in his journal entry for 8 August, 1852:

> The entertaining a single thought of a certain elevation makes all men of one religion, I know, for instance, that Sadi entertained once identically the same thought that I do, and therefore I can find no essential difference between Sadi and myself. He is not Persian, he is not ancient, he is not strange to me. By the identity of his thought with mine he still survives ... Sadi possessed no greater privacy or individuality than is thrown open to me ... Truth and a true man is essentially public, not private. If Sadi were to come back to claim a personal identity with the historical Sadi, he would find there were too many of us; he could not get a skin that would contain us ... By sympathy with Sadi I have embowelled him. In his thought I have a sample of him, a slice from his core, which makes it unimportant where certain bones which the thinker once employed may lie.[89]

America's greatest poet, Walt Whitman, also became acquainted with Persian Sufi literature through Emerson. In his *Leaves of Grass* he even refers to the whirling dervishes:

I hear dervishes monotonously chanting,
  interspersed with frantic shouts,

---

[86] *Ibid.*, p. 233.
[87] H.D. Thoreau, *The Writings*, 20 vols (Boston: Houghton & Mifflin 1906), II, pp. 87–8.
[88] Quoted by J.D. Yohannan, *Persian Poetry in England and America*, p. 137.
[89] H.D. Thoreau, *The Journals*, ed. Francis H. Allen (Boston: Houghton & Mifflin 1906), IV, p. 290 (8 August, 1852).

> as they spin around turning always to Mecca,
> I see the rapt religious dances of the Persians and the Arabs …
> I hear from the Mussulman mosque the muezzin calling,
> I see the worshippers within, nor form nor sermon, argument nor word,
> But silent, strange, devout, raised, glowing heads, ecstatic faces.[90]

That Whitman knew something about Sufism is demonstrated in his poem entitled "A Persian Lesson:"

> For his o'erarching and last lesson the greybeard Sufi,
> In the fresh scent of the morning in the open air,
> On the slope of a teeming Persian rose-garden,
> Under an ancient chestnut-tree wide spreading its branches,
> Spoke to the young priests and students.
>
> Finally my children, to envelop each word, each part of the rest,
> Allah is all, all, all – is immanent in every life and object,
> May-be at many-a-more removes –
> yet Allah, Allah, Allah is there.[91]

VI. CONCLUSION

For the first time since the expulsion of the Muslims from Spain during the period of the Reconquest, Islam is again making its presence felt in the West. There are now some eight million Muslims living in Europe and probably some five or six million Muslims in the United States. In addition to millions of immigrants who come from North Africa to France, from Turkey to Germany and from the subcontinent, Iran and the Persian Gulf to the countries of the European Union, we are witnessing the beginning of some conversions of native Europeans to Islam.

I mentioned earlier on that Sufism has acted as a bridge between Islam and Christianity. It has shown to the West the mystical face of Islam and has helped reduce religious prejudice. At the same time, it has helped Muslims develop their own form of ecumenical consciousness, enabling them to look at other religions not as heresies, but as expressions of one divine truth. In this regard, "the comprehensive humanity from which a Sufi could preach," as Marshall Hodgson pointed out, "gave the Sufi tradition an often spectacular advantage."[92] Ḥāfiẓ's verse alludes to the inclusivist nature of this Sufi outlook on religious diversity:

---

[90] Walt Whitman, *Leaves of Grass*, ed. Harold W. Blodgett and Sculley Bradley (New York: New York University Press 1965), "Proud Music," p. 408.

[91] *Leaves of Grass*, p. 553. For a good discussion of this poem see Massud Farzan, "Whitman and Sufism: Towards 'A Persian Lesson' ," *American Literature*, 40/4 (1976), pp. 572–82.

[92] *The Venture of Islam* (Chicago: University of Chicago Press 1977), II, p. 209.

[93] *Dīwān-i Ḥāfiẓ,* ed. Parwīz Nātil Khanlarī (Tehran: Sahāmī 'ām 1362 A.Hsh./1983; 2nd edn), ghazal 78: 3; p. 172.

Every man longs for the Friend, the drunkard as much as the sober;
Every place is the House of Love, the Synagogue as much as the Mosque.[93]

When Henry Martyn, one of the first Anglican missionaries to Iran, reached Shīrāz in 1811, he found his most attentive listeners among the Sufis. "These Sufis," he writes in his diary, "are quite the Methodists of the East. They delight in everything Christian except in being exclusive. They consider they all will finally return to God, from whom they emanated."[94]

If Islam is to have a permanent impact in the West – as I believe it will – its appeal will surely be mainly due to the mystical writings of Rūmī, Ḥāfiẓ, Ibn 'Arabī and other Muslim Sufis, rather than to the more narrow and limited appeal of Islamic militants and fundamentalists. As the result of the great efforts of many Western scholars, Sufism has already made its presence felt in the spiritual and intellectual life of the West. Incredibly, some translations of the poems of Rūmī are becoming best-sellers in the United States and Europe.[95] One can find clear examples of the influence of Sufi poetry on the work of some leading contemporary Western poets, including the beautiful poems of Peter Russell.[96]

However, it is interesting that even non-specialist Western scholars and scientists are turning towards Sufism as a source of spiritual guidance. C.J.S. Clarke, Professor of Applied Mathematics and Dean of the Faculty of Mathematical Studies at the University of Southampton, ends his recent book on *Reality Through the Looking-Glass*, a kind of refutation of the materialistic view of life, with a chapter on Rūmī, concluding with these words:

> When the logic of criticism has led you through the void of Derrida's scepticism then the only way forward is to follow the heart. And it is here that the poetry of Rumi carries its own stamp of authenticity. Houseman's test of the poem that described reality was whether or not it made his beard stand on end if he recited the poem while shaving. Rumi's poems, for many of his readers, pass this test, leaving one physically gasping at what is revealed, raising every hair of the body in a tingle of recognition. I hope that some of my readers will also share that recognition:
>
> Totally conscious, and apropos of nothing, he comes to see me.
> Is someone here? I ask.
> *The moon. The full moon is inside your house.*
> My friends and I go running out into the street.

---

[94] Quoted by Claud Field, *Mystics and Saints of Islam* (London: Francis Griffiths 1911), p. 207.

[95] E.g. the recent unparalleled sale of some 100,000 copies of an anthology of Persian Sufi poetry entitled *The Essential Rumi* (trans C. Barks and J. Moyne; New York: HarperCollins 1995) in North America.

[96] Parvin Loloi, "Islamic Influences on Peter Russelli's Poetry," unpublished paper delivered at the international conference "British and Irish Poetry in the Making," University of Salzburg, November 1996. A copy of the article was kindly sent to me by Peter Russell.

I'm in here, come a voice from the house, but we aren't listening.
We're looking up at the sky.
My pet nightingale sobs like a drunk in the garden.
Ringdoves scatter with small cries *Where, Where.*
It's midnight. The whole neighbourhood is up and out in the street, thinking
The cat-burglar has come back.

The actual thief's there too, saying out loud,
Yes, the cat-burglar is somewhere in this crowd.
No one pays attention.

Lo, I am with you always, means when you look for God,
God is in the look of your eyes,
in the thought of looking, nearer to you than your self,
or things that have happened to you.
There is no need to go outside.
Be melting snow.
Wash yourself of yourself.

A white flower grows in the quietness.
Let your tongue become that flower.[97]

If I may be allowed to borrow Rūmī's image, Sufism has truly arrived and is finally inside our house.

---

[97] C.J.S. Clarke, *Reality Through the Looking-Glass: Science and Awareness in the Postmodern World* (London: Floris Books 1996), p. 199.

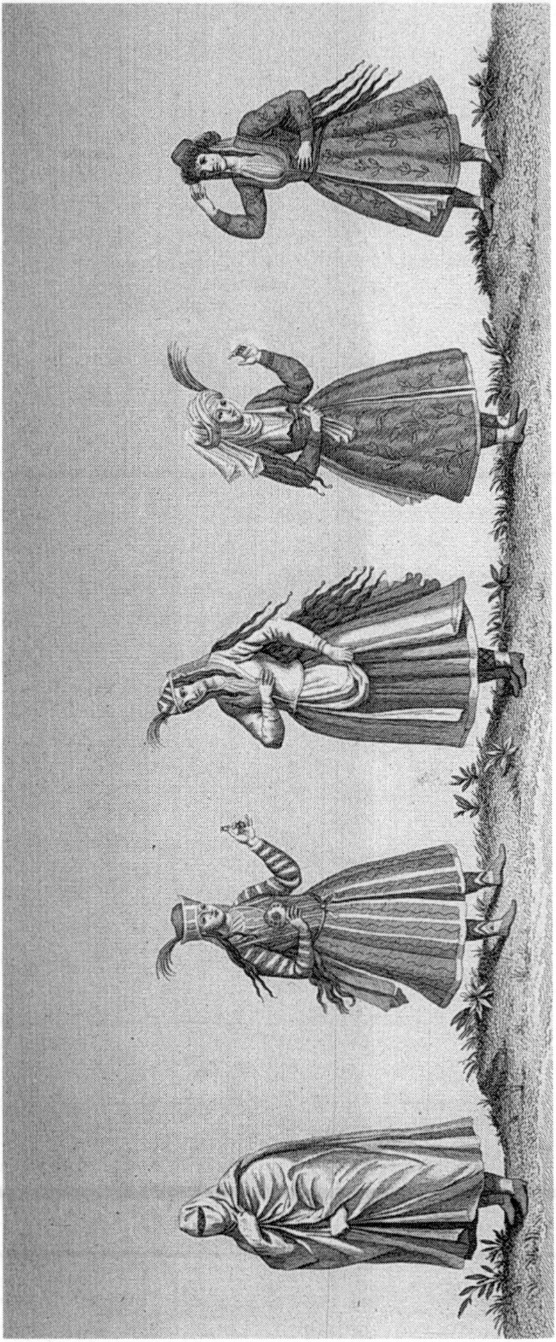

Plate 4: Persian Female Attire, From Chardin, *Voyages*, Pl. 23.

III

SUFISM AND SOCIETY IN SAFAVID PERSIA

هوالعزیز

روزی که برفتند حریفان پی هر کار

زاهد سوی مسجد شد و من جانب خمار

من یار طلب کردم و او جلوه‌گه یار

حاجی بره کعبه و من طالب دیدار

او خانه همی جوید و من صاحب خانه

That day our friends set out, each went his separate way:
The pietist into his mosque; I went the vintner's way.
I sought the Friend; he sought her sheen and radiant display:
The pilgrim's quest is just as far as the Ka'ba House;
My quest is always only Her: the Visio Dei*;*
The Manor-house is what he'll seek and find;
But I – my quest is only for the manor's Lord.

Sufism and the School of Iṣfahān

Taṣawwuf *and* 'Irfān *in Late Safavid Iran ('Abd al-Razzāq Lāhījī and Fayḍ-i Kāshānī on the Relation of* Taṣawwuf, Hikmat *and* 'Irfān)*

LEONARD LEWISOHN

I. INTRODUCTION

It is generally agreed today that the claim made by both E.G. Browne and Mīrzā Muḥammad Qazwīnī that hardly a single Persian poet of merit may be found during the entire Safavid period, such that "under this dynasty, learning, culture, poetry and mysticism completedly deserted Persia,"[1] is no longer tenable. Although the patronage and support which Persian poets were offered in Iran were "inadequate compared to India," for Hindustan "appeared to offer better opportunities of economic gain to the Persian poets," scholars generally acknowledge that the claim made by Browne that poetry and Sufism in Iran vanished from Persia during this period is greatly exaggerated.[2] Yet there is no escaping the fact that the flag of Persian mystical poetry hung at half-mast in Iran under the Safavids,[3] while in Mughal India, at least down to

---

* I am extremely grateful to Dr Andrew Newman, M.R. Juzi and Terry Graham for their many constructive comments on earlier drafts of this essay.

[1] Browne's *Literary History of Persia* (Cambridge: Cambridge University Press 1956–9), IV, p. 26, cited by both E. Yarshater, "Safavid Literature: Progress or Decline," *Iranian Studies* (1974 pp. 217, and 'Abd al-Ḥusayn Zarrīnkūb in his *Dunbāla-yi Justujū-yi dar taṣawwuf-i Īrān* (Tehran: Amīr Kabīr 1362 A.Hsh./1983), p. 223.

[2] Aziz Ahmad in his study of "Ṣafavid Poets and India," *Iran*, 14 (1976), pp. 118–19, thus argues that "there is considerable evidence that most of the Ṣafawīd monarchs from Ismā'īl I to 'Abbās II continued to write poetry and to patronize religious as well as non-religious verse."

[3] "With the exception of Muḥtasham Kāshī and Waḥshī Bāfqī, all the great poets of Ṣafawīd Iran migrated to India, and only one of them, Ṣā'ib, returned permanently to his homeland," Aziz Ahmad points out in his 'Ṣafavid Poets and India," p. 122. "In Persia the Safavid period was a generally unfavourable time for Persian language and literature," concluded Dhabīḥu'llāh Ṣafā, *Tārīkh-i adabiyāt-i Īrān*, II (Tehran: Intishārāt-i Firdaws 1373 A.Hsh./ 1994, 13th edn), V/I, p. 422; regarding which he supposes that the fact that Turkish and not Persian was the mother tongue of the founder of the dynasty, played a key role (*ibid.*, p. 424).

the reign of Awrangzīb the Puritan, Persian poets and poetry flourished with greater lustre (being provided with considerably more lucre there, as well[4]).

Since Browne's researches over three-quarters of a century ago, the development of Persian Sufism and Sufi poetry in Safavid Persia has been reappraised by scholars such as Ehsan Yarshater,[5] Aziz Ahmad,[6] Roger Savory,[7] 'Abd al-Ḥusayn Zarrīnkūb,[8] Dhabīḥu'llāh Ṣafā[9] and, more recently, Kathryn Babayan.[10] Examining the situation of Sufism in Safavid Iran in general and in the seventeenth century in particular, though no doubt it was a period of "unfavourable conditions for *taṣawwuf*",[11] what remains to be adumbrated is the peculiar social typology of the Sufism in Safavid Iran, both popular and 'high', *'amm wa khāṣṣ*, during and despite the theocratic regime.

In his classic study of *Sufism and the Sufi Literature* composed in the first half of the twentieth century, Y.E. Bertels was right to point out that "to date only the basic contours of the intellectual history of Sufism has been mapped out. Although substantial work has been done on the classical period which allows one to vaguely imagine its circumstances, next to nothing has been written about Sufism of the late classical [Safavid] period."[12] While the

---

[4] There are some quite contrary views about the reputed decline of Safavid-period poetry. On the contrast between the discouragement of Persian *belles-lettres* in Iran and their encouragement in India, see Ṣafā's *Tārīkh*, V/I, pp. 491–97 on Iran as a *kishvar-i bī-ravāj*, 'a land gone out of circulation' for Persian letters, as well as his similar discussion on pp. 421–4. On the other hand, the *Tuḥfa-i Sāmī* by Sām Mīrzā remains, as Aziz Ahmad pointed out, "an incontestable proof of the early Ṣafawīd interest in poetry" ("Safawid Poets and India," p. 120). The baroque *quality* of the poetry also needs re-examination (cf. the views of Shiblī Nu'mānī, *Sha'r al-'ajam*, Persian trans. by Muḥammad Taqī Fakhr Dā'ī Gīlānī [Tehran: Ibn Sīnā 1335 A.Hsh./1956; 2nd ed], translator's introduction, pp. ḥ–ṭ.) For further discussion of the position of poetry in Safavid times, see Roger Savory, *Iran Under the Safavids* (Cambridge: Cambridge University Press 1980), pp. 203–14; Ṣafā, *Tārīkh*, V/I, pp. 497–502.

[5] Article cited in n. 2 above and also revised version of the same: "The Indian or Safavid Style: Progress or Decline," in *Persian Literature*, ed. E. Yarshater (Albany: SUNY Press 1988), pp. 249–88.

[6] Aziz Ahmad, "Ṣafavid Poets and India," pp. 117–32.

[7] *Iran Under the Safavids*, pp. 203–15.

[8] Cited in note 2 above.

[9] Ṣafā, *Tārīkh*, V/I, *passim*.

[10] Kathryn Babayan, 'Sufis, Dervishes and Mullas: The Controversy over Spiritual and Temporal Dominion in Seventeenth-Century Iran', in *Safavid Persia: The History and Politics of an Islamic Society*, ed. Charles Melville (London: I.B. Tauris 1996), pp. 117–39; *idem*, "The Safavid Synthesis: from Qizilbash Islam to Imamite Shī'ism," *Iranian Studies*, 27/1–4 (1994), pp. 135–62; *idem*, "The Waning of the Qizilbash: The Spiritual and the Temporal in Seventeenth Century Iran" (University of Princeton doctoral dissertation 1993). I would like to thank Dr Babayan for providing me with a copy of her thesis.

[11] Ṣafā, *Tārīkh*, V/I, p. 201.

[12] *Taṣawwuf wa adabiyāt-i taṣawwuf*, Persian trans. by Sīrūs Īzādī (Tehran: Amīr Kabīr 1976), p. 661. Y.E. Bertels also pointed out here that Browne's treatment of Sufism in the fourth volume of his celebrated history was disappointingly meagre.

present volume in general aspires to rectify the omission of Safavid Sufism from the intellectual history of Iranian Islam, this chapter merely aims to illumine a small, but significant, aspect of the subject, namely the tense and difficult relationship between the Mujtahid cult and the Persian Sufism of late seventeenth-century Iran, as reflected in the school of Iṣfahān in general and the writings of 'Abd al-Razzāq Lāhījī and Fayḍ-i Kāshānī in particular.

Without understanding the political climate of the contemporary religious debates within which Safavid intellectual currents flowed, one can hardly hope to understand the attitudes towards Sufism which prevailed in seventeenth-century Persia. No literature – or indeed any art form – is created in a contextual vacuum, but closely mirrors the political views and social concerns of the age which nurtured it; the mind of intended audience plays an equal role in shaping a literature's rhetorical patterns of expression with the author's independent intellect. Just as one cannot divorce the poetry of John Milton (1608–74) from, for instance, his anti-Presbyterianism, republicanism, support for Cromwell and advocacy of civil liberties against the despotism of Charles I in England, so it is impossible to separate the politico-theological works of the thinkers of the seventeenth-century school of Iṣfahān from their philosophical, mystical and poetic writings.[13] For this reason, it is necessary briefly to trace the contours of the Safavids' suppression of Sufism (section II below) and the rise of the *mujtahid* cult (section III) in order to understand the political currents which affected the development of *taṣawwuf* and *'irfān*.[14]

At first sight, Safavid Sufism appears to be a completely different world from pre-Safavid Sufism. It is infused with extremism (*ghuluww*) and fuelled by fanatical Qizilbāsh *dervichisme*,[15] repackaged, decked out in a parti-

---

[13] In the introduction to *Prometheus Unbound*, Shelley made this clear: "We owe the great writers of the golden age of our literature to that fervid awakening of the public mind which shook to dust the oldest and most oppressive form of the Christian religion. We owe Milton to the progress and development of the same spirit: the sacred Milton was, let it ever be remembered, a republican and a bold inquirer into morals and religion."

[14] In his pioneering work on the history of the khānaqāh institution in Iran *Tārīkh-i khānaqāh dar Irān* (Tehran: Kitābkhāna Tahūrī, 1369 A.H.sh./1990), M. Kiyānī, while tracing the cause of the suppression of Sufism in Safavid Iran, insightfully observes that "the acceptance or rejection of Sufism in any society is, aside from historical circumstances, the product of the flucuations in the relations of the clergy, rulers and political authorities with the Sufis. The average man in the street will form an opinion either favourable or adverse to the Sufis on the basis of the pronouncements of his religious authorities and the acceptance or rejection of the Sufis by the political leaders of his day" (p. 500).

[15] This is a term coined by Jean Aubin ("La Propriété foncière en Azerbayjan sous les Mongols," in *Le Monde iranien et l'Islam*, 4, 1976–7), p. 128, to describe an essential component of a type of hereditary Sufism passed down by lineages of 'sacred families' during the Mongol period, so that "spiritual authority and material management was transmitted, hand to hand, hereditarily, with their morally privileged status and their ancestry assuring the social position of the inheritors." The social contexts of Safavid *dervichisme* are discussed by Zarrīnkūb, *Dunbāla*, pp. 232–3; Savory, "Some Reflections on Totalitarian Tendencies in the Safarid State," p. 229; *idem.*, *Iran under the Safavids*, p. 25ff.

coloured cloak of Shīʿite piety, its most celebrated exponents' diction and lexicon tainted by their Arab colleagues in the *madrasa*, all of whom are steeped in the semi-alien language of Lebanon from whence so many Safavid *ʿulamā'* hailed.[16] Seldom now does one imbibe the fresh highland air of the ecstatic and wild beauty of ʿAṭṭār and Rūmī, almost as if one had crossed a mountain pass and suddenly descended into a strange foreign gorge: that misty clime of Shīʿite theological speculation.[17] *Stricto sensu*, one now feels outside the realm of classical Persian Sufism;[18] most of the Safavid mystics discourse in a different tongue from that of Seljuk, Mongol and Timurid-period Sufism, basing themselves on Shīʿite imāmology and writings. Suffering under the growing pressure of puritan militancy, these writings

---

[16] Referring to the Arabization of Persian culture (due to the Safavid's desire for competent Shīʿite clerics) which ensued in the sixteenth century, Dhabīḥu'llāh Ṣafā notes how Al-Ḥurr al-Āmulī in his *Amal al-āmil* listed 1,100 Arabic-speaking scholars who migrated to Iran during the period, a statistic which indicates among other factors "the deep effect on Iran of the renewed propagation of Arabic language and culture" (*Tārīkh-i adabiyāt-i Īrān*, V/I, p. 128; see also n82 below). Ṣafā devotes an entire sub-chapter, based on detailed primary-source evidence, to the "severing of national ties" which occurred under Safavid rule, noting that because of the influx of Arabic-speaking clerics from Lebanon and Iraq, "Persian culture during the period was, in many respects, under the direct influence of Arab culture. Academic lessons and studies would begin and end in Arabic, and until the end they were involved with that language, in which most of their works were written. ... So it is no surprise if we find that these clerics are far from liking Persian culture." (*Tārīkh*, V/1, p. 187; also cf. 126–8; 366–8 for further comments on the Arabization of Persian culture). The great Persian literary critic and poet M.T. Bahār in his *Sabk-shināsī* (Tehran: Chāp-i tābān 1337 A.Hsh./1958) points out that the destruction of and corruption in the style and expression of Persian prose writing during the Safavid period is "without equal in any other historical period in Iran" (III, p. 301). He devotes an entire section of this study to 'the decline of Persian prose', where he observes how "sweet and subtle Persian terms and words are replaced by dry Arabic compounds and expressions" (*ibid.*, III, p. 256). For further comments about the Arabization of Persian culture during this period, see Ali Banuazizi, *Iranian Nationality and the Persian Language 900–1900: The Roles of Court, Religion and Sufism in Persian Prose Writing*, trans. J. Hillmann (Washington: Mage 1992), pp. 140–2. Of course, the 'Arabization' thesis advanced here by Ṣafā, Bahā and Meskoob has limited value, being restricted to the fields of theology and literature. It can be conceded that Safavid government maintained the same high level of Persian culture in other areas such as book painting, textiles and carpet manufacture as any previous dynasty in Iran.

[17] Discussing the disastrous impact of Shīʿism on Iran, M.T. Bahār notes that from the accession of Shāh Tahmāsp onwards, "in the space of fifty years, the condition of Persian literature was turned upside down; a new culture takes over which gives its own weird form to everything. Even if the Safavids came to power under the pretence of [Sufi] guidance (*irshād*), the gates of guidance during their reign are shut down, such that only one Sufi order (*silsila*) is allowed to exist ... an order whose adherents lacked all faith in Sufism (*taṣawwuf*). ... The true Sufis having suffered defeat at the hands of jurists and Akhbārīs, in Shīʿite books Sufis are now called irreligious and labeled heretics, such that even the works of Rūmī are reviled and fatwas for the death of the Sufis frequently given" (*Sabk-shināsī*, III, p. 255).

[18] On which, see the previous two volumes of *The Heritage of Sufism*, ed. L. Lewisohn (Oxford: Oneworld 1999).

reflect the suppressed nightmare of religious antagonisms which afflicted them. Such mystics, steeped in the rational tradition of legalistic scholarship, emphasize the socially acceptable nomocentric over the ecstatic and erotic aspects of *taṣawwuf*. Generally speaking, they all express themselves in a consciously esoteric philosophical language, the works of Avicenna and the Ishrāqī master Suhrawardī featuring as often, if not more frequently, than those of the great Sufis such as Ibn ʿArabī and Rūmī, whose works had all but succumbed to the *mujtahid*s' efforts culturally to expurgate *taṣawwuf* from the Persian psyche.

Even the highest adepts of the Iṣfahān School of theosophers generally seem to show scant respect for institutional Sufism and the traditional *khānaqāh*s. They rigorously insist on distinguishing between the "vulgar" or "popular" (*ʿawāmm*) generality of dervishes and the "high" and "elect" (*khāṣṣ*) Sufis. In spiritual method, they are also usually sober in orientation, after the fashion of an Abū Ḥāmid al-Ghazālī rather than an Abū Saʿīd ibn Abi'l-Khayr or an ʿAyn al-Quḍāt Hamadhānī. The rage of Ḥallāj, the ecstasy of Kharaqānī, the visionary transports of Bayazid, even the selfless *samāʿ* of Ṣafī al-Dīn Ardabilī, are now all considered politically incorrect – or at least a social embarrassment to the state-owned *faqīh*'s dignity.

Then perhaps the dearth of studies on Sufism in Safavid Persia – as the academic silence on the subject would implicitly imply – is simply because one can, or should, view Safavid Sufism as an epiphenomenon of politics and history? Perhaps the soul fled from Safavid Sufism, a lifeless social body left as heir to the vanished loves of the Mongol and Seljuk Sufis? One glimpse of the *Dīvān* of Ḥātif Iṣfahānī or the verse of Fayḍ-i Kāshānī, however, indicates that this is but a half-truth.[19]

II. THE SUPPRESSION OF SUFISM IN SAFAVID PERSIA

Nor happiness, nor majesty, nor fame
Nor peace, nor strength, nor skill in arms or arts,
Shepherd those herds whom tyranny makes tame;
Verse echoes not one beating of their hearts,
History is but the shadow of their shame

Shelley

Say to the Court it glows
And shines like rotten wood,
Say to the Church it shows

[19] Cf. S.H. Nasr's comments in his article "Spiritual Movements, Philosophy and Theology in the Safavid Period," *The Cambridge History of Iran* V (Cambridge: Cambridge University Press 1968), pp. 661–2.

What's good, and doth no good.
If Church and Court reply
Then give them both the lie.

Sir Walter Ralegh[20]

Although the Safavid theocracy arose "in the milieu of Sufism and of extremism,"[21] its "totalitarian state" as Roger Savory termed it,[22] was based on a politicalization of the master–disciple relationship, focusing upon an idolatrous cult of personality built around the ruler as both 'perfect master' (*murshid-i kāmil*) and absolute monarch.[23] Apotheosized as a divine incarnation, the first Safavid ruler Ismā'īl I (reg. 1501–24) was glorifed as the Mahdi[24] and even as God himself[25] by his zealous Qizilbāsh army. A Venetian merchant who visited Iran in the early sixteenth century reported:

> The name of God is forgotten throughout Persia and only that of Ismael remembered; if any one fall when riding or dismounted, he appeals to no other God but Shiac (Shaykh), using the name in two ways: first as God Shiac, secondly as prophet: as the Mussulmans say "laylla, laylla Mahamet resuralla [*lā ilāha ilāllāhu wa Muḥammadun rasūlullāhi*], the Persians say "Laylla yllala Ismael velialla" [*lā ilāha ilāllāhu* (*va*) *Ismā'īl valī allāhi*]; besides this, everyone, and particularly his soldiers, consider him immortal."[26]

In this attitude, Ismā'īl was faithful to the extremist cults of personality instituted by his Safavid forefathers Junayd (1447–60) and Ḥaydar (1460–88), who had transformed the originally peaceful Safavid order into "a militant ghāzī movement,"[27] thus beginning what was to become one of the darkest chapters in the entire history of Islamic Sufism. As S.A. Arjomand has

---

[20] Cited in *Elizabethan People*, ed. J. Hurstfield and A.G.R. Smith (London: Edward Arnold 1972), p. 164.

[21] Savory, *Iran Under the Safavids*, p. 77.

[22] "Some Reflections on Totalitarian Tendencies," pp. 226–41.

[23] For further discussion of Isma'īl's messianic self-divinization, see S.A. Arjomand, "Religious Extremism (*Ghuluww*), Sufism and Sunnism in Safavid Iran (1501–1722)," *Journal of Asian Studies*, 15/1 (1981), pp. 4–5; R. Savory, "The Consolidation of Power in Safavid Persia," *Der Islam* (1976), p. 91; R. Canfield, "Theological 'Extremism' and Social Movements in Turko-Persia," in *Turko-Persia in Historical Perspective*, ed. R. Canfield (Cambridge: Cambridge University Press 1991), pp. 132–60; K. Babayan, "Sufis, Dervishes and Mullas," pp. 117–19.

[24] A.K.S. Lambton noted that "As representative of the Mahdī, the Safavid shāh was closer to the source of absolute Truth than were other men, and consequently opposition to him was a sin. This theory led to the assumption of kingly infallibility," "Quis custodient custodes?," *Studia Islamica*, (1956), p. 129.

[25] Savory, *Iran Under the Safavids*, p. 17.

[26] *Travels of Venetians in Persia* London 1873: Hakluyt Society, p. 206; cited by Savory, *Iran Under the Safavids*, p. 24.

[27] Arjomand, *The Shadow of God and the Hidden Imam* (Chicago: University of Chicago Press 1984), p. 79.

observed, the main result of this movement was that "action govened by ethical norms became devoid of significance for salvation." The "Islamic normative order became inoperative," since the Safavid leader's stance

> implied the suspension of all Islamic normative influences which, for their efficacy, depended critically on the transcendence of God and mediation of the sacred law between God and man. It amounted to the abolition of all normative order independent of the personal will of the supreme leader, who was, at the same time, the Sufi murshid, the Shi'ite Imam, and the primordial godhead.[28]

Addressing the question how such extremist beliefs found acceptance in Anatolia and Kurdistān in the fourteenth century, Roger Savory posits the view that the Mongols' rule of Iran had displaced orthodox Islam and allowed the conditions for religious extremism or *ghuluww* to become normalized:

> The religious tolerance (some might say indifference) of the Mongol rulers deprived Sunnī or "orthodox" Islam of its dominant position and created conditions which facilitated the development not only of Shī'ism but of popular relgious beliefs of every kind.... Anatolia in particular became a veritable melting pot of religious ideas. The two principal ingredients in this pot were Shi'ism and Sufism, and in the course of the fourteenth century these two ingredients became permanently blended.[29]

However, the tolerance of the Mongols, modelled on the religious pluralism of Sufism,[30] which was the chief characteristic of Persian mystical topography from the thirteenth to the fifteenth century, as Hodgson makes clear,[31] was all but snuffed out under Ismā'īl[32] who not only insisted on sectarian conversion

---

[28] Arjomand, *The Shadow of God*, pp. 81–2.

[29] Savory, *Iran Under the Safavids*, pp. 23–4, whose general observations are borne out by M. Mazzaoui's more detailed analysis of primary-source material in his *The Origins of the Ṣafavids: Šī'ism, Ṣūfism, and the Ġulāt* (Wiesbaden: Franz Steiner 1972), pp. 59–80.

[30] See my *Beyond Faith and Infidelity: The Sufi Poetry and Spiritual Teachings of Maḥmūd Shabistarī* (London: Curzon 1995), chap. 3, for an extended discussion of the Mongols' attitude towards Sufism.

[31] "The Sufis tended to be as naturally tolerant of local differences as the Shar'ī 'ulamā' tended to be intolerant. The 'ulamā' had to concentrate on matters of external conformity, as dictated by the Shari'ah, in order to maintain the legal and institutional framework for social unity ... For the Sufis, on the contrary, externals were secondary. For many of them, especially by the Earlier Middle Period, even the difference between Islam and other cultural traditions such as Christianity was of secondary importance in principle; of still less moment were the various differences in social custom within the community of Muhammad. What mattered was the inner disposition of the heart to God" (*The Venture of Islam* [Chicago: University of Chicago Press 1977], II, p. 203).

[32] Referring to Shāh Ismā'īl I's (*reg.* 1501–24) reign of terror against those who did not conform to Safavid dogma, Tomes Pires, the Portuguese ambassador to China who visited Iran in 1511–2, noted: "He (i.e. Shāh Ismā'īl) deforms our churches, destroys the houses of all Moors who follow (the Sunnah of) Muḥammad and never spares the life of any Jew" (Tomé Pires, *The Suma Oriental: 1512–1515,* trans. from Portuguese by Armando Cortesao

to Shīʿism but believed Sufism to be incompatible with Sunnism.[33] The form of Shīʿism which Shāh Ismāʿīl's followers professed, even the form which his immediate father and grandfather espoused, merged with the vulgarized *dervichisme* of his armed Qizilbāsh quasi-Sufi followers to produce "the same sort of claims and beliefs which typify the *ghulāt* Shīʿites."[34] "Because of the oppositional stance of both the Imāmīs and the *ghulāt*, the ʿAlīd cause came to be the rallying cry around which both groups united;"[35] and in this manner, as Kathryn Babayan points out, exactly like the Fatimids who rose to power by use of similar revolutionary utopian slogans, "Shāh Ismā'īl too played on the *ghulāt* spirit of the *Qizilbash* to establish the Safavi empire. In his poetry Ismā'īl refers to himself as Farīdūn, Rustam, Alexander, Jesus, and the son of ʿAlī . . . He saw himself as the reincarnation of a host of holy and heroic figures from Islamdom's cultural past."[36]

Shāh Ismāʿīl's Shīʿitized reorientation of Sufism was tinged with his self-conception as not only a Sufi master, but the veritable hand and shadow of God on earth. He inherited the bloodthirsty and ruthless nature of his father and grandfather, and was notorious for his readiness to massacre those who disagreed with his political or religious views.[37] Shelley's verse:

> He loathed all faith beside his own and pined
> To wreak his fear of Heaven in vengence on mankind.[38]

best portrays the religious archetype at play. Hence, in examining the rise of the Safavid order from the mid-fifteenth century onwards, one is no longer studying *taṣawwuf* in the classical sense of the word, but rather an absolutistic despotism and theocratic autocracy masquerading with the mannerisms of

---

London: Hakluyt Society 1944, I, p. 27. Cited by David Yeroushalmi (ed.), *The Judeo-Persian Poet ʿEmrānī and his Book of Treasure: Emrānī's* Ganj-nāme, *A Versified Commentary on the Mishnaic Tractate Abot* [Leiden: Brill 1995], introduction, p. 20. The great hatred that Shāh Ismā'īl bore for Jews is especially striking for its intolerance. Raphaël du Mans, *Estat de la Perse en 1660*, ed. Ch. Schefer (Paris: Ernest Leroux 1890), p. 274, reported that "So deep is his hate that whenever he sees a Jew he orders to put out his eyes." (Cited by Yeroushalmi *The Judeo-Persian Poet Emrānī*, introduction, p. 20.)

[33] Rasūl Jaʿfariyān, *Dīn va siyāsat dar dūra-yi Ṣafavī* (Qum: Intishārāt-i Anṣāriyān 1370 A.Hsh./1991), p. 225.

[34] Zarrīnkūb, *Dunbāla*, p. 228.

[35] Babayan, "The Waning of the Qizilbash," p. 28.

[36] *Ibid*., p. 33; *idem*, "Safavid Synthesis," p. 143.

[37] When someone objected that the Sunni peasants might protest at the imposition of Shīʿism, he replied: "If they do, we will not leave a soul of them alive." Cited by Zarrīnkūb, *Dunbāla*, p. 224 (citing Abū Bakr Tihrānī, *Tārīkh-i Jahān-ārā*, quoted in Naṣru'llāh Falsafī, *Zindagī-yi Shāh ʿAbbās Awwal* [Tehran: 1332 A.Hsh./1953], I, p. 167). M.T. Bahār has compared the effect of Shāh Ismāʿīl on Persian culture to a "nest of wasps more deadly than all the Tartar hosts" (*Sabk-shināsī*, III, p. 250), for, in the pursuit of his own Shīʿite extremist faith, "he had no qualms at all in massacring, murdering, and wreaking mayhem, in which policy he exercised no degree of restraint" (*ibid*., III, pp. 253–4).

[38] Shelley, "The Revolt of Islam," XXXII.

taṣawwuf put on as a social facade;[39] in a word, the ideologization of mysticism to suit a particular religio-political agenda.[40]

Just as the shadow-self of puritanism is prurience, even the purest faith being prone to hypocrisy, so no religious sect or party exists whose piety and politics cannot be tainted and corrupted:

> The same ambition can destroy or save
> And make a patriot as it makes a knave.[41]

Despite its grand ideals, Sufism is no exception to this rule. Sir John Malcolm's remarks on the decline of Sufism under Zand rule in nineteenth-century Iran apply equally well to the Sufi sulṭāns of sixteenth-century Safavid Persia:

> There is no path to fame and power, however unseemly and rugged, on which man will not enter; the same passions which excite the worldly votary of ambition to the attainment of royal robes and a sceptre, fill the breast of the mendicant devotee, striving for the holy staff and sacred mantle that are to vest him with power over the minds of the multitude.[42]

---

[39] The Safavid sovereigns' economic exploitation and politicitized truncation of the master–disciple relationship in Sufism appears in the accounts given by contemporary European travellers to Persia. Michele Membré, a Venetian envoy to the court of Shāh Tahmāsp, for one, observed at first hand the absolutist tyranny which the king exercised over his dervish subjects. In Membré's description of the dervish dances of the "sophians" (i.e. Qizilbāsh Sufis) in the early sixteenth century, he relates that they play and sing praises to God and Shāh Tahmāsp "For they say that the said Shah receives the tenth of what they earn each year, for being their prophet. And there are those of them who, when a daughter is born to them, say, 'She will be *nadhr* for the Shah', that is a gift for a vow. And when she is of a suitable age, many bring her and show her to the said Shah, who keeps those who please him and lets the others go" (Michele Membré, *Mission to the Lord Sophy of Persia (1539–1542)*, trans. A.H. Morton [London: SOAS Publications 1993], p. 32).

[40] As Professor Ṣafā (*Tārīkh*, V/1, p. 201) points out: "The tinpot sect of Safavid Sufis who flourished during the uprising and expansion of power and under the rule of Shāh Ismā'īl and his son Shāh Tahmāsp were devoid of all the disciplines of classical Sufism; not only were they unaware of the higher ideals of Sufism, they had only a vulgarized apprehension of the existence of such ideals, their understanding being based on popular, watered-down beliefs followed without any deeper awareness. Since they followed the *ṭarīqat* of their own shaykhs in such an ignorant manner, no wonder that they readily condemned all other intellectual movements besides their own as heretical, and endeavoured to eliminate everyone else . . . These pseudo-Sufi Turkish *Qizilbāsh*, from the time that Sulṭān Junayd and Sulṭān Ḥaydar had decked them out in coats of mail and stripped them of their dervish robes, forging their pious strings of beads into sabres and spears . . . were in reality, no longer Sufis, although we can see, incredible as it appears, that they still insisted on calling themselves Sufis."

[41] Alexander Pope, *An Essay on Man*, II, 201–2.

[42] *History of Persia* (London 1829), II, p. 287. Lamenting similar conditions prevailing in Christianity in England a century later, while criticizing those who use "religion as a stalking horse to get and enjoy the world," the seventeenth-century English Nonconformist preacher John Bunyan told the same truth when he observed in *The Pilgrim's Progress* (ed.

The decline and descent of the Safavid *dudmān* into the Hades of political cultism had begun in late Timurid times when Shāh Ismā'īl's grandfather Junayd (1447–60), the first Safavid master to assume the title of Sulṭān "indicative of temporal authority ... introduced a militant note into the peaceful Safavid Order[43] by inciting his disciples to war against the infidels."[44] The Sunni theologian Faḍlullāh b. Rūzbihān Khunjī-Iṣfahānī in his *Tārīkh-i 'ālam-ārā-yi Amīnī* recorded Junayd's change of policy as follows:

> He had altered the character of his ancestors. In the nest of fantasy, the bird of temptation had laid the egg of the desire for temporal rule. Of course, as a consequence, it set flight in the air of his deranged desires. He allowed the falcon of his thoughts to soar every hour in a different direction, towards conquests of lands and climes.[45]

Junayd was chased out of Ardabīl by Jahānshāh and took refuge in Syria with the Āq Quyūnlū leader Ūzūn Ḥasan whose sister he married, thus cementing "his political alliance."[46] Khunjī-Iṣfahānī again wonders why

> instead of raising the flag of spiritual guidance, did he unfold the banner of military command, changing his mantle of renunciation (*khirqa-yi parhīz*) for bloodsoiled garments. Why did he switch the staff of ascetic restraint (*zuhādat*) for a death-dealing javelin, he wondered:
>
> What was it, what was it you missed in life,
> To gain what name or fame, or rank you wished
> Which made you switch your dervish robe for it,
> Change your Sufi cell for the barracks?

Roger Sharrock: Penguin 1987; Harmondsworth) that "the man that takes up religion for the world will throw away religion for the world; for so surely as Judas designed the world in becoming religious, so surely did he also sell religion and his master for the same. ... The Pharisees were also of this religion, long prayers were their pretence, but to get widows' houses was their intent" (pp. 154–5).

43 The contrast between the religious idealism of the original Safavid Sufi masters and the militant fundamentalism of the later Safavid sovereign *pīr*s is extraordinary. It is said that when the founder of the Safavid order, Shaykh Ṣafī al-Dīn Ardabilī was once challenged by Amīr Chūbān, the most formidable vizier at the court of the last Īlkhānid Sulṭān Abū Sa'īd (*reg*. 1317–35), with the question: "Who are more numerous, your disciples or my men?" Shaykh Ṣafī shamed him by his reply, "In Iran today, for every man at arms there are one hundred men of devotion" (Qaḍī Aḥmad Ghaffārī, *Tārīkh-i Jahān-ārā* [Tehran: 1343 A.Hsh./1964], p. 260; cited by Mazzaoui, *The Origins*, p. 71).

44 Savory, *Iran Under the Safavids*, p. 16. Michael Mazzaoui, in his *The Origins of the Ṣafavids*, noted that "From contemplative *ṣūfism* under *Śaiḫ* Ṣafī ad-Dīn to open heresy of the *ġulāt* type under Ğunaid and Ḥaidar is a long way and a far cry. The only explanation that could be offered (and this only by looking at the consequences rather than at the causes) is that by assuming this super-human and divine role, the new-type leaders of the Order could rally their followers and lead them to *ġazā* and conquest. ... In other words, the religious change was simply a pretext for political ends" (p. 273).

45 Faḍlullāh b. Rūzbihān Khunjī-Iṣfahānī, *Tārīkh-i 'ālam-ārā-yi Amīnī*, ed. John Woods (London: Royal Asiatic Society 1992), p. 266.

46 Savory *Iran Under the Safavids*, p. 17.

With the sword cut your focus on Oneness off,
Leave your Sufi refuge and slash all ties
With holiness, to toss away your staff
of pious righteousness, and raise the axe?[47]

The answer to the question posed in this *dūbaytī*, of course, had been given half a century earlier by Ḥāfiẓ in famous verses exposing the dark side of the Pharisitical hypocrisy lurking within Islamic piety:

I have a difficulty, and submit it to the wise men of this assembly:
Those who exhort to penitence, why aren't they penitents themselves?
One could say that not longer believing in the day of the last judgement,
They corrupt, by their fraud, the work of the supreme Judge.[48]

Contrary to the customary historical platitude, Shāh Ismā'īl, the first Safavid ruler, did not establish the new religion of Persia on the basis of either Shī'ism or Sufism. His religion was a kind of sectarian religious totalitarianism focused on *ghulāt* Islam, the doctrines and practices of which are completely alien to both traditional Shī'ism[49] and classical Sufism.[50] As Zarrīnkūb, Savory, Amoretti and so many other scholars have pointed out, the tone of his movement was primarily that of a personality cult based on his apotheosis "as a divine incarnation;"[51] while his claims were so fantastic and exclusivistic that he had no choice but to strive to expel every other Sufi order from the arena lest they be tempted to make similar claims.[52] If Sa'dī's tolerant Sufi ideal expressed in his famous maxim contrasting the simple piety of spiritual poverty to the grandious pretensions of temporal power –

---

47 *chih shud kaz faqr mayl-i jāh kardī*
bijā-yi khānaqah khargāh kardī
bih tīgh az khalwat-i waḥdat burīdī
'aṣā afkandī u nayza guzīdī

(*Tārīkh-i 'ālam-ārā-yi Amīnī*, p. 269.)

48 *Dīwān-i Ḥāfiẓ*, ed. Parwīz Nātil Khanlarī (Tehran: Sahāmī 'ām 1362 A.Hsh./1983; 2nd edn.), p. 404; Ghazal 194; vv. 2, 3; translation by Peter Russell.

49 Dhabīḥu'llāh Ṣafā in his *Tārīkh-i adabiyāt-i Īrān* (V/1, p. 170) underlines the fact that "the political milieu of the Safavid Redhat autocracy is one completely at variance with traditional Twelver Shī'ism, or in fact with any other Shī'ite denomination. More than anything, it was composed of popular beliefs professed without any intellectual verification or analysis of the religious subject-matter." Although Kathlyn Babayan is right to state that he "came to place his messianic claims within an Imami framework" ("Sufis, Dervishes and Mullas," p. 119) this is but an alibi for the crime already committed.

50 On which, see Javad Nurbakhsh's informative essay: 'The Key Features of Early Persian Sufism', in L. Lewisohn, *The Heritage of Sufism*, I:, pp. xvii–xli.

51 Savory *Iran Under the Safavids*, p. 23; Zarrīnkūb, *Dunbāla*, p. 227; Amoretti, "Religion in the Timurid and Safavid Periods," in *Cambridge History of Iran*, V, pp. 634–40.

52 Zarrīnkūb, *Dunbāla*, p. 228.

Two dervishes sleep in peace beneath a single sheepskin
But a single country is too small to contain two kings.[53]

– pithily sums up what Marshall Hodgson referred to as "the comprehensive humanity from which a Sufi could preach," which "gave the Sufi tradition an often spectacular advantage,"[54] – then Shāh Ismā'īl's conquest of Iran illustrates the perversion of this ideal and the forfeiture of this historical advantage.

Recognizing that his position as the cult leader of a radical religio-political party was far too left of centre to obtain a popular vote of confidence,[55] shortly after his seizure of Tabrīz, the capital of Iran in 1501 at the age of 14, Shāh Ismā'īl proclaimed nominal 'Shī'ism' to be the state religion of Iran. However, in the frenzy of his adolescence, and apparently in order to conserve and redirect the momentum of his revolutionary followers[56] who were attracted by "the vehemence of a fascinating ideology,"[57] he decreed that his supporters introduce the ritual cursing of the three other caliphs: Abū Bakr, 'Uthmān and 'Umar. Thus, Safavid party members known as *tabarrā'iyyān* were instructed to pace the streets and marketplaces, cursing three of the four 'righteous caliphs' (besides 'Alī). Whoever did not respond

---

[53] As Ṣafā notes (*Tārīkh*, V/I, pp. 203–4), the real reason behind the opposition of the Shī'ite *'ulamā'* to the Sufis centres on a power struggle based on a theological divergence of interpretation regarding the Islamic doctrine of 'sainthood and the sacrosanct' (*wilāyah*). "The Shī'ite divines (*'ālimān*) understood *walāyah* and guidance of people as part of the exclusive domain of the Imām, and in his absence, those appointed by him. The Sufis, on the other hand, included their own 'poles' (*aqṭāb*) and shaykhs among the number of the saints, considering both implicit and explicit obedience to *them* as incumbent, effectively disregarding the legalist scholars who claimed to be successors of the prophet. So it is evident that even two kings cannot rule a single clime although the dervish is ready to sleep under a single blanket with the rest of humanity" (see also n. 65 below).

[54] *The Venture of Islam*, II, p. 207.

[55] Both V. Minorsky and R. Savory have appropriately noted the resemblances between the *ahl-i ikhtiṣāṣ*, and Lenin's Politburo of 1919 which controlled the Bolshevik movement. See V. Minorsky, *Tadhkirat al-mulūk* (London 1942), pp. 1–3; Savory, "Some Reflections on Totalitarian Tendencies," pp. 226–41.

[56] Arjomand points out that when Shāh Ismā'īl proclaimed Shī'ism as the state religion in Tabrīz, "that city, like the rest of Iran, was predominantly Sunnī. It was only after much searching that a book containing the basic tenets of Imāmī Shī'ism, the *Qawa'id al-islām* by Ibn al-Muṭahhar al-Ḥillī (1250–1326) was found in the library of a qāḍī, and was made the basis of the new religion." (S.A. Arjomand, "Religious Extremism (*Ghuluww*), Sufism and Sunnism in Safavid Iran (1501–1722)," *Journal of Asian Studies*, 15/1 [1981], p. 3). Also cf. Zarrīnkūb, *Dunbāla, p.* 224. Shī'ites existed in pre-Safavid Iran but were constituted a very small minority living in Qum, Kāshān, Rayy and Sāva. On the Sunni origins of the Safavids, see Aḥmad Kasravī, "Tabār va kīsh Ṣafaviyān," *Iran Nameh*, 13/3 (1995), pp. 377–86; Mazzaoui, *The Origins of the Safavids*, pp. 46 ff.

[57] Hans R. Roemer, "The Qizilbash Turcomans: Founders and Victims of the Safavid Theocracy," in *Intellectual Studies on Islam*, ed M. Mazzaoui and V. Moreen (Salt Lake City: University of Utah Press 1990), p. 30.

with the slogan, "Sing more abuse of them, not less!" (*Bīsh bād, kam mabād!*) was put to death immediately.[58]

Under the spell of superficially disguised shamanist concepts, Ismā'īl himself – who was of Turcoman not Iranian descent[59] – advocated even more barbarous customs; he made himself a cup out of the skull of a defeated enemy, and instructed his cannibal Qizilbāsh followers to roast their defeated foes alive and eat their flesh to acquire strength![60] A special national holiday to celebate the murder of 'Umar was invented by the adolescent Shī'ite autocrat,[61] still faithfully observed in the Islamic Republic of Iran today![62]

This proclamation of Shī'ism:

> symbolized Shāh Ismā'īl's move away from *ghuluww* toward orthodoxy. The *ghuluww* had served its purpose in carrying the Safavi brotherhood into statehood. From the outset of his rule, Shāh Ismā'īl had realized that to unify and centralize his domains, it would be imperative to alter the nature of his legitimacy and to forge a uniform religion: heterodoxy had to be eliminated. The tensions, however, persisted between the contradictory functions of *pīr* and *shāh*, and the conflicting nature of *ghuluww* and Imamism.[63]

These tensions, with the psychological contradiction that dual recourse to interior sources of spiritual power and the exterior forces of a temporal potentate entail,[64] were resolved with unrighteous might when the Grand Sophy, as Europeans referred to the Safavid sovereigns, like his father and grandfather before him, switched the traditional interpretation of the Sufi doctrine of 'sainthood' (*wilāyah*: the saint's friendship with God) to imply the sanctification of his own political sovereignty on the basis of such extreme Shī'ism,[65] thereby excluding all other Sufis, or indeed, any dissenting expressions of religious belief, from their inhumane 'divine' plan.

---

[58] Cited by Zarrīnkūb in his *Dunbāla*, p. 224; also see Savory, *Iran Under the Safavids*, pp. 27–8.

[59] See Ṣafā, *Tārīkh*, V/I, p. 495.

[60] Hans R. Roemer, "The Qizilbash Turcomans: Founders and Victims of the Safavid Theocracy," in *Intellectual Studies on Islam*, ed. M. Mazzaoui and V. Moreen, p. 31.

[61] This holiday was celebrated annually on the 26th of Dhū'l-Hujjat. See Ṣafā, *Tārīkh-i*, V/1, p. 168.

[62] *Ibid.*

[63] Babyan, "The Waning of the Qizilbash," p. 37.

[64] On which, see Zarrīnkūb's interesting discussion and analysis, *Dunbāla*, pp. 230ff. and also Rasūl Ja'fariyān, *Dīn va siyāsat*, pp. 225–6.

[65] Hermann Landolt drew attention to this change in interpretation of the *wilāyah* doctrine, insofar as once the early Safavid rulers "assumed rule of Iran (with Shāh Ismā'īl I in 1501) they introduced Twelver Shiism, in a form hardly compatible with 'orthodox' Shī'ī doctrine, as state religion; their prayer carpet (*sajjādah*), symbol of the dignity of the Ṣūfī *shaykh*, or Ṣūfī *wilāyah*, became the symbol of the quasi-divine throne of Persia (*qālichah-i salṭanat*). Their success also brought about . . . the establishment of a real Shī'ī 'clergy' and its eventual politization" ("Walāyah," in *The Encyclopedia of Religion*, ed. M. Eliade [New York: Macmillan 1995], XV, p. 320). See also Ṣafā's comments on the clerical reinterpretation of the doctrine of *wilāyah* by Safavid *'ulamā'*, *Tārīkh*, V/I, pp. 203–4.

"Isma'il's hostility towards the non-Shī'ites," Kamil Shaibi reveals, "was based on the Musha'sha'a view of considering all their opponents disbelievers. This was why the graves of Jami, a Nasqhbandī Sufi, and Abū Ishan of Kazarun, a Sunni Sufi, were despoiled."[66] The Sufi chronologer Ḥāfiẓ Ḥusayn Ibn Karbalā'ī described how Shāh Ismā'īl I "eradicated, destroyed and extirpated most of the initiatic lineages [*silāsil* = Sufi Orders] of the Sayyids and Shaykhs' in Persia,[67] and how "the Sufi lineages (*silsilas*) were crushed by him."[68] Furthermore, during this period most of the great Sufi orders were forced to flee to Mughal India or Ottoman Turkey, or to go underground. The Naqshbandiyya were ferociously suppressed; Sufis of the Khalvatiyya order fled to Ottoman protection in Anatolia; the Dhahabiyya, Nūrbakhshiyya, and Nimatullāhiyya Orders survived, true, but with none of their former glory, remaining mostly underground and persecuted, increasing subjected to fanatic anathema by the theocratic establishment.[69] In 909/1503, after a massacre of 4,000 people, he drove the followers of the Kāzarūnī Sufi order out of Fars and desecrated the tombs of the Sufi shaykhs of that region.[70] As for the Nasqhbandiyya, all trace of this order "was extirpated from Western and Central Iran by the Safavids, for whom the slaughter of Sunni scholars and shaykhs was an essential part of establishing Shi'i supremacy."[71] As mentioned above, when Ismā'īl I conquered Herāt in 1510, he desecrated Jāmī's tomb.[72] The Khalwatī Order fled the Shī'ified Safavid regime for the more congenial Ottoman domains and the Nūrbakhshī branch of the Kubrawī order also declined sharply, with the great-grandson of Sayyid Muḥammad Nūrbakhsh, Qawām al-Dīn being executed by Shāh Tahmāsp (*reg.* 1524–76).[73]

Towards the end of Tahmāsp's reign, while overt Sufi practices on the part of the official Ṣafawiyya were gradually abandoned as politically inexpedient, the Sufi tradition continued in a purely ceremonial capacity. Just as the Safavid Shāhs appointed *'ulamā'* to the post of 'archbishop' (Shaykh al-Islām), to regulate religious affairs, they also created a 'general state secretariat for Sufi affairs' in the office of *Khalīfat al-khulafā'*, as is evident from *firmān*s issued from the reign of Shāh Tahmāsp right to the very end of the reign of Shāh Sulṭān Ḥusayn.[74] With the succession of Tahmāsp's son, Ismā'īl II (d. 985/1577) further

---

[66] Kamil Mustafa al-Shaibi, *Sufism and Shī'ism* (London: LAAM 1991), p. 319.
[67] *Rawḍāt al-janān wa jannāt al-jinān*, ed. Ja'far Sulṭān al-Qurrā'ī (Tabrīz, BTNK, 1344 A.H.sh./1965), II, p. 159.
[68] *Ibid.*, I, 491.
[69] A. Arjomand, "The Suppression of Sufism," in *The Shadow of God*, pp. 112–19.
[70] *Ibid., p.* 112.
[71] H. Algar, "The Naqshbandī Order: A Preliminary Survey of its History and Significance," *Studia Islamica* 44 (1976), p. 139.
[72] Arjomand, *The Shadow of God*, p. 112.
[73] *Ibid.*, p. 115.
[74] These are cited by Ja'fariyān, *Dīn va siyāsat*, pp. 113–18. On the office of *Khalīfat al-khulafā'*, see Zarrīnkūb, *Dunbāla*, pp. 240–1.

efforts to eradicate Sufism from Persia were made when he massacred the Sufis of Qazwin.[75] 'Abbās the Great (1587–1629) continued this anti-Sufi policy with the massacre in 1023/1614 of his Safavid Sufi followers in Qarājadāgh, accused of collaboration with the Ottomans. Just as Ismā'īl II before him had massacred the Sufis in Qazwin, so he also destroyed their Sufi centres there after blinding his Sufi grand vizier (*Khalīfat al-khulafā'*), jealously apprehensive of the loyalty held to him by his Qizilbāsh Sufi followers.[76]

Although the beginning of the destruction of institutionalized Sufism was largely a political act by the early Safavid Shāhs, aimed at eradicating any opposition from their own folk Shī'ite-*ghāzī* background, their initiative was largely supported by the Shī'ite clerics from Iraq, Lebanon and Syria who were welcomed to Iran at the end of the sixteenth century when the Safavid state turned to consolidating Shī'ism as the official religion. Aside from the actual historical factors, the survival of institutional Sufism in any Islamic society depends upon public opinion, which is susceptible to the vagaries of changing relations between the ruling authorities and the *'ulamā'* with the mystics. The fundamentalist religious policies of the Safavid sovereigns combined with a bitter propaganda campaign carried out by the Shī'ite clerics against Sufism effectively signalled the social obliteration of the *ṭarīqa*s and their traditions from the frontiers of Persia. And even if "out of political expediency, Isma'īl did compromise with some of the Sufi shaykhs – notably those of the Ni'matullāhī order, there can be no doubt about his relentless hostility towards most rival Sufi orders, a policy continued by his successors."[77]

It has been argued by one scholar that the main reason behind Shāh Ismā'īl's wish to eradicate Sufism was that "the *ghuluww* of the Qizilbash became equated with sufism partly because of the *tarīqat* tradition characteristic of the early phase of the Safavi brotherhood. This particular equation prompted the Safavis to foster the liquidation of sufism."[78] (Partially) true as this may be, the cardinal cause of the purge of the rival orders was the animosity of the formalist *'ulamā'*, those pseudo-orthodox Shī'ite clerics who viewed Sufism itself as a type of *ghuluww*, and whose bitter prejudice was thus largely responsible for its eradication.[79]

---

[75] See *Tārīkh-i khānaqāh dar Irān*, p. 239.

[76] Arjomand, *The Shadow of God*, p. 111.

[77] *Ibid.*, p. 112. The Safavids' relationship with the Ni'matu'llāhiyya is discussed by Terry Graham in this volume.

[78] Babayan, "The Waning of the Qizilbash," p. 40.

[79] 'The reason behind the shari'a-minded ulama's attacks on *ghulāt* and sufism are clear', Kathryn Babayan ("The Waning of the Qizilbash," p. 69) underlines: "The *'ulamā'*were attempting to convert the masses to Imamism. The religiosity of the masses and certainly that of the *oymāq*s was imbued with popular colorings of *ghulāt* and *ṭarīqat* sufism." Both Zarrīnkūb (*Dunbāla*, p. 224) and Dhabīḥu'llāh Ṣafā (*Tārīkh*, V/I, pp. 201ff.), basing themselves on primary-source evidence, also convincingly argue this point.

III. THE RISE OF THE *MUJTAHID* CULT

> The orthodox hierarchy of Persia have from the first made an open and violent war on this sect [of Sufis]; and though they have often failed to rouse the bigotry of the sovereign in their defence, then have always succeeded in convincing them that the established religion was necessary to the support of the state, and that nothing could be more dangerous than the progress of infidelity, which, by unsettling men's minds, was calculated to throw them into doubt and ferment.
>
> Sir John Malcolm[80]

> For he was of that stubborn crew
> Of errant saints whom all men grant
> To be the true church militant
> Such as do build their faith upon
> The holy text of pike and gun;
> Decide all controversy by
> Infallible artillery,
> And prove their doctrines orthodox
> By apostolic blows and knocks;
> Call fire sword and desolation
> A godly-thorough reformation
> Which always must be carried on,
> And still is doing but never done,
> As if Religion were intended
> For nothing else but being mended.
> A sect whose chief devotion lies
> In odd perverse antipathies,
> In falling out with that and this
> And finding something still amiss
>
> Samuel Butler (1612–80)

There were no major centres of Shīʿite learning in pre-Safavid Iran, so clerics had to be imported by the new regime from Arabic Iraq, greater Baḥrayn and Jabal ʿĀmil in the Lebanon.[81] As a consequence, the educational *madrasa*

---

[80] Sir John Malcolm, *History of Persia* (London 1829), II, p. 292.

[81] I am grateful to Andrew Newman for having brought to my attention the ongoing academic discussion about the relative demographic extent, social and theological importance of this migration. In his article on "The Myth of Clerical Migration to Safawid Iran," *Die Welt des Islams*, 23 (1993), pp. 66–112, Newman argues that the migration is mostly a myth and that there is little evidence to support the contention that any Arab Twelver scholars migrated in large numbers to Iran or, in fact, ever supported the Safavids. Devin J. Stewart re-examined Newman's thesis and evidence and came to slightly different conclusions, claiming the existence of a direct "influence of ʿĀmilī scholars in government policies… even in the early sixteenth century …," while pointing out that "it cannot be

system of seventeenth-century Persia became limited to two fields of learning: Shī‘ite theology and the Arabic language, and all other fields "were consigned to the shelves of oblivion, or else only made use of when required for religious purposes."[82] Despite the institutionalization of Shī‘ism in Iran, during Ismā‘īl's reign at least, the Safavid state managed to keep a firm hand on the clerical class. During the reign of Shāh Ṭahmāsp (1524–76), however, religious policy was changed to allow the Shī‘ite *mujtahids* to assume supreme spiritual authority, so that under his rule "the intellectual struggle of Shī‘ite clerics with Sufism began."[83]

Ṭahmāsp "turned to the further strengthening of Twelver Shi‘i institutions, forbidding art forms such as poetry and music which did not in some way praise ‘Alī and the Twelve Imams."[84] He interrupted the Friday prayer in all mosques connected with the Sunni community, often replacing prayer with ritual cursing.[85] Eighteen-year-old Ṭahmāsp, son of demi-god Ismā’īl, had fallen prey to the priestcraft of ‘Alī ibn al-Ḥusayn ibn ‘Abd al-‘Alī al-Karakī (d. 940/1533–4) whom he appointed to the post of "Deputy of the Hidden Imām" (*nā'ib al-imām*). To ensure that Karakī's word was considered infallible and incontrovertible in all matters of religion, Ṭahmāsp even issued the following decree:

construed as an accident that the leading jurists in the Empire during its first 120 years were all ‘Āmilīs' ("Notes on the Migration of ‘Āmilī Scholars to Safavid Iran," *Journal of Near Eastern Studies*, 55/2 [1996], p. 85 (see also p. 102, *infra*). However, Stewart agrees with Newman that very few ‘Āmilī scholars emigrated to Iran during the first fifty years of Safavid rule and that "the main influx of Bahraini scholars did not occur until the seventeenth century, and most ‘Āmilīs came during the latter half of the sixteenth century or later" (*ibid*., p. 86). The same debate is also critically appraised, with some different conclusions, by Rula Abisaab, "The Ulama of Jabal ‘Amil in Safavid Iran, 1501–1736: Marginality, Migration and Social Change," *Iranian Studies*, 27/1–4 (1994, pp. 103–22). However, with all its uncertainities and questions, this debate remains mostly peripheral to the purview of this chapter, being only marginally relevant to my argument here, the basic point of which remains that, as Ja‘fariyān succinctly puts it: "With the invitation extended by the Safavid shāhs to Shī‘ite *‘ulamā'* from Jabal-‘Āmal [to come to Iran] and their acquisition of control over the populace's intellectual and religious life, Sufism was marginalized and the work of directing the intellectual development of society effectively taken out of their hands. Although in the beginning, some *‘ulamā'* held the Sufis in esteem and addressed themselves to their needs, in the end through the power of the Shī‘ite *‘ulamā'*, Sufism, thus degraded, was generally unable to act as an effective force in politics or society, the activities of its *khānaqāhs* and centres being curtailed" (*Dīn va siyāsat*, p. 77).

[82] Ṣafā, *Tārīkh*,V/1 p. 172.

[83] Ja‘fariyān, *Dīn va siyāsat*, p. 225. See also Mangol Bayat's discussion, "The Rise of the Mujtahid to Power," in *Mysticism and Dissent: Socioreligious Thought in Qajar Iran* (Syracuse: Syracuse University Press 1982), pp. 19–25; and Ṣafā, *Tārīkh*,V/1 pp. 174–6.

[84] Rosemary Stanfield Johnson, "Sunni Survival in Safavid Iran: Anti-Sunni Activities during the Reign of Tahmasp I," *Iranian Studies*, 27/1–4 (1994), p. 126. Ṭahmāsp, did, however, patronize calligraphy and painting, for which he had "a lively enthusiasm" as Ebadollah Bahari, *Bihzad: Master of Persian Painting* (London: I.B. Tauris 1996), p. 189, points out.

[85] Johnson, "Sunni Survival in Safavid Iran," p. 129.

> It is clear and obvious that opposition to the rule of the *mujtahids* who are Protectors of the Canon Law (*sharḥ*) of the cardinal of the messengers (Muḥammad] is equivalent to polytheism (*shirk*). Therefore, whoever opposes the Seal of the *Mujtahids* [= Karakī] who is the heir of the knowledge of the cardinal of the messengers ... and does not become his follower is without doubt accursed and worthy to be denunciated, and excommunicated from this blessed court.[86]

As the author of the first polemical tract against Sufism in Safavid Persia,[87] Karakī played an instrumental role in arousing the animosity of the orthodox to Sufism. He can thus be considered as the inaugurator of a genre of writings that was later popularized by other dogmatic religious professionals of his class; he was, at the same time, the reviver of the ancient feud with Sufi philosophy which Shī'ite divines had begun many centuries earlier.[88]

The doctrine of 'making legal exertion' (*ijtihād*) in Shī'ism[89] first obtained canonical acceptance in the writings of 'Allāma al-Ḥillī (d. 726/1325) who defined it merely as the exertion by the jurist in obtaining a 'probably correct opinion' (*ẓann*) on specific matters in specific fields of law.[90] Under Karakī however, the decisive judgement was delivered that it was illegal to follow (*taqlīd*) a dead jurist (*mujtahid*). Although in theory this meant that tradition was being perpetually remade and renewed by living legal authorities, in practice a dynamic doctrine had become reified, creating a class of clerical hierocrats who assumed supreme religious authority to be their sole and exclusive property. It also assured "the continued transitiveness of juristic authority and precluded its exclusive attribution to eminent jurists of the past

---

[86] Al-Khwānsārī, *Rawḍāt al-jannāt fī aḥwāl al-'ulamā' wa'l-sādāt* (Tehran: 1970), IV, pp. 362–3; cited by Ṣafā, *Tārīkh*, V/1, p. 176; this *firmān* and a similar *firmān* by Tahmāsp are also cited by Ja'fariyān, *Dīn va siyāsat*, pp. 407–11) Although this post continued to be passed down patrimonially within the Karakī family for several generations, after Ṭahmāsp's death it declined in importance and was replaced by the *Ṣadr* function. See Arjomand, "The Mujtahid of the Age and the Mullā-bāshī," in *Authority and Political Culture in Shī'ism*, ed. S.A. Arjomand (Albany: SUNY Press 1988), pp. 82–3. For other relevant decrees concerning Karakī, see *idem*, "Two Decrees of Shāh Tahmāsp Concerning Statecraft and the Authority of Shaykh 'Alī al-Karakī," *Authority and Political Culture in Shī'ism*, pp. 250–62. The rise of the *mujtahid* cult coincided with a decline in public ethics, Ibn Karbalā'ī notes. Writing in 975/1567 during the reign of Shāh Ṭahmāsp, Ibn Karbalā'ī notes that he "has been wandering throughout Islamic countries for the past thirty years but I have not found one single judge (*qāḍī*) who is immune from these vices of fraud, bribery, mendacity and seizure of charitably endowed properties" (*Rawḍāt al-jinān va jannāt al-janān*, ed. Ja'far Sulṭān al-Qurrā'ī [Persian Texts Series no. 20; Tehran 1344 A.Hsh./1965], I, p. 128.

[87] Ja'fariyān, *Dīn va sīyāsat*, pp. 225–6; Babayan, "The Safavid Synthesis: from Qizilbash Islām to Imāmite Shī'ism," *Iranian Studies*, 27/1–4 (1994), p. 144, n. 27.

[88] See Safā"s provocative and erudite discussion of this phenomenon, *Tārīkh*, V/I, p. 203ff.

[89] For the historical development of this doctrine, see Aron Zysow, "Ejtehād," *Encyclopædia Iranica*, VIII, pp. 281.

[90] Arjomand, *The Shadow of God*, p. 140.

as in Sunnism."[91] Karakī was thus nicknamed the "inventor of Shī'ism" by the Sunnis.[92] His central role in the institutionalization of the jurists' hierocracy in Safavid Persia recalls the key position of Al-Qāḍī al-Nu'mān (d. 363/974) as codifier of Fātimīd legal theory and founding father of the Ismā'īlī theory of the imāmate (professing that knowledge can only be derived from the rightful Imāms from the Prophet's family).[93]

Space does not permit nor our subject allow anything but a brief discussion of the various currents in legal theory which flowed through the intellectual life of members of the school of Iṣfahān who were legatees of Karakī's heritage.[94] When one considers the social classes relevant to this essay, it is important to note that during Shāh 'Abbās's reign (1588–1629), one finds several groups competing for power in Persian society: (1) the exoteric Imāmī *mujtahid*s, usually of non-Iranian descent; (2) the Imāmī clerics of the Akhbārī school opposed to the *mujtahid*s, usually of Persian descent; (3) the Qizilbāsh Safavid Sufis, and finally; (4) groups of Sufis who had survived the previous pogroms against their orders. In respect of the significant sectarian developments in Shī'ite theology, by the mid-seventeenth century the first two groups of learned clerics in Safavid Iran had divided themselves into two distinct schools of thought.

The first of these was the Akhbārī school, the traditionalist *'ulamā'* comprising *sayyids* who belonged to the Persian "clerical estate"[95] firmly rejected *ijtihād* and condemned all recourse to the so-called *mujtahid*s. 'Akhbārīs "believed that all major theological questions had already been answered by the Imāms in the canonical collections of traditions, and that 'without the exegesis of the Imams the Koran would remain beyond human comprehension.'"[96] All believers who knew Arabic and studied these traditions might thus be considered independent *muqallidūn* (followers) of the rules previously established by authorities now dead (*taqlīd al-mayyit*).[97] Such clerics "tended to prefer philosophy and hermeneutics and devotional mysticism, centering around the figures of the Imams, to the syllogistic hairsplitting of the jurists."[98] Amongst these one finds the central figure in this

[91] *Ibid.*
[92] Shaibi, *Sufism and Shī'ism*, p. 320.
[93] See Ismail Poonawala, "Al-Qāḍī al-Nu'mān and Isma'ili Jurisprudence," in *Medieval Isma'ili History and Thought*, ed. Farhad Daftary (Cambridge: Cambridge University Press 1996), pp. 117–43.
[94] Good discussions are provided by Arjomand, *The Shadow of God*, chap. 5; Shaibi, *Sufism and Shī'ism*, chap. 8.
[95] My analysis here is based on Arjomand's interesting and provocative discussion, *The Shadow of God*, pp. 143–59.
[96] E. Kohlberg, "Akbārīya," *EIr*, I, p. 717.
[97] *Ibid.* See also A. Newman, "The Nature of the Akhbārī/Uṣūlī Dispute in Late Ṣafawid Iran," *BSOAS*, 55/1–2 (1992), part 1: 22–51; part 2: 250–61.
[98] Arjomand, *The Shadow of God*, p. 146.

essay, Fayḍ-i Kāshānī who, in his treatise devoted to the refutation of *ijtihād*, the *Safīnat al-najāt* (Ark of Salvation), as S.A. Arjomand points out, "adduces the 'authority verse' of the Qur'an to condemn all recourse to *mujtahids*. As obedience is due to God, the Prophet, the Imams, and none else, the norms of the sacred law can be directly obtained from the traditions (*akhbār*) of the infallible Imāms."[99]

The second school of thought consisted of the exoteric Taqlīdī (later called *Uṣūlī*) school of formalist *mujtahid*s who favoured the establishment of hierocratic authority in the person of the jurist rather than the individual believer. The main members and founders of this school were Mullā Aḥmad 'Muqaddas' Ardabīlī (d. 993/1585), better known for his politicization of the doctrine of imitative obedience (*taqlīd*) to the Shī'ite bishop (*mujtahid*), pronouncing it "incumbent with the existence of proof upon the *ijtihād* of the Mujtahid"[100]. Many of the theosophers of the Iṣfahān school discussed in section IV below, such as Shaykh Bahā' al-Dīn al-'Āmilī (953/1547–1030–1/1621), who held the position of Shaykh al-Islām in Iṣfahān under Shāh 'Abbās I (*reg*. 1588–1629), and Mīr Dāmād, were advocates of the *Uṣūlī* legal position.[101]

With the above discussion in mind, we can now turn back to the extremist religious milieu of late sixteenth-century Safavid Persia.

The four Safavid shāhs prior to 'Abbās had been riding on a wave of messianic expectations harboured by their subject-disciples.[102] By clerical exertion (ijtihād) certain *ḥadīth* were discovered or concocted, and advocated to support claims by Safavid kings to be the Mahdī, or at the very least, his deputy.[103] Yet, by the beginning of the seventeenth century, "the messianic yearning remained unfulfilled for those disillusioned *qizilbāsh* whose ancestors had taken up arms to help Isma'īl."[104] Consequently, the primary domestic opposition with which Shāh 'Abbās had to contend consisted of his own devoted followers, the Qizilbāsh Sufis who had brought his dynasty to power. Ismā'īl II (*reg*. 1576–77), who systematically killed and/or blinded all members of his father's original power elite,[105] had been murdered by the

---

[99] *Ibid*.

[100] Cited from his *Zubdat al-biyān* by Arjomand, *The Shadow of God*, p. 138; for a translation and elaboration of his views on the matter in the *Zubdat al-biyān*, see John Cooper, "The Muqaddas al-Ardabīlī on *Taqlīd*" in Arjomand, *Authority and Political Culture in Shī'ism*, pp. 263–6.

[101] For futher discussion, see Arjomand, *The Shadow of God*,, pp. 139ff.

[102] As Kathlyn Babayan put it: "The mahdīst nature of Shāh Ismā'īl I's rise to power shaped the way in which Imāmī scholars initially legitimized Safavi rule. ... [Thus] Imāmī clerics implied that Safavi rule was legitimate on the basis of mahdist rather than shar'ī legitimacy" ("The Waning of the Qizilbash," p. 38) cf. Shaibi, *Sufism and Shī'ism*, p. 319

[103] Even Shaykh Bahā'ī tailored his narration of *ḥadīth* to fit the Safavid pretentions that Shāh Ismā'īl was the Mahdi. See Babayan, "The Waning of the Qizilbash," pp. 38–9.

[104] *Ibid*., p. 40.

[105] Savory, *Iran Under the Safavids*, p. 69.

Qizilbāsh before he could murder his eldest brother: Muḥammad Khudābanda, father of 'Abbās. Then, disillusioned with Ismā'īl II as a king and spiritual master, the Qizilbāsh Sufis crowned Khudābanda king. He adopted the title of Sulṭān Muḥammad Shāh (1577–88). Infighting between the Iranians and the Turcoman Qizilbāsh characterized his reign, and eventually the meddling Qizilbāsh under the leadership of Murshid Qulī Khān forced the Shāh to abdicate in favor of his son 'Abbās.

Adept by virtue of birth – he was of noble Turcoman ancestry – in the courtly arts of intrigue, fratricide and assassination, from youth 'Abbās had been privy to the barbarous stratagems of his clannish Qizilbāsh disciples; he was skilled in the politics of ethnic factionalism – which in the specific Qizilbāsh milieu meant understanding how to use the disguise of pious devotion to contest and undermine one's opponents. As if reincarnating the vices of his grandfather, 'Abbās killed four of his own sons, while in 1589, only a year after he assumed power, he assassinated Murshid Qulī Khān, his Qizilbāsh regent who had brought him to power,[106] before assuming absolute control himself.

Obviously, such a summary historical excursus cannot sufficiently illuminate the extent which Qizilbāsh extremist mystical devotionalism had infected the social body of the Safavid state in particular and Persian culture in general. Only by suppressing the radical forces which had created, yet continued to challenge, the Safavid revolution could Shāh 'Abbās unify his government.[107] In practice, this meant the betrayal of the Qizilbāsh Sufis. Thus, in the 'Year of the Tiger' (1023–4/1614–16) "Abbās massacred scores of the veteren Lāhījānī Sufis of Qarājadāgh,[108] an act which the court historian Iskandar Beg Munshī justified by explaining that 'the Shah, by ordering this purge, wished to indicate that this group from now on was no longer to be included in within the circle of the Sufis, and to make a clear distinction between Sufis and non-Sufis."[109] Although the pretext used to launch the purge had been the Sufis' collaboration with the Ottomans, in reality 'Abbās merely intended to terrorize his own party into submission, thus indicating his disassociation from the politics of Qizilbāsh Sufi extremism.[110]

---

[106] Babayan, "The Waning of the Qizilbash," p. 44.

[107] For an excellent discussion of the political forces at play, see *ibid.*, chapter 5.

[108] See Jean Aubin, "Révolution chiite et conservatisme: Les Soufis de Lahejan, 1500–14 (Études Safavides II)," *Moyen Orient et Océan Indien* (1984), pp. 2–9.

[109] Iskandar Beg Munshī, *Tārīkh-e 'Ālamārā-ye 'Abbāsī, History of Shah Abbas the Great*, trans. R. Savory (Colorado: Westview Press 1978), II, p. 1097.

[110] For an account of which, see Munshī, *Tārīkh* II, pp. 1096–7. Babayan points out ("The Waning of the Qizilbash," p. 63) that "In classical Safavi usage the sūfī and the sufiesque *ghulāt* (*Qizilbash*) were one. For 'Abbās I to demonstrate the way in which he distinguished 'the sūfī from the non-sūfī,' he massacred the group that epitomized the classical meaning of the Safavi sūfī: those who gave Shāh Ismā'īl shelter in times of trouble, who venerated him as a pīr/god, and who had precedence over other sūfīs due to their particular devotion. That

Yet, in the process of unleashing Shī'ite orthodoxy and turning towards the *mujtahid* cult to rescue himself from his fanatical Safavid Qizilbāsh subjects, Shāh 'Abbās – applying Ḥāfiẓ's erotic metaphor to the political arena – fled the pit only to fall into the snare, suppressing *ghulāt* extremism by strengthening hardline Shī'ite dogmatism. As Kathlyn Babayan points out:

> In supressing the *ghulāt* Shāh 'Abbās I came to divorce religion from politics, relying on orthodoxy in this process, for orthodoxy provided him with a forum through which to attack *ghuluww*. It also awarded him the legitimacy with which he could become an absolute shāh. The public image 'Abbās I was cultivating reflects his attempts to seperate temporal from spiritual rule. ... Publicly, 'Abbās I was not playing on his legitimacy as *pīr* of the Qizilbāsh. Although the chroniclers continue to refer to the shāh as the *murshid-i kāmil* and to the Qizilbāsh as sūfīs, these titles were ceremonial, retaining perhaps only the element of obedience that was required of a disciple toward his spiritual guide.[111]

Contaminated with extremism, debilitated by its association with temporal party politics, Sufism in the second half of the seventeenth century – when the *mujtahid* cult reached the height of its power – became easy prey for the doctrinaire Shī'ite clerics for whom mysticism, illuminism, faith interiorized by divine love and contemplative vision have always been fuel for the fire of their Holy Inquisition.

IV. THE SCHOOL OF IṢFAHĀN: 'ABD AL-RAZZĀQ LĀHĪJĪ AND FAYḌ-I KĀSHĀNĪ ON THE RELATION OF *TAṢAWWUF*, *ḤIKMAT* AND *'IRFĀN*

In the third volume of *The Venture of Islam*, Marshall Hodgson remarked that the sixteenth century "undeniably marks the peak of Muslim political power," and opines that "the whole age from Bihzād the painter (b. c. 1450) through Mullā Ṣadrā the philosopher (d. 1640), in which the cultural forms associated with the Persian language culminated, ranks as something of a golden age and may usefully be called the 'Persianate flowering'." The intellectual and literary fabric of this "flowering," even when better studied, he remarked, will still remain difficult to define, since "if the age was a great age, its greatness lay largely in its finesse and subtlety, its culminations of refinement, rather than in feats more immediately obvious to a human being whatever his cultural background."[112]

The philosophical aspect of this 'flowering' is the 'school of Iṣfahān' outlined by Professor Nasr in the introduction to this volume. Its members

---

element of past loyalty and spiritual comradeship meant little in the politics of the Isfahānī age of Safavi rule." For an excellent discussion of the political significance of the massacre, see Arjomand, *The Shadow of God*, p. 111.

[111] Babayan, "The Waning of the Qizilbash," p. 52.

[112] Hodgson, *The Venture of Islam*, III, p. 49.

Plate 5: The Caravanserai of Kāshān. From Chardin, *Voyages*, Pl. 18.

comprised a group of theosophers who flourished in this city from the late sixteenth century down to the last three-quarters of the seventeenth century, and who created a unique synthesis of theological, mystical and philosophical thought which tolerated, or at least, interpreted Sufism's spiritual method (*tarīqa*) as integrally Islamic in the sense understood by traditional Islam.[113] The school of Iṣfahān counts as the most significant intellectual activity of the reigns of Shāh 'Abbās I, Shāh Ṣafī and Shāh 'Abbās II (1588–1666). Although the teachings of the theosophers who belonged to this school are individually distinct, they unite on common ground, justifying the definition of their collective views as a 'school' on four fronts.

1. *Sufism.* While all its members exhibited a profound respect for the ethical, intellectual and spiritual ideals of classical Persian Sufism,[114] few of them seem to have openly accepted the necessity of following the *ṭarīqa* discipline involving obedience to a living master (*pīr*, *murshid*). Most of these theosophers also wrote mystical poetry of varying quality, indicative of their devotion to Sufi literature.
2. *Shī'ism.* Their writings are permeated with Shī'ite piety, imāmology and theology. Where an ecumenical side of their theosophy does exist, the specificity of the Shī'ite social milieu wherein their works are situated, however, may tend to obscure this.
3. *Islamic Platonism.* On the other hand, the philosophy of the school often tended to stress what was "humanistically universal," as Hodgson pointed out.[115] Their teachings stemmed from the revival of the Illuminationist (Ishraqī) theosophy of Shaykh Shihāb al-Dīn Yaḥyā Suhrawardī (d. 587/1191), who had claimed his theosophy to be an Islamic synthesis of several ancient wisdom traditions: "the religion of the ancients adhered to by the Babylonians, the [Persian] Khusrawaniyyūn sages, the Indians, and all the ancients from Greece, as well as others."[116]
4. *Islamic Rationalism.* Philosophers in this school combined Peripatetic rationalism with Islamic Platonism. For the Iṣfahānī Safavid philosophers, "the term 'Peripatetic' does not have the same connotation which it has for us," Henry Corbin reveals, "if only because of no other reason than the

[113] Referring to S.H. Nasr's distinction here between traditional and non-traditional Islam in his *Traditional Islam in the Modern World* (London: Kegan Paul International 1987), prologue.
[114] The sole exception here is Mīr Dāmād, the founder of the school who had scant use for Sufism; on which, see section IV.2 below.
[115] Hodgson, *The Venture of Islam*, III, p. 51.
[116] See S.H. Nasr (ed.), *Shihaboddin Yahya Sohrawardi*: *oeuvres philosophiques et mystiques*, (Tehran: Institut Franco-Iranien 1970), I, p. 493. Cited by Hossein Ziai, "The Source and Nature of Authority: A Study of al-Suhrawardī's Illuminationist Political Doctrine," in *The Political Aspects of Islamic Philosophy*, ed. Charles Butterworth (Cambridge, Mass: Harvard University Press 1992), p. 328.

fact that they cherished the *Theology* attributed Aristotle.[117] From another point of view, and for the same reason, it is quite exceptional to find a philosopher who is purely and solely Peripatetic among them, a philosopher not thoroughly absorbed in neo-Platonism and who is not *eo ipso* in one way or another somewhat of an Ishrāqī."[118]

This amalgam of Sufism, Shī'ism, Platonist Ishrāqī theosophy and Islamic rationalism produced the unique philosophical collegium of Iṣfahān. While scholars have generally devoted considerable study to the religious, juridical, theosophical and philosophical background of this school, the orientation of its members to traditional Sufism has been relegated to the footnotes rather than integrated into the text of such studies. One need not search far afield to find the reason why Sufism has been marginalized: it lies in the crisis of cultural identity experienced by Sufis in late seventeenth-century Iran when confronted by an evil even worse than the Qizilbāsh warriors[119] of Ismā'īl: the rise of the cult of the Uṣūlī *mujtahid*s, creating a trend which, amongst its latter-day fundamentalist heirs, has carried on right down to the present day in Iran.[120]

As will be seen below, while most members of the school were inclined towards *'irfān* and Sufism, owing to the politically charged anti-Qizilbāsh climate and 'Abbās's denigration of *ghulāt*-type folk-Sufism, institutionalized *khānaqāh* Sufism no longer held the same place in the hearts of mystically oriented intellectuals that, for instance, it had had with earlier Sufi theosophers

---

[117] Translated from Greek into Arabic, this work was actually Books 4–6 of the Enneads of Plotinus, but was attributed to Aristotle by Islamic thinkers down to modern times.

[118] Henry Corbin, *Histoire de la philosophie islamique* (Paris: Gallimard 1964), p. 463.

[119] On the origins and history of the Qizilbāsh, see Roemer, "The Qizilbash Turcomans," pp. 27–39.

[120] Nikki Keddie and Juan Cole have pointed out that while Uṣūlī clerics were initially "important agents in legitimizing Safavid rule throughout Iran," the very same Uṣūlī-*mujtahidī* arguments "were used to express the independence of the ulama in relation to the shahs. The doctrine of the need of laymen to emulate mujtahids had the potential of putting the claims of the mujtahids higher than those of the shah, and such claims are recorded in the late Safavid period. Few, if any, Shi'i mujtahids before Khomeini seriously proposed that the ulama should actually rule, but in some ways this stance is the logical (though not inevitable) development of the Usuli school of jurisprudence, which sees the ulama as the general representative of the twelfth imam" (Nikki Keddie and Juan Cole [eds.] *Shi'ism and Social Protest* [New Haven: Yale University Press 1986], introduction, p. 8). In his discussion, "Khumayni's Concept of the Guardianship of the Jurisconsult," (in *Islam in the Political Process*, ed. J. Picatori (Cambridge: Cambridge University Press 1983), p. 160, Hamid Enayat finds a direct historical antecedent to this doctrine in Karaki's position as Shaykh al-Islām (paramount religious leader) and conception of the role of the jurisprudents in the Safavid state under Shāh Ṭahmāsp. For further discussion and comparison of the contemporary Iranian with the Safavid *mujtahid* cult, see Martin Riesèbrodt, *Pious Passion: The Emergence of Modern Fundamentalism in United States and Iran*, trans D. Reneau (Berkeley: University of California Press 1993), pp. 100–75; Bayat, "The Rise of the Mujtahid," pp. 18–19.

such as 'Abdu'llāh Anṣārī, Abū'l-Qāsim Qushayrī or Abū Ḥāmid Ghazālī. A century and half of Sufism's embroilment in Qizilbāsh fanaticism and Shī'ite *ghuluww* had tarnished the intellectual creditability and smudged the moral reputation of the Persian dervish ethos; the image of the mystic *faqīr* had taken on a sinister *double entendre*: the dervish saint was also now a barbarous brute, the holy pauper's mantle concealing an arrogant, ambitious parvenu.[121]

Many of the prominent philosophical and mystical figures of the school of Iṣfahān have already been mentioned by Professor Nasr in his introduction to this volume, but there are six thinkers who directly concern our present study: Mīr Dāmād (d. 1041/1631), Mullā Ṣadrā (d. 1050/1640), Bahā' al-Dīn 'Āmilī (d. 1030/1621), Mīr Abū al-Qāsim Findiriskī (d. 1050/1640–1), Muḥsin Fayḍ-i Kāshānī (d. 1091/1680), 'Abd al-Razzāq Lāhījī (d. 1072/1661–2). Each of these philosophers had his own individually nuanced and distinct understanding of the relation of Sufism (*taṣawwuf*), philosophy (*falsafa*), philosophical mysticism (*ḥikmat*) and theosophy (*'irfān*) to normative Islam.

Before entering into the main subject of discussion, an analysis of the thought of the mystical philosophers Muḥsin Fayḍ-i Kāshānī and 'Abd al-Razzāq Lāhījī, it will be useful to examine briefly the particular positions towards Sufism adopted by the four chronologically earlier figures mentioned above: Bahā' al-Dīn 'Āmilī, Mīr Dāmād, Mullā Ṣadrā and Mīr Abū al-Qāsim Findiriskī.

1. Bahā' al-Dīn 'Āmilī (d. 1030/1621)

Shaykh Bahā'ī's father, Ḥusayn al-'Āmilī, had emigrated from Lebanon to Iran where a student of Karakī introduced him to Shāh Tahmāsp, who later appointed him to the post of Shaykh al-Islām in Herāt.[122] When both his father and Tahmāsp died in 984/1576, Shaykh Bahā'ī inherited his father's position.[123] In theology, he supported the 'Uṣūlī school and advocated increasing the "growth in clerical authority with the secular state and supported the delegation of the Imām's power to the clergy,"[124] backing

---

[121] Babayan in this context cites an interesting story to illustrate the denigration of the dervish ideal: "The Waning of the Qizalbash," pp. 53ff.

[122] Andrew Newman, "Towards a Reconsideration of the 'Iṣfahān School of Philosophy:" Shaykh Bahā'ī and the Role of the Safawid *'Ulamā"*, *Studia Iranica*, 15/2 (1986), p. 169; Devin J. Stewart, "A Biographical Notice on Bahā' al-Dīn al-'Āmilī (d. 1030/1621)," *Journal of the American Oriental Society*, 111/3 (July–Sept. 1991), p. 566.

[123] Under 'Abbās I, Shaykh Bahā'ī was made Shaykh al-Islām of Iṣfahān, the new capital of Persia, in which capacity he performed immeasurable services to the Safavid state, was one of the key architects of the new capital city, and was a constant companion and advisor to 'Abbās the Great. See Newman, "Towards a Reconsideration," pp. 176–8.

[124] Newman, "Towards a Reconsideration," p. 168.

Karakī's cause and views on *ijtihād*.[125] John Cooper has pointed out that 'it is difficult to classify him [Shaykh Bahā'ī] along the normal faqīh/ṣūfī/faylasūf lines."[126] Although the studies of Andrew Newman and Devin Stewart which delineate Shaykh Bahā'ī's role as an 'Uṣūlī jurisconsult illuminate an important and neglected side of his personality, "his great leanings towards Sufism"[127] as exhibited in his Persian poetry, among other sources, are a no less significant aspect of his character and contribution to Islamic culture.[128]

The fact that Shaykh Bahā'ī affiliated himself, intellectually at least, with the Sufis is demonstrated at length by Edmund Bosworth.[129] Sa'īd Nafisī presents reliable evidence to assert that "it is absolutely certain that he adopted Sufism as his theosophical persuasion (*mashrab-i taṣawwuf dāsht*), being by nature inclined to mystical thought and conduct (*'irfān u sulūk*)."[130] Numerous passages from his Persian *mathnawiyyāt* in which he addresses the relation of Sufism to the theological sciences, and in which makes the latter succumb to his bitter critique, leave no doubt regarding his sympathy to Sufism.[131] Although such passages have yet to be analysed and studied in relation to his Uṣūlī theological views – which obviously reveal the more nomocentric side of his personality – on their own they rank as some of the finest Persian Sufi *mathnawī*s of the post-Mongol period, being some of the best examples of the theosophical perspective and ethical ideals of Persian Sufism in the annals of Persian literature.[132]

---

[125] "In two essays written during the early years of 'Abbās" reign ... Bahā'ī supported the exercise of *ijtihād* by Īmāmī clerics, and in the second, actually misrepresented criticisms offered by his father and others of 'Alī al-Karakī's exercise of *ijtihād*, both to defend the exercise of *ijtihād* and stress his own solidarity with al-Karakī, who, like Bahā'ī's father and Bahā'ī himself, had served the Safawid court, practiced *ijtihād* on its behalf, and supported the growth in the authority of the 'ulamā' within the community" Newman, "Towards a Reconsideration," (pp. 179).

[126] John Cooper, "Rumi and *Ḥikmat:* Towards a Reading of Sabziwārī's Commentary on the *Mathnawī*" in Lewisohn, *The Heritage of Sufism*, I, p. 418.

[127] Al-Khwānsārī, *Rawḍāt al-jannāt*, VII, p. 56. These are the words of his student Ḥusayn ibn Ḥaydar al-Karakī, cited by Devin J. Stewart, "A Biographical Notice," p. 570.

[128] Concerning primary and secondary sources which discuss his Sufism and attitude to *taṣawwuf*, see *Kulliyāt-i ash'ār va āthār-i fārsī Shaykh Bahā' al-Dīn Muḥammad al-'Āmilī* Ghulām Ḥusayn Jawāhirī, ed. (Tehran: n.d.), introduction, pp. 16–18.

[129] *Bahā' al-Dīn al-'Amilī and His Literary Anthologies* (Journal of Semitic Studies Monograph, no. 10 Manchester: Manchester University Press 1989), pp. 55–60, a work which presents the best summary of his Sufi affiliations to date. For other remarks see Devin J. Stewart, "A Biographical Notice," pp. 563–71. E. Kohlberg, "Bahā' al-Dīn 'Amelī," *Encyclopaedia Iranica*, III, pp. 429–30; Newman, "Towards a Reconsideration," pp. 188–9.

[130] Cited by Jawāhirī (ed.), *Kulliyāt-i ash'ār*, introduction, p. 17.

[131] See the references in his three *mathnawī*s (*Shīr u shakar*; *Nān u panīr*; *Nān u ḥalwā*) published in *Kulliyāt-i ash'ār-i farsī u mūsh u gurba-yi Shaykh Bahā'ī*, ed. Mihdī Tawḥīdīpūr (Tehran: Intishārāt-i Kitābfurūshī-yi Maḥmūdī 1336 A.Hsh./1957), on pp. 18–19; 41–4.

[132] For this reason I cannot agree with Ṣafā's damning opinion (*Tārīkh*, V/2, p. 1043) of the literary worth of his poems, which he describes as possessing "mystical taste (*dhawq-i*

2. *Mīr Dāmād (d. 1041/1631)*

Muḥammad Bāqir Astarābādī, popularly known as Mīr Dāmād (d. 1041/1631–2) has been accounted by S.H. Nasr and Henry Corbin respectively "the central figure in the school of Iṣfahān,"[133] and "the name who heads the list [of thinkers] in the School of Iṣfahān."[134] 'Abd al-Ḥusayn Zarrīnkūb described him as the foremost "philosophical Sage (*ḥakīm*), transcendentalist (*mutā'ala*) and jurisprudent (*faqīh*) of the Safavid era ... [who] comprehensively combined in himself the legacy of transcendental theosophists (*ḥikmat-i muta'āllihīn*), the ascetical qualities (*zuhd*) ascribed to the Sufis with the legal rank of *ijtihād* in the affairs of the *Sharī'a*."[135] He was the author of some forty works in Persian and Arabic,[136] nearly all of them written in a particularly dense, impenetrable style, devoted mostly to Peripatetic and Ishrāqī philosophy, as well as Shī'ite juridical issues. Occasionally, he expressed his metaphysics in poetry, as is evident from his *Dīwān* of Persian and Arabic poems, including the *mathnawī Mashāriq al-anwār* in which he uses 'Ishrāq' as his *takhalluṣ*. Mīr Dāmād's works[137] on philosophical mysticism (*ḥikmat*) include *Qabasāt, Taqdīsāt, Jadhawāt* (in Persian), *Sidrat al-muntaha*, and *Khalsat al-malakūt*.

In his *Tārīkh-i 'Alam-ārā-yi 'Abbāsī*, Iskandar Beg Munshī sings his praises, exclaiming that "today the rays of his illuminations (*ishrāqāt*) of his enlightened learning and accomplishments casts its glory upon students of knowledge, and the flashes of light sparkling from the constellation of his sunlike nature shine down upon all terrestrial beings."[138] Munshī also noted his deep erudition in the occult sciences and mathematics, while his attainment of *ijtihād* in the fields of *fiqh*, *tafsīr* and *ḥadīth* was such that "the jurisprudents of this day consider their legal decrees (*fatāwā-yi shar'iyya*) legally valid only if

---

'irfānī)," but being "absolutely devoid of originality or freshness, their only importance lying in the fact that an influential legalist scholar has composed them with complete liberty during an age dominated by bigoted puritans and formalist Mullās."

[133] S.H. Nasr, "The School of Iṣfahān," in *A History of Muslim Philosophy*, ed. M.M. Sharif (Wiesbaden: Harrassowitz 1966), II, p. 909.

[134] Corbin, *Histoire de la philosophie islamique, p.* 463. See Hamid Dabashi, "Mīr Dāmād and the Founding of the 'School of Iṣfahān'," in *History of Islamic Philosophy*, ed. S.H. Nasr and O. Leaman (London: Routledge 1996), I, pp. 597–634, which gives the best overall treatment of his position in this school.

[135] Zarrinkūb, *Dunbāla*, p. 246.

[136] See Andrew Newman's article "Dāmād, Mīr ...," *EIr*, VI: 623–6 for a list of his works.

[137] For a general review of his works, see Nasr, 'The School of Iṣfahān', pp. 915–6; Dabashi "Mīr Dāmād and the Founding of the 'School of Iṣfahān'."

[138] From the notice on Mīr Dāmād by Iskandar Beg Munshī in his *Tārīkh-i 'alam-ārā-yi 'Abbāsī*, reproduced in the Persian introduction to the *Kitāb al-Qabasāt*, ed. with an introduction by Mehdi Mohaghegh; Toshiko Izutsu, 'Alī Musawī Bihbahānī and Ibrāhīm Dībājī (Wisdom of Persia Series 7; Tehran–Montreal: Institute of Islamic Studies 1977), p. xxv.

he approves them."[139] Belonging to the 'Uṣūlī school and fully accepting the notion of the deputyship of the *faqīh*,[140] Mīr Dāmād himself was glad to second their praise, and in his *Mashriq al-anwār*, with hyperbole touching on the ridiculous and a mysticism melting into bathos, he boasts:

> From my Canon of Medicine (*Shifā*) Aristotle's learning has benefited;
> By way of my esoteric mysteries (*rumūz*),
> Plato sets foot in the realm of Ideas.
> ... Without my word how could Reason instruct and teach?
> Without my reason around, how could the world spin round?[141]

Mīr Dāmād's philosophy, like that of most of the other *ḥakīm*s of the school of Iṣfahān consisted, as T. Izutsu points out, "in a kind of harmonious combination

---

[139] *Ibid.*

[140] Newman, "Dāmād, Mīr," *EIr*, p. 625.

[141] Akbar Hādī, *Sharḥ-i ḥāl-i Mīr Dāmād va Mīr Findariskī* (Iṣfahān: Intishārāt-i Mītham Tamār 1363 A.Hsh./1984), pp. 104, 105. Although his high self-esteem apparently did not shock his contemporaries, posterity has yet to confirm the probity of Mīr Dāmād's smugness about the importance of his own compositions. In a letter to one of his associates who had asked him his opinion of one of his critics, Mīr Dāmād replied that he thought it strange how "idle souls whose individual character consists in base matter can allow themselves to boast and brag and lay senseless claims before holy minds and sacrosanct spirits [like mine]. Such folk do not even have the discrimination to realize that the mere *understanding* of my words is in itself an art, but *to quarrel* with me and call that 'learned discussion' (*baḥth*) is the utmost absurdity. For it's obvious that apprehension of higher levels of spirituality and the mature understanding of subtle matters is not available to just any feeble-minded and poorly endowed person. Hence, to dispute with me in intellectual matters just exhibits the weakness of my critic's nature – certainly, such a disputation cannot be undertaken by the analytical faculties of a bunch of folk who imagine, with their bat-like ambition, that sensual understanding is the height of wisdom and learning" (Hādī, *ibid.*, p. 36). In the exordium of one of his Mathnawī, *Mashriq al-anwār* (written in the same metre – of *baḥr-i sarī'* – and in imitation of, Niẓāmī's *Makhzan al-asrôt*, Mīr Dāmād boasts:

> I am the lord of learning, the king of knowledge,
> reclining on a pillow of Reason and Wisdom:
> My reflections comprise the Canon of Art;
> My thoughts inscribe the mysteries of Fate.

Perhaps one of the reasons that Mīr Dāmād's status in philosophy is so highlighted by Safavid-period chroniclers was his powerful political influence and connections. Henry Corbin notes: "In Iran his name is familar to everyone who possesses even a minimum of philosophical and theological culture. Although there are certain currents of popular piety which equally venerate him as a saint, his notoriety ever hardly seems to have crossed the frontiers of the 'Iranian world' – understood in the wider sense of the word – as the totality of those regions where the Persian language predominated as the main language of culture (thus, one still finds numerous manuscripts of Mīr Dāmād's works in libraries in Pakistan, while rarely elsewhere)" (*En islam iranien* [Paris: Gallimard 1972], IV, p. 17). The fact that he reportedly blessed the coronation of the 18-year-old Shāh Ṣafī I (1038/1628–1052/1642) in Iṣfahān in 1038/1628 (*Dīvān-i Fayyāḍ Lāhījī*, Jalīl Misgarnizhād's introduction, p. 25) and died while accompanying the Safavid monarch to the shrines in Iraq (Newman, "Dāmād, Mīr" *EIr*, p. 625), certainly indicates his influence and power in the Safavid hierocracy.

of rational thinking and visionary experience."[142] Although he adhered to the Peripatetic tradition, beneath the surface of his dry rational approach lay something quite akin to mysticism where one witnesses:

> the presence of swarming visions originating from an entirely different source, the living experience of a mystic. Mīr Dāmād was in this respect a perfect embodiment of the fundamental principle of philosophy as conceived by Ibn 'Arabī and Suhrawarī, namely, thinker in whom the rational-philosophical analysis of reality and the spiritual perfection to be attained through contemplative discipline proceed hand in hand with each other – a characteristic shared by most of the leading philosophers of the Safavid period.[143]

Shāh 'Abbās regarded him highly and, in fact was so in awe of his influence[144] that he tried to have him killed, according to the *Salāfat al-'aṣr*,[145] and from such royal malice alone Zarrīnkūb deduces that "in addition to his rank in philosophy (*ḥikma*) and religious law, he was regarded by his disciples and devoted followers as possessing to a degree the rank of spiritual guidance (*irshād*)."[146] In the *Tadhkira-yi Naṣrābādī*[147] Mīr Dāmād is described as conscientious in his efforts at self-purification (*tazkiya-yi nafs*); he assiduously performed superogatory prayers and for some forty years never slept on his side in a bed, a traditional picture which accords quite well with that of "venerable Sufi shaykh and master," and yet, as Zarrīnkūb suggests:

> Mīr Dāmād considered the rank of 'Sufi master' – which in that age of Sufism's decline, in fact hardly befitted his spiritual and intellectual stature – to be beneath his dignity. His claim to philosophical mysticism (*ḥikmat*) and erudition in that field, led him to consider himself third in rank to Fārābī as a teacher, in actual fact, to call himself the "third (after Fārābī and Aristotle) teacher" (*mu'allim-i thālith*). Although Mīr Dāmād followed the Peripatetic method in speculative philosopical mysticism, in his practical philosophical mysticism he tended to adopt the path of the Illuminationist school (*ishrāq*). In fact, Peripatetic philosophical mysticism combined with Illuminationist intuitionism in the teachings of the Iṣfahān school of Philosophy. The idea of attaining the goal of 'disembodiment' and 'transcending the flesh' (*khal'-i badan*) which Shaykh Ishrāq had ascribed to Plotinus, is also expounded by Mīr Dāmād in his *Jadhawāt* where the idea is attributed to Pythagorus. However, from Mīr Dāmād's standpoint, as is evident from both his *Qabasāt* and *Rawāshiḥ al-samāwiyya*, this is the principal condition for reaching the station of wisdom (*ḥikmat*). Of course, in the teachings of Najm al-Dīn Kubrā [d. 618/1221] and some of the masters of the Kubrawī order, this type of 'disembodiment' and abandonment of human corporeality was considered to be a necessary condition for realizing

[142] T. Izutsu, "Mīr Dāmād and his Metaphysics," in *Kitāb al-Qabasāt*, introduction, p. 2.
[143] Izutsu, "Mīr Dāmād and his Metaphysics," p. 3.
[144] Corbin, *En Islam iranien*, IV, p. 23.
[145] *Salāfat al-'aṣr*, p. 477. Cited by Zarrīnkūb, *Dunbāla*, p. 246
[146] Zarrīnkūb, *Dunbāla*, p. 246.
[147] *Tadhkira-yi Naṣrābādī, p.* 149. Cited by Zarrīnkūb, Dunbāla, p. 246.

> contemplation of the world of invisible realities (*'ālam-i ghayb*), and thus Mīr Dāmād's ideas in this respect are related to Sufi teachings. In any case, what makes Mīr Dāmād's Ishrāqī methodology most resemble Sufism is his emphasis on pure Unity, rather than merely attaining union (*ittiḥād*) in the intermediary stages and process of spiritual wayfaring. This is because he did not consider the Sufis – apparently because of their refusal to involve themselves with dialectical mysticism (*ḥikmat-i baḥthī*) – worthy of his attention. Hence, he occasionally criticizes their expressions, in his *Qabasāt* and *Rawāshiḥ al-samāwiyya*, among other works, and accuses them of deficiency in understanding and lack of deep investigation into philosophical issues.[148]

One may wonder if it was due to Mīr Dāmād's disdainful attitude towards classical Sufism[149] that the famous anti-Sufi Shī'ite cleric Muḥammad Bāqir Majlisī (d. 1070/1699–1700) saw fit to consecrate a long notice in his *Bihār al-anwār* to him, mentioning him with many laudatory comments, and even transcribing the philosopher's *Risālat al-khal'īya*, his Diary of Visions, in which he reflected that this treatise indicates "the deiformity (*ta'alluh*) of his innermost conscience." When, apropos of Majlisī's remarks, Henry Corbin wondered how "the same theologian who was a vehement adversary of the Sufis, could have rendered homage to Mīr Dāmād the ecstatic,"[150] he resolved the question as follows:

> If Majlisī voiced such an eulogy of Mīr Dāmād, it was because he had, in fact, opened up another horizon [of thought] beyond that of literal exoteric religion. Religious phenomenology must proceed here with extreme delicacy, in order to discover what is hidden (*bāṭin*) under the appearance (*zāhir*); thence certain oppositions resolve themselves which, on the level of the *zāhir* may appear insurmountable. It seems particularly necessary to let the spirit be presented with the nuance which reflects the theological usage current in Iran which distinguishes between *tasawwuf* and *'irfān*, between Sufism proper and mystical gnosis. The reserve with which Majlisī approached the former can also be found among the greatest spiritual and mystical figures in Shī'ism. The allusion here is essentially to *a certain type* of Sufism, the same type against which Mullā Ṣadrā, who himself might have easily passed for a Sufi, composed an entire treatise. We have already suggested the reasons for their opposition: the *ṭarīqat* organization, the role of the Shaykh, a certain sort of metaphysical monism interpreted in a sense least favourable for moral self-reformation, certain practices, etc. From

[148] *Dunbāla*, pp. 246–7.

[149] In a passage in his *Jadhawāt* concerning the imaginal realm he notes that while "the Sufi shaykhs have penetrated deeply into this matter," their views are incorrect from a strictly logical point of view "though they seem sweet and pleasant from the standpoint of ordinary aesthetic taste, discursive sensibility and poetic logic" (*Muntakhabātī az āthār-i ḥukamā'ī ilāhī-yi Īrān az 'aṣr-i Mīr Dāmād u Mīr Findariskī tā zamān-i ḥāḍir*, edited, introduced and annotated by Sayyid Jalāl al-Dīn Ashtiyānī, French introduction by Henry Corbin [Paris: Adrien-Maisonneuve/Tehran: Departement d'Iranologie de'Institut Franco-Iranien de Recherche 1972), I, pp. 55–7).

[150] Corbin, *En Islam iranien*, IV, p. 22.

> this, one may deduce that these spiritual figures were not in accord with the same paradox articulated by Haydar Āmulī: that Sufism is the true Shīʿism. However, if one could substitute the word *'irfān* for the word Sufism, then one finds a general accord among all the *'urafā'*. Hence, important points of difference lie concealed even within lexical matters. In the West, one often adopts the habit of considering Islamic mysticism to be, purely and simply, Sufism. Doubtless that is true in Sunnism, where the spiritual aspirant must 'enter Sufism' in order to go beyond the level of literal religion. However, a similar parallel does not exist in Shīʿism, wherein it suffices to follow the teachings of the Imāms to the very end in order to 'enter *'irfān*'. Such is the type of Shīʿite mystic which Mīr Dāmād and his spiritual posterity exemplify quite perfectly.[151]

Granted that Mīr Dāmād was a singular, if not idiosyncratic, type of Shīʿite mystic, Corbin's views about the relationship of Sufism to *'irfān* are, on several other counts, simply mistaken. Although both words vary in meaning, according to the context, from the point of view of traditional Persian Sufism *ma'rifat* or *'irfān* (mystical knowledge), constitutes the supreme goal of the path of *taṣawwuf;* it cannot, however, constitute a separate path or methodology either above or independent of *taṣawwuf.*[152]

As we have seen from the discussion in parts I and II in this essay, Sufism had been debilitated and vulgarized by its association with the *dervichisme* of the Qizilbāsh. The mystics (see part III) were subjected to state-sponsored harassment at the beginning of the Safavid period, and then, at the end of the seventeenth century (see below), the Sufi tradition itself, succumbing to successive waves of polemics and persecution by the mullās, became discredited and ultimately marginalized in the intellectual milieu. Majlisī's "reserve" about Sufism, is thus less a trait held in common by "the greatest spiritual and mystical figures in Shīʿism" than a by-product of the anti-Sufi climate of his own epoch. His attitude is less infused with genuine Shīʿite spirituality than belched up by his own active participation in the low-life politico-theological debates raging in seventeenth-century Iṣfahān. Lastly, conceding the view that it sufficed merely "to follow the teachings of the

---

151 *Ibid.*

152 Shaykh Bahā'ī, for example, had made this clear in his definition of *taṣawwuf* in the fifth book of his *Kashkūl:* "The science of Sufism deals with the One Essence and with Its names and Attributes inasmuch as they link the loci of their outward manifestation together with all related phenomena, to the Divine Essence. Thus, the subject of this science is the One Essence and its beginningless and eternal attributes. The questions it investigates include; 1) the emanation of multiplicity from the One Essence and its return thence, 2) the loci of manifestation a reflections of the divine Names and Attributes, 3) the return of God's people to him, 4) their wayfaring, spiritual warfare and ascetic practices, and 5) the fruits of each work and remembrance and the actual results in both this world and the next. Finally, the principles of this science are the knowledge of its definition and aim and the technical terminology of the Sufis." Cited by J. Nūrbakhsh, *Ma'ārif-i Ṣūfiyya* (London: Intishārāt-i Khāniqāh-i Niʿmatullāhī 1983), pp. 43–4.

Imāms to the very end in order to "enter ''*irfān*''", is characteristic of a certain sectarian theosophical doctrine peculiar to the Safavid School of Iṣfahānī *'irfān*, there is no prefiguring of this doctrine in the Sufism of pre-Safavid Persia, in which the role of a living master is, and has always been, unquestionably axiomatic.

In sum, if in Mīr Dāmād one finds the hubris of a Peripatetic philosopher who is infused with Shī'ite *'irfān* – the trunk of his visionary thought being grounded in Persian mystical *belles-lettres* in general and Ishrāqī Illuminationism in particular – it seems apparent that his spiritual roots received scant nourishment from the profound undercurrent of the Sufi tradition. Mīr Dāmād's misunderstanding or misappreciation of traditional Sufism is apparent from the feeble satire he composed to belittle Rūmī[153] discussed by Professor Nasr in his introduction to this volume. While the tree of Mīr Dāmād's philosophical *'irfān* may have flourished in the arid hyper-orthodox Shī'ite climate of seventeenth-century Iṣfahān, it was certainly never nourished by the same soil from which grew the Sufi schools of Khurāsān and Baghdad. Fortunately, his intellectual bias against Sufism was generally uncharacteristic of the school of Iṣfahān. It was Dāmād's illuminationist mysticism, rather than his independence from Sufism, which was conveyed to his foremost student, Mulla Ṣadrā.

3. Mullā Ṣadrā (d. 1050/1640)

The most important *ḥakīm* of the era of Shah 'Abbās I was no doubt Mullā Ṣadrā (also known as 'Foremost of the Theosophers', Ṣadr al-Muta'allihīn) whose place in the school of Iṣfahān has already been discussed in detail elsewhere in this volume.[154] However, since Mullā Ṣadrā was not only the physically related to (as father-in-law), but the main intellectual master of, the two main personages discussed in this essay, Muḥsin Fayḍ-i Kāshānī and 'Abd al-Razzāq Lāhījī, a few comments on his views about Sufism are required.

The 'Foremost of the Theosophers'' treatise 'Smashing the Idols of Paganism through Refutation of Contemporary Pseudo-Sufis' (*Kasr aṣnām al-jāhiliyya fī 'l-radd 'alā Mutasawwafa*) is one of the most important documents

[153] Cited by Hādī, *Sharḥ-i ḥāl-i Mīr Dāmād*, p. 42. The great Dhahabī master Quṭb al-Dīn Muḥammad Shirāzī wrote an eloquent rebuttal of Mīr Dāmād's critique in which he pointed out the errors in Dāmād's critique of the *Mathnawī*, revealing the learning Mīr Dāmād lacked and the uninformed nature of his *'irfān*.

[154] Works on Mullā Ṣadrā include S.H. Nasr, *Ṣadr al-Dīn Shīrāzī and his Transcendent Philosophy* (Tehran: Iranian Academy of Philosophy 1978); James Winston Morris, *The Wisdom of the Throne: An Introduction to the Philosophy of Mullā Ṣadrā* (Princeton, NJ: Princeton University Press 1981); Fazlur Rahman, *The Philosophy of Mullā Ṣadrā* (Albany: SUNY Press 1975). John Cooper's above-cited article "Rūmī and *Ḥikmat*" also contains some useful observations.

for the understanding of seventeenth-century Persian Sufism and the causes of the clerical persecution of Sufism during the period.[155] Composed in 1027/1617–18, *Kasr aṣnām*, contrary to the title's literal connotation, is not a tract against Sufism *per se* but only opposes certain corruptions in the Safavid *ghulāt* version of *taṣawwuf*. In fact, the first chapter of the book is devoted to commendation and praise of the genuine and traditional practices of Sufism, which he qualifies as being integrally 'Islamic'.[156] As Kathlyn Babayan reveals, *Kasr asnām* "attacks the darvish cultists who had pretentions to sufism. Mullā Sadrā had realized that mystically inclined *'alim*s like himself were in danger; for the shari'a-minded *'ulamā'* who engaged in the production of polemics against these assumed sūfīs did not distinguish between the sufiesque *ghulāt* and philosophers."[157] In composing this treatise to defend himself against foes of Sufism and the pseudo-orthodox clericalism and hardline Shī'ite exclusivism that had manifested themselves in the early seventeenth-century,[158] as Corbin points out:

> Mullā Ṣadrā had to confront a double category of 'ignoramuses': on the one part, he had to deal with the pious agnosticism of the *foqahā* of the legalitarian religion (cf. those addressed in the *Seh Asl*), on the other part, he had to face up to the obscurantism of certain Sufis who affected to scorn all books, education, intelligence, and knowledge as such. Mullā Ṣadrā's blame was not aimed at Sufism as such but at a certain degenerate sort of Sufism in his own time, without indicating precisely whom he had in mind.[159]

Perhaps for this reason, in the first volume of his monumental historico-philosophical work on Sufi orders, theosophy and traditions, the *Ṭarā'iq al-ḥaqā'iq*, the great nineteenth-century Sufi historian Ma'ṣūm 'Alī Shāh Shīrāzī (d. 1344/1926) pointed out that this work should be considered as penned in *praise* rather than in *condemnation* of the Sufis, as exemplifing a venerable tradition of criticism of vulgarized Sufism which also appeared in the *Kashf al-maḥjūb* of Hujwīrī, the *Mathnawī* of Rūmī and the *Gulshan-i rāz* of Shabistarī.[160] To illustrate Mullā Ṣadrā's method of critical appraisal combined

[155] *Kasr aṣnām al-jāhiliyya fī al-radd 'alā Mutasawwafa*, ed. Muḥammad Taqī Dānishpazhūh (Tehran: Dānishkadih-i 'ulūm-i ma'qūl va manqūl 1340 A.Hsh./ 1962).
[156] *Ibid*., pp. 7–8.
[157] "The Waning of the Qizilbash," p. 138.
[158] Kathlyn Babayan notes that "The withdrawal to Kahak of Mullâ Sadrâ (1021/1612–13), a product of the Ishrâqî school of philosophy, signals the existence of an orthodox undercurrent that was beginning to gain credence. In the first half of the seventeenth century, the mainstream current among the Imâmî ulama in Isfahan considered all three paths toward the knowledge of God (Sharî'at, Haqîqat, and Tarîqat) as legitimate" (*ibid*., p. 69).
[159] Mullā Ṣadrā, *Le Livre des pénétrations métaphysiques* (*Kitāb al-Mashā'ir*), Arabic text edited with a Persian version and French translation and annotation by Henry Corbin (Tehran: Tahūrī, 2nd ed 1363 A.Hsh./1984), p. 33, n.16 (French text).
[160] *Ṭarā'iq al-ḥaqā'iq*, ed. M.J Maḥjūb (Tehran: Kitābkhāna-i Bārānī 1345 A.Hsh./1966), I, pp. 182–3.

with informed praise of Sufism, Ma'ṣūm 'Alī Shāh cites the following passage from the *Kasr asnām*:

> Whoever considers the circumstances of the present day and the living conditions of its people, regarding with scrutiny and insight with knowledge born of certitude [will know] concerning the 'people of God' (*ahl Allāh*) and the masters of Sufism (*arbāb al-taṣawwuf*) and those who are perfect in their spiritual state (*al-kamāl al-ḥāl*) will prevent any of them from giving verbal expression [to their condition] but rather, will require them to keep it hidden.
>
> In brief, the 'Sufi' insofar as he is actually a 'Sufi' is concealed from [the apprehension of ordinary] human intelligence, and though he be visible in his bodily form, the rest of his states are hidden from public scrutiny . . . Those who are privy to His gnosis (*ahl 'irfānahu*), and who are His select servants and devotees are unknown to the people of the world, such that those who follow fleshly lusts cannot comprehend their states, and even if they did long to apprehend their rank, their degree is too lofty for benighted minds and the base natures to reach. Such adepts are becurtained within God's august Presence, and beneath the domes of His Majesty are hidden from the apprehension of villians and corrupt folk.[161]

The Sufi dimension of Mullā Ṣadrā's personality revealed by Ma'ṣūm 'Alī Shāh here becomes more pronounced in his Persian treatise entitled 'The Three Principles' (*Sih 'aṣl*),[162] where Mullā Ṣadrā introduces himself as *Khādim al-fuqarā'* – an obvious allusion to his affiliation to the Sufis.[163] This affiliation, or at least, sympathy for the Sufis is confirmed a few sentences later where he proceeds to cite a couplet from a ghazal of Ḥāfiẓ which states: "I do not travel this path through my own self-volition" – another indirect allusion to the need for spiritual direction and Mullā Ṣadrā's own probable affiliation to a Sufi master. Following this quotation of Ḥāfiẓ, Mullā Ṣadrā complains of the false scholars who "make repudiation of *the Dervishes* their motto in life, continually mocking the Path of divine wisdom (*ḥikmat*) and Unity (*tawḥīd*), and reviling the science of the Way to God and disengagement from

---

[161] Ma'ṣūm 'Alī Shāh, *Ṭarā'iq al-ḥaqā'iq*, I, p. 182; for the original passage, see *Kasr aṣnām*, pp. 103–04. This definition of the state of the true Sufi seems to be based on Rūmī's discussion of the real dervish in the *Mathnawī* (ed. R.A. Nicholson, London: Luzac & Co. 1925–40, III: 3669ff.). For a good discussion of *Kasr aṣnām*, see Babayan, "The Waning of the Quzilbash," chap. 5, notes 156–62.

[162] *Risāla-yi Sih aṣl*, ed. by S.H. Nasr (Tehran: Tehran University Press 1340 A.Hsh./1961), p. 5, line 5.

[163] The phrase *Khādim al-fuqarā'* 'caretaker of the poor' has an implicitly Sufi connotation. Besides the socially deprived, the unemployed, and beggars, no other group in Islamic society beside the Sufis are usually ever specifically referred to as the *fuqarā*. See the extended discussion of *faqr* and *faqīr* in Aḥmad 'Alī Rajā'ī Bukhārā'ī, *Farhang-i ash'ār-i Ḥāfiẓ* (Tehran: Intishārāt-i 'Ilmī, n.d.), pp. 509–23, as well as J. Nurbakhsh's book on this subject, trans. by L. Lewisohn, *Spiritual Poverty in Sufism* (London: Khaniqahi Nimatullahi Publications 1984).

[164] *Ibid.*, p. 6, lines 1–4. Italics mine. This complaint against *'ulamā'* who hate "the Dervishes" appears later in (and in fact, throughout) the treatise (cf. p. 93, lines 7–8).

materiality (*tajrīd*)."[164] This same aversion to anti-Sufi scholars appears again later on in the same chapter, where he explicitly expresses his intense dislike for "those scholars (*'ulamā'*) who deny the spiritual wayfarers (*sālikān*) and the brethren of purity … reviling divine wisdom (*ḥikmat*) and rejecting the truthful sages and the *Sufis"*.[165]

Examination of these pages (and other sections of the *Sih aṣl*) leads to only one conclusion: Mullā Ṣadrā, in this work at least, is an advocate of specifically *Sufi* philosophical mysticism (*ḥikmat*), rather than some independent Shī'ite philosophical mysticism divorced from the Sufi tradition. His *ḥikmat* is thus undeniably the fruit of his philosophical affiliation with the Sufi gnostic tradition – both that of the Akbarian theosophical school and the purely lyrical Persian Sufism of Rūmi – a fact demonstrated by his continual citation of Rūmī's *Mathnawī*[166] and Shabistarī's 'Garden of Mystery' (*Gulshan-i rāz*)[167] to illustrate the key concepts and ideas in this treatise. Many passages in his treatise appear specifically written *by way of exegesis on* the *Mathnawī*, rather than merely to provide a pleasant poetic illustration of or background for his own ideas.[168] Aside from his frequent citation of certain Shī'ite authorities such as Ja'far Ṣādiq, who is equally respected by the Sufis, as a thinker and master,[169] and some of the famous Shī'ite *ḥadīth* collections, such as Kulaynī's *'Uṣūl- kāfī*, there is little to distinguish the *Sih aṣl* from a classic Sufi tract on mystical psychology and spiritual discipline, composed after the fashion of a Jāmī or a Farghānī, cautioning the reader to abandon a life of passion and pursue a course of piety and religion. Having said this, though, it should be noted that Mulla Ṣadra explicitly denied his affiliation to any particular Sufi teacher.[170]

In brief, if his main mentor Mīr Dāmād distinguished, as Henry Corbin probably rightly maintained, between gnosis and Sufism, *'irfān* and *taṣawwuf*, for Mullā Ṣadra, the one is the other and the other the One.[171]

---

[165] *Ibid*., p. 10, lines 1–2. Italics mine.

[166] He cites Rūmī's *Mathnawī* some nine times in the treatise, citing varying numbers of couplets on each occasion, on the following pages: 2, 12, 30. 37, 41, 71, 72, 96, 109.

[167] He cites the *Gulshan-i rāz* some eight times on the following pages: 9, 19, 46, 73, 76,105, 111,112, 113.

[168] See for example, *ibid*., p. 96, lines 6–18.

[169] On which, see John Taylor, "Ja'far al-Sadīq, Spiritual Forbear of the Sūfīs," *Islamic Culture*, 40/1 (1966), pp. 97–113.

[170] In his *'Arshiyya*, the last work which Mullā Ṣadrā wrote (edited with a Persian translation by Ghulām Ḥusayn Āhanī, Iṣfahān: Kitābfurūshī-yi Shahriyār 1341 A.Hsh./1962), often considered an abbreviation of the *Asfār*, the author claims to have received his teaching from "the lamp of prophecy and sainthood; its substance derived from the fountainheads of the celestial Scripture and the way of the Prophet without recourse to study or discussion and without the teaching of any teacher" (p. 2).

[171] Cf. Ṣafā's (*Tārīkh*, V/1, pp. 215–16) provocative discussion of his relationship to *taṣawwuf*.

4. Mīr Abū al-Qāsim Findiriskī (d. 1050/1640–1)

Comparing the Platonists of Iṣfahān with their contemporaries, the Cambridge Platonists of England, Marshall Hodgson observed that Persian philosophy of the Safavid period "was alert to sources of pre-Islamic 'pagan' wisdom which might make it more humanistically universal."[172] One of the most important representatives of this humanistic univeralism in the school of Iṣfahān was Mīr Findiriskī, who had numbered Mullā Ṣadrā among his students.

The fact that he spent several years in India, where he frequented the company of Hindu yogis and ascetics, and composed a commentary on the Persian translation of the *Yoga Vasiṣtha* by Niẓām al-Dīn Pānipatī, is indicative of his wider ecumenical interests.[173] Findiriskī "tried to make peace in the war raging between the 'seventy-two sects', in which he achieved a measure of success through composition of a commentary on the work."[174]

Although the eminent contemporary Persian theosopher Jalāl al-Dīn Ashtiyānī describes Mīr Findiriskī as essentially an Islamic Peripatetic of the school of Avicenna, professing himself in the dark as to whether or not he professed any particular "mystical method in his heart (*dar bāṭin dārā-yi mashrab-i 'irfānī*),"[175] many scholars of Persian literature and philosophy have

---

[172] Hodgson, *The Venture of Islam*, III, p. 51.

[173] Nasr, "The School of Iṣfahān," p. 922; Ṣafā, *Tārīkh*, V, p. 311.

[174] Hādī, *Sharḥ-i ḥāl-i Mīr Dāmād* p. 57.

[175] *Muntakhabātī az āthār-i ḥukamā'ī ilāhī-yi Īrān*, I, p. 62. Ashtiyānī apparently based his views on Mīr Findiriskī's treatise on arts and sciences (*Risāla-yi Ṣanā'iyya*), in which the various types of professions and trades, and the metaphysical and moral reasons underlying the necessity for human employment are ennumerated and delineated, and in which there is little or no trace of philosophical mysticism (*'irfān*) and an entirely Islamic Peripatetic point of view prevails. For instance, the highest profession is that of the Prophet which is, in essence, good and beneficial, and the human profession which serves and benefits all the other professions is the blacksmith's trade (*ibid.*, I, p. 67), a truth which finds its scriptural confirmation in the Koran (LVII: 25). It is interesting to note that the first of his twelve professions of which "the subject is universal and general felicity its main concern" is described as being either "prophethood (*payghambarī*), deputyship [of a prophet] (*imāmī*), the juridical (*mujtahidī*) or philosophical (*faylsūfī*) profession" (*ibid.*, p. 68). In this description he communicates his belief that the prophet, theologian, jurisprudent and philosopher share similar moral and social responsibilities. The sole distinction between philosophers and prophets is that the former sometimes fall into error through their use of human reason and reflection, whereas the prophet, whose knowledge is through revelation (*waḥy*) and inspiration (*ilhām*), never errs. (*ibid.*, I, pp. 71–2). However, "when the philosopher reaches the farthest extent of his knowledge, this point is the generatrix (*mabdā'*) of Prophecy." Like Avicenna, Mīr Findiriskī maintained that the best example of such a philosopher is Aristotle (*ibid.*, p. 73). On Avicenna's views, see Fazlur Rahman, *Prophecy in Islam: Philosophy and Orthodoxy* (New York: Midway Reprint 1979), chap. 2. Despite these similarities in their function, Mīr Findiriskī is careful to note that there are serious differences and distinctions to be maintained between the abilities of the prophet and philosopher, making the latter but a pale reflection of the former.

remarked on Findiriskī's inclinations towards Sufism.[176] While E.G. Browne reflected that "while more a philosopher than a poet, and more a *darwīsh* than a philosopher, he does not exactly fall into any one of these three classes,"[177] Dhabīḥu'llāh Ṣafā, on the other hand, characterized Findiriskī as being "of a Sufi temperament (*Ṣūfī-manish*)."[178]

Whether apocryphal or not, the tales told of Mīr Findiriskī's habit of frequenting the meeting places of local dervishes in Iṣfahān became legendary in his own lifetime. Such stories, indeed, may be the basis of his reported affiliation with several of the orders in Safavid Iran.[179] Shāh 'Abbās once chided him, "I have heard it said that certain religious students, notables and scholars have been frequenting the company of rogues and listening to their rubbish." Without hesitation, Mīr Findiriskī retorted: "That's strange, because I spend most every day with jugglers and dervishes, yet never once noticed any seminary students or notables among them!"[180]

Mīr Findiriskī's alignment with Sufis in his daily life is reflected in his famous *qaṣīda* on the reality of gnosis,[181] in which he puts himself in an anti-philosophical, or at least an anti-Peripatetic camp in several verses, as, for example:

> *īn sukhan rā dar nayābad hīch fahm-i ẓāhirī*
> *gar Abū Naṣr-astī va'gar Bū 'Alī Sīnā'stī*
>
> The gist of words such as these
> no mind bound by exterior sense
> can know, be you the greatest sage,
> be you a Fārābī or Ibn Sīnā.[182]

The doctrine of mystical gnosis found in this *qaṣīda,* which criticizes the Peripatetic use of philosophical logic and reason (*'aql*) as an insufficient

[176] Likewise Nasr points out ("The School of Iṣfahān," p. 922): "As a Sufi, in spite of his having advanced very far upon the Path and having reached the state of pure contemplation and illumination, he mingled with the common people and wore the coarsest wool, and yet he was one of the most respected men in the Ṣafawid court. His manner resembled that of the Hindu Yogīs with whom he had had so much contact. He was a real man among men and one of the most striking Sufis of his time. While completely detached from the world and even from purely formal learning, he composed several important treatises including one on motion (*al-ḥarakah*), another on the arts and sciences in society (*ṣanā'iyyah*) . . . *Uṣūl al-fuṣūl* on Hindu wisdom, and a history of the Ṣafawids."
[177] *A Literary History of Persia*, IV, p. 258.
[178] *Tārīkh* V/1, p. 310.
[179] Ma'ṣūm 'Alī Shāh Shīrāzī claims that he was affiliated to the Nūrbakhshī and Ni'matullāhī orders: *Ṭarā'iq al-ḥaqā'iq*, I, p. 183.
[180] *Rayḥānat al-adab*, IV, p. 358.
[181] This poem is written in answer to *qaṣīdas* in the same metre by Nāṣir Khusraw and Shāh Ni'matullāh.
[182] See Hādī, *Sharḥ-i ḥāl-i Mīr Dāmād*, p. 66; Ṣafā, *Tārīkh*, V, p. 312–13 and the abbreviated translation given by Nasr, "The School of Iṣfahān," pp. 923–4.

means to apprehend reality is propounded in exactly the same manner as in the celebrated classical Persian Sufi poets such as Rūmī. In his exegesis of this couplet, the nineteenth-century Ḥakīm and pupil of Sabzivārī, Shaykh Mīrzā 'Abbās Dārābī, author of an important commentary on this *qaṣīda* , makes it quite clear that Findiriskī's thought is unapproachable through modes of Peripatetic analysis: only the Ishrāqī ascetic method or Sufism offers insight.[183]

Ultimately however, the same tensions between speculative philosophy and mystical poetry present in Shaykh Bahā'ī also appear in the writings of Mīr Findiriskī; the wrangling between the contrasting methods *'irfān*, *taṣawwuf* and *falsafa*, apparently resolved in the realm of their Sufi gnostic lyricism, in his thought still remain problematic in the prose of the world.

5. *'Abd al-Razzāq Lāhījī (d. 1072/1661–2)*

'Abd al-Razzāq b. 'Alī b. Ḥusayn Lāhījī (d. 1072/1661–2)[184] was the son-in-law of Mullā Ṣadrā and brother-in-law of Muḥsin Fayḍ-i Kāshānī (see section 6 below). In his Persian *Dīvān* one finds much interest in and reference to Sufism.[185] 'Abd al-Razzāq, whose pen-name 'Fayyāḍ' was given him by Mullā Ṣadrā, wrote several *qaṣā'id* celebrating his teacher Mullā Ṣadrā[186] and one in praise of Mīr Dāmād. However, he was not above writing occasional political panegryrics in praise of, among others, Shāh 'Abbās II, Shāh Ṣafī Murtaḍa Qulī Khān ('Abbās II's commander-in-chief) as well as many religious *qaṣā'id* in praise of the Prophet and the Imāms. "His poetry," Zarrīnkūb states, "although it follows the conventions of the period from a stylistic point of view, is not devoid of a passion for Sufism – 'Sufism', that is in the sense of speculative mysticism (*'irfān-i naẓarī*) rather than spiritual practice or

---

[183] *Tuḥfat al-murād: sharḥ-i qaṣīda-yi Mīr Findiriskī*, ed. Muḥammad Akbarī Sāvī (Tehran: n.p., 1372 A.Hsh./1993), pp. 54–8.

[184] One of the best accounts of his life and works is given in Jalīl Misgarnizhād's introduction to his edition of *Dīvān-i Fayyāḍ Lāhījī* (Tehran: Dānishgāh-i 'Allāma ḥabāṭabā'ī 1373 A.Hsh./1994). Other accounts include Muḥammad 'Alī Mudarris Tabrīzī, *Rayhānat al-adab* (Tehran 1331 A.Hsh./1952), IV, p. 361; Riḍā Qulī Khān Hidāyat, *Riyāz al-'ārifīn*, ed. Mehr 'Alī Gurkānī, (Tehran: n.d.), p. 382; Mīrzā Muḥammad Bāqir al-Musavī al-Iṣfahānī, *Rawḍat al-jannat* (Qum: 1391/1971), IV, p. 196; Ādharbīgdilī, *Ātashkada*, ed. Ḥasan Sādāt Nāṣirī, (Tehran: Amīr Kabīr 1336 A.Hsh./1957), II, p. 846. (All the above sources are also utilized by Jalīl Misgarnizhād in his introduction.).

[185] Recently published by Jalīl Misgarnizhād with an extentive and valuable introduction on the historical and literary background of his poetic work (see note 184 above). There is also an excellent edition with a comprehensive introduction to the same *Dīvān-i Fayyāḍ Lāhījī* (Tehran: Dānishgāh-i Tihrān 1372 A.Hsh./1993) edited by Amīr Bānū'ī Karīmī (references to Sufism are discussed on pp. 16–19).

[186] In a long *qaṣīda* entitled *Mu'jazat al-shawq* in reply to 'Urfī Shīrāzī's qaṣīda *Tarjumat al-shawq*, Fayyāḍ includes a panegryric to Mullā Ṣadrā, see *Dīvān-i Fayyāḍ*, pp. 423–4. He also wrote three other separate *qaṣīda*s in praise of Mullā Ṣadrā; pp. 458–60, 462–4, 465–8.

comportment (*sulūk-i 'amalī*) particular to adherants of a *khānaqāh* – demonstrating his spiritual inclination towards the reality of Sufism (*ḥaqīqat-i taṣawwuf*)."[187]

Like most of his contemporaries he expressed his admiration for Mīr Dāmād's spiritual and intellectual stature with unrestrained hyperbole, even claiming that "through you [Mīr Dāmād] the land of Iran is the universe's summation; through you the city of Iṣfahān has become the best of all climes."[188] "Just as on the Day of Judgement all human beings return to their Origin and Terminus, so to you they must refer in this world."[189]

His panegryrics in praise of Mullā Ṣadrā provide some important details about their relationship; one learns, for instance, that he enjoyed Mullā Ṣadrā's close personal company for many years and that he spent nearly every spring (Nawrūz is a sacred occasion for Persian extended family reunions) with him;[190] that his sense of physical separation from him was worse than being cast out of Heaven.[191] From the three lengthy panegryric *qaṣīda*s to Mullā Ṣadrā, his genuine love for this master are evident, and despite the flowery rhetoric, a characteristic of so much Safavid literature, his sincerity shines through. The following lines from a *qaṣīda* in praise of Mullā Ṣadrā recall the passionate love of Rūmī for Shams-i Tabrīzī:

> If till Judgement Day I were to worship the earth on which he walked, that would thus be meet: he's both teacher, father and spiritual Mentor . . . He's master of all the world (*ṣadr-i jahān*); and Excellence itself his universe; a Universal Mind: Perfection itself to him is beholden. Learning itself through him is dear. . . His mind like Plato's the solitude of mystical vision. In the company of academic debate his wit's as sharp as Aristotle. The Peripatetics all walk on foot; among them he alone is mounted. The Ishrāqīs are cast upon the earth and he alone left afoot.[192]

Even a superficial examination of such verses reveals Lāhījī's advocacy of a kind of gnostic Sufism, albeit devoid of many elements of the classical tradition. In many of his other works direct references to classical Sufi authors, sources, and citation of mystical doctrines can be found. This is most obvious in his *Gawhar-i murād* (The Essence of Spiritual Intention or Crown Jewel of Desire) a general work on theology, *kalām*, ontology and mystical theology (*'irfān*). Unfortunately, no critical edition of this work exists: the best copy in print is accompanied by an introduction which endeavours to manipulate the philosopher in political terms to meet the needs of "our [Islamic Republic's]

---

187 *Dunbāla Zarrīnkūb*, p. 254.
188 *Dīvān-i Fayyāḍ*, ed. Misgarnizhād, p. 462, v. 42.
189 *Ibid.*, p. 461, v. 29.
190 *Ibid.*, p. 463, v. 23.
191 *Ibid.*, p. 463, v. 25.
192 *Ibid.*, p. 467, vv. 50, 51, 52, 54, 59.

revolutionary spirit."[193] Since the thought of 'Abd al-Razzāq is prone to misinterpretation and distortion by both fundamentalist and modern ideological adversaries of Sufi mysticism, I shall try to rectify their bias in what follows.[194]

Avicenna is undoubtably the most frequently cited and celebrated author in the *Gawhar-i murād*. Thus, if 'Abd al-Razzāq Lāhījī appears at first sight to be nothing but an Islamic Peripatetic and follower of Ibn Sīnā – contrary to Madelung[195] – this is somewhat understandable, since he often terminates and confirms the validity of his own views and proofs by quoting what the "Shaykh in the *Shifā* states …" However, on closer investigation, Fayyāḍ's personal rapport with Avicenna has nothing to do with a rationalist orientation: his delight in the works of the Shaykh al-Ra'īs rather reflects the devotion and *dhawq* of a mystic for the founder of Islamic *ḥikma* (making one recall, in a different historical context, the same high respect accorded by 'Ayn al-Quḍāt Hamadhānī to Avicenna in his *Tamhīdāt*). Fayyāḍ's Avicenna is an *'ārif* who – above and beyond all his great philosophical achievements – is primarily the author of the ninth chapter of the 'Book of Philosophical Allusions' (*Ishārāt*) entitled 'Way Stations of the Gnostics' (*Maqāmāt al-'arifīn*).

One passage in the *Gawhar-i murād*, devoted to "Exposition of the way of the spiritual scientists (*muhaqiqqān*) among the legal scholars (*'ulamā'-yi sharī'at*), who are the objective of the Sufis and the gnostics, whether or not this name be

[193] This is the edition edited by Z. Qurbānī Lāhījī (Tehran: 1372 A.Hsh./1993), which features an introduction heavily spiced with quotations from Khomeini and Rafsanjani (e.g. introduction, pp. 12ff.). Although pp. 8–10 of this introduction, for example, are devoted to 'Abd al-Razzāq's *'irfān*, no reference is given to any of the (apparently politically incorrect) pro-Sufi passages in the *Gawhar-i murād* which I have discussed below. The same religious bias and partisanship is also evident in Jalīl Misgarnizhād's introduction to Fayyāḍ's *Dīvān* in which one section (on pp. 30–3) devoted to Lāhījī's *kalām*, *'irfān* and *taṣawwuf* utterly fails to deliver on the subtitle's promise – neglecting to mention the latter subject at all!

[194] Most modern Shī'ite religious dons, following the Safavid *mujtahid* cultists who are their ideological forbears, still consider Sufism, as Yann Richard insightfully pointed out, "as nothing more than an illegitimate competitor in the marketplace of religious values" (*Shi'ite Islam*, trans. A. Nevill [London: I.B. Tauris 1995], p. 54). Carl Ernst's analysis of the motivation of such biased selectivity is worth quoting in this regard: "Like the spin doctors who attempt to mold public opinion through commentary, fundamentalist spokesmen attempt through their rhetoric of total confrontation to claim representation of Islam. For this effort to succeed, they must discredit and disenfranchise all other claimants to the sources of authority in the Islamic tradition. There is no stronger rival claim on these sources than in Sufism" (Carl Ernst, *The Shambhala Guide to Sufism* [Boston: Shambhala 1997], pp. 212–13). Also cf. "Sufism and Fundamentalist Islam," in *ibid.*, pp. 211–15.

[195] It is true, as he points out, that 'Lāhījī's thought appears, throughout his works, dominated by his conviction of the continued validity of the integral teaching of Ibn Sīnā as against later critics', but this is not sufficient reason, as is shown below, to argue that the "internal evidence" that can be found in this works to show that he inclined to Sufism is "not convincing" (W. Madelung, "'Abd al-Razzāq," *Encyclopaedia Iranica*, I, p. 157).

ascribed to them," reveals the true breadth of Lāhījī's support for Sufism and advocacy of mystical Avicennanism. His introduction of Avicenna to defend the cause of philosophical mysticism (*'irfān*) in this passage simultaneously furnishes us with the truest account of – what is for him – the reality of Sufism.[196]

In Peripatetic ethical teaching, Lāhījī initially declares, the chief virtue is "Justice: denoting a harmonious balance and equity in all acts and works so as to incline to no one extreme." Lāhījī musters up a citation from Avicenna's 'Tract on Ethics' in support of this idea, adding that "without a complete awakening and broad-based self-consciousness causing one to enter deeply into, and become aware of, one's changing subjective humours, inner states, alterations experienced by the heart and the subtle minutiae of the soul's passions" no application or attainment of ethical virtues is possible.[197] "Many of the spiritual scientists (*muḥaqqiqān*) among the legal scholars (*'ulamā'-yi sharī'at*)," in order to realize such an understanding, Lāhījī explains, have chosen to retire into seclusion, a practice which can be traced back to the followers of the Prophet (*tāba'īn*) who from the earliest days of Islam had chosen to isolate themselves for the purposes of devotion and worship of God. Since their day an entirely new phenomenon has come into play, such that:

> in blind imitation of their practice, a group have established rites at variance with [the Prophet's] custom, and have decked themselves out in a special costume, considered it necessary to give themselves a special name, enacting peculiar rituals and coining their own separate terminology. In this fashion, the [customs of] 'masterhood and discipleship' (*pīrī va murīdī*) have became prevalent, good is combined with evil and wet and dry compounded. However, in relation [to the spiritual life] the closest thing to rectitude is to content oneself with worshipping and serving God without presuming to adopt any but the most ordinary names and denominations such as 'believers', 'sincere devotees', 'righteous servants', and 'pietists' (*mu'minīn va mukhliṣīn va ṣāliḥīn va muttaqīn*) mentioned in the Koran and the sacred Tradition (*sunna*), such that one not presume to adopt any other apparel and appearance than that of [simple] spiritual poverty and self-denial (*faqr va fanā'*), whatever its outer dress may be.[198]

---

[196] Contemporary Western scholars whose eyes are blinded by the dearly cherished orientalist fallacy that a *non-mystical* Islamic 'orthodoxy' actually exists – an entity no medieval Muslim ever subscribed to and which has largely been echoed by the modern media – are quite bewildered by the Sufi tendencies in a high-ranking Safavid theologian such as 'Abd al-Razzāq. To such distortions one can only respond that Islamic Sufism is, as S.H. Nasr emphasizes, "the inner dimension or heart of the Islamic revelation ... The attitude of traditional Islam to Sufism reflects that which was current during the centuries prior to the advent of puritanical and modernist movements in the 12th/18th century" ("What is Traditional Islam" in Nasr, *Traditional Islam in the Modern World*, p. 15). The donnish partiality to legalistic Islam and tacit acceptance of fundamentalist denunciations of Sufism as marginal or foreign to Islam, to which many Islamicists still uncritically subscribe, is raised by Carl Ernst in his *Shambhala Guide to Sufism*, pp. 8–18, 200.

[197] *Gawhar-i murād*, ed. Z. Qurbānī Lāhījī (Tehran 1372 A.Hsh./1993), p. 687.

[198] *Ibid*., p. 688.

This passage is a *locus classicus* for understanding, representing a key statement reflecting Fayyāḍ's sympathetic – yet not uncritical – approach to Islamic mysticism. That an ordained priest rails against priestcraft, or a monk assails the corruption of the clergy and their abuse of monastic ideals, does not imply that either priest or monk has repudiated the validity of the monastic way or has deserted his parish. Likewise, "if Fayyāḍ does not voice his approval of the master–disciple method (*ṭarīqa-yi pīr wa murīdī*) and the conventional Sufi discipline," as Professor Zarrīnkūb underlines (perhaps referring to this same passage), "this cannot be interpreted in any case as a denial and refutation of Sufism itself."[199] Criticism of Sufism *from within the tradition of Sufism*, in fact, has quite an ancient provenance.[200]

Having thus voiced his opinion about the corruption of the high ideals of Sufism, Fayyāḍ then briefly explains his view of what constitutes 'authentic' Islamic mysticism:

> The spiritual scientists (*muḥaqqiqān*) belonging to this class[201] are lords of high aspiration whose sights are fixed their sights exclusively on the Unique Divine Essence, and whose attention is directed to no other Aim than That . . . In the path of their spiritual wayfaring to God (*sulūk-i rāh-i khudā*) this group have delineated certain spiritual stations (*maqāmāt*), the first of which, after awakening (to the Quest) is repentance (*tawba*) from abandoning devotional practices and indulgence in sin, and the last is forsaking everything other than God, and repenting from the real sin (*gunāh-i ḥaqīqī*) which is one's fictional self-existence (*wujūd-i majāzī*), for it has been said 'Your existence is a sin worse than all other sin.'[202]

While in the first passage cited above, 'Abd al-Razzāq Lāhījī appears critical of both traditional and contemporary *ṭarīqa* Sufism, he also hardly differs from classical Sufi authors such as Hujwīrī or Qushayrī in expounding the traditional

---

199 *Dunbāla*, p. 254.

200 See Ernst, *The Shambhala Guide to Sufism*, pp. 18–31. One has only to recall these lines by Sa'dī to realize that the criticism of Sufism lies itself within an entire tradition of criticism through which the mystics strove to purify their high ideals from vulgarization:

Surat-i ḥāl-i 'ārifān dalq ast   īn qadar bas kay rū'ī dar khalq-ast
dar 'amal kūsh va har chih khwāhī pūsh   tāj bar sar nay u 'alam bar dūsh

murād-i ahl-i ṭarīqat labās-i ẓāhir nīst   kamar bih khidmat-i sulṭān biband u Ṣūfī bāsh

I also doubt that few Sufis would disagree with Sa'dī's statement

'Ālim u 'ābid u ṣūfī hamah ṭiflān-i rahand   mard agar hast bijuz 'ārif-i rabānī nīst

Yet, at the same time and in the same ghazal, Sa'dī enjoins the novice:

dārū-yi tarbiyat az pīr-i ṭarīqat bisitān   k'ādamī rā batar az 'illat-i nādanī nīst

201 *Ṭabaqa*: i.e. the class of scholars versed in *sharī'a* learning as well as the lore of the *ḥaqīqa*.

202 *Gawhar-i murād*, p. 688. The adage is ascribed to Rābi'a.

Sufi categorization of the spiritual stations. The predominately Sufi orientation of his doctrine becomes evident in his next paragraph, in which he briefly describes the categorizaton of the spiritual stations given by 'Abdu'llāh Anṣārī's in the *Manāzil al-sā'irīn* (Stations of the Wayfarers), an elaborate Islamic *Pilgrim's Progress* upon which, as A.G. Ravān-Farhādī pointed out, "Anṣārī's subsequent reputation in the annals of Sufism primarily rests."[203] The penultimate station in Anṣārī's categorization is the annihilation (*fanā'*) of the false Selfhood. In describing this concept, Lāhījī is careful to comment that at this station *fanā'* cannot be understood to properly "exist" in itself, "but rather this station implies an *annihilation from annihilation*. For at this level the utmost depths of divine Union become manifest and the wayfarer becomes endowed with all the divine Attributes, becoming eternal in God's own Eternity."[204]

To explain the highest reaches of Avicennan mysticism, Lāhījī takes a cue from Shaykh Abū 'Alī bin Sīnā's account of the "Waystations of the Gnostics," the ninth chapter of his 'Book of Philosophical Allusions' referred to above, first citing with approval the commentary on this text by Imām Fakhr-i Rāzī, who, he states, praised "this chapter as having arranged the sciences of the Sufis in a far better manner than any of his forebears and, to tell the truth, better than anyone subsequent to him." Interestingly enough, the approbation of the word 'Sufi' by the great Sunni theologian Fakhr al-Dīn Rāzī in this passage causes Lāhījī no alarm. 'Abd al-Razzāq's evident veneration of Avicenna's *Maqāmāt al-'ārifīn* renders him oblivious to both the anti-Sunni and anti-Sufi bias of his age. Neither Sunnism nor Shī'ism seem to matter in this context; what is of overall importance is the sublimity of the proper *philosophical presentation* of the Sufis' spiritual stations, and despite the obvious theological divergence of *madhhab* between Avicenna and our author, there is no disagreement about the transcendental *reality* of *'irfān*. Fayyāḍ's own Shī'ism disappears in the overwhelming light of the mystico-philosophical tradition, dissolving all sectarian exclusivism in its transcendental wisdom (*ḥikmat*).

The next few pages of the concluding chapter of his 'Crown Jewel of Desire' are devoted to further commentary on Avicenna's *Maqāmāt al-'ārifīn*. Quoting heavily from Nāṣir al-Dīn Ṭūsī's *Sharḥ* of this work, he concludes that Avicenna and Ṭūsī are only expressing in "different words (*taqrīrī dīgar*) the notion of the 'Unity of Being (*waḥdat-i wujūd*) which idea is the quintessence of the Gnostics' objectives and fruit of the hearts of saints." Lāhījī sums up his own opinion of the relation between philosophical mysticism (*ḥikmat*) and gnosticism (*'irfān*) as follows:

> From what has been mentioned above it is evident that the degree of gnosis (*ma'rifat*) is higher than that of philosophical mysticism (*ḥikmat*) and the Object

---

[203] See his article "The *Hundred Grounds* of 'Abdullāh Anṣārī (d. 448/1056) of Herāt," in L. Lewisohn, *The Heritage of Sufism*, I, p. xxx.
[204] *Gawhar-i murād*, p. 688.

> sought by the gnostics (*'urafā'*) is more dear than that of the philosophical mystics (*ḥukamā'*). For the latter aims to detach the rational soul from corporeality and attach it to the heavenly pleroma and the realm of pure immateriality. The aim of the gnostics, on the other hand, is severance of their attention from aught but God and realization of the station of annihilation (*fanā'*), merging into the World of Eternal Subsistence (*'ālam-i baqā'*).
>
> Yet, the aims of both the gnostics and the philosophers are more exalted than those of the ascetics and religious devotees (*zuhād va 'ubbād*), for the latter group does not aim to transcend corporeality, but only strives to overcome physical pleasures in expectation of attaining joys hereafter.[205]

Lāhījī distinguishes in this passage between a lower Shī'ite philosophical mysticism divorced from the Sufi tradition and a 'higher' knowledge present in Avicennan gnosis. He places the theosophy of Ibn 'Arabī and the philosophical gnosis of Avicenna – which aim to denude the imagination of all but God – on a higher level than an *Ishrāqī* type of *ḥikmat* whose aim is primarily body-denying and ascetic. He concludes the chapter with further citations from the *Maqāmāt al-'ārifīn*, noting with approval how Avicenna distinguished between three religious types: ascetics, devotees and gnostics. Every gnostic is necessarily an ascetic and a religious devotee, whereas many, if not most, ascetics and religious devotees lack gnosis. The highest rung of spiritual achievement, however, is that of the gnostic "whose inner being (*bāṭin*) is like a burnished mirror held up before the Almighty's visage whereupon is cast the image of divine manifestations, enlightening him with genuine spiritual pleasures such that he experiences a joy beyond all temporal things."[206]

Gnosis (*ma'rifat*), in a word, is the 'Crown Jewel of Desire'. *Ma'rifat*, states 'Abd al-Razzāq, the mystical Peripatetic, is the supreme desire, the highest aim, the *Gawhar-i murād* of the sage, whether philosopher, ascetic or Sufi. This philosophical truth is understood only by the *'ārif* who transcends all sects and names.[207]

From the above summary, it is evident that if 'Abd al-Razzāq Lāhījī did not subscribe to the practice of contemporary Sufis, his philosophical mysticism is quite Sufi in tenor.[208] Perhaps this is the reason that Mīrzā 'Abdullāh Afandī

---

205 *Ibid.* p. 691.

206 *Ibid.* p. 693.

207 Fayyāḍ's *Dīvān* is riddled with apophatic utterances which express this axiomatic mystical truth, of which the following couplets are a good example: "O Muslims, if being Muslim is merely this, then I'm a Jew, an infidel, a Zoroastrian: I am not a Muslim" (*Dīvān*, ed. Karīmī, p. 644, no. 516: 2); "If you have no taste to be a dervish, flee away, become a king; if you have no taste for inner peace then flee away into the melée. ... The taste for people's praise turns poison into sugar: if you are a man, renounce holy piety and into monkhood flee"(*Ibid*., p. 593, no. 452: 1, 5).

208 Jalāl al-Dīn Ashtiyānī thus described 'Abd al-Razzāq Lāhījī as "inclined to Sufism (*taṣawwuf*)," noting that "his principle method was that of the spiritual wayfarers (*ahl-i sulūk*) and that his spiritual attitude was exactly the same as that of his teacher" (*Muntakhabātī az āthār-i ḥukamā'ī ilāhī-yi Īrān*, I, p. 285).

described ʻAbd al-Razzāq as "harboring a Sufi's theosophical sensibility (*kāna Ṣūfī al-mashrab*)"[209] and why Henry Corbin pointed out that it was evident from this work alone that "he certainly had realized a personal experience of Sufism."[210]

A look at the second part of the introduction to the *Gawhar-i murād*, in which he vigorously argues that the practical gnostic method of the Sufis constitutes the *only authentic path to God* in Islam, reveals the full extent of ʻAbd al-Razzāq's sympathies with the theosophical ideals, if not with the actual practices of, *taṣawwuf*:

> It should be understood that the *via mystica* which leads to God Almighty is a way upon which none should ever imagine any methodical progress (*sulūk*) can be made except by means of humble entreaty and self-abnegation (*ʻajz va nīstī*). Indeed, what relation does a clod of dust and dirt have to the pure Creator?[211] What likeness does an earthborn being have with the Lord of Lords? For there is no kinship between the creature and the Creator, or between the possible and the Necessary Being, the temporally created and the Eternal Being and the perishing and the Everlasting One, such that by betaking oneself to the former one should be able to attend the latter's Court. The only way to that Court is through negation of all relationships (*ṣalb-i hama-yi nisbathā*), for when all relationships and ties are abolished and the veils of fantasy and imagination are removed from one's sight, such that one utterly despairs of all things, then the good tidings of hope in all things is issued. When the dust settles and the air is cleared, then the visible is clearly evident to the eye. Now, all beings, through their phenomenal contingency, are like a swirling cloud of dust polluting the atomosphere of thought. As long as it does not settle, nothing but dust can be seen.
>
> Thus, the object of those who have personally verified the Truth among the Sufis (*muḥaqqīn az Ṣūfiyya*)[212] in professing the 'Unity of Being' (*waḥdat-i wujūd*) and complete self-annihilation (*fanā'-yi muṭlaq*) cannot be anything above and beyond the idea here alluded to. Whatever else you hear about this matter, beware, pay it no heed!

---

[209] *Riyāẓ al-ʻulamā'*, p. 114.

[210] *Histoire de la philosophie islamique*, p. 471.

[211] This sentence seems to be a direct paraphrase of Shabistarī's hemistich in *Gulshan-i rāz*, ed. Ṣamad Muwaḥḥid, *Majmūʻa-i āthār-i Shaykh Maḥmūd Shabistarī* (Tehran: Kitābkhāna-i Ṭahūrī 1365 A.Hsh./1986) pp. 71–2, v. 125 "What relation does dust have to the pure realm: for apprehension is nothing but [to realize one's] incapacity to apprehend."

[212] The terminology adopted by Fayyāḍ in this passage is indebted to the spiritual typology proposed in Ṣā'in al-Dīn Turkah Iṣfahānī's (d. 830/1427) *Risāla-yi Shaqq al-qamar*. After discussing the various intellectual groups in Islamic society (philosophers, jurists, etc.), Iṣfahānī describes the Sufis. To cite here Henry Corbin's précis of his argument, he writes, "Les soufis dont il s'agit ici ont une haute culture théosophique, ils sont imprégnés aussi bien de la spiritualité de Sohrawardī que de celle d'Ibn ʻArabī. Deuṣ attributs les qualifient: ce sont des *Mohaqqiqān*, terme que indique une double *vérification personelle* à la fois spéculative et expérimentale. Ce sont 'ceuṣ qui ont compris' au sens propre du mot, correspondant à l'acception technique où nous prenons ice le mot *herméneutique:* un acte de 'comprendre' qui est acte de prendre conscience due fait *que* l'on 'implique' et de *ce que* l'on implique. … D'où la seconde qualification de nos soufies: ce sont des *Ahl-i shohūd*, des témoins oculaires, des initiés admis à la contemplation du mystére" (*En Islam iranien*, III, p. 247).

> In a word, the path to God (*rah-i khudā*) is a strait and narrow one; it can neither be discovered by oneself alone nor traversed solely with the aid of reason (*pāyimardī-yi 'aql*). One can only hope in divine grace, that in His Beneficent Mercy, He will open the way to his servants. Although he has sent the prophets to reveal this way, after they expounded and exposed it, one still must traverse the way which one is shown; and yet, despite the fact that one must proceed on the way oneself [by freewill], unless He conduct you, traversing it will be impossible.
>
> It should be also understood that all men have two ways to approach God: an exoteric (*rāh-i ẓāhir*) and an esoteric way (*rāh-i bāṭin*). Although one only can *reach* God by the esoteric way, one may *know* God through the exoteric way – albeit a wide gap between [theoretically] knowing God and actually reaching Him exists. It is because of this that so many allusions have been made to the hardships of the esoteric way – in contrast to the exoteric way which involves much less hardship insofar as the latter is based on rational demonstrations within the intellectual reach of every intelligent person capable of discerning effect from cause.
>
> The way of rational demonstration should proceed the way of spiritual conduct (*sulūk*).[213] for as long as a person does not know that there are posting houses on a road he never will make a journey to any destination.[214]

In part 3 of the introduction to the *Gawhar-i murād*, 'Abd al-Razzāq addresses the subject of the spiritual path (*taṣawwuf*) in a less oblique manner, noting that are basically only two divisions among Islamic scholars in theology (*ma'ārif-i ilāhī*): Mu'tazilites and Ash'arites. Such theological distinctions, however, don't appear in Sufism (*taṣawwuf*), where they are largely irrelevant, insofar as such scholastic differences:

> exist only among those who pursue the exoteric way (*sulūk-i rāh-i ẓāhir*) and the path of rational speculation and demonstration (*ṭarīqa-yi naẓar va istidlāl*), whereas the reality of Sufism (*ḥaqīqat-i taṣawwuf*) relates to one's conduct on the esoteric way (*sulūk-i rāh-i bāṭin*) alone. Whereas the final objective of the former is knowledge, the ultimate aim of the latter is known to be Union with the divine Essence.
>
> However, having said that, it should be added that the esoteric way is informed by the mode of conduct maintained upon the exoteric way (*masbūq-ast bar sulūk-i rāh-i ẓāhir*). Therefore, the Sufi must first be either a philosopher (*ḥakīm*) or a scholastic theologian (*mutakallim*). Making claims to Sufism (*ida'ā-yi taṣawwuf*) before being firmly grounded in mystical philosophy (*'ilm-i*

---

213 *Sulūk* denotes methodical progress on the *via mystica* or *ṭarīqa*, the process of ascension and advancement – psychical, ethical and spiritual – which the Sufi 'wayfarer' (*sālik*) experiences in his pursuit (*ṭalab*) of God. For further discussion of this term in Sufism, see L. Lewisohn, *EI*², s.v. *sulūk*.

214 *Muntakhabātī az āthār-i ḥukamā'ī ilāhī-yi Īrān*, I, pp. 285–6; *Gawhar-i murād*, pp. 33–4. Henry Corbin commented that this passage "ne laissent aucun doute sur l'inclination secrète et profonde de Mollā Abdorrazzāq pour le soufisme et sur conviction que les prophètes et les *awliyā'* ont été missionnés pour communiquer et expliquer le secret de cette voie *Muntakhabātī*., I, French introduction, p. 124).

> *ḥikmat*), *kalām* and, generally speaking, before being perfectly accomplished in rational and theoretical methods (*ṭarīq-i naẓar*), whether this be according to the lexicon of the orthodox theologians (*'ulamā'*) or not, is nothing but imposture and deliberately pulling the wool over the eyes of the common people.
>
> Our discourse here does not concern either the term *taṣawwuf* or the word *ṣūfī*; rather, our purpose is 'spiritual conduct' (*sulūk-i ma'nawī*), the quest for true union and the self-denying annihilation of all but Him, thus becoming eternal in His Eternity. The *ḥadīth* [where God declares that] "I am his ear . . . and eye"[215] alludes to this degree and in respect to the Holy Canon (*shar'*), this is what is referred to as true devotion and piety. Whatever the Sufis profess to have attained through interior intellectual revelations (*mukāshafāt-i 'ilmiyya*), their intention is not the attainment of speculative knowledge (*'ilm-i naẓarī*) without requiring proofs and demonstrations – since it is impossible to acquire speculative knowledge without certain intermediary means. Rather, the purpose of contemplative vision (*mushāhada*) is that it be the result of rational demonstration (*burhān*) without the interference of fantasy and delusive imagination.[216]

It is clear from this passage that 'Abd al-Razzāq did not approve of mystics who lacked prior training in either theology or philosophy. At the same time, he maintained the pre-eminence of *taṣawwuf* and endorsed the probity and piety of the Sufi path among other Islamic intellectual and spiritual sciences. Several centuries earlier, a similar if not identical doctrine was clearly enunciated by the Kubrāwī Sufi Shaykh 'Azīz Nasafī (d. between 1281 and 1300), who suggested that no good could come of a mystic without a prior theological education.[217] Thus it is clear that 'Abd al-Razzāq's opinion that the possession of a thorough philosophical or religious education is the *sine qua non* of practical Sufism was not by any means an independently developed doctrinal innovation original to the Safavid Shī'ite theological milieu in which he flourished: the doctrine has definite resonances, if not its entire origin, in the classical Persian Sufi tradition itself.

Later on in this chapter, while comparing Ishrāqī theosophy with Sufism in order to underline their similarity, 'Abd al-Razzāq clearly maintains the pre-eminence of the latter tradition. If Ishrāqī spirituality is not entirely spurious,

---

[215] "When I love a servant, I, the Lord, am his ear so that he hears by Me, I am his eye, so that he sees by Me, and I am his tongue so that he speaks by Me, and I am his hand, so that he takes by Me." Cited by Annemarie Schimmel, *Mystical Dimensions of Islam* (Chapel Hill: University of N Carolina 1975), p. 43.

[216] *Muntakhabātī az āthār-i ḥukamā'ī ilāhī-yi Īrān*, I, pp. 287–8; *Gawhar-i murād*, pp. 38–9.

[217] In the fifth treatise in his *Kitāb al-insān al-kāmil*, entitled *Risāla-yi dar biyān-i sulūk* (ed. Marijan Molé, Tehran–Paris 1962), p. 92, Nasafī states that the novice should "first go to the *madrasa* and acquire of Islamic legal knowledge (*'ilm-i sharī'at*) what is necessary . . . Then, he should study beneficial knowledge so that he becomes quick-witted and fathoms subtle expressions, since the understanding of learned discourse which is acquired in the *madrasa* is an extremely important pillar of this subject. Then, he goes to the *khānaqāh* and affiliates himself as a disciple to a shaykh, devoting himself to his threshold, contenting himself with one shaykh alone, learning what is necessary of the 'science of the mystical path' (*'ilm-i ṭarīqat*)."

he states, it is but a pale reflection of the major tradition in Islamic mysticism, which is *taṣawwuf*:

> The difference between the Sufi and the Illuminationist philosopher (*ḥakīm-i ishrāqī*) is that the path of Sufism (*ṭarīqa-yi taṣawwuf*) is traversed only *after* becoming completely versed in the principles of philosophical theology (*qawā'id-i kalāmī*) and grounded in the science of the *sharī'a*. For this reason, the fundamental teachings found in the books of the [Sufi] gnostics (*'urafā'*) are more comprehensive than those of the Illuminationist sages.[218]

Ishrāqī and Sufi mysticism, however, are both considered to be species of "spiritual conduct on the esoteric path" (*sulūk-i rāh-i bāṭin*). The Ishrāqī path, he stresses, is not one which involves acquisition of exoteric knowledge (*taḥṣīl-i 'ilm*), but rather is only "informed by" one's "conduct on the exoteric path" (*sulūk-i rāh-i ẓāhir*).[219] For this reason:

> There is no difference between Illuminationism and Sufism except that Sufism is juxtaposed to the discourse of the scholastic theologians (*takallum*) whereas Illuminationism (*ishrāq*) is juxtaposed to philosophical mysticism (*ḥikmat*). That is to say, whenever the mystic's spiritual conduct on the esoteric path *comes after* his conduct on the exoteric path – pursued according to the principles of philosophical mysticism (*ḥikmat*), it is known as the 'Path of Illuminationism' (*ṭarīqa-yi ishrāq*); but if his conduct [on the esoteric path] *comes after* his conduct on the exoteric path – followed according to the principles of philosophical theology (*kalām*) – it is known as the 'Path of Sufism'.
>
> Both the *Ishrāqī* sage's condemnation of the Peripatetics and the Sufi's censure of philosophical theologians and conventional religious scholars relate to the fact that both [those denounced] groups have limited themselves to formal conduct on the course of the exoteric way (*sulūk-i rāh-i ẓāhir*); and have based their studies on mere acquisition of intellectual concepts, disregarding and dismissing the essential goal – spiritual conduct on the esoteric path and quest for divine Union.
>
> [On the other hand], the Peripatetic philosophers and the philosophical theologians' censure of the Ishrāqīs and Sufis relate to the fact that the latter groups have set foot on the esoteric path without the adequate acquisition of exoteric knowledge and in-depth inquiry according to methods based on logical inference (*ṭarīq-i burhān*). But in reality, both groups are right in what they say, for true universality (*kamāl-i ḥaqīqī*) lies in the adornment of both one's inner and outer being, and, just as disregarding the inner being and contenting oneself with formal learning constitutes aberration and arrogance, so undertaking the interior journey without proper conduct in exoteric matters (*sulūk-i ẓāhir*) is a deviation and defect.[220]

'Abd al-Razzāq Lāhījī's sophisicated and subtle understanding of the relationship betweeen *taṣawwuf*, *ḥikmat*, *falsafa* and *'irfān* in these passages

---

[218] *Muntakhabātī az āthār-i ḥukamā'ī ilāhī-yi Īrān*, I, p. 289.
[219] *Ibid.*, I, p. 289; *Gawhar-i murād*, p. 40.
[220] *Muntakhabātī az āthār-i ḥukamā'ī ilāhī-yi Īrān*, I, pp. 289–90; *Gawhar-i murād*, p. 40.

reveals his deep sympathy and respect for Sufism, the foundation of which, however, he insists must be philosophically sound. He concludes:

> Sufis and Qalandars who do not have a firm grounding in discursive theosophy (*ḥikmat-i baḥthiyya*), who lack acquaintance with philosophical theology, traditional commentaries and exoteric knowledge concerning the ontological origin and end of creation (*mabda' u ma'ād*), while introducing themselves as masters (*murshid*) and spiritual guides of people – as do the *aqṭāb* of our own period and [some in] previous epochs – are nothing but brigands who waylay the common folk. The supreme theosopher [Ṣadr al-Mutā'allihīn = Mullā Ṣadrā] in his treatise *Kasr aṣnām al-jāhiliyya* took such people to task and exposed the [un]learning of this group, revealing the extent of their decadence.[221]

Lāhījī's intellectual attitude is thus fundamentally that of a theosopher personally inclined to Sufism, as careful to observe respect for classical Sufism as he was to preserve his aloofness from certain benighted representatives of pseudo-Sufism in Safavid Iṣfahān, making his sympathy with the classical Sufi tradition as manifest as is his intellectual distance and independance from the vulgarized *dervichisme* of the Qizilbāsh.

6. *Muḥsin Fayḍ-i Kāshānī*

Mullā Muḥsin Fayḍ-i Kāshānī (d. 1090/1679–80), pupil and son-in-law of Mullā Ṣadrā was "one of the most eminent theologians, philosophers, jurisprudents and mystics of the Safavid period, known for his prolific compositions in subjects ranging from Peripatetic philosophy to Ishrāqī 'oriental' theosophy, mysticism (*'irfān*) and both speculative and practical Sufism (*taṣawwuf-i naẓarī wa 'amalī*)."[222] One of the most important Shī'ite theosophers of seventeenth-century Persia, there was hardly any field of knowledge among the sciences of his day that he did not examine and discuss in his works.[223] Despite his fame and accomplishments, he preferred to live the life of a simple teacher in his home town of Kāshān, the 'City of Faith' (*Dār al-īmān*), and even turned down an invitation by Shāh 'Abbās to assume the post of archbishop of Iṣfahān (*Shaykh al-Islām*).[224] This cautious avoidance of centres of political power probably played a key role in ensuring Fayḍ's success as a writer on philosophical and mystical subjects. Born into a highly literary family in Kāshān, where his father possessed a large library, he composed some 200 works over the 65 years of his life.[225]

---

[221] *Ibid.*, pp. 290–1.

[222] *Muntakhabātī az āthār-i ḥukamā'ī ilāhī-yi Īrān az 'aṣr-i Mīr Dāmād u Mīr Findariskī tā zamān-i ḥāḍir*, ed. II, p. 118 from Ashtiyānī's Persian introduction.

[223] Bertels, *Taṣawwuf wa adabiyāt-i taṣawwuf*, Persian trans. by Sīrūs Īzādi (Tehran: T Amīr Kabīr 1976), p. 664.

[224] *Ibid.*, pp. 118–20.

[225] See Fayḍ's *Risāla-yi Mishwāq* (Tehran: 1348 A.Hsh./1969), Muṣṭafā'ī Fayḍī Kāshānī (ed.), introduction, p. 31.

In his autobiography written in 1065/1654 when he was 58, and appropriately titled 'The Heart's Tale' (*Sharḥ-i ṣadr*), Fayḍ related how he spent years wandering from city to city in Persia, in search of esoteric knowledge (*'ilm-i bāṭin*). In Shīrāz he had studied theology and *ḥadīth*, initially under "the supreme jurisprudent of his age" Sayyid Majīd Baḥraynī, from whom he received a diploma,[226] before going on to Iṣfahān, where he then memorized *ḥadīth* under Bahā' al-Dīn 'Āmilī (see section 1 above), from whom he received another diploma. Following an ill-fated Ḥājj to Mecca, on the return journey of which his beloved younger brother was killed by brigands, he ended up in Qum where he encountered Mullā Ṣadrā, who became his main teacher. He soon became one of the most passionate followers of Mullā Ṣadrā's transcendentalist philosophy,[227] describing Ṣadrā as "cardinal among the theosophists (*ahl-i 'irfān*), a moon in the firmament of certitude [one] ... who in the varieties of esoteric knowledge (*'ilm-i bāṭin*) was unique in his age, the supreme authority of his time."[228] Remaining in Qum eight years, he eventually married his teacher's daughter, from whom he received his *takhallus* 'Fayḍ' (Grace), recalling that given to his brother-in-law, 'Fayyāḍ-i' (Overflowing grace, 'Abd al-Razzāq) Lāhījī.

Unfortunately, as with 'Abd al-Razzāq Lāhījī, the study of the works Fayḍ-i Kāshānī has been dominated by *sharī'a*-minded Iranian Shī'ites who portray him as a foe of mysticism and Sufism:[229] a viewpoint which is both uninformed and inaccurate, belying his own quite powerful support for *'irfān* and respect for classical *taṣawwuf*. However, in one way, the disdain and distrust which Iranian theologians have shown towards Fayḍ-i Kāshānī's Sufi oeuvre is comprehensible; he was, after all, prodigiously active in the composition of

---

[226] *Sharḥ-i ṣadr*, in *Dah risālah-yi Muḥaqqiq-i Buzurg-i Fayḍ-i Kāshānī*, (Iṣfahān: Markaz-i taḥqīqāt-i 'ilmī va dīnī Imām Amīr al-Mū'minīn 'Alī 1371 A.Hsh./1992), ed. R. Ja'fariyān, p. 59.

[227] Bertels, *Taṣawwuf wa adabiyāt-i taṣawwuf*, p. 663.

[228] *Sharḥ-i ṣadr*, p. 61.

[229] A typical example of this intense anti-Sufi bias is found in a work on so-called 'Shī'ite Philosophy,' which claims that "Fayḍ often attacked the Sufis in his writings, calling them charlatans, cheats, liars, and heretical innovators. In any case, Mullā Muḥsin Fayḍ was an eminently celebrated man of learning, philosophy, ethics and *ḥadīth* and devoted his whole life to knowledge ... so it is extremely far-fetched to think that such a great mind could ever subscribe to such superstitious rubbish as Sufism and dervishism ..." (Shaykh 'Abdu'llāh Ni'mat, *Falāsafat al-Shī'a*; cited from the Persian translation of this book entitled *Falāsafa-yi Shī'a* by Sayyid Ja'far Ghaḍabān [Tabriz: n.d.], p. 557). For a similarly biased treatment see the introduction by Ḥusayn Qashāhī to Fayḍ's *Ḥaqā'iq dar sayr wa sulūk*, Persian trans. Muḥammad Bāqir Sā'idī Khurāsānī (Shīrāz: Intishārāt-i 'ilmiyya Islāmiyya 1340 A.Hsh./ 1961), pp. 1–35. The traditional clerical Shī'ite bias and wariness of Sufism is often reflected in scholarship of the Safavid period, in which regard Bertels' wise remarks (*Taṣawwuf*, *p.* 668) about the many *Pia fraus* or *durūgh-i maṣlaḥat-āmīz* written by Safavid historians such as Khwānsārī in the *Rawḍāt al-Jannāt* (who endeavoured to conceal Fayḍ's relation to the Sufis) are still worth bearing in mind. See also notes 193, 194, 196 above.

theological works, having virtually rewritten Ghazālī's *Iḥyā 'ulūm al-dīn* from a Shī'ite standpoint. That the philosophical and theological bent and aspect of his character tends to be emphasized over his mysticism is not difficult to comprehend, therefore, even if he was generally well disposed, if not personally inclined to, Sufism (as his lesser-known writings discussed below demonstrate).

In what amounts to a small monograph devoted to the question of the relationship of Fayḍ-i Kāshānī's theology to Sufism, Zarrīnkūb draws attention to the resemblances between his intellectual orientation and that of Abū Ḥāmid al-Ghazālī:

> Most of his works tend to support the fundamental principles of the Sufis, and thus gave credence and confirmation to the results of their doctrinal teachings. In his treatise on 'The Wayfarer's Sustenence' (*Zād al-sālik*) he cites the *exempla* and *dicta* of the Shī'ite Imāms which resemble those of the Sufis. He favourably interpreted such practices as the wearing of wool and the sitting in periods of retreat for forty days without involving himself in any juridical debate on the legality of such practices. Although the truth of the matter is that he did not look favourably upon conventional Sufism as practised by those who frequented *khānaqāh*s and disapproved of the Sufi tenets and disciplines as professed and propagated by the established mystics of his day, at the same time he did not share the same intense interest and preoccupation with philosophical mysticism (*ḥikmat*) and the peculiar issues in scholastic theology as 'Abd al-Razzāq Lāhījī and Mullā Ṣadrā, who were attached to such debates. Despite the fact that he wrote a number of philosophical treatises, such as his commentary [on Mīr Dāmād's] *Ḥāshiyya bar rawāshiḥ al-samāwiyya*, *Risāla al-imkān wa'l-wujūd*, *Anwār al-ḥikma*, *Risāla 'ayn al-yaqīn fī uṣūl al-dīn*, as well as several other treatises on theology, ontology, the concept of perpetual creation in nature and the imagination, like Ghazālī he apparently was concerned with the examination of religious problems, matters related to spiritual conduct (*sulūk*) and theosophy (*'irfān*). Perhaps, one can say that his intellectual methodology and mode of spirituality in the Shī'itized climate of the Safavid era, is completely reminiscent of the figure of Ghazālī in the Sunni milieu of Seljuk Iran.[230]

However, unlike Ghazālī, who gave his total endorsement of the Sufi method in his *al-Munqidh min al-ḍalāl*, Fayḍ-i Kāshānī stopped short of fully committing himself to practising the *ṭarīqa* of the traditional Muslim mystics.[231] In many ways, he is the best example of the sober, highly intellectual and nomocentric Shī'ite Sufism of the Safavid period. He was, as

[230] Zarrīnkūb, *Dunbāla*, p. 257.

[231] In one ghazal in which Fayḍ frankly records his spiritual achievement and realization, he concludes with this couplet: "A thousand thanks to God: my heart now rests from being pulled to and fro; for it, like Fayḍ is neither barrister, master or disciple" (*chūn Fayḍ nay pīr u nay faqīh u nay murīdīm*) (*Kulliyāt-i ash'ār-i Mawlānā Fayḍ-i Kāshānī*, ed. Muḥammad Paymān [Tehran: n.p. 1354 A.Hsh./1975], p. 260). Zarrīnkūb (*Dunbāla, p.* 251) notes that although both Fayḍ-i Kāshānī and Fayyāḍ pursued their own intellectual odysseys, they did

Bertels judiciously put it, "without any doubt a Sufi, but not a dervish."[232] Aside from the obvious Sufi tendencies in his works which are analysed below, Fayḍ-i Kāshānī was considered by many historians contemporary with him to harbour serious inclinations towards, perhaps even practical affiliations with, Sufism. Thus, Mīrzā Muḥammad Ṭāhir Naṣrābādī opined that "in his intellectual method Fayḍ integrated philosophical mysticism (*ḥikmat*) and Sufism (*taṣawwuf*),"[233] while the author of the *'Abbās-nāma* noted how, on one occasion, when Shāh 'Abbās II wished to benefit from the society of the dervishes, "he ordered the chief *mujtahid* of the age Mawlānā Muḥammad Muḥsin Kāshī, who is 'a wayfarer on both paths' (*sālik-i ṭarīqayn*) and 'intoxicated in both realms" (*mast-i nashā'tayn*), to be summoned to his presence'.[234] Both the reigning monarch and the educated elite of the Safavid period, as these remarks indicate, considered Fayḍ to be a leading authority on Sufism. If the Nūrbakhshī Sufi affiliation[235] which the Sufi chronologer Ma'ṣūm 'Alī Shāh Shīrāzī felt necessary to grant him remains unconfirmed in either his own writings or other contemporary sources, it is easy to understand how such an affiliation could be proposed. Let us then take a closer look at his views on Sufism, by examining his own writings.

In "The Heart's Tale"[236] Fayḍ-i Kāshānī's understanding and appreciation of Sufism is clearly manifest. At the beginning of the treatise he gives a stirring account of Shāh 'Abbās II's summoning of him to the royal court, his hesitation about accepting a position there and his aversion to the exoteric clerics controlling the court, who, while feuding amongst themselves, tried to make him the butt of their intrigues, culminating in his refusal to sacrifice his intellectual independence and accept any politico-religious posts (such as that

---

follow in the footsteps of the Sufi theologian Abū Ḥāmid Ghazālī, "for whose works they had a great regard:" "However, in accordance with the needs of their own age, they were at variance with Ghazālī on one point, and that was that they did not subscribe to any of the contemporary Sufis. This was especially the case, since in contradistinction to the Sufis of Ghazālī's age, neither the spiritual states nor the ethical practices of Sufis of the Safavid era hardly merited either support or defence."

The contemporary Persian critic 'Abd al-Karīm Surūsh has written a profoundly illuminating study (in his *Qiṣṣa-yi arbāb-i ma'rifat* [Tehran: Mi'raj 1373 A.Hsh./1994], pp. 1–131) of Fayḍ's relationship to Ghazālī, highlighting his opposition to Ghazālī's Sufi tendencies and his differences of opinion with the great Ash'arite theologian on the subject of *taṣawwuf.*

232 Bertels, *Taṣawwuf*, p. 673.

233 *Tadhkira-yi Naṣrābādī*, ed. V. Dastgirdī (Tehran: Furūghī 1352 A.Hsh./1973), p. 155; cited by Zarrīnkūb, *Dunbāla-yi* p. 254.

234 Mīrzā Muḥammad ḥāhir Vaḥīd Qazwīnī, *'Abbās-nāma*, ed. I. Dihgān (Tehran 1329 A.Hsh./1951), p. 255. Cited by Zarrīnkūb, *Dunbāla*, p. 254. I would interpret the terms "seeker in both paths" and "intoxicated in both realms" as denoting respectively the paths of *ḥikmat* and *taṣawwuf*, the two realms being this world and the next.

235 Ma'ṣūm 'Alī Shāh Shīrāzī, *Ṭarā'iq*, III, p. 115. This affiliation is often cited as historical fact, as in e.g. Al-Shaibi, *Sufism and Shī'ism*, p. 322.

236 In *Dah risālah-yi Muḥaqqiq-i Buzurg-i Fayḍ-i Kāshānī*, pp. 47–73.

of Shaykh al-Islām) offered him by the Safavid regime.[237] He then situates the Sufis at the nexus of the Islamic tradition, describing them as the chief representatives of the Way of Muḥammad. Taking Koran II:269 as his text, he comments that the supreme goal of all human knowledge is "philosophical mysticism (*ḥikmat*)" through which "the reality of things is revealed, in particular, the apprehension of the workings of one's own soul, itself the main resource in understanding all other divine truths and sciences." Although the science of *ḥikmat* existed in the revealed traditions of other inspired prophets long before the appearance of the Prophet Muḥammad, it only attained its perfection following his demise, whereupon, Fayḍ-i Kāshānī explains:

> A group of clever adepts from his noble community who felt it incumbent and required by conscience in their aspiration to follow him through the cherished traditions which remained after him, arrayed their inner and outer beings with contemplative vigilance and intimacy with God, and in this fashion became repositories of amazing types of wisdom (*badāyi'-yi ḥikmat*). From their blessed breaths occult modes of knowledge (*gharā'ib-i 'ulūm*) were manifest. . . . And by the science of Sufism (*'ilm-i taṣawwuf*) is meant precisely such marvellous types of wisdom (*badāyi'-yi ḥikmat*) and occult modes of knowledge (*gharā'ib-i 'ulūm*) which are of so sublime a rank. And to this wisdom the Muḥammadean Sunna and the ordinances of the last Prophet bear witness.[238]

Exactly as in the works of Ghazālī, Sufism here is presented as the supreme Islamic science: *ḥikma* = *taṣawwuf*. Keeping in mind that in most of Fayḍ-i Kāshānī's writings, and in particular, his poetry, 'worldliness' is depicted as the worst vice and pre-eminent mark of immorality, it is not surprising that at this point in "The Heart's Tale" the Sufis' notorious enemies the mullās are introduced and portrayed as worldly ignoramuses, asses in turbans,[239] not to mention several other unflattering epithets. The Sufis themselves, on the other hand, are described in glowing terms as perfect beings totally immersed in God; "folk of the hereafter and men of gnosis."[240]

> The wayfarers on this path are drowned in the ocean of certitude: in all they may hear or see, they audit and they perceive only God. The *tabula* of their apprehension is unblemished by association with ungodly matters . . . nor can the mirror of their hearts become tainted by rust; colourless the hue of the wine of divine unity they imbibe.

---

[237] See the introduction by Muṣṭafā'ī Fayḍī Kāshānī (ed.) to Fayḍ's *Risāla-yi Mishwāq*, p. 30, n. 3.

[238] *Sharḥ-i ṣadr*, p. 49.

[239] The association of mullās with donkeys was proverbial in Persian culture of the Safavid period. Sir John Chardin notes that the mullās "are false, envious, avaricious, and untrustworthy, as the Persian proverb goes 'Be careful of the front of a woman, the rear of a mule and all sides of a mollah.'" Cited by Ronald Ferrier, *A Journey to Persia: Jean Chardin's Portrait of a Seventeenth-century Empire* (London: I.B. Tauris 1996), p. 105.

[240] *Sharḥ-i ṣadr*, p. 52

> I'm servant of that man's wilful mind
> beneath heaven's azure-tinted dome
> who's free of all that interest stains,
> all designs, all hues attachment wears.[241]

> … Yet such a "man" is quite rare, quite hard indeed to come by – in any given age there are never more than two or three such men alive.[242]

This Sufic knowledge is described as being "beyond the understanding of the base, above the apprehension of sensualists"[243] – i.e. the dull-witted common clerics characterized as the Sufis' "natural foes," who are, like "most men, creatures of this world, devotees of ignorance and passion." Fayḍ-i Kāshānī now provides a vivid description of the mulla–Sufi conflict, characterizing it as the innate and primordial battle in Islamic society between the forces of sophisicated enlightenment and fundamentalist obscurantism. While his remarks – certainly at least for the social historian – shed light on the uneasy relations between clerics and mystics in late seventeenth-century Persia, they also illuminate his own views on the generally high place of Sufism in the Iranian body politic and the devastating effect of the influence of the malevolent mullās on late medieval Persian culture:

> Now because of these basic principles and natural hostility [i.e. between mullā and Sufi], from that time [i.e. since the Prophet's death] until today [i.e. 1654], the common folk in every age, and in particular, this troupe who've togged themselves up in turban and headband (*ahl-i 'imāma va dastār*) – the worldly savants and the common religious scholars (*'ulamā-yi 'awām*) – in every age and time in keeping with their normal habit and character, have always taken up the sword of spiteful partiality, conspiring and intriguing among themselves. For the sake of factionalism and creating division, they have repudiated the divine scholars (*'ulamā-yi rabānī*), hurling abuses at the gnostics familiar with spiritual realities and mystical lore. For the knowledge which is inscribed of the pages of passing ages and derived from the works of the prophets and the mysteries of the saints cannot be understood by all and sundry, but only by those sagacious wisemen who are the folk of the hereafter, who have traversed this path by compliance with the holy Law (*sharī'at*) and pursuit of the Sufi Path (*ṭarīqat*).[244]

Next is offered a glimpse into the worsening position of the Sufis in Safavid society in the face of the rising opposition to mysticism on the part of the corrupt and worldly Shī'ite clergy. Kāshānī continues his plaint that very success of the Sufis in Islamic society has caused them to become the butt of the envy of such pseudo-pietists:

---

[241] This verse is from *Dīwān-i Ḥāfiẓ*, ed. Parwīz Nātil Khanlarī (Tehran: Sahāmī 'ām 1362 A.Hsh./1983; 2nd ed), p. 90, no. 37:2.

[242] *Sharḥ-i ṣadr*, pp. 51–2.

[243] *Ibid.*, p. 52.

[244] *Ibid.*, p. 54.

In any case, such worldly scholars (*'ulamā-yi dunyā*), the leaders of the common herd, whose minds always have been, and still are, afflicted with rancour, drawing the blades of their tongues like swords, have cut up [the Sufis with] calumnies, scorn and abuse. In the meantime, the divine scholars (*'ulamā-yi rabānīyin*) have scored success on the field of fortune, vanquishing all their peers and contemporaries in both the practical and speculative arts, and hence they have been slandered, stigmatized and accused of heresy [by the mullās]. Refutations of their sublime compositions have even been composed:

> If the fool and failure who's fortune's victim
> Find faults and holes in us, no wonder – since in
> His purse all he's got are flaws and faults.

By such conduct their sole purpose is to attain celebrity and gain prominence and renown among the common folk.[245]

In the second section of his "Heart's Tale," Fayḍ-i Kāshānī first introduces his own particular type of socio-spiritual anthropology, propounding a religious hierarchy grading humankind into three classes: (1) those exclusively versed in exoteric knowledge; (2) those exclusively versed in esoteric knowledge; and (3) those versed in both exoteric and esoteric knowledge. The first class are described as those "who while enlightening others, burn themselves up," being on the whole totally corrupted by worldliness: "they have sold the hereafter for the sake of this world since they have no comprehension of either realm. Why? Because both realms can be understood only through esoteric, not exoteric, knowledge."[246] This group "are unworthy to rule the people, and even if they crown themselves with turbans, are mostly such of a mediocre and base nature, so drowned in error ... and thus followed only by the common riff-raff and ruffians who seek to benefit from them out of ulterior motives."

The second class, however, resemble stars; they illumine their immediate surroundings and contemporaries, but since they have access only to esoteric knowledge, they are unable to guide people to perfection.

The third class cast sun-like illumination on the world; they alone are worthy to rule and guide people, such that "one such person may illumine both East and West and become the pole (*quṭb*) of his age."[247] From his description of the highest rung in the religious hierarchy, there can be no doubt that this group are the Sufis – since one of the characteristics of this group is their ecstatic disposition, a trait peculiar to the Sufis in Islamic society. "The

---

[245] *Ibid.*, p. 55. It is interesting here to note that European travellers who visited Iran during this period echoed Kāshānī's sentiments. Jean Chardin thus notes: "The *Persians* are very civil and honest in manners of religion ... [yet] the clergy of the Country, who, as in all other places, hate to a furious degree, all those who differ from their opinion" (Sir John Chardin's *Travels in Persia*, a reprint of the edition of 1720 [London 1927], II, p. 185). Cited by Byron Porter Smith, *Islam in English Literature* [New York: Caravan Books 1977; 2nd ed], p. 24.
[246] *Sharḥ-i ṣadr*, p. 55.
[247] *Ibid.*, p. 56.

statements" of such esotericists, states Fayḍ, "which are spoken from a state of inspired enthusiasm (*dhawq*) and drunkenness (*mastī*) are of such a high level that, superficially understood, appear as heresy (*kufr*)." Hence, such utterances rouse the ire of common folk, so that:

> A group of vain persons who have never risen above their animal natures, whose outer characters are tainted by sin and whose inner natures are full of various sorts of rancour, envy and malice, make these statements an excuse to declare that 'All is God' (may God forbid that they become infidels and heretics!) – thus thinking that the poetry and verse of the great masters have this meaning. When they claim that the masters followed their [heretical] sect, another group in all sincerity suppose them to speak correctly, because, of course, they have heard the exoteric jurisprudents (*fuqahā-yi ẓāhir*) already denounce them as infidels. So when they see this group behave in this manner, they of course repudiate them. And truth is on their side since the words of the great masters are extremely difficult to fathom, while the actions and character of this latter group, are extremely despicable and vile.[248]

In this classic description of the mullā–Sufi controversy which has characterized Islamic culture throughout the centuries it is clear that Fayḍ is on the side of the Sufis. However, perhaps echoing his brother-in-law Fayyāḍ's views in the *Gawhar-i murād* cited above, equally reproachable in Fayḍ's eyes are those who blindly imitate the Sufis, pretending to leadership of the common folk without any qualification or training in *taṣawwuf*.[249] Fayḍ's opinion in this respect is very much in accord with the dictates of the Sufi tradition in which the necessity of combining contemplation with action, knowledge with spiritual practice, has always been axiomatic.[250]

It is relevant in this regard to point out that Fayḍ wrote a separate treatise, entitled 'The Judgement' (*al-Muḥākama*) in which he directly addressed the background of the conflict between the exoteric and esoteric authorities in Safavid Persia.[251] It may be recalled that almost all the major Shī'ite clerics were engaged in writing refutations of Sufi mysticism, delivering sermons from their pulpits on the evil ways of the dervishes, at this time (the late

---

248 *Ibid.*, p. 56.

249 As Rasūl Ja'fariyān points out in his introduction to *al-Muḥākama*, in *Dah risālah*, p. 95, Fayḍ endeavoured to expose the faults of both groups; "while defending *'irfān*, he did not hesitate to expose some of bad behaviour and misdemeanors of the Sufis as well."

250 Thus, in the opening chapter of one of the earliest Persian Sufi manuals of Sufism (Hujwīrī's *Kashf al-maḥjūb*) devoted to "the Affirmation of Knowledge" in Sufism, the author attacks "ignorant pretenders to Sufism who have never associated with a spiritual director (*pīr*), nor learned discipline from a shaykh, but without experience thrown themselves among the people" (Alī al-Hujwīrī, trans. R.A. Nicholson, *Kashf al-maḥjūb: The Oldest Persian Treatise on Sufism* [London: Luzac & Co. 1976], p. 17).

251 See also another edition of this treatise entitled "Muḥākama bayn al-mutaṣawwifa wa ghayrihim," *Nashriyya-yi Dānishkada-yi Adabiyāt-i Tabrīz*, II/i (1336 A.Hsh./1957). Cited by Babayan, "Sufis, Dervishes and Mullas," p. 137.

seventeenth century).[252] At the beginning of the treatise, he divides the Muslim community into two camps, one of those who "are renowned for knowledge and wisdom (*'ilm u ma'rifat*), and the other of those characterized by asceticism and worship (*zuhd u 'ibādat*)."[253] These two groups, as indications later in the treatise reveal,[254] are respectively the exoteric religious scholars and the esotericists/Sufis. However, if followed in the traditional manner, both ways advocate equally valid methods of approaching God, and both are in mutual need of the other, Fayḍ maintains.[255]

> While the scholars (*ahl-i 'ilm*) engage in psychological asceticism through contemplation (*fikr*), study (*ta'allum*) and humility (*khushū'*), the ascetics (*ahl-i zuhd*) undergo corporeal asceticism through invocation of God (*dhikr*), supererogatory acts of worship (*tahajjud*) and hunger (*jū'*). While the former group pursues the work of God, the latter group also turns to God, confessing their helplessness and need. "For at this court, the back of both are bent double in devotion to him."[256]

Following this passage, Fayḍ-i Kāshānī gives a formidable defence and fascinating description of the tolerant face of Islam. Considering the backwardness of the mullocracy of his day and age, his views exhibit an extraordinary degree of religious inclusivism. Citing several *aḥādith* of the Shī'ite Imāms and commenting on certain Koranic passages, he interprets the Koranic imperative to "dissuade others from evil" as implying the *covering up* of faults, the conscious forgiving and forgetting of sins. The purpose of these remarks, he asserts, is to demonstrate that "those who have really perfected themselves in knowledge and wisdom have never laid any blame on the practitioners of asceticism and devotion. In the same way, those who have really perfected themselves in ascetic practices and devotion never reproach and always regard the scholars (*ahl-i 'ilm*) with nothing but the greatest esteem."[257] 'Authentic Islam' as practised by its fully committed believers, declares Fayḍ, has tolerance and respect for differing opinions at its foundation; in his view, backbiting, slander and infighting are abnormal

[252] See Babayan, "Sufis, Dervishes and Mullas," pp. 117–39; and also Andrew Newman's chapter in the present volume.

[253] *Al-Muḥākama*, p. 97.

[254] Fayḍ designates them as "dervishes," and traces their practice back to the days of the *ahl-i ṣuffa*, who were dervishes of the Prophet's day. This characterization of the Sufis as the modern-day representatives of the ancient *ahl-i ṣuffa* has a long genealogy in Sufi writings; cf. 'Izz al-Dīn Maḥmūd Kāshānī (d. 735/1334) in his Persian textbook and manual of Sufi theosophy and practice, the *Miṣbāḥ al-hidāya*. Fayḍ also states clearly that "today the ascetics are the Sufis" (*al-Muḥākama*, p. 104).

[255] *Al-Muḥākama*, p. 98.

[256] *Ibid.*; the last phrase is the second hemistich from a famous ghazal of Sa'dī: see Nūrullāh Īzad-parast (ed.), *Ghazalhā-yi Sa'dī* (Tehran: Dānish 1362 A.Hsh./1993), p. 126, v. 2.

[257] *Al-Muḥākama*, pp. 101–2.

deviations from and perversions of both the intellectual and the spiritual traditions of Islam.

The problematic socio-political situation that now prevails, in which the ascetic-Sufi scorns the scholar, while the scholar in turn reviles the Sufi, stems from a vulgarization of the fundamental tenets of both movements. Among members of both groups, Fayḍ wisely reflects, one always finds those who wear their colours under false pretences:

> Whenever people who are supposedly affiliated to a certain group are seen to misbehave, one should not automatically judge the entire group to be bad. In every group of people both good and bad exist. This is especially true of these two groups [religious scholars and Sufis]. Most of the people outwardly affiliated to either group do not, in truth, belong among them. Rather, most of them are merely impersonaters seeking through their affiliation to acquire celebrity, wealth and social status. If one contemplates the situation deeply, one sees that the majority are not seeking spiritual perfection.
>
> One group of people, because they've learned some rubbish, consider themselves to be 'perfect', even counting themselves as *'ulamā'*. In fact, although they are content with the bare name and hollow rites of the articles of faith and the principles of religion, they taunt each other, sometimes making others the target of their censure, spraying the venom of their wrath onto the wounded victims' chests. Day by day, they become more injurious in their repudiation, vituperation and denunciation, scratching the countenance of kind fraternity with the rough barbs of spiteful hostility, and just to be troublesome cast the dust of their baleful rancour over the face of fidelity.
>
> Another group, wearing gowns of dissimulation and hypocrisy, have drunk the cup of pride from Satan's hand, and in following their sensual appetites and passions, contented themselves with a few idle cries and exclamations. Those who actually worship God among this group are few and far between. Few are those who find the path to Him, and yet – one must still irrigate a thousand thorns for the sake of a single rose.
>
> Oftentimes in beggars' rags one finds enlightened men;
> Draped in felt and sackcloth are hid the men of heart.
> Amid the dervish crowd, one man alone is meant
> But do not scorn the rest – that they be ignorant.[258]

Fayḍ's fair-mindedness in this passage is remarkable, instilling, beyond the specific topicality of the issue, a trans-social timelessness into the Safavid Sufi–mullā conflict. What pre-Enlightenment European thinkers called 'religious superstition' and modern Western scholarship (and journalism) refers to as 'fundamentalism', Fayḍ outlines as the basic socio-spiritual malaise of religious man. For fundamentalism assumes multiple religious disguises: his poeticized depiction of the conflict is more of the order of the discovery of the spiritual archetype of religious obscurantism than what Owen

---

[258] *Ibid*., pp. 102–3.

Chadwick calls 'stereotyping' (in which religious groups are pigeonholed by a reified perception of their beliefs).[259]

Fayḍ concludes the treatise with a shortlist of the some of the faults committed by both the pseudo-Sufis and the ignorant clergy,[260] citing Prophetic and Imāmite *ḥadīth*, while adducing Koranic references to prove that their practices have no basis in classical Islam. In sum:

> It should be understood that although the abominable acts which issue from the ignorant people among both groups are numerous, none of their behaviour reaches the point that it may be considered as legally allowable that any of them be comdemned as heretics (*takfīr*) or subjected to religious denunciation (*ṭa'n*). Slander of both groups is not permitted except regarding sins which they profess openly in public.[261]

Fayḍ-i Kāshānī's sober-minded temperance, his patient tolerance of the foibles of both the exoteric scholars and the Sufis in this treatise, has all the hallmarks of the traditional Islamic perspective of a religious tolerance which, as Mujtabā Mīnuvī[262] – and recently, an entire team of anthropologists[263] – pointed out, has always typified the Persian dervish ethos. As Rasūl Ja'fariyān has commented on this passage, "Fayḍ appears here as a herald of tolerance and unity – and that, at this particular period of Safavid history when sectarian divisions and conflicts were at their height."[264] While his critique of corruptions in Sufism (as in the reference to those clothed in "dissimulation and hypocrisy" in the last paragraph of the passage cited above), like that made by 'Abd al-Razzāq, is quite in accord with the classical Sufi tradition,[265] his dismissive attitude towards contemporary Sufism also echoes similar views of other clerics in the Safavid period.

---

[259] Owen Chadwick, *The Secularization of the European Mind in the Nineteenth Century* (Cambridge: Cambridge University Press 1975) p. 44.

[260] The Sufis' faults include excessively loud *dhikr-i jallī* (vocal invocation); mixing their devotions with poetry devoid of cognitative value, misunderstood by the audience, or else repeated in blind ignorance (*taqlīd*). The faults of the *'ulamā'* include the denunciation and cursing of the Sufis and ascetics; rebuking them for recitation of strange and unconventional sayings which "may have a spiritual veridical meaning, and in particular poetry, the axis of which revolves on metaphor and simile, so to abuse Muslims [for their poetry] is a daunting task" (*al-Muḥākama*, p. 107).

[261] *Al-Muḥākama*, pp. 108–9.

[262] See his "Āzādigī va tasāmuḥ," *Iranshenasi*, 4/1 (1992), p. 179.

[263] See M.C. Bateson, J.W. Clinton, J.B.M. Kassarjian, H.Safavi, M. Soraya, "Ṣafā-yi Bāṭin: A Study of a Set of Iranian Ideal Character Types," in *Psychological Dimensions of Near Eastern Studies*, ed. L.C. Brown and N. Itzkowitz, (Princeton: Princeton University Press 1977), pp. 257–73.

[264] Ja'fariyān, *Dīn va siyāsat*, p. 291.

[265] In the two treatises on Sufi chivalry by Shihāb al-Dīn Suhrawardī, co-founder of the Suhrawardiyya *ṭarīqa*, for example, one finds the same tolerant perspective on "dissuading others from evil" and the forgiveness of sins. See my translation of several passages from

However, Fayḍ-i Kāshānī's harshest stricture is reserved for the religious inquisitions of Sufis conducted by Safavid mullās. As if to underline the intensity of his feelings, the following passage, devoted to exposing their corruption, was even reproduced verbatim by Fayḍ in two different essays:

> They are a group who have cast off the halter of religious obedience (*taqlīd*) from their necks, having overturned their primordial natures, who excessively revile the saints and dervishes, and who reject everything which reaches their ear. Not contenting themselves with externalities and derivatives of Prophecy, they prefer to utilize absurd expressions of their own making. Neither do their passions allow them to engage themselves in obedience (*taqlīd*) nor has divine fortune favoured them with the scent of experimental verification (*taḥqīq*).
>
> To debase and corrupt but one sect of poor men,
> For the sake of spite, discord, of conflict and war,
> On the broadway of error, they've all gone lost, astray.
> So in college whatever the knowledge they'd saved
> It has been of no benefit, and to their detriment down in the grave.[266]

Over the following centuries, Fayḍ-i Kāshānī was celebrated among the Persian Sufis as a theologian supportive of and sympathetic towards Sufism. Thus, the Ni'matullāhī Sufi master Majdhūb 'Alī Shāh (d. 1238/1823) cited Fayḍ's *Al-inṣāf fī bayān al-firāq bayn al-ḥaqq wa'l-i'tisāf* (A Fair Exposition of Religious Denominations and Differentiation of their Truth from Error), an autobiographical tract written half in Arabic and half in Persian, in his book 'The Mirror of Truth' (*Mīrāt al-ḥaqq*),[267] to articulate and buttress his own version of Shī'ite Sufism. It is apparent from certain essays and letters written by Fayḍ-i Kāshānī in his old age, and particularly from statements in *al-Inṣāf*, that he experienced considerable disillusionment with Sufism and was overtaken in later years by a more critical attitude towards both *taṣawwuf* and *'irfān*. In order to illustrate this change of mind, it is necessary to examine some of the important passages and doctrines found in *al-inṣāf*. This treatise,[268] a kind of confession or manifesto of personal faith, was composed near the end of his life, in 1083/1672 – seven years before his death in 1090/

---

one of these treatises, in *Windows on the House of Islam: Muslim Sources on Spirituality and Religious Life*, ed. J. Renard (Berkeley: University of California Press 1998), pp. 235–44. Also cf. Ja'fariyān's comments, *Dīn va siyāsat*, *p*. 290. This aspect of Fayḍ's social views on mysticism is a central theme in his 'Tract on Friendship' (*Ulfat-nāma*), as well (in *Dah risālah*, pp. 203–19).

266 The translation is from the Persian text in his *Rāh-i ṣawāb* (p. 134), although a nearly identical passage also occurs in his *al-Inṣāf*, *p*. 190.

267 See chap. 9 of the *Mīrāt al-ḥaqq*, ed. Javād Nūrbakhsh (Tehran: Intishārāt-i Khānaqāh-i Ni'matullāhī 1353 A.Hsh./1974), pp. 247–65.

268 My analysis below makes use of both the recently published version edited by Rasūl Ja'fariyān: *Dah risālah*, pp. 183–99 as well as the version cited by Majdhūb 'Alī Shāh, *Mirāt al-ḥaqq*, pp. 247–61.

1679. The author's purpose in composing this treatise, as Majdhūb 'Alī Shāh pointed out, was "to combine and summarize the key concepts of the philosophers and the Sufis (*mutafalasafa* and *mutaṣawwafa*)."[269]

Al-Inṣāf begins on an autobiographical note, apparently modelled after chapter 3 of Ghazālī's *al-Munqidh min al-ḍalāl*,[270] explaining that he had perfected his theological education to such a degree in his youth that "in no problem did I have the need to follow (*taqlīd*) anyone else other than the 'one who is free from error and sin' (*ma'ṣūm*)" – referring here to his devotion and faith in the books and lore of the Shī'ite Imāms. However, he still felt a need to acquire the deeper gnosis of the "secrets of religion (*asrār-i dīn*);" despite the fact that his passions were – he admitted – opposed to this mystical tendency, and his reason remained unable to grasp any of these mysteries by its own efforts. To "satisfy his curiosity," he examined the possibilities available in various fields of knowledge:

> I spent a period of time absorbed in the disputations of the scholastic theologians, trying to remove my ignorance by the very means of ignorance. Another period of time I followed the discursive method of the philosophers (*mutafalsiffīn*), occupied in learning and pondering [their writings]. Another period I observed the high-flying exertions of the Sufis (*buland-parvāzīhā-yi mutaṣawwafa*) through their sayings. For still another period, being swept up in a light-headed fashion from one to the other in order to explain the sayings of each of these four schools,[271] I composed books and tracts. Other times, in order to collect and systematize these sayings I intertwined them all together, neither verifying the truth of all of them nor being committed in heart to any of them on the whole. Rather, I descended to these matters only to obtain information, writing what I wrote as an exercise in criticism, finding neither in their symbolic allusions[272] anything to cure my ailment, nor in the clamour of their words any Bilāl [the Prophet's muezzin] who could quench my thirst. Then, at last my soul was relieved, since I saw that what was embodied in these things may be likened to what the adage says: "They deceived me, they plundered me, they seized me, they overwhelmed me, and they attacked me, they led me astray: so my lot was to suffer abuse."[273]

---

[269] *Mirāt al-ḥaqq*, p. 261.

[270] Ed. Farid Jabre (Beirut: Libraire Orientale 1969), p. 22. See also W. Montgomery Watt's translation of this treatise as *The Faith and Practice of al-Ghazālī* (Oxford), where, on pp. xxff., Ghazālī describes his intellectual vacillations between the differing methodologies of the theologians (*Mutakallimūn*), Ismā'īlīs, philosophers and Sufis.

[271] I.e. the teachings of the Shī'ite Imāms, the scholastic theologians, the philosophers and Sufis.

[272] *Ishārātahum*: probably referring here to the symbolic allusions of the Sufis. "Sufism is the science *par excellence* of the Sufis . . . The term 'allusion' is given to this science for this reason: the contemplations enjoyed by the heart," states Kalābādhī, *Al-Ta'arruf li-madhhab ahl al-taṣawwuf*, trans. A.J. Arberry, *The Doctrine of the Sufis* (Cambridge: Cambridge University Press 1989), p. 76.

[273] *Dah risālah-yi Muḥaqqiq-i Buzurg-i Fayḍ-i Kāshānī*, pp. 183–4; *Mirāt al-ḥaqq*, p. 241.

Several pages are then devoted to giving the details of his disillusionment, enumerating the vanity of the various types of theological learning, criticizing the divisiveness and hypocrisy of the sects and the schools. At long last, Mullā Kāshānī takes safe refuge in the Koran and *ḥadīth*, concluding that the only truth that can be salvaged from all such studies, with faith intact and probity upheld, is following the directions of the Shīʿite Imāms. Here, Fayḍ succumbs to bewilderment, amazed at his philosophizing contemporaries "who have been sent the best of prophets for the sake of guidance, who have been given the best of religions, and who, by way of divine grace and kindness and this prophet, have been given a book and had wise successors (*khalīfa*) appointed for them, one after another to interpret it . . . and still they do not pay attention to its guidance, knocking on the doors of bygone nations in order to beg knowledge, seeking succour from the moisture still dribbling from their streams."[274] Summing up his attitude towards philosophy and Sufism vis-à-vis the teachings of the Koran, the Mullā of Kāshān now exclaims:

> Thus, this group of people suppose that there are certain sciences of religion which cannot be found in the Koran and *ḥadīth* and yet can be known by studying the books of the philosophers or Sufis, and that we must seek them there. Wretches! Why, they can't even understand that there isn't any fault or shortcoming in the Koran or *ḥadīth* – rather the fault lies in their own understanding and deficiency in the degree of their faith! As God Almighty has said: "And We reveal the Scripture unto thee as an exposition of all things and a guidance and a mercy and good tidings for those who have surrendered to God."[275] If any deficiency or shortcoming arises in their understanding and faith, no study of the books of the philosophers and Sufis will be of any avail, since they will never understand such material as the truth really demands. "I could fill the world full of precious pearls, but if you're unfit, if it is not your lot, so what?"[276] "Oh you whose sleeves are too short, how long will you stretch out your hands."[277]
>
> Furthermore, they should realize that even if they ascended to the heavens, they will understand no more about celestial matters than that which their capacity allows and their degree of faith permits. If they could but increase their capacity by strengthening their faith, perhaps they would be able to ascend higher "if they but knew."[278] Otherwise, however much they may investigate and ponder these subjects, they will only be that much more astray.
>
> . . . O brother, strive to strengthen your faith and increase your certainty by means of ascetic self-restraint (*zuhd*) and godfearing piety (*taqwā*) so that your knowledge and wisdom (*ʿilm va ḥikmat*) increase. "And fear God; God is

---

274 *Dah risālah-yi Muḥaqqiq-i Buzurg-i Fayḍ-i Kāshānī*, p. 187; *Mirāt al-ḥaqq*, p. 2.
275 Koran XVI:89, Pickthall translation.
276 Rūmī, *Mathnawī*, ed. Nicholson, I, 2390.
277 *Dīwān-i Ḥāfiẓ*, ed. Khanlarī, p. 868, no. 426: 10.
278 Koran II:102, 103. Two passages here relate to the occult sciences of the Jews which, according to the Koran, have neither profit nor harm, but "if they had but believed and been god-fearing, a recompense from God would be better, if they but knew."

> teaching you."[279] But otherwise, do not push yourself forward so much nor attempt matters that are beyond your scope. "Since you are undeserving of the Beloved's regard, do not seek consummation. Not even Jamshid's holy grail[280] avails the blind."[281]

Fayḍ-i Kāshānī's diatribe peters on for a few more paragraphs, in the course of which he cites more verses from Ḥāfiẓ, his favourite poet[282] and Rūmī's *Mathnawī*. What is the gist of the above passage? Authentic spirituality, true religiousness, is obtained solely by strengthening piety, deepening the life of contemplation by means of prayer, religious study of the *ḥadīth* and reading the Koran. Only then, *after* exertions in works of piety will any benefit accrue from study of the works of the Sufis and reading the tracts of the philosophers.

Having given both the Sufis and philosophers short shrift, he now turns on the philosophical theologians, the *mutakallimūn*, attacking them in even stronger language.[283] His treatise concludes with some remarks summing up his own position, followed by a verse from Ḥāfiẓ, a beautiful ghazal of his own, and lastly an invocation in Arabic entreating God for guidance. At the end of the treatise he summarizes his own position as follows:

> I am neither a scholastic theologian (*mutakallim*), philosopher (*mutafalassif*), Sufi (*mutaṣawwif*) nor formalist (*mutakallif*). Rather, I am a follower (*muqallid*) of the Koran, *ḥadīth* and the Prophet's family (*ahl-i bayt*). I am weary of the bewildering discourse of the four schools. I have forsworn them all. I am a stranger to all else except the Glorious Koran and the words of the Prophet and his Family; I am alien to all except whoever and whatever is conversant with them.
>
> Whatever I have read I have now forgot
> Except for the words of the Friend I ever reiterate.
>
> The reason for this is that during this period which I spent in academic discussions (*baḥth*), research and investigation into wide-ranging speculations and ideas, I personally tested out the paths of various schools, and penetrated into the quintessence of each of their doctrines. Then, with the eye of inner vision I saw that the eye of Reason is incapable of comprehending the august majesty of the Self-sufficient Eternal Being, and by the light of rational thought no one is able to penetrate into the court of the majestic all-encompassing divine Unity.[284]

---

[279] Koran II:282.

[280] *Jām-i Jam:* Jamshīd was a mythological Persian king of the Pishdadian line, who according to legend could behold all the affairs in his kingdom by gazing into his grail or cup.

[281] *Dah risālah-yi Muḥaqqiq-i Buzurg-i Fayḍ-i Kāshānī*, pp. 188–9; *Mīrāt al-ḥaqq*, pp. 251–2. This verse is from *Dīwān-i Ḥāfiẓ*, ed. Khanlarī, p. 902, ghazal 443, v. 2.

[282] In his *Dīvān*, Fayḍ devotes an entire ghazal in praise of Ḥāfiẓ, beginning: *Ay yār makhwān zay ash'ār ilā ghazal-i Ḥāfiẓ'* (*Kulliyāt-i Fayḍ, p.* 220).

[283] *Dah risālah-yi Muḥaqqiq-i Buzurg-i Fayḍ-i Kāshānī*, pp. 190–5.

[284] *Ibid.*, pp. 196–7.

While the spirituality of Fayḍ-i Kāshānī as expressed in this treatise is radically anti-traditional and anti-sectarian, the intellectual motivation behind his distancing himself from the Sufis near the end of his life remains an enigma. If his basic argument is that knowledge of God is too transcendent to be approached by the inferior means employed by any of the traditional Islamic philosophical, theological or mystical schools, this argument is ultimately unconvincing as a valid criticism of traditional Sufis, who, in fact, always maintained precisely the same thing![285] It also appears rather hypocritical of him to cite passages from the various Sufi authors such as Sanā'ī, Sa'dī and Rūmī to illustrate his ideas while belittling the Sufism of those very same authors – who also held that reason is incapable of understanding the transcendental Nature of God! Willing, indeed, to use the poetry of Rūmī, whose Sufi affiliations none contests, to expound an idiosyncratic type of Islamic mysticism, but snobbishly disdaining to acknowledge the validity in Rūmī's Sufi methodology![286] Regarded from the standpoint of this treatise alone, his 'mysticism' is that of a sober pietist whose sole consolation is the Muslim Scripture and the Shī'ite canon of *ḥadīth*.

My personal opinion is that this treatise represents the unfortunate – but fortunately momentary – disillusionment of an old man who despairs of all friends but the Friend, who, while struggling to shed all ties but the eternal bond with the divine, allowed himself to charge visionaries with deceiving; conceiving saints to be fools, he called men wise for not believing.[287] Quoting some of the same passages from this treatise, Bertels also points out that his statement cited above, that he merely wished to intertwine the writings of various groups together – "neither verifying the truth of all of them nor being committed in heart to any of them on the whole," is refuted by his own poetry,

---

[285] Fayḍ's statement, for example, about the transcendence of divine knowledge, and the incapacity of human reason to access it is echoed exactly by Hujwīrī's comment: "The perfection of human knowledge is ignorance of divine knowledge" (*Kashf*, p. 18). The theosophical doctrine of mystical agnosis is repeated endlessly by most later Sufis: cf., for instance, Muḥammad Lāhījī, *Mafātīḥ al-'ijāz fī sharḥ-i Gulshan-i rāz*, ed. R. Khāliqī and I. Karbāsī (Tehran: Zawwār 1371 A.Hsh./1992), p. 66.

[286] Fayḍ was in fact, deeply devoted to Rūmī, and frequently modelled his ghazals on the *Dīvān-i Shams* (e.g. his *Kulliyāt*, p. 260, *infra*).

[287] This would be a mistake repeated by too many of his clerical compatriots over the next 200 years, until under the leadership of some the late nineteenth-century Ni'matullāhī masters such as Mast 'Alī Shāh and Ṣafī 'Alī Shāh, the Persian Sufis regained some of their bygone glory. Fayḍ composed another essay similar to this one, entitled *al-Kalamāt al-ṭarīqa fī manshā' iktilāf al-ummat al-marḥūmat* (summarized by Ja'ariyān, *Dīn vasiyāsat*, pp. 357–65), in which he criticizes all the various schools in Islam, including the Sufis, for their extravagant claims, the tenor of which is echoed in his *Dīvān* almost exactly (see *Kulliyāt*, p. 107).

which venerates and celebrates the Sufi tradition and reflects a heartfelt admiration for its masters.[288]

It is interesting to note that later Persian Sufis such as Majdhūb 'Alī Shāh, while recognizing the apparent sincerity of Fayḍ-i Kāshānī's convictions in this treatise, clearly hesitated to condone them. In a postscript to chapter 9 of the *Mīrāt al-ḥaqq* (added for the reader's sake after citing the treatise in full), Majdhūb 'Alī Shāh penned a mildly critical note about Fayḍ-i Kāshānī's religious position, stating that "while one can appreciate that some of the matters (which he discussed) cannot to be taken absolutely seriously, neither should its author be anathematized or condemned for his opinions." But, pronounces Majdhūb, there is a strong mystical dimension in Fayḍ-i Kāshānī's works which must not be ignored, a dimension which is best revealed in his poetic works: "It is clear from a ghazal included at the end of the treatise that this venerable master had realized some very high degrees in his flight of spiritual vision and methodical progression (*sayr u sulūk*) [on the Path], for his *Dīvān* of ghazals and his *mathnawī*s contain many gnostic adages and truthful verities (*ma'ārif u ḥaqā'iq-i ḥaqīqiyya*), bearing witness to his advancement to the stages of divine closeness."[289]

In support of Majdhūb's contention, it should also be noted that Fayḍ wrote eight ghazals concluding with the rhyme-word 'love' (*'ishq*), all devoted to Sufi themes.[290] Although he confessed that in Rūmī's[291] poetry, "many mysteries lie hidden," he personally professed to follow the style (*tatabu'*) of, and prefer above all other poetry, the "ghazals of Ḥāfiẓ."[292] His appreciation and advocation of Sufi poetic hermeneutics is clearly evident in his *Risāla-yi Mishwāq*, a treatise devoted to defending the mystical aesthetics and poetic symbolism of the Sufis. This treatise is a commentary on certain sections of Maḥmūd Shabistarī's famous 1,000-line mystical epic *Gulshan-i*

---

288 Bertels, *Taṣawwuf*, p. 671. The fact that Fayḍ's pronouncements in this treatise stand in complete opposition to opinions expressed in his *Dīvān* concerning the Sufis is demonstrated by this ghazal confessing that the various great classical Persian Sufi poets all spoke of the mysteries in their own distinct manner:

kashf-i asrār-i ḥaqā'iq rā bih qadr-i fahm-i khwud
har kasī dar parda-yi ash'ār mīgūyad sukhan
gāh Mawlānā u gah 'Aṭṭār un gāhī Maghribī
gah zi shawqish Qāsim-i Anwār mīgūyad sukhan
man ki bāsham ar zanam dam az thanā-yi kardigār?
dar thanā-yish Aḥmad-i Mukhtar mīgūyad sukhan
Guft "Lā-aḥṣā," Muḥammad. Kīst dīgar dam zanad
līk qadr-i khwīsh har hushyār mīgūyad sukhan.

(*Kulliyāt-i ash'ār-i Mawlānā Fayḍ-i Kāshānī*, p. 318)

289 *Mīrāt al-ḥaqq*, p. 261.

290 *Kulliyāt*, pp. 228–33.

291 S.H. Nasr cites a commentary on the *Mathnawī* by Fayḍ, which, however, remains unpublished. "The School of Isfahan," p. 927.

292 See n. 283 above.

rāz,[293] drawing heavily on the brillant exegesis of this work by the Kubrawī master Muḥammad Lāhījī. *Risāla-yi Mishwāq* is, in fact, an elegant and eloquent précis of the *Gulshan-i rāz*'s contents, revealing Fayḍ's deep absorption in the classical Persian Sufi tradition.[294] Following in the footsteps of the classical Persian Sufis of the school of Ibn 'Arabī such as Fakhr al-Dīn 'Irāqī (d. 688/1289) and 'Abd al-Razzāq Kāshānī (d. 730/1329) who wrote tracts in defence of the Sufis' use of mystical terminology (*iṣṭilāḥāt*),[295] Fayḍ-i Kāshānī in this work also firmly defends the traditional view that each of the Sufis' occult poetic images has a symbolic correspondance to an archetypal meaning in the imaginal realm. Thus, in the introduction to the *Mishwāq* he notes that "words (*sukhan*) are but a form and their meaning (*ma'nā*) is as their spirit. In other words, words are like a cup and their meaning like wine; or, to use a different simile, words are like musk and their meaning like their fragrance."[296] Since the contents of a word's meaning far exceeds its phonic form – the literal letter – the Sufi poets "in giving the veiled ladies of these archetypal meanings (*ma'ānī*) verbal expressions, have employed subtle devices to interpret each reality, matching sensate forms and shapes with appropriately corresponding words to express 'that' through 'this'. In this manner, those with insight into the spiritual meanings (*ahl-i ma'nā*) delight in the realities so illustrated while those who solely perceive the figurative form (*ahl-i ṣūrat*) will suffer no ill."[297]

As Bertels points out, Fayḍ-i Kāshānī was favourably inclined to audition-with-music of Sufi poetry (*samā'*) and his positive views on this practice became the subject of controversy after he was attacked by a certain Mullā 'Alī al-Shahīdī al-'Āmulī who condemned his opinions as "smacking of blasphemy."[298] There are several passages in his *Dīvān* alluding to the practice of *samā'*,[299] and his ghazals are steeped in a melopoeia which Bertels finds unique in the history of Persian literature.[300] It would seem that Fayḍ was

---

[293] On which, see my *Beyond Faith and Infidelity.*

[294] Thus, the gnostic theosophy and the *Garden of Mysteries* of Shabistarī – a follower of Ibn 'Arabī and a Sunni Sufi who belonged to the Sunni Ash'arite *madhhab*, whose influence also pervades many of Fayḍ's other works – is the main inspiration throughout his *Risāla-yi Mishwāq*. See also Fayḍ's *Ḥaqā'iq dar sayr wa sulūk*, Persian trans. Muḥammad Bāqir Sā'idī Khurāsānī (Shīrāz: Intishārāt-i 'ilmiyya Islāmiyya 1340 A.Hsh./1961), pp. 585–6 where he cites long passages from the *Gulshan-i rāz* to illustrate certain matters concerning the meditation of the spiritual heart.

[295] See 'Irāqī's *Risāla-yi lamā'at wa risāla-yi iṣṭilāḥāt*, ed. J. Nūrbakhsh (Tehran: Intishārāt-i Khānaqāh-i Ni'matu'llāhī 1353 A.Hsh./1974); and Kāshānī's *Iṣṭilāḥāt al-ṣūfiyya*, ed. M. K. Ibrāhim Ja'far (Egypt 1981).

[296] *Risāla-yi Mishwāq*, pp. 36–7.

[297] *Ibid.*, p. 43.

[298] Bertels, *Taṣawwuf*, p. 665.

[299] *Kulliyāt*, *p*. 324, *infra*., where he describes Sufis dancing in *samā'*.

[300] Cf. Bertels' fascinating discussion of this, *Taṣawwuf*, pp. 676–83.

also not completely opposed to having his poetry sung in Sufi gatherings during the audition/music ceremonies and his lyrics were thus set to music to concentrate the faculties of the soul. One of his ghazals even begins by heralding his spiritual mission with Sufi music:

bāz āmadam bā nuql u may, sar-mast az jām-i alast
bāz āmadam bā chang u nay, sar-mast az jām-i alast.

I have returned again with wine and sweets
Drunk from the cup of Pre-eternity.
I have returned again with harp and flute
Drunk from the cup of Pre-eternity.

In another ghazal, whose rhyme-word is *ḥarf* (speech, letter, word), he states:

ṣāḥib-i dil rā-st fahm-i rāzhā az sāzhā   ṣāḥib-i dil shū, shinū az nāy u mūsīqār harf

Men of heart comprehend mysteries by instruments of music.
Be a man of heart then and hear the words of the organ.[301]

In fact, most of his life, Fayḍ-i Kāshānī, exactly like Ghazālī, had struggled to defend the tenets of classical Sufism from its foes among religious formalists and exoteric jurists, and the dominant tenor of his thought seems to be that found in his Persian *Dīvān*, *Sharḥ-i ṣadr*, *Risāla-yi Mishwāq*, *al-Muḥākamat*, *Rāh-i ṣawāb* and *Alfat-nāma*[302] rather than the world-wearied and disillusioned voice of the author of *al-Inṣāf.* Rasūl Ja'fariyān's remarks about the environmental causes underlying Fayḍ's disillusionment with Sufism merit citation in this regard:

> In the first few decades of his mature life, and even up to 60 years of age, Fayḍ displayed passionate enthusiasm for *'irfān* and *taṣawwuf.* Afterwards, however, he considerably distanced himself from these intellectual movements. In one respect, his Akhbārī religious inclinations had an adverse effect upon his effort to interpret Shī'ite traditions and *ḥadīth* in a light favourable to *'irfān*, ultimately inducing him to turn his attention to exoteric subjects. The academico-intellectual climate of his day cannot have been without its influence on this intellectual transformation, insofar as the last two decades of his life coincided with the peaking of the anti-Sufi movement that featured personages such as Mullā Muḥammad Ṭāhir Qumī and 'Allāma Majlisī as its leaders.[303]

In sum, in his approach to Sufism, Fayḍ-i Kāshānī maintained an intellectual independence; he is perhaps best described as an a *ḥakīm* who expoused an

---

[301] *Kulliyāt*, p. 227, *infra*. For a good discussion of Fayḍ's critical, yet not unfavourable, attitude to *samā'*, see 'Abd al-Karīm Surūsh, *Qiṣṣa-yi arbāb-i ma'rifat* (Tehran: Mi'raj 1373/ A.Hsh./1994), pp. 26–7.

[302] These treatises, which for reasons of space cannot be discussed here, are found in Ja'fariyān's edition of *Dah risālah*.

[303] Ja'fariyān, *Dīn va siyāsat*, p. 276.

unconventional type of philosophical mysticism, which was also, paradoxically, *au courant* with his age.

V. CONCLUSION

In religion,
What damnèd error but some sober brow
Will bless it and approve it with a text,
Hiding the grossness with fair ornament?

Merchant of Venice, III.ii

Zay Iblīs bih Bū'l-bashar chih inkār rasīd?
"Ḥaqq", guft Ḥusayn – bar sar-i dār rasīd.
Az shūmi'ī-yi sharr nafs-i mullāyān-ast
bā har nabī u walī kay āzar rasīd.

Dārā Shikūh

If the discussion above (sections IV. 5 and 6) has established that both Fayḍ-i Kāshānī and 'Abd al-Razzāq Lāhījī, who – after their father-in-law Mullā Ṣadrā – can be considered the foremost theosophers of the late Safavid school of Iṣfahān, did both harbour definite inclinations towards Sufism, the question remains as to why their contribution to late classical Persian Sufism has been so consistently ignored. The best answer to this enigma still remains these remarks penned by Y.E. Bertels:

> One need not search far afield to find the reason why such a highly celebrated author [Fayḍ-i Kāshānī], whose works deserve an independent monograph, suddenly passed into oblivion. The reason lies hidden in the severe opposition to him on the part of most of the '*ulamā'*. The central, most visible pretext for their antagonism to Mullā Muḥsin lay in his inclination to Sufism, a philosophy which in this period was subject to the harassment and persecution by the jurists (*faqīh*). Shaykh Yūsuf b. Aḥmad al-Baḥraynī, author of the biographical work *Lū'lū' al-Baḥrayn*, states that "Mullā Muḥsin had inclinations towards Sufism and approved to the concept of *waḥdat al-wujūd*. Now, since Persians always have had a great passion and attachment to the doctrines of Sufism, and achieved enormous progress by means of their passion and enthusiasm for Sufism, the works of Mullā Muḥsin thus enjoyed wide diffusion and brought him great popularity." Baḥraynī also adds that his popularity was brought to a sudden end through the efforts of Mullā Muḥammad Bāqir Majlisī (d. 1111/1699–1700).
>
> From the above, it is evident that the *'ulamā'* used all the formidable powers which they had at their disposal to bar the publication of his works, which makes it quite clear why his works are now so rare. The ascendancy of the *'ulamā'* has always been one of the most important political factors in Iranian political life, and so many other affairs are dependent for success on their will.[304]

---

[304] Bertels, *Taṣawwuf*, pp. 667–8.

Considering the policy of forced conversions and persecution of religious minorities at the end of the seventeenth century,[305] the gag-orders and *fatwās* issued by the late Safavid *mujtahids* against the Sufis[306] and the general ascendency of religious conservatives in the poltical landscape, it is not surprising if we should return here to a theme recurring throughout this essay, a theme which features as the tonic note of a dirge on the demise of religious tolerance and the consequent suppression of the Sufi mystical vision in Persia, namely the baleful influence of the *mujtahid* cult and the ideologization of religion to suit their particular political agenda – the same doleful tone which remains, unfortunately, the dominant characteristic of the Safavid dynasty (as it does also – not incidentally – of the contemporary Islamic [*sic*] Republic of Iran[307]).

As Bertels' comments above inform us, the ascendancy of the hardline Shī'ite clergy in the late seventeenth century no doubt has had much to do with both past- and present-day neglect of the Sufi literature of the Safavid period. In fact, it was less than a decade after Fayḍ's death in 1679 that Sufism in Iran was dealt a deadly blow, when, in 1098/1687, Muḥammad Bāqir Majlisī (1037/1627–1111/1700) was appointed Shaykh al-Islām in Iṣfahān.[308] Majlisī's exclusivist Shī'ism and puritanical policies during his tenure of this post when

---

[305] Walter Fischel's article "The Jews in Mediæval Iran from the Sixteenth to the Eighteenth Centuries: Political, Economic, and Communal Aspects," *Irano-Judaica* (1982), pp. 265–96, provides an account of the persecution of Jews both from the mid-seventeenth century onwards and Christians.

[306] See Babayan, "The Waning of the Qizilbash," chap. 4; Ja'farīyān, *Dīn va siyāsat*, pp. 221–60. A good account of the persecution of Sufis in late Safavid Persia is given by the last master of the Dhahabī Order under this dynasty, Quṭb al-Dīn Nayrīzī (1100/1688–1173/1759), in the introduction to the fourth section of his celebrated Arabic poem *Faṣl al-khiṭāb*, in which he assails the corruption of the Safavid clerical establishment, recording in detail the persecution endured by the Sufis and the destruction of their *khānaqāhs* at the hands of the *'ulamā'-yi ẓāhir*. The relevant passages are cited by Iḥṣānu'llāh 'Alī Istakhrī, *Uṣūl-i taṣawwuf* (Tehran: Kānūn-i Ma'rifat 1338 A.Hsh.1959), pp. 433–9.

[307] Cf. Arjomand's epilogue to *The Shadow of God*, pp. 269–70, in which he observes that while "the mahdistic principle enabled the founder of the Safavid empire to conquer Iran and establish Shī'ism … in the long run it clashed with the juristic principle of authority, … [producing] a crisis of legitimacy. … Khumaynī's followers have reacted by coining the phrase, highly reminiscent of early Safavid legitimatory motifs, 'O God, keep Khumaynī until the revolution of the Mahdi.'" In his *The Turban for the Crown: The Islamic Revolution in Iran* (Oxford: Oxford University Press 1988), the same author points out that the millenarian tenet of "the belief in the appearance of the Twelfth Imam as the Mahdi to redeem the world … was most convenient for Khomeini's revolutionary purpose, as it had been for the founder of the Safavid Empire in 1501." For other interesting parallels between the current Iranian hizbollah and Safavid hierocracies, see Hamid Dabashi, *Theology of Discontent: The Ideological Foundation of the Islamic Revolution in Iran* (New York: New York University Press 1993), pp. 111, 119, 296, 389–90, 492.

[308] Although Majlisī was the main instigator of anti-Sufi polemics in late Safavid Persia, his writing merely continued a tradition of attacks which can be traced back to Karakī, and are,

he effectively controlled the religious policy of Persia[309] – during the final years of the reign of Shāh Sulaymān (1077/1667–1105/1694) and under the reign of Shāh Sulṭān Ḥusayn (1105/1694–1135/1722) until his death in 1111/1699–70 – marked "the beginning of the decline of good relations between Shī'ism and Sufism."

In this respect Majlisī's role in the suppression of Sufism in late Safavid Persia can be compared to that of Henry VIII's vicar-general Thomas Cromwell (1485–1540) in the dissolution of the monasteries in medieval England. "It is interesting to note how Muhammad Baqir al-Majlisi fulfilled his programme of turning against Sufism," Kamil M. al-Shaibi observed: "first he denied that his father was a Sufi at all; then he attacked the chiefs of Asceticism and Sufism, deplored the wearing of woollen clothes and considered the Sufis disbelievers. ... The government persecuted the Sufis so violently that they were driven out of the capital Isfahan."[310] Majlisī established a religious trend that can at best be called a "vulgarization of Shī'ite faith (*tashayyu'-i 'ammā-girā*),"[311] in which endeavour he enlisted the support of the state, "not only to destroy to eradicate and murder the Sufis and destroy the *khānaqāh*s, but also to attack the learned traditions of the Sufis and their presence in Persian society."[312] In his *Jawāhir al-'uqūl*, Majlisī pronounced the murder of one Sufi to be equivalent to the performance of a 'righteous deed' (*ḥusna*).'[313]

Thus, Fayḍ-i Kāshānī's rather derogatory attitude towards the classical Sufism in *al-Inṣāf* may be seen to echo the governing party's line and reflect

---

as Rasūl Ja'fariyān points out, in essence "nothing particularly original" (*Dīn va siyāsat*, p. 254) to him. However, this does not mitigate the fact that Majlisī was the Sufis' most formidable opponent, whose polemics, notes, "bore the prosaic stamp of Shari'ah-mindedness" (*The Venture of Islam*, III, p. 54), based on an innate spleen and bigotry animating his theological crusade against Sufis and philosophers. He articulated his mission to be the sole authentic custodian of the Islamic tradition as an attempt to confront, discredit and refute the rival claims of Sufism: "When I saw that the common people were occupied with the heretical innovations of the Sufis and blasphemous philosophers, in face of them I diffused and propagated the works of the Shī'ites (*imāmām*) amongst them, even though I have heard that my enemies and opponents refer to me as being but 'periphrastic marginalia." (*Fihrist-i Nuskhahā-yi Kitābkhāna-yi Dānishgāh*, III, p. 126, as cited in Ja'fariyān, *Dīn va siyāsat*, p. 256).

[309] See W.C. Chittick's introduction to his translation of Fayḍ's "The Imperial Mirror," *Ā'īna-yi shāhī* in Arjomand, *Authority and Political Culture in Shi'ism*, p. 268.

[310] Al-Shaibi, *Sufism and Shī'ism*, pp. 322–3.

[311] Aḥmad Kāẓimī Musavī, "Jāyigāh-i 'ulamā' dar ḥukūmat-i Qājār," *Iran Nameh*, 15/2 (1997), p. 200.

[312] Musavī, *ibid.*, p. 202; see also Mehdi Keyvani, *Artisans and Guild Life in the later Safavid Period* (Berlin: Klaus Schwarz Verlag 1982), pp. 205–11 for a good discussion of the persecution of the Sufis.

[313] Muḥammad Bāqir Majlisī, *Jawāhir al-'uqūl* (Tehran: lithograph edition, n.p. 1303 A.Hsh./1885), p. 9. cited in *ibid.*, p. 223 n. 6; also cf. Ja'fariyān's discussion of Majlisī's anti-Sufi activities, *Dīn va siyāsat*, pp. 254–8.

the unpopularity of the Sufi movement in late seventeenth-century Persia.[314] Whether his disillusionment with Sufism at the end of his life was merely a way to blow with the political wind of his age and to survive the fundamentalist Shī'ite despotism raging around him by self-censorship, or whether it represented a genuine change in his intellectual orientation, is hard to know. Nonetheless, despite his criticism of all classes of the religious hierarchy – dervishes included – his harshest criticism is directed at the popular preachers.

* * *

In sum, the Safavid state was born in a climate of Shī'ite extremism, using Sufism as a facade to build up a cult of personality around the monarch as supreme Sophy, *murshid-i kāmil*. Given this betrayal of principles and profound political inversion of spiritual values, it is understandable that Sufism, despite its glorious history, featuring the richest poetic literature in the entire history of Islamic culture, should have been marginalized by philosophers such as Mīr Dāmād, and hardly acknowledged in many of the prose writings of the philosophers of the period (even when utilized in the poetic works of Mīr Findiriskī, for instance).

However, that *taṣawwuf* remained, despite the dominant cult of 'Uṣūlī *mujtahid*s who opposed Sufism and the Turcoman Qizilbāsh factionalism which had corrupted it, a – if not *the* – fundamental intellectual current of late classical Persian culture is evident when we consider the mystical persuasion of most of those gnostics from whom the school of Iṣfahān derives its principal name and fame: Bahā' al-Dīn 'Āmilī, Mullā Ṣadrā and his two sons-in-law, 'Abd al-Razzāq Lāhījī and Muḥsin Fayḍ-i Kāshānī. *Taṣawwuf* in their works remains the fundamental element. Extract Sufism from their theosophy (*'irfān*) and the entire Persian intellectual tradition will be seriously lacking in both 'wisdom' (*ḥikmat*) and 'philosophy' (*falsafa*).

---

314 Cf. Ṣafā's discussion (*Tārīkh* V/1, pp. 207ff.) of Fayḍ's relationship with the anti-Sufi polemics conducted by theologians during his later years.

Clerical Perceptions of Sufi Practices in Late Seventeenth-Century Persia

Arguments Over the Permissibility of Singing (Ghinā')*

ANDREW J. NEWMAN

Earlier in its life, Safavid studies viewed the 'long' seventeenth century as having begun with a "burst of cultural and intellectual achievement, in an atmosphere of military, political and economic stability" only to end "in the darkness of fanatical religious orthodoxy amid military, political, and economic chaos." A key aspect of this paradigm of decline is said to have been the rise of a ferocious anti-Sufi polemic over the period.[1]

There are now substantial bodies of secondary-source literature charting, respectively, both the complex, changing nature of the anti-Sufi polemic and the complex, changing nature of the underlying political and socio-economic dynamic of this period. Examining these two together reveals links between that polemic and that dynamic and suggests that a socio-economic and political rather than a "fanatical" explanation may be more useful in understanding the trends and events of this period of Iranian history generally and rise of the anti-Sufi polemic in particular.

The present discussion seeks to locate specific attacks on *ghinā'* (singing) within the broader anti-Sufi polemic, and to portray its rise as the response of middle-ranking clerics to a rejection of orthodoxy by certain elements in Iranian, and especially Iṣfahānī, society and the appearance of an alliance between the court of Shāh 'Abbās II (1052/1642–1077/1666) and certain philosophically inclined senior clerics, similar to that which had dominated the later years of the reign of 'Abbās I (997–8/1588–1038/1629). Examination of the debate over the legality of *ghinā'*, as consideration of the broader anti-Sufi

* The author is grateful to Dr Leonard Lewisohn for both his editing of this paper and his attention to the translation of Sufi terminology throughout. Errors herein are the responsibility of the author alone.

[1] See my "Towards a Reconsideration of the 'Isfahan School of Philosophy:' Shaykh Bahā'ī and the Role of the Safawid 'Ulamā'," *Studia Iranica*, 15/2 (1986), p. 165.

polemic itself, reveals as much about disputes among the Uṣūlī branch of the Twelver clergy as it sheds light on the actual practice of *ghinā'*, let alone other Sufi doctrines and practices, in this period.[2]

THE SEVENTEENTH-CENTURY SAFAVID SOCIO-POLITICAL AND RELIGIOUS DYNAMIC

Broadly speaking, the anti-Sufi polemic of the early and mid-seventeenth century appears to have expressed itself in two waves. The first included a series of essays directed mainly against the messianic veneration of Abū Muslim (d. 136/754), the Iranian 'Alid agent of the Abbasid movement in Khurāsān, in Iṣfahān from the late 1030s/1620s to the mid-1060s/1650s while the second focused on Sufi doctrines and practices.[3] In between there were several 'bridging' works which addressed both concerns. The attacks on *ghinā'* featured prominently both in those essays that bridged the two waves and in those of second wave itself.

All these works were the product of their authors' concerns with trends and events in the larger society of which they were a part. The earlier period, which produced the first wave of anti-Abū Muslim tracts, was marked by a series of general and specific socio-economic crises and political changes which, if they did not directly and chronologically follow on from each other, were clearly associated. Taken together these developments affected most adversely the commercial and skilled artisan classes in Iṣfahān, the very elements whose numbers and influence had experienced such growth during the reign of 'Abbās I as the result both of direct state intervention and indirect association with broader economic forces outside the realm's immediate borders.[4]

---

[2] On the dynamics between and among Uṣūlis and Akhbāris during this period, see my edition of and comentary on *Munyat al-mumārisīn* of 'Abdu'llāh al-Samāhijī (d. 1135/1723) in "The Nature of the Akhbārī/Uṣūlī Dispute in Late-Safawid Iran," *Bulletin of the School of Oriental and African Studies*, 55/1 (1992), pp. 22–51; 55/2 (1992), pp. 250–61.

[3] For the best discussion of this phenomenon, and these two waves, to date, see K. Babayan, "The Waning of the Qizilbash: The Spiritual and the Temporal in Seventeenth Century Iran," unpublished Ph.D. thesis, Princeton University, 1993; *idem*., "Sufis, Dervishes and Mullas: The Controversy over the Spiritual and Temporal Dominion in Seventeenth-Century Iran," in *Safavid Persia*, ed. C. Melville (London: I.B. Tauris 1996), pp. 117–38; *idem*, "The Safavid Synthesis: From Qizilbash Islām to Imāmite Shī'ism," *Iranian Studies*, 27/1–4 (1994), pp. 135–62. See also the sources cited below in notes 8 and 24. Aspects of Babayan's analysis have been questioned by W. Floor in his "The Rise and Fall of Mirza Taqi, the Eunuch Grand Vizier (1043–55/1633–45), *Makhdum al-Omara va Khadem al-Foqara"*, *Studia Iranica*, 26/2 (1997), pp. 237- 66, not available at the time of writing.

[4] In the works cited above Babayan also details the key political developments. On the socio-economic crises described herein, see R. Matthee, "The Career of Muhammad Beg, Grand Vizier of Shah Abbas II (r. 1642–1666)," *Iranian Studies*, 24 (1991) pp. 17–36; *idem*, "Administrative Change and Stability in Late 17th c. Iran: The Case of Shaykh Ali Khan Zanganah (1669–89)," *International Journal of Middle Eastern Studies*, 26 (1994), pp. 77–98.

Both Sufi orders and interest in Sufi-style inquiry had been extant and had provoked clerical concern in the sixteenth century. These were mainly based among the Qizilbāsh tribal elements whose support was crucial to the rise of the Safavid state.[5] In the later years of 'Abbās I's reign interest in and affiliation with these orders and their practices, coupled with a strong messianic veneration for Abū Muslim, became sufficiently widespread among the most distressed of the urban classes to generate attacks on Abū Muslim and such clerics as Muḥammad Taqī Majlisī (d. 1070/1659–1660) for their apparent embrace of this veneration. Counter-attacks – literary and physical – against Abū Muslim's detractors followed, as did further essays censuring Abū Muslim and defending such clerics as Mīr Lawḥī who had condemned this veneration in the first place.

These developments in the socio-economic and religious spheres coincided with, if they did not neatly correspond to, disturbance in what Babayan has described as the Shaykhāvand cabal, as the alliance between the harem, individual *oymaq* members and Tajīk *'ulamā'* which had dominated 'Abbās I's court gave way to the political grouping she termed the Rustam Beg cabal in 1041/1632. The former alliance of forces included the small coterie of rationalist, *'irfānī*-oriented clerics – Sulṭān al-'Ulamā' (d. 1064/1654), Mīr Dāmād (d. 1040/1630) and Shaykh Bahā'ī (d. 1030–1/1621), for example – names frequently identified with the cultural vitality associated with this period of Safavid history.[6] With the fall of this alliance, as exemplified by the Mab'as massacre in 1041/1632, its associated clerics, including most prominently the vizier Sulṭān al-'Ulamā', suffered accordingly. The dominance at court of the Rustam Beg cabal through the reign of Shāh Ṣafī (1038–52/1629–42) past the accession of 'Abbās II facilitated the open assault by middle-ranking clerics on the Abū Muslim tradition and its supporters, in that the former knew that Abū Muslim's partisans were without advocates at court.

The new political configuration which ascended to power *c.* 1054/1644, and included some elements of that coalition which had dominated the court of

---

See also his earlier "Politics and Trade in Late Safavid Iran" (unpublished Ph.D. thesis, University of California, Los Angeles, 1991). The growing *darvīsh*/merchant-class connection can be traced as early as Mullā Ṣadrā's *Kasr al-Aṣnām*, completed in 1027/1617–8, and in the latter years of the century in *Ḥadīqat al-Shī'a*, discussed below, and *Tadhkīra-yi Naṣrābādī*, completed in 1090/1679, on which see n. 36 below. See Babayan, "The Waning," pp. 262, 253, and also my "Anti-Sufi Polemics in Safavid Iran: *Ḥadīqat al-Shī'a*," forthcoming in *Iran*.

[5] See Babayan, 'The Waning of the Qizilbash', pp. 202ff.; Newman, "Towards," pp. 88–90. See also n. 12 below.

[6] Characterizations of the *'irfānī* inclinations of such clerics as Shaykh Bahā'ī as manifestations of their interests in *ṭarīqa* or 'popular' Sufism had been veiled challenges to the alliance between the court and this clerical coterie. See Newman, *ibid.* Taqī Majlisī was a student of Bahā'ī and thus also an 'associate' of this cabal. An attack on him was thus an attack also on his teachers and their court affiliations.

'Abbās I, attempted afresh to grapple with the continuing underlying socio-economic crises and the associated religious schisms affecting the realm. Sulṭān al-'Ulamā' returned as grand vizier the following year, in 1055/1645. The reappearance of the previous political alliance, especially including Sulṭān al-'Ulamā', could only have signalled the re-emergence of the court–clergy alliance which had sustained, if not always successfully defended, philosophical inquiry on the elite level and tolerated, at least, *darvīsh*-style inquiry and practices on the 'popular' level.

BRIDGES TO A NEW POLEMIC: *ḤADĪQAT AL-SHĪ'A* AND *SALVAT AL-SHĪ'A*

To the opponents of philosophical inquiry and Sufi-style practices, the reappearance of this earlier alliance demanded a reappraisal of strategy. The ascendance of the Rustam Beg cabal had resulted in the forcible, sometimes bloody, removal of the clerical associates of that earlier grouping, and the continued – perhaps politically expedient – presence at 'Abbās II's court of such well-known opponents of Sufism as the Ṣadr Ḥabīballāh Karakī (1041/1632/1063–1652/3) and the capital's Shaykh al-Islām 'Alīnaqī Kamrā'ī (d. 1060/1650) gave Sufism's opponents limited confidence to express their opposition.[7]

Two works in particular manifest this reassessment process and the limitations of its expression. The first, the Persian-language *Ḥadīqat al-Shī'a* attributed to Aḥmad b. Muḥammad Ardabīlī (d. 993/1585), was likely completed between 1058/1648 and 1060/1650, that is, within years of the reappearance of the alliance which underlay the return of Sulṭān al-'Ulamā'. The text itself was a history of Islam and Twelver Shī'ism – a self-contained work written in 1058/1648 in the Deccan – into which was inserted a diatribe against the Abū Muslim tradition and Sufism. The attack on the latter included a ferocious assault on the doctrines and practices of twenty-one different Sufi groups, unprecedented in the anti-Abū Muslim literature to this date. Thus, the text at once continued the existing anti-Abū Muslim agenda and set the parameters for a new one which focused on specific doctrines and practices.

The ascription of extreme behaviour – and even derogatory names – to the Sufi groups attacked in *Ḥadīqa* only resonated among the commercial and artisan elements witnessing the failure of the state, in alliance with the elite practitioners of philosophical inquiry, to alleviate their distress, and challenged them to redirect their spiritual energies and inquiries to orthodoxy. Such a polemic also implicitly challenged the court's clerical associates – Sulṭān al-'Ulamā', for example – to distance themselves from such doctrines and

---

[7] On these figures, see the sources cited in n. 15 below.

practices. The attribution of the work to the well-known Ardabīlī reflected the concern for self-preservation among these clerical critics given the apparent re-establishment of the alliance between the court and the philosophically minded clerics at the court of ʻAbbās II.[8]

To those familiar with anti-Sufi polemic, some of the criticisms levelled in *Ḥadīqa* against the Sufi groups are doubtless decidedly well known. Thus, for example, these groups are accused of embracing such heretical doctrines as *ḥulūl* (incarnation), *ittiḥād* (unitive fusion) and *waḥdat-i wujūd* (the unity of existence). Some are accused of claiming achievement of *mushārika* (partnership) with God, while others are said to have embraced theological errors such as *jabr* (predestination), claim *kashf* (mystical illumination) and *karamāt* (miraculous grace), and rejected the authority of the *ʻulamā'* and formal theological knowledge (*ʻilm*) in favour of esoteric knowledge (*ʻilm-i bātin*). Other groups are accused of abandoning such required practices as daily prayer, fasting and other *farā'iḍ*, as well as wearing unsuitable clothing – wool and felt hats, for example – and associating with the insane.

However, *Ḥadīqa* also included some quite extreme criticisms, attributing to these groups patterns of behaviour which were clearly deviant, if not degenerate. These aberrant practices were mainly of a sexual nature, e.g. adultery, sodomy, and sexual relations with children or Sufi novices. The author states, for example, that the Wāṣiliyya members call any sect member who refuses the advances of another a *kāfir*, while one who accepts attains the level of *wilāya* (friendship with God).

The author made little overt distinction between such practices and other unorthodox practices including *raqṣ* (dancing), *ghinā'* (singing) and *samāʻ* (spiritual audition, i.e. listening to poetry or music), and taking part in gatherings where there was handclapping. The latter were attributed to such groups as the Ḥāliya, Kāmiliyya, the Ilhāmiyya, the Nūriyya, the Jūriyya, the Jumhūriyya, and the Zarāqiyya (the ninth, fourteenth, fifteenth, sixteenth, eighteenth, twentieth and twenty-first of the groups, respectively). The Ilhāmiyya, for example, were said to disdain pursuit of theological learning (*amūkhtan-i ʻilm*) and knowledge of the science of the afterlife (*hashr va nashr*) in favour of the study of poetry and witticisms, popular ditties (*tarannumāt*), melodies (*naghmāt*), minstrelsy (*muṭribī*), singing and songs (*surūd*). They were said to memorize poetry noted for its blasphemous (*mulḥid*) tendencies, to claim that "we learn in an instant all that which the exoteric scholar (*ʻālim*) understands during his entire life reading and studying and considering," and to argue that, for them, the licit (*ḥalāl*) and illicit (*ḥarām*) are the same.

---

[8] The authorship of this work, the detailed anti-Sufi polemic therein, and the list of names of the different groups censured in this work are discussed in my "Anti-Sufi Polemics."

The criticisms levelled against *Ḥadīqa*'s twentieth group, the Jumhūriyya, typify the blending of the clearly aberrant with the 'merely' unorthodox. Members of this group allegedly considered that within everyone is something of the divine. Thus, Imām Ḥusayn and his murderer Yazīd, oppressor and oppressed, Musā and Pharaoh are all "one and the same (*yak*)." Similarly pigs and dogs, unclean according to the law, are pure (*pāk*). The author adds that this group also believe in the unity of existence (*waḥdat-i wujūd*), predestination (*jabr*), and the comparability of God to creation (*tashbīh*), and espouse a doctrine of incarnation (*tajassum*, *sūrat*). He says that this group are those most prevalent in the present day. They call love for God *'ishq*, and claim that the religious sciences (*'ulūm-i dīniyya*) are all merely exoteric (*ẓāhir*) disciplines to be disdained in favour of esoteric knowledge (*'ilm-i bātin*). They have sex with boys, girls and men, claiming, states the author, that thereby they are actually achieving union with God since everything visible contains some aspect of God. They practise forty-day retreats and encourage others to do so as well, and they act like crazy people, calling themselves the greatest of the saints of God (*akābir-i awliyā'-i Allāh*). They classify singing and songs (*ghinā'*, *surūd*) as religiously permitted (*ḥalāl*) and employ tambourines (*daf*), flutes and other instruments in their ceremonies (*majlis*). They attribute to each other miracles and revelation (*karamāt va kashf*). Most of them wear unsuitable hats and clothes. Some acknowledge that singing (*ghinā'*) is illicit (*ḥarām*) but claim that if no instrument is played, there is no *ghinā'*, even if there is chanting (*tarjī'*).

The twenty-first group, given the pejorative name Zarāqiyya (charlatans, hypocrites), was also accused of a pot-pourri of both deviant and heretical beliefs and practices. Members of this group wear felt hats, yellow clothes like the Magians (Majūs), and otherwise dress like Sunnis and heretics (*mulḥad*), so that they can recognize each other. They promote dancing and *samā'*, and their beliefs are simply a combination of those of other Sufi groups such that they form their own unique group. In this, says the author, they resemble the Jumhūriyya. Their masters (*pīr*s), well known among the people, censure the *'ulamā'* and those who do not like Sufis.

Like other groups, members of this group are said to lay claim to miracle-working powers (*karamāt*) and divine illumination (*kashf*), deceive the foolish, and enjoy witticisms and singing popular tunes (*tarannumāt*), melodies, musical entertainment (*muṭribī*), singing (*ghinā'*) and songs (*surūd*) – the word order paralleling condemnations of these practices by other groups elsewhere in *Ḥadīqa*. They chant the profession of faith (*shahāda*), sing popular melodies (*naghmāt*) and read poetry, either couplet by couplet (*bayt* by *bayt*) or hemstitch by hemstitch (*miṣra'* by *miṣra'*), according to poetic metre (*awzān*) and scansion (*taqṭī'āt*).

The author notes there is "no doubt that *ghinā'* consists in the raising of the voice (*madd al-ṣawt*) and that it includes the entertainer's ballad (*tarjī'-i muṭrib*), even if there is no *taqṭī‘* (scanning)" and that this group combines the former with *taqṭi‘āt*. The *‘ulamā’*, he says, agree that *ghinā’* is religiously prohibited (*ḥarām*), and that anyone who performs it or listens to it is a sinner (*‘aṣī*) and debauchee (*fāsiq*). This sort of invocation (*dhikr*), he continues, contravenes what the Prophet did and is heretical innovation (*bid‘a*) and error (*ḍilāl*). Some ignorant people, he continues, believe that the *ḥadīth* of the Prophet which enjoins: "Hurry to the gardens of paradise" and his definition of the latter as "the circle of *dhikr*"[9] refers to the gatherings of such debauchees (*majālis* of these *fāsiqūn*). They should remember Sūra VII:55 ("Call upon your Lord humbly and in secret") as well as the Prophet's injunction against shouting, creating a tumult (*‘arbada*), singing and songs (*surūd*), handclapping, dancing and swooning. This sort of *dhikr* is condemned by Shī‘ī and Sunni alike as innovation (*bid‘a*) of the sort widespread at the end of the Umayyad period and during the early ‘Abbāsid period. The meaning of the above-cited *ḥadīth* has been corrupted, says the author. *Dhikr*, he explains, refers to prayer and the Koran, adding that there is also the reference to Sūra XXI:7 ("Ask the followers of the Reminder [*ahl al-dhikr*, i.e. the Jews]…"). There are many, he continues, who form a dervish circle (*ḥalqa*), reciting the *shahāda* from the Koran together with verses of poetry along with singing popular tunes (*tarannumāt*), melodies (*naghmāt*), making use of poetic metre (*awzān*) and scansion (*taqṭī‘āt*). These are lazy, gluttonous individuals who lead the ignorant masses astray.

He also imputes to the Zarāqiyya sexual relations with boys, girls and men. They busy themselves, he says, with reading the Koran to make it appear that they seek religious knowledge (*‘ilm*) whereas in reality their aim is to deceive. Most of them, he says, are in fact the Talqīniyya – his thirteenth group. Most Sufis, he continues, wear hats and give their disciples old rags, making them sit in seclusion for forty days, forbidding them to eat meat and ordering them to seek esoteric knowledge (*‘ilm-i bāṭin*). Many go to the homes of the weak-minded and tempt them. Others go to the shops of certain merchants who are ignorant of the basic tenets of the faith (*qawā’id-i dīn*) to deceive them – a clear indication of the presence and activity of this group in the author's own time and of the link between these groups and the commercial and artisan classes. The author also notes the Zarāqiyya have allied with the Jūriyya "in our own time" to deceive the common people (*‘awwām*).[10]

---

[9] For the full text of this Prophetic *ḥadīth*, see Abū Ja‘far Muhammad b. ‘Alī al-Qummī, Ibn Bābawayh (d. 381/991–2), *Ma‘āni al-akhbār* (Qum: Intishārāt-i Islāmī, 1361 A.Hsh./1982), p. 321. I am greatly indebted to Dr H. Modarresi for directing me to the full text of this *ḥadīth*.

[10] Muqaddas-i Ardabīlī, *Ḥadīqat al-Shī‘a* (Tehran: Intishārāt-i ‘Ilmiyya-yi Islāmiyya 1343 A.Hsh./1964), pp. 584, 589–90, 594, 596–7. Other groups spoken of as ‘active’ included the first group, the Waḥdatiyya; the seventh group, the Mubāḥiyya; the Kāmiliyya; the fourteenth group; the eighteenth group, the Jūriyya; and the twentieth group, the Jumhūriyya.

The condemnation of singing and related practices was thus an element of a larger, more detailed polemic against unorthodox doctrines and, especially, behaviour. That critique continued the attack on Abū Muslim. However, insofar as the author added a detailed diatribe against the doctrines and practices of specifically named Sufi groups in which he ascribed to most, if not all, beliefs and customs aberrant in the extreme, *Ḥadīqa* also laid new ground in the anti-Sufi polemic in this period.

In 1060/1650, at most two years after the completion of *Ḥadīqa*, appeared the Persian-language *Salvat al-Shī'a*, also the product of this period of revaluation. The author calls himself Muṭahhar b. Muḥammad al-Miqdādī, but Rasūl Ja'fariyān has suggested that the essay was written by the same Mīr Lawḥī who figured in earlier attacks on Taqī Majlisī.[11] If, at sixteen pages, this work was much shorter than the anti-Sufi section of *Ḥadīqa*, which covered forty pages in its published version, like the author of the earlier work, Mīr Lawḥī utilized both elements traditionally identified with the anti-Sufi polemic as well as those newer ones utilized in *Ḥadīqa*.

The essay opens with a discussion of the treatises which preceded Mīr Lawḥī's own composition, including the rebuttal of earlier works by Taqī Majlisī. In the first chapter, Mīr Lawḥī notes that the worst of the Ḥallājiyya are the Zarāqiyya. Most Sufi shaykhs and Sunni clerics have tolerated this group, he says, but all Shī'ite clerics have condemned it. It is a group, he says, whose profession is singing (*khwānandigī kardan*), horseplay (*uṣūl gereftan*), handclapping, whirling (*charkīdan*) and, like drunken brawlers, roaring aloud (*na'ra zadan*) and swooning openly. There have been Sufis and Sunnis who have condemned the Zarāqiyya, he adds.

Reviewing these denunciations, the author focuses especially on their amusement-making (*ṭarab kardan*), handclapping, crying aloud and swooning. Such practices deceive the common people, states Mīr Lawḥī, citing a series of writings in which censure of such practices appears. In the process he refers to *Ḥadīqa*, attributing it to Ardabīlī, as well as *Mutā'ūn al-mujrimiyya* of 'Alī al-Karakī (d. 940/1534) and *'Umdat al-maqāl* by the latter's son Shaykh Ḥasan[12] as being among the more recent works that have denounced such practices and quoted prophetic traditions cited by earlier authors censuring such practices as seclusion, *samā'*, dancing and swooning.

[11] Rasūl Ja'fariyān, *Dīn va siyāsat dar dawreh-yi Ṣafavī* (Qum: Anṣāriyān 1370 A.Hsh./1991), pp. 246–51. On the essay itself see R. Ja'fariyān, ed., *Mīrāth-i Islāmī-yi Irān* (Qum: Mar'ashī Najafī Public Library 1374 A.Hsh./1995), II, pp. 339–59, and the very useful introduction, pp. 339–42. See also Babayan, "The Waning of the Qizilbash," p. 141, n. 342.

[12] On these two, see Babayan, "The Waning of the Qizilbash," p. 43, n. 78, pp. 139, 241, n. 577; Ja'fariyān, *Dīn va siyāsat*, pp. 226, 231–2, n. 5. Shaykh 'Alī cited the latter work in his *al-Sihām* (fo.27b). In one of the works cited is reference to the Wāṣiliyya, among those groups discussed in *Ḥadīqa*, p. 576. See my "Anti-Sufi Polemics in Safavid Iran," esp. n. 15.

Mīr Lawḥī also notes that there are many *ḥadīth* texts condemning the illicit actions of this group, especially *ghinā'*, which he defines as *khwānandigī* and raising the voice (*madd-i ṣawt*), along with the entertainer's ballad (*tarjī'-i muṭrib*). Ḥasan 'Alī – probably a reference to Ḥasan 'Alī Shūshtarī (d. 1075/1664–5), a teacher of Taqī Majlisī himself, and on whom see further below – condemned *ghinā'*, Mīr Lawḥī adds. Citing an essay by Muḥammad Bāqir Khurāsānī,[13] he also notes that recent scholars have composed essays against *ghinā'* in which they cite both Koran and *ḥadīth* texts against it. It is clear, he says, that the *'ulamā'* censure this group – still referring to the Zarāqiyya – for its practice of singing (*khwānandigī*), handclapping, amusement-making (*ṭarab kardan*), whirling (*charkīdan*) and feigning unconsciousness. This group clearly either did not believe in the Koran or *ḥadīth* or else were foolishly ignorant of the condemnations of such practices found therein. He then links the Zarāqiyya with the veneration of Abū Muslim and the traditions of such heretics as Sufyān-i Thawrī (d. 161/778) and Ḥallāj (d. 309/922).[14]

Since earlier Shī'ī clerics have condemned this group, and "in this age" scholars have composed many *fatwās* condemning their actions, Mīr Lawḥī then includes some of the latter in his essay, citing rulings by Aḥmad 'Alawī, who in 1043/1633–4 composed *Iẓhār al-ḥaqq*, one of the earliest anti-Abū Muslim essays; 'Alīnaqī Kamrā'ī, a religious judge (*qāḍī*) in Shīrāz during the reigns of 'Abbās I and Ṣafī and Shaykh al-Islam of the Safavid capital under 'Abbās II; Mīrza Habību'llāh Karakī, descendant of 'Alī al-Karakī, and Ṣadr under both Ṣafī and 'Abbās II; Rāfi' al-Dīn Nā'inī, a student of Shaykh Bahā'ī and also identified with mystical (*'irfānī*) tendencies and Muḥammad Bāqir Khurāsānī.[15]

If these judgements, like the essay itself, are brief, they allege a connection between those who venerated Abū Muslim and certain Sufi doctrines, practices, and orders – if only one of the latter – even if such a connection is not 'objectively' documented. Nevertheless, the work's subtext is clearly the

---

[13] *Salvat al-Shī'a* in Ja'fariyān, *Mīrāth-i Islāmī-yi Irān*, II, p. 353. On this essay, see notes 15, 21, 44, below.

[14] At this point (p. 355) he refers to the time between 1051/1641–2 and 1060/1650, calling the latter date "this time."

[15] Mīr Lawḥī, *Salvat al-Shī'a*, in Ja'fariyān, *Mīrāth-i Islāmī-y Irān*, II, pp. 355–9. The text of Khurāsānī's ruling reads: "There is no dispute among the Imāmī *'ulamā'* that *ghinā'* and *surūd* are religiously prohibited (*ḥarām*). From numerous *aḥadīth* it is clear that they are a great sin (*kabīra*). It makes no difference that in the Qur'ān there is *ghinā'* or poetry or something else. The *fatwās* of some earlier *'ulamā'* condemning dancing and handclapping (*taṣfīq*) are known. No *fatwā* of anyone who permitted that has been handed down is known. God is most knowledgeable in the truths of [these] matters."
On these rulings and their authors, see also Babayan, "The Waning of the Qizilbash," pp. 141, 145, 283–4, 129, 283, notes. 721, 284, and her list of their postings in an appendix. On S. Aḥmad, see my "Anti-Sufi Polemics," n. 7.

existing Abū Muslim polemic specifically attacking Taqī Majlisī, whose denunciation by Mīr Lawḥī as a partisan of Abū Muslim was now infamous. As such, *Salvat al-Shī'a*, as much as *Ḥadīqa*, was more a continuation of the reappraisal process discussed above than a fundamental break with the preoccupation with the veneration of Abū Muslim.[16]

OPENING THE SECOND WAVE: ṬĀHIR QUMMĪ'S *RADD-I ṢŪFIYYA*

During the years immediately following these two essays, however, much happened which further fanned the flames of anti-Sufi diatribe. At the death of Sulṭān al-'Ulamā' in 1064/1654 – after a harsh winter marked by severe inflation and famine – efforts continued to deal with both the growing underlying socio-economic crises and the concomitant rising interest in Sufi doctrines and practices. The outreach to Sufi and "popular" *darvīsh* modes of piety expanded under 'Abbās II's personal stimulus[17] as part of a larger strategy to bring the more radical of the contemporary spiritual schisms under the influence, if not the control, of the court and thus minimize their danger to the stability of the realm, and the capital city in particular. The latter culminated in 'Abbās II's call in 1064/1654 to Muḥammad Taqī Majlisī and Fayḍ-i Kāshānī (d. 1091/1680). Both were identified with *'irfānī* spirituality and, in the former's case, reverence for Abū Muslim. Both were also students of associates of the earlier politico-religious coalition dominant under 'Abbās I and loyal to the political establishment. Both were now asked to undertake assignments for the court. These commissions in particular could only have underscored the re-emergence of the court–clergy alliance and its tolerance, if not outright promotion, of the same philosophical inquiry on the elite level and *darvīsh* tendencies and practice on the 'popular' level that had been characteristic of 'Abbās I's reign.

Muḥammad Ṭāhir Shīrāzī Najafī Qummī composed his *Radd-i Ṣūfiyya* sometime before Taqī Majlisī's death in 1070/1659. Like the relevant portions of *Ḥadīqa*, this two-part essay both attacked Sufism in a general sense and included detailed descriptions of some twenty Sufi groups. The fact that the later work was a much-abridged but otherwise virtual copy of *Ḥadīqa* suggests Qummī's concern to bolster his credentials at this early stage of his career by openly associating himself with the substance and style of the polemic of Ardabīlī, a better-known scholar whose authorship of *Ḥadīqa* was already

---

16 Indeed, Ja'fariyān (*ibid.*, pp. 246–51) argues that *Salvat al-Shī'a* was a synopsis of an earlier anti-Sufi work by Muhammad Ṭāhir Shīrāzī Najafī Qummī (d. 1098/1687) himself, as part of an exchange with Taqī Majlisī, and was written by Mīr Lawḥī replying to the former's son Bāqir Majlisī (d. 1110/1699) over charges of his father's Sufi tendencies. See also n. 11 above.

17 Babayan ("The Waning of the Qizilbash," p. 271) cites a contemporary chronicle on the presence of two *darvīshes* from Rūm at a court *majlis*.

Plate 6: Royal Marketplace and Imperial Military Orchestra Building in Iṣfahān. From Chardin, *Voyages* Pl. 37.

being asserted from other quarters, via its attribution by Mīr Lawḥī.[18] Insofar as all *Ḥadīqa*'s references to the Abū Muslim tradition were excised in *Radd-i Ṣūfiyya*, however, this foray into polemic also betokened a break from the polemic's fixation with Abū Muslim to focus on certain, specific heretical doctrines and practices among Sufi groups. Indeed, it may be no exaggeration to suggest that Qummī alone was responsible for this shift in the nature of anti-Sufi polemic.[19]

For present purposes it remains to consider briefly the descriptions of Sufi groups in which Qummī's *Radd* addresses singing and related practices and compare these with corresponding descriptions in *Ḥadīqa*. The reports on the Ḥāliyya, *Ḥadīqa*'s ninth and Qummī's fifth group, for example, closely parallel each other. Both works censure handclapping, *samā'*, dancing, playing instruments and swooning, the latter said to effect nearness to God.

Qummī's twelfth group was *Ḥadīqa*'s twentieth, the Jumhūriyya. Less than five lines long, Qummī's description is, as usual, the shorter of the two. The first lines of each are parallel, but where *Ḥadīqa* – whose entry is six times as long – then added much detail, Qummī deleted much, including all the above-mentioned references to singing.

The Kāmiliyya are Qummī's sixteenth and *Ḥadīqa*'s fourteenth group. Abridging the earlier work, Qummī dropped references to their present activity noted in *Ḥadīqa* but retained mention of singing (*khwānandigī*) and dancing. On balance, the few variations between the two entries are not significant.

Qummī censures his seventeenth group, the Ilhāmiyya – *Ḥadīqa*'s fifteenth – for exactly the same reasons as did *Ḥadīqa*, and as briefly. Qummī includes among their heretical practices those related to singing which were cited in *Ḥadīqa* – and noted above – using the same wording, with but minor exceptions.

Qummī's eighteenth entry, on the Bāṭiniyya, abbreviates the first section of *Ḥadīqa*'s long eighteenth entry, on the Jūriyya. Both mention musical instruments (*sāzhā*), wine (*khamr*), and storytelling, though Qummī drops *Ḥadīqa*'s reference to the recital of the *Shāhnāma*.

---

[18] In addition, the association of Muḥammad Beg, appointed grand vizier at the death of Sulṭān al-'Ulamā' in 1064/1654, with Mullā Qāsim, who favoured direct clerical rule, may have given Qummī some confidence to express his dissent more openly than before. See Babayan, "The Waning of the Qizilbash," p. 89, citing the Mullā as launching such an attack in 1057/1664. See also pp. 145–6.

[19] My forthcoming "Anti-Sufi Polemics" discusses Qummī's career and contributions in greater detail, including especially the care he took to demonstrate his Uṣūlī proclivities and loyalty to the court even as he attacked its clerical associates, his willingness to "come out" at this stage, his subsequent, relative, retreat from the extreme attack on offer in both *Radd* and the relevant sections of the earlier *Ḥadīqa*, and examines comparatively the relevant sections of his *Radd* and *Ḥadīqa* to suggest Qummī himself authored both.

Qummī's nineteenth, the Nūriyya, is *Ḥadīqa*'s sixteenth group. The two entries are nearly identical with each other, including the passing references to *samā'*.

Qummī's twentieth group was *Ḥadīqa*'s twenty-first, the Zarāqiyya; the same group was targeted by Mīr Lawḥī in his *Salvat al-Shī'a*. If both entries were long, *Ḥadīqa*'s was, as usual, much the longer. The differences in the references to singing and associated practices typify the broader variations between *Radd-i Ṣūfiyya* and *Ḥadīqa*. Both note that, like many other Sufi groups already mentioned, this group lays claim to visionary powers and experiences (*karamāt va kashf*), engages in witticisms, intones measures (*tarannumāt*) and melodies and engages in musical entertainment (*muṭribī*), singing (*ghinā'*) and songs (*surūd*) – the word order parallel in both works.[20]

Ḥadīqa had mentioned the chanting of the *shahāda* by the Sufis, defined *ghinā'*, cited *ḥadīth* texts and Koran VII:55, noted alternative meanings of *dhikr* and censured the laziness of those engaging in such practices. In phrasing that matches almost word-for-word, both noted condemnations of this and other Sufi groups, linking these practices with drunkenness. *Ḥadīqa*, however, had claimed that its members had sex with boys, girls and men, and noted that most are like the Talqīniyya – Qummī's fourteenth and *Ḥadīqa*'s thirteenth description – and that most Sufis wear hats, give their disciples old rags to wear, sit in retreat for forty days, do not eat meat, and proselytize in homes and shops.

There seems an indisputable link between *Ḥadīqa* and Qummī's *Radd*: the latter is a much shortened version of the former, and we have suggested that Qummī authored both. However, where *Ḥadīqa* and *Salvat al-Shī'a* – the latter especially, because of its author's position within the polemic – address certain problematic Sufi practices still from within the anti-Abū Muslim critique, Qummī's *Radd* demarcates the shift from a concern with the Abū Muslim tradition to focus on problematic Sufi doctrines and practices.

This new polemic offered as little objective information on the Sufi doctrines and practices in the period which ostensibly occasioned it as the original anti-Abū Muslim polemic. The recourse to ascription of heretical beliefs and, especially, deviant behaviour and unflattering names mainly served to challenge urban elements to rechannel their spiritual attention to orthodoxy and to invite the court's clerical associates to stand aloof from such doctrines and practices. If the essays concerned drew no distinction between clearly perverted practices and the 'merely' unorthodox, that is, those of a less serious moral nature, references to the latter might, if taken carefully, have some ring of historical authenticity. Such behaviour included, for example, the wearing of distinctive clothes, self-imposed periods of seclusion, abandonment of certain of the *farā'iḍ* and various practices associated with singing. Indeed, in that all three of the

[20] Ardabīlī, *Ḥadīqat al-Shī'a*, p. 594; Qummī, *Radd*, Mar'ashī MS. 4014/7, fo. 29a. On the several manuscripts of this text consulted, see my "Anti-Sufi Polemics," n. 26.

above mentioned works refer to *ghinā'*, *Ḥadīqa*, especially, addressing associated practices, singing might be taken to have been a common, if not widespread, feature of the search for spiritual meaning in the midst of socio-economic and political turmoil, particularly in the urban setting. In their references to and refutations of spirited defences of the practice, later essays specifically attacking singing – representative of the second anti-Sufi wave's focus on specific practices – only further confirm singing's popularity.

AN UṢŪLĪ CRITIQUE OF SUFI DOCTRINE AND PRACTICE: SHAYKH 'ALĪ'S CRITICISMS

In 1073/1662, three years after Taqī Majlisī's death, Shaykh 'Alī b. Muḥammad b. Ḥasan (d. 1103/1691–2) included a brief attack on *ghinā'* in the first volume of his *al-Durr al-manthūr*. Sometime later he composed *al-Sihām al-māriqa min 'irād al-zanādiqa*, which addressed *ghinā'* as part of a larger discussion in which he also censured other Sufi doctrines and practices. As the discussion on *ghinā'* in the latter is a more detailed version of the criticisms in the former work, *al-Sihām* repays the greater attention.[21]

---

[21] As to the dating of these works, I'jaz Ḥusayn al-Kanturī (*Kashf al-Ḥujub*, Calcutta 1914, p. 313) and M.T. Dānish-pazhūh in his *Fihrist-i Kitābkhāna-i … Sayyid Muḥammad Mashkāt bi Dāneshgāh-i Tehrān* (Tehran 1335 A.Hsh./1956), V/1796, both claim *al-Sihām* was completed in 1070/1659, the year of Majlisī's death. References in *al-Sihām* to *Al-Durr* as completed, however, suggest that *al-Sihām* was finished sometime after 1073/1662, if not 1092/1681–2, when the second volume of *al-Durr* was completed. See also Āghā Buzurg Muḥammad Ṭihrānī, *al-Dharī'a ilā taṣānīf al-Shī'a* (Tehran–Najaf pp. 1353–98), XII, pp. 260–1. Cf. my earlier reference to the two works in "Anti-Sufi Polemics," and Tihrānī, *ibid*; Ja'fariyān, *Dīn va siyāsat*, pp. 231–2. Babayan ("The Waning of the Qizilbash," p. 244, n. 590) suggests that *al-Sihām* was completed between 1060/1650 and 1075–6/1664.

Sabziwārī's essay on singing, discussed at length below, was likely composed sometime before 1087/1676–7 since, in that year Shaykh 'Alī composed his *Tanbīh al-ghāfilīn* in reply to it. The copy of the latter work consulted (University of Tehran MS Film 3653) includes Sabziwārī's essay, discussed below, and Shaykh 'Alī's *Tanbīh;* the first folio of the MS gives the date of writing of *Tanbīh* as 1087. Khwānsarī's summary of Shaykh 'Alī's reply to the essay of Sabziwārī discussed below is a summary of the text of *Tanbīh* in hand. See Muḥammad Bāqir al-Khwānsarī, *Rawḍāt al-jannāt*, ed. M.T. al-Kashfī and A. Ismā'īlīyān (Tehran Qum, 1390–2 A.Hsh./1970–2), II, pp. 71–8. Ja'fariyān (*ibid*., pp. 202–3, esp. 203, n. 1) also refers to Shaykh 'Alī's *Tanbīh* as a reply to Sabziwārī's essay on *ghinā'*. While Shaykh 'Alī is known to have addressed *ghinā'* in several works, Sabziwārī, aside from his above-cited *fatwā* (see n. 15 above) and the essay on singing below, is not known to have specifically addressed *ghinā'* in any other context. Thus, Mīr Lawḥī's reference to such an essay by Muḥammad Bāqir Khurāsāni in his *Salvat* is unclear and may, in fact, refer to a longer version of the *fatwā* cited in *Salvat*. That Shaykh 'Alī addressed arguments raised by Sabziwārī in his essay, as will be seen, may suggest, however, that he was replying to an earlier essay by Sabziwārī, such as that mentioned by Mīr Lawḥī.

For the portions of *al-Sihām* in *al-Durr*, see 'Alī b. Muḥammad b. al-Ḥasan b. Zayn al-Dīn al-'Āmilī, *al-Durr al-manthūr* (Qum 1398/A.Hsh./1977), I, pp. 25–47.

Born in 1013 or 1014/1605–6, Shaykh ʻAlī was the great grandson of al-Shahīd al-Thānī ("the second martyr," d. 965/1559), who had avoided contact with the newly-established Safavid state. On his mother's side, he was related to ʻAlī al-Karakī, one of the earliest and best-known of the Arab clerics to serve the Safavid throne and author of the anti-Sufi tract cited above by Mīr Lawḥī. Like Qummī, Shaykh ʻAlī spent his formative years outside the Safavid realm and the orbit and influence of the proponents of rationalist, philosophical inquiry supported by ʻAbbās I's court. Coming from a strongly Uṣūlī background, Shaykh ʻAlī was a fierce opponent of both Muḥammad Amīn al-Astarābādī and the Akhbārī school[22] as well as of philosophical inquiry and Sufism.

Shaykh ʻAlī journeyed to Iran several times early in his career, initially, it would seem, to replace books in the family library destroyed by fire. About the time of the Mab'as massacre in 1041/1632, he settled in Iran, perhaps more at ease with the downfall of the alliance between the state and the philosopher-clerics of the Iṣfahān school.[23] Once there, however, Shaykh ʻAlī appears neither to have sought nor been offered any position at court, either during the heyday of the Rustam Beg cabal or following the resurgence of the court–clergy alliance in 1054/1644. Indeed, in distinct opposition to such clerical associates of the court as Fayḍ-i Kāshānī, Majlisī, and Sabziwārī, and even Qummī himself – albeit for different reasons – Shaykh ʻAlī opposed the performance of Friday prayer during the occultation. This was a stance not likely to win court favour.[24] Moreover, in 1074/1663, following completion of volume I of *al-Durr*, he began composing challenges to criticisms which Sulṭān al-ʻUlamā', whose identification with the court had been long-standing, had levelled against al-Shahīd al-Thānī.[25] Taking these together, his rejection

Shaykh ʻAlī wrote another essay on *ghinā'* in which he attacked Fayḍ-i Kāshānī. On these essays see also Tihrānī, *ibid.*, X, p. 229 XI, pp. 138–9. On the second volume of *al-Durr*, see Dānish-pazhūh, *ibid.*, V, pp. 1302–4; Tihrānī, *ibid.*, VIII, pp. 76–7. See also below, notes 43, 44. Tihrānī (*ibid.*, IV, pp. 443–7) does not list any *Tanbīh al-Ghāfilīn* for Shaykh ʻAlī.

22 On his essay rebutting Astarābādī's *al-Fawā'id al-madaniyya*, see al-Kanturī, *ibid.*, p. 183; Tihrānī, *ibid.*, VI, p. 168; and his own mention of the essay in *al-Durr*, II, p. 245. For references to Astarābādī in *al-Sihām*, see also n. 34 below.

23 This is apparent from the statement in an essay written *c.* 1087/1676–7, that he had been in Iran for some forty years, i.e. the mid-1040s/1630s. See al-Khwānsarī, *ibid.*, II, p. 73, and also *al-Durr*, II, pp. 238ff., esp. 241–2.

24 On Shaykh ʻAlī and Friday prayer, see Ja'fariyān, *Dīn va siyāsat*, pp. 122–23. He thus opposed the rulings of his ancestors ʻAlī al-Karakī and al-Shahīd al-Thānī. On Friday prayer generally, see my "Fayḍ al-Kāshānī and the Rejection of the Clergy/State Alliance: Friday Prayer as Politics in the Safavid Period" in a forthcoming collection of papers edited by L. Walbridge. On Sabziwārī, see further below. A reference in *al-Durr* (I, p. 176) suggests that Shaykh ʻAlī had written on the Friday prayer question before he completed volume I of this work in 1073/1662.

25 These were written during the years 1073–4/1663–5. See Tihrānī, *ibid.*, XII, pp. 67–8; V, pp. 174–5; X, pp. 200–1. Portions of volume I of *al-Durr* (I, pp. 168ff.) address issues in al-Shahīd al-Thānī's reading of the earlier work by al-Shahīd al-Awwal.

of court affiliation was – if only implicitly – clear, even if this was a safe time to make such a statement.[26]

Both *al-Sihām* and *al-Durr*, in that portions addressed such specific practices as *ghinā'* and the remainder dealt with other unorthodox Sufi beliefs and practices, paralleled both *Ḥadīqa* and *Radd*. However, comparing the attacks on *ghinā'* in *Radd* and *al-Sihām* it is clear that by the time of the latter's composition, and even by 1073/1662 when much of that critique was first offered in *al-Durr*, the critique of *ghinā'* as a specific, heretical practice had developed its own distinct momentum. That Shaykh 'Alī devoted his introductory remarks and the first chapter in *al-Sihām* to attacking *ghinā'* and that these remarks reproduced nearly verbatim the opening remarks on *ghinā'* in *al-Durr* suggests the debate on the issue had attained only greater consequence over the intervening years, to the point where a separate, if not entirely new, essay was required to address first the legality of this practice in particular and then other Sufi doctrines and practices in general. The continuing, and growing, debate on *ghinā'* further suggests that singing and associated practices were increasingly widespread over the period. Indeed, the arguments and rebuttals offered in both this essay and that of Bāqir Sabziwārī discussed below further confirm that *ghinā'* and its legality was an issue contested as much among late-Safavid-period Uṣūlī scholars as between practitioners of *ghinā'* and its critics. Furthermore, and finally, in keeping with the attacks of this second wave, neither *al-Sihām* or Sabziwārī's essay contain references to the Abū Muslim tradition.

Shaykh 'Alī opens his essay – and his remarks in *al-Durr* – by citing a statement of the sixth Imām, Ja'far al-Ṣādiq (d. 148/765), in which the Imām quoted the Prophet as saying:

> Recite the Koran with the melodies (*alḥān*) of the Arabs and their sounds (*aṣwāṭ*), and beware the melodies of the people of iniquity (*fisq*) and those who commit grave offences (*ahl al-kabā'ir*). After me will come people who chant (*yuraji'ūn*) the Koran in the cantillation of singing (*tarjī' al-ghinā'*) and wailing (*al-nūḥa*) and monastic practices (*al-rahbāniyya*). Following them is not permitted and their hearts and the hearts of those who follow them are turned inside out (*maqlūba*).[27]

---

[26] Sulṭān al-Ulamā' had died some ten years before, in 1064/1654, Majlisī died in 1070/1659; Kāshānī – plagued by chaos in the capital – was on the verge of resigning his post in Iṣfahān, and Mullā Qāsim launched his attack against Safavid legitimacy in 1075/1664. Moreover, and finally, 'Abbās II had accepted the futility of trying to influence, let alone control, the religious turmoil in the capital – if not also the socio-economic and political problems exacerbating it – and had withdrawn into the haram. For greater detail on these trends and events, see my "Fayḍ al-Kāshānī" and "Anti-Sufi Polemics."

[27] Muḥammad b. Ya'qūb al-Kulaynī, *al-Kāfī*, ed. A.A. al-Ghaffārī, (Tehran 1377–9/A.Hsh./1957–9), II, p. 614/3.

Shaykh 'Alī argues this text proves that *ghinā'* occurs when there is *tarjī' al-Qur'ān* in the manner well understood at that time, that *ghinā'* is defined as enraptured cantillation (*al-tarjī' al-muṭrib*), and that according to the philologists (*ahl al-lugha*) the root word from which the latter derives, *al-ṭarab*, describes a person in the extreme stages of sadness or happiness. This definition, he states, is clear to anyone who considers the matter. It is well known and customary, he maintains, that this prohibition applies to non-Koranic singing, as in the case of the Sunni Sufis and their heretics (*mulḥad*). If singing involves the cantillation (*tarjī'*) of which the Twelver *'ulamā'* speak, than this definition of singing, and consequent prohibition, applies to it.

To an opponent who argues for reference to common practice (*'urf*)[28] Shaykh 'Alī replies that in fact, in the Arab countries, when someone is heard reciting poetry in this manner, they say "he is singing" or "this is a singer." The Sufis, he says, admit that rapture and the condition which the disciple achieves is concomitant with *ghinā'*, sometimes claiming that *ghinā'* causes this state. Shaykh 'Alī notes that Imāmī scholars have allowed the singing that is the chanting of the leader of a caravan of camels (*al-hudā*) by a special reason (*dalīl*). Indeed, the meanings of melodies and tunes (*naghmāt*) and sounds (*aṣwāt*) approximate each other. In the *ḥadīth*, the key is the distinction between the melodies of the Arabs and those of corrupt, irreligious motives (*ahl al-fisq*).

Following these remarks Shaykh 'Alī's first chapter deals solely with *ghinā'*. All the Imāmī *'ulamā'*, he says, agree that *ghinā'* is forbidden. The prohibition is so clearly based in the Koran and the Sunna that it is not necessary to repeat the evidence from these two sources. The *'ulamā'* define *ghinā'* as raising of the voice (*madd al-ṣawt*) which comprises enraptured chanting or what popular usage (*'urf*) calls *ghinā'*, even if there is no rapture (*ṭarab*), in respect to poetry or the Koran or anything else. The *ḥadīth* cited above makes clear the prohibition as far as the Koran is concerned, but also requires prohibition in associated instances.

In an attempt to discover a middle, permitted position on *ghinā'* and its associated practices, his opponent then suggests there are forms of *ghinā'* not covered in the *ḥadīth* and therefore not forbidden, that is, something between the melodies of the Arabs and those of corrupt secular folk and grave sinners (*ahl al-fisq wa kabā'ir*). Likewise, continues his opponent, because something is similar to *tarjī' al-ghinā'* does mean it is *ghinā'*. The *ḥadīth* forbids only the

[28] The "If it is said ... I say" formula used here suggests such a claim had actually been advanced. Indeed, that *al-Sihām* was composed in Arabic signifies that its intended audience was an educated clergy. This is confirmed by the detailed, legalistic nature of his opponent's arguments in this essay. Reference to *'urf* (customary practice), not likely to be advocated by Akhbārīs, suggests an Uṣūlī opponent.

singing of the Koran. Anything else, his opponent concludes, requires a rational proof (*dalīl*) for its prohibition. Again, the manner of the objection suggests an Uṣūlī opponent.

Tarjī', Shaykh 'Alī replies, is *ghinā'*, and it is also specifically musical cadence (*laḥn*) and the musician's drawn-out voice (*madd al-ṣawt al-muṭrib*). Cantillation of the Koran (*tarjī' al-Qur'ān*), in fact, refers to ordinary vocal cantillation (*tarjī' al-ghinā'*) just as singing the Koran is like singing anything else. Therefore, there is, Shaykh 'Alī argues, no intermediate position between the melodies of the Arabs and those of profane and sinful corrupt folk (*ahl al-fisq wa' l-kabā'ir*). Moreover, he says, the latter acknowledge that *ghinā'* is among the causes of the state which the Sufi novice (*murīd*) attains; it is exactly what they do.

His opponent then offers a text:

> It is related from Abū 'Abdu'llāh [Imām Ja'far] that a man came to him and said: 'I have some neighbours and they have neighbours who sing and play the lute (*'ūd*). It's possible that I have come in at the door and have sat for a while listening to them.' The Imām said: "Don't do that."[29]

This text, argues the opponent, forbids *ghinā'* if it is accompanied by the lute, whilst *ghinā'* by itself is not forbidden.[30]

Shaykh 'Alī replies that one must extend the unqualified (*al-muṭlaq*) to the qualified (*al-muqayyad*), a formulation clearly Uṣūlī in nature, paralleling the distinction between 'general'(*'āmm*) and 'particular' (*khāṣṣ*) categories. Although accompaniment by the lute alone is mentioned, on this principle the answer lies in forbidding any instrument at all. Shaykh 'Alī also criticizes another effort to define *ghinā'* as the embellishment (*tazyīn*) of the voice such that the term *ghinā'* does not apply.

Sufism (*al-taṣawwuf*), he says, originally referred to a group of heretics (*zanādiqa*) and schismatics (*ahl al-khilāf*) who were enemies of the house of the Prophet after the appearance of Islam. This included Sufyān al-Thawrī and Ghazālī, the head of the enemies of the Shī'ite *ahl al-bayt*. It was never used by the Imāmīs during the time of the Imāms or even after this during the occultation. These days, he says, beginning a reference to contemporary practice, some Imāmis have studied Sufi books. While some adhere to the laws of the *sharī'a*, others have become affiliated with Sufi groups, to the point where they consider dancing, clapping of hands and *ghinā'* among the acts of worship (*'ibādāt*), and indeed perhaps preferable. These people have abandoned the *sharī'a*, and tried to convert the weak of intellect, the masses

---

29 With minor variations, this is Kulaynī, *ibid.*, VI, p. 432/10.

30 This argument paralleled that of the Jumhūriyya who, according to *Ḥadīqa*, claimed that if no instrument were played, then there was no forbidden *ghinā'* even if there were *tarjī'*. See n. 10 above.

and the riff-raff to the soundness of this path. They claimed that they were possessed of illumination and charismatic abilities (*kashf wa karamāt*), and caused people to abandon the study of the faith and its practices, including most of the religious obligations (*takālīf*), for sitting in one place for forty days in isolation and pursuing the pleasures of the self. The Sufis claimed that matters would be revealed to them without a human or other intermediary, and the riff-raff followed them and immersed themselves in forbidden ascetic practices (*al-riyāḍāt*). The Sufis used all this as a pretext for getting close to their followers, to take their money.

The remaining chapters of *al-Sihām* consider other, broader aspects of Sufism, with pertinent citations to the original sources. In the next chapter, for example, Shaykh 'Alī states that Sufism, regardless of its origins, soon became less conditional on knowledge *per se* and more dependent on a special knowledge to which its practitioners laid claimed for themselves. Indeed, he continued, it focused on externals, such as wearing distinctive clothes recognized by most people, and leaving off concern for the interior spiritual dimension of religion (*al-bāṭin*). Its practitioners claimed they spoke directly with God, the Prophet or the Imāms whereas, in reality, they had seen the jinn or Satan.[31] In another chapter Shaykh 'Alī criticizes Ghazālī (d. 505/1111) and Ibn 'Arabī (638/1240), suggesting a tendency among current practitioners to identify themselves with such figures. The Shaykh, with several folios of citations, devotes special attention to Ghazālī, citing his rejection of 'Alī's claim to the caliphate, his hatred of the Imāms, and his attacks on the Twelver clergy.[32] In another chapter he notes that during travels between Syria and Baghdad and in Mecca, he observed Sufis rejecting fasting and prayer and indulging in singing. Discussing the rise of doctrines such as indwelling of the divine (*ḥulūl*), unification (*ittiḥād*) and the 'unity of being' (*waḥdat al-wujūd*), the Sufis, he says, have abandoned any pretence of following the law and denied the existence of the Creator. The last few chapters include citations of *ḥadīth*, including that about Sufyān al-Thawrī, elsewhere described by Shaykh 'Alī in the same breath as Ḥasan al-Baṣrī (d. 110/728) as an enemy of *ahl al-Bayt*, who came into Imām Ja'far's presence wearing unsuitable clothing.[33] The singing of the Sunnis is also mentioned twice, and condemned.

---

[31] This may have been directed against Taqī Majlisī himself. See Babayan, "The Waning of the Qizilbash," pp. 279–80, where she describes his reported dream of Imām 'Alī, from Khwānsarī, *ibid*., II, p. 121.

[32] Shaykh 'Alī's citations in *al-Sihām* can be traced in W.M. Watt's translation of Ghazālī's *al-Munqidh* in *The Faith and Practice of al-Ghazālī* (London: George Allen & Unwin 1970), pp. 59–61, 68, 44–5, 49–50, 52–3.

It will be remembered that in 1046/1636, early in his career, Fayḍ-i Kāshānī wrote a commentary on Ghazālī's *Iḥyā 'ulūm al-dīn*.

[33] Cf. Kulaynī, *ibid*., VI, p. 442/8. On the references to Sufyān al-Thawrī and Ḥasan al-Baṣrī, see fo. 8a.

At the same time, the citing of *ḥadīth* texts, references to the importance of the written sources, and Shaykh 'Alī's explicit denunciation of Amīn Astarābādī further on in the essay might suggest that Shaykh 'Alī's opponent was of the Akhbārī persuasion. However, reference to the texts and their importance itself was not a mark of adherence to Akhbārism.[34] Indeed, the arguments presented in Shaykh 'Alī's essay, when considered together with those in Sabziwārī's essay, owed less to the Akhbārī than the Uṣūlī tradition.

At the same time, while abhorrence of singing may have inspired this essay, as evidenced by its being the subject of his opening remarks, both these remarks on *ghinā'* and the balance of the essay contain few details on then-current Sufi practices and beliefs generally, let alone particular remarks pertaining to *ghinā'*. Furthermore, there are no references to specific Sufi groups or to examples of extreme deviant behaviour of the sort noted by Qummī. Nevertheless, in being inspired by *ghinā'*, the essay does imply the continued popularity of singing and related practices in this period.

EVIDENCE FOR AN INTRA-'ULAMĀ' DISPUTE: MUḤAMMAD BĀQIR SABZIWĀRĪ'S UṢŪLĪ REBUTTAL

Sometime prior to 1087/1676–7, the anti-singing polemic elicited a response from Muḥammad Bāqir Sabziwārī (d.1090/1679). A student of Shaykh Bahā'ī, himself a loyal member of the political alliance which had dominated 'Abbās I's court, Sabziwārī's career paralleled that of the clerical associates of the court in that earlier period. Sabziwārī came to Iṣfahān sometime during the reign of 'Abbās II[35] when the earlier court–clergy alliance reappeared. He was a close colleague of Sulṭān al-'Ulamā', who had also studied with Bahā'ī and had been a prominent member of the earlier alliance. When Sulṭān al-'Ulamā' regained that prominence under 'Abbās II he appointed Sabziwārī a teacher at Iṣfahān's 'Abdu'llāh Shūshtarī school, built by 'Abbās I for Shūshtārī. Sabziwārī was also appointed leader of the Friday congregational prayers (*imām-i jum'a*) and Shaykh al-Islām in the city. Finally, Sabziwārī was an associate of Fayḍ-i Kāshānī, also a student of the clerical associates of 'Abbās' court. Much as Bahā'ī and Kāshānī, Sabziwārī was also interested in elitist mystical theosophy (*'irfān*) and philosophical inquiry.[36]

---

[34] On the denunciation of Amīn Astarābādī, see *al-Sihām*, fo. 20a. See also n. 22 above. On the disputes between Akhbārīs and Uṣūlīs in this period, see my "The Nature of the Akhbārī/Uṣūlī Dispute."

[35] For a *firmān* dated 1068/1658 to Sabziwārī, see Ja'fariyān, *Dīn va siyāsat*, p. 433.

[36] Babayan ("The Waning of the Qizilbash," p. 85, n. 195) notes a reference in Muḥammad Ṭāhir Naṣrābādī's *Tadhkira-yi Naṣrābādī* (ed. V. Dastgirdī, Tehran 1352 A.Hsh./1973, p. 151) (completed between 1083/1673–4 and 1090/1679) to Sabziwārī as an *'ārif*, suggesting the more exclusive nature of his pursuits. Other contemporary sources such as Muḥammad b. Ḥasan Ḥurr-i 'Āmilī, *Amal al-āmil* (Baghdad 1385/A.Hsh./1965–6, II, p. 250), and Mīrzā

Like these clerics, Sabziwārī too was on the 'court' side of many of the key issues of the day. Thus, for example, early in his career Sabziwārī adopted a position on Friday prayer similar to that of Fayḍ-i Kāshānī and Taqī Majlisī, both of whom also received court appointments under 'Abbās II.[37] That this was the preferred position was further demonstrated by the fact that Sabziwārī replaced as teacher at the Shūshtārī school 'Abdu'llāh's own son Ḥasan 'Alī, who opposed the performance of Friday prayer during the occultation.[38] Sabziwārī was also committed to an expansive role for the *faqīh* in the community as representative of the Hidden Imām during the latter's occultation.[39] Finally, he also dedicated several essays to the shāh, including *Rawḍat al-anwār*, a work in the 'mirror for princes' genre, written in 1073/1662–3.[40] Sufficiently endeared to the court thereby, Sabziwārī played a conspicuous role in Shāh Sulaymān's coronation following 'Abbās II's death in 1077/1666.[41]

Like Bahā'ī and his students Kāshānī and Majlisī, Sabziwārī was subjected to a series of withering attacks on a variety of issues, especially Friday prayer.[42] Where under similar attacks, Bahā'ī and Kāshānī had resigned their

---

'Abdu'llāh Afandī in his *Riyāḍ al-ulamā'* (Qum 1980, V, pp. 44–5) call him a *mutakallim, faqīh* and, in the nineteenth century, Khwānsarī (*Rawḍat al-jannāt*, II, p. 68) calls him *ḥakīm, mutakallim, faqīh, uṣūlī, muḥaddith*. All these epithets suggest his interests tended toward the elite-oriented philosophical inquiry identified with the scholars of the reign of 'Abbās I, rather than 'popular' inquiry. On Sabziwārī's Uṣūlī inclinations, see further below.

[37] Kāshānī completed his well-known Friday prayer essay *al-Shihāb al-thāqib*, in which he ruled that the prayer was *wujūb 'aynī*, in 1057/1647 – three years after the fall of the Rustam Beg cabal in 1054/1644 – and therein mentioned Sabziwārī's position on this issue as supportive of his own. As an Uṣūlī cleric – as will be discussed further below – Sabziwārī's example on this issue counters Ja'fariyān's suggestion (*Dīn va siyāsat*, pp. 126–8) that most of those who supported the *'aynī* position were Akhbārīs. The religio-political implications of the various positions on this issue, and the court appointments of Taqī Majlisī and Kāshānī, are discussed more fully above and also in my "Fayḍ al-Kāshānī." See also Tihrānī, *ibid.*, XV, p. 66. Sabziwārī had composed a commentary on a work of 'Allāma Ḥillī (d. 726/1325) in 1050/1640–1 (Tihrānī, *ibid.*, X, p. 19).

[38] Khwānsarī, *ibid.*, II, p. 68; Ja'fariyān, *Dīn va siyāsat*, pp. 156–7, 173; Tihrānī, *ibid.*, XV, p. 69. 'Abdu'llāh himself had, in fact, taken the position later adopted by Majlisī, Fayḍ-i Kāshānī, and Sabziwārī. See Tihrānī, *ibid.*, XV, p. 73; Ja'fariyān, *ibid.*, p. 128.

[39] See Norman Calder, "Legitimacy and Accommodation in Safavid Iran: The Juristic Theory of Muḥammad Bāqir al-Sabziwārī (d. 1090/1679)," *Iran*, 25 (1987), pp. 91–105. See also references to Sabziwārī in Babayan's "The Waning of the Qizilbash," pp. 85, 88, 246, notes 595, 283.

[40] See Tihrānī, *ibid.*, XI, pp. 289–90; XXI, p. 308; V, p. 57.

[41] S. 'Abd al-Ḥusayn Khātūnābādī, *Waqā'i al-Sinīn* (Tehran 1352 A.Hsh./1973), pp. 525–8, 529–30. Sabziwārī subsequently dedicated several essays to the new Shāh. See M.T. Dānish-pazhūh, ed., *Fihrist-i Kitābkhāna-i Markazī-yi Dānishgāh-i Tihrān* (Tehran 1340 A.Hsh./1961), X, pp. 1863–4; Hermann Ethé, *Catalogue of the Persian, Turkish, Hindustani and Pushtu Manuscripts in the Bodleian Library* (Oxford: Clarendon Press 1889), I, pp. 942–3.

[42] On attacks on Sabziwārī by 'Alī Riḍā Tajullī (d. 1085/1674), in an essay written sometime after 1081–2/1670–1, in which he argued for the prohibition (*taḥrīm*) of the prayer, criticized Fayḍ-i Kāshānī, and attacked Sabziwārī's philosophical tendencies, see Tihrānī, *ibid.*, XV,

court appointments, Sabziwārī did not. Instead, based at least on his essay on singing, he went on the offensive. Examination of Sabziwārī's essay on singing shows that he attempted to steer an intermediary course on the issue, between those unorthodox practices attributed to Sufi groups by Qummī, Mīr Lawḥī and Shaykh 'Alī and the complete forswearing of such expression as urged by all three scholars, even as he took special care to re-assert the authority of the key sources of Shī'ite Islam as interpreted according to the Uṣūlī school, and to affirm his own special capacity in that process. As Sabziwārī's essay in the main was devoted to discussion and rejection of the Uṣūlī-style arguments on offer in Shaykh 'Alī's *al-Durr* and *al-Sihām*, the controversy over singing seems to have been as much of an issue between Uṣūlis as between opponents and practitioners of singing and associated practices more generally.

Sabziwārī opens his Arabic-language essay[43] with a statement of his intention to cite both Koranic verses and *akhbār* from the Imāms on the prohibition of *ghinā'*, and statements from earlier Imāmī jurisprudents defining *ghinā'*. He notes that although Sunni jurisprudents have disagreed on the prohibition of *ghinā'*, Imāmī Shī'ites – citing, for example, Shaykh Ṭūsī (d. 460/1067), Ibn Idrīs (d. 598/1202), and 'Allāma Ḥillī – have prohibited it. Thus, citing Shaykh Tabrīsī's (d. 548/1154) condemnation of lying speech (*al-zūr*), Koran XXII:30 and XXV:72 were understood to refer to singing and Koran XXXI:6 was also held to have referred to and condemned *ghinā'*.

---

p. 77. See also Ja'fariyān, *Dīn va siyāsat*, pp. 128, 168. Ja'fariyān (pp. 170–1) suggests Tajullī held with the *takhyirī* position, whereas Tihrānī (*ibid.*) maintains he forbade the prayer.

Tajullī studied with the philosopher Ḥusayn Khwānsarī (d. 1099/1688), a student of Sabziwārī, husband of Sabziwārī's sister and close confident of the court. Khwānsarī opposed the performance of Friday prayer during the occultation, thus disagreeing with Sabziwārī, and also attacked him on certain philosophical issues. On Khwānsarī and Friday prayer, see Ja'fariyān, *Dīn va siyāsat*, pp. 40, 123. On Khwānsarī's philosophical dispute with Sabziwārī, see Dānish-pazhūh, *Fihrist-i Kitābkhāna*, III, pp. 242–3.

Sabziwārī encouraged another student, Surāb Tanukābunī (d. 1124/1712–13), to reply to Tajullī's Friday prayer essay. See Tihrānī, *ibid.*, XV, p. 80. He also took Sabziwārī's side in the philosophical dispute with Khwānsarī. See Dānish-pazhūh, *ibid.*, III, pp. 213–14. Surāb also defended his Friday prayer stance against 'Abdu'llāh Tūnī (d. 1071/1660–1), a *faqīh* who had opposed Friday prayer in an essay composed in 1058–60/1648–49, authored the Uṣūlī *al-Wāfiyya* in 1060/1649, and had been based in Iṣfahān and then Mashhad. See Tihrānī, *ibid.*, XV, pp. 80. On Tūnī, see Tihrānī, *ibid.*, XV, p. 74–5. See also Khātūnābādī, *ibid.*, p. 516. 'Abdu'llāh's brother Aḥmad was an opponent of both singing and Sufism generally. See Ḥurr-i 'Āmilī, *ibid.*, II, p. 23. Aḥmad Tūnī was alive when Ḥurr-i 'Āmilī penned the latter entry, but nothing is known of his death date. See also Tihrānī, *ibid.*, XI, p. 138; X, p. 204. In Aḥmad the circle is completed, from Friday prayer and philosophy back to anti-Sufi and anti-singing tracts.

[43] On the essay, see Tihrānī, *ibid.*, XVI, p. 61. That this essay was written sometime before 1087/1676–7 is attested to by Shaykh 'Alī's composition in that year of his *Tanbīh* in reply to this essay. It may also have been composed after the 1068/1658 *firmān* to Sabziwārī, referred to above, which made public the depth of his support at court. See also notes 15, 21 above.

Sabziwārī then cites nearly thirty *akhbār* from the Imāms attesting that in these instances the Prophet was referring to *ghinā'*,[44] adding that the occasional weakness in the chain of transmission (*isnād*) of these texts did not weaken the points being made therein.[45]

What about, says an opponent, those *akhbār* that praise a good voice and the embellishment (*ḥilya*) of the Koran therewith? The opponent then cites a number of texts.[46] This question, similar to that raised and dismissed by Shaykh 'Alī, suggests that at least some proponents of *ghinā'* were knowledgeable about the relevant textual evidence.

Sabziwārī, carefully distancing himself from supporters of such arguments, replies to each text cited. The first, he says, has a weak chain of authority (*sanad*) to support it. In any case, a good voice and the commendation of such a voice does not necessarily mean making musical entertainment (*iṭrāb*) and cantillation (*tarjī'*), which are what singing (*ghinā'*) involves. The second text was problematic, mainly because of the inclusion of Sahl ibn Ziyād, whom al-Najāshī (d. 450/1058–9) had denounced as an extremist (*ghālī*) and not a true Shī'ite. The third text he also condemned as weak, citing Ibn Idrīs. The fourth is best explained, he says, as an example of pious dissimulation or *taqiyya*, noting that the Umayyads and 'Abbasids would listen to music. The fifth had a weak chain of authority. The sixth, he says, does not in fact indicate what was claimed. The Sunni traditionalists, he adds, make many statements, but none of them really relate to *ghinā'*. Indeed, the Sunnis quote the Prophet as saying "embellish (*zayyinū*) the Koran with your voices," but this is a misquotation and Ibn al-Athīr (d. 606/1210) himself, he says, stated that it did not refer to either *taṭrīb* (vocal chanting) or *taḥzīn* (vocal ornamentation). The Sunnis have practised *ghinā'* in the past, and Ghazālī also made some statements about *ghinā'* being composed of a pleasant voice. But, Sabziwārī continues, *ghinā'* is not being forbidden on the basis of its being pleasant or melodious (*mawzūn*). Nor is there harm in causing understanding or moving the heart.

Having dismissed this argument, clearly reflective of the available arguments for singing, and thus put some distance between himself and its practitioners,

---

[44] His citations include many from Kulaynī's chapter on *ghinā'* and other sections. See Kulaynī, *ibid.*, 6: 431/6; 6: 431/3; 6: 431/4; 6: 433/13; 6: 433/15; 6: 433/16; 6: 432/10; 6: 431/2; 6: 432/8; 6: 432/9; 6: 433/12; 6: 434/18; 6: 434/23; 6: 435/25; 2: 614/3; 5: 120/5; 5: 120/4; 5: 120/6; 5: 120/7; 5: 119/1; 4: 41/7; 6: 434/19; 6: 435/ 2; 6: 436/7.

[45] It is perhaps such statements that led – or allowed – Mīr Lawḥī to cite Sabziwārī as having forbidden *ghinā'* when, as will be seen, in fact he argued for an intermediate position. See also Babayan, "The Waning of the Qizilbash," p. 246, n. 595, citing this reference. Alternately, given that this ruling must have been made before Mīr Lawḥī's composition of this essay in 1650 and that only later did Sabziwārī achieve the real prominence at court that perhaps allowed some 'flexibility', Sabziwārī may later have 'refined' his position to that on offer in the present essay. See also n. 15 above.

[46] These include Kulaynī, *ibid.*, II, p. 615/4; II, p. 616/11; part of *ibid.*, II, p. 616/13; *ibid.*, II, p. 614/2.

Sabziwārī then attempts to broaden the categories of what is permitted by defining carefully exactly what was forbidden. In the process he addresses many of Shaykh ʿAlī's own arguments. Sabziwārī notes that a number of matters must be addressed. First, citing ʿAllāma Ḥillī and al-Shahīd al-Awwal (d. 786/1384), Sabziwārī states that the Shīʿite *ʿulamāʾ* have clearly declared that the *ghināʾ* which is forbidden is the raising of the voice (*madd al-ṣawt*), comprising enraptured cantillation (*al-tarjīʿ al-muṭrib*) whether of poetry or the Koran, though all allow for the chanting of a camel driver. Sabziwārī cites Shaykh ʿAlī's own ancestor ʿAlī al-Karakī as stating that al-Shahīd al-Awwal had said that the issue was not merely the raising of the voice but the heart's inclining to the point where it is *muṭrib,* or enraptured, because of the song (*tarjīʿ*).

Sabziwārī cautions that the term *al-ṭarab* ('emotion and delight', from whence the word *muṭrib*, musician is derived) is not merely happiness (*al-surūr*), as some claim. Indeed, he says, the experts in language are careful to define *al-ṭarab* as what is induced by extremes of sadness or happiness, and cantillation (*tarjīʿ*) as the wavering of one's voice (*taraddud al-ṣawt*) in the throat. Sometimes, he notes, the jurisconsults (*fuqahāʾ*) consider these two restrictions in their definitions of *ghināʾ*, sometimes they merely forbid musical entertainment (*iṭrāb*) – citing Ibn Idrīs – and sometimes they focus on *al-tarjīʿ*, citing ʿAllāma Ḥillī. The grammarians – most of whom, it should be noted, were Sunnis – focus on the connection with *iṭrāb*. Terms such as *al-taghannin* (serenading), *al-taṭrīb* (vocal chanting), *al-tarjīʿ* (cantillation) and *al-laḥn* (melody, rhythm, mode) have similar meanings and are defined by reference to the other terms, Sabziwārī states. Thus, when some Shīʿite scholars discuss *ghināʾ* they refer to the common linguistic usage (*ʿurf*) to define what constitutes *ghināʾ* and declare it forbidden (*ḥarām*) – an argument put forth by Shaykh ʿAlī – even if no musical delight (*ṭarab*) is experienced. Al-Shahīd al-Thānī, one of Shaykh ʿAlī's own forbears, asserts Sabziwārī, states that singing (*ghināʾ*) is the raising of the voice (*madd al-ṣawt*), comprising enraptured cantillation (*al-tarjīʿ al-muṭrib*), which is called *ghināʾ* in the common usage (*ʿurf*) even if there is no rapture (*ṭarab*), whether this involves poetry or the Koran.

Second – again addressing a point advanced by Shaykh ʿAlī – it is claimed that the chanting of camel drivers is an exception. There are some who do not recognize this exception and declare even such singing to be illicit (*taḥrīm al-ghināʾ*). Sabziwārī, in a remark clearly designed to point to the unorthodox nature of his opponent's sources, says he knows no proof for this exception except some Sunni *akhbār*.

Third, there is the practice of hiring a female singer for a wedding. If she does not prattle and men do not have intercourse with her, Shaykhs Mufīd (d. 413/1022), Ṭūsī and Ibn Idrīs permit this. Here Sabziwārī cites a supporting text from Shaykh Ṭūsī.[47]

---

[47] The text is found with similar *akhbār* in Kulaynī, *ibid.*, V, p. 120/3.

Fourth, Shaykh Ṭūsī notes that some scholars have made an exception of the elegies to Imām Ḥusayn. Sabziwārī says he has not found anything on this except what Ṭūsī claimed, but that the generality of the *akhbār* forbid this.

It is Sabziwārī's fifth point which perhaps repays the most consideration. Here, by rigorously asserting what is forbidden in some detail, Sabziwārī leaves room for such associated practices as are not specifically covered by that prohibition. Thus he directly challenges Shaykh 'Alī's effort to extend the general prohibition to so many specific, associated practices.

Sabziwārī states that it is a common practice in his own time among ordinary people for the Koran, devotional supplications (*adhkār*), and other prayers to be sung with musical melodies (*alḥān*), tones (*naghmāt*) and ornamental vibrato (*taḥrīrāt*). This may, he says, lead to the reading of pseudo-Sufi poetry and such types of melodies. This practice, in turn, may be transmitted from the common people (*'awwām*) to the educated intelligentsia (*khawāṣṣ*), learned in natural sciences and religion (*ahl al-'ilm wa'l-diyāna*), and then onto those endowed with piety and justice (*al-'adāla*). The latter sometimes tend to the view that the singing of the Koran, devotional prayers (*adhkār*) theosophical poetry (*ash'ār al-ḥikma*) and religious exhortation is not *ghinā'*. Rather *ghinā'* is particular to the people of entertainment (*al-laḥw*) and debauchery (*al-fujūr*) in their profane gatherings (*majālis*) for sinful purposes (*al-mā'ṣī*), wine-drinking and such like, or, more generally, pertains to the utterances common among the community of professional musicians (*ahl al-musīqa*) in their exultations (*al-ta'zīmāt*). Sometimes, they define *ghinā'* according to common linguistic usage (*'urf*) – again, an argument offered by Shaykh 'Alī. But the specialists in this usage (*ahl al-'urf*), says Sabziwārī, do not consider this to be *ghinā'*. Sometimes they say the meaning of *ghinā'* is not known, without certifying that these things constitute *ghinā'*.

Where Shaykh 'Alī had argued for the extension of the prohibition on *ghinā'* to cover all associated practices, Sabziwārī notes that the legal principle (*al-aṣl*) on which all such things depend is permissibility (*al-ibāḥa*) until prohibition is established for certain.[48] It is essential, he claims, that one know Arabic to understand what is intended by a term. Continuing the emphasis on Uṣūlī methodology as imperative in such analyses, Sabziwārī states that the non-Arab must refer to the Arabs and language specialists (*ahl al-lisān*). The non-Arab cannot speculate and say that such and such an Arabic word is from the common Arabic parlance (*'urf al-'Arab*) or that it means this or that in Arabic unless his arguments are based on the evidence of the language specialists. The latter derive their understanding from such Arabic-language sources as the Koran, *ḥadīth*, the poetry of those who are eloquent, sermons, treatises, and reliable books. Al-Jawharī (d. 393–400/1002–10), Sabziwārī

---

[48] An Akhbārī might well have been more cautious on such a controversial issue. See my "The Nature of the Akhbārī/Uṣūlī Dispute," pt. 1, p. 39, notes 9, 51.

states, says the non-Arabs consider rhyming couplets of poetry (*dubayt*) to be *ghinā'*, as, in fact, they do most poetry. Again, responding to arguments raised by Shaykh 'Alī, Sabziwārī continues that most of "our jurisconsults (*fuqahā'*) say that *ghinā'* includes more than just the Koran and poetry, as do many Sunnis." Indeed, Sabziwārī notes that in his definition of *ghinā'*, Ghazālī – who had been attacked at length by Shaykh 'Alī – in seven sections of his *Iḥyā'* only once referred to emotions. He then notes that al-Sharīf al-Murtaḍā (d. 436/1044), a teacher of Shaykh Ṭūsī and himself a great rationalist scholar, detailed this disagreement among the Sunnis about Sufi *samā'* and the use of musical tones (*naghmāt*) and pleasant voices during the recitation of prayers (*adhkār*) and at other times. There are some who cite traditions and texts showing that *ghinā'* is forbidden. Others reject these texts as weak. The latter, he says, know the Arabic language and consider such invocations (*adhkār*) and poetry to be religious exhortation. He notes that Ghazālī's *Iḥyā'* details the disagreement between the two. Sunni *ḥadīth* are often cited as forbidding *ghinā'* since they contain evidence that the use of pleasant musical melodies (*alḥān*) in recitation of the Koran constitutes *ghinā'*. Musicians' statements support this thesis, as they account melodies composed in musical modes (*al-alḥān al-muṭriba*) as *ghinā'*.

This, he says, is what he has learned from study of the prohibition of *tarjī'* (cantillation) in the Koran in some of the aforementioned traditions and the censure of *taghannin* (chanting) in the Koran in others. There is no doubt, he concludes, that these citations support the dominant opinion.

Then, placing the discussion squarely on the level of what constitutes proper jurisprudence, Sabziwārī states that the objective (*ghayya*) in knowing religious terminology (*al-alfāẓ al-shar'iyya*) and its religious directives (*aḥkām*) in his own age is rational deduction (*al-ẓann*), but only rarely is the pursuit of the path of religious learning (*'ilm*) regarding the ordinances (*aḥkām*) not subject to corruption, and whoever claims the opposite is in error.

An opponent suggests that perhaps the philologists (*ahl al-lugha*) – who have been heretofore cited as cautious about the definition of *ghinā'* – may not be either correct or just in their faith, and therefore not reliable. Sabziwārī replies that the wise of every age agree that it is correct to refer to the skilful practitioners of a particular field (*aṣḥāb al-ṣinā'a*). This applies to language as well, in the past or present, in every age and period. Indeed, he continues, Shī'ite *'ulamā'* – citing the traditionist Ibn Bābawayh and Shaykh Ṭūsī and Ibn Idrīs – base their explanations of Arabic terminology on these specialists and refer to their statements to formulate religious directives (*aḥkām*). The Sunnis also referred to language specialists.

But, his opponent persists, in effect again appealing to common linguistic parlance (*'urf*), in the present time what Sabziwārī is discussing is not currently called *ghinā'* by the Arabs in their countries or territories. Sabziwārī replies that his opponent is listening to those unable to define *ghinā'*. Present-day references contain many falsifications and therefore cannot be used as definitive proof (*ḥujja*). Finally, he says these people are deviating from what was professed by their predecessors. It might be possible, he continues, based on the previous Koranic references to *al-zūr*, and considering the traditions (*akhbār*) defining this as singing (*ghinā'*) and the consequent injunction to avoid it, that each individual conscious of his religious duties (*mukallif*) was thus enjoined to abstain from *ghinā'* as well as its associated components. This would be based on definitive knowledge (*'ilm*). On rational deduction (*al-ẓann*), however, these other components are not forbidden because the underlying principle (*al-aṣl*) is the exclusion from prohibition of components about which there may be doubt.

His opponent then challenges Sabziwārī that religious duty (*taklīf*) requires avoidance of all those activities deduced (*madhnūna*) to be associated with *ghinā'* – perhaps the key argument advanced by Shaykh 'Alī. Sabziwārī replies that duty is a single entity made up of multiple parts, that the command to avoid may refer to one or the other part, but the principle requires definitive knowledge (*'ilm*). In sum, Sabziwārī concludes, the ideal in "our own time" is being cautious and limiting oneself to what is certain (*al-yaqīn*) – a principle often identified with the Akhbāris, but here used by an obviously Uṣūlī scholar. Indeed, citing the universally accepted *ḥadīth* (*maqbūl*) of 'Umar b. Ḥanẓala, Sabziwārī says the believer is enjoined to hesitation (*wuqūf*) when facing uncertainties (*shubahāt*).[49]

Sabziwārī then resorts to a statement of the Uṣūlī view of the nature of the community during the Occultation, thereby reasserting the authority of the *mujtahids* in this period. "Know," he says, "that the people are divided into two groups, a qualified authority on Divine Law (*mujtahid*) who has attained the ability to engage in rational demonstration (*istidlāl*) and is therefore deserving of being referred to on issues, and the follower of authority (*muqallid*) who has not attained this ability. It is the task of the *mujtahid* to make every effort of his own to consider the issues and take note of all the various reasons (*dalā'il*) and evidences (*madārik*) available and study different aspects of opinions and the facets of thoughts, avoiding caprice and refraining from prejudice and intolerance and idle chatter."

"The *muqallid* who has not reached the degree of rational demonstration must refer to the directives (*aḥkām*) of the '*ulamā*'." He must be careful from whom he takes these rulings, however, as corruption and hypocrisy abound in man. As he must act on the basis of the statements of the *'ulamā'*, the *muqallid* must distinguish between clerics who are knowledgeable and those who are ignorant. In this process, the *muqallid* is reminded that he is not to content

[49] This text, usually noted as having been cited by Uṣūlīs, has been shown to have been of use to both Akhbārīs and Uṣūlīs in this period. See my "The Nature of the Akhbārī/Uṣūlī Dispute," part 2, p. 255, n. 15.

himself with reference to one single statement, but must also examine the secondary issues and expend time in consideration and investigation to understand the different dimensions of opinions. He is then to be cautious and follow the path of certainty, and in this path there is salvation. Much of the remaining argument – including the many statements of the Imāms cited – similarly reasserts the authority of the *'ulamā'*.

Sabziwārī's essay reveals an effort to steer a middle course on *ghinā'* in particular and within the anti-Sufi polemic more generally. Like Shaykh 'Alī, Sabziwārī had an educated opponent – indeed at least two. Their arguments, one opposing and the other favouring a ban on singing, reflect different positions on the matter within the community of the day. In response to these, on the one hand Sabziwārī is clearly concerned to distance himself from the proponent of singing, to avoid being tarnished with the allegations of Sufistic, *darvīsh* behaviour – indiscriminately involving more than merely an interest in singing – being wielded against those inclined to philosophy and gnostic theosophy (*'irfān*) in both *Ḥadīqa* and *Radd*. Sabziwārī was conscious that his own interest in *'irfān* and his links to *'irfānī* clerics, as detailed above, had left him just as vulnerable to such allegations as Shaykh Bahā'ī had been. As such, Sabziwārī's essay paralleled efforts by his contemporaries, such as Fayḍ-i Kāshānī, to avoid association with the *darvīsh* practices common and, indeed, on the rise in this period.[50]

At the same time, the Uṣūlī-style arguments and analyses offered in Sabziwārī's essay, either by Shaykh 'Alī himself or a like-minded figure in another setting, suggest that the confrontation in this period over such Sufi-style practices and doctrines was as much between Uṣūlī scholars as, in this instance, between the allegedly *darvīsh* practitioners of *ghinā'* and their detractors. Underlying Sabziwārī's rebuttal of his opponent is a clear adherence to and utilization of Uṣūlī modes of analysis, together with an implicit assertion of his own superior position both jurisprudentially and in terms of his own court status, scholarly affiliations and credentials, as compared with those of his opponent.

---

[50] See, for example, Fayḍ's *Muḥākama* (composed *c.* 1072/1660–1) in which he condemned Sufi excesses and also his *al-Inṣāf*, finished in 1083/1672, wherein he continued his anti-Sufi polemic but, clearly on the defensive after his resignation from his court-appointed post, admitted that he had himself shown perhaps too much interest in *taṣawwuf* in his younger days. The polemic's continuation, the attention given the *darvīsh* cults in such sources as *Qiṣāṣ al-Khāqānī*, and the comments of Chardin over this period suggest the millenarian/ Sufi movement retained its vitality well past the death of 'Abbās II, in conjunction with the worsening socio-economic crises. On these essays of Fayḍ, see Ja'fariyān, *ibid.*, pp. 292–5. See also the sources cited in n. 4 above and the essay by L. Lewisohn in this volume, pp. 119–28.

CONCLUSION

As it developed throughout the middle and later years of the seventeenth century, anti-Sufi polemic was the product of a combination of socio-economic, political and spiritual trends and events specific to the Safavid period. The polemic expressed itself in a series of essays written by middle-ranking clerics over two phases, with several essays forming a 'bridge' between the first and the second. The first wave focused mainly on the messianic veneration of Abū Muslim among the urban commercial and artisan classes, the product of a spiritual quest generated by the impact on these groups of socio-economic and political trends and events already set in motion by the death of 'Abbās I in 1038/1629, and the apparent support given this veneration by certain clerics – especially Taqī Majlisī – who were part of the larger alliance between the court and certain *'irfānī*-oriented clerics. In the Mab'as massacre of 1041/1632 its affiliated scholars suffered accordingly.

The underlying socio-economic crises continued apace, however, culminating in 1054/1644 in further political change, the rise of a reconfigured court–clerical alliance which attempted afresh to grapple with both those crises and the concomitant spiritual turmoil. The evolving spiritual crises and the re-appearance of this alliance between the court and *'irfānī*-oriented clerics necessitated a reappraisal of the anti-Sufi polemic by its promoters. In response to these, and indeed provoking further changes in both, there ensued among middle-ranking clerical critics a gradual shift away from concentration on the veneration of Abū Muslim to attacks specifically directed against the unorthodox doctrines and practices of Sufi orders that were appearing on the urban scene as part of the spiritual malaise. Much as the old, the new polemic served both as a challenge to the disaffected urban elements to redirect their attention to orthodoxy and – as part of the attack on the clergy–court alliance – a challenge to those clerics inclined to *'irfān* and to serving the court to repudiate such interests and connections.

Several of the essays of this period which formed the new polemic, *Ḥadīqat al-Shī'a*, *Salvat al-Shī'a* and *Radd-i Ṣūfiyya* – the first two traversing the first and second waves, and the third marking the second wave – featured a series of allegations of unorthodox behaviour among these orders. In *Ḥadīqat al-Shī'a* and *Radd-i Ṣūfiyya*, the Sufis were accused of bizarre, if not clearly deviant, sexual practices. The attention given to *ghinā'* in this evolving polemic shows that music, singing and associated practices were among the many unorthodox practices attributed to the Sufi orders.

While it is clear from these, and other sources, that there was widespread, growing interest in *darvīsh*ism in this period, there is little "disinterested" information to corroborate the aberrant sexual behaviour alleged in these works. Both the frequent references in these works to, and the subsequent development of a separate polemic on *ghinā'* – relatively less objectionable –

and associated practices, may well, however, point to the popularity of singing and music in this period of socio-economic and political – and therefore spiritual – turmoil.

This separate polemic on *ghinā'*, typified by the confrontation between Shaykh 'Alī and Bāqir Sabziwārī discussed above, unfortunately reveals less about the details, let alone the popularity, of the practice itself on the 'popular,' or any other, level, than it does about the predilections of the protagonists. Sabziwārī's disavowal of the legality of the more extreme aspects of *ghinā'*, using overtly Uṣūlī analytical tools, demonstrates that the middle-ranking clerics' ascription of *darvīsh* tendencies to members of the court–clergy alliance, in effect to challenge the latter's *'irfānī* inclinations, had touched a nerve in one such cleric. Sabziwārī's defensiveness on this matter may account for his earlier *fatwā*, cited by Mīr Lawḥī in his *Salvat al-Shī'a* – and perhaps an earlier essay as well – on *ghinā'*, as well as the *fatwā* of Nā'inī, another student of Bahā'ī, also cited therein. At work in this polemic, then, is a conflict within Usūlism, the differentiation perhaps usefully understood by the positioning of the likes of Qummī and Shaykh 'Alī, and Sabziwārī himself, within the hierarchy of the religious community of the time.

One may observe a non-Persian connection to the latter wave of anti-Sufi, and especially anti-singing, polemic. Qummī spent his formative years outside Iran, as did Shaykh 'Alī. Neither was involved in the maelstrom of court/clergy politics which informed the careers and contributions of Bahā'ī, Majlisī, Fayḍ and Sabziwārī. In the end, these practitioners of elite 'high theosophical' *'irfānī* discourse in the later part of the seventeenth century – Usūlis to the core – were as much put on the defensive by other Usūlis not linked to the same political alignments, particular discussions or levels of inquiry. While these divisions do not apparently correspond to the divisions among Uṣūlis charted by al-Samāhijī in the early eighteenth century, they reveal interesting splits within Safavid Uṣūlism in this earlier period, which merit further study.

The Ni'matu'llāhī Order Under Safavid Suppression and in Indian Exile

TERRY GRAHAM

I. INTRODUCTION

When in the city of Tabrīz in the summer of 1501 Ismā'īl Ṣafavī (d. 1524), teenage hereditary leader of the Safavid Sufi order, declared himself shāh of Iran, he established the Twelve-Imām Shī'ite sect of Islam as the state religion. Up to that time, for nearly two and a half centuries of Mongol Īlkhānid and Timurid rule, religion had been relatively free, with the majority of Sufi orders existing within the Sunni community. However, with the advent of the Safavid dynasty, one of the world's first ideological dictatorships was founded – its most important predecessor having been Catholic Spain. Every Muslim organization was required to declare itself conformist with the state ideology. As a result, the Sufi orders had two choices: either declare themselves officially adherent to the Twelve-Imām Shī'ite sect or else quit Persian soil altogether and relocate somewhere else. The Qādiriyya and the Naqshbandiyya chose the latter course, while the Dhahabiyya, the Nūrbakhshiyya and the Ni'matu'llāhiyya opted for the former alternative.

As the tail of dogma wags the dog of the purpose for which the dogma was designed, so the Safavids' ideological zeal made them oblivious to their dervish origins, politicizing their once-mystical purpose to the point where, contrary to the Sufi principle of universal tolerance, they came to suppress any expressions which were different from their own extremist Shī'ite doctrinal position. As their grip tightened, from the time that their chief Shāh Ismā'īl seized power in 1501 they forced the existing Sufi orders to choose whether or not to accept the new Imāmite dispensation.[1] If the Orders were committed to Sunnism, as the Qādirīs and Naqshbandīs were, they were driven into the

---

[1] See A. Arjomand, "The Suppression of Sufism," in *The Shadow of God and the Hidden Imam* (Chicago: University of Chicago Press 1984), pp. 112–19.

mountainous or desert fringes of Iran, such as Kurdistān. Baluchistan, and the Khurāsānian border region with Afghanistan.

The Safavid accession to the throne came some three-quarters of a century after the death of Shāh Ni'matu'llāh Walī (834/1431), founder of the order bearing his name.[2] At the time of Shāh Ni'matu'llāh's death his following encompassed the entire Persianate world, from Anatolia to the Caucasus and Central Asia over to the frontiers of China down to the Persian Gulf and across into the heart of India. The core lay principally in a crescent running from northern Khurāsān and its principal cities of Mashhad and Herāt, the latter being the Timurid capital, governed by the benign Shāhrukh Shāh who, if not a disciple, was deeply, if not affectionately, respectful of Shāh Ni'matu'llāh, while his son Muḥammad Bāysunghur was almost certainly an initiate of the founder's son Shāh Khalīlu'llāh.[3] It then ran southwards to the region of Kirmān then swept eastwards to Yazd and ultimately Shīrāz, the city where the founder had pursued his studies steeped in the jurisprudence of the Sunnite Shāfi'ī school[4] which was the "intellectual milieu frequented by Shāh Ni'matu'llāh."[5] Beyond this east–southeast–southern crescent there was an important following in the northwestern region of Azerbaijan, centred on the southern metropolis of Tabrīz and the northern one of Shirvan (in the former Soviet republic of Azerbaijan).

Though the Kirmān–Māhān area had the advantage of being accessible to both Herāt and the subcontinent, the Timurid regime was weakening and the region became afflicted with growing disorder, vulnerable to raids by restless Baluchi tribesmen and under a hostile governor increasingly flexing his own

---

[2] See Terry Graham, "Shāh Ni'matullāh Walī: founder of the Ni'matullāhī Sufi Order," in *The Heritage of Sufism*, II: The *Legacy of Medieval Persian Sufism*, ed. L. Lewisohn (Oxford: Oneworld 1999), pp. 173–90.

[3] Ma'ṣūm 'Alī Shāh Shīrāzī, *Ṭarā'iq al-ḥaqā'iq*, ed. M.J Maḥjūb (Tehran: 1345 A.Hsh. / 1966), III, p. 104.

[4] His in-law, 'Aḍud ad-Dīn Ījī (d. 756/1355), was author of the classical summa of Sunni Ash'arite theology *Kitāb al-Mawāqif*, and would have been teaching at the same Shāfi'ite school attended by the founder; while his grandson Nūr ad-Dīn Aḥmad Ījī, who considered Shāh Ni'matu'llāh to be part of the Sunni Shāfi'ī elite of Shiraz, married his granddaughter Khadīja (d. Mecca 1469–70), that is, the daughter of the founder's son Shāh Khalīlu'llāh. A cousin of the jurisprudent, Sayyid Nūr ad-Dīn Muḥammad Ījī (d. 1394) was a shaykh of Shāh Ni'matu'llāh, impressed no less a figure than the awesome Ṭaymūr-i Lang (Tamerlane) with his spiritual authority, while his son Shaykh Abū Sa'īd Ījī, as a deputy of the founder, became a spiritual guide of the poet Ḥāfiẓ' beloved ruler Shāh Shujā' Muẓaffarī. Another Ni'matu'llāhī shaykh in Shiraz was the leading commentator on the *Mawāqif*, and one of the founder's closest friends, Mīr Sayyid Sharīf Zayn ad-Dīn 'Alī b. Muḥammad Jurjānī (d. 816/ 1413), who was appointed to a teaching post at the same Shāfi'ite school in 1377 by Shāh Shujā'. His other famous work is his *Ta'rīfāt* (Definitions), a sourcebook for terminology in a number of disciplines, amongst the most valuable being the terms relating to Sufism.

[5] Jean Aubin, *Matériaux pour la biographie de Shah Ni'matullah Wali Kermani* (Tehran–Paris: Institut Français d'Iranologie de Téhéran 1982; rprt), p. 2.

muscles in a bid for autonomy. Thus, when the founder's powerful friend and Timurid family-member, Sikandar b. 'Umar Shaykh, the governor of the region of Yazd at the time, offered Shāh Ni'matu'llāh land and tax relief in Taft, a town in the vicinity of the city of Yazd, he snapped it up as an alternative base. The governor eventually consigned four years of tax revenue to aid in the construction of the *khānaqāh* in Taft.[6] The site was a country estate around the town of Taft, 25 kilometres from Yazd and hence accessible to that city's famous silk-weaving workshops, so that silk cultivation could provide a product that Ni'matu'llāhī merchants were able to market at home and export abroad.

The tracing of the presence and activities of the Ni'matu'llāhī Sufi order in both Persia and India from the beginning of the sixteenth to the end of the eigthteenth century poses very much the challenge of serious detective work. We have clear, well-documented histories of the fifteenth century from the time of the founder, Shāh Ni'matu'llāh's, death in 834/1431 to the establishment of the Safavid dynasty of rulers in Iran in 1502. Thereafter, the vicissitudes of the order in Iran have still received a reasonable amount of documentation, insofar as it had made a pact with the ideologically oriented Shī'ite government, in declaring itself officially Shī'ite, a reverse of the situation elsewhere in the Muslim world, where normally the minority Shī'ite sect was forced to adopt a policy of *taqiyya* (pious dissimulation) in order to survive.

As if with a certain prescience, Shāh Ni'matu'llāh set about laying down principles of practice so that the order could maintain itself on the practical plane, whatever the pressures brought to bear on it; and at the same time, he went about ensuring the persistence of the basic structure of the order. When he was invited to the Deccan in central India he encouraged the immediate members of his family, including his son and successor, to take up residence in exile there under the protection of the court of Aḥmad Shāh Bahmanī (*reg.* 1422–36), his disciple. As a result, the heads of the order, the *quṭb*s, or 'poles', carried on in exile, while the 'rump' of the order remained in Iran. A situation perhaps unique in the history of Sufism developed, in which the body of an order continued to operate shorn of its head, which survived separately in a distant clime.

Well before the end of the seventeenth century in both Iran and the Deccan the Ni'matu'llāhīs dropped out of history. In Iran the headless order had made a pact with the establishment, which ultimately chose not to observe its end of the agreement, forcing the order to make a show of closing up shop. In India the bodiless heads had actually become part of the establishment of the successive regimes which ruled the site of their *jāgīr*s, or 'land-grants'. These regimes were predominantly Shī'ite in orientation and naturally sympathetic to, though not actively allied with, Safavid Iran, reinforcing the identification

[6] Aubin, *Matériaux*, p. 8.

of the order with Shīʿism by virtue of a twofold association with that sect, though sectarianism had been actively rejected as a principle by the Sunni Shafiʿi Shāh Niʿmatu'llāh himself.[7]

It is only with the first glimmerings of a potential revival from its moribund state that the order begins to emerge from the shadows of its dormancy in the mid-eighteenth century. The earliest hint for the researcher is a shrine called the *Takht-i Maḥmūd* (Palace of Maḥmūd) near Hyderabad in the east-central Deccan. This turns out to be the tomb of the first *quṭb* of the order who was not a descendant of the founder. The imposing nature of this tomb, which is also the burial place of the next two successors, who are also the last heads of the order in India before its restoration in Iran, foreshadows, as it were, the head being planted once again on the body during the great revival at the end of the eighteenth century.

Thus, we have a tale with a glorious beginning and an equally brilliant end, but with a comatose mid-section. Of course, this obscure middle part, being fraught with mystery, presents its own intrigue, enticing the researcher to play the detective in sorting out whatever evidence is unearthable.

II. POLITICS OF PRIMOGENITURE: THE FAMILY OF SHĀH KHALĪLU'LLĀH

Although it is the response of the Niʿmatu'llāhīs to the course of events in Safavid Persia and Mughal India which is at issue, a word on the role of Shāh Khalīlu'llāh, the founder's only child and his designated successor, is in order here. He was born in January 1374 in the village of Kūhbanān, the first place where Shāh Niʿmatu'llāh settled when he arrived in the Kirmān region after leaving Herāt. When Shāh Khalīlu'llāh acceded to the position of mastership on his father's death, it was purely pro forma, for from early on it was clear that Shāh Niʿmatu'llāh had his son in mind to succeed him. The founder entertained long-held intentions in this respect, as indicated in several verses of his poetry, such as this paternal counsel:

> Travel the Way, my noble Khalīlu'llāh;
>   in every way together with everyone.
> Gather disciples and cheerfully proclaim,
>   "There is no god but God, just He alone!"[8]

The son was thus groomed during the course of half a century for the successorship, and when he finally succeeded his father he was already a

---

[7] As he himself wrote in his *Dīvān;* see Sayyid Nūr al-Dīn Shāh Niʿmatu'llāh Walī-yi Kirmānī, *Kulliyyāt-i Shāh Niʿmatu'llāh Walī*, ed. J. Nūrbakhsh (Tehran: Intishārāt-i Khānaqāh Niʿmatu'llāhī 1361 A.Hsh./1982), p. 859.

[8] Cited by Javād Nūrbakhsh, *Zindagī u āthār-i Quṭb al-muwaḥḥidīn Janāb-i Shāh Niʿmatu'llāh-i Valī-yi Kirmānī*, ed. Hasan Kubārī (Tehran: 1337 A.Hsh./1958), p. 93.

Plate 7: The Chaukhandī of Ḥaḍrat Khalīl'ullāh. From G. Yazdani, *Bidar: Its History and Monuments*. Delhi: Barsidass 1995. Pl. 84.

respected figure in Timurid government and intellectual circles. In his own relationship with his son, Shāh Ni'matu'llāh seems to have concentrated on the more material familial and administrative matters, keeping him by his side to the very end. Even when such an important mission as a representation of his spiritual presence in India came up, when Aḥmad Shāh requested that Shāh Khalīlu'llāh come to his court in the Deccan, the founder sidestepped the request by sending his eldest grandson, Mīr Ḍiyā' al-Dīn Nūr-Allāh instead. Aḥmad Shāh gave his daughter's hand in marriage to Mīr Ḍiyā', who in turn undertook the spiritual training of her brother, the crown prince 'Alā' al-Dīn.

Historians and scholars are at variance in their apprisal of Shāh Khalīlu'llāh's personality. Jean Aubin remarks how "between a father dying at the age of 100 and sons and grandsons embarking on an active political life, in Iran, as well as India, Burhānuddīn Ḫalīlullah leaves the impression, perhaps erroneous, of not having a very distinguished personality."[9] In contrast, 'Alī Ṭabāṭabā'ī in his *Burhān al-ma'āthir* depicts Shāh Khalīl as a "stone-drunk ecstatic (*sarmast*)," so he seems to have had a rapturous dimension, as well.[10] Whatever his personal qualities or lack of them, the selection of the son as successor could certainly not be attributed to any lack of worthy candidates, for there was plenty of spiritual talent among the founder's many followers. It was probably simply a matter of the politics of primogeniture, for Wā'iḍī lists forty-two *khalīfa*s, that is deputies of the master of the Order, who were given permission to initiate and to train disciples.

Amongst these individuals Wā'iḍī mentions first the founder's son Shāh Khalīlu'llāh, then his four sons, the third of whom is Shāh Muḥibbu'llāh, who ultimately became his successor, and then Aḥmad Shāh Walī ('the Friend of God' or 'Saint' in conventional Western usage), the royal patron of the founder's family in the Deccan, whose tomb is still a site of visitation, as those of other saints throughout the subcontinent.[11] After these six individuals comes a list of thirty-six more names, including the formidable Shāh Qāsim Anwār. The roster indicates the broad reach of the discipleship in the founder's time, with names representing such far-flung cities as Tirmidh to the north-east (in present-day Tajikistan) to Shirvan in the north-west (now in the former Soviet republic of Azerbaijan) down to Shīrāz in Fars to the south-east, and specifying individuals with authority in regions even farther afield, such as Kabul towards the Indian border, Badakhshan on the Chinese frontier, and Anatolia towards the Mediterranean, two areas still within the range of Timurid control. There are shaykhs from Mashhad and Ṭūs in Khurāsān, from Tūn and Ṭabas in the middle of the barren Kavir, from Iṣfahān in central Iran, nearly a century away from being the Safavid capital; from Gilan on the

---

[9] Aubin, "La Famille Ni'matullahī," *Studia Iranica* 20/2 (1991), p. 245.

[10] 'Alī Tabataba'ī, *Burhān-i ma'āthir*, ed. G. Yazdani (Hyderabad 1936), p. 271.

[11] Yazdani, *Bidar: Its History and Monuments* (Delhi: Barsidass 1995), pp. 105–14.

Caspian Sea in northern Iran. This wide geographical scope indicates that had the order had the potential to encompass the vastness of the entire empire at the time.[12]

It is also clear that the family politics of primogeniture played the fundamental role in the selection of the masters of the Ni'matu'llāhiyya from its inception. In terms of the establishment, however, such legitimacy based on familial filiation was to continue to be a feature of the leadership of the order for the entire period of its existence under Safavid repression and Indian exile.[13] By intermarrying with royalty in India and carrying the cachet of *sajjāda-nishīn*ship[14] there, and through acquiring status as landowners and merchants in south-eastern Iran, the 'holy family' of the founder and his kin were able to maintain the hollow political framework which could be filled in due course by those truly charismatic figures who were to arise to revive the order in the early eighteenth century. Hereditary successorship, in those Persian orders that adopted it – namely, the Ni'matu'llāhiyya, Dhahabiyya, Ṣafawiyya and the Nūrbakhshiyya – became identified with the Shī'ite idea of the leader being either a representative of the imāmate, as in the case of Twelve-Imām Shī'ism, or the actual embodiment thereof, as in the case of the Ismā'īlīs, or Seven-Imām Shī'ites.[15]

After the respective deaths of Timur and Shāh Ni'matu'llāh, the succession of Shāhrukh brought a slackening of the reins of government and the resultant assertion of interests on the part of provincial governors. In particular, the governor of Kirmān, jealous of the favours heaped by the Timurid rulers on the Ni'matu'llāhīs, took advantage of the weakening of the central power to cut back the tax exemptions which had been the monarchs' policy towards Sufi organizations, apparently even seizing finances and expropriating goods and sending them on to the capital, Herāt.

Thus, Shāh Khalīlu'llāh had every reason to go to the Timurid court at Herāt to fight his corner and retrieve the benefits accruing to the family and the following of the order. However, Shāhrukh himself anticipated this move and invited him on his own behalf in the early 1430s.[16] The invitation had been

---

[12] Wā'iḍī in Aubin, *Matériaux*, p. 308.

[13] As 'Abd al-Ḥusayn Zarrīnkūb, *Dunbāla-yi Justujū dar taṣawwuf-i Īrān* (Tehran: Amīr Kabīr 1983), pp. 199–200, demonstrates.

[14] The term *sajjāda-nishīn* means literally 'one who sits on the prayer-carpet', denoting the hereditary successor to a Sufi saint, who maintains the endowments connected with the shrine of the ancestor.

[15] For further discussion of which, see Leonard Lewisohn, "An Introduction to the History of Modern Persian Sufism, Part 1: The Ni'matu'llāhī Order: Persecution, Revival, and Schism," *BSOAS*, 61/3 (1998), pp. 456–7; and esp. part 2 of the same article entitled "A Socio-cultural Profile of Sufism, from the Dhahabī Revival to the Present-Day," *BSOAS*, 62/1 (1999), section VII (d), pp. 17–18.

[16] Muḥammad Mufīd Mustawfī Yazdī, *Jāmi'-i mufīdī*, ed. Iraj Afshār (Tehran: Asadī 1961), pp. 200–1.

prompted by a legacy of respect, even affection, left by his father, but the son was an impressive enough figure to attract the humble respect of both the sovereign and the heir apparent, Prince Muḥammad Bāysunghur, of whom it is said that the prince actually poured the water for Shāh Khalīlu'llāh to wash his hands at meals.[17] The chronicler Ṣun'ullāh Ni'matu'llāhī makes much of the monarch's munificent and super-respectful treatment of Shāh Khalīlu'llāh, recounting that he sent an elegant litter every day to bring the Ni'matu'llāhī leader to court and seated his honoured guest by his side on the golden throne. The prime minister, Jalāl al-Dīn Fīrūz-Shāh, took exception to this coddling of the royal guest and confronted him in the ṣultān's presence with three questions. The first two had to do with his permitting all this cosseting, that is, the transport in the litter and the sharing of the throne; but it was the third question which revealed what was really eating at the minister: namely, why he presumed to pay no tax on his land in Kirmān.

Shāh Khalīlu'llāh riposted that Shāhrukh was no greater than his father, who had treated his own father, Shāh Ni'matu'llāh, with the same respect, quoting the founder's verse spoken to Timur:

> My domain is a world
>   that has no frontier,
> While yours but stretches
>   from Cathay to Shiraz.[18]

In answer to the second question, he also quoted his father but this time using blunt, forthright prose, saying simply, "Whoever has doubts about the precedence of my offspring over them is a bastard, and I am quite certain that King Shāhrukh is no bastard."[19] Then he cast doubt on the minister's opinion, putting him on the spot, before proceeding to the real issue behind the blind, namely, the matter of the tax exemption. Continuing to claim the high ground as a spiritual figure, he compared his situation with respect to the minister with the contention between the "tyrant caliph Yazīd and my ancestor, Ḥusayn b. 'Alī." Then, in true Sufi spirit, though not without a touch of mock liberality, he declared, "Whatever you want is yours for the asking. Go and take it in hand!"[20]

Despite the fact that Shāhrukh had invited Shāh Khalīlu'llāh to Herāt and held the family in considerable respect, he seems to have had too much respect for the stern spiritual figure to interfere and attempt to wield the political weight of his position in this confrontation with the prime minister. The tax exemption on the Kirmān–Māhān estates had been abrogated after Timur's

---

[17] Aubin, *Matériaux*, p. 201.
[18] *Ibid.*
[19] *Ibid.*
[20] *Ibid.*

death by a treasury critically in arrears because of mismanagement in Shāhrukh's time.[21] Whatever the outcome of the contention, Shāh Khalīlu'llāh must have enjoyed some success, but the struggle would have to be constantly renewed by successive generations of the family, with its centre relocated in the Yazd area, until the Safavid conquest in 1501 ended the rule from Herāt and brought in a whole new dispensation.

When Shāh Khalīlu'llāh finally departed for India sometime between 1433 and 1435 in the wake of his eldest son Mīr Nūru'llāh, who was now wedded to Aḥmad Shāh's daughter and thus firmly ensconced in the Bahmanid court, he left his second son Mīr Shams al-Dīn Muḥammad in charge of the order in Iran and custodian of the shrine at Māhān. He took with him his other two sons: the third, Muḥibb al-Dīn Ḥabību'llāh, and the youngest, who was to be his successor, Shāh Ḥabīb al-Dīn Muḥibbu'llāh. We know the latter's birth-year to have been 1427, so the future *quṭb* was still a young boy when he accompanied his family to the Deccan, never to return to Iran, yet to enjoy a distinguished career both materially and spiritually in the Bahmanid kingdom.

The king died soon after in 1436, and Shāh Khalīlu'llāh presided over the enthronement of the heir apparent as 'Alā' al-Dīn Aḥmad II, to another of whose sisters he married his son Ḥabību'llāh. (Eventually Muḥibbu'llāh was to marry a daughter of 'Alā' al-Dīn, sometime in the decade between the latter's accession to the throne and his own assumption of the *quṭb*ship.) At this point the order still enjoyed great prestige in Iran and Shams al-Dīn was commissioned with maintaining its status. Shāh Khalīlu'llāh went back to Iran in 1441, and in the brief time he spent there before returning to the Deccan – where he died in 1447 – he oversaw a signifcant expansion of the discipleship in Iran, the only time and area in which such a development occurred before the eclipse of the order in the Safavid period. In fact, 1447 was a critical year for the Ni'matu'llāhīs, because it saw the loss of both their last reasonably charismatic leader, Shāh Khalīlu'llāh, and their most powerful patron, Aḥmad Shāh Walī Bahmanī.

In a word, the brief period of expansion enjoyed by the order during Khalīlu'llāh's presence in Iran was testimony enough to his effectiveness as a spiritual leader and capable administrator, but with his death the momentum showed to a halt – well before the Safavids took over.

III. SUFI COURTIERS: THE NI'MATU'LLĀHIYYA IN INDIA

There is no evidence that the Ni'matullāhī Order as such was ever established in India; indeed, references to the heads of the order in the Deccan context

[21] Aubin, *Matériaux*, p. 16, citing Samarqandī, *Maṭla' as-sa'dayn*, I, p. 316.

tend to refer to them as 'Qādirīs',[22] not identifying them as Ni'matu'llāhīs at all![23] In fact, as the line of transmission passed from Shāh Khalīlu'llāh (d. 1455), the son of Shāh Ni'matu'llāh, to the third generation, the role of mastership seems to have become so attenuated that the ensuing generations of family-related successors had come to fit into the Indian subcontinental model of *pīrzādas* (hereditary Sufi masters) serving as *sajjāda-nishīns* (occupiers of the prayer-carpet [of authority]), in other words, hereditary keepers of the shrine of the saint from whom they were descended. This was an elegant building constructed on the site of the progenitor's *khānaqāh*; what becomes, in subcontinental terms, the *darbār* (court) or *dargāh* (atrium [to a higher domain]): terms for a place of pilgrimage. The descendants of Shāh Ni'matu'llāh in the Deccan were taken care of by their court connections, resulting in land being granted to them as *jāgīrs* under the Bahmanids, which stood them in good stead when the Bahmanid kingdom disintegrated and the family dropped out of history, retiring to tend their own gardens.[24]

Thus, by the time Shāh Khalīlu'llāh's youngest son, Shāh Muḥibbu'llāh, acceded to the *quṭbship*, the family were already, in effect, grandees in the

---

[22] K.A. Nizami points out in "Sufi Movement in the Deccan," in *History of Medieval Deccan (1295–1724)*, ed. H.K. Sherwani and P.M. Joshi (Hyderabad: Government of Andhra Pradesh 1974, p. 188) that "The descendants of Shāh Ni'matu'llāh Qādirī, who settled in the Deccan, were probably the first important Qādirī saints to enter India," this being stated in the context of a section on the arrival of the Qādirī order in that region, from which the Ni'matu'llāhīs are not distinguished.

[23] M.S. Siddiqi (*The Bahmani Sufis* [Delhi: Idarah-i Adabiyat-i Delli 1989], p. 78), mentions the Ni'matu'llāhī order as a sub-branch of the Qādirī order. He points out (p. 85) that the influence of the Ni'matu'llāhīs in the Deccan does not seem to have extended beyond the royal house of the Bahmanids and the foreign resident community of the Bahmanid capital Bidar. Hence, there does not seem to have been any activity of the Ni'matu'llāhī order as such amongst the populace of the Deccan. On the tomb of Aḥmad Shāh Walī Bahmanī in Bidar there are two chains represented: the conventional Ma'rūfiyya and a line of the Qādiriyya, thus associating the king and saint, along with his master Shāh Ni'matu'llāh and his master's master Shaykh 'Abdu'llāh Yāfi'ī with the lineage descended from Shaykh 'Abd al-Qādir Gīlānī, founder of the Qādiriyya, directly with the latter order quite specifically (Yazdani, *Bidar*, pp. 115, 119). According to the testimony of M.Z.A. Shakeb, the descendants of the Ni'matu'llāhī family with whom he had been in contact use the surnames 'Ḥusaynī' and 'Kirmānī' (personal communication, April 1997), not 'Ni'matu'llāhī', as claimants to descent from Shāh Ni'matu'llāh in Iran still do. These two surnames refer to their ancestor's full name Nūr ad-Dīn Ni'matu'llāh Ḥusyanī Kirmānī. Whether nominally Sunni or Shī'ite, the Indian branch of the family has long since abandoned any formal connection with Sufism, though there is some indication that if any definition of the 'order' had existed at all in the Deccan, it would have been as a 'Qādirī–Kirmānī' *silsila*, like the 'Qādirī–Yāfi'ī' line that continues to be active in present-day Yemen (cf. J.S. Trimingham, *The Sufi Orders in Islam* [Oxford: Oxford University Press 1973 (1971)], pp. 42, 273).

[24] M.Z.A. Shakeb, a contributor to this present volume, indicated in a personal communication to the author that they have retained these properties right down to the present day, and it is still this role of being landed gentry that provides for them today.

Shī'ite establishment of the Bahmanid court, though in no way connected with the clergy or involved in any canonical or theological officialdom.[25] However, they became deeply involved politically, on the whole in support of immigrant Persian groups. This political stance resulted in Muḥibb's brother, Shāh Ḥabību'llāh opposing the successorship of Humāyūn Shāh (1458–61) and, though having been honoured as a *ghāzī* (holy warrior) for his achievements on the battlefield under the preceding ruler Aḥmad II (*reg.* 1436–58), he was ignominiously arrested, then after escaping, killed in a treacherous manner by agents of the new king, resulting in a setback in family relations during Humāyūn's brief reign.

The situation was rectified by the next three kings, Niẓām al-Dīn Aḥmad III (1461–3), Muḥammad Shāh III (1463–82) and Maḥmūd Shāh (1482–1518), all of whom were ceremonially enthroned by Shāh Muḥibbu'llāh together with the resident Chishtī *sajjāda-nishīn*, with the Ni'matu'llāhī *quṭb* having the position of honour to the right, in escorting the king.[26] 'Ceremonial' is the key word, for the family in the Deccan after its brilliant early start, has no record of having done anything particularly distinguished, apart from maintaining its dignity and, especially after the Ḥabību'llāh escapade, keeping a low profile, literally, 'down on the farm', tilling the lands that had been generously granted them in their heyday with the Bahmanid court. As Siddiqi puts it:

> The Kirmānī sufis' proximity to the royal family due to matrimonial ties and their nativity were factors strong enough to make them popular among the aliens [i.e., the Persianate immigrants]. Their influence among the local people was less, who still associated themselves with the descendants of the earlier sufis [i.e., the Junaydīs and Chishtīs]. ... The members of the Ni'matu'llāhī family who were closely related to the royal family, accompanied them into the battlefields [and] had in fact become part of the administration. The nature of their activities thus manifests a clear departure from the policy of the earlier sufis of the Deccan.[27]

Siddiqi also adds, "The high profile of the Ni'matu'llāhī family in the Bahmani society was more due to their royal family connections, as they were steadily losing their spiritual and mystic values."[28] The fact that there are both Sunnis and Shī'ites among the descendants of the family living in the Deccan today is proof of the wisdom of their pragmatic policy, in which even the choice of sectarian affiliation must have been governed by the particular powerholder a

---

[25] It is said that when 'Alā' al-Dīn Aḥmad II mounted the throne in 1436, "Shāh Khalīlu'llāh Kirmānī, representing the Iranian Sufis, to the right and a native Deccani Sufi to the left, escorted the new king to the throne" (Muhammad Suleman Siddiqi, "Sufi–State Relationship under the Bahmanids [A.D. 1348–1538]," *Rivista degli Studi Orientali*, 64/1–2 [1991], pp. 90–1 [20–21]).

[26] *Ibid.*, pp. 93–4 [23–4].

[27] *Ibid.*, p. 90 [20].

[28] Siddiqi, *The Bahmani Sufis*, p. 162.

given ancestor may have been serving at a given time, since the thrust between the two sects has constantly shifted back and forth in that region.

In Iran, on the other hand, there was active interaction with the government during the Safavid period on the part of the descendants of Shāh Ni'matu'llāh, mainly with a view to reaping social benefits from the authorities, ranging from attempts to assure tax exemptions to efforts to increase their political status by intermarriage with the Safavid royal family (see section, IV below). The entente between order and government in Iran eventually, however, took a new twist in the seventeenth century, with the accession of Shāh 'Abbās II (1642–66), who fell under the power of the exoteric clerics and consequently launched a programme of repression comparable to that of his Mughal Sunni counterpart Aurangzīb in India. The documents dwindle to virtually nothing during this 'dark era' in both regions, afflicted by dogmatic oppression on both sides. In Persia, most of the Sufi orders had to close down their *khānaqāh*s and go underground or else retreat to the geographical fringes, the more out-of-the-way areas, this being an alternative taken by the Nurbakhshīs in Mashhad and the Ni'matu'llāhīs in Yazd and Kirmān, while the Dhahabīs adopted an ever more fervent Shī'ite, that is, 'official', colouration.

In the subcontinent it was the equally fanatical Sunnism of Aurangzīb that forced the Shī'ite governments of the post-Bahmanid Deccan to kowtow, changing their *khuṭbas* from enumerating the Imāms to citing the four Righteous Caliphs. The last Bahmanid king, the ineffectual Kalīmu'llāh Shāh, died in 1538, leaving the field to the five successor kingdoms in the fragmented region which had once been encompassed by the all-embracing Bahmanid realm. So little is known of the Ni'matu'llāhī *quṭb*s in this period that not even their birth, accession and death dates are recorded.

Monuments commemorating the family's existence, however, do exist in India – in fact, more is known of architecture of the mausoleums of the Ni'matu'llāhī descendants in the Deccan than of the biographies of the masters entombed therein.[29] In Bidar, for instance, stand four monuments to the Ni'matu'llāhī presence in the heyday of its court-life and artisanry: the tomb of Aḥmad Shāh Bahmanī (d. 1436), Shāh Ni'matu'llāh's prize disciple in the Deccan; the Chaukhandi (lit.,'four-storeyed building', see Plate 7, p. 169),

[29] Although of all the tombs in the Deccan none of those of the Ni'matu'llāhī family members seems to be a site of visitation; hence Yazdani does not use the terms *darbār* or *dargāh* with reference to them, whereas the joint tomb of the three non-family masters in Hyderabad, a popular point of visitation today, known as the *Takht-i Shāh Maḥmūd* locally, is referred to as the *Dargāh-i Maḥmūd-i Dakanī* by Ma'ṣūm 'Alī Shīrāzī (*Ṭarā'iq*, III, pp. 513). Interestingly enough, the author states that the mausoleum is taken care of by descendants of Riḍā 'Alī-Shāh Dakanī (d. 1214/1799) (*ibid.*), not any descendent of the Ni'matu'llāhī family. Siddiqi (*The Bahmani Sufis*), refers in this context to Mīrzā Ḍiyā' ad-Dīn Beg, *Aḥwāl wa āthār-i Shāh Ni'mat Allāh-i Walī* (Karachi 1975), pp. 190–213, which, judging by the title, may be nothing more than an Urdu rendition of Aubin's *Materieux*.

tomb of the founder's son Shāh Khalīlu'llāh (d. 1455); the *Takht-i Kirmānī*,[30] and the now ruined, but still grand, *madrasa* completed in 877/1472 by the brilliant Ni'matu'llāhī Sufi Maḥmūd Gāwān, the great Bahmanid prime minister (d. 886/1481) who hailed from Gilan in Iran's Caspian north.[31] While the two tombs, which are actually located in the complex of Bahmanid royal mausoleums by the village of Āshtūr, in the lowlands a mile and three-quarters to the east of Bidar, are fundamentally Persian in design and construction, they are blended with native Hindu elements, whereas the *madrasa* is almost purely Persian, being the only Tīmūrid structure of its kind in the subcontinent, that is, a four-porticoed edifice with a central courtyard, distinguished by tile revetments typical of Iranian architecture of the period.

As for the other buildings, the *Takht-i Kirmānī* (Kirmāni Palace), which is a ruin today,[32] seems to have originally been all or part of the residence of Shāh Khalīlu'llāh, built in connection with his arrival in 834/1431 at the invitation of Aḥmad Shāh Bahmanī. The building's name comes from its association with the family, many of whose descendants bear the name Kirmānī today, this having been the surname of Shāh Ni'matu'llāh himself. In keeping with the period of its construction, the building was constructed on generally Persian lines but by a combination of Persian and native Hindu craftsmen. The arches

---

[30] Writing in 1944 and describing conditions from a first visit in 1915 up to the time of publication, while reporting work in progress towards restoration of the historical buildings of Bidar in general, Yazdani states, "Some descendants of Shāh Khalīl Allāh still live in Bidar" (*Bidar*, p. 143, n. 1), though he gives no indication that they had anything to do with even the Takht-i Kirmānī by this time. In his thorough-going treatment of the *khānaqāh*s and tombs of the Chishtīs and the other Qādirī chains, Yazdani is careful to note if there is a sitting *sajjāda*, so one can conclude from his thoroughness and the lack of such indication with respect to the Ni'matu'llāhī tombs that no shrines of this family exist, the only tomb being so considered being that of Aḥmad Shāh Walī himself. Furthermore, it is very likely that there never were any *khānaqāh*s of the Ni'matu'llāhīs in India, for the actually practice of Sufism seems to have been confined to the court circle and the family, itself a merger of the Ni'matu'llāhī clan and the Bahmanid dynasty; any vestige of popular practice seems to be confined to the treatment of the *Takht-i Kirmānī* as a centre for Shī'ite ritual.

[31] See section II of the essay by M.Z.A. Shakeb in this volume (EDS).

[32] In his *Ṭarā'iq al-ḥaqā'iq* (III, p. 514), Ma'ṣūm 'Alī Shīrāzī recounts that during his travels through the Deccan in 1297/1879, he visited what he calls the *dihlīz* of Shāh Khalīlu'llāh, in other words, the building we know of as the *Takht-i Kirmānī*, and reports that in those days it was being cared for by a "*sajjāda-ṣāḥib*, a descendant of that worthy, residing there" and keeping it in good condition, even though many of the old buildings in the town were still in ruins from Awrangzib's depredations in the seventeenth century. The author spent some time chatting with the caretaking descendant and plying him with questions. He was told, "This couch which you see here is the Shāh's, he who still shines like the full moon," referring, of course, to his ancestor Shāh Khalīlu'llāh. As for the mausoleum of that ancestor, Ma'ṣūm 'Alī simply says that it and those of "certain of his progeny and descendants are in a complex of royal tombs outside of town," dismissing them with a mere mention and providing only the barest description and concluding that, apart from pleasant gardenlike surroundings, they were in an abandoned, ruined state.

have an Indic, pointed quality, for the advent of the Niʿmatu'llāhīs in the Deccan was part of a process of stepping up the Iranian influence which was to replace the local input for a time and lead to a peak of truly impressive Persianate architecture.

IV. THE NIʿMATU'LLĀHĪ FAMILY IN SAFAVID PERSIA

The decline of the Niʿmatu'llāhī order in Persia from a dynamic spiritual institution into a moribund dynastic family tradition set in around 1450, when Shāh Khalīlu'llāh's son Mīr Shams al-Dīn died prematurely at the age of forty,[33] leaving three sons, of whom we have no further report. His death removed the last figure of any spiritual weight from the Persian scene, for as his father's deputy in charge of spiritual and administrative matters in Iran, from the centre at Māhān, he had contributed heavily both to the initiation of new disciples and to maintenance of the order as an institution of influence and wide reach, both socially and geographically.

The loss of two key Niʿmatu'llāhī figures in Iran – Shāh Khalīlu'llāh departing to India in 1447 once and for all and his son Mīr Shams al-Dīn, the paramount shaykh of Iran, dying in 1450, predeceasing his father by five years – coincided with the loss of Timurid power in the Kirmān/Yazd area.[34] The death of Mīr Shams al-Dīn occurred at a time when the Kirmān area was in a particular state of tumult and disorder, so that when the seat of spiritual authority in Māhān was vacated there was no immediate will to fill it. For the next three centuries spiritual authority resided in Māhān only sporadically, although the site of Shāh Niʿmatu'llāh's tomb remained as a point of visitation, the grandeur and beauty of the complex being contributed to by sovereigns of the Bahmanid and, later, even the Safavid dynasties. As a spiritual centre, however, except for a brief time under Nūr ʿAlī Shāh Iṣfahānī during the early nineteenth-century revival period, it would never again play a major role in the operation of the order on any level.

The shrine complex had been built up over the centuries. The first structure, the tomb chamber itself, was begun immediately after the founder's death in 1431 at the command of the his devoted disciple Aḥmad Shāh I Walī Bahmanī (*reg.* 1422–36) and completed within the five years remaining of this Deccan king's own life. The final touches to the edifice were supervised by his son ʿAlā' al-Dīn Aḥmad Shāh II (*reg.* 1436–58), thus ensuring that the year 840/1436 was inscribed with a commemoration of Aḥmad Shāh's beneficence in the tilework over the grand entrance, set in an intricately stalactiform recessed arch. This forms a sublime portal which rises to the full height of the building, while opening into the majestic hall of lofty column-supported

[33] Aubin, *Matériaux*, p. 205; Yazdī, *Jāmiʿ-i mufīdī*, III, p. 48.
[34] Aubin, "La Famille Niʿmatullahī," p. 249.

arches in which the tomb is placed. The builders funded by the shāh made sure that great taste was invested in the enamel tile design, the craftsmanship and the calligraphy done in porcelain relief, and the exquisite patterning in ivory and sandalwood parquet-work of the panelling of a structure which soars upwards, storey upon storey of vaulted levels, surmounted by a turquoise dome, flanked by a pair of towering minarets to match.[35]

Following the death of Mīr Shams al-Dīn, and throughout the Safavid era, the geographical focus of the order's authority in Iran was to become Yazd, principally the centre at Taft, where the holder of the seat increasingly became more of a country-dwelling squire, wielding a degree of political power varying with the swing of the family's fortunes, sometimes including a kind of titular spiritual authority, often shared with another family member, generally a brother.

Even during the time of Khalīlu'llāh's brief return to Iran in 1441, there seems to have been a two-pronged policy in force, involving a spiritual thrust and a material drive, the former led by his son Mīr Shams al-Dīn in the spiritual centre at Māhān and the latter involving a joint enterprise of his grandsons, managing the economic centre at Taft, around which the main estates and business-cum-agricultural activities were focused.[36] While Shāh

---

[35] Nurbakhsh, *Zindagī*, pp. 128–9; Shīrāzī, *Ṭarā'iq*, III, p. 15.

[36] On the struggle with the Timurid bureaucracy to retain the tax exemptions and other privileges valuable for successful enterprise, there is the documentation of a valuable collection of letters (*Munsha'āt*, cited by Aubin, "La Famille Ni'matullahī") assembled by Sharaf al-Dīn 'Alī Yazdī, involving a correspondence between a certain Nūru'llāh, variously in the Deccan and in Iran (whom Aubin assumes to be the son of Khalīlu'llāh, contrary to evidence of the person's early death in the Deccan which the scholar himself cites, but who is more likely to be a son of Muḥibb, travelling back to Iran to work with his cousins), and key figures in the Timurid establishment. These missives not only shed light on what the family was up to at the time, but also provide insights into economic life and the socio-political scene in late-Timurid Iran and the Yazd region at the time.

Besides a vivid account of a stormy sea voyage, involving a boarding by pirates and subjection to serious privation, by Nūru'llāh, providing a rare piece of nautical writing in classical Persian (*ibid.*, pp. 247–8), there is an exchange of letters with the powerful Timurid minister Ghiyāth al-Dīn Pīr-Aḥmad Khwāfī, who fell from grace as early as 1441, whereupon the family and the order were deprived of an important patron at a critical juncture. Another protector with whom a correspondence was conducted was Ẓayn al-'Ābidīn Gunābādī, a high functionary in the Timurid tribunal, the highest judicial body in the empire.

There is a letter to another tribunal official, Sayyid Ghiyāth al-Dīn 'Alī Yazdī, with the month Rabi' I, clearly indicated but the year maddeningly missing, in which Nūr-Allāh reports his arrival in Taft very ill, apparently as a result of his harrowing voyage. The letter importantly indicates that the steps taken by his son Ẓahīr al-Dīn 'Alī before his arrival to obtain a ruling from the tribunal to protect the family's fiscal privileges were being followed up by Nūru'llāh himself, now that he had arrived on the scene (*ibid.*). Unfortunately, his condition deteriorated so seriously that he died in 1442. The lesson apparently learned from the unreliability of government patronage was that one had to be as economically independent as possible. Thus, there was all the more reason for the Ni'matu'llāhīs, whether family or order, to devote themselves to 'cultivating their garden' in the Voltairean sense.

Ni'matu'llāh himself had initially assigned this critical centre with its *khānaqāh* to someone outside the family, mismanagement eventually caused it to revert to the family.[37]

In Iran, the spiritual element seems to have become less and less significant in the maintenance of the order's identity as the years of Safavid rule went on and the ideological oppression tightened. Nonetheless, certain vestiges of spiritual form seem to have been maintained, such as reference to the leader of the order based in Yazd as the *murshid*, one of the Sufi terms for 'master' and the one which the Safavids themselves most favoured.[38] Where the head of the Ṣafawiyya was known as the *murshid-i kāmil* (perfect master), a simple *murshid* could be thought of as some sort of deputy or local governor,[39] which, in terms of power and influence, was certainly the case with the Ni'matu'llāhī family heads in the Yazd region during the sixteenth century, as we shall see.

At some stage, two of Shāh Muḥibbu'llāh's sons, 'Abdu'llāh and Ṣafī al-Dīn, moved from Bidar to their ancestral homeland to take over the family estates,[40] followed by a third brother, Ẓahīr al-Dīn. As the *Ṭarā'iq* puts it, "Ẓahīr al-Dīn 'Alī came from the realm of the Deccan to Yazd, settling in the site of Taft, where he engaged in guiding devotees. The progeny of this noble family resided variously in Yazd, in Taft, in Kirmān and in Māhān."[41] Of the first brother, 'Abdu'llāh, nothing further is heard. The second, Ṣafī al-Dīn, is notable solely for being the father of Mīr Niẓām al-Dīn 'Abd al-Bāqī and for belonging to the principal line of holders of the domain of Taft/Yazd. It is the third, Na'īm al-Dīn Ni'matu'llāh Baqī (Ni'matu'llāh III), however, who has made the greatest imprint in the annals.

While Mīr Shams al-Dīn was still alive and attracting and training disciples in Māhān, his grand-nephew Ẓahīr al-Dīn 'Alī was busy managing the estates and the *khānaqāh* at Taft. In fact, he had been so effective in his industry, both in the productivity of his work and his exercice of political influence with the Timurid government, that he had become one of the most important personages of the Yazd region.[42]

---

[37] Aubin, "La Famille Ni'matullahī," pp. 246–7.

[38] See Roger Savory, *Iran under the Safavids* (Cambridge: Cambridge University Press 1980), pp. 16, 46 and 235, for Safavid references to *murshid-i kāmil;* Yazdī, *Jāmi'-i mufīdī*, III, pp. 56, 65 and 67 for Ni'matu'llāhī references as *murshid*.

[39] *Ibid*., p. 32.

[40] The first two sons of Muḥibb who came from Bīdar to settle in Taft/Yazd, namely, 'Abdu'llāh and Ṣafī al-Dīn, seem to have intended to keep the family business – agriculture and the silk industry – running until their brother Ẓahīr al-Dīn 'Alī appears on the scene later on, to assume both the spiritual and the managerial roles. Both 'Abdu'llāh and Ṣafī al-Dīn apparently shared in the leadership functions until their brother came along (cf. Yazdī *Jām'-i mufīdī*, III, p. 49).

[41] Shīrāzī, *Ṭarā'iq*, III, p. 99.

[42] Aubin, "La Famille Ni'matullahī," p. 249.

Because of the affection between the Timurid rulers, from Shāhrukh onwards, and the Ni'matu'llāhī family, when Prince Iskandar b. 'Umar Shaykh was governing the Yazd region and Fars, the family supported Ẓāhir al-Dīn.[43] Declaration of allegiance to Muḥammad ibn Bāysungur, another grandson of Shāhrukh, who had attempted to establish independent rule in north-western Iran, on the part of Ḍiyā' al-Dīn Nūru'llāh II in 1442 seems to have been less well conceived, since it meant a momentary lapse from full accord with the legitimate government in Herāt, but this mistake was soon rectified by his father Ẓāhir al-Dīn, family head and legitimate authority, who had throughout maintained his loyalty to the incumbent Shāhrukh. He probably sent his son Ḍiyā' al-Dīn packing, for the latter was off straight away back to the Deccan, where he died in 1450.[44] Ḍiyā' al-Dīn's declaration of allegiance had apparently been encouraged by his grandfather's disciple, the poet Ādharī Ṭūsī who, after a spell singing the praises of Aḥmad Shāh as poet laureate of the Bahmanid court, had retired to the northern Khurāsānian town of Isfarāyin.[45] The theory had been that Shāhrukh was getting too senile to govern and the time was ripe to support his sympathetic son, to head off any move from a more hardline candidate supported by the fundamentalist clergy (obviously Sunni in this case).

The move having failed, Bāysunghur's son Muḥammad tried to seize power in 1447 upon the virtually simultaneous deaths of both his father and grandfather, this time making a bid for power in central Iran. Now Ẓahīr al-Dīn, as head of the family, joined a party of notables to greet the prince in Iṣfahān.[46] Again the motive was a mixture of policy and piety. A close family friend, his father's correspondent and collector of letters Sharaf al-Dīn 'Alī Yazdī, was a personal adviser to the sultan, thus giving greater impetus to his declaration of fealty. With the changing government and warring parties raiding the Yazd region, the Ni'matu'llāhī family had to decamp from their rural domicile at least twice and take refuge behind the walls of the city.[47]

Before entering into further detail about the history of the Ni'matu'llāhī male pedigree in late Timurid Persia, a brief word on the maternal line of descent from Shāh Ni'matu'llāh Walī and female scions of the founder is in order here. Only two names appear to have been noted during the late Timurid period. One of them is Khadīja (d. 874/1469–70), a daughter of Shāh Khalīlu'llāh (d. 860/1455), son of the founder and second *quṭb* of the Order. As younger sister of the third *quṭb*, Shāh Muḥibbu'llāh, she married the grandson of one of the founder's shaykhs, Sayyid Nūr al-Dīn Muḥammad Ījī (823/1420–896/1490), a prominent figure in the Shāfi'ite juridical and

[43] *Ibid.*, p. 237.
[44] Aubin, "La Famille Ni'matullahī," p. 249, n. 93.
[45] Dawlatshāh Samarqandī, *Tadhkirat al-shu'arā'*, ed. Muḥammad Ramaḍānī (Tehran: Khāwar 1959), p. 304.
[46] Aubin, "La Famille Ni'matullahī," p. 249.
[47] *Ibid.*, p. 250.

educational establishment of Shirāz and relative of the distinguished jurisprudent and theologian Qāḍī 'Aḍud ad-Dīn 'Abd ar-Raḥmān b. Aḥmad Ījī (d. 756/1355), author of the classical Shāfi'ite–Ash'arite summa of theology *Mawāqif*.[48] The other female scion of the family mentioned by name is a certain Jawāhira, cited in the *Tārikh-i Firishta* in a passage quoted in the *Ṭarā'iq*. This recounts that she sprang from a Ni'matu'llāhī father and a Bahmanid mother. She is mentioned in the context of the court of Yūsuf 'Ādil-Shāh (d. 916/1510), Shī'ite founder of the 'Ādil-Shāhī dynasty ruling the Bahmanid successor kingdom of Bijapur, to the west of Bīdar, with the circle of whose daughter, Sitī Khānum, she is associated. Bijapur was only just emerging as a separate entity within the frontiers of the Bahmanid kingdom, which after Yūsuf still had twenty-eight years to run, although with increasingly weak figurehead kings.

Back in Iran, if with Bāysunghur's ultimate accession to the throne and his father Shāhrukh's decease, the Ni'matu'llāhīs had, as it were, won the battle, they had really lost the war, for the new sultan had even less of a grip on the reins of government than his father had had. As the treasury became bankrupt through irresponsible expenditure and there ceased to be a single back-up patron to support them, the family, as the nucleus of the Order, became more and more subject to the vicissitudes of administrative changes, their subsidies both threatened by financial exigencies and subject to the fluctuating loyalties of administrators.[49]

In rising to the challenges presented by the uncertainities of the economic and political climate, there is every indication that Ẓahīr al-Dīn was a remarkable man. Not only was he shrewd enough to build up the agricultural and trade interests of the family holdings as well as deal with the intricacies of the Timurid bureaucracy, but he was also a good practitioner of his grandfather's teaching on the social plane, a man of generosity and chivalry (*jawānmardī*). Even as his coterie of dervish devotees in Taft was more and more reduced to an intra-family affair, he made sure that the family supported a *khānaqāh* along the highway serving travellers.[50]

When Ẓahīr al-Dīn died in 1450 (the same year as his uncle Mīr Shams al-Dīn), his son Na'īm al-Dīn Ni'matu'llāh II (d. after 906/1500) was more than

---

[48] While 'Abd al-Razzāq Kirmānī (Aubin, *Matériaux*, pp. 110–11) gives the name of the shaykh as Abū Sa'īd b. (i.e., 'son of') Sayyid Nūr al-Dīn Ījī, Shīrāzī (*Ṭarā'iq*, III, p. 60) erroneously gives Sayyid Nūr al-Dīn himself as the shaykh, where the "ibn" is omitted through apparent oversight. Aubin dates Nūr al-Dīn Muḥammad Ījī as dying in 796/1394, giving the dates of his grandson (Khadīja's spouse), Nūr al-Dīn Aḥmad as 823/1420–896/1490, completely consistent with the generational correspondence ("La Famille Ni'matullahi" p. p. 257). The fact that Nūr al-Dīn Ījī was an intimate of both the Walī and the paramount shaykh Shāh Qāsim Anwār is indicated in an anecdote by Kirmānī (*Matériaux*, pp. 43–4).

[49] *Ibid.*

[50] *Ibid.*, pp. 235–6.

capable of standing in the political shoes of his father, readily taking on the responsibilities for maintaining the family estates and whatever remained of administrative matters with the loss of the seat in Māhān. By now, the spiritual side of the two-pronged policy was losing its vitality, becoming merely a pro forma reason for the order to exist at all. In fact, the titular spiritual authority became once again integrated into the material 'business' – once again, in one person, although the emphasis was on keeping the economic operation going, immediately as a family enterprise, perhaps, in the long run, as a Sufi order.

Although he was also the paramount shaykh of the order in Iran, Ni'matu'llāh II's priorities were to keep as much of the family-cum-order's stipend as possible and to preserve the prestige of the family's connection with the Timurid establishment. Basically, he was concerned with maintaining links. Muḥammad Bāysunghur ruled for only two years before he was killed in the spring of 1452 in battle with his brother Bābur, who thus succeeded him. Fortunately, Bābur too had great respect for Sharaf al-Dīn, who was noted as an astronomer and intellectual in Timurid circles and so he granted him Taft as his territory.[51] Since Sharaf al-Dīn by now was living in the *khānaqāh* with Ni'matu'llāh II, Bābur's boon redounded to the benefit of the Ni'matu'llāhī estates as a whole, so that when Sharaf al-Dīn died two years later the grant of Taft came under Ni'matu'llāh II's name, giving further substance to his towering stature in the region of Yazd. It was for such reasons that this scion of the family became, as Aubin puts it, "the dominant personage of Yazd over the ensuing decades and a figure to be reckoned with in the whole of central Iran."[52]

Ni'matu'llāh II was in a position to make a good match, marrying Khānum Sulṭān, daughter of Amīr Jahānshāh, a khān of the Qarā-quyūnlū (Black Sheep) clan, which was connected in its religious persuasion to Shāh Ismā'īl Ṣafawī, a link that would be vital in the coming years. Ni'matu'llāh II's prestige was not gained lightly. It involved both political shrewdness and a reputation for spiritual authority, both of which were apparently factors in his having been offered the powerful khān's daughter in marriage. When responding to the khān's wedding invitation, he passed through Tabrīz on the voyage of return from Mecca to meet his Turcoman bride and be wed. Perhaps there was also a less worldly side to his journey, for an account is given of a certain Qarā-Yūsuf, one of Jahānshāh's intimates, who was a disciple of Ni'matu'llāh II, which suggests that he also had a following in Azerbaijan, some of it perhaps inherited from his illustrious forebear, Shāh Ni'matu'llāh Walī.

Mustawfī Yazdī gives some indication of Ni'matu'llāh II's fame as a Sufi by citing a poem in which he is hailed as "Pole (*quṭb*) of the World" and

---

[51] *Ibid.*, p. 250.
[52] *Ibid.*

"Supreme Recourse (*ghawth-i a'ẓam*),"[53] quoting the account of an episode involving a disciple of his, an intimate of his father-in-law Amīr Jahānshāh, who tells of calling on "the esteemed mystical guide Shāh Na'īm al-Dīn Ni'matu'llāh II, with whom I had a master–disciple relationship on the Path."[54] According to this account, Ni'matu'llāh II took some gold coins out from under his prayer carpet and, handing them to his disciple, told him that this was the seed-money to fund his career in India, to where he advised him to migrate. Qarā Yūsuf, heeding this counsel, settled in the Bahmanid kingdom, entering the service of the reigning sovereign of that dynasty, Shihāb al-Dīn Maḥmūd Shāh (reg. 1482–1518), under whom he became a distinguished general and ancestor to the Quṭb-Shāhī dynasty ruling Golconda, one of the Deccan successor kingdoms to the Bahmanid.[55] When Ni'matu'llāh II's father-in-law died, this shaykh and notable made a move early in 1468 to support his brother-in-law's claim to the succession and, consequently, to the rule of central Iran, including the regions of Iṣfahān and Yazd.[56]

Ni'matu'llāh II continued to manage the estates inherited from Yazdī's fief in Taft until in 906/1500–1, on the basis of a vision directing him to quit the world, [57] he decided to retire to Māhān, where he commissioned Sadīd al-Dīn Ṭāwusī to write the biography of his forebear Shāh Ni'matu'llāh Walī. He turned the care of the properties, their orchards and the silk enterprise over to his son and successor Ẓahīr al-Dīn 'Abd al-Bāqī who, taking whatever Sadīd al-Dīn had written in 911/1505–6, suggested that 'Abd al-Razzāq Kirmānī should finish it. Ẓahīr al-Dīn thus, like his father and predecessor, became both head of the family in Iran and the Order's paramount shaykh – a representative, that is, of the *quṭb*, the supreme head of the Order dwelling in the Deccan.

The following year Shāh Ismā'īl, the Safavid, completed his conquest of Iran, imposing his Shī'ite ideology on all its inhabitants. This led to a key development in Ni'matu'llāhī sectarian orientation, for "after the advent of Ismā'īl," as Amir Arjomand put it, 'the Order declared itself to be Shī'ite, and made a lasting alliance with the Safavids'.[58] Since, by this time the *ṭarīqa* was as much a political entity shaped around a small family clan as a Sufi order and, as such, constituted a virtual replica of the Safavid family dynasty-cum-order, this alliance presented few difficulties – accommodation to the ideological realities of sectarian politics merely being the flip-side of the coin of the Order's full-scale tribal patrimonialism.

Mīr Shāh Burhān al-Dīn Khalīlu'llāh II, the fifth master of the Order after Shāh Ni'matu'llāh was murdered in Herāt in 925/1518, after which his corpse

---

[53] Yazdī, *Jāmi'-i mufīdī*, III, p. 50.
[54] *Ibid*., p. 53.
[55] *Ibid*., pp. 53–4.
[56] Aubin, 'La Famille Ni'matullahī', p. 251
[57] Yazdī, *Jāmi'-i mufīdī*, III, p. 52.
[58] Arjomand, *The Shadow of God*, p. 116.

was transported to Taft in the Yazd region.[59] We can only speculate as to why he was back in Iran at this time; on the basis of the little the annals tell us, either his sectarian persuasion or his family politics may have been suspect. To begin with, Khalīlu'llāh II was the only one of the family to have acceded to the leadership without being the son of the incumbent. The murder of Shāh Khalīlu'llāh II may have been the decisive factor in prompting the Ni'matu'llāhīs in Iran to declare themselves Shī'ite for protective colouration, availing themselves of *taqiyya* (politic dissimulation), the very device which the Shī'ites had traditionally used when their existence was threatened by repressive elements in Sunni-dominated regimes. It was almost certainly the conclusive incident convincing them to keep their *quṭb*s in India for the time being, where there was no pressure for them to make an unambiguous declaration of sectarian commitment.

Despite the fact that the third *quṭb* following the founder, Shāh Muḥibbu'llāh, was – for all his pious asceticism – the prolific progenitor of seventy-three children, of whom seventeen boys and fifteen girls survived into adulthood, only his son Kamāl al-Dīn 'Aṭiyyatu'llāh (d. unknown), acceded to his father's position (thus becoming the fourth Ni'matu'llāhī *quṭb*). The appointment of Khalīlu'llāh II, a grandson of Khalīlu'llāh I's son Mīr Shams al-Dīn Muḥammad I – the sole son of the founder to remain in Iran and the only one of his four sons who did not marry into the Bahmanid royal family – to succeed 'Aṭiyyatu'llāh as *quṭb* may well have represented, therefore, an attempt by the Taft-based family branch to keep the leadership within the Ni'matu'llāhī clan in Persia. One may also speculate that the second Khalīlu'llāh's assassination may have posthumously prompted the decision to keep his son and successor – a third Shams al-Dīn Muḥammad I (after his grandfather and uncle) safely in the Deccan.

The fact that so little is known about the six family-connected successors to Shams al-Dīn Muḥammad I, purportedly directing disciples in the Deccan (see figure 1), while a great deal is known about their brothers and cousins operating in Iran (see figure 2), suggests that the former may have been little more than figureheads, and that the vitality of the order was contained, albeit increasingly in the material rather than the spiritual sense, within the Taft contingent.

Only a decade passed between Shāh Ḥabīb al-Dīn Muḥibbu'llāh's death in 914/1508 and that of Shāh Khalīlu'llāh II in 925/1518 – the only two dates for Ni'matu'llāhī masters which we have for this period.[60] Whether Muḥibb's son Kamāl al-Dīn 'Aṭiyyatu'llāh died during a brief period of incumbency and the

---

[59] It is because of a plaque discovered in the mausoleum of the Taft *khānaqāh* that we know when he died; see Nurbakhsh, *Zindagī*, pp. 103–9.

[60] Javad Nurbakhsh, *Masters of the Path: A History of the Masters of the Nimatullahi Sufi Order* (New York: Khaniqahi Nimatullahi Publications 1980), pp. 70–3.

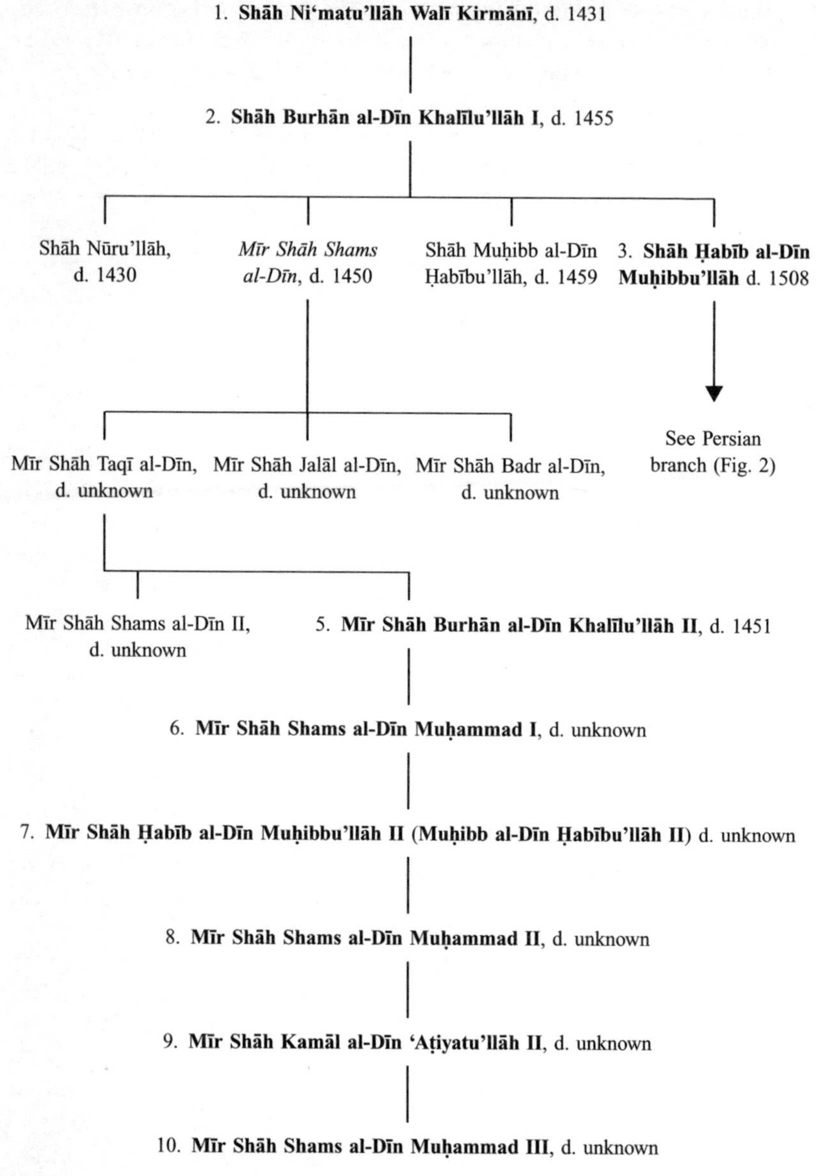

Figure 1: The Ni'matu'llāhī Family from Timurid Persia to Mughal India. Names in bold indicate *quṭbs* in the order's family pedigree; names prefaced by numerals indicate the succession of masters; vertical lines indicate father–son connections; names in italic indicate shaykhs (family heads with spiritual authority).

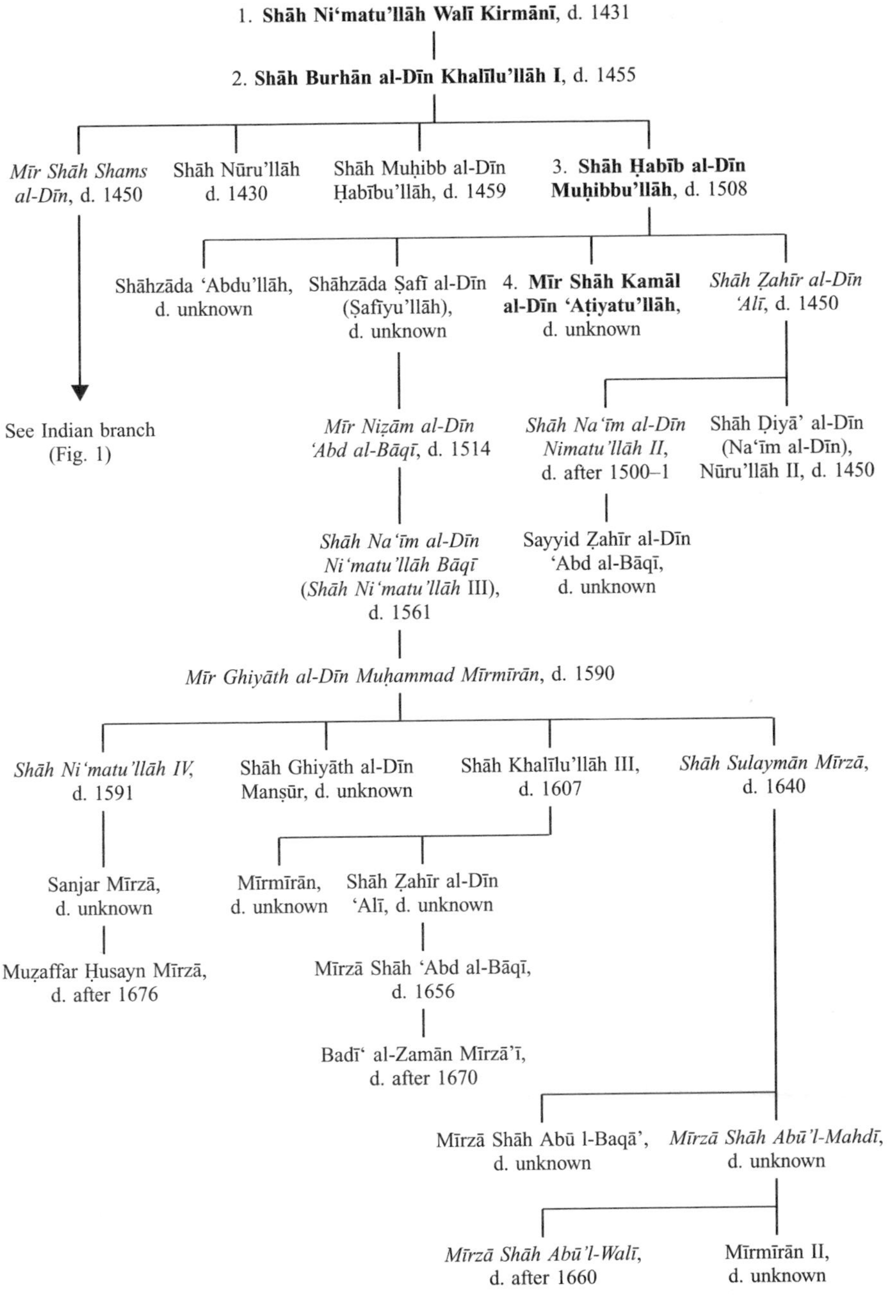

Figure 2: The Ni'matu'llāhī Family in Safavid Persia. (See note to Fig. 1.)

*quṭb*ship was passed on to Shāh Khalīlu'llāh II through a shaykh while he remained in Iran, or whether he went to the Deccan to receive the mantle directly from the incumbent, one can only guess. There is simply no record, as is also the case with all the remaining *quṭb*s in the family. It is only when the *quṭb*ship leaves the family and passes through two non-family members down to Riḍā 'Alī Shāh Dakanī (d. 1211/1796), that the Order re-enters history and dates reappear.

In the meantime, back on the Iranian front, it is now in the early days of the Safavid Sufi police state, and the Ni'matu'llāhī family clan has opted to dance to the same tune of family politics and dervish piety that had brought Ismā'īl such worldly notoriety and temporal success. Another grandson of Shāh Muḥibbu'llāh, the son of Ṣafī al-Dīn, by the name of Mīr Niẓām al-Dīn 'Abd al-Bāqī Yazdī, soon becomes so prominent that he is invited to assume the highest administrative office in the land, that of *wakīl*, the equivalent of vizier or prime minister in other Islamic governments. The office had been created in 1502 with the declaration of the monarchy, and the first holder of the position was a Turcoman Qizilbāsh, but after seven years Ismā'īl dismissed him and adopted a policy of appointing only Persians to offset the power of the Turcomans who had fought with him and helped propel him into power.[61]

Appointed in 1512, 'Abd al-Bāqī was the third Persian to hold this position. Indeed, he was so trusted by Shāh Ismā'īl that he was soon promoted to a more powerful and more confidential position, that of the Sufi king's plenipotentiary deputy, roughly equivalent to a Lord Chamberlain (*wakīl-i nafs-i nafīs-i humāyūn*).[62] Like his great-uncle Mīr Ḥabību'llāh, who had been dubbed 'Holy Warrior' (*ghāzī*) by the Bahmanid king 'Alā' al-Dīn Aḥmad II (*reg.* 1436–58), 'Abd al-Bāqī had military capability, but it was his sincere Sufi nature rather than his military prowess that brought about his martyrdom on the field of Chāldirān in 1514, when the Safavids experienced their most resounding defeat, this being at the hands of the Ottomans under Sulṭān Salīm. As the person closest to the shāh, this Ni'matu'llāhī dervish warrior took his position so seriously that he donned the king's armour and fought under his banner: the enemy mistook him for Ismā'īl and slew him without knowing that the shāh had actually escaped.[63] It is said that Mīr 'Abd al-Bāqī and another Ni'matu'llāhī Sufi, Mīr Sayyid Sharīf Shīrāzī, who died on the field of Chāldirān were so well respected by the enemy that Sulṭān Salīm himself expressed his regret at their demise.

In determining the succession following 'Abd al-Bāqī's martyrdom, one faces a problem in identifying the key descendant of the Ni'matu'llāhī family. Because of the conflict of information in the sources, often within a single

---

[61] See Savory, *Iran Under the Safavids*, pp. 42, 46–8.

[62] *Ibid.*, p. 42.

[63] Nūrbakhsh, *Zindagī*, p. 113.

source, perhaps as much to do with the scribe's copying of a manuscript as through any unreliability of informants or data-gathering, there is uncertainty about the identity of some of the individuals cited. The greatest puzzle concerns the identity of the chief personages who flourished during the first decades of the Safavid period. For instance, the son of Mīr Niẓām al-Dīn 'Abd al-Bāqī is identified in virtually the same way as the son of Ẓahīr al-Dīn 'Alī Yazdī. Both their cognomens are given variously as 'Nūr al-Dīn' and 'Na'īm al-Dīn',[64] and both have the first name 'Ni'matu'llāh', frequently used with the title 'Shāh'. However, the son of Mīr 'Abd al-Bāqī is more commonly identified as Ni'matu'llāh Bāqī. The *Jāmi'-i mufīdī* gives both this form[65] and that of 'Bāfqī'[66] (the latter probably being a scribal error, confusing the ascription relating to the regional town of Bāfq with that of the poet Waḥshī Bāfqī, who came to be an associate of the family in the following generation[67]).

This matter concerns the most awkward area in reconstruction of the lineage, namely, the successorship of Ni'matu'llāh II, involving the confusion of him with Ni'matu'llāh Bāqī, who must be assumed to be Ni'matu'llāh III, given the indication[68] that the son of Ghiyāth al-Dīn Mīrmīrān was Ni'matu'llāh IV. Despite his power and his propitious marriage, Ni'matu'llāh II has no progeny recorded in his name other than Ẓahīr al-Dīn 'Abd al-Bāqī, the chronology of whose life, as Aubin states,[69] is documented solely on the basis of the year 911/1506–7,[70] when he received a copy of the manuscript of the biography of the

---

64 Shīrāzī, *Ṭarā'iq*, III, p. 99, the most recent of the traditional sources, actually cites the issue of the confusion of cognomens.

65 Yazdī, *Jāmi'-i mufīdī*, III, p. 57.

66 *Ibid.*, II, p. 686. This context is interesting, for it occurs in a portion of the history which is not reproduced from the document of Ṣunu'llāh Ni'matu'llāhī, being rather a section describing the buildings and gardens of Yazd and its environs, with pp. 685–8 devoted to the *khānaqāh* complex at Taft, including mention of the connected mosque commissioned by the Safavid princess Khānash Baygum, Na'īm Ni'matu'llāh Bāqī's wife, and the *dīwān* = *khāna* (local administrative building) built by their great-great-grandson Mīrzā Shāh Abū'l-Mahdī, the *naqīb* in the mid-seventeenth century.

67 The former ascription makes particular sense when one thinks of it as a contraction of Ni'matu'llāh b. 'Abd al-Bāqī, since 'Bāqī' by itself is never used as a name, *al-Bāqī* with the Arabic article being a Name of God, meaning 'the Subsistent', and *'Abd al-Bāqī* having the sense of 'Devotee of the Subsistent'. The designation would probably have been brought in by early chroniclers and genealogists to distinguish this person from Ni'matu'llāh II, with whom he seems to have been confused from the beginning, given the alternate ascriptions of their cognomens, whether 'Nūr al-Dīn' or 'Na'īm al-Dīn'. It seems most likely that the latter cognomen belonged to both of these Ni'matu'llāhs: the first – hereafter referred to as 'Ni'matu'llāh II' – to distinguish him from his forebear, the founder; the second, having been given it as a matter of course, needed the suffix 'Bāqī' to distinguish him from his predecessor. He will be referred to as 'Na'īm ad-Dīn' or simply 'Na'īm' hereafter.

68 Notably by Arjomand, *The Shadow of God*, p. 116.

69 Aubin, "La Famille Ni'matullahī," p. 233.

70 Aubin, *Matériaux*, p. 4.

founder of the Order from Sadīd al-Dīn Naṣr Allāh Ṭā'ūsī Abarqūhī,[71] solicited in order to be turned over to 'Abd al-Razzāq Kirmānī for completion.

The assumption is, that on retiring from a very active life to one of quiet meditation in Māhān (perhaps in part to fill the gap left by the decease in 854/1450 of Mīr Shams al-Dīn), in briefly reconstituting the shrine as the spiritual seat of the order in Iran, Ni'matu'llāh II left something of a vacuum in the area of political and economic managerial authority, which his son Ẓahīr al-Dīn 'Abd al-Bāqī, either through lack of competence or early decease, was unable to fill. Elsewhere Aubin, without annotation, states that a certain Ẓahīr al-Dīn 'Alī was the son of Ḍiyā' al-Dīn Nūru'llāh (i.e. the brother of Ni'matu'llāh II).[72] If Ẓahīr al-Dīn 'Alī is one and the same as the aforementioned Ẓahīr al-Dīn 'Abd al-Bāqī (whose name really looks like a misnomer, another scribal error), then it would have been perfectly reasonable for Ni'matu'llāh II, on retiring from the world either without issue or without any heir on whom he could rely, to have designated his nephew (or son, depending on who he actually was) to succeed him in the short term.

Ni'matu'llāh Bāqī's political prominence inherited from his father, who held the office of prime minister, and his martyrdom – demonstrating the highest form of loyalty towards the Safavid ruler Shāh Ismā'īl – no doubt gave considerable weight to the Safavid sovereign's promotion of him and his branch of the family as *murshid*s, a title carrying political, as well as spiritual, weight in the region of Yazd under Safavid government. In any case, to take the generally accepted designation, Na'īm al-Dīn Ni'matu'llāh Bāqī succeeded his father as family head and paramount shaykh in Iran,[73] specifically entitled *murshid*.[74] This term traditionally denoted 'master of the Path' amongst the Sufis, but in the course of the transmutation of the Ṣafavid Sufi order into the Safavid political autocracy, "the Safavid shahs … transferred to the political plane what was essentially a religious and mystical relationship between a spiritual director and a traveler along the *via purgativa*."[75] Exploited for the purposes of an alien political agenda, the disciplic ideal consequently suffered corruption, becoming exploited to exact unquestioning obedience to the king as the putative *mushid-i kāmil* (perfect spiritual master).[76] The title could, by implication, be extended to other Sufi orders aligned to the Safavid's dervishdom, most notably to the Ni'matu'llāhiyya, which featured the most high-profile leader, buttressed officially by royal honours and physically by a provincial power base.

---

[71] Himself the son of a shaykh of Shāh Ni'matu'llāh Walī, by the name of Shaykh Burhān al-Dīn Khalīlu'llāh Ṭā'ūsī, cited in Shīrāzī, III, *Ṭarā'iq*, p. 60.
[72] Aubin, "La Famille Ni'matullahī," p. 246.
[73] Aubin, "La Famille Ni'matullahī," p. 256.
[74] Yazdī, *Jāmi'-i mufīdī*, II, p. 686.
[75] Savory, *Iran Under the Safavids*, p. 235.
[76] *Ibid.*

Due both to the trust and respect in which his father had been held and to his own formidable abilities, Na'īm al-Dīn Ni'matu'llāh al-Bāqī also enjoyed a position whose spiritual and political significance was confirmed by a grateful Shāh Ismā'īl, who went so far as to offer the hand of his daughter Khānash Baygum (more a title than a name, meaning 'Her Lord's Lady') in marriage to the new lord of Yazd. Ismā'īl died in 1524 at the age of 37, and as the new lady was, of course, the sister of the new king, Shāh Ṭahmāsp (who enjoyed the longest reign, from 1524 to 1576, of all the Safavids), the forging of such marriage ties with the Safavid regime came to stand the family in good stead; kinship connections, after all, guaranteed long-term security for Safavid cronies and confidantes, not to mention benefits, boons and honours given to extended kin, family and trusted allies.

So when Ṭahmāsp acceded to the throne, it is hardly surprising that he officially confirmed Na'īm as *naqīb* (chief religious leader, foremost *sayyid*) and governor of the province (*wilāyat*) of Yazd.[77] Na'īm's spiritual regency as Ni'matu'llāh III and political reign as Sufi *naqīb* were particularly distinguished for building activity and the development of the orchards and centres of production in this province.[78] His wife, Ṭahmāsp's sister Khānash Baygum was also a considerable figure in her own right, taking a keen interest in the ongoing construction work and beautification of both the the city of Yazd and the Ni'matu'llāhī centre at Taft, personally supervising the plan and erection of a mosque connected to the *khānaqāh* at the family seat.[79]

The Safavid–Ni'matu'llāhī alliance was put to the test when in 1534 the Ni'matu'llāhī lord demonstrated the power of his position by negotiating with a brother of the Shāh Ṭahmāsp, who had betrayed him by defecting to the hostile Ottomans. His intervention mitigated the king's wrath, so that the prince, Alqāṣ Mīrzā, merely went to prison rather than being executed.[80] It is clear that the Ni'matu'llāhī grandee, as brother-in-law of the shāh, was close enough to the immediate family to take up the cause of errant siblings who must have been intimates of his at one time or another.

These marriage links forged with the Safavids were made all the more binding when Na'īm's daughter married Ismā'īl Mīrzā,[81] the son of the shāh, who ultimately became Shāh Ismā'īl II (*reg*. 1576–7). Given Ismā'īl II's flirtation with a return to Sunnism and other caprices, his rule was virtually a fluke in Safavid history,[82] although the Ni'matu'llāhīs seem to have been in accord with the

---

[77] Yazdī, *Jāmi'-i mufīdī*, III, p. 57.
[78] *Ibid*.
[79] *Ibid*., II, p. 686; III, p. 60.
[80] Arjomand, *The Shadow of God*, p. 298, n. 65.
[81] Yazdī, *Jāmi'-i mufīdī*, III, p. 67.
[82] See M. Mazzaoui, "The Religious Policy of Safavid Shah Isma'il II," in *Intellectual Studies on Islam*, ed. M. Mazzaoui and V. Moreen (Utah: University of Utah Press 1990), pp. 49–56.

majority of the nobles in supporting the claims of his older brother, Muḥammad Khudābanda, who acceded to the throne as Shāh Sulṭān Muḥammad (*reg.* 1577–88) after the brief incumbent had been duly dispatched.[83]

Na'īm passed away in 969/1561, making way for his imposing son, Mīr Ghiyāth al-Dīn Muḥammad Mīrmīrān, who has been characterized as "one of the most influential and wealthiest of the provincial nobles in the second half of the sixteenth century."[84] He presided over major constructions and improvements in the Yazd region, developing the Maydān-i Shāh ('Royal Square' – no doubt inspired by its namesake in the capital), building numerous palaces and caravanserais, along with the grand Dawlatkhāna-yi 'Abbāsī.[85] At the same time, Ghiyāth al-Dīn Mīrmīrān does not seem to have been devoid of spiritual qualities, for as Mustawfī Yazdī's encomium went: "the flame of the lights of his spiritual guidance (*irshād*) melted the eye of seekers of love and loving-kindness in the crucible of asceticism and spiritual striving (*mujāhadat*)."[86] Even allowing for the author's renowned penchant for hyperbole, the specific employment of Sufi terms here and his warm emphasis on guidance involving love, rather than the dry monitoring of canon law predominating in later descriptions, does imply a feeling for Persian *taṣawwuf* which becomes gradually attenuated as the fundamentalist Shī'ite policy of the Safavid regime begins to bite in.

Under Mīrmīrān the region of Yazd was virtually a principality in its own right, powered fundamentally by its silk industry and its weaving of the still famous fine *tirma*, an intricately figured satin brocade.[87] This Ni'matu'llāhī notable even had his own poet laureate, one of the most distinguished poets of the Safavid era, Waḥshī Bāfqī (939/1532?–991/1583), who composed a good thirty eulogies in his honour, many of considerable length,[88] in contrast to a paltry one or two extended to the King of Persia, his royal uncle Shāh Ṭahmāsp.[89] The golden age of the Ni'matu'llāhīs and their promotion of the prosperity of Yazd lasted through the eleven-year reign (1577–88) of Shāh Sulṭān Muḥammad, whose sister, a second Khānash Baygum, was given in marriage to Mīrmīrān's eldest son Ni'matu'llāh IV, thus further cementing the interrelationship between the two families.

However, in the political firmament of Safavid Shī'ite clericalism the moon of the Ni'matu'llāhīs' hereditary Sufi patrimonialism was soon to wane. A hint

---

[83] Savory, *Iran under the Safavids*, pp. 68–70.
[84] Arjomand, *The Shadow of God*, p. 116.
[85] Yazdī, *Jāmi'-i mufīdī*, III, pp. 65–6. Cf. also II, pp. 677, 678 and 690 in the geographic section for further descriptions of Ghiyāth al-Dīn Mīrmīrān's constructions.
[86] Savory, *Iran under the Safavids*, p. 72.
[87] Still famous for what the West calls the 'Paisley' pattern, the 'park-bush' (*buta-jirqa*), an ancient Persian symbol representing both fire and the tree of life.
[88] Shams ad-Dīn Muḥammad (Waḥshī) Bāfqī, *Dīvān-i kāmil-i Shams ad-Dīn Muḥammad Waḥshī Bāfqī*, ed. Iraj Afshār (Tehran: Amīr Kabīr 1956), pp. 32–71.
[89] *Dīvān-i Waḥshī Bāfqī*, pp. 27–32.

of the turn in their fortunes came when Shāh Sulṭān Muḥammad abdicated in 1588 in favour of his dynamic 17-year-old son 'Abbās (*reg.* 1588–1629; known as 'the Great'), who was to mount the throne as the Safavids' greatest ruler, but one not disposed to tolerate minor powers under his dominion.[90] Mīrmīrān had only two years to live when the teenaged prince acceded as Shāh 'Abbās I. During this period trouble erupted when a certain Ya'qūb Khān, a fractious general of the shāh's Qizilbāsh military elite began making forays into the region of Yazd.[91] Initially, this seems to have been a policy indirectly encouraged by Shāh 'Abbās, who was mounting a campaign of conquest east and west, one result of which would be the ultimate recapture of Baghdad and its retention for a time in Persian hands. For this, the king had to be assured of complete docility on the part of his provincial notables.

The venerable Mīrmīrān did not pose a threat to the central government, but his third son, Shāh Khalīlu'llāh III, who was to succeed him on the material front, was more inclined to deal actively with the general, with whom he was shrewd enough to ally himself, until Ya'qūb, in his overweening zeal, having secured Fars to the west of Yazd and assuming that he had the latter domain and, hence, the southern tier of Iran, in his hands, declared his defiance of the shāh.[92] At this point, Shāh Khalīlu'llāh III opted for the establishment and proclaimed his allegiance to the shāh, so that when Ya'qūb's rebellion was put down, the shāh, on returning from the field could be invited and feted by the new lord of Yazd on a lavish scale.[93]

The year is now 999/1591. Mīrmīrān died last year. Khalīlu'llāh III is well ensconced in his possession of the fiefdom.[94]

Insofar as his two older brothers were concerned, the eldest, Ni'matu'llāh IV, was content to take on the spiritual role alone, thus providing for the two – temporal and spiritual – functions to be divided once again. The second brother, Ghiyāth al-Dīn Manṣūr, had died in his father's lifetime, and the grieving Mīrmīrān had built a mosque in his name.[95] Even in his father Mīrmīrān's lifetime Khalīlu'llāh III, though the third son, had been seen as the heir apparent – perhaps one reason why the Ni'matu'llāhī poet laureate Waḥshī Bāfqī chose him, rather than his brothers, to be the object of expansive eulogy.[96] Shāh 'Abbās's visit to Yazd and his entertainment by Shāh Khalīlu'llāh III marked, as Amir Arjomand pointed out, "the height of Ni'matu'llāhī prominence in Safavid

[90] Savory, *Iran under the Safavids*, pp. 79–81, on Shāh 'Abbās's policy of reorganizing the provinces for more direct central control and reducing the power of the Qizilbāsh.
[91] Arjomand, *The Shadow of God*, p. 116.
[92] *Ibid.*
[93] Yazdī, *Jāmi'-i mufīdī*, III, pp. 68–70.
[94] *Ibid.*, p. 64.
[95] *Ibid.*
[96] See Waḥshī Bāfqī's eulogy entitled "In Praise of the Liberal Prince Shāh Khalīlu'llāh," *Dīvān-i Waḥshī Bāfqī*, p. 7.

national politics. Shāh Khalīlu'llāh entertained Shāh 'Abbās in his capacity as the political head of the Ni'matu'llāhī family, while his brother, Shāh Ni'matu'llāh IV, received him as the spiritual representative of the head of the Order."[97] Thus, the most powerful shāh in the history of Safavid Iran was at this point so well disposed towards the Ni'matu'llāhīs that he had already endowed the construction of a magnificent portico around the founder's tomb in Māhān the year before, possibly in homage to the just deceased Mīrmīrān.[98]

Shāh Khalīlu'llāh III was the last Ni'matu'llāhī notable of Yazd to make a power-broking marriage match with the ruling Safavids in his capacity as a provincial authority in his seat of government. Just as his elder brother Ni'matu'llāh IV had married Shāh Sulṭān Muḥammad's daughter Khānash Baygum, so he married Shāh Muḥammad's other daughter Ṣafiyya Sulṭān Baygum – apparently a formidable woman, for her name occurs repeatedly in the accounts of the couple's descendants.[99] As Ma'ṣūm 'Alī Shāh sums up the socio-religious purpose underlying such marital ties: "it was by order of Shāh Sultan Muḥammad Ṣafawī that Ṣafiyya Baygum was betrothed to Shāh Khalīlu'llāh, and the dynasty of Shāh Ni'matu'llāh and the dynasty of the Ṣafawiyya, both being Ḥusaynī, became merged."[100]

At the banquet thrown by the Yazdī lord for his sovereign guest, Shāh 'Abbās used the occasion officially to decree his distinction amongst the nobility of the region, proclaiming his *niqābat* (chieftainship) and *sarfarāzī* (superiority), but being careful to avoid assigning any gubernatorial position to Shāh Khalīlullāh, for he was bent on a programme of reorganizing the provinces of Iran with a view to tightening the state's central authority, as well as rationalizing the means of tax levy, so that funds could be easily procured to finance his newly created standing army.[101] In the course of this policy, he was dealing the final *coup de grâce* to even the fiction of any non-Safavid Sufi presence in his kingdom.[102]

In pursuit of his centralizing policy, Shāh 'Abbās was anticipating the approach of the French king Louis XIV half a century later, drawing the nobles of the provinces into the capital and creating a new order. While the Persian sun-king did not use the formal terms employed by his French counterpart, he did, in effect, have a *noblesse de la robe*, an order of those rewarded for civil

---

97 Arjomand, *The Shadow of God*, p. 116.

98 Nurbakhsh, *Zindagī*, p. 129; Shīrāzī, *Ṭarā'iq*, III, p. 15.

99 Yazdī, *Jāmi'-i mufīdī*, III, p. 83, provides a good example.

100 Shīrāzī, *Ṭarā'iq*, III, p. 101. Mustsawfī Yazdī's report (*Jāmi'-i mufīdī*, III, p. 67) that the princess was daughter of Sulṭān Muḥammad's brother Ismā'īl II is clearly erroneous on a number of counts which need not be entered into here.

101 Savory, *Iran under the Safavids*, pp. 79–80.

102 The vestigial Ṣafavid Order, once having been the nucleus of maintaining the old Qizilbāsh troops whose forebears had put the Safavids in power in the first place, now posed the greatest threat to the power of the shāh's police state.

achievement, and a *noblesse de l'épée*, a category of those distinguished for valour on the field. While the Ni'matu'llāhīs' forebear Mīr Niẓām 'Abd al-Bāqī would have qualified for the latter, his comfortable descendants from the time of Shāh 'Abbās I on would have been beguiled with the former.

So, out went the by-now empty Sufi terms – *murshid, murshid-i kāmil* and so forth, along with any pretence of Sufi organization – and in came a formal army and a conventional administrative structure,[103] along with confirmation of the rule of Islamic law governed by Shī'ite theological doctrine, in which spirituo-political, as well as canonical, authority was vested in the exoteric clergy, serving as the ideological as well as the judicial arm of the government (very much a throwback to the pre-Islamic Sasanian Mazdean hieratic system). At the same time, consistent with the shāh's long-term policy, while the monarch appeared to be honouring his provincial host with all sorts of encomiums, he was actually to demonstrate his true intentions by inducing him to join the court circle, where, though elevating him to the primacy of all nobility, dubbing him "the most eminent *sayyid* of the realm"[104] – the *naqīb al-nuqabā'*, archduke or chief courtier, as it were – he would actually pursue a policy of divesting him of any political power remaining in his fiefdom. The move to the capital may have been virtually immediate, because the only date we have for the period is that of the death of his sister-in-law, the second Khānash Baygum, who died in Iṣfahān the very year of the banquet, suggesting that the family were already there when the lady passed away.[105]

Shāh 'Abbās's program of emasculating the lords of far-flung fiefs by distancing them from their bases of provincial authority and retaining them at court under the royal eye became particularly evident when, in 1001/1593, the king humiliated Khalīlu'llāh III by bestowing public honour on another ranking noble.[106] In the end, the lavish entertainment that Khalīlu'llāh had extended to the king may have rebounded, ironically, against him, causing the monarch to find it all the more imperative to take measures to curb his local powers. The Ni'matu'llāhī archduke survived another decade and a half, languishing in pampered exile, until he died in 1016/1607.[107]

With the decease of Khalīlu'llāh III, a new figure emerges into prominence, his younger brother Shāh Sulaymān Mīrzā, who survives his sibling by a productive further quarter of a century, dying in 1050/1640. However, being an obscure younger brother, he seems to have had the stature to run the affairs of the family from the capital, quietly going about the business of managing the estates and endowments of Taft and Māhān, while at

---

[103] *Ibid.*, p. 78.
[104] Arjomand, *The Shadow of God*, p. 116.
[105] Yazdī, *Jāmi'-i mufīdī*, III, p. 67.
[106] Arjomand, *The Shadow of God*, pp. 116–17.
[107] Yazdī, *Jāmi'-i mufīdī*, III, p. 64.

the same time giving spiritual guidance – hence, once again combining the twin roles incumbent upon the Niʿmatu'llāhī family leaders.[108] In addition to his apparent managerial talents, Sulaymān is praised for his spirituality and ability to provide guidance with "his tongue uttering the rhetoric of transcendent inspiration, unveiling the mysteries of divine cognition," such that "the flame of the lights of his spiritual guidance (*irshād*) dissolved the vision of the seekers of the aims of love and loving-kindness, while through his spiritual guidance, with a single breath the elixir of discipline transformed the copper of the being of those who enjoy ecstasy and engage in spiritual striving (*mujāhadat*) into coin of the purest gold."[109] Indeed, Sulaymān is the last Niʿmatu'llāhī family chief to be connected to Sufi activity in the historical accounts. According to Mustawfī Yazdī, as well as his social duties as the *kalāntar* (district chief) and *naqīb* of Yazd, he vouchsafed *irshād* ('spiritual guidance' from the Sufi point of view) and was associated with *'irfān* (gnosis).[110] While the foregoing extolling of Sulaymān's spiritual qualities, like the general run of the author's descriptions, borders on hyperbole, it actually indulges less in purple prose than most and does employ terms from the Sufi lexicon which he reserves strictly for those involved in Sufi guidance, thus indicating that, at least from the author's point of view, the capability of gnostic training was still alive in members of the Niʿmatu'llāhī family right down to his own time, the last quarter of the seventeenth century.

Reading between the lines, one may infer that the accession of Shāh Ṣafī (*reg.* 1629–42) to the throne brought some relief from Shāh 'Abbās's oppression, so that, with the mantle of both the Niʿmatu'llāhī clan authority and the family's 'spiritual' leadership falling on the shoulders of Sulaymān Mīrzā, the new king was happy to alter his father's policy to some extent, releasing his sons to return to their home district and resume direct control of their estates, while at the same time guaranteeing the maintenance and support of the family members who continued to be detained in the capital. The shah's liberality and open-handedness was not confined to those family members who preferred the luxuries and high life of the capital, but extended to the offspring of Sulaymān back in provincial Taft/Yazd, where, according to Mustawfī Yazdī, "every day he bestowed a new grace, generously adding [to the ancestral] Ḥā'irī, Malikatī and Nūrī endowments."[111]

While Khalīlu'llāh III's son Ẓahīr al-Dīn 'Alī is marked out with special praise for his virtues, neither he nor his brother Mīrmīrān seem to have been considered for the succession, probably being retained in the capital as part of the sequestering of their father and, thus, their father's line. Mustawfī's source,

[108] *Ibid.*, p. 72.
[109] *Ibid.*
[110] *Ibid.*
[111] *Ibid.*, p. 73.

Ṣun'ullāh Ni'matu'llāhī seems to be saying this between the lines in which he repeats laudatory mention of this scion of the old stock along with his mother.[112] On his deathbed in 1640 Sulaymān Mīrzā enjoins his sons to "revive attention to strengthening the pillars of the religious law (*shari'at*)," look after "the interests of the *sayyid*s and the clerics," and "reinforce the lofty Imāmite [i.e., Shī'ite] sect."[113] The emphasis is now placed on exoteric Shī'ite functions rather than Sufi mystical ones.

On their father's death Shāh Ṣafī (*reg*. 1629–42) sent the sons back to Yazd.[114] Mīrzā Shāh Abū'l-Mahdī, the eldest son of Sulaymān Mīrzā who inherited the post of *naqīb* at his father's bequest,[115] was said to be committed to "looking after the wayfarers of the path of sincerity and integrity (the Sufi expression *yak-rangī*, literally, 'one-colouredness')," [116] as well as being in charge of the *suyūrghāl*s (fiefs), these generally registered as *awqāf* (endowments), and thus responsible for both the spiritual and economic affairs of the Ni'matu'llāhī Sufi clan and farming estate. At the death of his father, Abū'l-Mahdī was authorized by decree of the young king Shāh 'Abbās II (*reg*. 1642–66) to "set about planting the sapling of stature with his steadfastness on the banks of the river of spiritual guidance (*irshād*)."[117] Mustawfī Yazdī praises Abū'l-Mahdī's industry and devotion to fulfilling the commitment enjoined by his father, as well as his humility and his "ardent eagerness to associate with dervishes and recluses (*gūsha-nishīnān*), along with his assiduous maintenance and reparation of the buildings and cultivation of the orchards in his domain in (Taft and elsewhere)."[118]

In 1065/1654, Abū'l-Mahdī set out on the pilgrimage to Mecca with his entourage of offspring and retainers as spiritual leader, in the exoteric sense, of his flock.[119] The expedition was endorsed by Shāh 'Abbās II, who gave the Ni'matu'llāhī chief a plenipotentiary status wherever he travelled. As a result, he was given a warm, even affectionate reception by Ḥusayn Pāshā, Ottoman governor of Baṣra, en route, indicating the importance of his position in the eyes of the Ottomans as a quasi-official envoy of the Safavids. On return from

---

[112] *Ibid.*, p. 70 gives mention of both this son and his brother, giving a glowing description of the former while leaving the latter undescribed. Then again, *ibid.*, p. 83, he mentions Ẓahīr's name, along with that of his mother Ṣafiyya, out of context, as if there were some role for them to play which was denied them either by fate or royal decree. The fact that the mother was a princess of the blood and a personality in her own right, combined with the matter of her husband Khalīlu'llāh III's formidable nature, may well have been key factors in the detention of them and their line on the part of the Safavid monarchs.

[113] *Ibid.*, p. 74.

[114] *Ibid.*, p. 76.

[115] *Ibid.*, pp. 74–5.

[116] *Ibid.*, p. 75.

[117] *Ibid.*, p. 76.

[118] *Ibid.*

[119] *Ibid.*

pilgrimage he visited the capital, Iṣfahān, where he was well received by the shāh. It is clear that Abū'l-Mahdī belonged to the circle of 'royals', with mutual friends amongst the capital's notables, as is indicated by the historian's statement that they "took leave of the court's intimates" before setting "out for the region of Yazd"[120], suggesting that they did not need the king's permission to come and go, simply going through the niceties of bidding farewell to their friends amongst the courtiers.

While Abū'l-Mahdī held the spiritual authority and managed the family's estates and endowments, his brother Mīrzā Shāh Abū l-Baqā' was appointed *kalāntar* of the Yazd region, probably indicating a certain restoration of the – now less threatening – Ni'matu'llāhī notables' position in the eyes of the Safavid monarchs succeeding Shāh 'Abbās I.[121] In fact, Abū l-Mahdī had no compunction about following in the footsteps of his august grandfather Ghiyāth al-Dīn Mīrmīrān and sponsored a host of buildings and developments. Indeed, the one date that we have in connection with him is the year 1074/1663, when he completed a pond to enhance the environs of his ancestor Shāh Ni'matu'llāh Walī's *khānaqāh* in Taft.[122]

As for the next generation, Abū l-Mahdī's son, Mīrzā Shāh Abū'l-Walī, inherited both the political position of *naqīb* and the spiritual rank of guide from his father.[123] By now, however, guidance is expressed in more exoteric terms, as religious 'direction' or *hidāyat* rather than Sufi guidance or *irshād*,[124] indicating that by this time the family's spiritual authority has more to do with their position as Ḥusaynī *sayyid* grandees in the system of official, state-sponsored Shī'ism than any connection to a living Sufi tradition. Emphasis is placed on the fact that the likes of Abū l-Walī and his brother Mīrmīrān II have inherited the lineage of Imām Ḥusayn – the most prestigious in the Shī'ite context – from both the paternal Ni'matu'llāhī and the maternal Safavid sides.[125] The irony here, of course, is that the founders of both lines were Sunnis in their sectarian persuasion,[126] and, particularly as Sufi masters, placed little importance on this genealogical connection – apparently leaving such concerns to the factitious religio-political agendas of their descendants!

Abū'l-Walī carried on the tradition of active construction and improvement inherited from his father and great-grandfather. Indeed, the sole date known in connection with him is 1070/1659–60, when in the Dārbandak quarter of the Yazd district of Ahristān he is recorded as having completed a mansion in a sumptuous

---

120 *Ibid.*, p. 81.
121 *Ibid.*, pp. 74–5.
122 *Ibid.*, II, p. 287.
123 *Ibid.*, III, pp. 82–4.
124 *Ibid.*, pp. 82–3.
125 *Ibid.*, p. 83.
126 On the Safavids' falsification of their Sunni origins, see Savory, *Iran Under the Safavids*, p. 2; on the Sunni origins of the Ni'matu'llāhiyya, see my "Shāh Ni'matu'llāh Valī."

garden, complete with an artificial lake.[127] As the year indicated is four years before the aforementioned year of his father Abū'l-Mahdī's construction of the lake, given the absence of any death dates, this suggests that he may have been active in sponsoring developments well before he officially acceded to his father's post. At some point, his brother Mīrmīrān II was appointed *kalāntar* by the king – probably 'Abbās I – succeeding his uncle Abū'l-Baqā'.[128]

In conclusion, while this side of the Ni'matu'llāhī Sufi fiefdom was clearly the most dynamic line of Ni'matu'llāhī family descent, it, like all the others, vanishes from history after this generation, the last to be mentioned in the *Jāmi'-i mufīdī*, the most authoritative historical source for the late period. It was the dominant line in Yazd at the end of the seventeenth century, holding the reigns of authority in the name of the Ni'matu'llāhī family and playing a vital part in the political, economic and cultural life of the region. We can date the period roughly by the dates of the composition of the history by Mustawfī Yazdī, who, though working in India, was constantly in touch with his home region. He started the work in the Deccan in 1087/1676 and finished it in Lahore four years later in 1091/1680 during the reign of 'Abbās II's successor Shāh Sulaymān (*reg.* 1666–94).[129]

Mustawfī does seem to have been more closely in contact with the two branches of the family which remained in Iṣfahān, for he writes more personally about his contemporaries in those lines. Concerning the offspring of Ni'matu'llāh IV, he mentions Sanjar Mīrzā as specifically born of his father's union with another Safavid princess, the second Khānash Baygum.[130] Then he speaks of his own contemporary, Sanjar Mīrzā's son Muẓaffar Ḥusayn Mīrzā, as "alive and well in Iṣfahān at the time of writing."[131]

As for the other line, the progeny of the powerful, but muzzled, Khalīlu'llāh III, the author first cites Mīrzā Shāh 'Abd al-Bāqī, the son of Ẓahīr al-Dīn 'Alī, giving the death date for this scion of the old stock as 1067/1656, in Iṣfahān.[132] This is followed by a report that his son, Badī' al-Zamān Mīrzā, was alive and resident in Iṣfahān in the year 1080/1669–70),[133] enjoying grace and favour at the hands of the king (Shāh Sulaymān), with the benefit of ample income-providing properties (*suyūrghālāt*).[134]

And that is the last word we have of the main line of the Ni'matu'llāhī family in Persia![135] Why have they disappeared virtually without a trace after

---

[127] Yazdī, *Jāmi'-i mufīdī*, III, p. 83.
[128] *Ibid.*
[129] *Ibid.*, I, intro. by I. Afshār, p. viii.
[130] *Ibid.*, III, p. 67.
[131] *Ibid.*
[132] *Ibid.*, p. 71.
[133] *Ibid.*
[134] *Ibid.*, pp. 71–2.
[135] The author of the *Ṭarā'iq* (III, p. 102) claims that in 1316/1898 he encountered

such an auspicious epoch of prominence? The answer is probably twofold. Those members of the family who remained in Iṣfahān were so thoroughly identified with the court-contaminated aristocracy that when the Safavids fell in 1722, they too tumbled into obscurity. As for the Yazd branch, being less identified with the regime, their fate may have been settled in a different way, at the hands of the intolerant regime itself, a hint of which is suggested by the following historical testimony:

> Under Shāh Sulaymān, who succeeded 'Abbās in 1666, a new and insistent voice entered the court, that of a doctrinaire Shī'a theologian, Muḥammad Bāqir Majlisī. By the time Shāh Sulṭān Ḥusayn succeeded Sulaymān in 1694, Muḥammad Bāqir had prepared the ground to become the real power behind the throne. He was not only fiercely opposed to the Sunnis, but also to the Sufis as well as a whole catalog of minority groups, embracing Mazdeans (Zoroastrians), Jews and Christians, forcing all he could reach to embrace his brand of Shī'ite Islam.[136]

The Ni'matu'llāhiyya of Yazd may well have still been carrying both the brand of patrimonial Sufi dynasticism and potential political autonomy, making them ready targets, after the benign eras of the shāhs Ṣafī, 'Abbās II and Sulaymān, to be suppressed by the true ruler of the country after 1594, the rabid, crusading fundamentalist Majlisī and his band of zealots.

In conclusion, in Persia, the very course the family took to preserve itself sowed the seeds of its ultimate dissipation, for through intermarriage with the royal dynasty, and by waging war with the Ottomans, in being worldly in its association with the temporal powers-that-be – the Safavid state – the Ni'matu'llāhī clan made itself vulnerable to the ways of the world, hence falling into decline when its state connections and links to royal patronage were broken. Similarly in the Deccan, the efforts of Shāh Ni'matu'llāh's descendants to maintain by hereditary means the order as the private preserve of their own family pedigree ultimately failed, serving solely as the conduit of a spirituality which could only be revived once the transmission had passed out of the family and into the hands of those who had purely spiritual motives.

---

descendants of Shāh Ni'matu'llāh in the city of Kirmān but did not specify whom they were. The present Ni'matu'llāhī *quṭb*, Dr Javad Nurbakhsh, himself a native of Kirmān, maintains that there are no extant descendants of the family in that city, stating that anyone with the Ni'matu'llāhī name would have taken it through association with the Sufi order or through identification with the saintly founder, whose shrine in Māhān is so close to the city. Dr Nurbakhsh reports that individuals living in the region of Iranian Baluchistan did come to him, offering credible testimony of descent from the founder, but these are the only people he can reliably say are descendants of Shāh Ni'matu'llāh still on Iranian soil (personal communication from Dr Nurbakhsh, London, UK, April 1997).

[136] Clive Irving, *Crossroads of Civilization: 3000 Years of Persian History* (London: Weidenfield & Nicholson 1979), p. 174. See also the essay by Leonard Lewisohn in this present volume, pp. 131–4.

*Rewriting Ni'matu'llāhī History in Safavid Chronicles**

SHOLEH A. QUINN

Sufism under the Safavids (907/1501–1135/1722) has received considerable attention from various contemporary scholars. A number of important monographs, articles and dissertations in the last several decades have all shed light on various aspects of this topic.[1] These studies have explored a wide range of themes, such as the decline of the Qizilbāsh during the rise of the Safavid state, the history of the Safavid Sufi order and its relationship with *ghulāt* movements and Shi'ism, the role Sufis played during the early years of Shāh Ismā'īl (*reg*. 907/1501–930/1524), the history and sociology of Shi'ism in Iran, and general discussions of the history of Sufism under the Safavids. Many of these works employ Safavid chronicles to trace the history of the Sufi orders, but these valuable records of the past cannot be fully utilized in the absence of a historiographic perspective.

The purpose of this chapter is to examine the Safavid chronicles and to discover how Safavid chroniclers wrote and rewrote the history of one of the

---

* I would like to thank Dr Ann Fidler and Dr Steven Miner of Ohio University for reading earlier drafts of this. I take full responsibility, of course, for all errors and oversights.

[1] The following list is by no means comprehensive, but includes some of the significant studies of Sufism under the Safavids: Hamid Algar, "Some Observations on Religion in Safavid Persia," *Iranian Studies* 7 (1974), pp. 287–93; Said Amir Arjomand, *The Shadow of God and the Hidden Imam: Religion, Political Order, and Societal Change in Shi'ite Iran from the Beginning to 1890* (Chicago: University of Chicago Press 1984); Jean Aubin, "L'avènement des Safavides reconsidéré (Études Safavides, III)," *Moyen Orient et Océan Indien*, 5 (1988): 1–130; Jean Aubin, "Études Safavides: Schah I Ismā'īl et les notables de l'Iraq: Persan," *Journal of Economic and Social History of the Orient*, 2 (1959), p. 3781; Jean Aubin, "La politique religieuse des Safavides," in *Le Shi'ism imamate: Colloque de Strasbourg (6–9 mai 1968)*, arranged by R. Brunschvig and T. Fahd (Paris: PUF 1970), pp. 235–44; Jean Aubin, 'Revolution Chiite et conservatisme: les Soufis de Lāhejān, 1500–1514 (Études Safavides, II)', *Moyen Orient et Océan Indieni,* 1 (1984), p. 1–40; Kathryn Babayan, "The Waning of the Qizilbash: The Temporal and the Spiritual in Seventeenth Century Iran" (Ph.D. diss., Princeton University 1993); Michel Mazzaoui, *The Origins of the Safawids: Ši'ism, Ṣūfism, and the Ǧulāt* (Freiburger Islamstudien, 3 Wiesbaden: Franz Steiner; 1972); and Seyyed Hossein Nasr, "Religion in Safavid Persia," *Iranian Studies* 7 (1974), pp. 271–86.

Sufi orders flourishing in Iran at the time the Safavids came to power in 1501: the Ni'matu'llāhiyya. By examining the rewriting of Safavid history in light of the several historiographical traditions prevalent in Safavid Iran, we learn a great deal about the legacy of various historical figures, and how that legacy changed over time.[2]

AN INTRODUCTION TO SAFAVID HISTORIOGRAPHY

Safavid historiography, like many areas of Safavid history, is an underdeveloped field. A current and comprehensive list of all Safavid chronicles, published or unpublished, does not exist, nor has the complex interrelationship between each history been fully established. Nevertheless, recent scholarship illuminates many formerly obscure topics. For example, the dating of the so-called "Ross Anonymous," previously considered the earliest of Safavid chronicles, has been established by Alexander Morton as the late seventeenth century, sometime in the 1680s.[3] As a result of Morton's careful research, we also now know the identity of the author as Bījan, 'the reciter of Safavid history (*Qiṣṣa-yi Ṣafavī-khwān*)', as well as the probable title of the work: *Jahān-gushā'ī-yi Khāqān-i Ṣāḥibqirān*.[4]

Other questions related to Safavid historiography are extremely complex, such as how Safavid chroniclers composed their histories, what methodologies they used, and what their underlying motives for writing were, and scholars are only now beginning to address them. Briefly, and very generally, Safavid chroniclers followed earlier established traditions of Persian historical writing, in particular the Timurid tradition, in composing their histories. For instance, nearly all early Safavid historians upheld a Timurid chronicle, Sharaf al-Dīn 'Alī Yazdī's *Ẓafarnāma*, as a model, and others considered another Timurid work, 'Abd al-Razzāq Samarqandī's *Maṭla'-i sa'dayn*, a work worthy of emulation.[5]

---

[2] For another example of this approach, focusing on a different place and time, see Denise A. Spellberg, *Politics, Gender, and the Islamic Past: The Legacy of 'Ā'isha bint Abi Bakr* (New York: Columbia University Press 1994). In this study, Spellberg is not as concerned with the 'history' of 'Ā'isha's life as she is with how the history of 'Ā'isha was rewritten over time. The legacy of 'Ā'isha evolved and developed through early and medieval Islamic history, just as the legacies of various Safavid Sufi leaders developed and changed through the course of Safavid history.

[3] See A.H. Morton, "The Date and Attribution of the *Ross Anonymous*: Notes on a Persian History of Shāh Ismā'īl I," in *Pembroke Papers* I, ed. Charles Melville (Cambridge: University of Cambridge Centre of Middle Eastern Studies 1990), pp. 179–212.

[4] See Morton, "Date and Attribution," p. 179. Bījan's history has recently been published. See *Jahān'gushā'ī-yi Khāqān* (*tārīkh-i Shāh Ismā'īl*), ed. Allāh Datā Muḍtarr (Islamabad: Markaz-i taḥqīqāt-i fārsī-i Īrān va Pākistān 1984).

[5] See, for example, Qaḍī Aḥmad Munshī Qummī, *Khulāṣat al-tawārīkh*, 2 vols, ed. Iḥsān Ishrāqī (Tehran: Dānishgāh-i Tihrān 1363/A.Hsh./1984), pp. 5–6 (hereafter cited as *Khulasat*); and Iskandar Beg Munshī, *Tārīkh-i 'ālam-ārā-yi 'Abbāsī*, ed. Iraj Afshār, 2nd

One important aspect of this established tradition of historiography, which we also see in the earlier Arabic, Ottoman, and Mughal historical traditions, is the practice of imitative writing. In his study of the rise of Timurid historiography, John E. Woods has shown how late Timurid chroniclers used early Timurid histories and 'updated' them in specific ways, while retaining the syntax and style of the earlier text.[6] Like their Timurid predecessors, Safavid historians, when narrating the past, chose a previously written work or works as imitative models which they would then modify in specific ways and for specific reasons. The motives behind these changes were often religiously and politically inspired, though the chroniclers no doubt altered texts for aesthetic purposes as well. In other instances, chroniclers would reproduce an earlier history word for word, usually without attribution, thereby making it difficult for us to pinpoint the original source. When narrating contemporary events, the historians were of course unable to imitate earlier works, and in these portions of their chronicles they utilized other methodologies, such as consulting with eyewitnesses, narrating events which they themselves participated in or witnessed, or paraphrasing contents of various sorts of official documents.[7]

There are a number of reasons why it is important to be aware of these historiographical issues. As often in the case of Safavid history, information in these narrative sources cannot be 'checked' by consulting archival-type documents. Therefore, it becomes necessary to look beyond using chronicles as non-contextualized 'pools of information' from which we extract names, dates, and places, and to explore strategies for how to read and use these narrative sources. Knowing, for instance, which earlier imitative models a particular chronicler used in his history allows us to see exactly how he rewrote the past, making it easier for us to understand why he made particular modifications. This also helps us 'date' the material in a particular chronicle, so we can distinguish what information is new, and what is being preserved from an earlier work. All of this in turn provides us with a better understanding of the changing political and religious climate of the time. In short, as our knowledge of how Safavid chronicles were written increases, so does our ability to read and interpret them.

In addition to knowing which sources the Safavid chroniclers used, it is also important to be aware of the general genres of Safavid historical writing.

---

edn, 2 vols (Tehran: Amīr Kabīr 1350 A.Hsh./1971), p. 373 (hereafter cited as *TAAA*). For an English translation of this text, see Iskandar Beg Monshi, *History of Shah 'Abbas the Great*, trans. Roger Savory, 2 vols, (Persian Heritage Series, 28 Boulder, Colorado: Westview Press 1978), p. 544, hereafter cited as Savory.

[6] John E. Woods, "The Rise of Timurid Historiography," *Journal of Near Eastern Studies* 46 (1987), pp. 81–107.

[7] For information on the writing of Safavid documents, see Muḥammad Ḥasan Simsār, "Farmān-nivīsī dar dawra-yi Ṣafaviyya," *Barrasīhā-yi tārīkhī* 2 (1346 A.Hsh./1967–8), pp. 127–52.

Unfortunately, we know very little about such schools of historiography aside from a few recent and preliminary hypotheses, and perhaps it is even too soon to use as definitive a word as 'genre' when we begin to categorize these texts. Tentatively, however, we can discern at least three traditions, although certainly more exist and the lines distinguishing them are, of course, extremely fluid.[8] The first is a 'high' literary tradition which follows models established by Khwāndamīr in his *Ḥabīb al-siyar* (930/1524), a work which bridges the Timurid and Safavid periods, since Khwāndamīr based his work on his maternal grandfather Mīrkhwānd's *Rawḍat al-ṣafā* (873/1469), a late Timurid work. Some of the characteristic features of this genre include ornate, adorned phrases and the use of numerous rhetorical embellishments. Many later Safavid chroniclers, including those who wrote during Shāh 'Abbās's reign and after, followed and imitated this style of historical writing. Examples include Qāḍī Aḥmad Qummī, author of *Khulāṣat al-tawārīkh* (999/1591) and Maḥmūd ibn Hidāyat Allāh Naṭanzī, author of *Naqāvat al-āthār fī dhikr al-akhyār* (1007/1598). This tradition originally centred in Herāt, since the earliest Safavid chroniclers, Ibrahīm Amīnī, author of *Futūḥāt-i shāhī* (927/1520–21), and Khwāndamīr, both wrote there. Khwāndamīr and Amīnī had both initially served the Timurids in Herāt, and their histories of Shāh Ismā'īl stylistically continued the Timurid literary tradition promoted during their time by Mīr 'Alī Shīr Navā'ī during the rule of Sulṭān Ḥusayn Bāyqara (875/1470–912/1506).[9]

Like their counterparts in the Ottoman empire, Safavid court astrologers (*munajjims*) were also involved in historical writing, and form a second historiographical strand.[10] During the reign of Shāh 'Abbās I (*reg*. 995/1587–1038/1629), Jalāl al-Dīn Munajjim Yazdī, author of *Tārīkh-i 'Abbāsī*, rose to prominence not only as Shāh 'Abbās's official court astrologer, but also as a historian, or at least a historical recorder. Yazdī always accompanied the king, participated in various political affairs, and had considerable influence on the

---

[8] Within these three broad traditions we can of course detect further sub-genres with distinguishable differences. Some chronicles, for instance, are 'world histories', some are local histories, others cover the history of the entire Safavid dynasty, and still others focus on the reign of one particular king or, occasionally, one campaign or battle.

[9] For more information on Herāt as a center of Timurid patronage, see Maria Szuppe, *Entre Timourides, Uzbeks et Safavides: Questions d'histoire politique et sociale de Hérat dans la première moitié du XVI*[e] *Siècle* (Paris: Association pour l'Avancement des Études iraniennes 1992).

[10] Part of the responsibilities of the court astrologer included following and recording the actions of the king in order to choose auspicious times for various events and activities. The anonymous *Tadhkirat al-mulūk* describes the duties of the *munajjim bāshī*, stating that this individual "is daily present at the palace in order to make his suggestions in case the sovereign or the muqarrabs should order him to ascertain a felicitous hour (*sā'at-i sa'd*) for the beginning of an affair or for starting on a journey, or for putting on, and cutting out new clothes …" (*Tadhkirat al-mulūk*, trans. and ed. V. Minorsky [E.J.W. Gibb Memorial Publications, New Series, 16; London: E.J.W. Gibb Memorial Series 1943], pp. 57–8.

shāh.[11] Yazdī's prose is characterized by his probable usage of official court documents in his narrative, and his style is relatively straightforward in comparison to that of chroniclers modelling their works on the early Herāt histories. Individuals from at least two subsequent generations of his descendants were also astrologers involved in historical writing: Yazdī's son Mullā Kamāl, and his grandson Jalāl al-Dīn Muḥammad, also wrote historical works. Together they form a second multi-generational family of Safavid historians, the first consisting of Mīrkhwānd and his grandson and great grandson, Khwāndamīr, and Amīr Maḥmūd (b. Khwāndamīr), respectively.[12]

A third historiographical strand has also been identified, and again, Morton has outlined its principal features, which point to what he calls an "invented tradition" of Safavid history. These include (1) dramatization; (2) invention of speech and heroic deeds; (3) emphasis on personal relationships; (4) negotiation; and (5) predictive dreams.[13] The existing texts associated with this genre were written late in the dynasty's history; they are all anonymous, with the exception of Bījan's history, and they exist in numerous related versions.[14]

SAFAVID CHRONICLES AND THE DECLINE OF THE SUFI ORDERS

Many scholars have noted the decline of most official Sufi orders as the Safavid dynasty gradually consolidated its power in Iran. This suppression began as early as during the reign of Shāh Ismā'īl and continued through the reign of Shāh 'Abbās. Of the many Sufi orders flourishing in Iran prior to the establishment of the Safavid state, such as the Naqshbandiyya, the Khalwatiyya, and the Nūrbakhshiyya, most did not survive through the Safavid era as organized orders.[15]

In comparison with these other orders, however, the Ni'matu'llāhīs lasted quite late into the Safavid period, even though some time between 836/1432–

---

[11] See Mullā Jalāl al-Dīn Munajjim Yazdī, *Tārīkh-i 'Abbāsī yā rūznama-yi Mullā Jalāl*, ed. Sayf Allāh Vaḥīd Nīyā (Tehran: Intishārāt-i Vaḥīd 1366 A.Hsh./1987). Yazdī probably came from a notable family in Yazd that belonged to the social class of bureaucrats (*dīvānī*), and most likely received the title of chief astrologer (*munajjim bāshī*) during Shāh 'Abbās's reign. Mossadegh cites as an of example Yazdī's influence at the court his role in the plan to suppress the *nuqṭavī* movement. See 'Ali Asghar Mossadegh, "La Famille Monajjem Yazdi," in Jean Calmard, 'Ali Asghar Mossadegh, M. Bastani Parizi, "Notes sur des historiographes de l'époque Safavide," *Studia Iranica* 16 (1987), pp. 125–6.

[12] See the works of Mullā Kamāl and Jalāl al-Dīn Muḥammad cited in Mossadegh, pp. 126, n. 4; 128, n. 15; and 128, n. 18.

[13] Morton, "Date and Attribution," pp. 203–4.

[14] See, for instance, *'Ālam-ārā-yi Ṣafavī*, ed. Yad Allāh Shukrī, 2nd. edn (Tehran: Intishārāt-i Iṭṭilā'āt, 1363 A.Hsh./1984) (hereafter cited as *AAS*); and *'Ālam-ārā-yi Shāh Ṭahmāsp*, ed. Īraj Afshār (Tehran: Dunyā-yi Kitāb 1370 A.Hsh./1991) (hereafter cited as *AAST*).

[15] For a general summary and history of these orders, see Arjomand, *The Shadow of God*, pp. 112–18.

840/1436, the leading shaykh had moved to the Deccan.[16] During Safavid rule, the city of Yazd became a prominent Iranian Niʿmatu'llāhī centre. The Niʿmatu'llāhīs had converted to Shīʿism and subsequently intermarried with the Safavid royal family, enjoying great prominence until one Niʿmatu'llāhī family member, Mīrmīrān Yazdī (d. 998/1589–90), came into conflict with the rebellious Qizilbāsh officer Yaʿqūb Khān Dhū al-Qadr, and Mīrmīrān's nephew, Khalīlu'llāh, subsequently fell from favour with Shāh ʿAbbās.[17] Said Arjomand cites a certain Shāh Sulaymān Mīrzā, Khalīlu'llāh's younger brother, as the last significant spiritual head of the Iranian Niʿmatu'llāhīs.[18]

Various historical strands have expressed the history of the Niʿmatu'llāhīs in different ways. The early chronicles following the Herāt tradition focus on the political alliances that the Safavids forged with the Niʿmatu'llāhī family, and narrate events associated with various Niʿmatu'llāhī individuals without discussing the Niʿmatu'llāhī Sufi order. The late popular tradition of Safavid historical writing, on the other hand, emphasizes the role of certain Niʿmatu'llāhīs in supporting various Safavid rulers, and provides evidence for a Niʿmatu'llāhī historiographical resurgence in the late seventeenth century. Below, we shall examine the history of the Niʿmatu'llāhīs in Iran during the Safavid period in light of these two very different historiographical traditions. A comparison of certain key episodes which appear in both genres help explain how both the early official chroniclers and the later popular historians viewed the Niʿmatu'llāhīs.[19]

THE HERĀT TRADITION

Our analysis of the Niʿmatu'llāhīs begins by examining the earliest chronicle to discuss the Niʿmatu'llāhīs, Khwāndamīr's *Ḥabīb al-siyar.* In his description of the Niʿmatu'llāhiyya, Khwāndamīr, like later official Safavid historians, does not emphasize the family's *ṭarīqa*-related activities, which seem to have disappeared during the reign of Shāh ʿAbbās I.[20] In fact, if one did not know who the Niʿmatu'llāhīs were, it would be difficult to know that individuals such as Mīr Niẓām al-Dīn ʿAbd al-Bāqī Yazdī (hereafter referred to as ʿAbd al-Bāqī), were even affiliated with a Sufi order. Probably owing to political alliances

---

[16] See Hamid Algar, *EI*², s.v. "Niʿmat-Allāhiyya."

[17] For information on how Safavid chroniclers narrated the episode of Yaʿqūb Khān, see Sholeh A. Quinn, "Historical Writing during the Reign of Shāh ʿAbbās I," University of Chicago Ph.D. thesis 1993. See also Arjomand, *The Shadow of God*, pp. 116–18.

[18] Arjomand, *Ibid.*, p. 117. See also the essay by Terry Graham in this volume (Eds).

[19] Since neither Yazdi nor his descendants discuss the early history of the Safavids in his chronicle, I will not discuss the astrologer tradition of historical writing in this study. Furthermore, other works, such as the *Jāmiʿ-i Mufīdī*, while providing significant information on the Niʿmatu'llāhīs, fall outside of the traditions of historiography discussed here.

[20] See Algar, *EI*², s.v. "Niʿmat-Allāhiyya."

Plate 8: The Coronation of Shāh Sulaymān (reg. 1666–94). From Chardin, *Voyages*, Pl. 81.

formed between the Safavid and Ni'matu'llāhī families, discussions of individual Ni'matu'llāhī family members, in particular the later Ni'matu'llāhīs, are primarily politically centred, such as mention of an individual receiving a particular official appointment, or marrying into the Safavid family.

The accounts of the Ni'matu'llāhīs begin with Khwāndamīr's description of Shāh Ni'matu'llāh (d. 834/1431), founder of the Ni'matu'llāhī order, as the 'chief of the lords of Arabs and Persians':

> In performing miracles and bringing about preternatural events (*aẓhār-i karāmāt va khwāriq-i 'ādāt*) he surpassed all miracle-working shaykhs. The sultans of the time and rulers of the age held their foreheads in devotion upon the threshold of his guidance, and the *'ulamā'* and great Sufis of the age considered his court (*dargāh-i ka'ba-ishtibāhash*) the focus of their needs (*qibla-yi ḥājāt*).[21]

Khwāndamīr uses similar phrases to describe *Sayyid* Na'īm al-Dīn Ni'matu'llāh II, a son of Shāh Ni'matu'llāh, as a lofty sayyid "who spent his days maintaining the customs of his glorious ancestors at the shrine frequented by rulers and sulṭāns."[22] He lists a third Ni'matu'llāhī family member, 'Abd al-Bāqī (d. 920/1514), as one of the nobles of Iraq and Azerbaijan who came to offer congratulations to Shāh Ismā'īl upon the victory of Khurāsān (916/1510).[23] Although 'Abd al-Bāqī was the spiritual as well as political head of the Ni'matu'llāhī order in Iran, Khwāndamīr only mentions his 'political' appointments, roles, and accomplishments as they related to the newly established Safavid state. We learn, therefore, that 'Abd al-Bāqī was later appointed to the post of Ṣadr, and then, after the death of Amīr Najm, Shāh Ismā'īl appointed him to the post of *vakīl* (*vikālat-i nafs-i nafīs-i humāyūn*).[24] After receiving this important appointment 'Abd al-Bāqī was involved in crushing a rebellion of "outlaws and brigands" who "had named Abu'l-Muḥsin Mirzā's son Sulṭān Muḥammad Bayqara Padshāh and were ravaging the area of Nasa and Yazar."[25] 'Abd al-Bāqī eventually died in 1514 in the Battle of

---

[21] Khwāndamīr, *Tārīkh-i ḥabīb al-siyar*, 4 vols, ed. Jalāl al-Dīn Humā'ī (Tehran: Kitābkhānah-'i Khayyām 1333/A.Hsh./1954), p. 7. All references here are to volume IV. hereafter cited as *Habib*. For a recent English translation of volume IV of *Habib*, see *Habib u's-siyar*, trans. and ed. W.M. Thackston, 2 vols (Sources of Oriental Languages and Literatures, 24; Cambridge, Mass.: Harvard University, Department of Near Eastern Languages and Civilizations 1994), p. 355, hereafter cited as Thackston.

[22] *Habib*, p. 606; Thackston, p. 626: "This lofty sayyid, who spent his days maintaining the customs of his glorious ancestors at the shrine frequented by rulers and sultans, was one of the sons of Sayyid Ni'matullah Wali."

[23] *Habib*, p. 517. For more information on 'Abd al-Bāqī, see P.P. Soucek in *EIr*, s.v. "'Abd-al-Bāqī Yazdī," and Roger Savory, "The Principal Officers of the Safawid State during the Reign of Isma'il I (907–30/1501–24)," *BSOAS* 23 (1960), pp. 91–105. In this article, Savory discusses 'Abd al-Bāqī's role as ṣadr.

[24] *Habib*, pp. 533–4.

[25] *Habib*, p. 542; Thackston, p. 604.

Chāldirān.[26] Subsequent chronicles falling within the Herāt tradition, such as *Dhayl-i Ḥabīb al-siyar*, *Nusakh-i jahān-ārā*, and *Takmilat al-akhbār* do not mention Shāh Ni'matu'llāh or Sayyid Na'īm al-Dīn Ni'matu'llāh II. Owing to the scopes of these texts, the primary focus is on 'Abd al-Bāqī, particularly in connection with his participation in the Battle of Chāldirān. We see one of many occurrences of imitative writing in three historiographically related Safavid chronicles: two written during the reign of Shāh Ṭahmāsp (930/1524–984/1576) – Qāḍī Aḥmad Ghaffārī's *Nusakh-i jahān-ārā* and Abdī Beg Shīrāzī's *Takmilat al-akhbār* – and one from the reign of Shāh 'Abbās I, Qāḍī Aḥmad Qummī's *Khulāsat al-tawārīkh*.[27] The fact that all three narratives mention 'Abd al-Bāqī's receiving the position of *ṣadr* in a similar fashion suggests that no significant ideological shifts related to the Ni'matu'llāhīs had taken place between the time that Ghaffārī and Qāḍī Aḥmad wrote their chronicles in 1570 and 1592, respectively.[28]

NJA	*Takmila*	*Khulāṣa*
va khidmat-i Mīr Sayyid Sharīf ṣadr az ān muhim isti'fā farmūda bi-ziyārat-i 'atabāt-i sidra- martabāt raft va ān manṣab-i 'ālī dar avāyil-i Dhū al-Ḥijjah bi-Murtaḍá-yi mamālik al-Islām aswat al-awlād Sayyid al-anām Mīr 'Abd al-Bāqī mufawiḍ gardīd.[29]	*va Amīr Sayyid Sharīf tark-i ṣadrāt karda bi ziyārat-i 'atabāt-i 'āliyāt raft va ān manṣab bi Sayyid 'Abd al-Bāqī Ni'matu'llāhī ki dar dār al-'ibāda-yi Yazd bar sarīr-i hidāyat mutamakin būd hawāla raft.*[30]	*va ham dar īn sāl Amīr Sayyid Sharīf Shīrāzī ki bi manṣab-i ṣadrāt sar afrāz būd, rukhsat-i ziyārat-i 'atabāt-i 'āliyāt-i sidra martabāt girifta mutavajjah-i ān amākin-i mushrifa shud va dar avāyil-i shahr-i Dhū Ḥijjah al-Ḥaram Ḥijjah-i madhkūr manṣab-i sāmī-i ṣadrāt bi Mīr 'Abd al-Bāqī Yazdī ki az awlād-i 'ārif-i ṣamadānī-i Shāh Ni'matu'llāh Kirmānī būd tafwīḍ būd.*[31]

[26] *Habib*, pp. 545–7.

[27] See *Khulasa*; Qāḍī Aḥmad Ghaffārī Qazvīnī Kāshānī, *Tārīkh-i jahān-ārā*, ed. Ḥasan Narāqī (Tehran: Kitāb-furūshī-i Ḥāfiẓ 1342 A.Hsh./1963), hereafter cited as *NJA*; and Zayn al-'Ābidīn 'Alī Abdī Beg Shīrāzī, *Takmilat al-akhbār*, ed. 'Abd al-Ḥusayn Navā'ī (Tehran: Nashr-i Nay 1369 A.Hsh./1990), hereafter cited as *Takmilat*.

[28] Qāḍī Aḥmad in particular was quite apt to depart from imitative writing if the political conditions deemed it necessary.

[29] 'And Mīr Sayyid Sharīf the Ṣadr was granted a resignation from serving that position and went on a pilgrimage to the heavenly shrines, and on 1 Dhū al-Ḥijjah, that post was given to the Murtaḍá of the Islamic lands, the leader of descendants, the sayyid of mankind, Mīr 'Abd al-Bāqī' (*NJA*, p. 274).

[30] "Amīr Sayyid Sharīf left the ṣadrate and went on a pilgrimage to the holy shrines, and that position [of *ṣadr*] was transferred to Sayyid 'Abd al-Bāqī Ni'matu'llāh, who was in the abode of obedience of Yazd, seated on the throne of guidance" (*Takmila*, p. 51).

[31] "And also in this year, Amīr Sayyid Sharīf Shīrāzī who was exalted with the position of *ṣadr*, received permission to go on pilgrimage to the holy and heavenly shrines, and headed for that holy region, and at the beginning of the mentioned month of Dhū al-Ḥijjah, the high position of *ṣadr* was entrusted to Mīr 'Abd al-Bāqī Yazdī, who was among the offspring of the eternally learned Shāh Ni'matu'llāh Kirmānī" (*Khulasa*, p. 117).

Later chroniclers such as Muḥammad Yūsuf Vāla Iṣfahānī, author of *Khuld-i barīn* (1078/1667–8) employed techniques of imitative writing to describe these incidents, with no major revisions to the narrative.[32]

THE POPULAR TRADITION

In contrast to the Herāt historiographical tradition, there is another more popular, or 'invented' genre of Safavid historical writing. Although scholars have demonstrated that there are connections between these chronicles and earlier standard accounts such as Ḥasan Beg Rūmlū's *Aḥsan al-tawārīkh*, these chroniclers employ a style which is overall direct, unadorned, and straightforward.[33] Morton has speculated that although early accounts representative of this tradition do not exist today, its origins might well go back at least to the time of Shāh Ṭahmāsp.[34] The histories from this genre to be discussed here are the *'Ālam-ārā-yi Ṣafavī* (1086/1675–6) and the *'Ālam-ārā-yi Shāh Ṭahmāsp*. Although I was unable to consult the *'Ālam-ārā-yi Ismā'īl*, it should be properly considered a recension of the *'Ālam-ārā-yi Ṣafavī*.[35] The *'Ālam-ārā-yi Ṣafavī* primarily focuses on the reign of Shāh Ismā'īl, and also includes an account of the dynasty's origins. The *'Ālam-ārā-yi Shāh Ṭahmāsp*, as the name suggests, is devoted to the reign of Shāh Ṭahmāsp, and the author does not mention the history of the dynasty's origins or the reign of Shāh Ismā'īl, at least in the portion that has survived today. For our purposes, these texts are particularly important not as sources of factual information, but as an indicator, perhaps, of what constituted popular appeal in the late seventeenth century. An examination of these two histories indicates that members of the Ni'matu'llāhī family were clearly one strong element of this popular appeal, because both narratives include significant 'new' information on the Ni'matu'llāhīs not found in the earlier chronicles of the Herāt tradition.

Although Bījan's history should certainly be considered part of this group of chronicles, his *Jahāngushā'ī-yi Khāqān* does not include 'invented' material on the Ni'matu'llāhīs. This could be due to the complex

---

[32] See Muḥammad Yūsuf Vāla Iṣfahānī, *Khuld-i Barīn (Īrān dar rūzgār-i Ṣafaviyān)*, ed. Mīr Hāshim Muḥaddith (Tehran: Bunyād-i Mawqūfāt-Duktur Maḥmūd Āfshār 1372 A.Hsh./ 1993), p. 211.

[33] See Morton, "Date and Attribution," pp. 185 and 188, for instance, for a discussion of the connections between Bījan's history and Rūmlū's *Aḥsan al-tawārīkh*.

[34] See A.H. Morton, "The Early Years of Shah Isma'il in the *Afzal al-tavārīkh* and Elsewhere," in *Safavid Persia: the History and Politics of an Islamic Society*, ed. Charles Melville (London: I. B. Tauris 1996), pp. 44–5.

[35] There are at least four, and probably more, anonymous Ismā'īl romances housed in various manuscript collections. Two have been published under the names of *'Ālam-ārā-yi Ṣafavī* and *'Ālam-ārā-yi Ismā'īl*. According to Morton, they should be considered two variants of the same work. See Morton, "Date and Attribution," pp. 187–8.

circumstances under which Bījan worked. He was apparently under pressure by his 'patron' Āqā Muḥammad Riḍa Beg, who may have been one of the court eunuchs, to incorporate at least some information from what he called an "incoherent text from Rasht," which Morton suggests may be similar to the *'Ālam-ārā-yi Ṣafavī*.[36] Although Bījan clearly used material from this work in his history, and indeed it has many of the characteristics of this genre as outlined by Morton, such as dialogue and speeches, Bījan also relied heavily on Rūmlū's *Aḥsan al-tawārīkh* and other official Safavid chronicles.

'Ālam-ārā-yi Ṣafavī

The *'Ālam-ārā-yi Ṣafavī* has been dated to 1086/1675–6, but it has not been used extensively as a source for Safavid history, owing to the fact that it too forms part of the late 'invented' tradition of early Safavid history. William Hanaway suggests that the *'Ālam-ārā-yi Ṣafavī*:

> is popular history, told in the style of a *naqqāl* and employing many of the narrative devices of popular storytelling. This book could well be called, in today's terms, an alternative history. Here the actions and the heroes are presented very differently from how they would have been found in a court history. Conversations are reconstructed (or invented) in popular language, and events are presented dramatically with a stress on the bravery and daring of individuals in bringing Shah Esma'il to power.[37]

In his description of the *'Ālam-ārā-yi Shāh Ismā'īl*, Robert McChesney hypothesizes that this and related histories in this genre have their origins in popular and oral traditions.[38] Both McChesney and Morton analyse specific episodes in *'Ālam-ārā-yi Shāh Ismā'īl* and Bījan's history, respectively, and conclude that despite the many factual errors, faulty chronology, and fantastic elements in these texts, they do tell us a great deal about Safavid society and how at least some elements of late seventeenth century Safavid society viewed their own earlier history.[39] Both are, consequently, extremely important and useful sources. The question which now remains to be answered is what role did the Ni'matu'llāhīs play in this altered or alternative tradition of Safavid history, and why?

The author of the *'Ālam-ārā-yi Ṣafavī* mentions a certain Shāh Ni'matu'llāh in connection with two main episodes: Shāh Ni'matu'llāh's contest against Muḥammad Karrah for Yazd, and Shāh Ni'matu'llāh's battle

---

[36] Morton, "Date and Attribution," pp. 194–5.
[37] William Hanaway, "Iranian Identity," in "Symposium: Iranian Cultural Identity," *Iranian Studies* 26 (1993), p. 150.
[38] See Robert McChesney in *EIr*, s.v. " 'Ālamārā-ye Šāh Esmā'īl."
[39] Morton, "Date and Attribution," p. 203.

with Jān Vafā Mīrzā. The individual mentioned here is probably Shāh Ni'matu'llāh Yazdī, also known as Shāh Nūr al-Dīn Ni'matu'llāh II (Bāqī) (1505–64).[40] The accounts, of course, include considerable discussion of Shāh Ismā'īl's role in both of these events. The standard histories which follow the Herāt tradition, and in which there is continuity between at least *Ḥabīb al-siyar*, *Aḥsan al-tawārīkh*, and *Tārīkh-i 'ālam-ārā-yi 'Abbāsī*, describe Muḥammad Karrah as a former Aq-Qūyūnlū local official (*dārūgha*) of Abarqūh, who was subsequently appointed governor of that town by Shāh Ismā'īl.[41] Although slight variations exist in these different versions of this episode, Iskandar Beg Munshī's *Tārīkh-i 'ālam-ārā-yi 'Abbāsī*, is generally representative. Writing during the reign of Shāh 'Abbās I, Iskandar Beg explains that when Shāh Ismā'īl was involved in the Rustamdār campaign of 909/1504, Muḥammad Karrah seized Yazd and had the governor executed. When Shāh Ismā'īl heard about this, he and his army went to Yazd. After a two-month siege, Muḥammad Karrah finally retreated to a citadel, which the Safavid army eventually overran. They found Muḥammad Karrah in "one of the towers which housed the military band." There, they seized him, put him in an iron cage and took him to the Naqsh-i Jahān square of Isfahan, where he was executed and burned.[42] Iskandar Beg notes the significance of this campaign as one that "consolidated Ismā'īl's power in Persian Iraq, destroyed all his foes, and swept the province clean of all rebellion and sedition."[43]

Although there are some similarities to Rūmlū's version of the episode in his *Aḥsan al-tawārīkh*, the *'Ālam-ārā-yi Ṣafavī* greatly expands on this account in extremely significant and interesting ways. In particular, as already mentioned, the author introduces a new character who plays a prominent role in the episode: a certain 'Shāh Ni'matu'llāh Yazdī', who is not mentioned in any of the earlier chronicles in relation to this episode. In the *'Ālam-ārā-yi Ṣafavī*, the author explains how Shāh Ni'matu'llāh wrote a letter to Shāh Ismā'īl, informing him that Muḥammad Karrah ('Karrahī' in *'Ālam-ārā-yi Ṣafavī*) had seized Yazd, captured him (Shāh Ni'matu'llāh), and demanded that he give him his daughter, otherwise he would kill him. The author then describes Shāh Ni'matu'llāh's escape from Muḥammad Karrah, Shāh Ismā'īl's

---

40 The problematic dates for this individual will be discussed below.

41 See *Habib*, pp. 478–80; *TAAA*, 30–1, Savory, p. 49; Ḥasan Beg Rūmlū *Aḥsan al-tawārīkh*, ed. 'Abd al-Ḥusayn Navā'ī (Tehran: Bābak 1357 A.Hsh./1978), pp. 76, 111–13. Hereafter cited as *Ahsan*. See also Ḥasan Rūmlū, *A Chronicle of the Early Safawis: Being the Ahsanu't-tawarikh*, vol. II, trans. C.N. Seddon (Baroda: Oriental Institute 1934), pp. 23, 35. Hereafter cited as *Ahsan*, Seddon. The term *dārūgha* can be translated as police chief, mayor, or local governor. See Ann K. S. Lambton in *Encyclopædia Iranica*, s.v. "Cities III. Administration and Social Organization."

42 *TAAA*, p. 31; Savory, p. 49. See also *Ahsan*, pp. 111–13; Seddon, p. 35. Rūmlū's account is generally similar to Iskandar Beg's.

43 *TAAA*, p. 31; Savory, p. 49.

advance into the city, and Shāh Ismā'īl's giving his own daughter to Shāh Ni'matu'llāh. Shāh Ni'matu'llāh's role in this episode includes trying to prevent Muḥammad Karrah from taking his daughter, his meeting the king when Shāh Ismā'īl came to Yazd, his writing a letter to the people of Yazd encouraging them to open the gates of the city to the king, and finally giving his daughter in marriage to the shāh.

This episode exemplifies the author's practice of reinventing portions of early Safavid history by inserting Shāh Ni'matu'llāh. In this account, the fact that the author mentions Shāh Ni'matu'llāh's name at all is significant because none of the earlier chroniclers refer to him in connection with this episode. Of course, this could be due to the fact that this individual was probably not yet born, thus indicating that this episode was indeed fabricated.[44] Also significant is the author's explanation that Shāh Ni'matu'llāh's sending a letter to Shāh Ismā'īl was the main reason that Shāh Ismā'īl marched on Yazd. Other texts, such as Rūmlū's *Aḥsan al-tawārīkh*, state that Shāh Ismā'īl simply "heard" of Muḥammad Karrah's actions and decided to head for Yazd.[45] Thus, when the author of *'Ālam-ārā-yi Ṣafavī* had the opportunity to explain how Shāh Ismā'īl learned about this, he stated that Shāh Ni'matu'llāh was the individual who informed the king of the situation. Furthermore, the entire segment of the story explaining how Muḥammad Karrah demanded Shāh Ni'matu'llāh's daughter does not appear in any of the other chronicles, either. Finally, the author explains how Shāh Ni'matu'llāh wrote a letter to the people of Yazd, urging them to open the gates of Yazd to Shāh Ismā'īl. When the people obliged, Shāh Ismā'īl's men were able to enter the city and eventually capture Muḥammad Karrah. As a result, then, of Shāh Ni'matu'llāh's plea for assistance to the king and the assistance he subsequently rendered the king once he arrived in Yazd, the king rewarded Shāh Ni'matu'llāh's loyalty and sincerity by making him the governor of Yazd and giving him his own daughter in marriage.

By explaining the events of Yazd in terms of Shāh Ismā'īl marching there to render aid to Shāh Ni'matu'llāh, the author of *'Ālam-ārā-yi Ṣafavī* assigns, perhaps, a more benevolent motive for Shāh Ismā'īl's actions. In other words, in this version, Shāh Ismā'īl responds to Shāh Ni'matu'llāh's request for aid and assistance. By stressing the various letters that were written and the diplomatic efforts that took place before the attack on Yazd, and placing a respectable individual, Shāh Ni'matu'llāh, at the centre of such efforts, the author shows that Shāh Ismā'īl exhausted all other means for settlement before

---

[44] The dates I have been able to find for this individual, 911/1505–971/1564 (based on Szuppe, below), mean that he could not have participated in the events of Yazd as described by the author of *AAS* because they took place in 910/1504. For a chart showing the marriage alliances between the Safavid and Ni'matu'llāhī family, see Maria Szuppe, "La Participation des femmes de la famille royale à l'exercice du pouvoir en Iran safavide au XVIe Siècle," *Studia Iranica* 23 (1994), p. 225.

[45] *Ahsan*, pp. 111–13; Seddon, p. 35.

he attacked. In the process, the author also provides an explanation for the marriage alliance which later took place between Khānish Khānum I (daughter of Shāh Ismā'īl) and Shāh Ni'matu'llāh. We can certainly detect similarities in the themes in this episode and two which Morton analyses in Bījan's history: one regarding Qanbar Āqā and the other about the siege of the castle of Fīrūzkūh. In both of these episodes, Bījan relies on sources similar to the *'Ālam-ārā-yi Ṣafavī*, which stress Shāh Ismā'īl's negotiating with his enemies. Morton concludes that this is one of the main themes or conventions of this particular tradition of Safavid historiography: that of justification by negotiation.[46] Morton further explains this in terms of notions of kingship, in which the 'righteous ruler' allowed enemies to submit before attacking, as Shāh Ismā'īl did in the episode of Muḥammad Karrah.[47]

The account of Jān Vafā Mīrzā's 'battle' with Shāh Ni'matu'llāh is likewise unique to *'Ālam-ārā-yi Ṣafavī*, yet contains conventional elements similar to the episode of Muḥammad Karrah. Here, the author provides details about Shāh Ni'matu'llāh's participation in the local affairs of Yazd when Jān Vafā Mīrzā, an Uzbek leader, attacked Yazd. In a manner very similar to his account of Shāh Ni'matu'llāh playing a key role in delivering the people of Yazd from Muḥammad Karrah, in this episode the author explains Shāh Ni'matu'llāh's involvement in defending Yazd from Jān Vafā Mīrzā.

Specifically, Shāh Ni'matu'llāh sent a message to Shāh Ismā'īl informing him that Jān Vafā Mīrzā had attacked. In response to the letter, Shāh Ismā'īl decided to send 5,000 troops to Yazd. In the meantime, however, Shāh Ni'matu'llāh did his best to protect the city and look out for the Uzbeks until the king's help arrived. This involved an elaborate ruse of 'feigning' to tax the people of Yazd by taking one *tuman* from each house to give to Jān Vafā Mīrzā in order to placate him until the king came. The idea was to make him so anxious to receive the money, that Shāh Ismā'īl's men could arrive unnoticed and take Jān Vafā Mīrzā by surprise. As a result of Shāh Ni'matu'llāh's assistance, Shāh Ismā'īl eventually did reach Yazd, and Jān Vafā Mīrzā was delivered to him.[48] Here again, Shāh Ni'matu'llāh was the initial cause of Shāh Ismā'īl's becoming aware of the situation in Yazd and sending help to that city. In the meantime, Shāh Ni'matu'llāh did not fight, but instead kept Jān Vafā Mīrzā preoccupied until Shāh Ismā'īl's arrival.

It is unclear why the author includes this episode in his account, since none of the other standard chroniclers mention it. It does show that the Safavids made, if not 'diplomatic' efforts to prevent war, then at least strategic efforts, and the author places Shāh Ni'matu'llāh at the centre of such plans. Shāh Ni'matu'llāh, again, appears as a staunch supporter of Shāh Ismā'īl, protecting

---

[46] Morton, "Date and Attribution," p. 204.
[47] *Ibid.*
[48] *AAS*, pp. 271–81.

Yazd from the Uzbek enemies and informing Shāh Ismā'īl of the events so that the king could take further action.

'Ālam-ārā-yi Shāh Ṭahmāsp

Still another anonymous history contains numerous references to the Ni'matu'llāhīs and amplifies the role of one Ni'matu'llāhī family member in particular. This text, recently published with the title *'Ālam-ārā-yi Shāh Ṭahmāsp*, is an account of the reign of Shāh Ṭahmāsp. Based on an analysis of the language used in this text, the editor, Īraj Afshār, concludes that the author was probably from Yazd. Although he notes the similarity between this chronicle and *'Ālam-ārā-yi Ṣafavī*, Afshār does not try definitively to date the text.[49] However, as we shall see, the author of this chronicle employs many devices similar to those of the *'Ālam-ārā-yi Ṣafavī* and Bījan's history. This, and the fact that the author alludes to an episode only found in the *'Ālam-ārā-yi Ṣafavī*, points to a probable connection between this text and the other anonymous Ismā'īl histories, and suggests that it was written some time after 1086/1675–6, when the *'Ālam-ārā-yi Ṣafavī* was composed.

The principal Ni'matu'llāhī family member mentioned in *'Ālam-ārā-yi Shāh Ṭahmāsp* is Shāh Ni'matu'llāh Yazdī, who is probably the same Shāh Ni'matu'llāh mentioned in *'Ālam-ārā-yi Ṣafavī*.[50] His name appears in connection with a number of episodes highlighting his involvement with the Safavid family, including the royal princes Alqās Mīrzā and Ismā'īl Mīrzā, the latter being his son-in-law, as follows: (1) 'Abd Allāh Khān [Uzbek] in Yazd; (2) episodes concerning Alqās Mīrzā, Shāh Ni'matu'llāh, and Shāh Ṭahmāsp; (3) the marriage between Ismā'īl Mīrzā (Shāh Ismā'īl II) and Shāh Ni'matu'llāh's daughter; (4) Shāh Ṭahmāsp's going to Yazd; and (5) Ismā'īl Mīrzā's attempt to be king, and Shāh Ni'matu'llāh Yazdī's role in persuading him to change his mind. In all of these episodes, Shāh Ni'matu'llāh is portrayed as a solid supporter of Shāh Ṭahmāsp: he helps defend the king from challenges to his rule by showing wayward members of the Safavid family the way to obedience and submission, and he marries his daughter off to Shāh Ṭahmāsp's son, Ismā'īl Mīrzā.

The account of the contest between Shāh Ni'matu'llāh Yazdī and 'Abd Allāh Khān Uzbek in *'Ālam-ārā-yi Shāh Ṭahmāsp* contains similar elements to the episode of Muḥamamd Karrah, and in fact the author alludes to the *'Ālam-ārā-yi Ṣafavī* in his narrative. He states that Shāh Ni'matu'llāh had sent a petition to Shāh Ṭahmāsp, asking him for assistance against Abdu'llāh Khān

---

[49] Afshār may have decided not to do so, perhaps understandably, in order to avoid another half century or so of confusion which occurred as a result of E. Denison Ross's erroneous dating of Bījan's history. See Morton, "Date and Attribution," pp. 179–81.

[50] See Szuppe, "La Participation des femmes," p. 225.

Uzbek: "When the shah read the petition of the *navvāb* [Shāh Ni'matu'llāh], it occurred to him that [since] in the time of Muḥamamd Karrah, the king [Shāh Ismā'īl] read the *navvāb*'s [Shāh Ni'matu'llāh's] petition and quickly went to him, Shāh Ṭahmāsp would also do the same thing."[51] Since the only history which includes this episode is *'Ālam-ārā-yi Ṣafavī*, we can assume that the author of *'Ālam-ārā-yi Shāh Ṭahmāsp* was familiar with this work, or at least one of a similar type. In the *'Ālam-ārā-yi Shāh Ṭahmāsp*, the author describes how Shāh Ṭahmāsp went to Yazd in order to rescue Shāh Ni'matu'llāh and his people from 'Abdu'llāh Khān and the Uzbeks. He eventually met the king, presented him with gifts, and accompanied him to Mashhad, where the king made the pilgrimage and then proceeded to Herāt, while Shāh Ni'matu'llāh remained in Mashhad, waiting for the king to return. When the battle with the Uzbeks ended, the king returned to Mashhad, intending to accompany Shāh Ni'matu'llāh back to Yazd. However, there the news arrived that the Ottomans were headed for Iran. With apologies to Shāh Ni'matu'llāh, Shāh Ṭahmāsp headed back for Qazvīn.[52] This episode, then, portrays Shāh Ṭahmāsp and Shāh Ni'matu'llāh in a co-operative relationship, with Shāh Ṭahmāsp rescuing the people of Yazd, and Shāh Ni'matu'llāh accompanying the king to Mashhad.

In the episode of Alqās Mīrzā's revolt, the author emphasizes Shāh Ni'matu'llāh's role in bringing Alqās Mīrzā to Shāh Ṭahmāsp after the prince's rebellion, in which he joined the Ottomans.[53] Although the official histories following the Herāt tradition mention this Shāh Ni'matu'llāh only briefly as Alqās Mīrzā's brother-in-law, the *'Ālam-ārā-yi Shāh Ṭahmāsp* greatly expands on this account.[54] The author adds numerous details of a sort that would fall under the category defined by Morton as "personalising relationships."[55] For instance, he describes how, in order to win the king's mercy, Alqās Mīrzā puts on dirty clothes and has Shāh Ni'matu'llāh put a chain on his neck and lead him to the king. The people at the palace park (*bāghistān*) of Qazvīn, as well as the *'ulamā'* at the court, began to cry upon seeing Alqās Mīrzā. Alqās Mīrzā eventually won the king's forgiveness after an emotional display in which he presented himself to the king in his dirty clothing and long, uncovered hair. His life was spared, and he was subsequently taken to the fortress of Alamut with a promise of a yearly stipend of 1,000 *tumans* from Shāh Ṭahmāsp.[56]

Another 'Safavid-family-related' episode in which Shāh Ni'matu'llāh was extensively involved was the marriage of his daughter to Ismā'īl Mīrzā. As in

---

[51] *AAST*, p. 46.
[52] The entire episode is in *AAST*, pp. 45–50.
[53] See Cornell Fleischer in *EIr*, s.v. "Alqās Mīrzā."
[54] See, for example, *TAAA*, pp. 74–5; Savory, pp. 123–4.
[55] See Morton, "Date and Attribution," p. 203.
[56] *AAST*, pp. 115–17.

the episode of Alqās Mīrzā's rebellion, Iskandar Beg and other chroniclers describe this event, but not in such detail as the *'Ālam-ārā-yi Shāh Ṭahmāsp*, in which the author provides a great deal of information about the negotiations and arrangements that preceded the actual marriage, and then describes the wedding feast itself in a similarly detailed manner. Shāh Ni'matu'llāh is portrayed as being honoured to have the king marry Ismā'īl Mīrzā to his daughter, and insists on offering some sort of modest '*darvīsh*-like' dowry to the king in exchange for the king's lavish dowry of 9,000 *tuman*s-worth of gold, jewels, and clothing.[57]

Among the striking themes in this episode is the author's description of the wealth displayed at this wedding feast. In the *'Ālam-ārā-yi 'Abbāsī*, Iskandar Beg Munshī describes this same event. He states that Shāh Ṭahmāsp had so much compassion for his son that he allowed him to get up and dance, even though it was a royal event.[58] He also makes that observation that "they made such a wedding celebration that Qizilbāsh feast and banquet is still the talk of everyone, high and low."[59] It is possible that the author of *'Ālam-ārā-yi Shāh Ṭahmāsp* based his narrative of that episode on those stories about the wedding that were still apparently circulating at the time of Iskandar Beg's writing, because he greatly expands on the episode in ways that could indicate that he wrote his history for popular audiences and for entertainment purposes.

The author elaborates on the tremendous preparations that went into the wedding feast. He describes how the confectioners and candle-makers prepared sweets and poured candles for an entire month, the great parties that were prepared in four separate gardens, and then the music, dancing, drinking, and festivities that took place at the celebration itself. Thus the author transforms an event barely mentioned by Iskandar Beg Munshi into one that certainly could have caught the interest of those who either read this account or had it recited to them.

The author also makes a point of describing the crown, the sword and dagger belts, and other items of clothing worn by Shāh Ṭahmāsp and Ismā'īl Mīrzā at the wedding, and states the value of each of these items in *tumans*. Thus he states that the 20,000 *tuman* crown (*tāj*) originally came from 'Alā' al-Dawla Dhū al-Qadr's treasury, and had then been transferred to Shāh Ismā'īl; Shāh Ismā'īl's 18,000 *tuman* vest (*khaftān*) had originally been sent by the Mamluk sulṭān Qāytbay (*reg.* 872/1468–901/1496) to 'Alā' al-Dawla; his 12,000 *tuman* sword belt had been given to Sulṭān (Ḥusayn) Mīrzā Bāyqara (*reg.* 875/1470–912/1506) by Sulṭān Abū Sa'īd (*reg* 855/1451–873/1469) and subsequently sent to Shāh Ismā'īl; and Shāh Ṭahmāsp's custom-made 12,000 *tuman* outer garment (*bālāpūsh*) was adorned with gold brocade on the

---

57 *AAST*, p. 136; see also Szuppe, p. 226, n. 68.
58 *TAAA*, p. 132.
59 *Ibid*.

outside, lined with three sable furs, and had twelve rubies and one-*mithqāl* pearls sewn onto it instead of buttons. Finally, Ismā'īl Mīrzā's 9,000 *tuman* dagger belt was given to him by his father Shāh Ṭahmāsp, along with his 1,070 *tuman* outer garment (*libās-i vīrāq*).[60] Then follows a description of music and dancing, and an account of how all of the amirs except for 'Abdu'llāh Khān and Shāh Virdī Sulṭān got drunk and danced. Ismā'īl Mīrzā became upset that these two individuals were not dancing, so he got up, grabbed 'Abdu'llāh Khān with one hand and Shāh Virdī Sulṭān with the other, and they all danced together.[61]

By including the catalogue of clothing and jewellery in his history, the author emphasizes the wealth of the Safavids at the time of Shāh Ṭahmāsp, and by naming the various items that were previously owned by powerful rivals to the Safavids, such as the Mamluk Sulṭān Qāytbay and the Dhū al-Qadr leader 'Alā' al-Dawla, and subsequently sent to the early Safavid rulers, he implies that these individuals and the dynasties they represented had submitted to the Safavids. It is also possible that the author was commenting on his contemporary situation by reflecting on the dynasty's past power and wealth, and the fact that Shāh Ni'matu'llāh's family had married into that power could only serve to increase the prestige of the Ni'matu'llāhīs at the time of writing. Finally, perhaps, even as they are today, people in the late seventeenth century would have been impressed with and entertained by descriptions of jewels, fancy clothing, expensive wedding parties, and names of the rich, the famous, and the powerful.

Later on, after the marriage, Shāh Ni'matu'llāh played a significant role in trying to stop Ismā'īl Mīrzā from rebelling. After the prince had situated himself in Herāt, some individuals tried to persuade him to make a bid for the kingship of the whole of Iran. Ismā'īl Mīrzā wrote a letter to Shāh Ni'matu'llāh, asking him for advice, and Shāh Ni'matu'llāh summoned the prince to Yazd. Shāh Ni'matu'llāh warned the prince that if he continued with such activities, his fate would be the same as that of Alqās Mīrzā, and both Shāh Ni'matu'llāh and his people would be killed. The king discovered Shāh Ni'matu'llāh's actions and sent him a robe of honour in gratitude, but the prince ultimately did not heed his father-in-law's advice. He proceeded to mint coins in his own name, and was ultimately seized. Shāh Ni'matu'llāh, upon learning this news, became very sad, and eventually the people of Ismā'īl Mīrzā's family were sent to Yazd.[62]

In all these episodes, the author of the *'Ālam-ārā-yi Shāh Ṭahmāsp* portrays Shāh Ni'matu'llāh as a 'hero' who figures significantly in early Safavid history. He shows complete loyalty to Shāh Ṭahmāsp, he helps deliver one

---

60 *AAST*, p. 135–8.
61 *Ibid*, p. 137.
62 *Ibid*, pp. 349–53.

rebellious prince to the king, and he tries to stop another prince, who also happens to be his son-in-law, from doing the same. He also participates in negotiations and diplomacy. If we assume a late date of composition, as for the other anonymous histories and for Bījan's chronicle, and if we also assume that the history was intended for more popular audiences than the chronicles based on the Herāt tradition, we may conclude that the Ni'matu'llāhī historiographical legacy continued to be extremely strong even into the late seventeenth century. The message in both *'Ālam-ārā-yi Ṣafavī* and *'Ālam-ārā-yi Shāh Ṭahmāsp* seems to be that various Ni'matu'llāhī leaders not only displayed loyalty and devotion to the Safavid ruling dynasty, but were also moral and right-minded individuals who had gained the respect of the people.

CONCLUSION

Perhaps the most important question in relation to these popular histories is why the authors would rewrite early Safavid history and assign such a prominent role to various Ni'matu'llāhī family members in that late-seventeenth-century re-imagined Safavid past. One factor could be the authors themselves and their backgrounds. Yadu'llāh Shukrī, editor of *'Ālam-ārā-yi Ṣafavī*, has suggested that its language indicates the author to be of Azeri background. He also hypothesises that he was a Shī'ite, and among those devoted to the family of Shaykh Ṣafī.[63] Īraj Afshār similarly examined the language of *'Ālam-ārā-yi Shāh Ṭahmāsp* and concluded that the author of this text was originally from Yazd, and provides a number of examples of words which reflect the Yazdī dialect.[64] We do not know where the authors wrote their histories, but we do know that, according to Arjomand, in the sixteenth century at least, the Ni'matu'llāhī *takīya* in Tabrīz (Azerbaijan) was "one of two or three supralocal ones (as distinct from the local convents, usually associated with families of *sayyids* with land holdings in the area) mentioned by Karbalā'ī."[65] Furthermore, we know that Yazd was traditionally one of several centres of Ni'matu'llāhī activity, and during the time of Shāh 'Abbās, it was the residence of the spiritual head of the order, Shāh Khalīlu'llāh.[66] Arjomand goes on to explain how "evidence suggests" that local youth and recreation groups took over these *takīya*s and were involved in factional fights such as the Ḥaydarī–Ni'matī conflicts. He further states that in the late Safavid period (the time, presumably, that *'Ālam-ārā-yi Ṣafavī* and probably *'Ālam-ārā-yi Shāh Ṭahmāsp* were written), "interfactional conflicts occurring during the Muḥarram processions represented an extremely serious problem for the

---

[63] *AAS*, pp. xx–xxi.
[64] *AAST*, p. 15.
[65] Arjomand, *The Shadow of God*, p. 117.
[66] See *TAAA*, p. 431; Savory, p. 606.

maintenance of law and order in the late Safavid period, one that remained unsolved until the fall of the dynasty and beyond."[67]

Could it be that both of these authors, presumably having lived through these kinds of events, were reflecting on and imagining a past in which the Niʿmatu'llāhī leaders were working in co-operation with the Safavid ruling dynasty to help keep order? Or could it be that they were writing for popular audiences who were involved in these sorts of Niʿmatī–Ḥaydarī town conflicts and would be interested in earlier Niʿmatu'llāhī history, in particular as the formal Sufi activities and practices of the order disappeared? At the very least, these texts suggest that the Niʿmatu'llāhī legacy in late Safavid Iran was more than simply 'destructive communal sport' as embodied in the Ḥaydarī–Niʿmatī factional fights.[68]

The fact that several histories which form a distinct school or genre of historical writing emphasize the origins and rise of the Safavid dynasty supports the hypothesis that at least some aspects of Safavid society were looking back, perhaps with a certain amount of nostalgia, to the past. It is interesting to note that Shaykh Ḥusayn ibn Shaykh Abdāl Zāhidī also dedicated his *Silsilat al-nasab-i Ṣafaviyya*, a hagiography drawing heavily on the *Ṣafwat al-ṣafā* (composed 759/1358, updated 940/1533), to Shāh Sulaymān.[69] Although we cannot consider this work to be part of the same tradition as the anonymous popular chronicles, it is still significant that it focuses on the earliest period of Safavid history, and its composition provides further evidence of a revival of early Safavid history during this time.

Standard accounts of the Niʿmatu'llāhiyya explain how, after the falling out between Shāh 'Abbās and Mīrmīrān Yazdī, the Niʿmatu'llāhīs ceased to exist as an active Sufi order, and it was only after Maʿṣūm 'Alī Shāh Dakkanī went from India to Iran in the late eighteenth century and reintroduced the order, that a resurgence took place.[70] More research needs to be done in order to understand why Dakkanī was so successful in his attempts to revive the order. It is possible that he was able to draw on some sort of Niʿmatu'llāhī legacy that still was quite alive at the time, and it is possible that the late seventeenth-century popular histories reflect that legacy and its resilience.

Certain aspects of Shāh Ṣafī II (Sulaymān)'s rule (1077 [1078]–1666 [1668]–1694) could also provide an explanation for the general characteristics of the late Safavid popular chronicles. The first has to do with the changing nature of kingship in the late Safavid period. After the reign of Shāh 'Abbās I,

---

[67] Arjomand, *The Shadow of God*, p. 118.

[68] See Hossein Mirjafari, "The Ḥaydarī–Niʿmatī Conflicts in Iran," trans. and adapted J.R. Perry, *Iranian Studies* 12 (1979), pp. 135–62.

[69] Shaykh Ḥusayn Abdāl Zāhidī, *Silsilat al-nasab-i Ṣafaviyya* (Berlin: Orientalischer Zeitschriftenverlag iranschahr 1924), p. 9.

[70] See, for instance, Algar, "Niʿmat-Allāhī," *EI*^{2}; and Arjomand, *The Shadow of God*, p. 244.

princes were increasingly confined to the harem, and as a result, the inner palace became a centre of focus and power.[71] Rudi Matthee has outlined the basic features of this harem system, in which Shāh Sulaymān relied heavily on a 'secret council of eunuchs' for advice.[72] It is therefore not surprising that Morton concluded that Bījan's history may have been commissioned by Āqā Muḥammad Riḍā Beg, probably a court eunuch, who ordered Bījan to insert portions of a text similar to the *'Ālam-ārā-yi Ṣafavī* into his history. If this is the case, we might conclude that the audience for this particular strand of historical writing was in the palace, and quite possibly the inner palace, and consisted chiefly of eunuchs and *ghulāms*.[73]

The economic situation of Shāh Sulaymān's reign, which can be financially characterized as broke, also explains some of the content of the popular chronicles. Matthee states that when Shāh Sulaymān came to the throne, the royal treasury was 'nearly empty' and out of necessity, the court had to be extremely frugal in its spending practices.[74] The situation was so severe that the shāh's grand vizier, Shaykh 'Alī Khān, implemented a strict financial policy that resulted in cutting down court spending, and courtiers, include the *ghulāms*, had to rely on the king's personal financial generosity.[75] Shaykh 'Alī Khān was a strict Muslim who disapproved, or at least did not himself participate in the popular pastime of drinking parties at the palace, and was disliked at the palace for his fiscal measures. This helps us understand the expanded wedding party account in the *'Ālam-ārā-yi Shāh Ṭahmāsp*, if it was indeed written during Shāh Sulaymān's reign. By describing the drunken dancing festivities, the writer of this chronicle could be indirectly commenting on and criticizing Shaykh 'Alī Khān, and the author's description of the values of items worn by Shāh Ṭahmāsp and Ismā'īl Mīrzā at the feast could be an indirect critique of the contemporary financial situation at the court. In other words, such a description might send a message to the king and his vizier that the Safavids had seen better, and certainly wealthier times.

In conclusion, this study has suggested strategies for how to read the Safavid chronicles in a way that enables us to learn not only about the period of time the authors narrate, but also about the times in which they wrote. In the case of the chronicles used in this study, we see the existence of two historiographical strands that depict the Ni'matu'llāhiyya in very different ways. One is an official tradition, which notes accomplishments of individual Ni'matu'llāhīs such as appointments to various official positions, and the other

---

[71] See Rudi Matthee, "Administrative Stability and Change in Late-17th–Century Iran: The Case of Shaykh 'Ali Zanganah (1669–89)," *International Journal of Middle East Studies*, 26 (1994), pp. 77–98.

[72] *Ibid*, p. 89.

[73] *Ibid.*, p. 89; Morton, "Date and Attribution," p. 185.

[74] Matthee, "Administrative stability," pp. 82–3.

[75] *Ibid.*, pp. 83, 88.

a popular tradition that seeks to rewrite key Ni'matu'llāhī leaders into early Safavid history, and perhaps glorify their role in that history. Although much has been made of the fictional nature of these histories, they are important sources that tell us a great deal about late seventeenth-century popular attitudes towards the early history of the Safavids, and as such we cannot afford to overlook them.

IV

SUFISM & ISHRAQI & AKBARIAN PHILOSOPHY

هو العزیز

هر در که زنم، صاحب آن خانه تویی تو

هر جا که روم، پرتو کاشانه تویی تو

در میکده و دیر که جانانه تویی، تو

مقصود من از کعبه و بتخانه، تویی تو

مقصود تویی کعبه و بتخانه بهانه

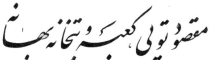

Whatever door I knock upon, the Lord within
The house is always you, and every place I go
The light that shines therein is always you.
The One beloved in bodega or convent you:
From Ka'ba or pagoda all my quest and aim
Again, is you. You, you are what I seek therein;
The rest – pagoda or the Ka'ba – all is but a ruse.

Suhrawardī's Heir? The Ishrāqī Philosophy of Mīr Dāmād

IAN RICHARD NETTON

INTRODUCTION

Mīr Muḥammad Bāqir b. Shams al-Dīn Muḥammad al-Ḥusaynī al-Astarābādī (d. 1041/1631–2), universally known as Mīr Dāmād, was one of the greatest luminaries of 'The School of Iṣfahān'.[1] His name alone would have been sufficient to contradict the venerable canard that Islamic philosophy ended with Ibn Rushd.[2] Yet with the exception of a few studies by scholars like Henry Corbin, Seyyed Hossein Nasr and, more recently, Hamid Dabashi,[3] little work has been done in the West on this great mystic and philosopher.

This essay attempts to identify, briefly, some of the major components of the classical Ishrāqī Sufi paradigm articulated so powerfully by Shihāb al-Dīn Yaḥyā Suhrawardī (549/1153–587/1191), the great Shaykh al-Ishrāq, and then goes on to examine the extent to which the thought of Mīr Dāmād conformed to that prototypical paradigm, with some reference to the Arabic *Kitāb al-qabasāt* of Mīr Dāmād. It analyses the latter's thought under the three headings of Platonism, Aristotelianism and Neoplatonic Sufism. The article concludes by examining the extent to which Mīr Dāmād's philosophy of time may be said to have enlarged the boundaries of classical Ishrāqism.

Of Mīr Dāmād, Henry Corbin wrote: "His name is familiar in Iran to everyone who has a modicum of philosophic and theological culture. Certain

---

[1] See Seyyed Hossein Nasr, "The School of Iṣpahān," in *A History of Muslim Philosophy*, ed. M.M. Sharif (Wiesbaden: Harrassowitz 1966), II, pp. 904–31; repr. in Seyyed Hossein Nasr, *The Islamic Intellectual Tradition in Persia*, ed. Mehdi Amin Razavi (Richmond: Curzon Press, 1996), pp. 239–70.

[2] See Henry Corbin's remarks in his *La Philosophie iranienne islamique aux XVIIe et XVIIIe siècles* (Paris: Éditions Buchet/Chastel 1981), p. 17; Nasr, *Islamic Intellectual Tradition in Persia*, p. 126.

[3] For the contribution of these three scholars see below.

currents of popular piety venerate him even as the equivalent of a saint."[4] Corbin retells a story to illustrate Mīr Dāmād's sense of humour, but perhaps the story also reveals the sage's own sense of his worth and eminence in philosophy. One day, in the temporary absence of Mīr Dāmād, his most famous pupil, Mullā Ṣadrā,[5] is asked: "Who do you think is the more eminent out of such and such a mullā and Mīr Dāmād?" Mullā Ṣadrā replies without hesitation that Mīr Dāmād, his master, is. The pupil's interlocuter then asks: "Who do you think is the more eminent out of Ibn Sīnā and Mīr Dāmād?" Again Mullā Ṣadrā replies without hesitation that it is Mīr Dāmād. Finally, he is asked to choose between the great Fārābī (*Magister Secundus* or *al-Mu'allim al-Thānī* as he was called) and his master. As Mullā Ṣadrā hesitates for the first time, a brusque voice replies behind him confirming that the correct answer is still Mīr Dāmād.[6]

Mīr Dāmād commonly rejoices in three principal designations. First, he is known as 'The Third Master (or Teacher)' (*Magister Tertius* or *al-Mu'allim al-Thālith*),[7] third, that is, after Aristotle and al-Fārābī. (Posterity was clearly not willing to give him the benefit of his own humour!). Second, Mīr Dāmād took the pen name *Ishrāq* to show in the most obvious way his adherence to the thought and spirituality of Suhrawardī.[8] Third, scholars are fond of designating Mīr Dāmād as 'a Shī'ite Avicennan'.[9]

There are other designations and honorifics as well: 'Master of Thought',[10] 'Perfect speculative theologian',[11] one of the "greatest *ḥakīms* of the period,"[12] even 'eleventh Archangelic Intellect'.[13] All bear witness to the lasting esteem in which Mīr Dāmād was – and is – held.

However, it is on the second major designation, that of *Ishrāqī*, that this essay will now dwell for a while. Our focus for comparison is Shihāb al-Dīn

---

[4] Henry Corbin, *En Islam iranien: aspects spirituels et philosophiques* (Paris: Gallimard 1972), IV, p. 17.

[5] See Nasr, *Islamic Intellectual Tradition in Persia*, p. 258.

[6] Corbin, *En Islam Iranien*, IV, p. 25 n. 20; see also Hamid Dabashi, "Mīr Dāmād and the Founding of the 'School of Iṣfahān'," in *History of Islamic Philosophy*, ed. S.H. Nasr and O. Leaman, (London, New York: Routledge 1996), I, p. 602.

[7] Corbin, *En Islam iranien*, IV, pp. 18, 25, 57; A.S. Bazmee Ansari, "Al-Dāmād," *EI*^{2},, II, p. 103; Dabashi, "*Mīr Dāmād*," p. 602; Nasr, *Islamic Intellectual Tradition in Persia*, pp. 61, 63, 248.

[8] Nasr, *Islamic Intellectual Tradition in Persia*, p. 164; see also Henry Corbin, "Confessions extatiques de Mīr Dāmād, maître de théologie à Ispahan (Ob.1041/1631–1632)," in *Mélanges Louis Massignon*, (Damascus: L'Institut Français de Damas/L'Institut d'Études Islamiques de l'Université de Paris, 1956), I, p. 335.

[9] See, for example, Corbin, *En Islam iranien*, IV, p. 51; *idem.*, "Confessions extatiques," p. 350.

[10] *Idem.*, "Confessions extatiques," p. 333; *idem.*, *En Islam Iranien*, p. 17.

[11] *Idem.*, "Confessions extatiques," pp. 338–39.

[12] Nasr, *Islamic Intellectual Tradition in Persia*, p. 247.

[13] Corbin, *En Islam iranien*, IV, p. 58.

Suhrawardī whose extraordinary impact and influence on Mīr Dāmād and many others has been frequently noted. Indeed, as Seyyed Hossein Nasr succinctly observes: "The whole intellectual effort of the Safavid period is unimaginable without the figure of Suhrawardī."[14]

THE LIFE OF SUHRAWARDĪ

Shihāb al-Dīn Abū 'l-Futūḥ Yaḥyā ibn Habash ibn Amīrak Suhrawardī was born in 549/1153. He bears a number of titles, which include 'The Executed' (*al-Maqtūl*) and 'The Martyr' (*al-Shahīd*). There is no doubt, however, that his most famous and most universal title is 'Master of Illumination' (*Shaykh al-Ishrāq*).[15] There is equally no doubt that his most famous book is *Ḥikmat al-ishrāq*[16] which we might render as 'The Wisdom of Illumination' but which has also been translated as *Théosophie orientale*.[17]

Suhrawardī was born in Suhraward in north-west Persia, near the modern city of Zanjān. He studied in Marāghah and Iṣfahān and later engaged in much travel, not only in Persia but in Syria and Anatolia as well, meeting many Sufis as he went. Eventually, he was invited to the Ayyūbid court at Aleppo by the prince al-Malik al-Ghāzī (also called Malik Ẓāhir Shāh). Malik Ẓāhir was the son of the Ayyubid sulṭān Ṣalāḥ al-Dīn. Just as Aristotle had been tutor to the heir of the throne of Macedonia, Alexander the Great, so Suhrawardī became tutor to Malik Ẓāhir. It was, however, an invidious position for anyone, much less the outspoken, headstrong and brilliant Shaykh al-Ishrāq, and his ideas, religious and political, roused much enmity and jealousy, especially among the *'ulamā'*. Orders were given for Suhrawardī's execution and he died in 587/1191 aged only 38. His thought, however, had a major impact on future generations of thinkers, philosophers and Sufis.[18]

---

[14] Nasr, *Islamic Intellectual Tradition in Persia*, p. 163.

[15] See Ian Richard Netton, *Allāh Transcendent: Studies in the Structure and Semiotics of Islamic Philosophy, Theology and Cosmology* (London: Routledge 1989, repr. Richmond: Curzon Press: 1994), pp. 256–7; Seyyed Hossein Nasr, *Three Muslim Sages* (Cambridge, Mass: Harvard University Press, 1969, repr. Delmar, New York: Caravan Books 1976) p. 55. The most recent monograph on Shihāb al-Dīn Suhrawardī is Mehdi Amin Razavi's *Suhrawardi and the School of Illumination* (Richmond: Curzon Press 1997).

[16] *Kitāb ḥikmat al-ishrāq* in *Oeuvres philosophiques et mystiques*, II (Académie Impériale Iranienne de Philosophie, publication no. 13, Bibliothèque Iranienne, N.S.; (Tehran: Académie Impériale de Philosophie/Paris: Librairie Adrien-Maisonneuve 1977), ed. Henry Corbin (hereafter referred to as *Ḥikmat al-ishrāq*), p. 256.

[17] Henry Corbin, *Histoire de la philosophie islamique* (Paris: Gallimard 1964), I, p. 287.

[18] See Nasr, *Three Muslim Sages*, pp. 56–8; Netton, *Allāh Transcendent*, pp. 256–7, p. 306 n. 8; *idem*, "The Neoplatonic Substrate of Suhrawardī's Philosophy of Illumination: *Falsafa* as *Taṣawwuf*," in *The Heritage of Sufism*, II, ed. L. Lewisohn (Oxford: Oneworld 1999); Hossein Ziai, "Shihāb al-Dīn Suhrawardī: Founder of the Illuminationist School," in S.H. Nasr & O. Leaman (eds) *History of Islamic Philosophy*, I, pp. 434–5.

Suhrawardī wrote in both Arabic and Persian. Hossein Ziai has identified three major groups of his works:

1. There are his four important philosophical works which are of outstanding significance for his *Ishrāqī* thought; best known is *Ḥikmat al-ishrāq*. The others are *al-Talwīḥāt* (*Intimations*), *al-Muqāwamāt* (*Apposites*) and *al-Mashāri' wa'l-muṭāraḥāt* (*Paths and Havens*).
2. Then there are his symbolic tales in Arabic and Persian like *Risālat al-ṭayr* (*The Treatise of the Birds*) and *'Aql-i Surkh* (*The Red Intellect*).[19] Ziai notes that 'in these writings Suhrawardi, as in Ibn Sīnā's Arabic tales before him, uses the symbolic narrative to portray philosophical issues, though usually simple ones intended for the novice. The tales are more significant in their use of language than in their philosophical content.'[20]
3. Finally, there is a group of "devotional prayers and invocations."[21]

Last in this thumbnail sketch of Shihāb al-Dīn Suhrawardī's life, works and milieu, we may identify briefly the kind of milieu in which he lived, if not flourished. It is clear from the bare details of his life adumbrated above that it was a milieu of great change, controversy, turbulence and warfare.[22] The Crusades were well under way. Between 1153, the date of his birth and 1191, the date of his death, Damascus submitted to Nūr al-Dīn (25 April 1154), Shirkuh, with the help of his nephew Ṣalāḥ al-Dīn, became *wazīr* of Egypt (18 January 1169), Ṣalāḥ al-Dīn himself won control of Egypt (1169), the latter proclaimed the 'Abbasid Caliphate in Egypt (10 September 1171), the last Fatimid caliph, al-'Āḍid, died (13 September 1171), Ṣalāḥ al-Dīn occupied Damascus (28 October 1174), Ṣalāḥ al-Dīn was formally invested as Governor of Egypt and Syria (May 1175), Aleppo submitted to Ṣalāḥ al-Dīn (11 June 1183), Ṣalāḥ al-Dīn defeated the Crusader army decisively at the Battle of Ḥaṭṭīn, captured Guy of Lusignan and executed Reginald of Kerak (4 July 1187); and, finally, Ṣalāḥ al-Dīn captured Jerusalem (2 October 1187). By the period between 1187 and 1189 nearly all the Latin states had been captured by Ṣalāḥ al-Dīn.[23]

This plethora of dates helps to put some flesh on Ziai's statement that, when Suhrawardī's death was demanded, "the great Sulṭān Saladin clearly had more pressing matters at hand than to bother with the execution of a wayfaring mystic, had he not been deemed to be a clear threat to political security."[24] As with Ḥallāj before him, it was probably Suhrawardī's political views, rather

[19] Ziai, "Shihāb al-Dīn Suhrawardī," p. 436.
[20] *Ibid.*
[21] *Ibid.*, p. 437.
[22] *Ibid.*, p. 435.
[23] Marshall W. Baldwin (ed.), *A History of the Crusades*, I: *The First Hundred Years* (Madison, Milwaukee–London: University of Wisconsin Press 1969), pp. 624–5.
[24] Ziai, "Shihāb al-Dīn Suhrawardī," p. 435.

than just his religious Ishrāqī philosophy, which precipitated his downfall: "The year of Suhrawardī's execution was turbulent with political and military conflict. England's King Richard the Lionheart had landed in Acre, and major battles were taking place between Muslims and Christians over the Holy Land."[25] It is clear that dissidents of any kind could easily be construed as a threat to the state itself.

In sum, the paradigm of Suhrawardī's life combines the following elements: he was a man of title (Shaykh al-Ishrāq), a man of intellect (writer, tutor) who travelled to sustain that intellect, a man of deep spirituality (Sufi), a man of deep philosophical originality and insight (*Ishrāqī*), and finally, a man of blood (al-Maqtūl/al-Shahīd). It was a short but very full life.

THE LIFE OF MĪR DĀMĀD

We do not know the exact date of birth of Mīr Dāmād but we do know that he was born in the second half of the tenth *hijrī* century.[26] We also know that he came from a very distinguished Shī'ite family.[27] Like Suhrawardī before him, he bore, as we have seen, a number of distinguishing titles, the most famous of which was 'The Third Master' (*al-Mu'allim al-Thālith*). And if we had to identify any single book as outstandingly typical of the man and his achievement, we could not go far wrong if we alighted on his Arabic *Kitāb al-Qabasāt*. Dabashi renders the word *qabas* as "a sparkle of fire"[28] but the word could also be translated as 'firebrand' or 'live coal',[29] and Henry Corbin's suggested rendition for the whole title is 'Le Livre des charbons ardents'[30] (The Book of Glowing Embers [or Live Coals]). Of *Kitāb al-Qabasāt* Hamid Dabashi notes: "*al-Qabasāt* has remained a central text of Islamic philosophy since its first appearance … [and] by the common consensus of many of his commentators, *al-Qabasāt* is Mīr Dāmād's most significant philosophical text."[31] I shall return to this text in a little while.

Mīr Dāmād was born in Astārābād but brought up in Mashhad. Here he gained his initial education. He visited Qazvīn and Kāshān before continuing his studies in Iṣfahān.[32] We know that he also spent some time in Qum.[33] Like

---

[25] *Ibid.*

[26] Corbin, *En Islam iranien*, IV, p. 22. For a brief survey and introduction to Mīr Dāmād, see Andrew J. Newman, "Dāmād," *EIr.*, VI, pp. 623–6.

[27] Corbin, *En Islam iranien*, IV, p. 22; see also *idem.*, "Confessions Extatiques," p. 340; Nasr, *Islamic Intellectual Tradition in Persia*, p. 247; *idem*, "The School of Iṣpahān," p. 914.

[28] Dabashi, "Mīr Dāmād," p. 609.

[29] See Hans Wehr, *A Dictionary of Modern Written Arabic*, 2nd printing (Wiesbaden: Harrassowitz 1966), p. 738 s.v. *qabas*.

[30] Corbin, *Philosophie iranienne islamique*, p. 26.

[31] Dabashi, "Mīr Dāmād," pp. 610, 612.

[32] *Ibid.*, p. 603; see also Corbin, *En islam iranien*, IV, pp. 22–3.

[33] Corbin, *En islam iranien*, IV, p. 23, n. 15.

Suhrawardī, again, Mīr Dāmād espoused the classical Islamic tradition of *riḥla fī ṭalab al-'ilm*. The end product was one who combined the gifts of a thinker with those of a spiritual guru,[34] and an academic expertise in *kalām*, *ḥikma* and *fiqh*, not to mention bees and their habits![35] Not only did he win the respect of many of the great scholars of the day in a range of disciplines such as philosophy, theology, law and Sufism[36] but Mīr Dāmād won the admiration of the secular authorities of his age as well. He was "held in great esteem, rather awe, by Shāh 'Abbas Ṣafawī I (996–1039/1587–1629), at whose court he wielded great influence, and his successor Shāh Ṣafī I."[37] Corbin even detects "a certain fear [by Shāh 'Abbās] in the face of his immense influence."[38] Like Suhrawardī, Mīr Dāmād wrote in both Persian and Arabic. Seyyed Hossein Nasr notes that these writings, to which we shall come in a while, "many of which are incomplete, are written in a very abstruse style which adds to the difficulty of understanding their contents."[39]

The death of Mīr Dāmād in 1041/1631–2 occurred after he became ill while travelling to Karbalā' with Shāh Ṣafī. They buried him in Najaf[40] and he was even venerated by some as a saint.[41] Mīr Dāmād's reputed last words were a quotation from the Koran: "O soul at peace, return unto thy Lord, well-pleased, well-pleasing."[42]

The age in which Mīr Dāmād lived was no less volatile than that of the *Shaykh al-Ishrāq*, Suhrawardī. The latter died at the age of 38; since we do not know the exact date of birth for Mīr Dāmād,[43] we cannot specify his age at

---

[34] Corbin, *Philosophie iranienne islamique*, p. 26.

[35] Nasr, "The School of Iṣpahān," p. 914 esp. n. 40; *idem.*, *Islamic Intellectual Tradition in Persia*, pp. 248; 266, n. 40.

[36] See Dabashi, "Mīr Dāmād," p. 606.

[37] Ansari, " 'Al-Dāmād," p. 104; see also Corbin, "Confessions Extatiques," p. 342.

[38] Corbin, "Confessions Extatiques," p. 342. Shāh 'Abbās may even have tried to have Mīr Dāmād killed, such was the awe in which the former held the latter. See Ibn Ma'ṣūm, *Salāfat al-'aṣr* (Cairo 1906), p. 477, cited in Zarrīnkūb, *Dunbāla-yi Justujū dar tasawwuf-i Īrān* (Tehran: Amīr Kabir 1362 A.Hsh./1983), p. 246. I am indebted to Dr Leonard Lewisohn for this reference.

[39] Nasr, *Islamic Intellectual Tradition in Persia*, p. 248.

[40] Dabashi, "Mīr Dāmād," p. 603; Ansari, "Mīr Dāmād," p. 104; Corbin, *En islam iranien*, IV, p. 24; *idem.*, "Confessions Extatiques," p. 342; Nasr, "The School of Iṣpahān," p. 248.

[41] Sayyid Jalāl al-Dīn Ashtiyānī and H. Corbin (eds), *Anthologie des philosophes iraniens*, I [Introduction Analytique par Henry Corbin] (Tehran: Departement d'Iranologie de l'Institut Franco-Iranien de Recherche/Paris: Adrien-Maisonneuve 1971), p. 16.

[42] Koran 89:27–8 trans. A.J. Arberry, *The Koran Interpreted* (London: Allen & Unwin/New York: Macmillan 1971), II, p. 338; Corbin, *En Islam iranien*, IV, p. 24.

[43] Nasr, "Spiritual Movements, Philosophy and Theology in the Safavid Period," in *The Cambridge History of Iran*, volume VI: *The Timurid and Safavid Periods*, ed. Peter Jackson and Lawrence Lockhart (Cambridge: Cambridge University Press 1986), p. 670 believes 969/1561–2 is "fairly likely."

death but he was very probably older than his *Ishrāqī* predecessor when he embarked on that last fateful journey to Karbalā'. We do know, however, that he served both Shāh 'Abbās Ṣafawī I (996/1587–1039/1629) and his successor Shāh Ṣafī 1 (1039/1629–1052/1642). A brief examination of their respective reigns highlights the nature of the age through which Mīr Dāmād lived, worked and wrote.

'Abbās I inherited a variety of constantly recurring problems. He was faced with the problem of Türkmen princes.[44] Shāh 'Abbās treated them ruthlessly to a degree that it is no exaggeration to say that his reign "saw the beginning of the end for the Türkmens, the decline of their military and political influence and the eclipse of their social status."[45] Furthermore, the Ottomans remained a problem for 'Abbās for the whole of his life. The Peace of Istanbul of 21 March 1590 ended twelve years of Ottoman–Safavid conflict, but the conditions imposed on the latter dynasty were draconian and, as with Versailles in the twentieth century, contained the seeds of further conflict, which eventually erupted with a Safavid reconquest of Azerbaijan, Nakhchivān and Erivan.[46]

If it is not too simplistic a comparison, the Ottomans were to Shāh 'Abbās what the Crusaders were to Ṣalāḥ al-Dīn. But by "the end of the 10th/16th and the beginning of the 11th/17th century, Shāh 'Abbās had mastered the crisis which had shaken his country at the time of his accession, in respect both of external enemies and of disruptive forces at home. Iran now enjoyed the greatest territorial extent it ever reached under the Safavids."[47]

In this volatile milieu Mīr Dāmād not only survived but flourished, as we have seen, wielding great influence at the Safavid court. Others were not so lucky: Shāh 'Abbās had his eldest son, the crown prince Ṣafī Mīrzā, murdered in 1024/1615, and three other princes, including a later crown prince, Imām Qulī Mīrzā, blinded.[48] On Shāh 'Abbās's death, the new ruler, a grandson, took the title of Shāh Ṣafī. The latter began his reign with the systematic murder of large numbers of the royal family, together with several leading generals and court officials.[49] It was a reign which saw conflict between the Safavids and the Ottoman Empire, Georgia, India and the Uzbeks.[50] It was a reign which ended in 1052/1642, about ten years after the death of Mīr Dāmād, with a country much reduced in size, territorially, from that which he had inherited.[51]

---

[44] H.R. Roemer, "The Safavid Period," in Jackson and Lockhart, *Cambridge History of Iran*, VI, pp. 262–3.
[45] *Ibid*., p. 264.
[46] *Ibid*., pp. 266–7.
[47] *Ibid*., p. 269.
[48] *Ibid*., p. 277.
[49] *Ibid*., p. 280.
[50] *Ibid*., p. 283.
[51] *Ibid*., p. 287.

It is clear that we do not need to press, further, the volatility of the milieu in which Mīr Dāmād lived and wrote. And if we compare Mīr Dāmād's life now with that of Shihāb al-Dīn Suhrawardī, we can see that the former adheres closely to the paradigm extrapolated for the latter: Mīr Dāmād, too, was a man of title (*al-Mu'allim al-Thālith*), a man of intellect who travelled in search of knowledge, a man of deep Ishrāqī spirituality who has been called both *Sayyid al-Ḥukamā'* and *Sayyid al-Falāsifa*,[52] and a man of deep and complex philosophical achievement, especially in his treatment of time, to which we shall presently come.

There are, of course, two profound and obvious differences between the lives of Shihāb al-Dīn Suhrawardī and Mīr Dāmād: the latter did not meet a violent death and he managed to maintain the favour, indeed awe, which he had won at court.

STRANDS IN THE SUHRAWARDIAN *ISHRĀQĪ* PARADIGM

Having identified this close resemblance between many essential features in the *lives* of Suhrawardī and Mīr Dāmād, it is appropriate to turn now to a comparative analysis of some of the essentials of their *thought*. This section will try to identify some of the key strands in the intellectual paradigm which might neatly be characterized as the Suhrawardian *Ishrāqī* paradigm. In the first place it was Platonic. Second, it was what I will term post-Aristotelian and third, it was Neoplatonic. It was never *solely* any of these but rather a distinctive mixture which imprinted a radical stamp on Iranian thought for centuries afterwards.

Now it has been well said that *Ishrāqī* wisdom "in the hands of Suhrawardī ... becomes a new school of wisdom integrating Platonic and Aristotelian philosophy with Zoroastrian angelology and Hermetic ideas and placing the whole structure within the context of Sufism."[53] The author might also have added Neoplatonism to the exotic and eclectic mixture outlined here. In what follows we shall concentrate briefly on delineating the Platonic, Aristotelian and Neoplatonic elements in the Surawardian Ishrāqī paradigm.

An examination of Plato's language uncovers three principal sources:

---

[52] Nasr, "Spiritual Movements," p. 669. Razavi (*Suhrawardī*, p. 125) sees the differences between Shihāb al-Dīn Suhrawardī and Mīr Dāmād as follows: "While Mīr Dāmād defended the rationalistic philosophy of the Peripatetics, he made a distinction between rationalism and illumination. Whereas Suhrawardī distinguished between Oriental and Occidental philosophy, Mīr Dāmād distinguished between *Yamānī*, the illuminative philosophy, and *Yūnānī*, the discursive philosophy of Greeks. *Yamānī* being the Orient represents the illuminative, while *Yūnānī* stands for discursive philosophy."

[53] Nasr, *Islamic Intellectual Tradition in Persia*, p. 131.

> First, he has a tendency to use visual imagery (e.g. the Sun and the Cave in *Republic* Books VI and VII) to illustrate the mind's progress in knowledge, and especially to describe the final attainment of knowledge in terms of clear vision (e.g. also *Symposium*). Second, he tends to talk of the person with knowledge looking at/to (*blepein*) the Forms. Third, in crucial passages (e.g. *Republic* Book V, 477) he tends to use the word 'gnosis' and its cognates, a term with overtones of recognition and acquaintance.[54]

It is the second source, with its looking at or to the Forms, which is of particular interest in our Suhrawardian analysis here. It has been observed that "Socrates" persistent pursuit of definitions led him to postulate Forms as the subject-matter of definitions and of true knowledge . . . beside the world of constantly changing particulars there is a world of unchanging meanings, or definables, which can be grasped once and for all by the mind.'[55] Now Suhrawardī's respect for Plato is well known;[56] in what follows we shall adumbrate Suhrawardī's own doctrine of Forms, with all the implications that has for a Suhrawardian epistemology. The aim, here, is not to cover every aspect of the Suhrawardian paradigm but simply to highlight important aspects of it.

Suhrawardī's complex hierarchy of lights, with its longitudinal (*ṭabaqat al-ṭūl*)[57] and latitudinal (*ṭabaqat al-'arḍ*)[58] orders is well known.[59] Indeed, I have characterized elsewhere what Suhrawardī established as "a deeply complex and heavily baroque structure of Neoplatonic Lights."[60] Associated with this structure is something akin to Plato's world of the archetypes. In a cosmology where there is "a radical identification of emanation, intellect, archangel and light,"[61] the development of the Latitudinal Order of Angels draws heavily on Plato's world of archetypes or *ideai*.[62] Suhrawardī tells us that everything in the universe is a "talisman" (*ṭilasm*) or an "image" (*ṣanam*) of the angels associated with the Latitudinal Order.[63] It is at this point that Suhrawardī's eclectic Ishrāqism is most apparent: the Latitudinal Angels in his cosmology bear names drawn from Zoroastrian angelology:[64] Khurdād governs the water and is its archetype (*ṣāḥib ṣanam*); Murdād's realm is the trees; while the "talisman" of Isfandārmudh is the earth.[65]

---

[54] J.C.B. Gosling, *Plato* (The Arguments of the Philosophers; London: Routledge & Kegan Paul 1983), p. 122.
[55] *Ibid.*, p. 141.
[56] See *Ḥikmat al-Ishrāq*, p. 10.
[57] See *ibid.*, pp. 145, 135–7, 178.
[58] See *ibid.*, pp. 142–3, 145, 177–9.
[59] See Netton, *Allāh Transcendent*, p. 267, fig. 8.
[60] *Ibid.*, p. 306.
[61] *Ibid.*, p. 260.
[62] *Ibid.*, p. 263.
[63] See *Ḥikmat al-ishrāq*, pp. 143–5.
[64] See Netton, *Allāh Transcendent*, pp. 263–4; Nasr, *Three Muslim Sages*, pp. 71–2.
[65] *Ḥikmat al-ishrāq*, pp. 157, 193, 199.

Plato then, or at least, Platonic influence, figures prominently in the Suhrawardian Ishrāqī paradigm. When we turn to Aristotle, and the impact of the Stagirite, we find that the reception of his thought is more mixed. What we have, basically, is an Aristotle whose "Peripatetic philosophy ... [has been] interpreted and modified by Suhrawardī."[66] There seems little doubt that, for Suhrawardī, the study of Aristotle, as articulated in the three major Aristotelian treatises (*Kitāb al-talwīḥāt*, *Kitāb al-muqāwamāt* and *Kitāb al-mashāri' wa'l-muṭāraḥāt*) constituted a primary or 'elementary' philosophical education, an essential substratum for the magisterial, and quite different, *Ḥikmat al-ishrāq*.[67] Another part of this primary education was clearly the study of Ibn Sīnā who had a considerable influence on Suhrawardī.[68] A similar debt would later be incurred by Mīr Dāmād.

Suhrawardī may be said to use and 'abuse', or at least criticize, Aristotle. Two examples must suffice. In logic "he follows mostly the teaching of Aristotle but criticises the Aristotelian definition. According to the Stagirite, a logical definition consists of genus plus differentia. Suhrawardi remarks that the distinctive attribute of the object which is defined will give us no knowledge of that thing if that attribute can be predicated of any other thing. A definition in *ishrāqī* wisdom is the summation of the qualities in a particular thing which when added together exist only in that thing."[69]

Suhrawardī was keen to transmute Aristotelian philosophy into a suitable foundation for ishrāqism. His specialism is a kind of philosophical alchemy. For the Muslim Peripatetics, being/existence (*wujūd*) was held to have a priority over essence (*māhiyya*). Essence was thus relegated to the status of accident.[70] Suhrawardī held this to be unacceptable, since, for him, existence could "not have any external reality outside the intellect which abstracts it from objects."[71] The existence of an object *was* its essence and should not be considered as "a separate reality."[72]

Ultimately, it is fair to say that "al-Suhrawardī moved from the traditional peripatetic mode of discourse to an altogether different register."[73] And that move away from traditional Peripateticism was continued in the school of Iṣfahān under such luminaries as Mīr Dāmād.

The third aspect of the Suhrawardian *Ishrāqī* Paradigm, which I would like to examine here briefly, before moving directly to the thought of 'The Third

---

66 Nasr, *Three Muslim Sages*, p. 58.
67 *Ibid.*; see also *idem*, *Islamic Intellectual Tradition in Persia*, p. 134.
68 *Idem*, *Islamic Intellectual Tradition in Persia*, p. 127.
69 *Ibid.*, p. 135.
70 *Ibid.*
71 *Ibid.*
72 *Ibid.*
73 Netton, *Allāh Transcendent*, p. 257.

Master', is Suhrawardī's Neoplatonism. He is not *just* a Neoplatonist but that aspect of his thought is of major significance.[74]

I have already referred to the "baroque structure of Neoplatonic Lights"[75] established by Suhrawardī and in this we see so many of the classical features of Plotinian Neoplatonism. There are the motifs of emanation, yearning, dominance, and ontological rather than temporal precedence.[76] From the *Nūr al-Anwār* emanates the First Light or First Intellect (*al-Nūr al-Awwal*, *al-'Aql al-Awwal*), and from the latter, other lights or intellects emanate.[77] In *Ḥikmat al-ishrāq*, "the lower lights are dominated by the higher and the former yearn for the latter. The whole of existence is ordered like this."[78]

THE THOUGHT OF MĪR DĀMĀD

It is abundantly clear that Mīr Dāmād was influenced both by Shihāb al-Dīn Suhrawardī and Ibn Sīnā before him. We have already noted earlier the designation of Mīr Dāmād as a "Shī'ite Avicennan." It is not proposed to examine here, at least directly, the Avicennan baggage borne by Mīr Dāmād,[79] but to rather explore briefly the same three elements we have just surveyed in the thought of Suhrawardī – the Platonic, Post-Aristotelian and Neoplatonic – with reference to the thought of Mīr Dāmād.

Henry Corbin reminds us that those he terms the "Platonists of Persia" (*Platoniciens de Perse – Ishrâqiyân-e Irân*) were contemporary with the Cambridge Platonists.[80] We may note here too that the life of the Italian humanist and Platonist, Giordano Bruno (1548–1600), overlapped with that of Mīr Dāmād (1561/2?–1631/2). (Like Shihāb al-Dīn Suhrawardī before him, Bruno met a violent death, executed for heresy in 1600[81]). The latter "held that human ideas are just the shadows or reflections of divine ideas."[82] And the same mixture of Platonism and (*Ishrāqī*) Neoplatonism, that we find in the school of Iṣfahān in the age of Mīr Dāmād, also prevailed in Europe at the

---

[74] *Ibid.*, p. 268

[75] *Ibid.*, p. 306.

[76] *Ibid.*, p. 261.

[77] See *Ḥikmat al-ishrāq*, pp. 128, 132–4, 137–40, 154, 178–9.

[78] Netton, *Allāh Transcendent*, p. 262.

[79] For this see Corbin, *Philosophie iranienne islamique*, pp. 19, 26; Nasr, *Islamic Intellectual Tradition in Persia*, p. 248; *idem.*, "Spiritual Movements," pp. 671, 672, 674; see also Corbin, *En Islam iranien*, IV, pp. 33–5.

[80] Corbin, *En Islam iranien*, IV, p. 11.

[81] See Michael J. Wilmott and Charles B. Schmitt, "Biobibliographies," in *The Cambridge History of Renaissance Philosophy*, ed. Charles B. Schmitt, Quentin Skinner, Eckhard Kessler and Jill Kraye, (Cambridge: Cambridge University Press, 1988), pp. 810–11, see also *ibid.*, p. 51; Corbin, *En Islam iranien*, IV, p. 11.

[82] Richard H. Popkin, "Theories of Knowledge," in Schmitt *et al.*, *Cambridge History of Renaissance Philosophy*, p. 677.

same time and earlier: a form of Platonism, which included much Neoplatonism, "was presented by Marsilio Ficino (1433–1499), who inaugurated the movement of Renaissance Platonism [in Europe]. One of his major undertakings was the *Theologia Platonica* (1474). In this and in his many commentaries on Platonic and Neoplatonic works, he tried to show that by contemplation we can reach illumination from Platonic ideas, thereby approaching ultimate knowledge, which is knowledge of God."[83] Platonism for Ficino was multi-dimensional and embraced the Platonic, the Plotinian and the Hermetic.[84] He had much in common here with Shihāb al-Dīn Suhrawardī and the later school of Iṣfahān.

Henry Corbin also insists that we cannot detect a rigid Aristotelianism among the *Ishrāqīs*.[85] Once again, this is a trait reflected in the West as well. As one author neatly puts it, writing of the humanist critique of Aristotelianism during the European Renaissance: "With the recovery of so much more classical learning during the Renaissance, some realised that Aristotle, rather than being 'the Master of them that know', was just one of many ancient thinkers, and that his accomplishment might actually be far less than had been claimed by his ardent scholastic followers."[86]

Now, in what follows, it is not intended to claim that Mīr Dāmād was an out-and-out Platonist[87] and nothing else, but simply that, like Shihāb al-Dīn Suhrawardī before him, he was influenced by the thought of the Greek Master, specifically in the area of the archetypes, and thereby conforms, in this respect, to the Suhrawardian *Ishrāqī* paradigm adumbrated above.

We shall return later in more detail to Mīr Dāmād's conception of time. Our brief references here are designed to locate and ground his own view of the archetypes. In his *Kitāb al-Qabasāt* Mīr Dāmād identifies a species of time which he calls *dahr*.[88] This seemingly innocuous Arabic word is usually rendered as "time; long time, age, epoch; lifetime; eternity; fate, destiny."[89] However, the extreme complexity of Mīr Dāmād's thought is notorious: according to one popular story, Munkar and Nakīr, the Angels of the Grave, and even God himself, had problems with Mīr Dāmād's sayings![90] It comes as no surprise, then, to find Izutsu rendering the term *dahr* as "Meta-Time." Izutsu explains:

---

[83] *Ibid.*, p. 674.
[84] *Ibid.*
[85] Corbin, *En Islam iranien*, IV, p. 17.
[86] Popkin, "Theories of Knowledge," pp. 671–2.
[87] See, too, the *caveat* in Ashtiyāni, *Anthologie*, I, p. 27.
[88] See Mīr Dāmād, *Kitāb al-Qabasāt*, ed. M.Mohaghegh, T. Izutsu, A. Mūsavī Bihbahānī and I.Dībājī, with English introduction by T. Izutsu (Wisdom of Persia Series no. 7; Tehran: McGill University Institute of Islamic Studies, Tehran Branch with Tehran University 1977), pp. 6–7.
[89] Wehr, *Dictionary of Modern Written Arabic*, p. 295, s.v. *dahr*.
[90] Nasr, "Spiritual Movements," p. 671.

> *Dahr*, the Meta-Time, is the metaphysical dimension of all non-material things. It is the domain where the eternally immutable Intelligences find their proper abode, which carry different names according to different schools of thought and different philosophical traditions, such as: the platonic Ideas, "eternal archetypes" (*a'yān thābitah*, Ibn 'Arabī), "lords of the species" (sg. *rabb al-nau'*, Suhrawardī) and Angels.[91]

Dahr, then, is the sphere or abode chosen by Mīr Dāmād for what parallels Suhrawardī's Latitudinal Order of Angels. Seyyed Hossein Nasr adds the following gloss, highlighting the *function* of the archetypes:

> The divine essence or ipseity (*dhāt*) is above all distinctions and qualities; yet it is also the source of the divine names and attributes which are both one with the essence and yet distinct from it. ... The names and attributes, which are the same as the archetypes, Platonic ideas, or the lords of the species (*rabb al-nau'*) as the Ishrāqīs call them, in turn generate the world of change. They are the immutable intelligences of this world, and each species in this world is a theurgy (*ṭilism*) for its archetype.[92]

The very world in which we live is brought into existence via the archetypes and so the creation of the world is characterized as *dahrī*.[93]

The Aristotelian and Neoplatonic substrata of Mīr Dāmād can detain us here more briefly. The terminology that is being used, or referred to, is often Aristotelian in origin. For example, Mīr Dāmād deploys the words *'aql mustafād* in his *Jadhawāt* several times.[94] This 'Acquired Intellect' (*'Aql Mustafād*) derives, of course, ultimately from Aristotle's *De Anima*.[95] But in the same text there are also references to Aristotle, together with the so-called *Theologia Aristotelis* (a Neoplatonic compilation).[96] As with Shihāb al-Dīn Suhrawardī, what we have in Mīr Dāmād is a post-Aristotelian, one whose thought is "very far from being a continuation of Muslim Peripatetic philosophy" but is rather a combination of illumination and ratiocination.[97]

The third aspect of the paradigm to be considered is the Neoplatonic. As with Suhrawardī, we may view this most easily through the lens of Mīr Dāmād's hierarchical cosmology and "chain" of Being.[98] This has much in common with

---

[91] Izutsu's Introduction to *Kitāb al-Qabasāt*, p. 5.

[92] Nasr, "The School of Iṣpahān," p. 916; see also Corbin, *La Philosophie iranienne islamique*, p. 253. For *ṭilism* see Mīr Dāmād, *Jadhawāt* (Bombay, lithographed edn, 1302/A.Hsh./1884), e.g., p. 92.

[93] Nasr, "The School of Iṣpahān," pp. 916–17.

[94] E.g. Mīr Dāmād, *Jadhawāt*, pp. 10, 11, 19.

[95] See *De Anima*, III.5.430^{a}10, 430^{a}18, 432^{b}26 for the various types of intellect in Aristotle's thought. Compare al-Fārābī, *Risāla fī'l-'aql*, ed. Maurice Bouyges (Beirut: Imprimerie Catholique 1938), p. 12.

[96] See Mīr Dāmād, *Jadhawāt*, p. 11. Izutsu (Introduction to *Kitāb al-qabasāt*, p. 3) reminds us that, for Mīr Dāmād, "the *Theology of Aristotle* was an authentic work of the Stagirite."

[97] Nasr, "Spiritual Movements," p. 672.

[98] See Mīr Dāmād, *Jadhawāt*, pp. 8–10.

the scheme established by Suhrawardī. At the very top is God, who, in typically Ishrāqī fashion, is characterized as *Nūr al-Anwār*.[99] In true Suhrawardian style there is a Longitudinal Order (*ṭūlī*) and a Latitudinal Order (*'arḍī*).[100] It differs from the Suhrawardian model in that the chain of Being is divided into two parts, "one in which there is an effusion or theophany (*tajalli*) away from the divine essence and the other in which there is a return to the origin: the first extending from the divine essence to prime matter or *hyle* and the other from the *hyle* back to the origin of all existence. Moreover, each chain is divided into a longitudinal (*ṭūlī*) order and a latitudinal (*'arḍī*) order."[101] The very first set of emanations in the Longitudinal Order of the chain of emanation is that known as *Anwār-i Qāhira* (the Victorial Lights), and the very first of these, making it the very first emanation from the *Nūr al-Anwār*, is *'Aql-i Kull* (the Universal Intellect).[102] The whole chain of Being is then elaborated in a characteristically Ishrāqī fashion.[103] "As is evident in both *al-Qabasāt* and *Jadhawāt*, for Mīr Dāmād being is circulated through a cycle of emanation from the Divine Presence to the physical world and then a return to It. In a progression of distancing emanations, the material world is gradually emanated from the Divine Presence."[104]

Mīr Dāmād's ontology is articulated using a vocabulary of Suhrawardian emanation.[105] And it is clear, looking back through this brief survey, that the thought of Mīr Dāmād, in its Platonic, post-Aristotelian and Neoplatonic aspects at least, has much in common with the Suhrawardian intellectual paradigm adumbrated above.

In much of this, we may note that the two major philosophical works of Mīr Dāmād, the Arabic *Kitāb al-Qabasāt* and the Persian *Jadhawāt*, are vital sources for Mīr Dāmād's metaphysics and cosmology. It is therefore useful to pause at this point (before moving to an area of almost profound singularity in his thought, his doctrine of time), and try to survey briefly the structure and content of the Arabic *Kitāb al-Qabasāt*, whose content provides the foundation for so much of what has already been observed, and which is of vital importance in any attempt to analyse his doctrine of time.

THE STRUCTURE AND CONTENT OF MĪR DĀMĀD'S *KITĀB AL-QABASĀT*

We may concur with Mīr Dāmād's commentators that "*al-Qabasāt* is Mīr Dāmād's most significant philosophical text."[106] It is, moreover, the principal

[99] *Ibid*., p. 8; Dabashi, "Mīr Dāmād," p. 614; Nasr, "The School of Iṣpahān," p. 918.
[100] Mīr Dāmād, *Jadhawāt*, e.g., pp. 8, 22.
[101] Nasr, "The School of Iṣpahān," pp. 917–18; see also Dabashi, "Mīr Dāmād," p. 614.
[102] See Mīr Dāmād, *Jadhawāt*, pp. 8, 21.
[103] See *ibid*., esp. pp. 8–10.
[104] Dabashi, "Mīr Dāmād," pp. 614–15.
[105] See, for example, "Mīr Dāmād," *Jadhawāt*, pp. 5, 19, 22, 25, 26, 27, 30, 31.
[106] Dabashi, "Mīr Dāmād," p. 612.

frame for his extraordinarily complex theory of time, with the treatment of which this essay will conclude.

Mīr Dāmād himself, somewhat vaingloriously one might feel, insisted on the worth of the *Qabasāt*, observing in verse that:

> In *al-Qabasāt* I became the sea of certitude

and insisting in a further, self-glorificatory, verse that:

> . . . I made the earth with my *al-Qabasāt*
> The envy of the heavenly abodes.[107]

As we have already seen, *Kitāb al-Qabasāt* may be rendered in English as 'Book of the Sparkles of Fire' or 'Book of the Live Coals',[108] while its sister Persian volume, the *Jadhawāt*, can be translated as 'Book of the Burning Brands',[109] or 'Book of Particles of Fire'.[110] These typically *Ishrāqī* titles[111] may indeed, in Corbin's words, be "fanciful" at first sight and "have no bearing whatever on the seriousness of the Text,"[112] but from a semiotic and intertextual perspective they reflect a corpus of *Ishrāqī* work with often shared values, cosmology and metaphysics. Mīr Dāmād is clearly fond of the images of light espoused by the Ishrāqī School: not only does he divide his *Kitāb al-Qabasāt* into ten *qabasāt*[113] followed by three conclusions,[114] but each individual *qabas* is divided by such rubrics as *wamḍa* (gleam of light)[115] and *wamīḍ* (sparkle).[116] In view of such light-inspired divisions it is perhaps useful to revisit Corbin's descriptions of titles such as *Qabasāt* and *Jadhawāt* as "fanciful." For what must be clear from all this is that Mīr Dāmād, deliberately and consciously, takes the metaphysical subject-matter of his text, which ranges from a discussion of "the variety of created beings and the divisions of existence"[117] in the first *qabas* to a discussion of "the matter of Divine Ordination (*al-qaḍā' wa'l-qadar*), the necessity of supplication, the promise of His reward and the final return of all things to His judgement" in the tenth[118] – and clothes it in the

---

[107] Akbar Hādī, *Sharḥ-i hāl-i Mīr Dāmād wa Mīr Findiriskī* (Iṣfahān: Intishārāt-i Mītham Tamār 1363 A.Hsh./1984), p. 134 cited and translated in Dabashi, "Mīr Dāmād," pp. 604–5.
[108] See notes 28, 29 above.
[109] Corbin, *History of Islamic Philosophy*, trans. Liadain Sherrard and Philip Sherrard (London–New York: Kegan Paul International in assoc. with Islamic Publications for the Institute of Ismaili Studies 1993), p. 339.
[110] See Nasr, *Islamic Intellectual Tradition in Persia*, p. 250.
[111] See *ibid.*, p. 165.
[112] Corbin, *History of Islamic Philosophy*, p. 339.
[113] *Kitāb al-qabasāt*, pp. 3–466.
[114] *Ibid.*, pp. 466–84.
[115] E.g. *ibid.*, pp. 3, 6, 15, 143, 146, 147.
[116] E.g. *ibid.*, pp. 16, 17, and *passim*.
[117] Dabashi, "Mīr Dāmād," p. 609; see *Kitāb al-Qabasāt*, pp. 3–36.
[118] Dabashi, "Mīr Dāmād," p. 610; see *Kitāb al-Qabasāt*, pp. 407–66.

classical *Ishrāqī* garb of light. The terminology of light thus used may have no direct bearing on the text, as Corbin intimates, but in semiotic terms it signals the *Ishrāqī* allegiance of that text in an unmistakable and intertextual manner. Shihāb al-Dīn Suhrawardī's *Ḥikmat al-ishrāq* and Mīr Dāmād's *Kitāb al-qabasāt* and *Jadhawāt* constitute a notable Ishrāqī intertext.[119]

THE PHILOSOPHY OF TIME OF MĪR DĀMĀD

To start with a simplification, the classical Islamic philosophers embraced, and grappled with, at least three distinct paradigms imbued with the interwoven topics of time, creation and eternity: there was, firstly, the Aristotelian model of God as an Unmoved First Mover 'complemented' by an eternal world; there was the Koranic model, which, like the Judaic and Christian paradigms, held to an eternal God who created the world *ex nihilo*; and, finally, there was the Neoplatonic model of eternal emanation from the One, who was unknowable, described in apophatic vocabulary, and who had an ontological, but not a temporal, priority over what emanated from Him. The concept of time, like the spectre at the feast, infused the discussion of all three classical paradigms. L.E. Goodman puts it like this:

> Islam displaces the ancient idea of time as an implacable enemy with the scriptural image of time as the stage of judgement, a narrow bridge of accountability stretched between creation and eternity. The stark contrast of temporal evanescence with all the immutability of eternity challenges Muslim theologians and philosophers of the classic age. The dialectical theologians of the *kalam* describe time and change atomistically[120] and even occasionalistically, seeking to preserve the absoluteness of the contrast and to avoid compromising the purity of God's creative act and the sheer facticity of its temporal effect. The *falasifa*, philosophers in the Greek tradition, use Platonic, Aristotelian, and Neoplatonic arguments to reconcile temporality with eternity. Stripped of argument, their emanative and archetypal schemes join the core symbolisms of Islam, but only when accomodated to the Qur'anic ideas of judgment and creation.[121]

---

[119] For more on concepts of intertextuality, see Ian Richard Netton, *Text and Trauma: An East–West Primer* (Richmond: Curzon Press 1996).

[120] "Atomism offered a concept of time which conceived of it as composed of a finite number of time-atoms or instants which are real entities. ... In every instant, God is thus creating the world anew [*ex nihilo* since each atom and its accidents last only for a moment] ... the Mu'tazila and Ash'ariyya made atomism an instrument of divine omnipotence and providence and held that each moment within time is the direct creation of the eternally active God" (Gerhard Böwering, "Ideas of Time in Persian Sufism," in *The Heritage of Sufism*, I, ed. L. Lewisohn (Oxford: Oneworld (1999), pp. 214–5.

[121] L.E. Goodman, "Time in Islam," *Asian Philosophy*, 2/1 (1992), p. 3. For an equally profound study which evaluates, *inter alia*, Bergson's arguments about time, see *idem*., "Time, Creation and the Mirror Of Narcissus," in *Divine Intervention and Miracles in Jewish Theology*, ed. Dan Cohn-Sherbok (Jewish Studies, 16; Lewiston–Queenston–Lampeter: The Edwin Mellen Press 1996), pp. 99–151.

Goodman notes that "one of the proofs that the *falasifa* believed cogently demonstrated the eternity of the world was an argument expounded by Proclus and based on the idea that if God is a creator, He must be a creator essentially (through His essential goodness and generosity) and so must create eternally."[122] He reminds us that "Plato defined time rather gnomically as the moving image of eternity. It was Aristotle who stood close enough to Plato to allow later readers to unfold a conceptual sense from these words, calling time the measure of motion (*Physics*, IV 14, 223^{a}19). When al-Kindi (d. 867), the first important philosopher to write in Arabic, wished to mark the boundary between time and eternity, he used the *kalām*-like expedient of a verbal formula, adding to Aristotle's four kinds of change a fifth – creation – God's bringing something (*aysa*) from nothing (*laysa*)."[123] But the Neoplatonists, al-Fārābī (*c.* 870–950) and Ibn Sīnā (980–1038), who succeeded al-Kindī, refused to accept that the world had an origin in time. For them, the Koranic doctrine of *creatio ex nihilo* represented "the much subtler ontic dependence of the temporal world upon a timeless God's eternal act."[124] Of course, the theologians, represented notably by al-Ghazālī (1058–1111), would have nothing to do with an eternal world: "If the world were eternal, al-Ghazali argues, an infinite time would have elapsed before today."[125]

The above remarks provide the merest hint of the medieval debates which raged among the *mutakallimūn* and the *falāsifa* over the concepts of time and eternity. They serve, however, as a useful backcloth against which we may conclude by examining briefly Mīr Dāmād's philosophy of time.

Mīr Dāmād was particularly preoccupied by the problems of time, and eternity.[126] This preoccupation is clearly visible from the start of *Kitāb al-Qabasāt*, and paramount among his ideas was that of "eternal creation, *ḥudūth-ī dahrī*,"[127] or, as Izutsu puts it more obscurely, "metatemporal contingency."[128]

It is in his concept and philosophy of time that Mīr Dāmād displays an astonishing versatility, if not total originality.[129] Basically, Mīr Dāmād's paradigm of reality embraces three divisions: *zamān*, *dahr* and *sarmad*. These terms have been variously translated (see table 1); but there is no doubt that, of

---

[122] Goodman, "Time in Islam," p. 9.
[123] *Ibid.*, p. 11.
[124] *Ibid.*, p. 13.
[125] *Ibid.*, p. 16, citing al-Ghazālī, *Tahāfut al-falāsifa,* I, ed. M.Bouyges (Beirut: Imprimerie Catholique, 1962), pp. 53–4.
[126] Corbin, "Confessions Extatiques," p. 334; Nasr, "Spiritual Movements," p. 673.
[127] Nasr, *Islamic Intellectual Tradition in Persia*, p. 248.
[128] Izutsu's Introduction to *Kitāb al-Qabasāt*, p. 8.
[129] *Ibid.*, p. 4; Nasr, 'Spiritual Movements', p. 674; although Mīr Dāmād's cosmology and concept of eternity, based on the triad of *zamān*, *dahr*, and *sarmad*, were unique, the actual distinction of the three terms by a single author was not his doing alone. Böwering ("Ideas of Time," p. 213, n. 33) reminds us that "Ibn Sina . . . refines the terminology by the distinction of *zamān*, *dahr*, and *sarmad*."

Table 1: *Zamān*, *Dahr* and *Sarmad*

	Zamān	*Dahr*	*Sarmad*
Nasr[130]	time	eternity	eternity
Dabashi[131]	temporality	atemporality	everlasting
Izutsu[132]	Time	Meta-Time	No-Time
Corbin[133]	*le temps*	*perpétuité*	*éternité*
Wehr[134]	time, fate, destiny	time, epoch, eternity, fate, destiny	endless duration, eternity
Böwering[135]	a long time having beginning and end (= Gk *chrónos*)	time from the beginning of the world to its end (= Gk *aión*)	incessant continuance
Afnan[136]	time	eternal duration	absolutely fixed time, perpetuity
Koran	Non-Koranic	K. 45: 24	K. 28:71

all these terms, it is the concept and vocabulary of 'eternity' that has caused, and continues to cause, the most problems.

St Augustine, classically, had problems with the notion of time: "What *is* this time? If no one asks me, I know; if I want to explain it to a questioner, I do not know."[137] But in antiquity, perhaps it is the Father of Neoplatonism himself, Plotinus, who best articulates the complexities of the notion of eternity: "Eternity, thus, is of the order of the supremely great; intuition identifies it with God: it may fitly be described as God made manifest, as God declaring what He is, an existence without jolt or change."[138]

Referring to the relationship between the members of Mīr Dāmād's triadic concept of time, Nasr points out that "*Sarmad* is the cause of *dahr* and *dahr* the cause of *zamān*, so that ultimately the Divine Essence is the cause of all

---

[130] Nasr, *Islamic Intellectual Tradition in Persia*, p. 249.
[131] Dabashi, "Mīr Dāmād," p. 613.
[132] Izutsu, introduction to *Kitāb al-Qabasāt*, p. 4.
[133] Corbin, *La Philosophie iranienne islamique*, p. 28.
[134] Hans Wehr, *A Dictionary of Modern Written Arabic*, 3rd edn (Ithaca, N.Y.: Spoken Language Services 1976), s.v. *zamān, dahr, sarmad.*
[135] Böwering, "Ideas of Time," pp. 212–13. See also Franz Rosenthal, *Sweeter than Hope: Complaint and Hope in Medieval Islam* (Leiden: Brill 1983), p. 6.
[136] Soheil M. Afnan, *A Philosophical Lexicon in Persian and Arabic* (Beirut: Dār al-Mashriq 1969), pp. 102–3, 117–8, 125.
[137] St Augustine, *Confessions*, Book Xl, trans. Frank Sheed (Indianapolis, Ind.–Cambridge, Mass.: Hackett Publishing Co. 1993), repr. in *Time*, ed. Jonathan Westphal and Carl Levenson (Hackett Readings in Philosophy; Indianapolis–Cambridge: Hackett 1993), p. 15.
[138] Plotinus, *Enneads* lll.5.V, trans. Stephen MacKenna, repr. in Westphal and Levenson, *Time*, p. 78.

things," since *sarmad* is the world of the Divine Essence,[139] while the archetypes inhabit the world of *dahr*.[140]

Corbin has summed up Mīr Dāmād's achievement in the following words:

> One of the problems that preoccupied him was that of finding a solution to the dilemma of cosmology; a world *ab aeterno*, or a world which came into existence in time (as the *mutakallimūn* professed) before there was any time? Between the eternally existing and the event which came into existence in time, he sought a solution in an eternal coming-to-be (*ḥudūth dahrī*), an eternally new event.[141]

For Aristotle, time was a measure of motion. For Mīr Dāmād, his triadic concept of time embraced a complex set of interlocking gradations of changelessness and change. The world is not a product of time in the sense of *zamān* where a divine *fiat*, at a given moment in time, creates that world *ex nihilo*. The world is the product of the immutable archetypes that inhabit the realm of *dahr*. For this reason creation is characterized as *dahrī*, not *zamāni*, and Mīr Dāmād's new concept is called *ḥudūth-i dahrī*, eternal creation.[142]

Izutsu, as we have noted, translates *dahr* as "Meta-Time," which may be defined as "a kind of eternity intermediary between the dimension of absolute timelessness and the dimension of Time."[143] And what Mīr Dāmād does is to hold that "although the world has no temporal beginning, it does have a meta-temporal beginning. And to say so is nothing other than saying that the existence of the world is preceded by non-existence."[144]

SUHRAWARDĪ'S HEIR?

Mīr Dāmād's extraordinarily difficult philosophy of time, with its tripartite division, renders him *sui generis*. He is, indeed, the heir of Shihāb al-Dīn Suhrawardī, but the philosophy of time articulated in his *Kitāb al-Qabasāt* ensures that he is also much more than that. He does, as we have seen, adhere in many ways to the essential features of the *Ishrāqī* intellectual paradigm; but his views on time transcend the boundaries of that paradigm in a radical and definitive fashion. His most famous pupil, who overshadowed him in fame, Ṣadr al-Dīn Shīrāzī, known as Mulla Ṣadrā (979/1571–1050/1640), rejected both "the view of the Peripatetics who believe the world to have been created only in essence or *in principio* but not in time and the view of Mīr Dāmād about *al-ḥudūth al-dahrī*" holding rather to a belief of creation in time (*al-*

---

[139] Nasr, *Islamic Intellectual Tradition in Persia*, p. 250; see *Kitāb al-qabasāt*, p. 7.

[140] Nasr, *Islamic Intellectual Tradition in Persia*, p. 250.

[141] Corbin, *History of Islamic Philosophy*, p. 339.

[142] Nasr, "Spiritual Movements," p. 674; *idem*, *Islamic Intellectual Tradition in Persia*, p. 249.

[143] Izutsu, introduction to *Kitāb al-qabasāt*, p. 5.

[144] *Ibid.*, p. 7.

ḥudūth al-zamānī).[145] However, Mulla Ṣadrā held this belief in *creatio ex nihilo* alongside a belief in the existence of changeless archetypes for the created world.[146] The terminology of archetypes and *ḥudūth* may be the same: their philosophical and cosmological patterning is very different.

ENLARGING THE BOUNDARIES

Mīr Dāmād's philosophy of time was but one of many diverse approaches to that complex subject, the overall history of which still awaits a substantial monograph. And it is the diversity as well as the complexity which still impresses. For example, G. Böwering concludes that:

> the journey through the world of time in Persian mysticism led from Bāyazīd's ecstasy, Tustarī's recollection of primordial time, Shiblī's paradox of the eternal moment and Kharrāz's annihilation of temporality and subsistence in eternity through theoretical notions of *waqt* and *wajd* and such select mediaeval expressions of time as 'Ayn al-Quḍāt's black light, Daylamī's past and future compressed into the present and Bahā'-i Walad's co-being of the Eternal with time expressed in the images of poetry, miracle stories and social institutions.[147]

Now it is indeed "a commonplace that time, not space, is the dimension of change."[148] And Aristotle's view that "time is the measure of change"[149] and motion, articulated in the *Physics*,[150] has cast a long shadow over the development of the philosophy of time. It may or may not be true "that there are conceivable circumstances in which the existence of changeless intervals *could* be detected."[151] What *is* true is that many of the conceptions of time in modern philosophy are just as radical, thought-provoking and complex as anything ever devised by Mīr Dāmād.[152] They range from Einstein's general theory of relativity through theories of cosmic time, parallel time-series and tree time.[153] However, these all have little in common with Mīr Dāmād's ideas.

---

[145] Nasr, *Islamic Intellectual Tradition in Persia*, p. 286.
[146] *Ibid.*
[147] Böwering, "Ideas of Time," p. 233.
[148] Robin Le Poidevin and Murray MacBeath, introduction to *The Philosophy of Time*, ed. Robin Le Poidevin and Murray MacBeath (Oxford Readings in Philosophy; Oxford: Oxford University Press 1995), p. 1.
[149] *Ibid.*, p. 5.
[150] See *Physics* Bk. IV 10, 218^b, 19–20, Bk. IV 12, 221^a.
[151] Sydney Shoemaker, "Time without Change," in Le Poidevin and Macbeath, *Philosophy of Time*, p. 79.
[152] See, for example, the chapters in Le Poidevin and MacBeath, *Philosophy of Time*.
[153] See Quentin Smith, "Physical Time in Current Cosmologies" in Quentin Smith and L. Nathan Oaklander, *Time, Change and Freedom: An Introduction to Metaphysics* (London–New York: Routledge 1995), pp. 185–214. See also the modern classic by Stephen Hawking, *A Brief History of Time: From the Big Bang to Black Holes* (London: Bantam Press 1988).

Slightly more profit might perhaps be gained from the ideas of the Rumanian historian of religion, Mircea Eliade (1907–86), who differentiates between sacred and profane time[154] and identifies "a mythical time [which] is made present"[155] and "the notion that time is periodically regenerated by symbolic repetition of the creation."[156] Eliade notes:

> What is true of time in Christian worship is equally true of time in all religions, in magic, in myth and in legend. A ritual does not merely repeat the ritual that came before it (*itself the repetition of an archetype*) [my italics], but is linked to it and continues it, whether at fixed periods or otherwise.[157]

If we are to make any other kinds of useful comparisons with Mīr Dāmād's thought, perhaps the way forward lies in classical and modern definitions of eternity. Here the very focus is Dāmādian.

In such definitions Dāmād, and other theistic philosophers of time, share the idea that "eternity is God's timeless mode of existence."[158] The latter differ over what kind of definition of eternity they wish to espouse. It might be:

- the 'non-temporal duration' definition according to which "God endures simultaneously with all instants of time, rather than exists instantaneously, but his duration does not consist of stages that succeed one another."[159]

or

- the 'present instant' definition according to which "God does not endure but exists only at one permanently present instant. This instant is not a part of time and is unlimited in the sense that there are no instants before and after it."[160]

or

- the 'tenseless duration' definition of eternity according to which "God's duration possesses successive parts, but the parts of his duration do not possess properties of being future, present or past. This definition requires the tensed theory to be true, i.e., that events in time possess properties of being future, present or past."[161]

or

---

[154] Mircea Eliade, *Sacred Time*, repr. in Westphal and Levenson, *Time*, pp. 197, 200.
[155] *Ibid.*, p. 201.
[156] *Ibid.*, 212.
[157] *Ibid.*, p. 200.
[158] Quentin Smith, "Eternity," in Smith and Oaklander, *Time, Change and Freedom*, p. 53.
[159] *Ibid.* See also the definitions of 'eternal' in L. Nathan Oaklander, "Fatalism and Tenseless Time," in Smith and Oaklander, *Time, Change and Freedom*, p. 128.
[160] Smith, "Eternity," p. 53.
[161] *Ibid.*

- The 'tenseless instant' definition whereby "God exists at one instant that is not a part of time. This instant is not present and it is not simultaneous with, earlier than or later than any other instant. The tenseless theory of time is true, so all successive events exist equally and are equally apprehended by God."[162]

None of these definitions directly parallels the cosmology of Mīr Dāmād, with its focus on *zamān*, *dahr* and *sarmad*. But in their preoccupation with the nature of God and the nature of eternity they share in a 'great tradition'.

In this essay I have surveyed the classical elements of the Suhrawardian *Ishrāqī* paradigm as they were articulated and extended by Mīr Dāmād. I endeavoured to confirm that the point at which Suhrawardī and Mīr Dāmād part company was in the latter's complex philosophy of time. I have suggested in conclusion that future scholars may wish to re-examine this philosophy of time in greater depth by reference to the development of modern ideas and definitions of eternity. As my notes demonstrate, the philosophy of time is a flourishing sub-specialism in modern philosophy and perhaps ideally suited to the re-examinations and reformulations necessary in any further study of Mīr Dāmād's magisterial *Kitāb al-Qabasāt*

---

[162] *Ibid.*

Travelling the Sufi Path
A Chishtī Handbook from Bijapur

WILLIAM C. CHITTICK

During the reigns of Akbar and Jahāngīr (963/1556–1037/1628), numerous Sufis were writing books and treatises that one might classify as belonging to the school of Ibn 'Arabī (d. 638/1240).[1] Indeed, by this time, it was difficult to write anything on Sufi theory without employing the technical terminology of this school. This is not to say that all these authors had necessarily read any of Ibn 'Arabī's works or considered themselves his followers, but rather that this school of thought had played a major role in shaping the intellectual language of the day. The well-known Sufi Shaykh Aḥmad Sirhindī (d. 1034/1624) is a case in point. Although he was critical of certain ideas that he attributed to Ibn 'Arabī, his own writings are full of the terminology and concepts of Ibn 'Arabī's perspective, as he often acknowledges.

Although Sirhindī may be the best-known Sufi author of this period, this should not lead us to think that he was also the most important or the most representative. 'Importance' depends upon one's choice of criteria. In terms of certain political and nationalistic ideas that have come to play a role in establishing Muslim identity in the present century, Sirhindī may indeed be considered to have special importance. But, if we are to judge by criteria internal to the Islamic tradition in general and the Sufi tradition in particular, we will find many other authors of the same period deserving serious study and perhaps much more worthy than Sirhindī of being considered important. Once the works of these authors have been published and analysed, and once their influence on later Sufis has been traced, we might well find that Sirhindī had little to offer to the tradition and that he was unknown except in a relatively

---

[1] The term 'School of Ibn 'Arabī' is problematic, and here I use it loosely to indicate a certain theoretical approach to Sufi teachings employing concepts and technical terminology that were highlighted by Ibn 'Arabī and his immediate followers, such as Ṣadr al-Dīn Qūnawī. See Chittick, "The School of Ibn 'Arabī," in *History of Islamic Philosophy*, ed. S.H. Nasr and O. Leaman (London: Routledge 1996), I, pp. 510–23.

small circle. In any case, the necessary research has not yet been carried out, so at this point I can offer this only as a hypothesis. I believe it may be true, because I have found many extremely interesting works from this period by authors who, for one reason or another, have been ignored by modern scholarship.[2]

One of the major reasons that most Sufi writing of India has remained unstudied is that modern scholars have focused on social and political history and have had little interest in the goals and intentions of the Sufi authors themselves. As Carl Ernst has well illustrated, three competing historiographical schools – the British, the Muslim, and the Hindu – with three distinct agendas, have provided us with a diversity of interpretations of the significance of India's past in terms of modern social and political concerns.[3] One of the results of the specific preoccupations of these scholars is that, by and large – and with certain obvious and important exceptions – they have made assumptions about the Sufi tradition and ignored the actual works of the authors. Very few have had the interest or the training to situate the Sufi writings in the context of Islamic intellectual history. When statements are made about content, these are typically based not on a study of the works, but rather on a superficial understanding of the Sufi tradition as found in the central Islamic lands.[4]

Among the many important Sufis writing in this period, probably the most careful student of Ibn al-'Arabī's works and the most faithful representative of his school of thought was Shaykh Muḥibb Allāh Mubāriz Ilāhābādī, who died twenty-four years after Sirhindī in 1058/1648. He wrote many works in Persian and a few in Arabic. Several of these works are based squarely on the text of Ibn 'Arabī's *Futūḥāt al-makkiyya*, which does not seem to have been much studied in this period; he also wrote two commentaries on the *Fuṣūṣ al-ḥikam*, a short commentary in Arabic and a much longer commentary in Persian. Here, however, I would like to look at one of the many other figures of the

---

[2] See Chittick, "Notes on Ibn al-'Arabī's Influence in India," *Muslim World*, 82 (1992), pp. 218–41.

[3] See Carl Ernst, *Eternal Garden: Mysticism, History, and Politics at a South Asian Sufi Center* (Albany: SUNY Press 1992), chap. 2. See also Ernst's important discussion of the term Sufism, as it came to be formulated by Western scholars working in the Indian context in his *Shambhala Guide to Sufism* (Boston–London: Shambhala 1997). This formulation, along with the reactions to it by modern-day Muslims, helps explain the peculiar ways in which various attempts continue to be made, both by Muslims and non-Muslims, to detach Sufism from the heart of the Islamic tradition.

[4] Rizvi's two-volume *History of Sufism in India* (New Delhi: Munshiram Manoharlal, 1978–83) is unfortunately no exception to this rule. Although it is an invaluable work for those who want to gain a rough idea of the important Sufi authors in the subcontinent, the statements about content are invariably superficial, and the information about the Sufi learned tradition that the author offers is based on the Western secondary literature, not his own reading of the texts that he enumerates.

period who deserve investigation. This is Shaykh Maḥmūd Khwush-Dahān (d. 1026/1617), who belongs to the Chishtī group that has been studied by Richard Eaton in *Sufis of Bijapur*. Eaton has made clear – if there was any doubt – that Sufism in various forms was flourishing in this west-central Indian province during this period. Among the most active Sufi groups was the Chishtī order to which Shaykh Maḥmūd belonged. It was centred on a famous family of Sufis that traced itself back to Shāh Mīrānjī Shams al-'Ushshāq (d. 1499), who was born in Mecca and appears to have been originally a Chaghatay Turk. According to the traditional accounts, as a young man he had a dream of the Prophet in which he was instructed to travel to Bijapur to find one Shāh Kamāl, who turned out to be Kamāl al-Dīn Biyābānī (d. 867/1462–3), the successor, with one intermediary, of the famous Chishtī shaykh Gīsū Darāz (d. 825/1422).

Having himself become the successor of Biyābānī, Shams al-'Ushshāq was then succeeded by his own son Burhān al-Dīn Jānam (d. 1005/1597), a prolific author of Persian works on Sufi theory and practice. Burhān al-Dīn was in turn succeeded by Shaykh Maḥmūd Khwush-Dahān, who derived from a well-known Qādirī family in Bīdar. Shaykh Maḥmūd also wrote many Persian works, one of which is *Ma'rifat al-sulūk* (The True Knowledge of Wayfaring). It has been described as "the summary work of all Bijapuri Chishtī teachings and a book upon which scores of later treatises were based."[5] In it, Shaykh Maḥmūd outlines, in an unusually simple and systematic manner, the basic teachings and practices that were being imparted to disciples by his shaykh, Burhān al-Dīn Jānam, and presumably by himself as well. Not only did this work play an important role in a major branch of Indian Sufism, but it also has a much wider significance, because, as far as I can judge, it is an especially clear presentation of the methods and goals of the later Sufi tradition throughout much of the Islamic world.

It needs to be remembered that Sufi authors had produced a wealth of works on both theory and practice over the centuries, and the Indian authors continued to write prolifically, mainly in Persian. By the beginning of this period, Indian Sufis had access to a plethora of writings and oral teachings, and they could easily become aware of the differing theoretical and practical frameworks of diverse Sufi authors. More than two hundred years had passed

[5] Richard M. Eaton, *Sufis of Bijapur: Social Roles of Sufis in Medieval India* (Princeton: Princeton University Press 1978), p. 146. I have chosen to present this work here not because I think it the most important or the most interesting of the period, but because I happen to have a copy of an adequate manuscript, the work is relatively short and clearly written, and its contents are especially instructive concerning the overall teachings of Sufism. The manuscript I am using is Osmania University 1047. Other manuscripts that I have seen include Osmania University 752; Salar Jung Museum, Tas 232/5 and Tas. 250; and Andhra Pradesh State Oriental Manuscripts Library 30682. The work is reported to have been lithographed in Lucknow (Nawal Kishore 1898), but I have not seen the edition.

since the enormous outpouring of Sufi writing in the twelfth and thirteenth centuries. Throughout the subcontinent, the more learned Sufis were familiar with the writings of Abū Ḥāmid Ghazālī and 'Ayn al-Quḍāt Hamadānī, not to mention the Persian Sufi poets, especially Rūmī, and the vast range of theoretical works by Ibn al-'Arabī and his followers. Scores of important Sufis of the central Islamic lands and India had produced works of significance, and each of the several Sufi orders flourishing in India had its own favourite authors, as well as shaykhs who themselves wrote many sorts of works on Sufi teachings. Then, as today, it was practically impossible for a single seeker to gain a complete overview of the diverse Sufi teachings that were available. Nonetheless, every seeker who made any attempt to visit Sufi shaykhs, study Sufi writings, and listen to Sufi poetry would have been exposed to a variety of ideas and conceptual schemes that were not always easy to interrelate.

In order to organize the received lore of Sufism and Islam, Sufi authors took different approaches. Even when the teachings of two authors seem to be the same, careful analysis often shows that there are important discrepancies. There is no single 'Sufi doctrine' accepted by all the Sufi teachers, other than the basic creed of Islam. What we usually see is that a given author will conceptualize the received wisdom in his own personal terms, on occasion idiosyncratically, and then offer his own theory to his students and readers as a guide to understanding the nature of things. In parallel texts written by philosophers or theologians we may be dealing with pure theory, but in the Sufi texts, the practical applications of the teachings are either stated explicitly or implied by the context of the writings, which are not aimed at 'thinkers', but at practitioners and adepts. The Sufis considered theory important – except in moments of rhetorical excess or poetical intoxication – but they always understood theory as a means to an end, not an end in itself. Hence, the theory is constantly being modified to fit the practical circumstances.

From early times, Sufi authors had offered various overarching schemes to organize the Islamic worldview and to situate Muslim practice within this view. In many Sufi works, and in many chapters of these works, one of these schemes is employed as the organizing principle. Typically, as anyone who has looked at the secondary literature on Sufism is well aware, these schemes present us with hierarchies, in keeping with the general Islamic idea that reaching God depends upon following a specific 'path' (*sharī'a*, *ṭarīqa*) or climbing a 'ladder' (*mi'rāj*). This is especially obvious in the many books written on the 'stations' (*maqāmāt*) or 'waystations' (*manāzil*) of the path, whether these be enumerated as seven, ten, forty, one hundred, three hundred, one thousand, or whatever. One of the most familiar of these schemes is that of *sharī'a*, *ṭarīqa*, and *ḥaqīqa* – Law, Path and Reality. Another is the ascending degrees of self or soul (*nafs*) – the soul that commands to evil (*ammāra*), the blaming soul (*lawwāma*), and the soul at peace with God (*muṭma'inna*); often a fourth is added, the 'inspired soul' (*mulhama*). Still another scheme, in a more theoretical realm, is the Five Divine Presences, which are enumerated in various ways. One common version presents us with the terms *nāsūt*, *malakūt*, *jabarūt*, *lāhūt* and *hāhūt*, which can be translated as Humanity, Sovereignty, Domination, Divinity and Ipseity. Another well-known scheme describes the ascending microcosmic degrees, sometimes called the 'subtle centres' (*laṭā'if*) and often considered to be seven in number. Thus, for example, we find body, soul, spirit, heart, mystery, hidden (*khafī*) and most hidden (*akhfā*).

* * *

The great richness of the Sufi tradition in the Mughal period and the variety of conceptual schemes found in Sufi texts may help explain Shaykh Maḥmūd's intentions in writing *Ma'rifat al-sulūk*. What he offers is a synthesis of various dimensions of Sufi thought and practice, or a way of correlating all the diverse technical terms that appear abundantly in the texts and the tradition. He makes clear in presenting his synthesis that all this conceptualization has the practical aim of guiding seekers on the path to God.

Shaykh Maḥmūd summarizes his book, which is relatively short – about 150 pages – in a circle divided into eight sectors (see Figure 3). The circle represents all and everything: the One and the many, God and the world, Lord and servant, macrocosm and microcosm, and the interrelationships among the various realities that can be conceptualized in the nature of things. Each of the eight sectors has five levels, for a total of forty sections (forty being the number of completion, as Professor Schimmel reminds us[6]). In fact, however, the fifth level is the same reality in each case, but it is given different names depending on the sector from which one enters into it.

The first sector is arranged in terms of *wujūd* – 'existence' or 'being' – and more particularly, according to the famous distinction between Necessary, Possible, and Impossible Existence. This gives us only three levels, so the Shaykh adds two more, *'ārif al-wujūd*, 'the Gnostic of Existence', and *wāḥid al-wujūd*, 'the One of Existence'. This last and highest level obviously points to the doctrine of *waḥdat al-wujūd*, 'the Oneness of Being', which by this time was identified with Ibn 'Arabī – even though this identification does not help us much to understand the actual historical development of the idea and the various meanings that were given to it by diverse authors.[7] In any case, Shaykh Maḥmūd names the circle and the other diagrams according to the level of existence, and he puts the One of Existence at the highest level. Thus he

---

[6] See Annemarie Schimmel, *The Mystery of Numbers* (Oxford: Oxford University Press 1993), pp. 245–52.

[7] See my article "Rūmī and *Wahdat al-wujūd*," in *Poetry and Mysticism in Islam: The Heritage of Rūmī*, ed. A. Banani, R. Hovannisian, and G. Sabagh (Cambridge: Cambridge University Press 1994), pp. 70–111.

Figure 3: The One of Existence

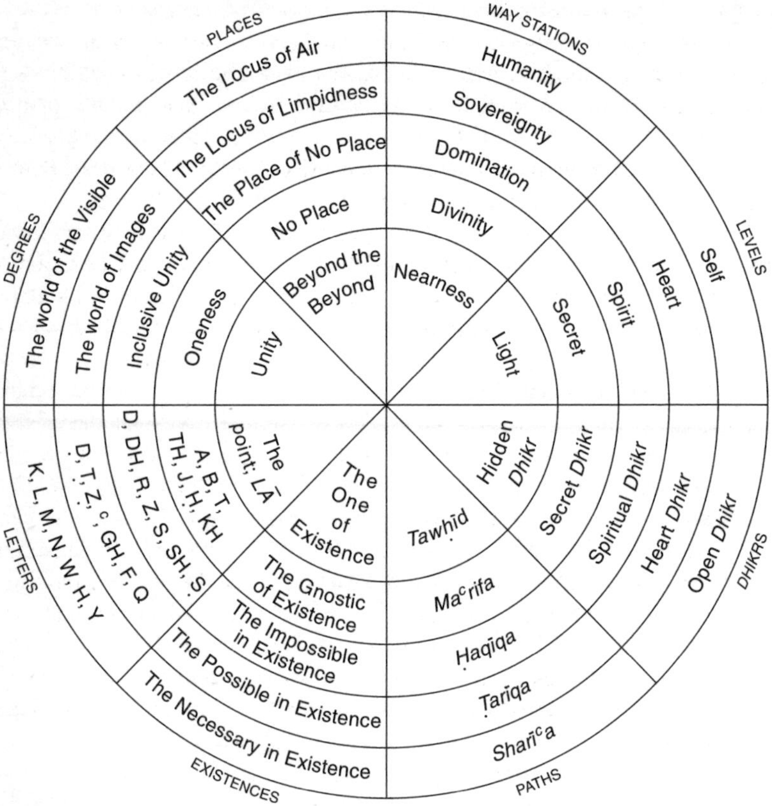

demonstrates that he belongs to the mainstream of Indian Sufism in terms of the central importance of *waḥdat al-wujūd*.

The second sector of the circle presents five 'paths' (*sabīl*), beginning with the *sharī'a*, then the *ṭarīqa*, then the *ḥaqīqa*, then *ma'rifa* and finally *tawḥīd*.

The third sector is organized in terms of different levels of the remembrance of God, beginning with the voicing of the formula (*dhikr-i jalī*), and ending with the innermost realization of what is being remembered (*dhikr-i khafī*).

The fourth sector deals with subtle centres, which the author simply calls 'levels' (*marātib*), that is, levels of the human microcosm – self or soul, heart, spirit, secret, and light.

The fifth presents us with 'waystations' (*manāzil*), four of them clearly inspired by standard terminology for the Five Divine Presences: *nāsūt*, *malakūt*, *jabarāt* and *lāhūt*. The fifth, however, which the author calls the way station of nearness (*qurb*) is, according to Ibn ʻArabī, the summit of the path, the highest stage attainable by anyone who is not a prophet.

The sixth sector designates 'places', and here various terms are offered through which one might speak of 'localization' at any level of reality. This particular scheme may be original with the Bijapuri school, though the individual terms are well enough known. The five places are the locus of air (*maḥall-i hawā*), the locus of limpidness (*ṣafā'*), the 'Place of No Place' (*makān-i lā makān*), 'No Place' itself, and 'Beyond the Beyond' (*warā' al-warā*).

The seventh sector offers us five 'degrees' (*darajāt*), and here the author seems to have taken inspiration from another standard method for explaining the Five Divine Presences: the world of the visible (*shahāda*), the world of images (*mithāl*), inclusive unity (*wāḥidiyya*), oneness (*waḥda*), and (exclusive) unity (*aḥadiyya*).

Finally, Shaykh Maḥmūd describes the five levels in terms of the Arabic alphabet, whose symbolism was often made use of in various contexts, such as delineating the twenty-eight degrees of the Breath of the All-Merciful that gives birth to the cosmos. The Shaykh ascribes seven letters to each of the four outer levels, beginning from the end (and following the *alif–bā'*, not the *abjad* order). Thus, the outermost level is made up of the seven letters beginning with *yā'* and ending with *kāf*. The fourth level ends with the first of the twenty-eight letters, *alif*. As for the fifth and highest level, this is identified both with the point, from which the *alif* is often said to be generated, and with the *lām–alif*, which is sometimes considered the twenty-ninth letter of the alphabet. More importantly, of course, *lām–alif* spells *lā* or 'no', so it can denote the utter undifferentiation and 'nonentification' (*lā taʻayyun*) of the Divine Essence – just as, mathematically, the point designates that which has no dimensions whatsoever.

To prepare the reader for the circle, which is the summation of his teachings, Shaykh Maḥmūd first offers four tables corresponding to the four outer levels of the circle (see Tables 2–5). In the tables, however, he does not offer exactly the same scheme as he provides in the circle. He presents each table as having thirteen levels, not eight, and only five of the eight sectors are mentioned in the table, leaving eight other ways of conceptualizing the four outer levels of the circle. (The tables in the manuscript I have seen have thirteen levels. However, the twelfth level is the same in each case – *haft shughl* or 'seven occupations'. I do not think that this is meant to be a level of its own, but rather the designation for the significance of the seven letters that are mentioned in the thirteenth level, given that each letter designates a specific 'occupation', that is, ritual form or duty, that the Sufi should employ).

In the four tables (Tables 2–5), Shaykh Maḥmūd first mentions the level of existence, then the archangel who is entrusted with the level. Then he turns to the levels of the human microcosm. In the circle (Fig. 3), he mentions the five

Table 2: The Necessary in Existence

The Knower *ʻālim*	The Necessary in Existence *wājib al-wujūd*	The Gnostic *ʻārif*
	Entrusted angel: Michael *muwakkal*: Mīkā'īl	
Watchfulness *murāqaba*	The growing spirit *rūḥ-i nāmī*	Annihilation *fanā'*
	The fleshly heart *qalb-i muḍgha*	
	The commanding soul *nafs-i ammāra*	
	Understanding: comparison *fahm-i qiyās*	
	Open remembrance *dhikr-i jalī*	
Disengagement *tajrīd*	*Tawhīd* through words *tawḥīd-i aqwālī*	Solitude *tafrīd*
	Path of the *Sharīʻa* *rāh-i sharīʻat*	
	Way station: Humanity *manzil-i nāsūt*	
Witnessing *mushāhada*	Martyrdom of origin *shahādat-i mabdā*	State *ḥāl*
	Seven occupations *haft shughl*	
Lover *ʻāshiq*	y, h, w, n, m, l, k	Arriver *wāṣil*

Table 3: The Possible in Existence

The Knower	The Possible in Existence *mumkin al-wujūd*	The Gnostic
	Entrusted angel: Seraphiel *muwakkal*: Isrāfīl	
Watchfulness	The motile spirit *rūḥ-i mutaḥarrik*	Annihilation
	The repenting heart *qalb-i munīb*	
	The blaming soul *nafs-i lawwāma*	
	Understanding: imagination *fahm-i wahm*	
	Remembrance of heart *dhikr-i qalbī*	
Disengagement	*Tawḥīd* through acts *tawḥīd-i af ʻālī*	Solitude
	Path of the *Ṭarīqa* *rāh-i ṭarīqa*	
Witnessing	Waystation: Sovereignty *manzil-i malakūt*	State
	Martyrdom of ecstatics *shahādat-i wujadā*	
	Seven occupations	
Lover	q, f, gh, ʻ, ẓ, ṭ, ḍ	Arriver

Table 4: The Impossible in Existence

The Knower	The Impossible in Existence *mumtani‘ al-wujūd*	The Gnostic
	Entrusted angel: Azrael *muwakkal*: ‘Azrā’īl	
Watchfulness	The rational spirit *rūḥ-i nāṭiqa*	Annihilation
	The healthy heart *qalb-i salīm*	
	The soul at peace *nafs-i muṭma’inna*	
	Understanding: conjecture *fahm-i gumān*	
	Remembrance of the spirit *dhikr-i rūḥī*	
Disengagement	*Tawḥīd* through states *tawḥīd-i aḥwālī*	Solitude
	The path of the reality *rāh-i haqīqa*	
Witnessing	Waystation: Domination *manzil-i jabarūt*	State
	Martyrdom of intenders *shahādat-i ‘umadā*	
	Seven occupations	
Lover	ṣ, sh, s, z, r, dh, d	Arriver

Table 5: The Gnostic of Existence

The Knower	The Gnostic of Existence *‘ārif al-wujūd*	The Gnostic
	The entrusted angel: Gabriel *muwakkal*: Jibrā’īl	
Watchfulness	The holy spirit *rūḥ-i qudsī*	Annihilation
	The witnessing heart *qalb-i shahīd*	
	The inspired soul *nafs-i mulhama*	
	Understanding: the aware *fahm-i āgāh*	
	Remembrance of the secret *dhikr-i sirrī*	
Disengagement	*Tawḥīd* through essence *tawḥīd-i dhātī*	Solitude
	The path of gnosis *rāh-i ma‘rifa*	
Witnessing	Way station: Divinity *manzil-i lāhūt*	State
	Martyrdom of witnessers *shahādat-i shuhadā*	
	Seven occupations	
Lover	kh, ḥ, j, th, t, b, a	Arriver

subtle centres as self, heart, spirit, secret, and light. But in the four tables (Tables 2–5), instead of this hierarchy, he provides four levels for each of spirit, heart, and soul. Thus, if the subtle centres can be viewed as specific realities from one point of view, from another point of view, each can be differentiated into levels. The four levels of spirit are the growing or vegetable spirit, the motile or animal spirit, the rational or human spirit, and the holy or prophetic spirit. The four levels of heart are the lump of flesh (*muḍgha*), the repenting heart (*munīb*), the healthy heart (*salīm*), and the witnessing heart (*shahīd*). The four levels of soul are the commanding soul (to evil), the blaming soul, the soul at peace, and the inspired soul.

Next the Shaykh turns to the path leading to God in broad terms. First, he mentions four ascending levels of *tawḥīd* – in words, acts, states, and essence. Second, he mentions the mode of understanding (*fahm*) that corresponds to each level: understanding by comparison (*qiyās*), by imagination (*wahm*), by conjecture (*gumān*), and by awareness (*āgāh*). These levels correspond to the four levels of the path, as mentioned in the circle, beginning with the *sharī'a*. The appropriate mode of remembrance and the corresponding waystations are the same as those mentioned in the circle. Finally, Shaykh Maḥmūd mentions four levels of 'bearing witness' or 'martyrdom' (*shahāda*). Although the discussion and terminology here are not completely clear to me, he seems to be saying that at each level there is a specific mode of dying in the path of God, a martyrdom through which one is reborn on the next higher level.

Finally, the Shaykh mentions in each table the words "the seven occupations," and these are followed by seven letters of the alphabet. In the text, he explains that at each level, the seeker has an appropriate supplication or short prayer, each of which corresponds to a letter of the alphabet. Hence, there are twenty-eight "occupations," with a twenty-ninth pertaining to the centre of the circle. I have arranged the twenty-nine levels in Table 6. Most of the supplications begin with the letter to which they pertain and address the bodily member or attribute that is mentioned in the table. For example, the supplication for the second level, pertaining to the letter *hā'* and to the knees, reads *Hadhdhib jalsatanā yā Allāh*, that is, "Refine our sitting, O God!" Shaykh Maḥmūd translates the saying into Persian and adds some commentary as follows: "O God, keep our knees sitting in this station so that they will not stand to worship anything else."

The supplication for the letter *'ayn*, which corresponds to hearing, reads *'allimna'l-qur'ān yā Allāh*, "Teach us the Koran, O God!" The Persian translation reads, "O God, teach us the Koran, which is Thy Speech, through our hearing, so that knowledge of Thee may be achieved."

The supplication for the letter *zā'* and the attribute of adornment is *Zayyinnā fī zīnatika yā Allāh*, "Adorn us with Thy adornment, O God." Shaykh Maḥmūd renders it, "O God, bestow upon our existence an adornment from Thy existence."

Table 6: The Twenty-Nine Occupations

LETTER	REALITY
Table 2	
Yā'	Feet
Hā'	Knees
Wāw	Navel
Nūn	Breast
Mīm	Throat
Lām	Forehead
Kāf	Nose
Table 3	
Qāf	Speech
Fā'	Smell
Ghayn	Eyesight
'Ayn	Hearing
Ẓā'	Intellect
Ṭā'	Heart
Ḍād	Satisfaction
Table 4	
Ṣād	God's decree
Shīn	Intercession
Sīn	Journey
Zay	Adornment
Rā'	Mercy
Dhāl	Tasting
Dāl	Path
Table 5	
Khā'	Vicegerency
Ḥā'	Love of God
Jîm	Beauty
Thā'	Laudation
Tā'	Blessing
Bā'	God's Name
Alif	God's Essence
Circle	
LĀ	Nonentification

Besides the mention of seven occupations, the four tables (Tables 2–5) have other common features. They begin with one sort of existence, and the order in each case is the same. Each has a centre column divided into thirteen levels. Each also has two side columns in which the same pair of terms is mentioned in the same position. Each of these pairs represents a basic relationship that has different connotations in the context of each table. The term on the left represents a lower stage on the spiritual journey, and the term on the right a higher stage. The left-hand term, in other words, represents a preparation for what is designated by the right-hand term.

In the first case, we have the knower and the gnostic. The learned knowledge of the knower will eventually turn into the tasted, witnessed knowledge of the gnostic.

Second are watchfulness and annihilation. Through the practice of watching one's own inner states in keeping with the instruction of the spiritual guide, one eventually achieves the annihilation of all individualized and self-centred attributes and the subsistence (*baqā'*) of the divine attributes, in the form of which human beings were created.

Third are disengagement and solitude. One disengages one's self from the world and the body and achieves a state of being alone with God.

Fourth are witnessing and state. Through witnessing the divine influxes within oneself one is transported into an altered state of consciousness.

Finally, at the bottom of the table, in the highest stage of realization for each level, are the lover and arriver. The adept who is transported by love for God achieves the station of arrival at or union with his Beloved.

The book is divided into two main sections. In the first section, Shaykh Maḥmūd offers the four tables as depictions of ascending stages on the path to God. Then he presents the circle as the culmination of the journey and the realization of *waḥdat al-wujūd*. The circle is the end of the first journey – the journey to God beginning from the world, or the ascending arc, the upward climb on the ladder of the *mi'rāj*. The circle is also the beginning of the second journey, which is the return from God on the descending *mi'rāj* to the world from whence one began. In the second part of the book, Shaykh Maḥmūd reviews the stages of the ascending journey, in reverse order from those of the descending journey, inasmuch as all the stages represent different dimensions of what the seeker realizes through the One of Existence.

Finally, I offer a few examples of Shaykh Maḥmūd's commentary on the four tables and the circle. I follow his discussions of the term *wujūd* as he moves through its various stages. As is obvious from the arrangement of the tables, Shaykh Maḥmūd considers *wujūd* – 'existence' or 'being' – as the primary reality, in terms of which everything else needs to be understood, and in this he is in perfect harmony with the later intellectual tradition in general.

Shaykh Maḥmūd calls his first three tables (Tables 2–4) *wājib al-wujūd* (the Necessary in Existence), *mumkin al-wujūd* (the Possible in Existence), and *mumtani' al-wujūd* (the Impossible in Existence). This classification of *wujūd* into three basic categories was, of course, standard in Islamic thought from Avicenna onwards. The fourth table (Table 5) is that of *'ārif al-wujūd*, 'the Gnostic of Existence' or the 'Knower of Existence', and this reflects the fundamental Sufi quest for the type of knowledge that is designated as *ma'rifa* (often *'irfān* in late texts from Persia), and which can best be understood as 'self-knowledge'. Shaykh Maḥmūd makes the primary importance of this self-knowledge completely explicit in his introduction to the work, immediately after citing his own *silsila* back to Gīsū Darāz. Here, he explains the purpose of the Sufi Path in terms of knowledge of the self, referring to the famous prophetic dictum, "He who knows (*'arafa*) himself, knows his Lord." This knowledge is not *'ilm*, or learned knowledge, but *ma'rifa* – tasted and realized knowledge of one's own self and one's own Lord, or, to use an English term, 'gnosis'. And, of course, this is the very word that the Shaykh employs in the title of his work, *Ma'rifat al-sulūk*, 'The Gnosis of the Wayfaring', or 'The Self-Knowledge Achieved by Travelling the Path'. He writes:

> O traveller, the path and method mentioned [in this work] was threaded on the string by a *silsila* such as this, and this blessing was passed down, hand to hand, until it reached our own shaykh. If the seeker wants God's path and the way of the Muhammadan *sharī'a*, he should study this treatise. Hopefully, he will lift the veil from the beauty of the object of his quest and his beloved ...
>
> O friend, in the path of realization, the traveller must find these four levels of existence in his own existence and he must arrive at them. He must pass, level by level, until he reaches the gnosis of the Essence of the Real – glory be to Him; high and exalted is He!
>
> However, each existence has conditions and necessities. Therefore, each existence has been written down in a table and each has been explained. The traveller must know all the conditions and put them into practice so that he may reach his goal.
>
> Now, if God gives success, let me elucidate the existences and explain their conditions. Thereby the reality of 'He who knows himself knows his Lord' will be clarified for the seeker in the most beautiful manner.
>
> I will depict the four existences of 'He who knows himself' in four rectangular tables to indicate directions, place, and time. Then the fifth table will be the circle of 'knows his Lord'. This is the circle of nonentification, non-directionality, no-place, and no-time. This is the One of Existence, which is the absolute Essence of the Creator.

Although the terms 'necessary', 'possible', and 'impossible' pertain to standard philosophical and theological vocabulary, they are redefined in the work. Clearly, the Bijapur Sufis wanted to appropriate familiar terms, but they were not especially concerned to use them in the usual meanings. Thus the term 'Necessary in Existence' normally refers to God, who is and cannot not be, but in the first table and in the circle, it has a completely different sense. Shaykh Maḥmūd himself explains the two meanings of the term. First, he tells us, the Necessary in Existence is God, who "abides through Himself for all eternity. He has no changing, no alteration, no new arrival, and no annihilation. He is 'the Living, the Self-Abiding" [Koran:254], while the existence of all existent things abides through Him.' Then he explains that his master, Burhān al-Dīn Jānam, applied the term to "the earthy, human existence (*wujūd-i khākī-yi insānī*)," and he explains the rationale for this as follows:

> This earthly, elemental, human existence is the necessary in existence (*wājib al-wujūd*), which is to say that it is the indispensable in existence (*lāzim al-wujūd*), because this corporeal existence is necessary and indispensable for the existence of the spirit. After all, without this corporeal existence, the spirit could not depart from the world of the absent (*'ālam-i ghayb*) to become manifest in the world of witnessing (*'ālam-i shuhūd*). If there were no corporeal existence, the spirit would remain hidden in the world of the absent. This is because, although the spirit was created on the Day of the Covenant, before this corporeal existence – for, as the *ḥadīth* tells us, 'God created the spirits 40,000 years before the bodies' – without this earthly existence, the spirit would not be able to gain a gnosis through which it knows the Real with all His attributes and perfections.
>
> Thus, for example, although the receptivity for the whole tree is found in the seed, if the seed is not planted in the ground, the receptivity will not become manifest and the tree will not come to exist. Hence, God created the frame of Adam and made the spirit of the Covenant descend into it. When the spirit and the frame were paired, the true existence became manifest from their junction as a receptacle for the divine Essence and attributes. This is the reality of the heart's substance.

After explaining that Adam's reception of knowledge from God – when God taught him all the names – was made possible only by the heart, the Shaykh concludes this discussion by repeating that this usage of the term 'necessary in existence' pertains specifically to his Shaykh's technical terminology. Otherwise, he says, if someone were to say that the earthly body is the necessary in existence, meaning the Essence of God, this would be blatant unbelief.

Shaykh Mahmud's second table (Table 3) pertains to *mumkin al-wujūd*, the 'possible in existence'. Normally, this term is applied to everything other than God that is not strictly impossible. In this sense, the term indicates that nothing but God has any claim on existence. When we consider any given thing, in and of itself, we cannot say that it must exist, only God has that attribute, because only God is identical with *wujūd* itself. The things, in terms of their own realities, may or may not come to exist. Their coming to be depends absolutely upon the necessary in existence. Here, however, Shaykh Maḥmūd applies the term 'possible in existence' to the second level of the ascending arc to God. Although he refers to it as 'spiritual existence', in fact it corresponds to the lower realms of the absent world, or to what many Sufis call the 'world of imagination', which lies between the world of bodies and the world of spirits. I quote Shaykh Maḥmūd's own explanation of why his Shaykh, Burhān al-Dīn, employed the term *mumkin al-wujūd* in this meaning:

O friend, let me tell you the whole of the true knowledge and the reality of the possible in existence so that this existence will become plain to you. Through it you may set out on the path of the *ṭarīqa* and through this possible in existence you may give indications of the waystation of the Sovereignty (*malakūt*) with all its conditions.

O traveller, the term 'possible in existence' is used for that which does not abide through its own existence. Sometimes it is, and sometimes it is not, within the [creative] command of the Real. It is the existence of everything in the cosmos, from body to spirit and from [earthly] carpet to [divine] Throne. This possible in existence abides through the Essence of the Real, but the Necessary in Existence that is God's abides through its own Essence, and He does not change, neither in His Essence nor in His attributes.

Then, O friend, in his technical terminology, our Shaykh named spiritual existence 'the possible in existence'. Within this earthly body, this spiritual existence takes the form and the shape of this same earthly body. It is this that becomes separate from the body during sleep. It is also called the 'flowing spirit' (*rūḥ-i jārī*). Thus it has been said, "The spirit is two – the flowing spirit and the abiding spirit." This flowing spirit is precisely the possible in existence that I mentioned. It was created at the time of the Covenant. The question, "Am I not your Lord?" [Koran VII:172], reached this very spirit, and the answer, "Yes indeed," was heard from this spirit. ...

This spirit is called 'the possible in existence' because it also does not abide through itself, but rather through the abiding spirit, and the abiding spirit is the holy spirit. The holy spirit is the ray of God's Essence, and it came to be settled at His command, as will be explained. The holy spirit abides through itself. Like the ocean, it is infinite; it does not slip and does not move. This [holy] spirit, which is the ray of the Necessary's Essence, is just like the Necessary. Hence, the possible in existence is the connection to that holy spirit.

O friend, the possible in existence is in the inner domain through form, for you will be correct to see it along with all the organs. The earthly existence has motion from this [possible] existence, and it constantly flows in a journey, without your command, going in accordance with the ancient habit.

O traveller, whatever form appears in your own inner domain – whether it is your form or the form of another – is the possible in existence. This is because the possible thing has two aspects, since it both comes into being and it turns into nothing, while it does not abide through itself. Thus it abides through the holy spirit. The holy spirit stands in the place of the Necessary, while the form stands in the place of the Possible.

The place of the 'possible in existence' is the heart, by which I mean every passing thought (*khaṭara*) that assumes form in the inner human domain, and this inner domain will be the heart, since the form appears in the heart.

This place is also called 'limpidness' (*ṣafā'*), for our Shaykh said, "The elemental, 'Necessary in Existence' is in the air, and the spiritual, 'possible in existence' is in the limpidness." So, O friend, the spiritual, possible in existence journeys in the world of limpidness, just like wind, which goes through the power of Seraphiel.

At the beginning of his third table (table 4) Shaykh Maḥmūd discusses 'the Impossible in Existence'. The usual example given by the theologians for an impossible thing is an associate for God. Shaykh Maḥmūd explains that the specific meaning he has in mind for the term corresponds with what is often called the 'world of the spirits' – the highest of the three created worlds – though the rationale for his use of the term in this sense is not as clear as it was in the two previous examples:

> O traveller on the path, the literal reality of 'the impossible in existence' is that in which nothing has existence. In other words, it withholds forms from the things. This impossible in existence is an associate for the Creator, just as has been written in the books.
>
> It is well known that the existences are of three sorts: first, the Necessary in Existence; second, the possible in existence; and third, the impossible in existence. The first two were explained briefly earlier. As for the impossible in existence, it is the fact that, in eternity without beginning, nothing except the Essence of God had existence. In other words, there was only the Essence of God.
>
> So, you should know that the Being (*hastī*) of the Real's Essence demands non-being (*nīstī*) since, other than God's Essence, there is nothing. This 'non-being' is the impossible in existence, which is the existence that abides neither through itself nor through the other. It has no mode (*i'tibār*).
>
> It is the impossible in existence that is called 'No Place' (*lā makān*), and that is neither the Essence nor the relation of the attributes. It is the place of all things, since all the existent things and all the possible things of both worlds appeared within this Impossible in Existence.
>
> So understand, O traveller, what this impossible in existence is within yourself, in keeping with 'He who knows himself knows his Lord', for our Shaykh explained it after having explained the possible in existence. You must find it within yourself, while it is not. Once you have heard the explanation of the possible in existence, which is the moving force within the earthly body, you must cast it far from your gaze. Instead, you must gaze until you give no movement to any of your own outward or inward passing thoughts. You must remain steady, as a still witnesser (*shāhid-i sākin*). Once this state has been turned over to you, you will have joined with the impossible in existence of yourself, which is a ray of the impossible in existence of the Real. Within this existence is the holy spirit, and this being is the ray of the Real's Being.
>
> O traveller, the impossible in existence and the being of the spirit are not separate from each other. On the contrary, the impossible in existence is identical with the holy spirit's being, just like, for example, fire and the heat of fire, for these two are not separate from each other. Understand this, for the heat of fire does not allow anything to arrive in the fire – such as scorpions, gnats, flies, ants, and various crawling things – without burning it as soon as it arrives. So, know that the heat is the majesty (*jalāliyyat*) of the fire, or rather, it is identical with the fire.
>
> O traveller, the holy spirit has a majesty such that it lets no passing thought of the heart come into it. It is said that this majesty that belongs to being is the impossible in existence. The being of the holy spirit stands in the place of the Real's Being, while this [majesty] stands in the place of the impossible. Understand this, for it is a marvellous, subtle intimation and the allusion of the perfect spiritual guide (*murshid*). Grasp it well within yourself, for "He who knows himself knows his Lord."

In such a way does the Essence of the Necessary abide in itself through itself, and through its own impossible in existence it has made all the existent things appear within this impossible in existence. Understand!

The fourth table (table 5) pertains to fully actualized self-knowledge and self-awareness, above even the world of the spirits. Perhaps it corresponds to what, in Ibn al-'Arabī's terms, would be the self-knowledge gained by the greatest of the Sufis when they know their own immutable and uncreated entity, just as it is known by God for all eternity. It is this immutable entity that responds to God's command to come into existence. Then spirit, imagination, and body represent its three basic levels of manifestation. Shaykh Maḥmūd writes as follows:

The term 'Gnostic of Existence' is used for him who knows his own existence. In other words, it is the being (*hastī*) that knows itself. This is the being that is knowing and free from all beings. This being itself abides in God's command, while the mentioned Necessary, Possible, and Impossible beings abide through the Gnostic of Existence. They have need of it, but it is totally independent of them ...

This existence is like and similar to the non-delimitation of the Being of the Real, which is free and holy beyond all the possible existences. ... O traveller ... find in your own existence the Gnostic of Existence, and recognize it, so that you may find and recognize God as non-delimited (*muṭlaq*). This level consists of "He who knows himself knows his Lord."

In explaining the circle (Figure 3), which summarizes his previous four diagrams and adds the all-inclusive level of unity, or *waḥdat al-wujūd*, Shaykh Maḥmūd begins as follows:

The fifth diagram is named 'the One of Existence'. In other words, the diagram of the previous existences was drawn from this diagram in respect of the descent and manifestation of the One Existence of the Real. This diagram is the centre and circumference of all the circles, and all the circles go back to it. This is because the Necessary in Existence abides through the possible in existence; the possible in existence abides through the impossible in Existence; the impossible in existence abides through the Gnostic of Existence; the Gnostic of Existence abides through the One of Existence, and the One of Existence abides through itself. Hence, the reality of all the circles goes back to it.

Every allusion written in those diagrams is also explained in this circle in keeping with the technical terminology of each sort. In order to explain in each case these technical terms, which are the language of the Sufis, the technical term of each level has been explained in eight sorts, in keeping with the eight paradises. In each term, five levels are explained, similar to the five treasures that become manifest from the storehouse of "I was a Hidden Treasure" ...[8] Know

---

[8] I am not yet sure what he has in mind by the term "five treasures" (*panj ganj*). Perhaps he means those enumerated in a short treatise of this name by Muḥammad Makhdūm Sāwī, a prolific Qādirī author, also from Bijapur, whose dated works were written between 1108/1696 and 1123/1711. Sāwī explains these five treasures as the treasure of Eternity and the Absent; the treasure of the created, non-delimited light, which is Muḥammad; the name Allah; the knowledge of self; and the Koran.

> also that each technical term is found in the path of a road through which one can reach one's own root, in keeping with "The paths to God are in the number of the breaths of the creatures." Thus each term and each road that is mentioned leads to the fifth circle, and the fifth circle is named 'the One of Existence', since nothing except the Holy Essence can be called 'the One of Existence', given that He is One through His own existence and He abides through His own Essence. He is One with no associate. …
>
> [Once the traveller passes beyond the first four circles], he reaches the fifth diagram, which is the One of Existence and which has no direction, no time, and no place. It is undelimited by any sort of binding and nonentified by any sort of entification. This is why the diagram was drawn as a circle, but those four diagrams, since they are connected with time, space, direction, and entification, were drawn as rectangles. However, when one looks at the first four diagrams from the last diagram with a gaze of nonentification, those four diagrams also appear as circular and nonentified. This is why those four circles have been drawn around the circle of the One of Existence, just like the circle of the One of Existence. Thus the traveller will be able to find the One of Existence in each circle. After all, when the traveller passes beyond the levels of the entifications and reaches the level of nonentification, he sees all the levels as nonentification. Since the form of nonentification cannot be understood save as a circle, all five tables have been drawn as circles.

After having explained why the central circle is called by eight different names, Shaykh Maḥmūd proceeds to explain each of the eight sectors in terms of the descent from the centre to the circumference. Thus, concerning 'existence', he writes as follows:

> Know, O traveller, that if the fifth circle is considered in terms of the technical language of existence, then it is called 'the One of Existence'. This is because the traveller, after wayfaring through the four existences, will arrive at the fifth existence, which is the Essence of the Real. … There, he will not see anything as present. All the external things, which are outside the Essence, will appear as obliterated in obliteration, annihilated in annihilation, and non-existent in non-existence. [Nothing will appear] save the Essence, which abides through Itself and causes all things to abide through Its attributes – whether this is called the One of Existence or the Necessary in Existence. After all, the Essence is One Being that abides in Itself through Itself, and this perfection of attribute is worthy for It.
>
> Then, through the ray of His own One Existence, the One brought the Gnostic of Existence into existence. It is the Muḥammadan Light, as defined earlier. Then, through the being of the Gnostic of Existence, a non-being appeared, and that non-being, which is the impossible in existence, made the possible in existence manifest. From the possible in existence, the necessary in existence appeared.
>
> Thus the necessary in existence is the locus of manifestation (*maẓhar*) for the possible in existence, the possible in existence the locus of manifestation for the impossible in existence, the impossible in existence the locus of manifestation for the Gnostic of Existence, and the Gnostic of Existence is the locus of manifestation for the One of Existence.

O traveller, whenever someone finds the One of Existence, by the same token he will find the locus of manifestation that is the earthly, necessary in existence, as explained earlier.

Know also that although we discussed the necessary in existence that pertains to earth in terms of the human being, the verified truth is that everything included among the kinds of corporeal things is necessary in existence in keeping with the existence of that thing. This necessary in existence then entails a possible in existence, which entails an impossible in existence. Within the last a Gnostic of Existence is concealed – however, it is concealed in the thing in keeping with the thing's entification. Whether things be plants, inanimate objects, or animals, these four existences are within them. However, they do not become manifest save in the existence of the human individual, who is a receptacle for the Essence and attributes of the Divinity. . . .

O traveller, it was said that "The paths to God are in the number of the breaths of the creatures." This is a meaning of which nothing's existence is empty. In each thing, these four existences are concealed. When God gives this existence awareness and self-knowledge, it finds the One of Existence, which is God, in its own existence. It has no need for any other existence, for it will not see God's Essence in anything else, only in its own existence. This is the reality of "He who knows himself knows his Lord." Everyone must seek God in his own self so that he may find Him – whatever sort the seeker may be, whether jinn, human being, plant, or animal. 'The paths to God are in the number of the breaths of the creatures.' In every existence, there is a path to God by which it can reach God.

Know, O traveller, that the encompassing of all existences by the One of Existence will be gained when the traveller reaches and recognizes the One of Existence. Just as he is the gnostic of his own existence and sees himself as encompassing all his parts, so he will see the Real as encompassing the whole universe, while no veil appears in the midst. He will gaze on nothing but the Essence of the existence of perfection, which has permeated the existence of the things through the self-disclosures in the species. Sometimes he will see the One of Existence identical with the Gnostic of Existence and the Gnostic of Existence identical with the One of Existence. Sometimes he will witness the Gnostic of Existence in the One of Existence; sometimes the possible in existence in the impossible in existence; the impossible in existence in the possible in existence; the possible in existence in the necessary in existence, and the necessary in existence in the possible in existence. Sometimes he will see all this as identical with the One of Existence, and sometimes he will see the One of Existence identical with all this. . . . Such is gazing upon the unity of the Essence – majestic is His majesty and all-inclusive His gifts!

This then is a brief introduction to the elaborate and coherent synthesis of Sufi teaching offered by Shaykh Maḥmūd Khwush-Dahān. I hope that before long the opportunity will arise to provide a complete translation and analysis of the treatise, but even more strongly, I hope that other scholars will take a closer look at some of the riches of the Persianate Sufi tradition that are now mouldering in the libraries of the subcontinent.

The Influence of Ibn ʿArabī's Doctrine of the Unity of Being on the Transcendental Theosophy of Ṣadr al-Dīn Shīrāzī*

MUHAMMAD REZA JUZI

INTRODUCTION

Ṣadr al-Dīn Muḥammad ibn Ibrāhīm Qawāmī Shīrāzī (d. 1050/1640), better known as *Ṣadr al-Mutaʾallihīn* (Foremost among the Theosophers) or Mullā Ṣadrā, ranks as the first major philosopher in the Islamic world in whose works the thought of Ibn ʿArabī was reflected. Although a thorough explanation of all the various aspects of the profound dialogue between these two Muslim thinkers is beyond the scope of this brief study, I will try to outline some of the views held in common by Ibn ʿArabī and Mullā Ṣadrā about the Reality of Being and its individual uniqueness.[1] Such a study, it is hoped, will in turn serve to clarify the influence of the Akbarian School on the thinkers of the Safavid era, especially after Ṣadr al-Dīn Shīrāzī.

The areas of consensus between Mullā Ṣadrā and Ibn ʿArabī are not only restricted to the doctrine of the individual uniqueness of Being. Mullā Ṣadrā supported Ibn ʿArabī's ideas on several other important issues, such as the notion of the imaginal world, the eternal archetypes, afterlife states, eschatology, as well as his hermenutical approach to the Koran.[2] Those who

---

* 'Transcendental theosophy' (*al-ḥikmat al-mutaʿāliyya*) was the term employed by Ṣadr al-Dīn Shīrāzī for his school of philosophy. It is also the title of his greatest book: *al-Ḥikmat al-mutaʿāliyya fī 'l-Asfār al-arbaʿa al-ʿaqliyya* (Qum: Intishārāt-i Muṣṭafavī 1344 A.Hsh./1965) (The Transcendental Theosophy in Fourfold Intellectual Journeys). Some scholars have speculated that Ṣadr al-Dīn Shīrāzī adopted the title of this book from one of Ibn ʿArabī's treatises, *Risāla al-asfar*, although there is insufficient evidence to support this. In any case, whereas Ibn ʿArabī's *Risāla al-asfār* solely concerns 'spiritual' journeys, Ṣadr al-Dīn Shīrāzī's *Asfār* is about both spiritual and intellectual journeys (see *Asfar*, I, pp. 1–15).

[1] See S.J. Āshtiyānī's *Hastī az naẓar-i falsafah va ʿirfān* (Mashhad: Intishārāt-i Zawwār 1345 A.Hsh./1966), pp. 6–15.

[2] Also see S.J. Āshtiyānī's concise forward to Mullā Ṣadrā's *al-Shawāhid al rubūbiyya fī al-manāhij al-sulūkiyya* (Mashhad: Mashhad University Press, 1346 A.Hsh./1967).

study Mullā Ṣadrā's writings carefully, especially his magnum opus *Asfār* and his commentary on the Koran, quickly realize that he honours Ibn 'Arabī's thought more than any other Sufi thinker, as is evident from his extensive and heavy quotations from the *Futūḥāt* and the *Fuṣūṣ al-hikam*.

In fact, the whole body of Mullā Ṣadrā's transcendental theosophy functions as the rational structure and logical articulation of Ibn 'Arabī's teaching, something which is clear if we examine the key notion of *ḥikma*.[3] One of the original meanings of this term, the understanding of which is the ultimate goal of both the the Sufis and philosophers, is the very 'wisdom' or 'esoteric sapience' mentioned in the Koran (II: 269): "God gives the wisdom on whom he wills and whoever is given wisdom, is given a great blessing." In a saying attributed to the fifth Shī'ite Imām Muḥammad al-Bāqir, such *ḥikma* is interpreted as *al-tanafaqquh fī'l-dīn*, namely, the struggle to understand the meaning of faith and religion.[4] It may be noted that the word *fiqh* or 'jurisprudence', from which *tafafaqquh* is etymologically derived, originally meant 'right understanding' and 'deep insight'. Since this type of *ḥikma* has its origin and the source in God himself, many Muslim philosophers understood 'wisdom' as the struggle to acquire divine qualities or attributes (*al-takhulluq bi-Akhlāq allāh*).

Needless to say, the *ḥikma* alluded to by the Koran is a sort of knowedge beyond the reach of the rational faculty, although human reason can apprehend its existence. In a passage at the beginning of his *Futūḥāt*, Ibn 'Arabī divides the sciences into three different ranks: rational or intellectual science, the science of taste and the science of mysteries. As far as intellectual science goes, human intelligence is the source as well as the master of its understanding and cognizance. In the science of taste, as its name indicates, the object of knowledge is known only through an indescribable intuition: a 'taste' which is like the taste of the sweetness of honey, to which the rational faculty cannot attain. Finally, the science of mysteries is considered to be the noblest and highest type of knowledge; it is realized only by prophets and saints, being a kind of divine grace, neither innate nor originating in human reason – which however, is still quite capable of understanding it.[5]

If, in the opinion of certain Sufis and mystics, especially those of Ibn 'Arabī's school, human reason (*'aql*) is depreciated and devalued, this is only in regard to its inability to know divine things, while its aptitude for knowing and understandintg in general has never been denied.[6] The wisdom or *ḥikma* espoused by the Koran is described as being a kind of divine effusion which God Almighty bestows upon the heart of one worthy of its bestowal.

---

[3] See 'Abdullāh Javādī Āmulī's commentary on the sixth volume of the *Asfār* (Tehran: Intishārāt-i Zahrā 1368 A.Hsh./ 1989), introduction, pp. 37–43.

[4] Muḥsin Fayḍ Kāshānī, *'Ilm al-yaqīn* (Qum: Intishārāt-i Bīdār 1358 A.Hsh./ 1979), II, p. 212.

[5] *Futūḥāt al-makkiyya*, ed. and annotated by O. Yahia (Cairo: Al-Hay'at al-Miṣriyyat al-'Āmma li'l-Kitāb 1972), I, pp. 138–44.

[6] See also S.H. Nasr's introduction to the present volume (EDS).

Juxtaposed to this wisdom vouchsafed by divine grace is another kind or wisdom which is generally acquired by man's own intellectual activity, which in Islamic philosophy has been divided into four branches: Peripatetic philosophy (*ḥikmat-i mashshā'ī*), scholastic theology (*kalām*), Illuminative metaphysics (*ḥikmat-i ishrāq*) and, finally, Sufism (*taṣawwuf*).[7]

While heavily influenced by Ibn 'Arabī, Mullā Ṣadrā's transcendental theosophy, in one sense, represents an attempt to combine and integrate all these various types of *ḥikma*. However, rather than acting as a disciple or commentator belonging to the Akbarian school, he was, contrary to the opinion of some contemporary scholars, more of an intellectual follower or advocate of Ibn 'Arabī, his transcendental theosophy being, in fact, the 'scale' or rational explanation of Ibn 'Arabī's speculative gnosis. Mullā Ṣadrā believed that mystical intuition must always be accompanied and defended by rational demonstration. He pointed out that although the mystics and Sufis were usually united in their views on asceticism and spiritual vision, they had almost no practice in rational sciences and discourses.[8] Mullā Ṣadrā strongly believed that every intuition or spiritual vision is demonstrable, for whatever is not absurd or impossible can certainly be proven, like a mathematical proposition. In a word, the comprehensiveness of the transcendental theosophy lies in its claim to satisfy the needs of both mystics and rational philosophers.

MULLĀ ṢADRĀ AND IBN 'ARABĪ ON THE UNITY OF BEING

Although some scholars have maintained that the term *waḥdat al-wujūd* (oneness or unity of Being) was not actually used by Ibn 'Arabī as a technical term in his writings, it has always been historically linked to his name. We know that the Shaykh's well-known pupil Ismā'īl ibn Sawdakīn, who often recorded his utterances, used this special term quite explicitly in his commentary on Ibn 'Arabī's *al-Tajalliyyāt al-illāhiyya*,[9] demonstrating that, in regard to its antiquity, usage of this term dates back to the lifetime of Ibn 'Arabī himself. Furthermore, considering the fact that Ibn Sawdakīn read his commentary on *al-Tajalliyyāt al-illāhiyya* aloud before Ibn 'Arabī, and that the Shaykh admired and appreciated his commentary, it seems quite unlikely that Ibn 'Arabī was not himself acquainted with this important term which later stirred up so much controversy, or that such a faithful disciple did not follow his master's vocabulary.

In the earliest phase of his philosophical development, Mullā Ṣadrā initially adhered to the philosophical position known as the 'principality of quiddity'

---

[7] 'Abd al-Razzāq Lāhījī, *Gawhar-i murād*, ed. Z. Qurbānī Lāhījī (Tehran: 1372 A.Hsh./ 1993), pp. 33–41.

[8] See *Asfār*, VI, p. 284.

[9] See *al-Tajalliyyāt al-illāhiyya*, with the commentary of Ibn Sawdakīn, ed. and annotated by O. I. Yahia (Tehran: Iran University Press 1988), p. 106.

(*aṣālat al-māhiyya*) held by Suhrawardī Maqtūl, but as his thought evolved he came to accept the doctrine of the 'principality of existence' (*aṣālat al-wujūd*) instead, and ended up maintaining the concept of the individual uniqueness of Being (*waḥdat al-shakhṣiyya al-wujūd*), although, of course, there were many other important phases which his thought underwent as it matured. At the beginning of the *Asfār*, Mullā Ṣadrā confessed that he had initially been a believer in the doctrine of the 'principality of quiddity'.[10] In fact, the only work in which one can witness his belief in this doctrine is a treatise entitled *Sarayān nūr al-wujūd al-ḥaqq fi'l-mawjūdāt*.[11] Written in his youth, this small treatise of sixteen pages expounds a theology of intuitionism (which he terms 'tasting divinity': *dhawq al-ta'ālluh*), a doctrine whose most distinguished exponent before him had been Jalāl al-Din Dawānī (d. 907/1501). Not mentioning the doctrine of the 'principality of existence' here, he puts his emphasis on the theory of the Unity of Being, considering the diversity of beings as a reality and rejecting the views of those mystics who considered it to be merely illusory.

In his more mature writings composed in later life, however, Mullā Ṣadrā repudiated the doctrine of the 'principality of quiddity' and based his ontology on the 'principality of existence', maintaining that the quiddities themselves were inherently perishable and subject to annihilation. To substantiate his views on this ontological question in the *Asfār*,[12] he invoked the thought of Ibn 'Arabī and Ṣadr al-Dīn Qūnawī (d. 673/1274), the foremost interpreter and systematic proponent of Ibn 'Arabī's teachings to the Persian-speaking world. He directly quoted from Ṣadr al Dīn Qūnawī's *Miftāḥ al-ghayb*, noting that the books of the mystics – especially those of Shaykh al-Akbar and his disciples like Qūnawī – were saturated with investigations into the non-existence of the possible essences. As if to underline the depth of the subsequent influence of Ibn 'Arabī on Mullā Ṣadrā's philosophical thought, it should be noted that the first work that he wrote after this radical change in metaphysical outlook was a treatise called 'The Design of the Cosmos' (*Ṭarḥ al-kawnayn*), whose expressions and words indicate the deep influence of the works of two major Akbarian thinkers: the *Tamhīd al-qawā'id* of Sā'īn al-Dīn Turka (d. 836/1432–33) and the commentary on Ibn 'Arabī's *Fuṣūṣ al-ḥikam* by Dā'ūd Qayṣarī (d. 751/1350).

However, despite such an important change of mind, Mullā Ṣadrā still had a long way to go before he reached the idea of the Unity of Being and managed to solve the problem of the diversity of possible entities. In this phase, he employed the concept of the existential hierarchy/gradation of being (*tashkīk al-wujūd*). Prior to Mullā Ṣadrā, Muslim philosophers had been acquainted with the metaphysical significance of this concept,[13] but only used it in the realm of

---

[10] *Asfār*, II, p. 49.

[11] Published in Ṣadr Al-Dīn Shīrāzī, *Majmū'ah-i maqālāt* (Qum: Intishārāt-i Muṣṭafavī, n.d.), p. 132.

[12] *Asfār*, II, p. 22.

[13] Originally used as a technical term in the science of logic, the term *tashkīk* was adopted by

quiddities. In their view, there were two types of universal concepts: (1) the equivocal universals: universals equally true for all their subjects; and (2) univocal universals: universals untrue for all their subjects, but rather applicable to them according to degrees of intensity and weakness, their most applicable instances being the categories of time and motion.[14] Although Mullā Ṣadrā propounded the idea of the gradation of Being in conscious opposition to the Peripatetic philosophers who believed in the essential diversity of the portions of Being, he took a major step towards unitarianism by attributing the phenomenon of multiplicity to gradation itself. Yet there still remained a few problems, which would not be solved until his philosophical views reached their final maturity.

First was the fact that the unity in which he believed at this stage was a typical Unity of Being in gradation, rather than the individual uniqueness of Being which Ibn ʻArabī and his followers advocated.

Second, under the influence of Suhrawardī, who believed in the hierarchical differentiation of the quiddities, Mullā Ṣadrā endorsed the concept of hierarchical grades of Being, considering Being as a reality with different stages of intensity and perfection.

Third, and lastly, contrary to the opinions of the mystics, he considered multiplicity to be a distinct reality rather than an illusion, and supposed that the negation of the multiplicity of Being entailed a denial of the existence of the prophets, divine revelation and all the precepts of religion. He surmised Being to be unique yet characterized by various hierarchical grades, with God, as the most perfect and supreme Being, situated at the highest grade, and possible beings placed in a hierarchy of levels below God in different grades of strength and perfection, according to their closeness or distance.

In this regard, it may be noted that Ibn ʻArabī and his disciples never totally rejected the concept of hierarchical grades of Being; rather, they held an analogous position which understood all phenomenon to be 'loci of manifestation' (*maḥall-i ẓuhūr*) for the Divine Names, according to the receptivity or preparedness (*istiʻdad*) of the permanent archetypes (*aʻyān thābita*) that are potentialities within the Divine Essence. In one of his treatises, called *al-Risālat al-hādiyya' al-murshidiyya*, Ṣadr al-Dīn Qūnawī states that "whatever is said about the multiplicity of Absolute Reality and its priority, intensity and perfection, all goes back to the loci of the self-manifestation of Being and the disposition of existential receptacles (*qawābil*)."[15]

Suhrawardī as a metaphysical term in his *Ḥikmat al-ishrāq* to explain the gradation of quiddities, and later applied to the domain of being and ontology by Ṣadr al-Dīn Shīrāzī. In his *Fundamental Structure of Sabzawārī's Metaphysics* (Tehran 1968), Professor Izutsu translated the term as 'analogical gradation'.

[14] See G.E. Dīnānī, *Falsafa-yi Suhrawardī* (Tehran: Intishārāt-i Ḥikmat 1364/A.Hsh./1985), pp. 261–7.

[15] See Ḥamza Fannārī's *Miṣbāḥ al-uns*, Persian trans. M. Khajavī, (Tehran: Intishārāt-i Mullā 1994), p. 156.

Therefore, while the *reality* of all possible beings is indeed one and the same, the difference among them stems from their varying degrees of receptivity for the self-disclosure of Being to them. According to Ibn 'Arabī there are three universal grades pertaining to the Reality of Being:

1. The level of the divine Essence (*dhāt*), also termed the 'Absolute Unseen' (*ghayb muṭlaq*). At this level, which has no name or sign by which it can be approached, man can neither recognize nor worship God; having no manifestation, this level is not qualified by any gradation.
2. The second stage is the first self-disclosure of the Essence, usually referred to as the first self-manifestion (*al-ẓuhūr al-awwal*) or 'the most holy emanation' (*al-fayḍ al-aqdas*) of the Absolute unto itself, which also encompasses the entire cosmos.
3. The third stage is called by Ibn 'Arabī and Mullā Ṣadrā 'the holy emanation' (*al-fayḍ al-muqaddas*), being the level in which limited or conditioned beings (*wujūdāt muqayyada*) emerge from potentiality in the Absolute into outward 'reality'.

THE GRADATIONS OF THE REALITY OF BEING

In respect to this theory of ontological gradations, the most difficult metaphysical issue resolved by Mullā Ṣadrā was that of the type of relationship which obtains between the Absolute Being and particular beings. Recognizing that as long as the issue of the gradation of Being between the Eternal Creator and creatures in time was not adequately addressed, the dispute between philosophy and mysticism would continue, Mullā Ṣadrā resolved the problem by utilizing three principal theses:

1. The notion that theosophers who have intimately experienced a mystical 'unveiling' (*kashf*) of the realities of the hierarchial gradation of Being are alone capable of providing a 'veracious proof' (*burhān al-ṣadīqīn*) or demonstration of these ontological stages;
2. the rule that 'the non-composite simplicity of the reality [of Being] encompasses and contains everything' (*basīt al-ḥaqīqa kull al-ashyā'*);
3. through referring the principle of causality to the creative act of Being's continuous self-disclosure.[16]

On these three principles Mullā Ṣadrā also grounded his concept of 'the individual uniqueness of Being." This concept, explained in the simplest language possible, implies several things:

1. That there is only one real instance of Being in creation;
2. all existence, all 'is-ness', is restricted to that reality of Being (*ḥaqīqat al-wujūd*);

[16] *Asfār*, II, p. 301.

3. all other 'beings' beside that 'reality of Being' have no independent or substantial reality of their own;
4. the existence of created phenomena, or 'what is other' than that 'reality of Being' entirely depends on the self-disclosure of Being, before which all phenomena are to be conceived of as various modes or determinations of Being;
5. what we call the cosmos or world, whether apparent or unseen, is but an appearance of that 'reality of Being'.

The best example that can be given for this gnostic experience of being is that which is also given by most of the great Persian Sufis: of the sea and its waves, wherein no real distinction between Reality – the sea – and its phenomenal appearance – as waves – can be found. The waves are the outward appearance of sea, and the sea is the inward reality of waves.

Following Qayṣarī's commentary on the *Fuṣūṣ al-ḥikam* – and thereby setting his seal of approval on all the precepts that Ibn 'Arabī held concerning Being – in the twenty-second chapter of the *Asfār*, Mullā Ṣadrā reexamines the meaning of the reality of Being, and in the twenty-fifth chapter he clearly and explicitly expounds the idea of the individual uniqueness of Being. He characterizes it as constituting the 'straight path' (*ṣirāṭ al-mustaqīm*), stating:

> God Almighty guided me on the straight path and showed me that Being and its existing phenomena are all one and the same. Whatever can be seen in the universe is nothing but the revelation of that unique reality and the manifestation of His attributes and divine Names. All created beings, from the Holy Spirit down to matter, with all their various forms and modes of existence, are nothing but various degrees of the one true Light and separate self-determinations of one divine Being.[17]

Following this passage, he emphasizes the fact that by presenting this demonstration of the individual uniqueness of Being, mystical theosophy has attained its final culmination, insofar as providing a rational justification for this theory was so complicated and difficult as to defy the intellectual efforts of previous philosophers.

Apart from the theory of the individual uniqueness of Being, in his commentary on the Koran and his interpretation of the sayings of the prophets and Shī'ite Imāms, Ṣadr al-Dīn Shīrāzī was also deeply influenced by Ibn 'Arabī. Thus, to underline what was stated at the beginning of this chapter, we may conclude that among previous Islamic philosophers, no philosopher had ever been so intimately steeped in and associated with Ibn 'Arabī as Ṣadr al-Dīn Shīrāzī, for no other philosopher had, up until his day, ever been able to bring about such a grand conformity between mystical intuition (*kashf-i 'irfānī*), intellectual demonstration (*burhān-i 'aqlī*), and divine revelation (*waḥy-i ilāhī*).

---

[17] *Asfār*, II, chap. 25, p. 292.

V

ESOTERIC MOVEMENTS & CONTEMPLATIVE DISCIPLINES

هو العزیز

بلبل بچمن زآن گل رخسار نشان دید

پروانه در آتش شد و اسرار عیان دید

عارف صفت روی تو در پیر و جوان دید

یعنی همه جا عکس رخ یار توان دید

دیوانه منم من که روم خانه به خانه

The nightingale singing on the green has seen
The sign: her rosy cheek; the flame in which the moth
Has flown has shown to it this arcane mystery.
In every youth and every elder, mystics see
Your face's lovely traits and hue, that is to say
That everywhere a likeness of her face reflected can be seen.
I am a lunatic – to wander house to house like this.

Ismā'īlī–Sufi Relations in Early Post-Alamūt and Safavid Persia

FARHAD DAFTARY

Until recently, the Ismā'īlīs were studied almost exclusively on the basis of evidence collected or fabricated by their numerous enemies, including especially the bulk of the Sunnī heresiographers and polemicists of medieval times, as well as the Crusaders and their occidental chroniclers. As a result, a multitude of myths and legends, rooted in either hostility or imaginative ignorance, had continued to circulate regarding the teachings and practices of this Shī'ī Muslim community. The field of Ismā'īlī studies has, however, witnessed nothing less than a revolution since the 1930s, resulting from the recovery and study of a large number of authentic Ismā'īlī texts. Modern scholarship has now succeeded in shedding light on all the major phases in the history of the Ismā'īlīs and their diverse literary and intellectual traditions of learning.

Nevertheless, aspects of Ismā'īlī history and thought continue to be shrouded in mystery due to a lack of reliable sources of information. Of the obscure periods in Ismā'īlī history, mention may be made of one of the foremost, the first five centuries following the fall of the Nizārī Ismā'īlī state in Persia in 654/1256, a period which partially overlapped with Safavid rule (907/1501–1135/1722) over Persia. It was precisely during the earliest centuries of this post-Alamūt period that relations of a particular kind developed in Persia between Ismā'īlism and Sufism. The purpose of this chapter is to convey a brief overview of the background and the nature of these Ismā'īlī–Sufi relations on the basis of the fragmentary findings of modern scholarship on the subject.

In 487/1094, the Ismā'īlīs of Persia, who were then under the leadership of Ḥasan-i Ṣabbāḥ (d. 518/1124), asserted their complete independence from the Fatimid regime in Cairo. Ḥasan had already launched an armed revolt against the Saljūq Turks, and he now effectively founded the independent Nizārī Ismā'īlī state and *da'wa* or mission in the midst of Saljūq dominions. This state, centred at the mountain fortress of Alamūt in northern Persia, controlled several territories in Persia and Syria, with a multitude of mountain fortresses and their surrounding villages. Despite the incessant hostilities of the Saljūqs and their successor dynasties, the Nizārī Ismāʿīlī state in Persia survived for 166 years until it was destroyed by the all-conquering Mongol hordes in 654/1256.[1]

The Mongols demolished Alamūt and its famous library as well as the other major Ismāʿīlī fortresses of Persia. They also massacred large numbers of Ismāʿīlīs in both northern Persia and in Khurāsān. Despite the claims of Juwaynī,[2] who had accompanied the Mongol conqueror Hūlāgū on his campaigns against the Persian Ismāʿīlīs, and other Persian historians of the Īlkhānid period, however, the Persian Ismāʿīlīs survived the destruction of their state and mountain strongholds. In the aftermath of the Mongol debacle, which permanently ended the political prominence of the Ismāʿīlīs, the Ismāʿīlī community became utterly demoralized and disorganized. Many of those who had survived the Mongol swords migrated to Badakhshān, in Central Asia, or the Indian subcontinent, where Ismāʿīlī communities already existed. Those who remained in Persia now began a new phase of their history, living clandestinely outside their traditional fortress communities. Moreover, they were once again obliged to strictly practise the Shīʿī principle of *taqiyya*, or precautionary dissimulation, which had become an integral part of Ismāʿīlī teachings.

With the exception of the Fatimid period, when Ismāʿīlism was adopted as the *madhhab* or system of jurisprudence for the Fatimid state and the Ismāʿīlīs enjoyed the protection of that state, the Ismāʿīlīs had by and large been persecuted throughout the Muslim world. As a result, from early on in their history during the third/ninth century, the Ismāʿīlīs had made extensive use of *taqiyya*, hiding their true religious beliefs to safeguard themselves under hostile circumstances. Indeed, the Ismāʿīlīs, like the Ithnāʿasharī or Twelver Shīʿīs with whom they shared the same early Imāmī heritage, including the observance of *taqiyya*, had become rather experienced in adopting different external guises as required. For a while during the Alamūt period, for instance, the Persian Ismāʿīlīs had even adopted the *sharīʿa* in its Sunni form. Be that as it may, in the aftermath of the fall of Alamūt, the Persian Ismāʿīlīs once again resorted widely to *taqiyya*, which soon took the form of Sufism.

---

[1] For an overview of the history of the Nizārī Ismāʿīlī state during the Alamūt period, see M.G.S. Hodgson, "The Ismāʿīlī State," in *The Cambridge History of Iran*: V: *The Saljuq and Mongol Periods*, ed. J.A. Boyle (Cambridge. Cambridge University Press 1968), pp. 422–82, and F. Daftary, *The Ismāʿīlīs: Their History and Doctrines* (Cambridge: Cambridge University Press 1990), pp. 324–434.

[2] ʿAṭāʾ Malik Juwaynī, *Taʾrīkh-i jahān-gushāy*, ed. M. Qazvīnī (Leiden: Brill/London: Luzac 1912–37), III, pp. 277–8; English trans., *The History of the World-Conqueror*, trans. J.A. Boyle (Manchester: Manchester University Press 1958), II, pp. 724–5. This translation has recently been reprinted, with the same continuous pagination in one volume, under the title of *Genghis Khan: The History of the World Conqueror* (Manchester: Manchester University Press/Paris: Unesco Publishing 1997), also containing a new introduction and bibliography by David O. Morgan.

Before investigating the early manifestations of the Ismā'īlī use of *taqiyya* in the garb of Sufism, it should be recalled that the disorganization of the Persian Ismā'īlī community of Īlkhānid times was all the more aggravated by the fact that the Ismā'īlīs had now also been deprived of the central leadership that they had previously enjoyed during the Alamūt period. After the initial leadership of Ḥasan-i Ṣabbāḥ and his next two successors at Alamūt, who acted as *dā'ī*s and *ḥujja*s of the then inaccessible Nizārī Ismā'īlī imāms, the imāms themselves had emerged from their concealment to take charge of the affairs of their state, *da'wa* and community. According to Nizārī traditions, Shams al-Dīn Muḥammad, the son and designated successor of the last ruler of Alamūt, Rukn al-Dīn Khurshāh (d. 655/1257), had been hidden by some Ismā'īlī dignitaries who in due time took him to Azerbaijan. Shams al-Dīn Muḥammad and his immediate successors seem to have remained in north-western Persia. There, they lived secretly, without direct access to their followers who were now scattered in different regions. Shams al-Dīn, who has been identified in legendary accounts with Shams-i Tabrīz, the spiritual guide of Mawlānā Jalāl al-Dīn Rūmī (d. 672/1273), evidently lived secretly as an embroiderer, hence his nickname of Zardūz. On Shams al-Dīn's death around 710/1310, his succession was disputed by his descendants. As a result, the Nizārī Ismā'īlī imāmate and community split into the rival Qāsim–Shāhī and Muḥammad–Shāhī branches.[3] Lack of evidence does not permit us to differentiate adequately and accurately between these Nizārī Ismā'īlī communities of Persia during the early post-Alamūt centuries; hence our discussion for those centuries may be taken to hold true for both communities. But for the Safavid period, unless specified otherwise, our references are to the Qāsim–Shāhī branch, which eventually emerged as the predominant one in Persia and elsewhere. The Muḥammad–Shāhī line of Nizārī imāms was actually transferred to India during the early decades of the tenth/sixteenth century, and by the end of the twelfth/eighteenth century this line had become discontinued.

It was in Mongol Persia that the Nizārī Ismā'īlīs began to use, under obscure circumstances, poetic and Sufi forms of expressions. It should be noted here that from the time of Ḥasan-i Ṣabbāḥ Persian had been adopted, in preference to Arabic, as the religious language of the Persian-speaking Ismā'īlīs. This explains why the literature produced during the Alamūt and post-Alamūt periods by the Ismā'īlīs of Persia, Afghanistan and Central Asia was entirely in the Persian language. In time, this commonality of language made Ismā'īlī–Sufi literary encounters all the more readily possible in Persia. Nizārī Quhistānī, a Persian Ismā'īlī poet who was born in Bīrjand in 645/1247 and died there in 720/1320, seems to have been the earliest post-Alamūt Nizārī

[3] On this post-Alamūt schism in Nizārī Ismā'īlism, see W. Ivanow, "A Forgotten Branch of the Ismā'īlīs," *Journal of the Royal Asiatic Society* (1938), pp. 57–79.

author to have chosen the verse and Sufi forms of expressions for camouflaging his Ismāʿīlī ideas, a model emulated by later Ismāʿīlī authors in Persia. Nizārī Quhistānī, in fact, served the Sunni Kart rulers of Herāt and was obliged to panegyrize them in many of his *qaṣīdas*. Nizārī Quhistānī travelled extensively, and certain allusions in his versified *Safar-nāma* (Travelogue), written in *mathnawī* form and containing about 1,200 verses, indicate that he actually saw the Ismāʿīlī Imām of the time, Shams al-Dīn Muḥammad, in Azerbaijan around 679/1280.[4]

During the earliest post-Alamūt centuries, the Persian Nizārīs increasingly disguised themselves under the mantle of Sufism, without establishing formal affiliations with any one of the Sufi orders or *ṭarīqas* which were then spreading in Persia. The origins and early development of this curious phenomenon, as noted, remain very obscure. However, modern studies of the meagre literary works of the Nizārīs of Persia and Central Asia dating to the early post-Alamūt period have clearly revealed that Nizārī Ismāʿīlism did become increasingly infused in pre-Safavid Persia with Sufi teachings and terminology. At the same time, the Sufis themselves used the Ismāʿīlī-related *bāṭinī ta'wīl* methodology, or esoteric exegesis, also adopting certain ideas which had been more widely ascribed to the Ismāʿīlīs. Indeed, a coalescence had now emerged in pre-Safavid Persia between Persian Sufism and Nizārī Ismāʿīlism, which represented two independent esoteric traditions in Islam. It is owing to this Ismāʿīlī–Sufi coalescence, still even less understood from the Sufi side, that it is often difficult to ascertain whether a certain post-Alamūt Persian treatise was written by a Nizārī author influenced by Sufism, or whether it was produced in Sufi milieus exposed to Ismāʿīlism.[5] As an early instance of this peculiar interaction, mention may be made of the celebrated Sufi treatise *Gulshan-i rāz* (The Rose-Garden of Mystery) composed by Nizārī Quhistānī's contemporary Maḥmūd Shabistarī (d. after 740/1339–40), and its later commentary by an anonymous Nizārī Ismāʿīlī author.[6] A relatively

---

[4] See Ḥakīm Saʿd al-Dīn Nizārī Quhistānī, *Dīvān*, ed. M. Muṣaffā (Tehran: ʿImī 1371–3/ A.Hsh./1992–4), I, pp. 105, 109; Ch. G. Baiburdī, *Zhizn i tvorcestvo Nizārī Persidskogo poeta* (Moscow: Izdatelistvo Nauk 1966), pp. 158, 162; I. K. Poonawala, *Biobibliography of Ismāʿīlī Literature* (Malibu, Calif: Undena Publications 1977), pp. 263–7, and J.T.P. de Bruijn, "Nizārī Ḳuhistānī," *EI*², VIII, pp. 83–4.

[5] See, for instance, W. Ivanow, *Ismaili Literature: A Bibliographical Survey* (Tehran: Ismaili Society 1963), pp. 127–31, and H. Corbin, *History of Islamic Philosophy*, trans L. Sherrard (London–New York: KPI in association with the Institute of Ismaili Studies 1993), pp. 95, 102–4, 304–6, 326.

[6] This anonymous Ismāʿīlī commentary entitled *Baʿḍī az ta'wīlāt-i Gulshan-i rāz* has been edited, with French translation, by H. Corbin in his *Trilogie ismaélienne* (Tehran: Institut Français de Téhéran/Paris: Librairie d'Amérique et d'Orient/A. Maisonneuve 1961), text pp. 131–61, translation pp. 1–174. See also W. Ivanow, "An Ismaili Interpretation of the Gulshani Raz," *Journal of the Bombay Branch of the Royal Asiatic Society*, New Series, 8 (1932), pp. 69–78, and Poonawala, *Biobibliography*, pp. 274, 351.

obscure Sufi master, Maḥmūd Shabistarī produced his *Gulshan-i rāz*, a *mathnawī* containing some one thousand couplets, in reply to questions raised about Sufi teachings, and it clearly shows its author's familiarity with certain Ismā'īlī doctrines. Many commentaries have been written on the *Gulshan-i rāz*. In fact, the Ismā'īlīs of Persia and Central Asia generally consider this treatise as belonging to their own literature, which may also explain why the *Gulshan-i rāz* was later commented upon in Persian by a Nizārī author. The authorship of this commentary, which comprises Ismā'īlī interpretations of selected passages, may possibly be attributed to Shāh Ṭāhir, the most famous Imām of the Muḥammad-Shāhī Nizārīs who did in fact write a treatise entitled *Sharḥ-i Gulshan-i rāz*.

As a result of the same Ismā'īlī–Sufi interactions of the post-Alamūt times, the Persian-speaking Ismā'īlīs have regarded some of the greatest mystic poets of Persia as their co-religionists and selections of their *dīvān*s have been preserved particularly in the private Ismā'īlī libraries of Badakhshān, now divided between Afghanistan and Tajikistan. Amongst such poets, mention may be made of Farīd al-Dīn 'Aṭṭār and Jalāl al-Dīn Rūmī, as well as lesser figures like Qāsim al-Anwār. Similarly, the Nizārīs of Central Asia consider 'Azīz al- Dīn Nasafī, the celebrated Sufi master of their region, as a co-religionist and they have numerous copies of his Sufi treatise entitled *Zubdat al-ḥaqā'iq* in their collections of manuscripts.[7] The Ismā'īlīs of Persia, Afghanistan and Central Asia, all belonging to the Nizārī branch of Ismā'īlism, have continued to use verses by the mystical poets of Persia in their various religious rituals and ceremonies, which often also resemble Sufi *dhikr*s or incantations; the origins of such traditions, too, may be traced to the Ismā'īlī–Sufi encounters of the early post-Alamūt centuries.

By the ninth/fifteenth century, the Persian Ismā'īlīs had begun to adopt Sufi ways of life even externally. Thus, the Ismā'īlī imāms, who were still obliged to hide their true identity, now appeared as Sufi masters or *pīr*s, while their followers adopted the typically Sufi guise of their disciples or *murīd*s. The adoption of a Sufi exterior, and indeed the Persian Ismā'īlīs' success in seeking refuge under the general mantle of Sufism, would not have been so easily possible if these two esoteric traditions of Islam did not share common doctrinal grounds. The Ismā'īlīs, too, had from early on developed their own *bāṭinī* tradition based on a fundamental distinction between the exoteric (*ẓāhir*) and the esoteric (*bāṭin*) dimensions of religion, or between the apparent, literal meaning and the inner, true significance of the sacred

---

[7] Nasafī's *Zubdat al-ḥaqā'iq* has been included in an edition of Ismā'īlī works recovered from Badakhshān; see *Panj risāla dar bayān-i āfāq va anfus*, ed. Andrei E. Berthels (Moscow: Izdatelistvo Nauk 1970), pp. 91–207, and A. Berthels and M. Baqoev, *Alphabetic Catalogue of Manuscripts found by 1959–1963 Expedition in Gorno-Badakhshan Autonomous Region* (Moscow: Izdatelistvo Nauk 1967), pp. 63–4, 81–2.

scriptures and the religious commandments and prohibitions. Accordingly, they held that every revealed scripture, including especially the Koran, and the laws or *sharīʻa*s laid down by them, had its literal meaning, the *ẓāhir*, which had to be contrasted to the inner meaning or true spiritual reality (*ḥaqīqa*) contained in the *bāṭin*. They further held that the *ẓāhir*, or religious laws enunciated by prophets, had undergone periodical changes, while the spiritual truths would remain immutable and eternal. From early on, the Ismāʻīlīs had also adopted a cyclical view of the religious history of humankind, teaching that religious laws were announced by different speaker-prophets (*nāṭiq*s), as recognized in the Koran, while it was the function of these prophets' successors, the *waṣī*s and imāms, to explain and interpret in every era (*dawr*) the hidden or true meanings of the revelations and the religious laws expressed by them. These hidden truths, or *ḥaqā'iq*, could be made apparent through *ta'wīl* (esoteric exegesis), the process of deducing the *bāṭin* from the *ẓāhir*. The Ismāʻīlīs further held that in every era, the esoteric world of spiritual reality could be accessible only to the elite (*khawāṣṣ*) of humankind, as distinct from the common masses (*ʻawāmm*) who were merely capable of perceiving and understanding the *ẓāhir*, the literal meaning of the revelation. Accordingly, in the era of Islam, initiated by the Prophet Muḥammad, the eternal truths of religion could be explained only to those who had been properly initiated into the Ismāʻīlī community and recognized the teaching authority of the Ismāʻīlī imāms who succeeded the Prophet and his *waṣī*, ʻAlī b. Abī Ṭālib; for they alone represented the true sources of *ta'wīl* in the era of Islam.

Initiation into Ismāʻīlism took place gradually, and the initiates were bound by their oath (*ʻahd*) to keep secret the *bāṭin* imparted to them by the imām or the hierarchy of teachers authorized by him. The *bāṭin* was thus not only hidden but also secret, and its knowledge had to be kept away from the uninitiated common people, the non-Ismāʻīlīs, who were not capable of understanding it. By exalting the *bāṭin* and the truths (*ḥaqā'iq*) contained therein, the Ismāʻīlīs were from early on regarded by the rest of the Muslim society as the most representative Shīʻī community expounding esotericism in Islam, hence their common designation as the Bāṭiniyya. However, this designation was often used abusively by anti-Ismāʻīlī sources which accused the Ismāʻīlīs in general of ignoring the *ẓāhir*, or the commandments and prohibitions of Islam, in a way similar to the general condemnation of Sufis by Muslim jurists.

During the Alamūt period, with the declaration of the *qiyāma* or resurrection in 559/1164, which was subsequently developed in terms of a doctrine and incorporated into the contemporary Nizārī Ismāʻīlī teachings, yet greater affinities were established between Ismāʻīlism and Sufism. The Nizārī Ismāʻīlī doctrine of the *qiyāma* thus prepared the ground even further for the coalescence that was to develop between these two esoteric traditions during the post-Alamūt centuries.[8] This doctrine exalted the autonomous teaching authority of the current Ismāʻīlī imām over that of any previous imām, while the declaration of the *qiyāma* also implied a complete personal transformation of the Nizārī Ismāʻīlīs, who henceforth were expected to see nothing else but their imām and the manifestation of the divine truth in him. In the spiritual paradise of the *qiyāma* into which the Nizārīs had been collectively admitted, the current Nizārī imām became the manifestation of the divine word (*kalima*) or logos. It was essentially through this vision of the imām that the Nizārī Ismāʻīlīs could find themselves in paradise. The imām had to be seen in his true spiritual reality, however, by penetrating the metaphysical and mystical significance of his person. Only then would one be enabled to view the whole world from the imām's perspective. As a result, one would be able to lead a totally spiritual life, a paradisal existence accessible only to the Nizārī Ismāʻīlīs who acknowledged the spiritual guidance of the sole legitimate imām of the time.

This viewpoint towards the universe, and the imām, would in fact lead the individual to a third level of being, a world of *bāṭin* behind the *bāṭin*, the ultimate reality or *ḥaqīqa*, contrasted to the worlds of the *sharīʻa* and its *bāṭin* as interpreted by ordinary Ismāʻīlī *ta'wīl*. In the realm of the *ḥaqīqa*, believers would turn from the *ẓāhirī* world of appearances to the spiritual realm of the ultimate reality and unchangeable truths. In the Nizārī Ismāʻīlī teachings of the Alamūt period, the *qiyāma* was thus identified with the *ḥaqīqa*, a realm of spiritual life, in close analogy to the *ḥaqīqa* of the Sufi inner experience. On that level of existence, the Nizārīs had only an inward spiritual life, and the imām was to serve for his followers in the same role that a Sufi *pīr* or shaykh did for his *murīd*s or disciples. By concentrating their attention on him, they could be made to forget their own separate beings; and through him they would merge into their idealized roles as expressions of cosmic harmony. However, the Nizārī Ismāʻīlī imām was more than a mere Sufi master, one among a multitude of such guides. The imām was a single cosmic individual who summed up in his person the entire reality of existence (*wujūd*); the perfect microcosm, for whom a lesser guide, or a Sufi *pīr*, could not be substituted. The cosmic position of the Ismāʻīlī imām, as the representative of cosmic reality, was also analogous to that of the Perfect Man (*al-insān al-kāmil*) of the Sufis, though again the latter could not offer a full equivalent of the Nizārī Ismāʻīlī imām, with whom the Nizārīs of the post-*qiyāma* times shared a joint spiritual existence.

Meanwhile, certain developments in the religio-political ambience of post-Mongol Persia were facilitating the activities of the Nizārīs and other Shīʻī

[8] On the controversial Nizārī doctrine of the *qiyāma* and its implications, see Daftary, *The Ismāʻīlīs*, pp. 386–96; see also Christian Jambet's *La Grande résurrection d'Alamūt* (Lagrasse: Verdier 1990), which is based on a phenomenological approach to the subject.

movements as well as the general Ismāʿīlī–Sufi relations. Īlkhānid rule, founded by Hūlāgū in 654/1256, the same year in which he destroyed the Ismāʿīlī state, was effectively ended in Persia with Abū Saʿīd (716/1316–736/1335), the last great ruler of that Mongol dynasty. Subsequently, Persia became politically fragmented, with the major exceptions of the reigns of Tīmūr (771/1370–807/1405), and that of his son Shāh Rukh (807/1405–850/1447). During this turbulent period, lasting until the advent of the Safavids, different parts of Persia were held by local dynasties, including the minor Īlkhānids, the Muẓaffarids, the Jalāyirids, the Sarbadārids, the later Timurids, the Qara Qoyunlu and the Aq Qoyunlu. In the absence of any strong central authority, the political fragmentation of Persia between the collapse of the Īlkhānid empire and the establishment of the Safavid dynasty provided more favourable conditions for the activities of a number of movements, most of which were essentially Shīʿī or influenced by Shīʿism. The Nizārīs and certain Shīʿī-related movements with millenarian aspirations, such as those of the Sarbadārids, the Ḥurūfiyya and the Mushaʿshaʿ, as well as certain Sufi orders, found a suitable respite in post-Mongol Persia to organize or reorganize themselves during the eighth/fourteenth and ninth/fifteenth centuries. It was under such circumstances that the Nizārī imāms, as we shall note, emerged more openly at Anjudān in central Persia, though still hiding their identity.

The same political atmosphere had been conducive to a rising tide of Shīʿī tendencies in Persia during the two centuries preceding the advent of the Safavids. This phenomenon, too, had rendered Persia's religious environment increasingly eclectic and more favourable to the activities of the Nizārīs and other crypto-Shīʿī or Shīʿī-related movements. Some of these movements, especially the radical ones with political agendas which normally also possessed millenarian or Mahdist aspirations, like those of the Ḥurūfiyya and their Nuqṭavī or Pisīkhānī offshoot, proved extremely popular. It is noteworthy that leaders of the majority of such movements in post-Mongol Persia hailed from Shīʿī-Sufi backgrounds. However, the Shīʿism that was then spreading in Persia was of a new form, of a popular type and propagated mainly through the teachings and organizations of the Sufis, rather than being promulgated by Twelver or any other particular school of Shīʿism. This popular Shīʿism spread mainly through several Sufi orders, hence its designation as "*ṭarīqah* Shīʿism" by Marshall Hodgson.[9] It is significant to recall that most of the Sufi orders in question, those founded during the early post-Alamūt period, remained outwardly Sunni for quite some time. However, they were at the same time devoted to ʿAlī and the *ahl al-bayt*, acknowledging ʿAlī's spiritual guidance and including him in their *silsila*s or chains of spiritual masters. All this led to a unique synthesis of Sunni-centred Sufism and ʿAlid loyalism.

---

[9] Marshall G.S. Hodgson, *The Venture of Islam: Conscience and History in a World Civilization* (Chicago: University of Chicago Press 1974), II, pp. 493ff.

Among the Sufi orders that played a leading role in spreading pro-'Alid sentiments and Shī'ism in Persia, mention should be made of the Nūrbakhshiyya, the Ni'matu'llāhiyya, and the Ṣafaviyya *ṭarīqa*s. All three orders eventually became fully Shī'ī. The Ṣafavī *ṭarīqa* played the most direct part in the 'Shī'itization' of Persia; it was indeed the leader of this order who ascended the throne of Persia in 907/1501 and at the same time adopted Ithnā'asharī Imāmī Shī'ism as the state religion of his realm. In this atmosphere of religious eclecticism, the 'Alid loyalism of certain Sufi orders and religio-political movements came to be gradually more widespread. As a result, Shī'ī elements began, in a unique sense, to be superimposed on Sunni Islam. By the ninth/fifteenth century, there had appeared a general increase in Shī'ī and pro-'Alid sentiments throughout Persia, where the bulk of the population still remained Sunni. Professor Claude Cahen has referred to this curious process as the "Shī'itization of Sunnism," as opposed to the propagation of Shī'ism of any specific school.[10] At any rate, it was in such an ambience of pre-Safavid Persia, characterized by *ṭarīqa*-diffused Shī'ī–Sunni syncretism, that the Nizārī Ismā'īlīs found it convenient to seek refuge under the 'politically correct' mantle of Sufism, with which they also shared many esoteric ideas.

Meanwhile, Twelver Shī'ism had been developing its own relations with Sufism in pre-Safavid Persia.[11] The earliest instance of this non-Ismā'īlī Shī'ī–Sufi rapport is reflected in the writings of Sayyid Ḥaydar Āmulī, the eminent Ithnā'asharī theologian, theosopher and gnostic (*'ārif*) from Māzandarān who died after 787/1385. Strongly influenced by the teachings of Ibn al-'Arabī (d. 638/1240), whom the Nizārīs consider as another of their co-religionists, Ḥaydar Āmulī combined his Shī'ī thought with certain gnostic–mystical traditions, as well as theosophy (Persian, *ḥikmat-i ilāhī*), also emphasizing the common grounds between Shī'ism and Sufism. According to Āmulī, a Muslim who combines the *sharī'a* with *ḥaqīqa* and *ṭarīqa* (the spiritual path followed by Sufis) is not only a believer but a believer put to test (*al-mu'min al-mumtaḥan*). Such a Muslim, who is at once a true Shī'ī and a Sufi, would preserve a careful balance between the *ẓāhir* and the *bāṭin*, equally avoiding

---

[10] Claude Cahen, "Le problème du Shī'isme dans l'Asie Mineure Turque préottomane," in *Le Shī'isme Imāmite: Colloque de Strasbourg (6–9 mai 1968)*, arranged by R. Brunschvig and T. Fahd (Paris: Presses Universitaires de France 1970), pp. 118 ff. See also M. Molé, "Les Kubrawiya entre Sunnisme et Shiisme aux huitième et neuvième siècles de l'hégire," *Revue d' Etudes Islamiques*, 29 (1961), pp. 61–142; S. Amir Arjomand, *The Shadow of God and the Hidden Imam* (Chicago: University of Chicago Press 1984), pp. 66–84, and H. Halm, *Shiism*, trans. J. Watson (Edinburgh: Edinburgh University Press 1991), pp. 71–83.

[11] See H. Corbin, *En Islam Iranien* (Paris: Gallimard 1971–2), I, pp. 74–85, III, pp. 149–213; *idem*, *History of Islamic Philosophy*, pp. 332–5; S.H. Nasr, "Le Shī'isme et le Soufisme," in *Le Shī'isme Imāmite*, pp. 215–33, and his *Sufi Essays* (London: George Allen & Unwin 1972), pp. 104–20.

the excessive literalist, judicial interpretations of Islam and the antinomian stances of the radical *ghulāt* Muslims.[12] Aspects of this fusion between Twelver Shīʻism and mysticism, or rather gnosis (*ʻirfān*) – in combination with different philosophical (theosophical) traditions, later culminated in the Safavid period in the works of Mīr Dāmād (d. 1040/1630), Mullā Ṣadrā (d.1050/1640) and other members of the gnostic-theosophical ʻSchool of Iṣfahān'. It should be added that with the Safavid persecutions of Sufi orders, the proponents of the mystical experience began to use the term gnosis or *ʻirfān* in preference to Sufism (*taṣawwuf*).

No details are available on the activities of the Nizārī Ismāʻīlī imāms succeeding Shams al-Dīn Muḥammad until the middle of ninth/fifteenth century, when they emerged at Anjudān posing as Sufi *pīr*s. Islām Shāh, the thirtieth imām, who was a contemporary of Tīmūr and died around 829/1425, may have been the first imām of the Qāsim-Shāhī Nizārī line to have settled in Anjudān. In fact, the Persian chroniclers of Tīmūr's reign do refer to earlier Nizārī activities in Anjudān, also mentioning a Timurid expedition sent against them in 795/1393.[13] It is, however, with Mustanṣir bi'llāh, the thirty-second imām of this line who succeeded to the imāmate around 868/1463, that the Qāsim-Shāhī imāms were definitely established at Anjudān, initiating what W. Ivanow (1886–1970), the foremost pioneer in modern Nizārī studies, designated as the Anjudān period in post-Alamūt Nizārī Ismāʻīlism.[14] Anjudān, situated thirty-seven kilometres east of Arāk and the same distance westward from Maḥallāt in central Persia, remained the seat of the Qāsim-Shāhī Nizārī imāms and their *daʻwa* activities until the end of the eleventh/seventeenth century, a period of more than two centuries, coinciding with the greater part of the Safavid period. It seems that the imāms had chosen Anjudān rather carefully: not only did the locality have a central position in Persia while still being removed from the main centres of Sunni power, but it was also close to the cities of Qum and Kāshān, the traditional Shīʻī centres of Persia designated as the *dār al-muʼminīn* (abode of the faithful). The Nizārī antiquities of Anjudān, discovered in 1937 by Ivanow, include an old mosque and three mausoleums containing the tombs of several imāms, with invaluable epigraphic information. The mausoleum of Mustanṣir bi'llāh, who died in 885/

[12] Ḥaydar Āmulī, *Jāmiʻ al-asrār*, ed. H. Corbin and O. Yahya in a collection of Āmulī's treatises entitled *La Philosophie Shiʻite*, Bibliothèque Iranienne (Tehran: Département d'Iranologie de l'Institut Franco-Iranien/Paris: A. Maisonneuve 1969), pp. 47, 116–17, 216–17, 220–2, 238, 388, 611ff. See also Āmulī's *Asrār al-sharīʻa wa-aṭwār al-ṭarīqa wa-anwār al-ḥaqīqa*, ed. M. Khvājavī (Tehran: Cultural Studies and Research Institute 1982).

[13] Niẓām al-Dīn Shāmī, *Ẓafar-nāma*, ed. F. Tauer (Prague: Oriental Institute 1937–56), I, p. 136, and Sharaf al-Dīn ʻAlī Yazdī, *Ẓafar-nāma*, ed. M. ʻAbbāsī (Tehran: Amīr Kabīr 1336 A. Hsh./1957), I, pp. 443–4; ed. A. Urunbayev (Tashkent 1972), p. 500.

[14] W. Ivanow, *Brief Survey of the Evolution of Ismailism* (Leiden: E.J. Brill, for the Ismaili Society 1952), p. 29.

1480, is still preserved there under the name of Shāh Qalandar, whose Ismāʿīlī identity remains completely unknown to the local inhabitants.[15]

The Anjudān period witnessed a revival in the *daʿwa* activities of the Nizārī Ismāʿīlīs. As noted, the general religio-political atmosphere of Persia had now become more favourable to the activities of the Nizārīs and other Shīʿī movements. As a result, with the emergence of the imāms at Anjudān, the Nizārī *daʿwa* was reorganized and reinvigorated, not only to win new converts but also to reassert the central authority and the direct control of the imāms over the various outlying Nizārī communities, especially in Central Asia and India where the Nizārīs had increasingly come under the authority of a number of hereditary dynasties of local leaders. The Anjudān renaissance in Nizārī Ismāʿīlism also brought about a revival in the literary activities of the community in Persia. The earliest fruits of these efforts were the works produced by Abū Isḥāq Quhistānī, who flourished during the second half of the ninth/fifteenth century, and Khayrkhvāh-i Harātī, a *dāʿī* and poet who died after 960/1553.[16]

The Nizārī imāms and their followers were still obliged, in predominantly Sunni Persia, to practise *taqiyya* in the guise of Sufism. In the course of the Anjudān period, it became customary for the Nizārī Ismāʿīlī imāms to adopt Sufi names; they often also added, like Sufi masters, terms such as Shāh and ʿAlī to their names. Mustanṣir bi'llāh, whose own Sufi name was Shāh Qalandar, may even have developed relations with the Niʿmatu'llāhī Sufi order, though concrete evidence is lacking. At any rate, the Persian Nizārī Ismāʿīlīs now clearly appeared as a Sufi *ṭarīqa*, one among many such orders then existing in pre-Safavid Persia. For this purpose, the Persian Ismāʿīlīs had readily adopted the master–disciple (*murshid–murīd*) terminology of the Sufis. To outsiders, the Nizārī imāms at Anjudān appeared as Sufi *murshid*s, *pīr*s, or shaykhs. They were evidently also regarded as pious Fatimid ʿAlid Sayyids, descendants of the Prophet through his daughter Fāṭima and ʿAlī. Similarly, ordinary Nizārīs posed as the imāms' *murīd*s, who were guided along a spiritual path or *ṭarīqa* to *ḥaqīqa* by a spiritual master. With Shīʿī ideas and ʿAlid loyalism then spreading in so many Sufi orders in Persia, the veneration of ʿAlī and other early ʿAlid imāms by Nizārīs did not cause any alarm regarding the true identity of this Shīʿī community. It is interesting to note that the Nizārīs still refer to themselves as their imām's *murīd*s, while the word *ṭarīqa* is used by them in reference to the Ismāʿīlī interpretation of Islam.

---

[15] W. Ivanow, "Tombs of Some Persian Ismaili Imams," *Journal of the Bombay Branch of the Royal Asiatic Society*, New Series, 14 (1938), pp. 49–62, and F. Daftary, "Anjedān," *EIr*, II, p. 77.

[16] Ivanow, *Ismaili Literature*, pp. 141–4, and Poonawala, *Biobibliography*, pp. 269–70, 275–7.

An extremely important book entitled *Pandiyāt-i javānmardī* (Admonitions on Spiritual Chivalry), containing the sermons or religious admonitions of Imām Mustanṣir bi'llāh, has survived from the early Anjudān period.[17] Copies of the Persian version of the *Pandiyāt*, which is also extant in a medieval Gujarati translation, are still preserved in the manuscript collections of the Ismā'īlīs of Badakhshān and adjacent regions, including Hunza and other areas of northern Pakistan. In the *Pandiyāt*, the Nizārīs are referred to by Sufi expressions such as *ahl-i ḥaqq* and *ahl-i ḥaqīqat*, or 'the people of the truth', while the imām himself is designated as *pīr*, *murshid* and *quṭb*.[18] The *Pandiyāt* is indeed permeated with Sufi ideas; the imām's admonitions start with the *sharī'at–ṭarīqat–ḥaqīqat* categorization of the Sufis, portraying the *ḥaqīqat* as the *bāṭin* of the *sharī'at* which could be attained by the faithful by following the *ṭarīqat*, or spiritual path. In accordance with the Nizārī teachings of the time, rooted in the doctrine of the *qiyāmat* of the Alamūt period, the *Pandiyāt* further explains that the *ḥaqīqat* essentially consists of recognizing the spiritual reality of the current imām. The *Pandiyāt* also stresses the duty of the faithful to recognize and obey the current imām. An equal stress is placed on the obligation of the Nizārīs to pay their religious dues regularly to the imām of the time. These admonitions are reiterated in the writings of Khayrkhvāh-i Harātī. By his time (the middle of the tenth/sixteenth century), the term *pīr*, the Persian equivalent of the Arabic 'shaykh', had acquired widespread Ismā'īlī application and was used in reference to *dā'īs* of different ranks as well as the person of the imām himself. Subsequently, the term *pīr* fell into disuse in Persia, but it was retained by the Nizārī Ismā'īlīs of Central Asia and India.

In the meantime, the advent of the Safavids and the proclamation of Twelver Shī'ism as the religion of Safavid Persia in 907/1501 promised yet more favourable circumstances for the activities of the Nizārīs and other Persian Shī'ī communities. The Nizārīs did, in fact, reduce the intensity of their *taqiyya* during the initial decades of Safavid rule. As a result, the religious identity of the Nizārī imāms and their followers became somewhat better known despite their continued use of the *murshid–murīd* and other Sufi guises. The new optimism of the Persian Ismā'īlīs proved short-lived, however, as the Safavids and their *sharī'a*-minded *'ulamā'* soon adopted a rigorous religio-political policy aimed at suppressing popular forms of Sufism as well as all the Shī'ī or Shī'ī-related movements which fell outside the boundaries of

[17] Mustanṣir bi'llāh, *Pandiyāt-i javānmardī*, ed. and trans. W. Ivanow (Leiden: E.J. Brill for the Ismaili Society 1953).

[18] *Ibid.* text, pp. 26, 27, 31, 32, 39, 57, 65, 86, 87, 90, 91, 99, translation pp. 7, 17, 19, 20, 24, 36, 40, 53, 54, 55, 56, 61, 62, and elsewhere.

[19] For an interesting analysis of this policy, see K. Babayan, "Sufis, Dervishes and Mullas: The Controversy over Spiritual and Temporal Domination in Seventeenth-Century Iran," in *Safavid Persia*, ed. Charles Melville (London: I.B.Tauris 1996), pp. 117–38. See also Arjomand, *Shadow of God*, pp. 109–21, 160–87.

Twelver Shī'ism.[19] This policy was even directed against the Qizilbāsh who had brought the Safavids to power. Most of the Sufi orders of Persia were in fact extirpated in the reign of Shāh Ismā'īl (907/1501–930/1524), who also widely persecuted various non-Ithnā'asharī Shī'īs.

The Nizārīs, whose increasingly overt activities had attracted the attention of Shāh Ismā'īl and his successor, Shāh Ṭahmāsp (930/1524–984/1576), as well as their Twelver *'ulamā'*, received their share of the Safavids' early religious persecutions. At the instigation of his *sharī'a*-minded *'ulamā'*, Shāh Ismā'īl eventually issued an order for the execution of Shāh Ṭāhir al-Ḥusaynī, the thirty-first imām of the Muḥammad-Shāhī Nizārīs who had become rather popular in Kāshān due to his learning and piety. However, Shāh Ṭāhir succeeded in fleeing from Persia in 926/1520. He eventually settled down in the Deccan, where he acquired a prominent position and rendered valuable diplomatic services to the Niẓām–Shāhīs of Aḥmadnagar. After Shāh Ṭāhir, who died around 952/1545, the imāms of his line continued to reside in Aḥmadnagar and then in Awrangābād. Meanwhile, in 981/1573, Shāh Ṭahmāsp persecuted the Qāsim-Shāhī Nizārīs of Anjudān in the time of their thirty-sixth imām, Murād Mīrzā. This imām who pursued a relatively active policy, possibly in collaboration with the Nuqṭavīs who were severely persecuted under the Safavids, was eventually captured and brought before Shāh Ṭahmāsp, who had him executed.[20]

The Safavids came to have their own dynastic disputes and domestic strifes during the reigns of Ismā'īl II and his successor, Muḥammad Khudābanda (985/1577–995/1587), providing a respite for the religious movements that had survived the earlier Safavid persecutions. This proved particularly timely for the Persian Ismā'īlīs who by then had already adopted a second tactical disguise, that of Twelver Shī'ism enforced by the Safavid regime. This new form of *taqiyya*, too, could readily be accommodated by the Nizārī Ismā'īlīs, who shared the same Ḥusaynid Fatimid 'Alid and early Imāmī Shī'ī traditions with the Twelvers. By the time of Shāh 'Abbās I (995/1587–1038/1629), who during his long reign led Safavid Persia to its peak of glory, the Persian Nizārīs had become very successful in their Twelver guise. Indeed, Shāh 'Abbās did not persecute the Nizārīs and their imāms, who had by then even developed friendly relations with the Safavids. Murād Mīrzā's successor as the thirty-seventh imām at Anjudān, Khalīlu'llāh I, who carried the Sufi name of Dhu'l-Faqār 'Alī, was in fact married to a Safavid princess, possibly a sister of Shāh 'Abbās. The success of the Nizārī imāms in practising *taqiyya* in the form of

---

[20] Qāḍī Aḥmad al-Qummī, *Khulāṣat al-tavārīkh*, ed. Iḥsān Ishrāqī (Tehran: Dānishgāh-i Tihrān 1359–63/A. Hsh. 1980–4), I, pp. 582–4, and A. Amanat, "The Nuqṭawī Movement of Maḥmūd Pisīkhānī and his Persian Cycle of Mystical-Materialism," in *Mediaeval Isma'ili History and Thought*, ed. F. Daftary (Cambridge: Cambridge University Press 1996), especially pp. 289–95.

Twelver Shīʿism is further attested to by an epigraph, recovered by the present author at Anjudān in 1976. This epigraph, originally attached, according to the then prevailing custom, to the entrance of an old mosque in Anjudān, reproduces the text of a royal decree issued by Shāh ʿAbbās in Rajab 1036/March–April 1627. According to this decree, addressed to Amīr Khalīlu'llāh Anjudānī, the contemporary Nizārī imām, the Shīʿa of Anjudān, cited as a dependency of the *dār al-mu'minīn* of Qum, had received an exemption from paying certain taxes, like other Shīʿa around Qum. It is significant to note that in this decree the Anjudānī Shīʿīs and their imām are clearly considered to have been Ithnāʿasharīs. Amīr Khalīlu'llāh, according to his tombstone in Anjudān, died in 1043/1634; and after him, the Nizārī imāms in Persia continued to practise *taqiyya* under the double guises of Sufism and Twelver Shīʿism until the end of the Anjudān period, though the Sufi cover seems to have become increasingly overshadowed by that of Twelver Shīʿism.

Similarly to the Qāsim-Shāhī Nizārī imāms of Anjudān, Shāh Ṭāhir and his successors in the Muḥammad-Shāhī line, too, observed *taqiyya* in India in the form of Twelver Shīʿism, which was more acceptable than Ismāʿīlism to the Muslim rulers of India who were interested at that time in cultivating friendly relations with the powerful Twelver Shīʿī Safavid dynasty of Persia. This may explain why Shāh Ṭāhir wrote several commentaries on the theological works of well-known Twelver scholars. However, Shāh Ṭāhir achieved his greatest religious success in the Deccan, when Burhān Niẓām Shāh (915/1509–961/1554), owing to the efforts of this Nizārī Ismāʿīlī imām, proclaimed Twelver Shīʿism the official religion of his state in 944/1537.[21] Subsequently, Shāh Ṭāhir's son and future successor, Shāh Ḥaydar, was dispatched on a diplomatic mission to the Safavid court in Persia. It is also interesting to note in this connection that in the *Lamaʿāt al-ṭāhirīn*, one of a few extant Muḥammad-Shāhī Nizārī works composed around 1110/1698, the author clearly hides his Ismāʿīlī ideas under the covers of Ithnāʿasharī and Sufi expressions; he also eulogizes the twelve imāms of the Ithnāʿashariyya while alluding occasionally to the imāms of the Muḥammad-Shāhī Nizārī line.[22]

By the final decades of the eleventh/seventeenth century, not only had the Persian Ismāʿīlīs managed to survive under their double Sufi–Ithnāʿasharī guises, but the Nizārī Ismāʿīlī *daʿwa* had successfully spread in remote regions such as Badakhshān, and in India, where the Nizārīs became known as Khojas. In these regions, too, the Nizārīs developed their own rapport with Sufism during the Anjudān period. It was in the time of Shāh Nizār, the fortieth imām

---

[21] On Shāh Ṭāhir, the most famous Nizārī Ismāʿīlī imām of the Muḥammad–Shāhī line, and his successors, see Daftary, *The Ismāʿīlīs*, pp. 448, 453–4, 472, 486ff., where further references are cited; Poonawala, *Biobibliography*, pp. 271–5, and his "Shāh Ṭāhir," EI^2, IX, pp. 200–1.

[22] See Ivanow, *Ismaili Literature*, pp. 165–7, and Poonawala, *Biobibliography*, pp. 270–1, 281.

of the Qāsim-Shāhī Nizārīs who succeeded his father Khalīlu'llāh II in 1090/1680, that the seat of this line of imāms was transferred from Anjudān to the nearby village of Kahak, bringing to a close the Anjudān period in post-Alamūt Nizārī Ismā'īlism. Shāh Nizār, who according to his tombstone in Kahak died in 1134/1722, the same year in which Safavid rule was effectively brought to an end by the Afghan invasion of Persia, seems to have established relations with the Ni'matu'llāhī Sufi order. At any rate, he adopted the Sufi name of 'Aṭā' Allāh. This explains why his followers in certain parts of Persia, notably in Kirmān, came to be known as 'Aṭā' Allāhīs.

From the second half of the twelfth/eighteenth century, when the Nizārī Ismā'īlī imāms emerged in Kirmān from their clandestine existence and began to play important roles in the political affairs of Persia, they also developed closer relations with the Ni'matu'llāhī Sufi order, which was then being revived in Persia by the thirty-fourth *quṭb* of the order, Riḍā 'Alī Shāh (d. 1214/1799) who, like his predecessors, resided in the Deccan. But these relations were now no longer cultivated for *taqiyya* purposes. By that time, the identity of the imāms had become generally known and they themselves often provided protection for various prominent Ni'matu'llāhī Sufis who were then frequently persecuted in Persia. It is, however, beyond the scope of this essay to consider post-Safavid Ismā'īlī–Sufi, relations which reached their climax during the long imāmate of Ḥasan 'Alī Shāh (1232/1817–1298/1881), the first of the modern Nizārī Ismā'īlī imāms to bear the title of Āqā Khān.[23]

[23] For Ismā'īlī–Sufi relations during the Zand and Qājār periods of Persian history, see N. Pourjavady and P.L. Wilson, "Ismā'īlīs and Ni'matullāhīs," *Studia Islamica*, 41 (1975), pp. 118–35, and Daftary, *The Ismā'īlīs*, pp. 498–503, 506–7, 517–18, where references to primary sources are cited.

The Rawshaniyya

A Sufi Movement on the Mughal Tribal Periphery

SERGEI ANDREYEV

INTRODUCTION

This study attempts to answer two questions posed by the history of the Rawshani movement.[1] The first is how and why a Sufi circle that originated in a remote area of the Mughal imperial frontier turned into a militant religio-political movement. The second is how this movement collapsed despite its initial success and a genuine religious appeal. The drama of the Rawshani movement unfolded against the background of Pashtun tribal frontier society that differed significantly from neighbouring India. Therefore, in order to understand the peculiarities of this predominantly Pashtun movement it will be essential to consider the main traits of Pashtun society.

In the country of the Pashtuns an individual outside tribal structure is absolutely defenceless. A Pashtun's inherited plot of land or share in a communal land property is the basis for his political and social participation in his kinship or alliance-based group. Since acquired property or residence rights cannot give an individual full tribal membership, migration from the ancestral land in effect signifies an important loss of social and political status and threatens personal security. Outside his own clan, a Pashtun or a non-Pashtun migrant can survive only as a client of a powerful patron, whether individual or collective, who provides him with protection and defence of his honour. Thus, the idea of clan and tribe symbolizes unity defined by descent. At the same time, individual political interests find their expression in the concept of politically corporate factions or blocs.[2] The breakdown into these factions or blocs can occur at any level, both individual and collective (i.e. clan-based). Under normal circumstances these blocs are headed by chiefs

---

[1] This is *rawshānī* in Persian and *rawx̌ānī* in Pashto. Given this discrepancy between Persian and Pashto renditions of the name of the movement, as well as my use of both Persian and Pashto materials, I shall always give this word as 'Rawshani' or 'Rawshaniyya'.

[2] *Gund* in Pashto, literally 'party'.

who, by increasing the number of their supporters and/or clients, boost their social and political status.

Pashtuns have no memory of a pre-Islamic past, asserting that they always were Muslims and that therefore all their customs are Islamic, even if these sometimes contradict the Koran. This attitude generates a low regard for the Muslim teachers among them, both mystical and non-mystical. Besides, Sufi guides as well as mullās and *'ulamā* are not usually a part of the native kinship structures, and thus do not qualify for the same high status as Pashtuns. Even the most prominent of them enjoy only the status of alien 'guests of honour' living in a tribal environment and serving a Muslim community.

In times of peace the Sufi guides mainly attract disciples from poor backgrounds, while men with claims to secular power or to any degree of religious piety and learning never take an active part in Sufi ceremonies.[3] The Sufi guide exercises his influence outside tribal organization and established patterns of social behaviour. Because of this, sociologically, not only genealogically, he is not a part of the tribal system. On the contrary, by the nature of his activity he constantly challenges this system. However, this paradigm of the troublesome, but nevertheless possible, coexistence of the Sufi guides and tribesmen cannot be applied to all tribes. Thus, the Mohmands do not follow any Sufi brotherhood, perceiving Sufism not as an acceptable alternative or supplement to traditional normative Islam but as a surrogate for it.[4]

If left unchecked by secular tribal authorities, whenever the religious leaders assume authority over large groups of people who are normally subject to another, the bonds between the guide and his individual followers have a latent tendency to evolve into the bloc-type relationships, challenging the regular system of authority based on a tribal lineage. As often happens in Pashtun society, individual relationships resembling the organization of a traditional Sufi brotherhood turn into a new kind of institution, usually identified as 'maraboutic Sufism'.[5] In this case, affiliation to the spiritual guide is based on the collective adherence of a clan or tribe to the *pīr*'s family. Otherwise, the number of a guide's individual followers is usually very low.

In times of political trouble, the main religio-political role of the *pīr*s is to reassert the unity and integrity of Islam when it is being challenged by tribal factionalism often combined with the threat of non-Muslim outsiders. This kind of political unification can be conditionally called 'supra-tribal' since the

---

[3] Richard Tapper, "Holier than Thou: Islam in Three Tribal Societies," in *Islam in Tribal Societies: From the Atlas to the Indus*, ed. Akbar S. Ahmed and David M. Hart (London: Routledge & Kegan Paul 1984), pp. 261–3.

[4] A. Ahmed, "Religious Presence and Symbolism in Pushtun Society," in Ahmed and Hart, *Islam in Tribal Society*, pp. 318–9.

[5] Olivier Roy, *L'Afghanistan: Islam et modernité politique* (Paris: Éditions du Seuil 1985), pp. 56–8.

tribesmen are united by charismatic religious leaders who appeal primarily to their religious feelings at the expense of their tribal identities. When the 'supra-tribal' model is applied, the message of unification is meant to be spread as widely as possible and membership in the political coalition is offered to everyone, regardless of his tribal or even ethnic origin.

Thus, it follows that when a Sufi guide leads a popular uprising on a supra-tribal basis, the relationships between spiritual guide and his personal followers turn into those between the leader of the 'holy war' and the warriors of Islam. However, as we shall see below, such religiously inspired movements based on the bloc principle do not usually last for long.

I. RAWSHANI POLITICS

Before proceeding to an analysis of Rawshani history it is necessary to give an outline of the main development of the movement and its founder.[6] Bāyazīd Anṣārī[7] (*c.* 927 or 931/1521 or 1552–980 or 983/1572 or 1575), the founder of the movement, belonged to the Anṣār family living among the Ormur people[8]

---

[6] The main source for this study is 'Alī Muḥammad Mukhliṣ, *Ḥālnamā-yi-Bāyazīd Rawshān* (Kabul 1986), a biographical account of Bāyazīd Anṣārī and his descendants down to the accession of Awrangzīb in 1068/1658, written in Persian by 'Alī Muḥammad ibn Abū Bakr Qandahārī, commonly known by his pseudonym Mukhliṣ. A devoted follower of the Rawshani doctrine, Mukhliṣ worked under the patronage of Rashīd Khān (d. 1058/1648), the grandson of Bāyazīd Anṣārī who joined the imperial service. Because his patron became a Mughal *manṣabdār*, Mukhliṣ played down contradictions between the Rawshanis and the Mughals. Afżal Khān Khaṫṫak (*c.* 1072–3/1661–3 – 1161/1747–8), who had no connections with the Rawshani movement, provided a more or less neutral account of the Rawshaniyya in a few *daftar*s of his book *Tārīkh-i-muraṣṣa'* (see *The Gulshan-i-Roh: Being Selections, Prose and Poetical, in the Pus'hto, or Afghan Language*, ed. Captain H.G. Raverty [London: Williams & Norgate 1860]). This work is mainly a history of Pashtun tribes through the eyes of a tribal chief written in Pashto. Afżal Khān brought his historical narration up to the year 1136/1723–4. Other major sources for the study of the Rawshani movement are *Tadhkira al-Abrār wa'l-ashrār* (Delhi 1892) and *Makhzan al-Islām* (Peshawar 1969), both by Akhūnd Darwīza (940/1533–1048/1638–9). He himself was probably a Chishtī *pīr* who, together with his teacher Sayyid Mīr 'Alī Ghawwās Tirmidhī (usually called Pīr Bābā and still highly venerated among the Pashtuns), bitterly opposed the Rawshaniyya from the legalistic point of view. Because of his hatred of Bāyazīd Anṣārī and his followers, Akhūnd Darwīza's account of the movement is not very reliable and should always be checked against other sources.

[7] For further details on Bāyazīd Anṣārī's biography see the present author's Oxford University doctoral thesis: "History and Doctrine of the Rawshani Movement," and his forthcoming book on the same topic: *Sufi Illuminati: The Rawshani Movement in Muslim Mysticism, Society and Politics* (London: Curzon Press 2000).

[8] The Ormurs (Ōrmur/Ōrmær or Barakī, as they call themselves) are a small group of people living in Afghanistan and Pakistan. They spoke a distinct language belonging to the South-East group of Iranian languages called Bargistā, or Bargastā which is now almost extinct. It is not a written language; except for a few songs, the Ormurs possess no literature. The Ormurs lived

in Kaniguram in the country of the Wazir Pashtuns who were the patrons of the subdued Ormurs.

During his childhood he was neglected by his father and humiliated by his stepmother. While a teenager, fascinated by religion, he ran away to perform *Ḥājj* but was caught by his relatives and returned home. As he matured in life, he developed a conviction that he had attained a knowledge of divine Unity (*tawḥīd*) which for him signified the realization of the all-embracing unity of God and his creation, achievable only under the guidance of the Perfect Guide (*pīr-i kāmil*) – Bāyazīd himself. Since people were still unaware of the true nature of *tawḥīd*, he proclaimed that the entire population of Kaniguram wallowed in polytheism (*shirk*), a declaration that obviously antagonized many of his compatriots.

---

mainly on trade and travelled widely. As a result, a few Ormur settlements were founded outside their homeland. According to the *Ḥālnāma*, the family of Bāyazīd Anṣārī was engaged in caravan trading and had some property in Ghazni and 'other parts' [of the country] (Mukhliṣ, *Ḥālnāma*, p. 22). Bāyazīd Anṣārī was taken by his father on business trips from his childhood (Mukhliṣ, *Ḥālnāma*, p. 19). According to Mountstuart Elphinstone (*An Account of the Kingdom of Caubul and its Dependencies in Persia, Tartary and India* [London 1839], I, p. 411), the Ormurs closely resembled the Pashtuns in their manners. H.A. Rose, however, supports a different view: "their [the Ormurs'] marriage ceremonies, general rites and customary laws differ widely from those of the surrounding [Afghan] tribes" (*A Glossary of the Tribes and Castes of the Punjab and North-West Frontier Province* [Lahore 1914]), III, p. 483. Pashtun neighbours of the Ormurs often accused them of fire-worship and membership of the non-existent sect of the *chirāgh-kush* or 'Lamp-Extinguishers', allegedly notorious for its debauchery. At the same time, and in spite of these accusations, it is possible that the Ormurs were in fact regarded as a group of people of some religious significance, since all Ormurs were reported by a native informant to be *sayyids* (see Georg Morgenstierne, *IndoIranian Frontier Languages,* I: *Parachi and Ormuri* [Oslo 1929], I, p. 311). Sir Olaf Caroe, *The Pathans 550 B.C.–A.D. 1957* (London: Macmillan/New York: St Martin's Press 1964 p. 201) also writes that many families among the Ormurs in Kaniguram call themselves Sayyid or Anṣār. In the *Imperial Gazetteer* of India (1908, v. XIV, p. 231), the emigrants from Kaniguram living in Jalandar suburbs were also described as Anṣār. Perhaps the terms *sayyid* and *anṣār* here do not mean specifically a descendant of the Prophet Muḥammad or a companion of the Prophet Muhammad from Medina but merely 'a noble man', and these titles were adopted by the Ormurs just as many Pashtuns took the title Khān. However, Bāyazīd Anṣārī was considered as a descendant of an *Anṣār* family and a list of his ancestors descending from Khwājah (Abū) Ayyūb Ansārī, a famous companion of the Prophet Muḥammad is given in the *Ḥālnāma* (pp. 23ff.). (For more details on the Ormurs, see Andreyev, "Notes on the Ormur People," *Peterburgskoe Vostokovedenie*, 4, [1993], pp. 230–8.) C.M. Kieffer ("La Maintenance de l'identité ethnique chez les Arabes arabophones, les Ormur et les Parācī en Afghanistan," in *Die ethnischen Gruppen Afghanistans*, ed. Erwin Orywalī [Wiesbaden: Dr Ludwig Reichert Verlag 1986], pp. 130–31) provides some extremely interesting information on the veneration of Bāyazīd Anṣārī among modern Ormurs and their distinct religious identity. According to his native informant, the Ormurs belong to a separate sect and consider Bāyazīd Anṣārī as one of their own religious authorities. Although it is difficult to agree with Kieffer's view that the Rawshani doctrine is a development of the native Ormur religious tradition based on Zoroastrian beliefs and practices, the information provided in his article deserves further investigation.

After Bāyazīd Anṣārī had started to preach his mystical doctrine, he formed a circle of his disciples and quarrelled with the members of the local religious establishment. The Ormurs of Kaniguram split into two factions: those of Bāyazīd's supporters and those of his adversaries. In spite of the protestation of Bāyazīd's Pashtun patron, the Pashtun overlords of Kaniguram ordered him to leave the area, fearing escalation of the conflict. After his expulsion, he travelled among Pashtun tribes for several years, acquiring more and more disciples among the tribesmen and gradually boosting his status. Finally, he received the highest possible honour a non-Pashtun can aspire to: he was allowed to marry a Pashtun girl of the Mohmandzay tribe and also given a plot of tribal land, a privilege usually reserved only for the *sayyid*s.

However, Bāyazīd Anṣārī's activities were constantly marred by the plots of envious Sufi masters whose authority he undermined by his insistence that he alone was the true *pīr*. It seemed that almost every time he changed his place of residence, events were destined to unfold according to the same pattern: envious religious teachers, afraid of losing their disciples to Bāyazīd Anṣārī, complained to the local secular authorities and described the founder of the Rawshani movement as a dangerous heretic who claimed to be the *Mahdī*, demanding his death or, at least, expulsion from the area.

The Sufi *pīr*s of the Khalil tribe were more successful than their colleagues elsewhere in making such accusations stick. They obtained the support of the local chief, Malik Ḥabīb who, unlike other tribal chiefs who were reluctant to get involved in religious conflicts, had decided to join ranks with the Sufi guides. However, it appears that Malik Ḥabīb had a political rather than a religious motive for entering into this alliance. As he explained to the governor of Peshawar, Jānish-Khān,[9] sooner or later Bāyazīd Anṣārī would "take up the sword;" therefore he should be killed promptly.[10] Thus, for the first time, the Rawshani movement was described as a serious political force to be reckoned with, since it was now in a position to take independent actions and undermine the *status quo*.

Arlinghaus speculated that Malik Ḥābīb opposed Bāyazīd Anṣārī because he was either afraid of the Rawshanis undermining the Khalils' alliance with the Mughals or else feared that Bāyazīd's association with another Khalil chief Malik Sānī, would dangerously increase the latter chief's prestige and power.[11] However, since the *Ḥālnāma* does not provide any ground for either of these

[9] Jānish-Khān (Jānis-Khān in the *Ḥālnāma*) is mentioned by Abū al-Faḍl, in the *Ā'in-i Akbarī* (*The Ain-i-Akbari by Abul-Fazl-i-Allami*, ed. in the original Persian by H. Blochmann, XII, [Bibliotheca Indica no 58; Calcutta 1872–7], pp. 537–38). Unfortunately this source does not provide any information on the time of his governorship in Peshawar.

[10] Mukhliṣ, *Ḥālnāma*, p. 332.

[11] Joseph Theodore Arlinghaus, "The Transformation of Afghan Tribal Society: Tribal Expansion, Mughal Imperialism and the Roshaniyya Insurrection, 1450–1600" (Duke University, Ph.D. thesis 1988), p. 286.

motives, they can therefore be considered merely as hypotheses. Contrary to Arlinghaus's opinion, Bāyazīd Anṣārī did not harbour an anti-Mughal position at that time.[12] Thus, his arrival among the Khalil tribe could not jeopardize its alliance with the Mughals.

The second theory fits the paradigm of Pashtun bloc politics. Indeed, if Bāyazīd Anṣārī, who by that time had acquired potential political and military force, enjoyed Malik Sānī's hospitality, he would inevitably enhance the social and political prestige of his host. Besides, if he stayed for a long time, politically speaking he would have become his host's client and thus would have had to provide Malik Sānī with political and military support when the need arose. However, it seems that this was not the case either. Malik Ḥabīb described the Rawshanis as an independent force that could pose a potential threat. Besides, Malik Sānī did not just provide shelter for a travelling Sufi; he himself became a disciple of Bāyazīd Anṣārī. Thus, in effect, he surrendered his political sovereignty as a Pashtun chief and became a member of Bāyazīd's own bloc based on religious identity.

Unlike the case in traditional 'maraboutic Sufism', in times of peace Bāyazīd Anṣārī and his successors did not limit their influence on the collective body of their *murīd*s to doctrinal issues. On the contrary, they actively interfered in the political and even the economic life of their followers. Thus, by the time Malik Ḥabīb realized its danger, the Rawshani movement was already capable of much more than merely undermining his individual tribal faction by throwing its weight in favour of Malik Sānī. From a band of exiles and loathed outcasts, the movement had developed into a political force threatening the whole fabric of tribal society.[13]

Thus, when Malik Ḥabīb successfully intrigued at the Kabul court, an order for the arrest of Bāyazīd Anṣārī was issued. However, it appears that he was not detained and travelled to the court of Muḥammad Ḥākim, the ruler of Kabul, voluntarily.[14] There he successfully defended himself against the

---

[12] Although this matter is very confused and it is impossible to identify when exactly Bāyazīd Anṣārī adopted his anti-Mughal rhetoric and policy, it appears that at that time he did not plan any anti-Mughal actions or, at least, did not publicize them. Otherwise, he would not have travelled to the court of the Mughal ruler Muḥammad Ḥakīm when he was requested to do so.

[13] For a discussion of the political significance of the Rawshani movement, see below.

[14] Mukhliṣ (*Ḥālnāma*, pp. 334–5). If the Mughal authority had tried to arrest and disgrace him, as Akhūnd Darwīza (*Tadhkira al-Abrār*, p. 153) maintained, contrary to the evidence of the *Ḥālnāma*, it would have certainly provoked a confrontation with the Khalil Pashtuns among whom Bāyazīd Anṣārī resided at that time. The tribesmen would have been bound to support the Rawshanis, not only as their hosts but also as followers of Bāyazīd Anṣārī. They would have considered this attempt as a serious infringement of their tribal sovereignty and honour and felt obliged to fight back in order to protect their spiritual leader. However, none of the sources dealing with the history of the Rawshani movement reports on a skirmish between the Peshawar authorities and the Pashtun tribesmen. The *Ḥālnāma* does not provide

charges of heresy before the chief *qāḍī* of the city and Muḥammad Ḥākim allowed him to return to the tribal area near Peshawar.

The release of Bāyazīd Anṣārī from captivity in Kabul proved to be an important political and religious asset for him.[15] Since the Rawshani leader refuted all charges and walked out a free man, his authority among the Pashtun tribes increased and he began to entertain far-reaching ambitions to expand his influence outside the tribal area. Thus, from the town of Kalladher in the country of the Mohmandzays (later known as Muhammadzays)[16] he sent his envoys to Balkh and Bukhara. His *khalīfa* Dawlat-Khān went to visit Emperor Akbar with the book *Ṣirāt al-tawḥīd* written by Bāyazīd Anṣārī. Another *khalīfa* visited the ruler of Badakhshan Mīrzā Sulaymān, with Anṣārī's other work *Khayr al-ṭālibīn*. According to the *Ḥālnāma*, both kings treated the Rawshani emissaries with honour and Mīrzā Sulaymān even declared himself a disciple of Bāyazīd Anṣārī. At the same time, the Rawshani preachers continued to propagate the Rawshani creed among the Pashtun tribes and at least one of them, Maudūd, moved to Sind and Baluchistan where he resided in the Sayyidpur near Hyderabad (Sind) and converted many people to the Rawshani tenets.[17]

However, the Rawshani success and security proved to be short-lived. Their safety was undermined by the eagerness of the Tu'i tribesmen, who turned into

---

any explanation as to why Bāyazīd Anṣārī decided to submit himself to the Mughal authorities. Since he did not respect the contemporary *'ulamā'* it is unlikely that he wanted to present his case for their examination. Thus, it looks plausible that Bāyazīd Anṣārī's behaviour was first of all motivated by political factors rather than religious considerations. At that time, he did not yet command any considerable political authority or military strength, and therefore an open confrontation with the Kabul authorities would have been too dangerous for him. However, religious considerations could also have partly contributed to his decision to go to Kabul. At that time, he entertained the idea of attracting contemporary rulers to his doctrine. Thus it is possible that he remained politically neutral towards the Mughals and even hoped to influence them while in Kabul. The *Ḥālnāma*'s account of the wish of Muḥammad Ḥākim to become Bāyazīd's disciple may indicate that his conversion was one of the initial goals of the Rawshani leader's trip to Kabul.

[15] In theory, the mullās and other Muslim clerics not associated with Sufi brotherhoods are supposed to distinguish between real and false Sufi guides for the benefit of the common Muslims (see M.G.S. Hodgson, *The Venture of Islam: Conscience and History in a World Civilization* [Chicago: University of Chicago Press 1974], III, pp. 201–54). Among Afghan Sunnis, learning is used as a measure of the *pīr*'s credentials. For the recognition of the claimant to the status of Sufi guide, besides his declaration of mystical experience, the *'ulamā'* require an additional proof, that of learning (Robert L. Canfield, "Ethnic, Regional, and Sectarian Alignments in Afghanistan," in *The State, Religion, and Ethnic Politics: Pakistan, Iran and Afghanistan*, ed. Alī Bannazizi and Myron Weiner [Lahore: Vanguard Books 1987], pp. 219–20). Thus, by passing the test before the highest Muslim authority, the chief judge of Kabul, Bāyazīd Anṣārī received a legitimizing boost to his initial claim of *karāma*.

[16] Darwīza, *Makhzan al-Islām*, p. 124.

[17] Mukhliṣ, *Ḥālnāma*, pp. 361–2, 366, 375.

Plate 9: Pashtun Warriors. Early Nineteenth-century Drawing. From J. Rattray, *The Costumes of the Various Tribes, Portraits of Ladies of Rank, Celebrated Princes and Chiefs, Views of the Principal Fortresses and Cities, and Interior of Cities and Temples of Afghaunistaun*. London, 1848. Frontispiece.

over-zealous followers of the doctrine. During the month of *Ramaḍān* they expected the end of the world to occur and decided to abandon their worldly pursuits. It appears that their ecstatic state reached a very high point, since some of them did not take any food and a newborn child was named 'Isā Thānī, apparently in the anticipation of the Second Coming of Christ. Their collective exaltation coincided with the passage of a trade caravan from India through their region. Annoyed by the devotion of the traders to worldly pursuits, the Tu'is rushed towards the caravan in order to explain to the merchants the inevitability of the Last Judgement. However, the latter, unaware of the Tu'is' pious intentions, abandoned their goods, which were destroyed by the Rawshanis, and ran away. According to the *Ḥālnāma*, they were afraid of the tribesmen since "they knew that all Pashtuns had united and Bāyazīd Anṣārī had taken up the sword."[18]

However, it seems that the fears of these unlucky merchants had some grounds, since other sources provide circumstantial evidence that by the time of the Tu'i incident the Rawshanis might have already begun their military activities. According to *Dabistān-i-Madhāhib*, Bāyazīd Anṣārī repeatedly received a divine command to fight against those who did not recognize God (i.e. non-Rawshanis). Three times, he declined to obey this order. Eventually, he was given the ultimate order to begin fighting. He felt compelled to comply and thus began the holy war (*jihād*). The *Dabistān* also reports that Bāyazīd Anṣārī and his sons were engaged in highway robbery for many years.[19] Rizvi thinks that this passage from the *Dabistān* refers to the first battle with the Mughal troops described in the *Hālnāma*.[20]

However, there is no indication in the *Dabistān* that this is the case. This paragraph is placed before the section dealing with the Kabul trial, which obviously pre-dated the above-mentioned battle. Although it does not necessarily imply that these events took place before Bāyazīd Anṣārī was summoned to the court of Muḥammad Ḥakīm, it also does not prove that it happened after the Kabul trial. Thus, it cannot be ruled out that even before the recorded skirmishes with the hostile tribes and the Mughal authorities, the Rawshanis had begun low-key military activities.

Akhūnd Darwīza also complains that for many years Bāyazīd Anṣārī plundered people and killed the *'ulamā'*.[21] Since Darwīza never spared a chance to disparage the Rawshanis, it is not possible to rely on his account unless it is

---

[18] *Ibid.*, pp. 376–9. S.A.A. Rizvi ("Rawshaniyya movement," *Abr-Nahrain*, 6, [1965–6], p. 85/7 [1967–68) interprets this passage, *kārawāniyān dānistand ka tamām-i-afghānān yagāna shudand wa pīr-i-rawshān shamshīr girift* (*Ḥālnāma*, p. 379) as "... [they] thought that Bāyazīd had taken up arms against them." This translation is not correct.

[19] Mūbad Kiykhusraw Isfandiyar, *Dabistān-i-Madhāhib*, edited in 2 vols by Riḍāzāda Malik (Tehran: 1362 A.Hsh./1983), pp. 283–4.

[20] Rizvi, "Rawshaniyya Movement," p. 86.

[21] Darwīza, *Makhzan al-Islām*, pp. 125ff.

supported by other evidence; in this respect, the testimony of the *Dabistān* appears to be more credible since its author occupied a neutral position regarding the movement. Thus, taking together all the above-mentioned statements concerning Bāyazīd Anṣārī's military strength and activity, it seems possible to suppose that the Rawshani military actions began before the first battle recorded in the *Ḥālnāma*. Whether these attacks were co-ordinated by Bāyazīd Anṣārī, as the *Ḥālnāma*'s account of the merchants' fears implies, or were undertaken independently, like the Tu'is' attack, cannot be established with any degree of probability. Perhaps the Pashtuns were engaged in their usual plunder of passing caravans and periodical raids but, since many of them were now associated with the Rawshani movement, their actions were perceived by unsympathetic contemporaries as a major Rawshani offensive. However, even if Bāyazīd Anṣārī may personally have wanted to repudiate these actions, he was bound to fail since plundering was an essential part of the Pashtuns' low-production economy.

Having heard the complaints of the terrified traders who insisted that Bāyazīd Anṣārī had led the tribal rebellion, Muḥammad Ḥākim sent 500 cavalrymen to punish the Tu'is. They defeated the tribesmen and took many of them back to Kabul as prisoners.[22] Bāyazīd Anṣārī tried to avoid a direct confrontation with the Mughal authorities and therefore wrote an apologetic letter to Muḥammad Ḥākim, in which he explained that the Tu'is had gone mad and that the prisoners should be released. However, as the *Ḥālnāma* puts it, because of the intrigues of the courtiers who claimed that Bāyazīd Anṣārī would complicate their relations with the Pashtuns, the ruler of Kabul ordered the governor of Peshawar to attack the Rawshanis. Although the Mohmandzays were prepared to fight for their religious leader, Bāyazīd Anṣārī intended to migrate to the country of the Yusufzays, which was beyond the reach of the Mughals, in order to avoid bloodshed. His plan did not materialize and with 313 of his followers[23] he was forced to confront the Mughal army. Before the counter-attack Bāyazīd Anṣārī addressed his soldiers, many of whom were unarmed, and explained that they fought only out of necessity. Despite their pitiful state, the Rawshani army led by Bāyazīd Anṣārī defeated the Mughals.

After this initial confrontation, the Rawshanis "began war in that region." It is noteworthy that Bāyazīd Anṣārī called the place of the battle Aghāzpūr (the place of the beginning) and those disciples who participated in this conflict, in imitation of the early Muslim practice, received the title (*laqab*) of Aghāzpūri[24]

---

[22] Mukhliṣ, *Ḥālnāma*, pp. 379–80.

[23] This number is probably symbolic since it is known that a force of slightly more than 300 Muslims fought in the battle of Badr.

[24] Cf. W. Montgomery Watt's point that "Those who had fought at Badr as Muslims – the Badriyyūn – came to be regarded as an aristocracy of merit, and in the most versions of the *dīwān* of 'Umar are said to have constituted the highest class of Muslims" ('Badr,' *EI*^{2}, I, p. 868).

and were given the larger part of the military booty.[25] According to *Dabistān-i-Madhāhib*, Bāyazīd Anṣārī retained one-fifth of the military loot to use for rewarding the worthiest members of his community:[26] this again is an imitation of the early Muslim practice.

With regard to the first Rawshani battle, it is noteworthy that apart from providing the *hijrī* year of the death of Bāyazīd Anṣārī the *Ḥālnāma* also gives another date, "the year two and a half from the beginning, that is, the war."[27] The meaning of this statement is quite ambiguous. On the one hand it could be a simple device for chronological co-ordination, but on the other it may indicate that the Rawshanis developed their own chronology. If this is the case – and the appellation of Bāyazīd Anṣārī's comrades-in-arms as 'the people of the beginning' proves that it may well be – it is strange that the first military confrontation with the Mughals was chosen as the watershed.

According to the *Ḥālnāma*, it seems that initially the Rawshanis tried to avoid an open confrontation with the Mughals. If so, the divine revelation to Bāyazīd Anṣārī, or the beginning of his active teaching, or, in imitation of the Prophet Muḥammad, his migration from Kaniguram, might have been more appropriate for the beginning of a new era. Obviously, 'Alī Muḥammad Mukhliṣ who resided in India and held pro-Mughal views, tried in his book to play down the anti-imperial sentiments and activities of the Rawshanis. Given this mitigation of the anti-Mughal ethos of the early Rawshani movement, it is strange that Mukhliṣ considered it necessary to mention that Bāyazīd Anṣārī named the first war with the Mughals 'the beginning'. However, it would appear that despite his attempts to present the Rawshani struggle against the Mughals as having ensued from a misunderstanding, he could not bypass the significance of this first battle, and given the appellation of the battle, it seems safe to conclude that the Rawshanis considered it as a watershed in the history of their movement. Thus it seems that Mukhliṣ involuntarily exposes the true importance of the military confrontation with the Mughals for the construction of the Rawshani identity.

Akhūnd Darwīza did not describe this battle with the Mughals. However, he mentioned that Bāyazīd Anṣārī wanted to spread his doctrine throughout the entire region and therefore planned to conquer both Khurāsān and India and divide his realm between his comrades-in-arms, after the fashion of numerous Turkic invaders of the region. In order to facilitate this expedition he purchased horses against promissory notes guaranteeing the payment of larger sums of money after the defeat of Emperor Akbar.[28] Although Akhūnd Darwīza never neglected an opportunity of slandering Bāyazīd Anṣārī, in this

---

[25] Mukhliṣ, *Ḥālnāma*, pp. 380–2, 385–6.
[26] Isfandiyar, *Dabistān-i-Madhāhib*, p. 283.
[27] Mukhliṣ, *Ḥālnāma*, p. 387.
[28] Darwīza, *Makhzan al-Islām*, p. 125.

particular case he had no reason to consider his anti-Mughal views as something compromising the Rawshani leader, since he himself abhorred Akbar and, as a Muslim scholar associated with the Pashtuns, held the Mughals in contempt.

His account of Bāyazīd Anṣārī's aggressive plans is provided only in his *Makhzan al-Islām* and is not given in *Tadhkirah al-Abrār*. However, when it comes to the main subject of the books – both of which are polemics attacking the Rawshani doctrine – the two sources are almost identical. Thus, if Akhūnd Darwīza found it possible to omit this episode from one of his books it is plausible that he did not consider it important enough for the purposes of condemning the Rawshani movement, and thus this fragment may well be true.

Furthermore, Bāyazīd Anṣārī's intention to lead his armies to India and Khurāsān was in line with the well-established Pashtun tradition of invading foreign countries. Even modern Pashtuns regret the loss of their domains in India; for the contemporaries of the Sur Pashtuns' confrontation with the Mughals it was a burning political issue. Bāyazīd's beloved uncle Khudādād took an active part in the Pashtuns' struggle against Bābur. Thus, in the implementation of his military plans, the Rawshani leader may have followed not only the traditional Pashtun policy but his own family tradition as well.

After a few years of fighting, in 1572 or 1575 Bāyazīd Anṣārī died.[29] His eldest son, Shaykh 'Umar, now assumed the leadership of the movement, whereupon occurred the first conflict between the Rawshanis and the Pashtun tribesmen, namely the Yusufzays. Although sources provide conflicting accounts about the motives for this conflict, it seems that the Yusufzays were antagonized by Shaykh 'Umar's attempt to levy taxes on them.[30] Under Shaykh 'Umar's successor Jalāl al-Dīn the movement reached its peak with the largest number of tribes joining it. After the death of Jalāl al-Dīn the movement was headed by other descendants of Bāyazīd Anṣārī who fought the Mughals with changing success. When the Rawshani movement became weakened due to their disagreements with the tribes,[31] the Mughal authorities applied their policy of stick and carrot and lured some prominent leaders of the movement into the imperial service with the promise of *manṣab*s and *jāgīr*s, so that by the end of the 1630s the Rawshani movement had all but disappeared as a political force.

The Mughals managed to defeat the Rawshani movement by a combination of overwhelming military strength and skilful diplomacy. However, this

---

[29] For a detailed discussion of Bāyazīd Anṣārī's possible date of death see Andreyev, *Sufi Illuminati*.

[30] Darwīza, *Tadhkirah al-Abrār*, pp. 155–6.

[31] For the account of these conflicts see below.

military and political victory cannot be explained only in terms of successful imperial power politics. It is a well-known fact that tribes can resist empires for centuries and small-scale guerrilla warfare can perpetuate itself almost indefinitely – to which the later history of Pashtuns bears ample witness. The Mughals defeated the Rawshani movement only because its own inner weaknesses undermined its integrity and led to many tribes deserting the movement. In order to understand the whole complexity of this situation it is necessary to consider the uneasy relationships between the Rawshani movement and the Pashtun tribes.

One of the most striking features of the Rawshani movement was the development of a non-tribal identity among its followers. As is the case with all religions and ideologies, the Rawshani identity was based on the co-sectarians' common beliefs. However, for the Pashtuns not affiliated with the Rawshani movement, their 'Pashtunness' usually took precedence over their membership of the Islamic community and affiliation with Sufi brotherhoods.

With regard to the development of the Rawshani identity, the following episodes recorded in the *Ḥālnāma* are worth considering: when in 989/1581, Emperor Akbar interviewed the Rawshanis – who, after their persecution and defeat by the Yusufzays, arrived at his invitation at the imperial camp near Peshawar – he asked them about their tribal affiliation. All of them named their tribes. However, one woman from the Khalil tribe refused to identify her tribe, claiming that she was only a Rawshani. When the emperor pressed her to identify her tribe, not her beliefs, she insisted that her tribe was Rawshani and she had no other.[32] Such renunciation of one's own tribe is usually not only unthinkable but also extremely dangerous, since by doing so one loses all protection and is put in a very vulnerable position. The Afghan saying speaks volumes of this situation: *bad qawm bāshī, bī qawm nabāshī* (It is better to belong to a bad tribe [solidarity group] than not to belong to any at all).[33] If one renounces one's tribe one must be confident of the all-embracing support of an alternative social and political body.

The behaviour of Bāyazīd Anṣārī's Pashtun *khalīfa*s also deserves some attention. It is reported in the *Ḥālnāma* that the brother of the maternal grandfather of 'Alī Muḥammad Mukhliṣ, the author of this book, was a son of the chief (*malik*) of a Khudaydad-Khel clan of the Dawlatzay tribe, of the Orakzay union of tribes. Having become a devoted disciple and *khalīfa* of Bāyazīd Anṣārī, he received the title of *Darwīsh-Dādū* (The Wandering Teacher) in acknowledgement of his services to the Rawshani cause.

---

[32] Mukhliṣ, *Ḥālnāma*, p. 438.

[33] Olivier Roy, "Groupes de solidarité au Moyen-orient et en Asie centrale: Etats, territoires et réseaux," *Les Cahiers du CERI*, 16 (1996), p. 3.

Before his death he appointed his non-Pashtun Tirahi[34] disciple as his *khalīfa*.[35]

---

[34] The Tirahis are a Dardic people who once populated the whole mountain country of Tirah. Nowadays a few thousand of them can be found only outside their ancestral homeland. The Tirahis, as well as the Pashtun newcomers of Tirah-Afridis and Orakzays, were converted to Rawshani doctrine by Bāyazīd Anṣārī's *khalīfa* Shaykh Bāyazīd Daur (Mukhliṣ, *Ḥālnāma*, p. 272). Later, the combined Rawshani Pashtun–Tirahi force repelled the Mughal attack on Tirah (*ibid*., p. 387). The *Ḥālnāma* does not provide any further information on the development of Pashtun–Tirahi relations. However, according to Akhūnd Darwīza the above-mentioned alliance of the Pashtuns and their non-Pashtun neighbours proved to be short lived. The Pashtuns began to persecute and kill their former Tirahi allies for conspiring with the Mughals to seize Tirah. The Tirahis found refuge in a mountain fortress. Bāyazīd Anṣārī took the side of the Pashtuns and explained to the Tirahis that they had sinned before their guide and must repent and come to him with their hands tied. Three hundred and twenty of them left the fortress and appeared before Bāyazīd Anṣārī, only to be killed by their spiritual master. After that the Afridis and Orakzays plundered Tirah. The remaining Tirahis fled to Nangrahar (Darwīza, *Tadhkirah al-Abrār*, p. 154; *Makhzan al-Islām*, p. 126), thus leaving their homeland, probably forever, in the hands of the Pashtuns.

At the first glance, it looks as if Akhūnd Darwīza's account of the war between Pashtuns and Tirahis contradicts the information provided by the *Ḥālnāma* on the Pashtun–Tirahi anti-Mughal alliance. Indeed, it seems unlikely that soon after repelling a dangerous assault, one party of the alliance of the co-sectarians would decide to conspire with their enemies. However, people are rarely driven exclusively by religious considerations, and the Tirahis were no exception to this rule. They were one of many non-Pashtun ethnic groups in the area subject to Pashtun invasion. For them, the increasing Pashtun dominance meant the imposition of foreign rule and a reduction of their status to that of clients. Thus, despite the fact that they shared the same beliefs with the Afridis and Orakzays and, like other non-Pashtuns, shared Islam with the Pashtun invaders, politically they were opposed to the Pashtuns. Moreover, they had a history of turning to the Mughals for help against the Pashtuns, and from the time of Bābur ("[they] had a secret sympathy for the Mughals" as Akhūnd Darwīza put it (*Makhzan al-Islām*, p. 126)). It appears that the Tirahis were allied to Bābur in 925/1519 during his campaign against the Pashtun tribes; as the *Bābur-nāma* testifies, at that time the Sulṭān of Tirah stayed in Bābur's camp (Ẓāhir al-Dīn Muḥammad Bābur Pādshāh Ghāzī, *Bābur-nāma*, trans. A.S. Beveridge [London 1969], p. 411). Therefore, their conduct seems to be logical and politically sound. Although because of his hatred of the Rawshani movement Akhūnd Darwīza often provided fabricated accounts of the Rawshaniyya, his remark on the Tirahis' old connections with the Mughals, which is substantiated by an independent source, namely the *Bābur-nāma*, indicates that in this instance his account of the Pashtun–Tirahi conflict can be given some weight. As for Bāyazīd Anṣārī, it is not surprising that he decided to take the side of the Pashtuns. It was politically more expedient to ally oneself with the powerful and victorious tribesmen than with a losing indigenous people, although Bāyazīd Anṣārī himself was one of them. Whether he went as far as massacring his Tirahi followers cannot be established with any degree of probability since Akhūnd Darwīza is the only author who records this event. It is also unknown whether the Tirahis were really expelled from their homeland at that time since later British Indian sources maintain that they were driven away only at the beginning of the nineteenth century (C.M. Kieffer, "Afrīdī," *EIr*, I, p. 79). Anyway, if the hypothesis that the Pashtun–Tirahi conflict really took place is correct, it is not surprising that 'Alī Muḥammad Mukhliṣ chose to keep silent about this incident since this occurrence would have been too embarrassing for the Rawshanis.

[35] Mukhliṣ, *Ḥālnāma*, pp. 299, 314–15, 317.

This seemingly ordinary story speaks volumes about the attitude of the closest associates of Bāyazīd Anṣārī towards their religion and social position. By becoming Bāyazīd's *khalīfa* Darwīsh-Dādū not only traded his privileged status – he was the son of a *malik* – for religious association; in effect, he ceased to be a member of his tribe. Politically speaking, he turned himself into a client of Bāyazīd Anṣārī and therefore dramatically decreased his status within his own tribe and moved into a different category of people, that of Muslim religious teachers.

This social and political transition is confirmed by his appointment of a Tirahi as his own deputy. For a Pashtun, close association with a non-Pashtun client is degrading, while for a scholar or Sufi it is absolutely acceptable. It is noteworthy that this appointment apparently took place after the conflict between the Pashtuns of Tirah, including Darwīsh-Dādū's own Orakzays, and the Tirahis. Thus, Darwīsh-Dādū, being confident in his new status of a Sufi master, found it possible to disregard not only the social conventions of the Pashtuns but political reality as well.

It is also mentioned in the *Ḥālnāma* that Jalāl al-Dīn had a special affection for 'the Kandaharis', for "all who came from the tribes of Kiwi, Baraki, Kaniguram, Lokhani, Gilzay, Kakar, Babar, Shirwani and Shirani were [in the group of] the Kandaharis. They called themselves the Kandaharis and considered the shame of each other as their own shame."[36] This sharing of each other's shame and honour is another typical pattern of tribal identity, usually unthinkable in a group of Pashtuns of mixed tribal origin. What makes this phenomenon even more interesting is the membership of non-Pashtuns, namely Ormurs, described in the *Ḥālnāma* as Barakis and Kaniguramis, in this community. Another noteworthy feature of this group of "the Kandaharis" is that all of them originated from tribes that never collectively joined the Rawshani movement.

With regard to the development of the Rawshani identity, certain parallels with early Islamic history are obvious. The first Muslims who united around the Prophet Muḥammad also severed their tribal ties, albeit temporarily, by the mere fact of leaving their hometown of Mecca. However, such was the case only with the Prophet's immediate associates, while the Arab tribes that converted to Islam *en masse* preserved their tribal identities for centuries to come. These identities disappeared in favour of a common Islamic identity in the time of the 'Abbasids when non-Arab clients (*mawlā*) were emancipated. This process affected only those Arabs who left the cradle of Islam in Arabia.

It seems that the Rawshani identity developed according to the same scheme: the core group of sectarians directly associated with Bāyazīd Anṣārī and his successors abandoned their tribal or communal affiliation in exchange for an all-embracing religious identity. However, the tribes that associated

[36] Mukhliṣ, *Ḥālnāma*, pp. 306–7.

themselves with the Rawshani doctrine on a collective basis preserved their sense of tribal uniqueness, as the Arab Muslim tribesmen had done many centuries before. Accounts of the Rawshani *khalīfa*s and of the woman, mentioned above, who denied any ethnic or tribal identity before Emperor Akbar fit this assumption. However, the case with "the Kandaharis" is more complicated. They were not immediate associates of the Rawshani leaders; on the contrary, they were described as the rank and file of the Rawshani movement. Nevertheless, they adopted a common Rawshani identity. Their self-appellation as "the Kandaharis" cannot be considered as an indication of a regional identity, which – in Pashtun-dominated society – was almost non-existent.

Perhaps the best explanation is to assume that the Kandaharis were composed of people of various tribes and ethnic groups that did not convert *en masse* and who, in order to join the Rawshani movement, had to abandon their tribal homelands, thus losing tribal support and eventually their tribal identity as well. In order to survive in the hostile world they had to establish some sort of community which could perform the same supportive and protective functions as did their respective tribes. Once they became Rawshanis, building this community on the basis of their new belief was the most obvious choice. The fact that the *Ḥālnāma* mentions Jalāl al-Dīn's special affection for "the Kandaharis" may indicate that this body of de-tribalized sectarians represents the socio-political ideal that the Rawshani leaders strived to achieve, either consciously or unconsciously.

Abandonment of normal social, family and kinship ties is typical of millenarian movements and charismatic cults, and in the Muslim world the Qizilbāsh followers of the Safavids provide a clear parallel with the Pashtun followers of the Rawshani movement. (In this context, it may be observed that despite certain typological similarities between the Safavids and the Rawshanis – both fit the paradigm of the incipient formation of state structures in the Muslim world – there was no historical relation between the two movements. In general, Pashtuns were under the influence of Indian–Persianate Islam and maintained very few contacts with Persians.) Like the Kandaharis, most of the initial supporters of the Safavids were organized, as Qizilbāsh, into new composite groups of heterogeneous ethnic and tribal origin.

It is a conventional wisdom among the students of the Rawshaniyya that the tribes abandoned the Rawshani movement because it threatened their authority.[37] However, the question of *how* the Rawshani movement could undermine tribal integrity remains unanswered. It seems that one of the

---

[37] Arlinghaus, "The Transformation of Afghan Tribal Society"; M.G. Aslanov, "Narodnoe dvizhenie roshani i ego otrazhenie v afganskoi literature XVI–XVII vv.," *Sovetskoe Vostokovedenie*, 5 (1955); V̦.A. Romodin, *Istoriia Afganistana*, II (Moscow: Nauka 1965).

'dangers' posed by the Rawshaniyya was the above-mentioned facilitation of the de-tribalization of Pashtun society. With regard to the process of de-tribalization and establishment of a new kind of political mechanism, the remark of the Jesuit envoy to the court of Akbar, Father Monserrate (who penned a short account of the Rawshani movement) that the Rawshanis abandoned "their lawful rulers"[38] is of particular importance.

On the other hand, this de-tribalization was not a universal phenomenon applicable to all followers of Rawshani doctrine. The Pashtuns who became Rawshanis simply because their entire tribe joined the movement did not have to leave their tribe in order to embrace a new doctrine. They did not become individual disciples of the Rawshani leaders, but on the contrary followed the pattern of 'maraboutic Sufism', which excludes the establishment of intimate *pīr-murīd* ties. Thus they continued to enjoy the full support of their fellow tribesmen, who also became their fellow co-sectarians. The author of the *Ḥālnāma* was quite aware of the distinction between individual disciples and collective converts. The former are always mentioned by name, even if after their conversion they did not play any role in Rawshani history. The latter, on the other hand, are briefly accounted for as mass converts belonging to a certain tribe or ethnic group. Pashtuns, and subordinated to them non-Pashtuns – the people who collectively joined the Rawshani movement – never developed a common identity which could help them to overcome their political differences, as the Pashtun–Tirahi conflict clearly illustrates.

In the course of time, the tribes began to desert the movement, and by the time of Jalāl al-Dīn's successor Aḥdād, the Rawshanis had lost the support of one of the most loyal tribes, namely the Orakzays. According to the *Tārīkh-i Muraṣṣa'*, Malik Tōr̂, the chief of the 'Abd al-Aziz Khel of the Orakzay tribe, who had initially wholeheartedly supported the movement, deserted to the Mughal camp because he would not give Aḥdād the power "over his house and field" although he was prepared to obey his orders.[39] According to L. White King, the Deputy Commissioner of Kohat in Political Charge of the Orakzays

[38] *The Commentary of Father Monserrate, S.J., on his Journey to the Court of Akbar* (Oxford: Oxford University Press 1922), p. 142.

[39] Afżal Khān, "*Tārīkh-i Muraṣṣa*", in *The Gulshan-i-Roh*, p. 31. The *Tārīkh-i Muraṣṣa* does not supply us with precise information on the nature of this 'power' over property which Malik Tōr̂ refused to grant to Aḥdād. However, Akhūnd Darwīza's remark that the Rawshani–Yusufzay conflict was caused by Shaykh 'Umar's attempt to levy taxes on the Yusufzays does shed some light on the nature of the Rawshani claims on tribal property. Thus it seems reasonable to assume that Aḥdād wanted to make Malik Tōr̂'s property subject to taxation. It is unlikely that Aḥdād would have risked an attempt of outright confiscation of Malik Tōr̂'s property, since he could hardly have justified this action. Besides, by doing so he would have unquestionably alienated the chief. Therefore, it is hardly possible to think about any other claim to the chief's property apart from taxation made by the Rawshani leader. This attempt to impose taxes obviously antagonized the chief. It is well known that no government has ever managed to levy taxes on all Pashtun tribes.

(whose term of service lasted from 1897 to 1900), who probably relied on an oral tradition, he was bribed by the Mughals.[40] It is quite possible that both versions are correct.

Before discussing the causes of disagreement between the followers of the Rawshani movement and the tribes in more detail, it is necessary to address the question of why so many tribes joined the movement, and also to review the place of Bāyazīd Anṣārī and his followers in the Pashtun tribal environment.

In the above account of the Rawshani movement the main emphasis was on the internal political dynamics of Pashtun society, but one cannot ignore the genuine spiritual appeal of the Rawshani doctrine which attracted many people to it on an apolitical basis. They then became individual disciples of Bāyazīd Anṣārī and formed a classical *pīr–murīd* relationship with him (see below). Nonetheless, in order to explain the mass conversion to the Rawshani doctrine and the support of whole tribes for the movement, it is necessary to also consider the socio-political implications of Rawshani activities.

I would suggest that it is possible to distinguish several stages in the political career of Bāyazīd Anṣārī. At the beginning of his religious activity, when he had not yet been recognized as an important spiritual guide outside the circle of his immediate disciples with whom he had established classical *pīr–murīd* relations, Bāyazīd was a mere client of Mīrzā Malik, the Pashtun head of his part of Kaniguram. Thus, his position was the same as that of his father, who was a *qāḍī*, as well as that of other Muslim scholars and mystics who flourished under the auspices of their patrons.

However, when the number of Bāyazīd's *murīd*s increased he formed his own bloc opposed to the networks of other Sufi guides. Although he now had his own followers, he did not cease to be a client of Mīrzā Malik. The chief-centred blocs and *pīr*-centred blocs – in other words, Sufi circles – coexisted in, so to speak, parallel social universes and an individual's position in one bloc rarely influenced his status in other blocs. Members of these secular and religious bodies freely crossed the boundaries of their respective groups and assumed various identities at the time of crossing. This model applied not only to rank and file members of the blocs but to the *pīr*s as well: thus, the heads of Sufi circles often remained the clients of tribal chiefs. However, these *pīr*s were important political assets for their patrons since they boosted the latter's authority and increased their political weight. Initially, such was also the case with Bāyazīd Anṣārī and Mīrzā Malik. However, because of Bāyazīd's radical criticism of the religious establishment he proved to be an

---

[40] *The Orakzai Country and Clans* (Lahore: Vanguard Books 1984 a reprint of L. White King, *Monograph on the Orakzai Country and Clans: A Government Report*, Lahore 1900), pp. 44, 140.

embarrassment to his patron as well as the source of his potential conflict with other chiefs.

Bāyazīd Anṣārī's initially relatively low status prevented the Wazirs who lived side by side with the Ormurs, for instance, from joining the Rawshani movement. The Wazirs did not oppose Bāyazīd's activities and even intervened sympathetically into his dispute with Shaykh Awriyā, a local Sufi guide of some authority residing in the neighbouring town of Sangtawi. It is likely that the best way of explaining the Wazirs' position with regard to Bāyazīd Anṣārī lies in the nature of tribal social relations. For the Wazirs, Bāyazīd Anṣārī was only one of their clients whom it was necessary to defend against outsiders. At the same time, it would be considered not only degrading but even dangerous for the established order itself to join a client. Bāyazīd Anṣārī succeeded in converting other tribes because for them he was a complete outsider. Since he had no hereditary status to define his position he could be more socially mobile, climbing the social and political ladder more easily only among the tribes that had no association with the Ormurs.

After his expulsion from Kaniguram, Bāyazīd Anṣārī gradually turned into the head of the 'Islamic coalition', a development facilitated by the arrival of a significant number of new disciples and isolated cases of the collective conversion of entire tribes. An 'Islamic coalition' may be described as a combination of various personal networks of the Sufi *pīr*s belonging to the same brotherhood who allied themselves in pursuit of a common cause. Although these coalitions can exercise significant political influence, they are usually short lived and arise only in special circumstances. Because of the all-embracing nature of Islam, such coalitions involve an association of ritual, social and political qualities, without any clear distinction between the religious and political spheres,[41] within a single entity established to address a particular Islamic political issue. Thus, any political problem also becomes a religious problem, and even those who are usually not directly associated with Sufi networks are often dragged into the coalition. The 'Islamic coalition' thus becomes the core of the process of 'supra-tribal' unification, the aim of which is to provide a response to a political challenge. This response is always dressed in Islamic rhetoric which by no means is an opportunistic political exercise based merely on formal lip-service, but rather a major unifying force of the coalition. As soon as the *raison d'être* of such a coalition disappears, it quickly disintegrates.

In the development of the Rawshani movement, the 'Islamic coalition' was only the intermediate stage. Unlike members of other conventional 'Islamic

---

[41] Robert L. Canfield, *Islamic Coalitions in Bamian: A Problem in Translating Afghan Political Culture, in Revolutions and Rebellions in Afghanistan Anthropological Perspectives*, ed. Nazif Shahrani and Robert L. Canfield (Institute of International Studies, Research Series no. 57; Berkeley: University of California Press 1984), pp. 224–5, 228; and *idem*., "Ethnic, Regional, and Sectarian Alignments," pp. 81–2.

coalitions', which are usually concerned with a single political challenge, the Rawshanis addressed a wide range of issues. They aspired to a new order and an 'Islamic coalition' could serve their purposes only for a short time. The early Rawshani movement was an 'Islamic coalition' only inasmuch as it was based on and confined to its own religion-based network and facilitated 'supra-tribal' unification. When the movement acquired considerable strength, it realized its potential, outgrew the limits of an 'Islamic coalition' and transformed itself into a new entity.

Thus, the next and the final stage in the development of the Rawshani movement and Bāyazīd Anṣārī's career was the establishment of a religio-political body which, depending on the discipline and the theoretical orientation of the individual researcher, is termed a 'nativistic movement', 'revitalization movement', 'charismatic movement' or 'messianic movement'. The modern consensus on this phenomenon is that the people who participate in such movements lack previous political organization. Since these movements are usually millenarian and messianic, their leaders claim to be prophets or God himself – in the case of Bāyazīd Anṣārī, 'the Perfect Guide'. Their political organization and activity is aimed at the expulsion of foreigners and the reassertion of native traditions. In the present context, what is important for the understanding of the Rawshaniyya is that the leaders of these movements usually formulate their ideas in the same religious language as is used by the adversaries (usually foreigners) against whom their message is directed.[42] Such religious movements could transform themselves either into isolated and marginalized communities like that of the Dhikrīs in nearby Baluchistan, or into incipient state structures, as was the case with the Naqshbandī imāmate in the northern Caucasus, the Mahdawī state in the Sudan and perhaps even the Safavid Qizilbāsh of Iran. It seems that the latter was also the case with the Rawshani movement. The message of Bāyazīd Anṣārī touched a chord in the collective Pashtun psyche and initially roused Pashtuns to rally around him and his successors.

The Pashtuns sought unification for two reasons: to secure their control over the recently conquered lands and peoples in the basin of the Kabul river, and to oppose the threat of the Mughal Empire which undermined their independence. Thus the Rawshani movement had a dual nature, being both expansionist and defensive in its political orientation. As a charismatic movement with nativistic aspirations, the Rawshaniyya provided an ideal ideological ground for unification. By adhering to their own religious tradition which differentiated them from other Muslims, the Pashtuns could effectively

---

[42] See Michael Adas, *Prophets of Rebellion: Millenarian Protest Movements against European Colonial Order* (Chapel Hill: University of North Carolina Press 1979); Ralph Linton, "Nativistic Movements," *American Anthropologist*, 45/2 (1943); Anthony F.C. Wallace, "Revitalization Movements," *American Anthropologist*, 58/2 (1956).

resist assimilation into the dominant power structure of the Mughal Empire. Adoption of the new and distinct creed also harmonized with the exclusivistic 'Pashtun-Islamic' piety characteristic for their *Weltanschauung*, as was briefly described above in the introduction to this chapter. At the same time, non-Pashtuns were attracted to the movement because it provided a new religious identity for all its members. By sharing the dogma of their Pashtun masters, non-Pashtuns reckoned to achieve equal status with the Pashtuns, however superficial this equality might be. Unlike the Pashtuns, who resisted political assimilation into the Mughal Empire, non-Pashtuns were eager to become assimilated. By being 'adopted' into tribal structures and genealogies, they became less disadvantaged vis-à-vis 'pure' Pashtuns. As opposed to the Pashtuns, who usually succeeded in resisting the remote and often ineffective power of the Mughals, non-Pashtuns had no hope of getting rid of their Pashtun masters, who – unlike the faraway Mughals – exercised firm control at a grassroots level.

Bāyazīd Anṣārī was eager to emphasize his Pashtun connections. When the ruler of Kabul Muḥammad Ḥakīm proposed that he sever his connections with 'his ignorant Pashtuns', he proudly asserted that "God made me to be born among these people in order that I could enlighten them" and refused to desert them.[43] Although initially the Rawshani movement catered to the Pashtuns' ethnic sentiments and corresponded to their political interests, very soon it began to undermine tribal power structures. Not only did it challenge the power of tribal authorities by imposing the leadership of religious guides, it also began to eradicate tribal identity, two simultaneous tendencies which could have led to the establishment of the first Pashtun state in the tribesmen's homeland. However, without expansion and colonization of the new territories, essential for the survival of tribal political formations, this embryonic 'state' was bound to collapse. By imposing taxes on the Pashtun tribesmen, or at least by their effort to control the tribesmen's property, the Rawshani leaders attempted to establish quasi-state structures.[44] But since there were no newly conquered rich subjects to exploit by the means of an authoritative state apparatus, free-minded Pashtuns could not tolerate the centralizing tendencies associated with the Rawshani movement: hence the tribes began to desert the movement.

If Bāyazīd Anṣārī could have initiated an expansion, the situation might have been quite different. Because of its political, state-building ambitions the Rawshani movement also lost its chance of survival on a more modest scale.

---

[43] Mukhliṣ, *Ḥālnāma*, p. 341.

[44] This hypothesis is supported by the evidence of the *Ḥālnāma*, in which (p. 519) at least one prominent Rawshani general, namely Abū Bakr, was given the title of *khān* by Aḥdād. Although usually the prerogative of granting titles is reserved exclusively for rulers, in Pashtun society the term *khān* is sometimes used as a self-proclamation. However, this was not the case with Abū Bakr.

If the Rawshanis could have limited themselves to spiritual matters exclusively they could have survived as a religious community on a par with the Dhikrīs. However, given the nature of the Rawshani movement, which was developing from an "Islamic coalition" into a religious movement with charismatic and nativistic characteristics, the abandonment of political ambitions was absolutely impossible, making the movement's eventual disintegration virtually inevitable.[45]

II. RAWSHANI SUFISM AND SPIRITUALITY

The Rawshaniyya was not only a political phenomenon: it began as a religious movement with its own agenda and gradually developed into a full-fledged mystical brotherhood with a religious hierarchy, corpus of theological writings, distinct ritual and cultural activities associated with its ideas.[46] The ultimate goal of the Rawshaniyya was the attainment of *tawḥīd*, that true monotheism which is the highest state of unity with God. Like many other Sufis, Bāyazīd Anṣārī called this state 'the true Islam' (*Islām-i-ḥaqīqī*) as opposed to formal Islam (*Islām-i rasmī*).[47]

The concept of man's communion with God and the inseparable unity of the divine and human is based on a metaphor comparing man with a fish and God with the ocean. The ocean has the fish within itself and the fish has the ocean within itself; they are thus one and the same. The relationship of man and God as analogous to that of the fish with ocean is a powerful image, often repeated in the writings of Bāyazīd Anṣārī. The constant flow of water in the ocean facilitates the disappearance (*maḥw*) and re-emergence (*raj'a*) of the eternal essence that finds its incarnation in different forms.[48] In order to realize this unity, man must open "the eyes of his heart" and "look not from inside at outside but from inside at inside."[49] This spiritual vision led to the realization that not only are man's existence and God's existence inseparable, but man cannot be distinguished from God since man observes God through God.

---

[45] On the problem of the possible survival of the Rawshani doctrine after the collapse of the movement see Sergei Andreyev, "British Indian Views (Nineteenth and Early Twentieth Centuries) of the Later Followers of the Rauxāniyya Sect in Afghanistan and Northern India," *Iran*, 32, (1994), pp. 135–8.

[46] The most important source of Rawshani doctrine is Bāyazīd Anṣārī's magnum opus *Khayr al-Bayān* (Peshawar 1967; there is also a facsimile edition of the Berlin manuscript of *Khayr al-Bayān* published in Kabul in 1975), a book composed in Pashto as a conversation between God and Bāyazīd Anṣārī. It is the oldest extant book in the Pashto language. Bāyazīd Anṣārī's treatise *Maqṣūd al-Mu'minīn* (Islamabad 1976), written in Arabic, and his autobiography in Persian, *Ṣirāt al-Tawḥīd* (Peshawar 1952) also provide interesting information on doctrinal issues. Scattered references to Rawshani doctrine can also be found in the *Ḥālnāma* by Mukhliṣ.

[47] Bāyazīd Anṣārī, *Ṣirāṭ al-Tawḥīd*, p. 112.

[48] Mukhliṣ, *Ḥālnāma*, p. 46.

[49] *Ibid.*, pp. 44–5.

Thus, he sees God not in His external manifestations but in His own actuality which is, at the same time, the very essence of man's existence.[50]

Only those who realize this unity are true monotheists, dwelling in the realm of *tawḥīd*. In order to achieve this state man must abandon his phenomenal self and annihilate himself in God, that is, reach the state of *fanā'* and "dwell in God," being in the state of subsistence in his Eternity (*baqā'*).[51] Like Ibn 'Arabī[52] Bāyazīd Anṣārī thought that the state of *baqā'* involved acquaintance with divine secrets.

Given his strong emphasis on the omnipresence of God and His inseparability from man and the entire created world, it is evident that Bāyazīd Anṣārī followed the *wujūdī* school of Sufism. His description of God and man's unity with Him strongly resembles a famous passage of Ibn 'Arabī's in which the famous Sufi thinker summarizes his concept of *waḥdat al-wujūd*:[53] "nothing exists other than God, His attributes and His acts. Everything is He, is through Him, proceeds from Him, returns to Him; and were he to veil Himself from the universe even for the space of the blinking of an eye, the universe would straightaway cease to exist, for it survives only through His protection and His care."[54]

Apart from the general *wujūdī* spirit of Rawshani teachings, there is one indication that Bāyazīd Anṣārī was aware of Ibn 'Arabī's works and considered him a reliable authority worthy of respectful reference. Thus in *Maqṣūd al-mu'minīn*, while describing the importance of remembrance of God (*dhikr*), Bāyazīd once refers to Ibn 'Arabī's remark in his *al-Futūḥāt al-Makkiyah* that "The *dhikr* of God is a duty of the seeker."[55] It is symptomatic that the only reference to Ibn 'Arabī deals with such a commonplace item of theological discourse as *dhikr*, and that Bāyazīd Anṣārī never referred – as might be expected from a conscious follower of Ibn 'Arabī – to this famous Sufi thinker in order to justify his own metaphysical ideas. Thus, it appears that Bāyazīd Anṣārī saw himself as inspired exclusively by his personal mystical experience rather than as a conscious follower of Ibn 'Arabī.

Ultimate and total unity with God must be attained through a gradual progress of ascension from one spiritual station (*maqām*) to another. The stages were as follows: (1) *sharī'a* (the Divine Law); (2) *ṭarīqa* (the Sufi Path); (3) *ḥaqīqa* (the ultimate Reality or Truth); (4) *ma'rifa* (Gnosis), (5) *qurba* (Nearness); (6) *waṣla* (Union); (7) *waḥda* (Oneness); and

---

[50] *Ibid.*, pp. 50–1, 60.

[51] *Ibid.*, p. 63.

[52] Ibn 'Arabī, *al-Futūḥāt al-Makkiyya* (Beirut: n.d.), II, pp. 220–21.

[53] Ibn 'Arabī himself never called his theory *waḥdat al-wujūd*. It was named so by his later followers.

[54] M. Chodkiewicz, *Seal of the Saints: Prophethood and Sainthood in the Doctrine of Ibn 'Arabī*, (Cambridge: ITS 1993), p. 149.

[55] *Maqṣūd al-mu'minīn*, p. 318.

(8) *sukūna* (Tranquillity), although sometimes the latter four stages (5–8) were considered as interior levels within the highest station of Gnosis. In his description of these stations, Bāyazīd Anṣārī focused on the changing nature of certain basic Islamic concepts, such that a varying interpretation of the five 'pillars of Islam' is directly connected with the nature of the knowledge received at each *maqām*. The spiritual advancement of the Rawshani novices is compared to the qualities of prophets, 'friends of God' and angels, whose character traits the Rawshanis are expected to imitate or acquire at almost every stage.

Description of the mystical states (*aḥwāl*) realized by the traveller of the path is also carefully geared to Bāyazīd Anṣārī's personal experience during his own advancement from one stage to another. In his mystical quest, the Rawshani master reached the highest possible stage of spiritual perfection and found himself in total unity with God, describing his relation with God in the following way:

> Sometimes [I am one with] Him and sometimes [I am] from Him; that is: sometimes having ascended I arrive to the level of [spiritual] subtleness [unity] and sometimes having descended I come to the level of [material] coarseness [separateness]; that is: sometimes I see myself as [one with] the sea and sometimes I recognize myself as being born and created out of the sea.[56]

The description of his state in this passage closely resembles the traditional Sufi concepts of *baqā'* (permanent subsistence in God) and *fanā'* (annihilation), both terms which are used by Bāyazīd Anṣārī, although rarely. It should also be pointed out that he constantly described the ultimate goal of his teaching as the attainment of the *tawḥīd*, a theological and metaphysical term which usually means monotheism or unity but is also often employed by the Sufis as a substitute for *fanā'*.[57] Having achieved the highest possible stage of spiritual perfection, Bāyazīd Anṣārī was considered by his followers as the spiritual leader or guide (*rāhnamā*) and the 'master of the time' (*ṣāḥib-i zamān*).[58] In line with the general Sufi tradition, Bāyazīd Anṣārī began to display miraculous powers which were traditionally associated with Sufi guides.

The writings of Bāyazīd Anṣārī and his followers put a strong emphasis on practical matters such as the importance of the spiritual guide and are less concerned with providing a coherent and detailed written account of ideas on the nature of God and spiritual perfection. Since the Rawshani description of

---

[56] *Gāhī ū wa gāhī az ū; ya'nī gāhī 'urūj namūda ba martaba-yi laṭāfat mīrasam, wa gāhī nuzūl kardah dar martaba-yi kathāfat mīāyam; ya'nī gāhī khūd rā daryā mībīnam wa gāhī az daryā zād wa būd mīdānam* (Mukhliṣ, *Ḥālnāma*, p. 268).

[57] See Fazlur Rahman, s.v. "Bakā" wa-Fanā', in *EI*^{2}.

[58] Mukhliṣ, *Ḥālnāma*, p. 240.

metaphysical problems resembles brief notes taken in order to remind the follower of the doctrine of the knowledge received from his *pīr*, it is next to impossible to study Rawshani dogma independently, by relying solely on the extant texts. For Bāyazīd Anṣārī, the main purpose of recording his thoughts was to describe his own mystical experience, not to present an elaborated system of philosophical concepts in the tradition of speculative Sufism. It was the spiritually inspired guide rather than the mystic-scholar trained in the interpretation of his school's legacy who was considered best qualified to explain the essence and specific peculiarity of each aspect of the new Rawshani doctrine. The Rawshani texts were there to serve only as a reminder of the guide's lessons, for without a mystical experience vouchsafed by the *pīr*'s guidance, the student of the Rawshani movement is often at a loss to understand the real meaning of its various concepts.

In this context, it should be pointed out that Bāyazīd Anṣārī's usage of the adjective 'perfect' (*kāmil*) for the description of the guide (*pīr-i kāmil*) is not a Rawshani innovation; this term as well as its modifications belongs very much to the Naqshbandī Sufi tradition, having been used in the works of previous Naqshbandī authors, namely 'Abd al-Khāliq Ghujduwānī's *Risālah-i ṣāḥibiyya*, 'Abd al-Raḥmān Jāmī's *Nafaḥāt al-uns*, and 'Alī ibn al-Ḥusayn al-Kāshifī's *Rashaḥāt-i 'ayn al-ḥayāt*.[59] However, as is usually the case with Rawshani works, no source gives direct reference to any outside influence, even including the Naqshbandī one.[60] Again, the absence of any written sources which give evidence of outside influences on Anṣārī's ideas confines the student of the Rawshani movement to mere speculation regarding the historical development of its doctrine.

With regard to the term *pīr-i kāmil*, the famous Sufi concept of *al-insān al-kāmil* (the Perfect Man) of course comes to mind, an expression that is usually

---

[59] See Johan G.J. ter Haar, "The Importance of the Spiritual Guide in the Naqshbandi Order," in *The Heritage of Sufism*, II: *The Legacy of Medieval Persian Sufism*, ed. Leonard Lewisohn (Oxford: Oneworld 1999), p. 318.

[60] It is possible that Bāyazīd Anṣārī never mentioned his predecessors in order to prove that he had received a genuine revelation and was not a compiler of the ideas expressed by other people. Given the fact that the *Ḥālnāma* emphasized that the founder of the Rawshani movement never received a proper education ("Bāyazīd Anṣārī was not intelligent enough to realize that education is important," as Mukhliṣ, *Ḥālnāma*, p. 12, put it), this approach appears to resemble the well-known tradition in the Muslim world in which the illiteracy of the founder of a new religious tradition proves the genuine character of his teaching. In this regard, one thinks of the numerous speculations on the illiteracy of the Prophet Muḥammad and Emperor Akbar which were used as a legitimizing means. On the other hand, if we give full credit to the *Ḥālnāma*'s account that Bāyazīd Anṣārī was poorly educated, it is possible to assume that having acquired his knowledge of sophisticated theological problems by hearsay, the founder of the Rawshani movement was both unable and unwilling to make proper references to various intellectual traditions, since he did not want to compete with the *'ulamā'* on their own ground.

thought to have been first used by Ibn 'Arabī[61] with the general meaning of a man who has fully realized his essential oneness with the Divine Being in whose likeness he is made. As Ibn 'Arabī himself put it: "It is through him that God looks at His creatures and dispenses His mercy upon them."[62] The class of Perfect Men comprises the prophets, all the saints or 'friends of God' (*walī*) including the *quṭb*.[63] For some Sufis, such as al-Jīlī, the real *al-insān al-kāmil* was only the *quṭb* himself[64] who headed the hierarchy of *walī*s. In this regard, Bāyazīd Anṣārī's usage of the term *pīr-i kāmil* instead of *insān al-kāmil* should be seen as reflecting the didactic concerns and the primarily homiletic nature of his teachings. Thus, he often compared the result of his activities with that of the Prophet Muḥammad, a claim which may be in line with another Sufi interpretation of the term *quṭb* as a manifestation of the 'Muḥammadan Truth' (*al-ḥaqīqat al-muḥammadiyya*).[65]

With the above remarks in mind, a reconstruction of Bāyazīd Anṣārī's concept might be attempted as follows. At any given time there may be only one

---

[61] There is also an opinion that the use of this term by Sufis antedated Ibn 'Arabī. The notion of the Perfect Man initially originated in non-Sufi esoteric or philosophical traditions. As adumbrated by the Ikhwān al-Ṣafā' and by Ibn Miskawayh in the late fourth/tenth century, the term was applied both to the Imām and to the secular ruler. Later, the concept was taken over by the Islamic 'chivalry' movement (*futuwwa*), and the subsequent merging of *futuwwa* with Sufism may have contributed to the further spread of this notion. Obviously, any discussion on the origin and development of the concept of the Perfect Man is outside the scope of this chapter.

[62] Ibn 'Arabī, *Fuṣūṣ al-ḥikam*, ed. A.A. Afifi (Beirut: Dār al-Kutab al-'Arabi 1946), I, p. 50; Eng. trans in Chodkiewicz, *Seal of the Saints*, p. 70. In order to become the 'Perfect Man', a man must develop spiritually to the degree of seeing God in everything (realizing *waḥdat al-wujūd*) and constantly adjust the shape of his heart according to the various forms of Divine manifestation. Through this constant changing of his heart man receives understanding of the totality of God's self-manifestation. This subject is dealt with extensively in Ibn 'Arabī's chapter on 'Adam' in the *Fuṣūṣ al-ḥikam*. For more details on the ultimate realization of a human being, i.e. attainment of the level of the Perfect Man see Masataka Takeshita, *Ibn 'Arabī's Theory of the Perfect Man and its Place in the History of Islamic Thought* (Tokyo: Institute for the Study of Languages and Cultures of Asia and Africa 1987), pp. 113–18.

[63] This general Sufi view as described by Nicholson may be an explanation why Bāyazīd Anṣārī used the terms *walī* and *quṭb* interchangeably.

[64] R.A. Nicholson, *Studies in Islamic Mysticism* (Cambridge: Cambridge University Press 1921), pp. 78, 86.

[65] de Yong, s.v. "Ḳuṭb," *EI*², V, p. 543. This concept was studied by R.A. Nicholson, who wrote that 'Abd al-Karīm ibn Ibrāhīm al-Jīlī, the fourteenth/fifteenth-century mystic and the author of *al-Insān al-kāmil*, thought that in every age the Perfect Man was an outward manifestation of the essence of the Prophet Muḥammad (metaphysically described as 'the Light of Muḥammad' or 'The Spirit of Muḥammad'), which had the power of assuming whatever form it would. The Perfect Man appears in different guises and receives various names, which vary with each epoch in harmony with the 'guise' of that epoch. Al-Jīlī described his own meeting with the Prophet who appeared to him in the guise of his own spiritual guide. Thus the Perfect Man is the 'pole' or *quṭb* around which the spheres of existence turn (Nicholson, *Studies*, pp. 87, 105; R. Arnaldez, "al-Insān al-Kāmil," *EI*², III, p. 1241).

true *pīr* who is the *pīr-i kāmil*, that is the Supreme Perfect Man – *al-insān al-kāmil* – whose special mission is to enlighten the people,[66] who is therefore the sole *quṭb* of his epoch[67] or 'master of the age'. It seems that Bāyazīd Anṣārī used the term *walī* as a synonym of *pīr-i kāmil/quṭb* insofar as it is mentioned in the *Ḥālnāma* that there can be only one *walī* at a time – a statement that contradicts the general Sufi view that there can be a number of *walī*s at any given time. This term was quoted in this context in a *ḥadīth* of unknown origin, here translated into Persian as *pīr*.[68] However, since *quṭb*s are *ipso facto* 'friends of God', one can assume that in the Rawshani context the single *walī* who appears in every epoch is the *quṭb* who is, for the Rawshaniyya, the only true guide.

Before he realized his own election through divine revelation, Bāyazīd Anṣārī, being an aspiring young mystic, had desperately sought for a suitable guide. He did not succeed in his search and was described by the *Ḥālnāma* as *ṭālib-i kāmil* (perfect disciple/seeker) who had no *pīr-i kāmil* (perfect master).[69] Eventually, Bāyazīd Anṣārī received an Uwaysī-type initiation directly from God without the mediation of any earthly teacher. Since he had failed to discover anyone who might possess the necessary qualities of a true guide, he developed a contempt for all traditional religious authorities. Bāyazīd Anṣārī's strong feelings towards traditional *pīr*s may be explained not only by their low knowledge and immorality but also by his rejection of the religious establishment which he had had no chance to join since, because of his lack of education and proper initiation into a valid Sufi tradition,[70] he was unable to meet the conventional criteria for a teacher of religion. He was

---

[66] In the case of Bāyazīd Anṣārī, the 'people' here are, in the first instance, the Pashtuns.

[67] "The *quṭb* who is *pīr-i kāmil* is single (*yak*) at anytime" (Mukhliṣ, *Ḥālnāma*, p. 143).

[68] Mukhliṣ, *Ḥālnāma*, p. 143.

[69] *Ibid.*, pp. 37, 38, 50, 94.

[70] Cf. "If anyone by means of asceticism and self-mortification shall have risen to an exalted degree of mystical experience, without having a Pīr to whose authority and example he submits himself, the Sufis do not regard him as belonging to their community" (Muḥammad ibn al-Munawwar, *Asrār al-tawḥīd fī maqāmāt al-Shaykh Abī Sa'īd*, ed. V. Zhukovskii [St Petersburg 1899], p. 55; partial English trans by Nicholson, *Studies*, p. 10). As Nicholson remarked: "In this way a continuous tradition of mystical doctrine is secured" and "[Sufis] do not allow any one to associate with them, unless he can show to their satisfaction that he is lineally connected in both these ways [personal connection with a recognised *pīr* and the recipient of the Sufi mantle (*khirqa*)] with a fully accredited pīr" (*ibid.*, pp. 10, 23). The Uwaysī tradition is obviously an exception to this strict rule. However, Bāyazīd Anṣārī resorted to the Uwaysī ideas only when he himself became a religious teacher. He never employed the argument served by Jalāl al-Dīn Rūmī, who recognized the possibility of a lone mystic's journey towards spiritual perfection but noted that even if, as a rare exception, somebody managed to attain perfection without the help of a worldly guide, in reality he had been helped by 'the hearts of many guides' (Jalal al-Dīn Rūmī, *Mathnawi*, ed., trans. and annotated by R.A. Nicholson, 8 vols [London 1925–40]; I: 2974). The founder of the Rawshani movement was probably familiar with the thought of Jalāl al-Dīn Rūmī whose poetry is quoted in the *Ḥālnāma*.

constantly reminded of this by his adversaries and sympathizers. The reasons given by the former and the latter were, of course, very different. It also seems that Bāyazīd Anṣārī's father 'Abdu'llāh's cynical words that only those disciples who pay their guide well gain knowledge, and the attempts of his Kaniguram antagonist 'Uthmān to deceive him in order to obtain knowledge of *tawḥīd* and proclaim himself *pīr*[71] triggered Bāyazīd Anṣārī's bitterness and discontent with contemporary religious authorities.[72]

CONCLUSION

Given a certain lack of consistent theology and its strong emphasis on the importance of the spiritual master, the Rawshani movement should be placed within the tradition of practical, devotional and the usually rather eclectic Sufism which concentrated not on metaphysical discourse but on everyday mystical practice under the attentive guidance of the *pīr*. Considering the realities of the highly illiterate Pashtun tribal society which lay far away from the centres of Muslim scholarship and was not directly influenced by sophisticated intellectual traditions, one could hardly expect anything different.

This type of Sufism agreed with the realities of the young Pashtun culture, which was at that time still internalizing the teachings of Islam and looking for inspiration in different directions, eager to imitate various intellectual and cultural traditions which in the tribal periphery of the Mughal Empire were mainly associated with Persianate Indian Islam. This imitation dealt not only with philosophical and mystical issues but with literary works as well. However, because of the peculiarities of tribal society, which set the Pashtuns apart from their neighbours, the results of their imitation and adoption of the elements of high Islamic culture were sometimes quite different from those achieved by their prototypes.

However, the fact that in many respects the Rawshani movement was an imitation of a foreign intellectual and cultural tradition does not diminish its significance for Pashtun history and culture. The Rawshaniyya not only became the vehicle for the expression of Pashtun spirituality, the movement also shaped the form of native artistic and intellectual articulation, eventually transforming Pashtunistan into a truly Muslim society which was concerned not only with exoteric Islamic rituals but with deeper spiritual matters as well.

---

[71] Mukhliṣ, *Ḥālnāma*, pp. 39, 102.

[72] The only exception is Bāyazīd Anṣārī's cousin Khwāja Ismā'īl. It is known that before he started preaching Bāyazīd Anṣārī wanted to become a disciple of this relative, whom he apparently considered a true guide worth following. However, Khwājah Ismā'īl did not possess the complete knowledge of *tawḥīd*, which was revealed only to Bāyazīd Anṣārī (Mukhliṣ, *Ḥālnāma*, p. 128).

As the *Ḥālnāma* confirms, apart from the knowledge of divine unity (*tawḥīd*), Bāyazīd Anṣārī left two more "treasures" for his Pashtun followers: music and poetry in Pashto, both art forms that were non-existent before him.[73] Just as the first Pashtun musicians were his disciples, and began to compose "elaborate melodies," Bāyazīd Anṣārī was the first person to compose *qaṣīda*s, ghazals, *mathnawī*s and *rubā'ī*s in Pashto. His children and disciples imitated him and also wrote *diwān*s in Pashto,[74] some of which were preserved for posterity.

In this fashion, Rawshani authors consciously initiated the use of the Pashto language. Although the reason for their writing in Pashto was doctrinal, the consequences of the deliberate decision to write theological works and poetry in this vernacular tongue, motivated by the view that Bāyazīd Anṣārī had a mission of enlightening the Pashtuns, ultimately influenced the whole of Pashtun culture, which, as a result of the Rawshani intellectual activities, acquired its own independent literary tradition.

---

[73] Although there is no means of verifying this claim of the *Ḥālnāma*, it is quite possible that it is true since there is no reliable evidence of pre-Rawshani poetry and theological works in Pashto. Besides, there is no stylistic difference between the writings of Bāyazīd Anṣārī and his antagonist Akhūnd Darwīza. Other Pashtun opponents of the Rawshani movement also imitated or at least admired the literary style and skills of Bāyazīd Anṣārī and his followers. It seems that if these enemies of the Rawshani movement could draw on a different Pashto literary tradition they would have done so, rather than imitate the style of their rivals, whom they sincerely hated.

[74] Mukhliṣ, *Ḥālnāma*, pp. 345, 359.

Contemplating Sacred History in Late Mughal Sufism

The Case of Shāh Walī Allāh of Delhi

MARCIA K. HERMANSEN

The following chapter is devoted to the study of certain texts of the Sufi thinker Shāh Walī Allāh against the background of Persianate Mughal Sufism, the eighteenth century, and conceptualizations of the so-called 'decline' of Sufism. Shāh Walī Allāh died in 1762 and is considered one of the most versatile and prominent intellectual figures of eighteenth-century Muslim India. The use of his writings is suggested by the fact that he composed such an extensive range of texts and that he does not exclusively present the perspective of a single Sufi order (*ṭarīqa*), although he has been most closely associated with the Naqshbandiyya. Unlike the earlier works of Sufis such as Ibn 'Arabī (d. 1240), his writings could not be considered as "text producers",[1] since they were rarely commented on by contemporaries and seemed to have raised little controversy in his own time.[2] Still, they are important, both in their own right and as indicative of tendencies internal and indigenous to Islamic thought at this time. Trends beginning to appear in these texts may signal a trajectory that would have occurred within the Islamic tradition on its own, had not the intensive upheavals associated with the colonial experience intervened.

I will take as a basis for discussion several texts, drawn from what we may term Shāh Walī Allāh's writings on 'practical' Sufism, rather than those explicitly on mystical theory[3] or on his well-known works in the fields of

---

[1] On "text producers" or literary watersheds see Ian R. Netton, *Allāh Transcendant: Studies in the Structure and Semiotics of Islamic Philosophy, Theology and Cosmology* (London: Curzon Press 1994), p. 300.

[2] Maḥmūd Aḥmad Barkātī, *Shāh Walī Allāh aur unkā Khāndān* (Delhi: Maktaba Jāmi'a 1992), pp. 31–40.

[3] For example, his *Lamaḥāt* (Arabic) (Hyderabad, Sindh: Shāh Walī Allāh Academy, n.d.). English translation by G.H. Jalbani (Hyderabad Sindh, 1970). Reissued and re-edited by D.B. Fry as *Sufism and the Islamic Tradition: Lamahat and Sata'at of Shah Waliullah of Delhi* (London: Octagon Press 1986) and *Saṭa'āt* (Hyderabad, Sindh: Shāh Walī Allāh Academy 1964). English translation by G.H. Jalbani (see above); Urdu translation with commentary by Muḥammad Matīn Hāshimī (Lahore: Idāra Thaqāfiyya Islāmiyya 1986).

ḥadīth, *fiqh*, or Koranic studies.[4] An examination of these and other of Shāh Walī Allāh's works in the genre of Sufi manuals seems to indicate that he wrote in various modes, sometimes invoking Koranic and *ḥadīth* citations, while at other times laying out historical discussions and analysis without having recourse to such proof texts. I will focus on several passages from Shāh Walī Allāh's works that deal more particularly with contemplative practices and the historical and existential significance of Sufism and its major figures. These are: *Hama'āt* (Outpourings)[5] and *al-Tafhīmāt al-ilāhiyya* (Divine Inspirations).[6]

On the basis of his portrayal of sacred history and its interaction with historical stages and figures in the development of Sufism, I argue that Shāh Walī Allāh represents a pivotal figure in the transition from pre-modern to modern ways of thinking and writing in Muslim religious literature. This is particularly important since he precedes contact with European thought and the advent of printing.

THE EIGHTEENTH CENTURY AND SUFISM

The idea of the eighteenth century as one whose main significance was as a precursor to reform has been standard in histories of the Muslim world covering this period, whether they focused on the Middle East or on Muslim South Asia. The idea that the content of Indian 'Persianate' Sufi texts of this period reflects a shift towards an orientation to reformism has been explored in a preliminary way for the nineteenth century by Warren Fusfeld in his work on the successors to the Naqshbandis Mirzā Maẓhar Jān-i Janān (1785) and Ghulām 'Alī Dihlavī (1824).[7] Arthur Buehler takes up this theme in his book

---

[4] For example, *Ḥujjat Allāh al-bāligha*, (Cairo: Multazim al-ṭab' wa-l-nashr dār al-kutub al-ḥadīth 1952–3); English translation M.K. Hermansen, *The Conclusive Argument from God* (Leiden: Brill 1996) and *al-Budūr al-bāzigha* (Arabic text) (Hyderabad, Sindh: Shāh Walī Allāh Academy 1970); English translations by J.M.S. Baljon, *Full Moon on the Horizon* (Lahore: Ashraf 1988) and G.H. Jalbani (Islamabad: Hijra Council 1985). For a bibliography of Shāh Walī Allāh's works as well as secondary studies see Marcia K. Hermansen, "The Current State of Shāh Walī Allāh Studies," *Hamdard Islamicus*, 11/3 (1988), pp. 17–30.

[5] Shāh Walī Allāh, *Hama'āṭ* (Persian original) (Hyderabad, Sindh: Shāh Walī Allāh Academy, 1964), formed the basis for much of Mīr Valiuddin's work, *Contemplative Disciplines in Sufism* (London: East–West Publications 1980).

[6] Shāh Walī Allāh, *al-Tafhīmāt al-ilāhiyya* (Hyderabad: Shāh Walī Allāh Academy 1967) is a two-volume collection of shorter pronouncements and treatises in both Persian and Arabic. The book was compiled by his disciples and does not follow any structural organizing principles. The vast majority of the entries have to do with mystical topics, and in general the discussions are more focused than one tends to find in the genre of letters to disciples. This work has never been translated into Urdu, unlike his other works, although it has been judged philosophically important for the understanding of his thought.

[7] Warren Fusfeld, "The Shaping of Sufi Leadership in Delhi: The Naqshbandiyya-Mujaddidiyya, 1750–1920," Ph.D. dissertation, University of Pennsylvania, 1981.

on the South Asian Naqshbandiyya.[8] The evidence of this shift is to be found, according to Fusfeld, in the emergence among Sufis of a legalism and style of argument traditionally more characteristic of the *fuqahā'* or legal scholars rather than mystics. Buehler further cites as evidence of reformist trends the increased use of proof texts from the *ḥadīth* and the Koran cited in texts in support of Sufi claims.[9] At the same time, this reformist influence has often been characterized as being symptomatic of that other feature associated with later Sufism, 'decline'.

The extension of this hypothesis, that is, that some sort of movement towards a change or decline in Mughal Sufism is already evident in eighteenth-century texts or even earlier, has been less closely examined, although some steps have been taken in this direction. For example, according to Buehler, Shāh Walī Allāh's works *al-Qawl al-jamīl* and *Intibāh fī-salāsil awliyā' Allāh* are precursors to the genre of *ma'mūlāt* works.[10] *Ma'mūlāt* are Sufi manuals on topics such as exercises, supplications, formulae for solving worldly problems, and so on, which would have traditionally been imparted by a shaykh personally and directly to his disciple. The production and dissemination of such materials in written form signals a shift away from a primarily oral tradition of personal instruction.[11] It is this depersonalization that marks a shift in the role of the shaykh from educator or director to charismatic mediator, as Buehler argues. One may further surmise that this shift indicates a lessening of confidence in the transformative impact of the tradition and its contemplative and other practices. Annemarie Schimmel noted a similar trend in her study of Khwājah Mīr Dard, a late eighteenth-century Sufi and Urdu poet, noting that by his time books and texts had begun to be substituted for oral *ṣuḥbat* (the company of the Sufi master).[12]

Putting formerly secret and initiatic contemplative practices into texts and ultimately into print could be seen as a watering down of their power. This lifting of the veil on esoteric thought and practices[13] could also be attributed to a loss of confidence, or at least a shift in faith in their efficacy or authority. For example, I have argued in an earlier study on Sufi cosmological diagrams through to the twentieth century that the depiction of the Sufi spiritual itinerary (*sulūk*) through a system of subtle centres known as the *laṭā'if* shifted over

---

[8] Arthur R. Buehler, *Sufi Heirs of the Prophet: The Indian Naqsbandiyya and the Rise of the Mediating Sufi Shaykh* (Columbia, South Carolina: University of South Carolina Press 1998).

[9] *Ibid.*, p. 170.

[10] *Ibid.*, pp. 235–6.

[11] *Ibid.*, p. 239 *passim*.

[12] Annemarie Schimmel, *Pain and Grace: A Study of Two Mystical Writers of Eighteenth Century Muslim India* (Leiden: Brill 1976), p. 73.

[13] For a discussion of the repercussions of print on the Sufi tradition see "the publication of the secret" in Carl Ernst, *The Shambhala Guide to Sufism* (Boston–London Shambhala 1997), pp. 215–20.

time from a format asserting the effectiveness of training procedures within a single Sufi order (*ṭarīqa*) to a broader and less specific design. This depicted and rationalized the manner in which multiple affiliations were pursued by individuals according to a more 'natural science' medically based model.[14] The reach of this literature describing contemplative practices beyond the circles of the initiates also meant that it had to contest other Muslim discourses for religious legitimacy. Thus Indian Sufis in the eighteenth and nineteenth centuries were to be drawn into the discourse of the legalists by projecting their claims to authority onto a broader space.

Reformist treatises such as the *Sirāṭ al-mustaqīm* of Shāh Ismā'īl Shahīd (1831), Shāh Walī Allāh's grandson, continued to represent contemplative practices as efficacious and connected with particular *ṭarīqa* affiliations while at the same time criticizing other aspects of 'popular' Sufism. Such writings might be taken to exemplify the contention between legalist and esotericist elements.[15] One possible conclusion is that these later texts in which legal and esoteric paradigms are reproduced in discrete spaces contrast with earlier works which attempt to integrate them or to elucidate the former in terms of the latter. Examples of this latter type would be the earlier works of Ibn 'Arabī or the works in the *asrār al-dīn* genre.[16]

It seems unlikely, however, that the mere writing down of spiritual practices and contemplative techniques would indicate a decline in "authentic" Sufism, already marginalized by reformist agendas, since earlier examples of this genre may be cited. Among many examples would be the manuals of the Chishtī Order, such as the *Muraqqa'* and *Kashkūl* of Kalīmullāh Jahānābādī (d. 1729)[17], the *Jawāhir al-Khamsa* of Muḥammad Ghauth Gwāliorī (d. 1562) or even some parts of Ibn 'Arabī's (d. 1240) *al-Futūḥāt al-makkiyya*. The fact that many Muslim thinkers, for example Ibn Sīnā (d. 1037) and al-Suhrawardī (d. 1191), would write discrete works in widely varying modes, depending on language and genre, seems also to work against this hypothesis.

Other possible observations pertinent to tracing developments in eighteenth-century Muslim thought can be extrapolated from Peter Gran's discussion of Egypt at this period. His study argues that broad patterns of

---

[14] Marcia Hermansen, "Mystical Paths and Authoritative Knowledge: A Semiotic Approach to Sufi Cosmological Diagrams," *Journal of Religious Studies and Theology*, 12/1 (1992), pp. 52–77.

[15] The legalistic and esoteric models coexist in works such as those of Ibn 'Arabī. In Shāh Walī Allāh's writings we find evidence of their increasing separation from one another although *Ḥujjat Allāh al-Bāligha* may be seen as a synthesis of the two modes.

[16] *Asrār al-Dīn* or 'secrets or inner meanings of religion' are works in which mystics explain the spiritual benefits of following the *sharī'a* injunctions. For example, al-Ghazālī's *Iḥyā' 'ulūm al-dīn*, 'Izz al-Dīn al-Sulamī's *Qawā'id al-aḥkām fī maṣāliḥ al-ānam* (Cairo: Maktaba al-kulliyya al-azhar 1968) and Shāh Walī Allāh's *Ḥujjat Allāh al-Bāligha*.

[17] *Kashkūl-i kalīmī* (Delhi: Mujtabā'ī 1890), *Muraqqa'-i kalīmī* (Delhi: Mujtabā'ī 1895).

text production and concerns raised within religious discussions may be understood as reflecting broader worldwide elements of economic and social change. For example, among the new patterns emerging in Egyptian society that impacted on participation in religious discourse and its formulation were the rise of a middle class of merchants and scholars. This led to a new interest in literature shared in middle class salons patronized by members of Sufi orders whose members were mercantile or scholarly rather than aristocratic.[18] Gran cites Murtaḍā Zabīdi's (d. 1791) writings as reflecting this "rise in critical consciousness;[19]" an intriguing association, given that Zabīdī studied with Shāh Walī Allāh at a young age before he migrated from India.

MUGHAL SUFISM

It is clear that waves of creativity in Sufi thought crested at varying periods in the Central Arab, Persian, and South Asian regions. The characterizations of eighteenth-century Sufism and its textuality presented here apply only to South Asia. However, it is likely that elements of the hypothesis that textuality in writings could be applied as an index of cultural change and intellectual shifts in patterns of thinking and writing may be applicable to developments in other regions. It should be observed that late classical Mughal Persianate Sufism remained a powerful force in the intellectual and social spheres in India until a comparatively late period.

The history of Mughal Sufism requires more detailed study before generalizations and categorizations can be applied with any degree of assurance. Standard issues are the extent to which cultural synthesis occurred, tracing its major strands and areas of influence, and the social history of Sufi orders in terms of their class and ethnic membership and patronage networks at the central court[20] as well as in various regional contexts. In terms of cultural synthesis, Wolpert observes that:

> The Great Mughals, whose reigns span the entire seventeenth century, have with good reason become universal symbols of power and affluence, of tenderness and cruelty, of ferocity and sensitivity; luxury loving, licentious, sentimental, brutal, and poetic; they were the embodiment of all those extremes characteristic of the Indian life-style known as Mughali. Jahangir, Shah Jahan, and Aurangzeb each in his own way epitomized some aspects of the complex cultural syncretism within

[18] Peter Gran, *The Islamic Roots of Capitalism: Egypt 1760–1840* (Austin: University of Texas Press 1979). Studies of late Mughal India which deal with some of these economic aspects are reviewed and extended in Muzaffar Alam's work, *The Crisis of Empire in North India: Awadh and the Punjab 1707–1748* (Delhi: Oxford University Press 1986), pp. 2–9.

[19] Gran, *Islamic Roots of Capitalism*, p. 54.

[20] Khaliq Ahmad Nizami, "Naqshbandi Influence on Mughal Rulers and Politics," *Islamic Culture*, 39 (1965), pp. 41–62 and "Shah Wali Ullah Dehlavi and Indian Politics in the 18th Century," *Islamic Culture*, 25 (1951), pp. 133–45.

> which they lived and over which they presided. The courts they maintained, the courtiers they chose, reflected a new syncretic patina of civilization that was a blend of Indian, Persian, and Central Asian manners and mores.[21]

During the period of Awrangzīb's reign contacts between India and the Hijaz were strengthened, owing to the religious interests of the emperor and improved trade and transport on European vessels.[22] The attitude to non-Muslim cultural influences and eclecticism in general became increasingly rigid. Since Awrangzīb did not patronize arts such as music, painting and architecture, these no longer were able to reflect such a synthesis of mystical elements in general to a wider public. At the same time, *'ulamā'* and scholars were beneficiaries of imperial support[23] and their influence increased with the patronage of works on law such as the *Fatāwa 'Ālamgīrī*, and *ḥadīth* studies.

During the reigns of the later Mughals, the Naqshbandī *ṭarīqa* seems to have spread more widely in society and to have become the movement of merchants, poets, and the lower nobility. This may help explain the vitality of the Naqshbandīs in intellectual, literary and education activities. As Peter Gran argued in the case of Egypt,[24] a wider social diffusion of participation of Sufism among literate classes may also have had an impact on the conceptualization of the texts and their internal discourses, even before the subsequent impact of the new technologies for mass dissemination.

In Indo-Muslim intellectual circles of this period religious writings reflect the linguistic mix of Arabic and Persian. The emergence of Urdu, initially as a language of poetry, was beginning to be felt, although it was not until the early 1800s that Urdu would gather the momentum to make the transition to a language of prose expression, tied to elements advocating religious reform and able to take advantage of the introduction of printing to Muslim South Asia.[25]

Locating Late Mughal Sufism

The eleventh *hijrī*/ eighteenth *milādī* century in Muslim history is one that poses a number of historical problems that have been recently addressed, but not satisfactorily solved. Traditionally, historians narrating Muslim civilization have seen this as a period of stagnation and decline before the encounter with European forces and ideas that occasioned stirrings of reform. More detailed

---

[21] Stanley Wolpert, *A New History of India*, 3rd edn. (New York: Oxford University Press 1989), p. 149.

[22] John F. Richards, *The Mughal Empire New Cambridge History of India*, I/5 (New York: Cambridge University Press 1993), p. 172.

[23] *Ibid*, p. 174.

[24] Gran, *Islamic Roots of Capitalism*.

[25] On the role of printing on the production of Islamic writings in South Asia see Francis Robinson, "Technology and Religious Change: Islam and the Impact of Print," *Modern Asian Studies*, 27/1 (1993), pp. 229–51.

study has traced the indigenous grounding for concepts of reform,[26] and some progress has been made in understanding the social and economic context engendering shifts in Muslim thought and activism of this period.[27] In terms of Sufism, the period is considered 'baroque' in the sense of a flowering and confluence of a number of intellectual styles, but also the last gasp before the decline into popularization and saint cults. Institutionalization and popularization were tendencies that diffused the ideas and practices of Sufism to wider and wider spheres of cultural influence in Muslim societies. Both Western scholars and the Sufis themselves, however, portray a qualitative 'decline' in Sufi standards along with this broadening of outreach. Hujwīrī's well-known statement that "At one time Sufism was a reality without a name, now it is a name without a reality,"[28] was made in the eleventh century![29] Correspondingly, many Western scholars defined the 'Golden Age' of Sufism[30] as the age of ascetic, wandering Sufis, many of whom challenged the normative 'routinized' Islamic practices of the jurists.

One influential model for periodizing the history of Sufism has been Trimingham's formulation of stages beginning with what he terms the *khānaqāh* stage of the tenth century. This period was characterized as individualistic and aristocratic in orientation.

In the second, *ṭarīqa* stage of 1100–1400, we have the transmission of a doctrine, rule, and method as well as collective methods for inducing ecstasy, which Trimingham associated with the bourgeois classes.

The third, pre-reform stage was that of the *ṭā'ifa* or sect whose inception Trimingham dates to the fifteenth century. This phase is marked by the founding of saint cults, defined by the transmission of allegiance and a popularization of participation and rituals.[31] Trimingham's account in *The Sufi Orders in Islam* then jumps to nineteenth-century revival, which to a certain extent might be considered a fourth stage.[32] What about the eighteenth century? According to Julian Baldick, "this period has traditionally been seen as one of decline, too late for the admirer of classical Islamic culture, and too

[26] John Voll, "Tajdid and Islah," in *Voices of Resurgent Islam*, ed. John L. Esposito (Oxford: Oxford University Press 1983), pp. 32–47.

[27] Nehemia Levtzion and John Voll, *Eighteenth Century Reform and Renewal in Islam* (Syracuse: Syracuse University Press 1987); Gran, *Islamic Roots of Capitalism*.

[28] Al-Hujwiri, *Kashf al-mahjub*, trans. R.A. Nicholson, reprint (Lahore: Islamic Book Foundation 1976), p. 44.

[29] For a discussion of internal Muslim concepts of decline, in particular the decline of Sufism, see Fritz Meier, "Sufisme et déclin culturel," in *Classicisme et déclin culturel dans l'histoire de la civilisation musulmane*, ed. R. Brunschvig and G.E. von Grunebaum (Paris: Chantemerle 1957), pp. 217–45.

[30] J. Spencer Trimingham, *The Sufi Orders in Islam* (Oxford: Clarendon Press 1971), p. 103.

[31] *Ibid.*

[32] On revival movements as a fourth stage see the new preface by John O. Voll to Trimingham's *The Sufi Orders in Islam* (New York: Oxford University Press 1998), p. ix.

early for the champion of modernity."[33] The very fact that the eighteenth century does not fall neatly into either category indicates its position as a time of transition, struggle, and discontinuity.

More recently, Ira Lapidus replicates the model of a Sufism that declined from the era of the charismatic individual to that of static tomb cult. According to his formulation, "charisma shifts from the personal religious insights of the founding teachers to the tombs. The shrines become centers of worship and lands are granted converting pirzadas into a petty gentry."[34] The difference between the class analysis of Lapidus and that of Trimingham is that for Lapidus the Sufi shrine custodians themselves become the gentry (and presumably distanced from 'authentic' Sufism) rather than the decline resulting from the diffusion of the tradition to the lower classes.

Another way of understanding historical changes in the style and concerns of Sufi writing and practice is offered by Fritz Meier.[35] He follows the indications of the Sufi master Ibn 'Abbād al-Rundī (d.1390) who differentiated between "teaching shaykhs" (*shaykh al-ta'līm*) and "directing shaykhs" (*shaykh at-tarbiyya*). Meier concludes that "teaching shaykhs" were typical of the earlier period of Sufism up to the tenth century while exemplary shaykhs were the norm up to the fourteenth century or even later.[36]

Further developing this trend of analysis, Arthur Buehler takes a neo-Weberian approach to understanding forms of Sufi leadership and focuses on styles of authority. His argument is that the classical period may be characterized by a transition from early teaching shaykhs to directing shaykhs who trained their disciples in spiritual exercises, allowing the followers to experience intimacy with God. This model persisted in Muslim South Asia into the eighteenth century, the time of the rise of the "Muḥammadan path" when veneration of the Prophet came into ascendancy. It seems that this veneration enhanced the shaykhs' own authority as mediators, since individuals were no longer felt to be capable of developing such intimacy on their own. The further shift, which some may see as a decline, occured in the nineteenth/twentieth centuries with the transition to 'mediator' shaykhs

---

[33] Julian Baldick, *Mystical Islam: An Introduction to Sufism* (New York: New York University Press 1989), p. 132.

[34] Ira Lapidus, *A History of Muslim Societies* (New York: Cambridge University Press 1988), p. 460.

[35] Fritz Meier, in particular, has taken an interest in questions of the 'decline' or shift in later Sufism. See his "Sufisme et déclin culturel," in Brunschvig and von Grunehaum, *Classicisme et déclin culturel* and "Khurāsān and das ende der klassischen ṣufik," in *Atti del convegno internazionale sul tema : La persia nel medioevo* (Rome 1971), pp. 545–70. This article has been reprinted in Meier, *Bausteine I: Ausgewahlte Aufsatze zur Islamwissenschaft*, ed. Erika Glassen and Gudrun Schubert (Istanbul: Steiner 1992), 94–130.

[36] Fritz Meier, *Meister und Schuler im Orden der Naqshbandiyya* (Heidelberg: C. Winter 1995), pp. 8–9. A discussion of Rundī may also be found in Buehler, *Sufi Heirs*, pp. 31–2.

rather than 'educator' or 'directing' shaykhs.[37] "Unlike directing shaykhs, however, there is no evidence that mediating shaykhs concerned themselves with the individual spiritual development of their disciples in the context of a rigorous spiritual discipline."[38] In the case of the South Asian Naqshbandiyya, political changes wrought in the context of British colonial power, as well as modern dislocations of traditional knowledge, reoriented the mediating function of the Sufi saint. The mediator shaykh is an object of love for the disciple. This is understood in later periods as the only means to achieve love for the Prophet and ultimately love for God. "The only way to God was through the mediation of a shaykh connected with Muhammad who in turn would intercede with God on behalf of the believer."[39]

This emphasis on the rise of prophetic veneration evokes the neo-Sufism hypothesis propounded by Fazlur Rahman,[40] espoused by John Voll and later contested by O'Fahey and for a time Radke.[41] Proponents of neo-Sufism contend that the veneration of the Prophet as an element of Sufi teaching assumed increased importance in the eighteenth century, leading to more devotional and popular styles of religious practice. In Sufi theory emphasis was correspondingly given to a conceptual dualism rather than earlier philosophical monism – the 'all is He' of *waḥdat al-wujūd*.[42] This parallels other theories of 'organic' religious change in which the 'great empire' stages of world religions as diverse as Hinduism, Christianity, and Islam gave rise to monistic philosophical trends. These, in turn, were later replaced or at least to a large degree superceded by dualistic devotionalism to more personally accessible objects of veneration. This development corresponds to the rise of greater individualism, itself grounded in historical shifts as profound as the fragmentation of empires, the rise of mercantile and other middle classes between the elites and the peasants, and the proliferation of vernacular expressions of religious ideas and piety.[43]

---

[37] *Ibid*., pp. 29–54, 199–210, 224–7.

[38] *Ibid*., p. 199.

[39] *Ibid*., p. 200.

[40] Fazlur Rahman, *Islam* (New York: Doubleday 1968), p. 240.

[41] The increasing prominence of the Prophet in Walī Allāh's visions may be related to one of the characteristics of 'Neo-Sufism' according to John Voll, "Hadith Scholars and Ṭarīqahs: An '*Ulema*' Group," *Journal of Asian and African Studies* 15 (July–October 1980), pp. 262–7. A review of this debate may be found in R.S. O'Fahey, *Enigmatic Saint: Ahmad ibn Idris and the Idrisi Tradition* (Evanston: Northwestern University Press 1990), pp. 1–9 and B. Radke and R.S. O'Fahey "Neo-Sufism Reconsidered," *Islam: Zeitschrift fur Geschichte und Kultur des Orients*, 70/1 (1993), pp. 52–87.

[42] William Chittick, "Rumi and *Waḥdat al-wujūd*" in *Poetry and Mysticism in Islam*: *The Heritage of Rūmī*, ed. A. Banani and G. Sabagh (New York: Cambridge University Press 1994), pp. 218–41 and Alexander Knysh, "Ibrāhīm al-Kūrānī (d. 1101/1690), an Apologist for *waḥdat al-wujūd*" *Journal of the Royal Asiatic Society*, 5/1 (1995), pp. 39–47.

[43] Robert Ellwood, *The History and Future of Faith: Religion Past, Present, and to Come* (New York: Crossroad 1988).

When considering indigenous models of the history of Islamic mysticism, Bruce Lawrence raises the important historiographical question of how Sufis in Mughal India understood their origins. "How did Sufi biographers in the pre-modern period recall the formation of those institutional structures, brotherhoods dedicated to preserving the Divine Trust, that had marked their lives?"[44] Lawrence indicates that their choice of whom to include in biographical compendia (*tadhkira*s), as well as the Sufis' own presentation of lineages, would be a source for deriving these views. For example, two histories of the Qādirī order produced during the seventeenth century by 'Abd al-Ḥaqq Muḥaddith Dihlavī and the Mughal prince Dārā Shikūh took very different perspectives on the history of that order.[45] In this vein, we may inquire as to whether the model of decline, so facilely applied to this period after the fact and in consonance with an overriding narrative of Muslim stagnation and European rise, was one which the Sufis themselves structured into their writings.[46] As we will see in the works of Shāh Walī Allāh, Sufi biographies and the histories of particular Sufi movements were being read in a developmentally progressive way in eighteenth-century India. This, in turn, helped provide a conceptual basis for the renewal espoused by revivalist movements.

There is no doubt that a general sense of criticism of contemporary society and religious life may be found in the contemporary texts, including the *Ḥujjat Allāh al-Bāligha*. In his work *al-Tafhīmāt al-ilāhiyya* Walī Allāh laments the fragmentation of political and intellectual authority pervasive in his times, citing divisive elements and fruitless disputes occurring in Muslim society.[47] As far as a spiritual trajectory is concerned, however, the idea of being heirs to prophecy continues in the Indian Sufi texts from Sirhindī through Walī Allāh and beyond.[48] The eighteenth-century Naqshbandīs reflected on their own exalted status and their authority in projecting new and more advanced formulations. In the case of Shāh Walī Allāh, formulating his own *ṭarīqa* based on a series of advancements through the subtle spiritual centres (*laṭā'if*),[49] and

---

[44] Bruce Lawrence, "An Indo-Persian Perspective on the Significance of Early Persian Sufi Masters," in *The Heritage of Sufism*, I: *Classical Persian Sufism from its Origins to Rumi*, ed. Leonard Lewisohn (Oxford: Oneworld 1999), p. 22.

[45] Bruce Lawrence, "Biography and the seventeenth-century Qadariyya of North India," in *Islam and Indian Regions*, ed. Anna Libera Dallapiccola and Stephanie Zengel-Ave Lallemant (Stuttgart: Franz Steiner 1993), p. 145.

[46] On the idea of permanent progress in Islam, see Meier, "Soufisme et déclin culturel," *passim*.

[47] Shāh Walī Allāh, *al-Tafhīmāt al-ilāhiyya*, I, pp. 110–1.

[48] Yohanan Friedmann, *Prophecy Continuous: Aspects of Ahmadi Religious Thought and its Medieval Background* (Berkeley: University of California Press 1989).

[49] This will be discussed later in the present chapter. On Shāh Walī Allāh's claims to spiritual status see J.M.S. Baljon, *Religion and Thought of Shah Wali Allah al-Dihlavī* (Leiden: Brill 1986), pp. 15–20.

in the case of Mīr Dard and his father, developing the concept of the *ṭarīqa Muḥammadiyya*.[50]

The issue of origins, relationships and transformations permeates Sufi texts of this period. Perhaps one hint of the mentality of the eighteenth-century Sufis of Delhi was that they reflect historical cycles while seeing themselves as being at the summit or completion of a spiritual trajectory. They were the heirs to a closed prophecy and the seals on the openings of new *ṭarīqa*s. In order to illustrate my contention that the eighteenth century represents a period of struggle in which new codes of thinking and writing were emerging in Muslim intellectual life, I am going to focus on several discussions of the history of Sufism according to Shāh Walī Allāh.

The reason that I would like to draw particular attention to this theme is that it reflects the major shift that I believe takes place in eighteenth-century Mughal Sufism. One indication of the importance of this theme is that Shāh Walī Allāh returns again and again to the idea of a historical development of the articulations of Sufi spirituality. This framing incorporates a concept of spiritual genealogy while situating it within broader frameworks of historical change.

I have been influenced in this approach of studying modes of representing historical frameworks by the explanations of the literary critic, Northrop Frye, on the development of "Great Codes" in Western literary/religious history. Taking the Bible as a starting point, Frye presents a thesis of three phases of shifting textual modalities which shaped major civilizational narratives into broader mythological and narratological frameworks. This emplotment of particular elements, persons, and events within larger, even cosmic, frameworks of time and its meaning, is an index of religious consciousness and the way in which it has structured textuality in particular epochs.

I cannot aspire to do more than briefly sketch out a relevant part of Frye's complex and fecund line of argument within the confines of this discussion. Frye sets out a tripartate model of the development of written language from that of sacred texts such as the Bible, to the interpretations of this text in what we might call classical or medieval thought, and finally to the more analytic or descriptive prose of the post-enlightenment period. Frye observes that "In sacred texts, for example, the Bible, imagery and narrative set up a mythological universe within which Western literature operated until the eighteenth century."[51]

The sacred text employs "hieroglyphic" or poetic language in which the subject and object are linked by a common power. This corresponds to the force of metaphor ("this is that") and narrates using a language of immanence with respect to the divine presence or ultimate reality.

---

[50] Schimmel, *Pain and Grace*, p. 32, *passim*.

[51] Northrop Frye, *The Great Code* (New York: Harcourt Brace & Co. 1983), p. xi.

The next phase of written language, generated by early literate elites who interpret sacred texts, features allegoric modes of expression and the form of metonomy in which "this stands for that."[52] According to Frye, the extended prose of "allegory smooths out the discrepancies in a metaphorical structure by making it conform to a conceptual standard."[53] In this phase of writing, it is the quality of divine transcendence that is emphasized.[54]

The third phase, which had always existed in brief conversational communication, is that of extended prose narration. This modern analytic prose reflects the stage at which human beings increasingly experience themselves as differentiated and separated from the world of nature and it is guided the concept of a mind that analyses, derives and tests hypotheses.

In the several examples from the writings of Shāh Walī Allāh that I will cite, it is this element of the broader framework of mythic, allegorical/analogical and analytic or historically descriptive writing that I am trying to excavate.

SHĀH WALĪ ALLĀH

Shāh Walī Allāh (1703–62) is felt by many to be the towering intellectual figure of his time in South Asia. The study of his works reveals a kaleidoscopic array of patterns of historicity. These he derives while attempting to order both objective historical facts and an inspired understanding of the meaning of these facts. The differences in the language and disciplines of his many works clearly vary with the concept of the works' purpose and audience. He wrote in many modes, ranging from Koranic interpretation and translation, *fiqh* and *ḥadīth* studies, and in the most technical Arabic as well as in Persian prose. His master work, the *Ḥujjat Allāh al-Bāligha*[55] has been compared to al-Ghazālī and al-Sulamī in the sense that it is a text on the inner meaning of religious practices (*asrār al-dīn*) explicated in a mystical mode while reinforcing the practice of the *sharī'a* and following the *sunna*.

(a) As my first example I take a passage from Shāh Walī Allāh's Persian work *Hama'āt* (Outpourings). In an attempt to frame the history of Sufism, Shāh Walī Allāh describes a rather Ibn Khaldūnian rise and fall of Sufi orders (*ṭarīqas*) and affiliations (*nisbas*). In the first paragraph, after the praise for God and the Prophet, he writes:

> This is a model of the affiliation (*nisba*) which God the Bestower had placed in my heart in traveling the straight path and an elucidation of the *ṭarīqa* which guides towards God.

---

[52] *Ibid.*, p. 7.
[53] *Ibid.*, p. 10.
[54] *Ibid.*, p. 15.
[55] See the Arabic text and my translation cited in n. 4 above.

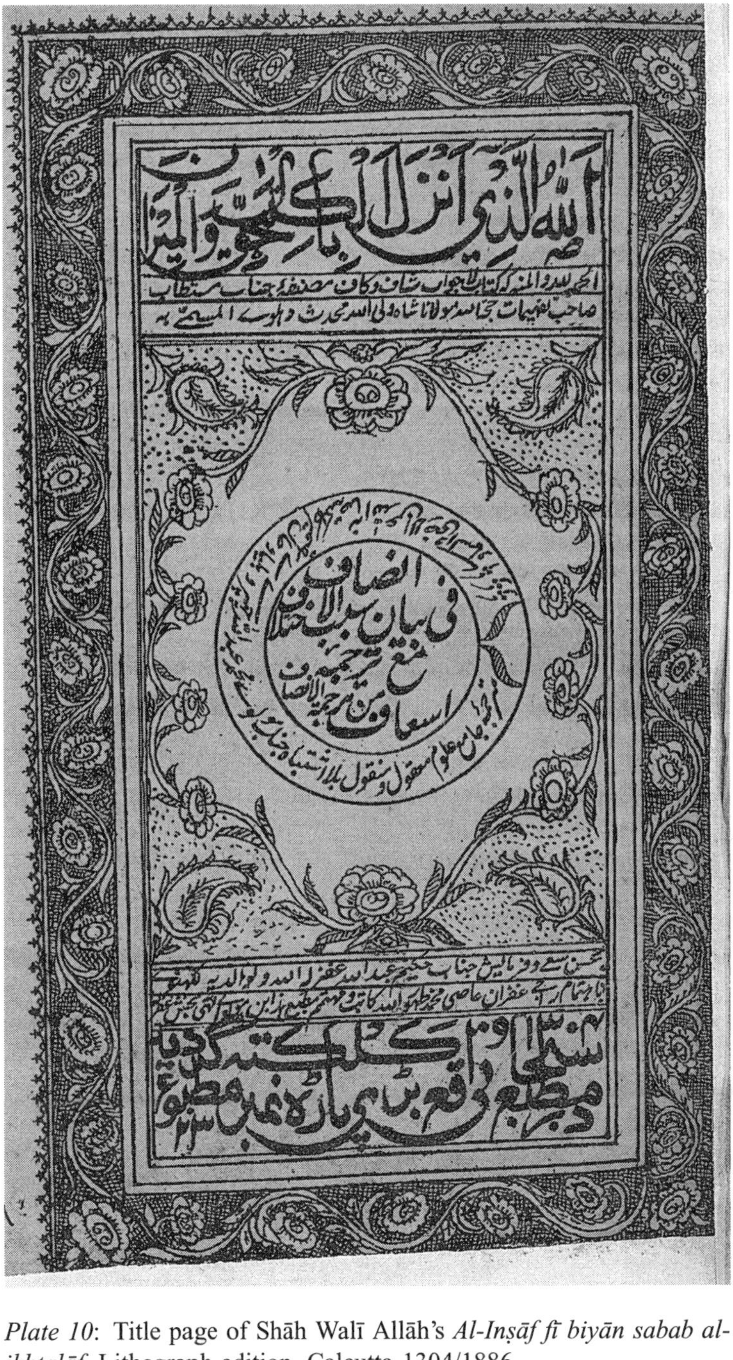

Plate 10: Title page of Shāh Walī Allāh's *Al-Inṣāf fī biyān sabab al-ikhtalāf.* Lithograph edition. Calcutta 1304/1886.

The Muḥammadan religion has an inner and outer aspect. The exoteric dimension derives from the beneficial purposes,[56] forms, expected sources, determined times, locations, and quantities for achieving these (purposes) and the effective support in propagating these and preventing their becoming changed.

The esoteric dimension involves obtaining the illuminations and effects of acts of worship, acquiring these qualities, and so on. Inevitably, the divine assistance and providence preserves the religion through both dimensions distributed across each of these divisions.

After the passing of the Prophet, peace be upon him, following his promise that the divine providence would be preserved among his heirs in accordance with the capacity of those who carried on the tradition, one of the two groups, on the basis of pre-eternal capacity and divine providence, took charge of upholding the exoteric dimension. These are the jurists, *ḥadīth* scholars, warriors (*ghāzīs*), and Koran reciters …

The other group (upholders of the inner dimension) possess in their pre-eternal constitution the connection (*nisbat*) of self-purification (*iḥsān*).[57] Thus, in every age the members of this group are the recourse of the people of that time, and they guide them through their quality of obtaining the illuminations of worship, realizing the benefits and sweetness of it, and taking on the noble virtues and refined states.

In sum, in every age a representative the saints will be born according to the divine providence, and charged with establishing and spreading the interiority of religion and its essence which is *iḥsān*. …

When this is actualized in a particular saint, it results in his being highly respected by the people around him who are drawn toward him and speak highly of him. He will have disclosed to his heart the spiritual practices of the religion of Muḥammad. His company and utterances will have an impact and attraction, and there will occur to him types of miraculous insights. He will have the ability to control and influence human affairs through the power given by God and his prayers will be answered. Seekers will gather around him and his functioning according to the requirements of that spiritual rank in laying out and appointing spiritual exercises, litanies, and so on will ultimately result in a spiritual lineage (*khānvādih*).[58] People will follow the itinerary of this spiritual lineage and achieve quick results. Those who aid it will be successful and its opponents will be repulsed. Both the masses and the elite will crave for it and be in awe of it. …

[This will persist] until such as time when the divine providence will direct itself to some other person, and take root there, bringing another lineage into being. In this case the initial family will be left like a body without a soul, and its spiritual itinerary (*sulūk*) will lose its attractive force (*jadhb*). In some ages there

---

[56] *Maṣāliḥ*: in Shāh Walī Allāh's thought this term refers to the beneficial interests that lie behind the rulings of the divine law.

[57] Muslim mystics often associate the term *iḥsān* (righteousness, self-purification, doing things beautifully) with their interpretation of the most interior or essential aspect of religious practice based on a *ḥadīth* in which the Prophet was asked to explain first Islam, then faith (*īmān*) and, finally, *iḥsān*. His answer was that "*Iḥsān* is to worship God as if you see Him, for even of you cannot see Him, He sees you" Muslim and Bukhārī, S.V. *īmān*).

[58] *Hama'āṭ*, p. 13.

are many spiritual masters (*aqtāb*) with a great master in every region. In reality the attraction to drawing nearer on the paths toward God is an effect of that divine providence, not a decree of any particular spiritual lineage. This is like the reflection of the stars in a stream of water, for if the water in a stream changes a thousand times, what effect will it have on the form.

> If the garments are changed from time to time,
> What harm does it do to the person wearing them

Still in every time the leaders and disciples speak to the effect that their lineage is the best, affirming its proximity and achievement of the objective, and they are correct to the extent that I have indicated.

In sum, there are many Sufi lineages, there have been many in the past, and there will be many in the future.[59]

Shāh Walī Allāh then discusses topics such as the revival of these Sufi 'families,' whether they constitute fourteen sub-groups,[60] and so on.

I would characterize this model of the rise and fall of Sufi movements as an explanation of historical processes. A pervasive theme in Shāh Walī Allāh's understanding of these phases in his historical depiction of Sufism is that all these *ṭarīqa*s basically agree on the basis of the path (*aṣl-i ṭarīqat*). He constructs the teachings of Sufi *ṭarīqa*s here as temporally reinvigorated and transformed inspirations of teachings that are constantly being renewed along the lines of 'Renewership' (*mujaddidiyya*). Thus, one may expect revivals and further spiritual attainments within Sufism to continue.

(b) In the next section or chapter of the same work,[61] Shāh Walī Allāh returns to the same theme, this time presenting another historical structure for the development of Sufism by laying out a model of four phases. "There have been four comprehensive changes during the path of Sufism," he declares:

> In the time of the Prophet and his Companions and for a number of later centuries, the focus of the people of perfection was usually on the primary objective of the external divine law, and all other dimensions were absorbed in that. The *iḥsān*[62] of this group consisted of performing prayer, fasting, rememberance of God, recitation of the Koran, pilgrimage, giving alms and participating in *jihād*. They did not intellectualize, although they experienced the spiritual pleasure of these practices and they did not incline to ecstatic or altered states of mind or make ecstatic utterances. Neither did they have knowledge of the divine theophanies and self-veiling. Their longing was for paradise and their fear hell-fire. If they exhibited mystical insights, miracles, intoxicated states, or being overwhelmed (by ecstasy), it was incidental, not intentional, or it may have been due to factors of personal inclination.[63]

---

[59] *Ibid.*, pp. 13–14.

[60] The precise number of Sufi sects is a topic that came to be broadly discussed in Sufi writings. Hujwīrī in his *Kashf al-maḥjūb* (p. 176) states that there were twelve Sufi lineages.

[61] Shāh Walī Allāh, *Hama'āt*, pp. 16–19.

[62] See n. 57 above.

[63] *Ibid.*, p. 17.

1. This first phase is sober Sufism, characterized by following the Islamic law (*sharī'a*), the absence of ecstatic states (*wajd*), and the fear of hell and desire for paradise.
2. The second phase, epitomized by the figure of Junayd (d. 298/910) is characterized by asceticism and the connection of the heart to God:

> In the time of the master of the Sufi school, Junayd, and slightly earlier, another tendency emerged. Generally the people involved maintained the same attitudes, but some of the elite ones obtained a special spiritual state after making great efforts, performing severe austerities, completely cutting themselves off from the world, and continuous practice. This state consists of total focus on the connection (*nisba*) of attaching the heart to God. Thus they directed their attention to Him and began to instruct in this way, and they remained for long periods in contemplation. They began to clarify the states of divine manifestation and self-veiling, intimacy and alienation, and they explained these states with anecdotes and allusions. It is truer of this state of Sufism to say that they only expressed what they had experienced personally. They began to like the audition of music. Ecstatic states and dance appeared among them for the first time, along with elaborate theories of thought processes and intuitions. They separated themselves from the masses and went to the mountains and wilderness. In food they sufficed with grass and tree leaves and they dressed in patched robes. Their sincerity was such that they worshipped God neither out of fear of hell nor ambition for paradise, but rather out of love for Him.[64]

3. Then came the phase of eradicating the lower soul or ego (*nafs*) represented for Shāh Walī Allāh by the Sufis, Abū Sa'īd ibn Abī'l-Khayr (d. 440/1049)[65] and Abū l-Ḥasan Kharaqānī (d. 426/1034).

> In the age of the ruler of the Path (*sulṭān al-ṭarīqa*), Shaykh Abū Sa'īd ibn Abī'l-Khayr, it (Sufism) took another form. The generality of people remained fixed on actions while the elite concentrated on the states. The elite of the elite achieved an attraction through which they were guided to a specific aspect of lifting the veils on the Essence sustaining all things, being absorbed into Him and taking on His qualities. Thus they were not so occupied with litanies and spiritual practices nor with austerities and difficult exercises, and they were not so concerned with recognizing the deceptions of the ego and the world. Their total concern was with perfecting that focus and all of these other spiritual experiences (*nisba*), they termed 'veils of light'. At this time they distinguished between the unity of witnessing (*tawḥīd shuhūdī*) and the unity of essence (*tawḥīd wujūdī*). However, their essential goal was achieving the state of annihilation or extinguishing the individual ego.[66]

---

[64] *Ibid.*, pp. 17–18.
[65] On whom, see Terry Graham, "Abū Sa'īd ibn Abī'l-Khayr and the School of Khurāsān," in Lewisohn, *Heritage of Sufism*, I, pp. 83–135.
[66] *Hama'āt*, pp. 8–19.

4. In the fourth stage, Ibn 'Arabī represents the culminating figure who is said to have penetrated the descending emanations (*tanzīlāt*) of the One.[67]

> After that, in the age of the Greatest Shaykh Muḥyī al-Dīn Ibn 'Arabī and slightly before him, their outlook broadened and they went from states of psychological ecstasy (*wijdān nafsāniyya*) to investigating the realities of the higher [commanding] self (*nafs al-amriyya*) as it really is, and to understanding the descending manifestations of the Necessary Being. They came to recognize the identity of the First Emanator, the process of emanation, and matters of this type.[68]

This depiction of the history of Sufism represents a shift in Shāh Walī Allāh's framing concept of sacred history. Here he is attempting to explain the success or even charismatic appeal of certain figures and movements based both on their own intrinsic spiritual makeup and on the suitability of that constitution or mission for a particular age. The development or succession of these ages is not random, but rather is evolutionary in terms of a particular divine plan or providence. The frameworks of myth and allegory can incorporate historical elements and personages, even fairly recent ones, into the system. This strategy can also be applied in explaining contemporary events.

The association of certain historical Sufis and their teachings with transitions of thought and practice within the tradition indicates that through extensive study of the Sufi biographical (*tadhkira*) literature and the original Sufi texts Shāh Walī Allāh had formed a developmental understanding of Sufi ideas and practice. This led him to the important analytical conclusion that, "It is necessary that the writings of each age of Sufis be interpreted in the light of the tastes and inclinations (*adhwāq*) of the contemporary period and that one [Sufi thinker] should not be judged according to the taste of another."[69]

(c) A further example of Shāh Walī Allāh's approach to Sufi history is his statement in *al-Tafhīmāt al-ilāhiyya* about the history and identity of his own *ṭarīqa*. Whether this passage indicates that Shāh Walī Allāh had the intention of starting a new movement or whether he was using the term *ṭarīqa* in a less specific sense may be questioned. It seems that the abstract nature of his formulation of this "method of the perfect one (*ṭarīqa al-kamāl*)" makes it likely that the concepts are esoteric rather than applicable to an organized movement. Its ideas are incipiently revivalistic when they suggest an optimism regarding further spiritual experience and practice. The fact that his approach is eclectic and decentralized, however, reflects the fact that he did not function

[67] In fact, in another location Shāh Walī Allāh sees Ibn 'Arabī's teachings as opening the highest levels of annihilation (*fanā'*) in the hidden spiritual centres. (*al-Tafhīmāt al-ilāhiyya*, I, p. 168).
[68] *Hama'āt*, p. 19.
[69] *Ibid*., p. 20.

as a reorganizer of any specific *ṭarīqa* organization. This may be taken as an indication of his transitional position between previous concepts of Sufi *ṭarīqa* identities and the reorganized or renewed Sufi movements of the nineteenth century.

The entire text of this passage is too lengthy to reproduce here in full. I will, however, quote extensively in order to illustrate its structuring through seven eras or cycles. What I would particularly like to highlight is his structuring of Sufi history as a new mythic narrative. The passage is particularly interesting and significant because in it Shāh Walī Allāh is formulating his own *ṭarīqa*, providing an insight into what this term meant for him. This *ṭarīqa* formulation, however, seems to be less about a specific identity and a series of practices than about the charismatic efficaciousness of a path and its founder at a particular historical moment. Some questions which are presented by the text are: was Shāh Walī Allāh moving toward a more eclectic sense of Sufi identity and affiliation;[70] did this map an institutionalized movement or set of practices, and was this an aspect of a broader *ṭarīqa Muḥammadiyya* movement?

The Way of Perfection (Kamāl)[71]

> God, blessed and exalted, bestows whatsoever He wills on whomsoever He wills. None can forbid His decree and there is no limit to His generosity. Among His greatest grace and kindness to me is that He bestowed upon me the way of perfection, and determined its rules for me and showed me its methods, after He had taught me the stations and states of those who have drawn near to God, both in detail and generally. Through it the Prophets, may peace be upon them, can be imitated in their states and stations. One of them [the stations] is 'perfection' which the Prophet indicated when he said, "Many men have been perfected."[72]
>
> You should know that our *ṭarīqa* can be explained proceeding through seven cycles. Whenever one of its cycles comes to an end another develops out of it.[73]

FIRST STAGE

At this juncture, Shāh Walī Allāh presents the first stage of his *tarīqa* as that of "True faith (*īmān ḥaqīqī*)." It consists of purifying the original nature (*fiṭra*) with which every person is endowed. This is described as the sphere of reason for which prophet Adam is the exemplary model.

---

[70] Hermansen, "Mystical Paths."

[71] *Al-Tafhīmāt al-ilāhiyya*, II, pp. 2–82. Discussed in Baljon, *Religion and Thought*, pp. 112–3, but only in terms of its prophetology, not as hagiology.

[72] The exact wording of this *ḥadīth* is not found in the standard collections but a commonly cited report mentions the perfection of many men as well as of two women, the wife of Pharoah and Mary, daughter of 'Imrān.

[73] *Al-Tafhīmāt al-ilāhiyya*, II, p. 72.

SECOND STAGE

He terms the second stage the "Opening of the Breast" (*sharḥ al-ṣadr*):

> God said, "And the one whose breast Allāh has expanded for Islam"[74] and "Did We not expand your breast,"[75] and the Prophet was asked about what they referred to and he answered, "Emptying oneself of the abode of pride and turning toward the eternal abode."[76]
>
> The true nature of this stage consists of breaking down the lowest level of the spirit (*nasama*)[77] in its essence (*jawhar*) through its clashing with the spiritual attraction (*jadhb*) [of being drawn to God]. This is because everything in existence has a connection to God. Thus it was legislated to worship God's Essence (*'ayn*), and to prostrate before Him in reality, from pre-eternity to post-eternity. In sum, the saints call this "the first stage of annihilation."

THIRD STAGE

The third stage is that of "drawing-near [to God] through supererogatory actions" (*qurb al-nawāfil*),[78] the core of which, he states, "is breaking down the essence of the ego:"

> There are various sorts of 'drawing-near to God' through supererogatory practices (*nawāfil*). It is understood by many of the wise persons that these share in certain verbal expressions. One case is that God theophanizes in the form of a person's lower soul (*nafs*) in an actualized, external way and this is the peak of the summit and the center of the circle. This is what is referred to in the *ḥadīth* when he said, "I become his hearing." It seems that it has not been bestowed on anyone of the community which we are investigating except one or two persons, who are al-Khiḍr and Shaykh 'Abd al-Qādir [Jīlānī].
>
> A second case would be when the blowing of spiritual attraction (*jadhb*) clashed against the rigidity of the ego (*nafs*) and the attraction would keep on struggling against the ego (*nafs*) until the person would become like burned out grass whose reality was gone but whose [external] form remained. Shaykh Bahā' al-Din Naqshband [d. 1390] is the epitome of this type, and his spiritual attraction (*jadhb*) kept him in this state [of annihilation] throughout his entire life.[79]

What merits our attention in this case is Shāh Walī Allāh's use of specific figures from the history of Sufism to illustrate certain spiritual conditions, which are then interpreted as signifying something further about a particular age. Thus, we see him operating a process of mythologizing Sufi history in

---

[74] Koran XXXIX:22.
[75] Koran XCIV:1.
[76] An unusual *ḥadīth* cited in Tirmidhī and Bayhaqī.
[77] The pneuma or the lowest level of the Spirit according to Shāh Walī Allāh. This breaking down is done in order to strengthen the power of the rational soul (*nafs al-nāṭiqa*), an intermediate stage on the way to the higher spirit.
[78] Some of the names of these stages or eras are commonly found in previous Sufi theories, for example the drawing near through obligatory and supererogatory practices.
[79] *Al-Tafhīmāt al ilāhiyya*, II, p. 76.

order to elaborate a broader framework of understanding. In this case, the cyclical nature of spiritual unfoldment, in which the gnostic recognizes or awakens to the contemplation of the One, is combined with a linear salvation history.

FOURTH STAGE

The fourth stage is wisdom (*ḥikma*):

> "Whoever is given the *ḥikma* is given the greatest good" [Koran II:269]
>
> The Prophet said about the characteristics of the substitutes (*abdāl*),[80] that "they are not preferred due to much praying nor fasting, but they are preferred due to magnanimity of soul."[81]
>
> According to us, wisdom is 'existential drawing-near' (*qurb al-wujūd*). Its essence consists of the person's remaining as he was pre-eternally insofar as his fixed essence (*'ayn thābita*) is worshipping and prostrating before God, drawn near to Him, transcending evil and corruptions. This represents the condition of the preceding types of knowledge, the place to find complete sinlessness, and the location of the previous positions.
>
> Once I had attained this station, the science of the divine names was disclosed to me, as well as the science of bringing into existence and drawing nearer to God, the divine legislation, the last days, the wonders of the human being. . . .The saints have continued to stand firm in their faith, and they have deeply sought out the annihilation of the rational soul. Annihilation (*fanā'*) is a garment and an inner aspect, and their state is never completely free from focusing on it. Faith is an outer dress and an overt thing towards which their references were directed and their expressions were targeted, until the Sufis came along.
>
> The first of them was *Dāwud al-Ṭā'ī* (d. 162–5/778–81),[82] then came *Ma'rūf al-Karkhī* (200/815),[83] and *al-Sarī* (*al-Saqaṭī*) (d. 253/867).[84] They were firmly established in the (stage of) the opening of the breast and their meanings pointed towards annihilation of the lower self. Thus, when they became grounded in annihilation (*fanā'*), it became apparent that comprehending it and reaching its core could not be achieved until the drawing-near through supererogatory practices (*nawāfil*) could transcend the drawing-near of obligatory worship in its rules and effects. Then there succeeded them in this persons who came after them until the generation of *Abū Sa'īd* (*ibn Abī'l- Khayr*) (d. 440/1049)[85] and *Aḥmad-i Jām* (d. 536/1141)[86] and the way was streamlined for them, and perfection

---

80 The *abdāl* are one of the ranks of the spiritual government of the saints according to one *ḥadīth*. There are either forty or seven of them at any time. Cf. Annemarie Schimmel, *Mystical Dimensions of Islam* (Chapel Hill: University of North Carolina Press 1975), p. 200.

81 This *ḥadīth* is not found in the standard collections.

82 On Dāwud al-Ṭā'ī see al-Dhahabī, *Siyar 'alam al-nubalā'* (Beirut: al-Risāla 1982), VII, pp. 422–5.

83 "He was among the first to speak of divine love, and his teaching that one cannot learn love, for it is a divine gift and not an acquisition, has had a great impact on mystical thought" (Schimmel, *Mystical Dimensions*, p. 53).

84 He was a disciple of al-Karkhī. "Biographers claim that Sarī was the first to discuss the various mystical states (*aḥwāl*)" (*Ibid.*).

> overflowed from their very selves. Then God theophanized to *Shaykh 'Abd al-Qādir* (d. 562/1166) and the storm of attraction (*jadhb*) carried away *Shaykh Bahā al-Dīn* (Naqshband).
>
> Then God, may He be praised, brought forth perfection in a new sense that mixed annihilation with wisdom for *Shaykh Muḥyī ud-Dīn Ibn al-'Arabī* and this resulted in various types of spiritual knowledge. Once it became apparent that comprehending them was completed, the intelligent ones continued to treat some part of them.
>
> Then *Shaykh Aḥmad Sirhindī* (d. 1035/1625) came along and foretold the reappearance of Jesus, peace be upon him, and the light of prophecy shone upon him in its generality. Then the lights of the unseen flowed over me and I attained the station of wisdom (*ḥikma*) and on that day I was made the deputy of Joseph,[87] because he is the one who possessed wisdom (*ḥikma*) among the Prophets.

The fourth stage, wisdom, is clearly of great importance in Shāh Walī Allāh's schema. Within this spiritual stage of 'existential drawing-near', he mentions all the stages in the development of Sufism: for example, the Sufis of Baghdad and Khurāsān, as well as the Indian Naqshbandīs, including himself.

FIFTH STAGE

This stage is called *qurb al-farā'iḍ*, or the 'drawing-near through the obligatory acts of worship':

> The fifth stage is the 'drawing-near' through the obligatory acts of worship. The Prophet said, in a *ḥadīth qudsī*, "I have not brought near to my servant anything dearer to me that performing what I had made obligatory on him."[88]
>
> My Lord made me understand, may His majesty be exalted, that whatever [divine] name should come to dominate a person, the signs of this would be that he would be able to effect his desire in the world and that he would be forced to some strong vision. When I had completed this cycle I made a covenant on the following matters:
>
> 1. That my heart and physical form would be totally devoted constantly to worship;
> 2. that if anyone needs me or is attracted to me for support, either in matters of faith only, or in other ways of drawing nearer to God [Sufism], I will prevent him from worshipping or asking for help from any other than God and from having doubts, fleeting thoughts,[89] and other related matters;

---

[85] Said to be the first Sufi to draw up a preliminary monastic rule for his disciples. He was also known for his austerities (*ibid.*, p. 241).

[86] Said to have received the Sufi cloak of succession from Abū Sa'īd. He seems to have been known for sternness rather than love, but like Abū Sa'īd could exemplify a period before formal Sufi orders came into existence (*ibid.*, p. 244).

[87] This reference to Yūsuf/Joseph may be associated with the title of the larger work since *al-tafhīmāt* can refer to Joseph's abilities in dream interpretation.

[88] *Ḥadīth* (Bukhārī, *Riqāq,* 38). This is the earlier part of the "*ḥadīth* of supererogatory prayers (*nawāfil*)."

[89] There is a problem in the text at this point, I read *khaṭir* rather than *khaṭm*.

3. that there can be no connection of love between me and another person unless this is permeated by the coloring of God;
4. to follow the path of the prophets and their practice;
5. not to be one of the *'ulamā'* thriving in worldly life, inclined to the world and its offspring in knowledge and dealings.

SIXTH STAGE

The sixth stage is the drawing nearer to God through the Angelic Realm (*qurb al-malakūtī*):

> The Prophet said, "God, when he loves a servant calls Gabriel and says, 'I love so and so, so love him'." "He said, 'Then Gabriel loves him, then he proclaims in the heavens saying, 'God loves so and so, so love him and the people of the heavens love him so that he will receive a good reception on the earth'."[90] God says, may He be praised, "Those who believe and do good works, the Merciful One will create love for them."[91]
>
> Once this cycle expanded, all of the world was put under our supervision, in management and control, and we became aware of the source of the divine law and the explanations of the prophets for it, elaborating and interpreting it.

SEVENTH STAGE

The seventh spiritual stage is the attainment of perfection (*al-kamāl*):

> The seventh is the stage of perfection. The Prophet said, "Many men have been perfected and among women only Khadīja bint Khawlaid, Miryam daughter of 'Imrān, Āsiya the wife of Pharaoh and Fāṭima daughter of Muḥammad."[92] Its essence is uniting the worshipper with his perfections that reach out towards God, imploring Him with the tongue of their capacities so that He bestows a new level of perfection obtained from mixing of these six [previous] elements in the emanation of a sanctified form upon them. The beloved of God [set out][93] in this cycle, then he kept on developing until he became the seal of the prophets.
>
> When this stage began for me, I saw [a vision] while I was sitting after the afternoon prayer, as if my clothing had been removed until I was completely naked. Then there appeared a theophany of the Prophet and he stood at my left side. I put on the clothing of validation, and the lowest level of the spirit (*nasama*) uttered a cry saying, "Truth, truth, truth." Then it became calm and this was an emanation of validation, comprehensively. Then an emanation of eternal blessing descended from above and on my right and on my left, transcending all verbal expressions and beyond all description, so praise be to God, Lord of the worlds. This is the end of what I wanted to explain with respect to the *ṭarīqa* that was bestowed on me, as a totality, on the basis of allusion and symbol.[94]

---

[90] A well-known *ḥadīth* found in Bukhārī, Muslim and other collections.
[91] Koran XIX:96.
[92] *Ḥadīth*. See n. 73 above.
[93] Blank space in the original manuscript according to editor's note in *al-Tafhīmāt al-ilāhiyya*, II, p. 81.
[94] *Al-Tafhīmāt al-ilāhiyya*, II, p. 82.

These passages from *al-Tafhīmāt al-ilāhiyya* can be taken to represent Shāh Walī Allāh's attempt to combine frameworks of sacred history with elements of the actual historical development of the Sufi tradition within Islam. Both Koranic and *ḥadīth* citations initiate his presentation of each of the eras, in a sense legitimizing the *sharīʿa* basis of the formulation. Here, Shāh Walī Allāh is adding something new to the discussion of sacred history: his prophetology lays out a theory of human spiritual development that parallels the sending of the prophets, building on the Islamic idea that each prophet has a certain speciality. This Sufi prophetology, derived from elaborating the structure of a Koranic narrative, follows a pattern established by classic mystical texts such as Ibn ʿArabī's *Fuṣūṣ al-ḥikam*. However, in the case of Shāh Walī Allāh we find an additional idea elaborated: that these progressive spiritual developments continue among the heirs to the prophets, specifically the Sufis. Thus, inner development, or *iqtirāb* ('drawing-nearer' to God), does not end with the seal of prophecy.[95] At the same time, this model still maintains the concept of the person of Muḥammad as the epitome of perfection towards which all improvements are directed, as he is the completion of both prophecy and sainthood.[96]

CONCLUSIONS

In the selections from the writings of Shāh Walī Allāh presented above, we find evidence of an eighteenth-century mystic's struggle to understand the development of the Sufi tradition in the light of a broader framework of 'Perfection History'. The actors in this history extend past the seal of prophecy to the saints, known to Shāh Walī Allāh through Sufi biographical literature. These historical figures are associated with styles of piety and qualities of experience based on their own writings, as well as on the way Sufi tradition has memorialized them.

The style of these writings is one in which the system of conceptual organization shapes the narrative. The allegory precedes and controls the understanding of any parts, even those derived from historical fact and empirical observation and analysis, a style typical of pre-modern analogical thinking and writing.

The eighteenth-century Mughal era may be understood as a transitional period in which the baroque and ornate Indian style of expression began to reflect new trends, evidencing a shift towards the enhanced role of the

---

[95] J.M.S. Baljon, "Prophetology of Shāh Walī Allāh," *Islamic Studies*, 9 (1970), pp. 69–79. Friedman, *Prophecy Continuous*, pp. 86–92, discusses the "people who are spoken to (*muḥaddathūn*)," among other types of "continuous prophecy."

[96] This idea is represented elsewhere in Shāh Walī Allāh's diagrammatic representations of the respective paths of sainthood and prophecy as discussed in Hermansen, "Mystical Paths."

individual. Elements typical of this movement include the use of symbols in the service of arguments reinforcing identity,[97] and a transition from intuitive to more cognitive forms of interpretive strategies.[98] In considering how these various systems are laid out by Shāh Walī Allāh in overlapping grids, we note that they are not jugglings along the line of the bricoleur or the kaleidoscope analogies given in structuralist explanations of mythological thinking.[99] The individual parts are not merely random elements that derive their meaning through incorporation into a mythic structure. Rather, each individual element has a religious and symbolic meaning as part of an earlier structure that must then make sense in a new configuration. Thus, the positioning of historical elements within mythic structures transforms both in a new act of interpretation. The fact that Shāh Walī Allāh's writings combine mythical or religious cosmologies with historical explanation makes them transitional between pre-modern and modern 'scientific' ways of understanding phenomena. Therefore, the characteristic of the eighteenth century as a period of transition from pre-modern to modern ways of thinking and writing is evidenced by Shāh Walī Allāh's attempt to reconcile the mythic structure of sacred cycles with the linearity of salvation history, historical fact and personal observation.

His scheme of systems of symbols which work together reminds us of a sort of divinatory system: it is not just a passive reflection capable of explaining the past, but also has a generative capacity for projecting the past into the future.[100] Far from being mechanistic, these symbols allow a certain imaginal or poetic approach to translating actual experience into patterns of progressive spiritual awakening (*laṭā'if*), the sequence of Prophetic revelations, and the mystical realizations of the Sufi saints.

Shāh Walī Allāh's efforts to systematize, as part of a broader project of reconciling divergent perspectives in Muslim theology, law and exegesis, have made his writings particularly fertile ground for those seeking evidence of transitional strategies of thinking and writing in eighteenth-century Islam. The Persianate milieu of late Mughal Sufism and its concerns with identity, authority, and cultural synthesis, no doubt, contributed to the emergence of these themes in his writings.

In his explanation of changing modalities of narrative, Northrop Frye takes note of the increasing separation of subject and object in modern eras of

---

[97] See Marcia K. Hermansen, "Citing the Sights at the Holy Sights: Visionary Pilgrimage Narratives of Pre-Modern South Asian Sufis," in *Discourses of American Islam*, ed. Earle Waugh and Frederick M. Denny (Atlanta: Scholars Press, forthcoming).

[98] Marcia K. Hermansen, "Mystical Visions as 'Good to Think': Examples from Pre-Modern South Asian Sufi Thought," *Religion*, 27/1 (1997), pp. 25–43.

[99] Claude Levi-Strauss, *The Savage Mind* (Chicago: University of Chicago Press 1966), p. 17.

[100] On the relationship between canonical schemes of organization and divinitory possibilities see Jonathan Z. Smith "Sacred Persistence: Towards a Redescription of Canon," in his *Imagining Religion* (Chicago: University of Chicago Press 1983), pp. 36–52.

textual expression. He correlates the prevalence of the concept of 'spirit' with the mythic or metaphorical character of early sacred texts influenced by oral traditions in which this subject/object separation is far from absolute. The subsequent emergence of the interpretive writings of pre-modern literate cultures is marked in thinking and narration by increased references to the 'soul'. This concept reflects an increased awareness of individual human identity. The transcendent referent is signified in such texts by the mode of metonomy and the form of allegory. Modern descriptive or analytic narrative, however, is inhabited by the human 'mind' in which the subject is separate from the world it observes. This clearly is not the same as the intellect (*'aql*) of classical Islamic writing nor even of Shāh Walī Allāh, for whom the intellect is still infused with elements of soul and spirit. In the passages cited above, the author maintains the role of the divine agent and purpose guiding the inner and outer events of human experience.

In terms of the motif of the decline of Sufism, the connection made in the earlier mystical texts through myth and allegory to transcendent realms of meaning is more difficult to sustain in later, more expository forms of prose, as well as in polemic or legalistic texts. We latter-day readers experience the shift as a flattening or decline in the quality of mystical writing occasioned by the retreat of these prior modalities. Ultimately, the extent to which these shifts in narration reflect historical changes in individual imagination and spiritual self-fashioning is a topic that remains to be investigated.

Chishtī Meditation Practices of the Later Mughal Period

CARL W. ERNST

How does one define a Sufi order? I would like to pose this question in relation to the Chishtiyya, the most widespread Sufi lineage in South Asia.[1] The organization of the Sufi orders as societies based on teaching lineages seems to have been largely the work of the twelfth and thirteenth centuries. Most Sufi orders are named after a famous figure who is viewed in effect as the founder. In this way the Suhrawardiyya Order is named after Abū Ḥafs al-Suhrawardī, the Aḥmadiyya after Aḥmad al-Badawī, and the Shādhiliyya after Abū al-Ḥasan al-Shādhilī.[2] The founders are generally those masters who codified and institutionalized the distinctive teachings and practices of the orders, although in many cases their reputations as saints go far beyond the circle of initiates. Most orders were localized to particular regions, though a few such as the Qādiriyya and the Naqshbandiyya are found widely distributed across many Muslim countries. The orders expanded as teaching networks based on initiatic genealogy; each master's authority derived from that of his predecessor, in a chain going back to the Prophet Muḥammad. Within each main order there are frequently sub-orders, sometimes designated by composite names with two or more elements to indicate how many levels of branching have occurred. In this way one sees the Ma'rūfī–Rifā'ī Order, the Jarrāhī–Khilvatī (or Cerrahi–Halveti) Order, and the Sulaymānī–Niẓāmī–Chishtī Order. Some of the main sub-branches were formed in the fifteenth and sixteenth centuries or even later.

The Chishtī Order is not named after a particular individual but rather a place that symbolizes an entire lineage. Chisht, not far from Herāt, is one of the two ancient Sufi centres in eastern Khurāsān (present-day Afghanistan),

---

[1] This essay has been written in the context of a larger study by Bruce B. Lawrence and myself: *Burnt Hearts: The Chishtī Sufi Order* (forthcoming from Curzon Press).

[2] The Arabic feminine termination '-iyya' found in, e.g., Qādiriyya, assumes the word *ṭarīqa* or 'way', in the phrase '*al-ṭarīqat al-Qādiriyya*', 'the Qādiriyya way'. One can also for convenience use the masculine form and speak of 'the Qādirī Order'.

along with Jām (home to the famous early master Aḥmad-i Jām [d. 1142], whose verses have been of particular importance to the Chishtīs). The historical origins of the shrine at Chisht are shrouded in obscurity, but it goes back at least to the early tenth century, when Abū Isḥāq of Syria was directed by his Baghdadian master 'Ulū Dīnawarī to go to this obscure outpost at the eastern edge of the Islamic world. Although he is reported to have returned to Acre to be buried, his disciple Abū Aḥmad Abdāl (d. 966) was buried at Chisht, thus inaugurating the first recognizable stage of the pre-Indian Chishtiyya.[3] But it is not until the thirteenth century, when Mu'īn al-Dīn Chishtī reached India, that the Chishtī order emerged into the light of history.

A Sufi order like the Chishtiyya can be looked at from a variety of perspectives. One way to chart this kind of tradition is through institutional forms, particularly the patronage structures that supported the development of shrine cults around the tombs of Sufi saints. Another perspective is the lineage itself. Within the Sufi tradition, after the formation of the orders, their articulation in the form of an initiatic lineage was to some extent a retrospective reconstruction. There are few examples of complete lineages going back to the Prophet prior to the eleventh century, and critics were suspicious of their historical authenticity.[4] Yet the symbolic importance of these lineages was immense; they provided a channel to divine authority through the horizontal medium of tradition. Regardless of their verifiability in external historical terms, the chains of masters and disciples were necessary for the transmission of spiritual power and blessings.

Nevertheless, the historical development of the Sufi orders is still imperfectly understood, since so many sources remain unstudied. This has not prevented some scholars from attempting to describe a historical pattern to the Sufi orders taken as a whole. The most ambitious attempt to provide a historiographical interpretation was provided by J. Spencer Trimingham, a specialist in the history of Islam in Africa, in his book *The Sufi Orders in Islam*. Trimingham enunciated a threefold theory of the development of Sufism which has more than a passing resemblance to the tripartite schemes that litter the landscape of Western historiography (ancient–medieval–modern, etc.). The valuable information collected in this sympathetic and learned compendium is marred by a theory of classicism and decline, divided into three periods. Trimingham called the first period of early Sufism "a natural expression of personal religion ... over against institutionalized religion based on authority." This stage was succeeded by a second period, of the formation of *ṭarīqa* 'ways' in groups based on chains of masters and disciples, around the

---

[3] Mutiul Imam, "Abu Esḥāq Šāmī," *EIr*, I, p. 280; *idem*, "'Abdūl Čestī, Abū Aḥmad," *EIr*, I, p. 175.

[4] J. Spencer Trimingham, *The Sufi Orders in Islam* (Oxford: Oxford University Press 1971), pp. 261–3.

twelfth century. The full institutionalization of Sufism into *ṭā'ifa*s or organizations was the third and final period, beginning about the fifteenth century. While the association of the orders with saints' tombs as state-sponsored centres of devotion ensured their popular success, Trimingham argues, this institutionalization led to a decline of Sufism from its original pure mysticism. After this point he sees no originality, but sterile repetition of the past and an unfortunate tendency to hereditary succession of authority. The result of this 'deeper spiritual malaise' was the transformation of the orders into hierarchical structures that, to him, were uncomfortably similar to the Christian church and its clergy.[5] Trimingham's observations contain a modern and strongly Protestant attitude that champions 'personal religion' over 'institutionalized religion', and his theory of decline logically derives from his assumption that mysticism must be a personal and individual phenomenon. The notion of historical decline is a rhetorical strategy for evaluating and classifying history according to what one considers to be of real value and what constitutes a departure from that. Most theories of the rise and fall of civilizations (from Gibbon to Toynbee) are very selective in the time-frames used for comparison, and their assumptions about the relationship between moral status and the success of political power are unprovable. The 'classicism and decline' model has long exercised a fascination over students of Islamic culture.[6] It is especially odd to notice that the 'decline' of Islamic civilization has been an unquestioned axiom accepted until recently by most orientalists, secular modernists and fundamentalists, but for different reasons. In all these cases, the colonization of much of the Muslim world and the consequent loss of political power by Muslims were interpreted moralistically as the judgement of either history or God upon a civilization that had become inadequate.[7] The notion of the decline of Muslim nations was especially attractive to the self-image of Europeans in the colonial period, since it provided a noble justification for conquest and empire on the basis of the 'civilizing mission' of the West (also known as 'the white man's burden'). If, however, we do not intend to support any of these agendas, then the notion of 'classicism and decline' is distinctly unhelpful in the study of a tradition such as Sufism.[8]

---

[5] Trimingham, *The Sufi Orders*, pp. 2, 70–1.

[6] Gustave E. von Grunebaum, ed., *Klassizismus und Kulturverfall; Vorträge* (Frankfurt am Main: V. Klostermanns 1960).

[7] For a fundamentalist 'golden age' view of Islam, see the historical charts in Isma'il R. al Faruqi and Lois Lamya' al Faruqi, *The Cultural Atlas of Islam* (New York: Macmillan 1986).

[8] Trimingham explicitly states that "the decline in the orders is symptomatic of the failure of Muslims to adapt their traditional interpretation of Islam for life in a new dimension" (pp. 256–7), i.e., the failure of Muslims to become totally Westernized. The most powerful critique of the notion of the 'decline' of Islamic civilization was provided by Marshall G.S. Hodgson in *The Venture of Islam: Conscience and History in a World Civilization* (Chicago: University of Chicago Press 1974), III.

When we come to the Chishtiyya, it is apparent that the 'golden age' syndrome so favoured by orientalists has had a very strong impact. The vast majority of studies of Chishtī Sufism concern a handful of 'great saints' from the thirteenth and fourteenth centuries, who in many cases are still treated with hagiographic reverence. It must be acknowledged that this classical approach to Sufism to some extent mirrors a strong golden age historiography that is deeply etched into Muslim piety, based on the model of 'pristine Medina' under the Prophet Muḥammad as the perfection which later generations can admire but never equal. Yet this backward-looking concept of history has always been balanced by a strong notion of renewal, which is typically embodied in at least one outstanding religious leader in each century. And while even the earliest handbooks of Sufism are notorious for proclaiming that true Sufism no longer existed in their day (a thousand years ago!), the ongoing reality of sainthood as a manifestation of divine mercy is simultaneously asserted.[9] The ironies generated by restricting true spirituality only to the past are demonstrated by the remarks of the Chishtī master Ḥasan Muḥammad in the late sixteenth century (which today would be considered the period of decline):

> It is related of the revered Shaykh Ḥasan Muḥammad that a man of Lahore came and said, "In this time there is no one worthy of listening to music (*samāʿ*)." He replied, "If there were no one worthy of listening to music, the world would be destroyed." The man said, "In times past, there were men like Shaykh Naṣīr al-Dīn [Chirāgh-i Dihlī], the Sultan of the Shaykhs [Niẓām al-Dīn Awliyā'], and the revered [Farīd al-Dīn] Ganj-i Shakkar. Now there is no one like them." He answered, "In their time, men said the very same thing."[10]

Writing in the early nineteenth century, the biographer who transmitted this conversation was keenly aware of the constant need for renewal of the tradition. Repeatedly he observes of masters of the later periods that they "gave life to the example (*iḥyā'-i sunna*) of the Chishtī masters."[11] We should be careful to distinguish this expression from the metaphor of revival or rebirth, which suggests a reanimation of something defunct. To give life to tradition is necessary in every generation.

Yet of even greater importance than the institutional and historical structure of a Sufi order was the transmission of distinctive practices that gave each order its character. For the Chishtī order, this transmission included distinctive practices associated with music. But the core of Sufi transmission

---

[9] Yohanan Friedman, *Prophecy Continuous: Aspects of Aḥmadī Religious Thought and Its Medieval Background* (Berkeley: University of California Press 1989), pp. 94–101.

[10] Gul Muḥammad Ahmadpūrī, *Takmila-i siyar al-awliyā'* (MS K.A. Nizami), fos. 43b–44a.

[11] *Ibid*. fols 19a (Kamāl al-Dīn 'Allāma, d. 1355), 24a ('Alam ibn Sirāj, d. 1406), 42a (Ḥasan Muḥammad, d. 1575).

was the complex of prayer and meditation practices associated with the recollection and recitation of the names of God.[12] The term for this recitation is *dhikr*, meaning 'recollection'. *Dhikr* (pronounced *zikr* by non-Arabs) is mentioned very frequently in the Koran, since humanity is often called upon in the sacred text to remember God and his commands. The movement towards interiorization of the Koran that was so decisive for the development of Sufism lent itself especially to the practice of meditation in which the names of God are chanted over and over again, either in solitude or in company, aloud or silently.

The practice of *dhikr* seems to have become well established by the eleventh century, though there are indications of it among earlier Sufis. In the description of *dhikr* by al-Ghazālī (d. 1111) it has assumed a great importance as the single technique best adapted to concentrate the heart exclusively on God. The first major treatise on *dhikr*, "The Keys of Salvation" by Ibn 'Aṭā'ullāh of Alexandria (d.1309), demonstrates the range of Sufi practices available in the Mediterranean region in the thirteenth century.[13] The principal formulas used in *dhikr* were based on the negation ('there is no god') and affirmation ('but God') of the Muslim profession of faith, and the ninety-nine Arabic names of God. Historical transmission, though inherently conservative in character, is also cumulative, however. Generations of Sufi teachers added their own formulations of new combinations of divine names and distinctive litanies (*awrād*) that were carefully preserved by their disciples. Specialized psychophysical techniques, including breath control were developed by each order; thus the Kubrawī order in Central Asia was known for its systematic forty-day retreats with elaborate forms of visualization to accompany *dhikr*.

One must be cautious, however, in attempting to generalize about the character of a Sufi order. The tendency of some recent scholarship is to treat membership in a Sufi order as something like an ideological commitment to a political party. It is often assumed in addition that membership in a Sufi order was exclusive. That is not in fact the case. Unlike the Christian monastic orders, which were divided by firm lines of authority and sacrament, Sufi orders could frequently overlap one another. Multiple initiation has been noted since the early fifteenth century, when a Chishtī like Ashraf Jahāngīr Simnānī claimed initiation in fourteen different orders. We can assume that one of these initiations would take precedence, but that did not by any means prevent one from receiving these additional initiations as a kind of supplement to the main teaching. The non-exclusive character of Sufi initiation has important implications for the social extension of Sufism. In this light, it is difficult to

---

[12] See my *Shambhala Guide to Sufism* (Boston: Shambhala Publications 1997), esp. chap. 4, for a discussion of Sufi practices associated with the names of God.

[13] Ibn 'Ata Allah al-Iskandari, *The Key to Salvation; A Sufi Manual of Invocation*, trans. Mary Ann Koury-Danner (Cambridge: Islamic Texts Society 1996).

regard the constitution of Sufi orders and sainthood as a zero-sum competition, which a purely political analysis would suggest. It is in fact this wide collection of techniques that makes Sufism a cumulative tradition rather than a series of isolated and private experiences.

A good example of both the distinctiveness of Chishtī practice and its augmentation from other orders is provided by two Chishtīs of the eighteenth century, Shah Kalīmu'llāh Jahānābādī (d. 1729) and his chief disciple Niẓām al-Dīn Awrangābādī (d. 1730). These two have been credited as being the leaders of a Chishtī 'renaissance' that restored the ethical principles of the early Indian leaders of the order.[14] As indicated above, it may be something of an exaggeration to regard the Chishtī order as moribund or in decline between the fifteenth and eighteenth centuries; it may be more useful instead to consider Kalīmu'llāh and his successor Niẓām al-Dīn as two prominent examples among many who strove to give life to the tradition. In any case, the letters from Kalīmu'llāh to Niẓām al-Dīn repeatedly touch upon what is simultaneously the tension between two Sufi orders and the multi-dimensional character of a single order. Kalīmu'llāh in these letters tells his disciple to avoid excessive and conspicuous practice of vocal *dhikr* and music, as these are controversial and are not shared by other Sufi groups; the Naqshbandīs, in particular, avoid music and have a silent *dhikr*. He urges Niẓām al-Dīn to cultivate the practice of meditation (*murāqaba*), which is common to all orders. Kalīmu'llāh observes that people of Central Asian ancestry (notably in the court and the military) are almost always attached to the Naqshbandī Order, and therefore it will be necessary in some public contexts to downplay distinctive Chishtī practices and highlight instead those that are common:

> The people of Central Asia (Turan) generally belong to the teaching of the Naqshbandī masters, and their way is the way of meditation (*murāqaba*). Previously in Central Asia there was much of the Kubrawiyya and Kāzaruniyya teaching; in both of these orders they go to the extreme in performing *dhikr*. But today, because they are submissive, the Naqshbandī path is very widespread. Since all the paths are found in you, why should you remain a stranger to the way of meditation? Train people in this way also, for by God! It is the shortest of paths. There is no doubt concerning the greatness of this order.[15]

Here Kalīmu'llāh is reminding Niẓām al-Dīn that he has been initiated into the Suhrawardī, Naqshbandī, and Qādirī orders alongside the Chishtiyya. Hagiographies of the nineteenth century stress that at certain strategic moments it was possible to integrate other Sufi orders into the structure of the Chishtiyya. Muḥammad Gul Aḥmadpūrī (d. 1827) composed in 1810 a supplementary biographical work on the Chishtī order which clarified these

---

[14] K.A. Nizami, 'Čishtiyya', *EI*², II, p. 55.

[15] Kalīmu'llāh Jahānābādī, *Maktbūbāt-i kalīmī* (Delhī: Maṭba'-i Mujtabā'ī 1315 A.Hsh./ 1897), p. 57; cf. also pp. 11, 19, 47, 77–8, 80.

other links.[16] He included a complete lineage of the Suhrawardī order under the entry on Maḥmūd Rājan (d.1495), a Qādirī lineage under Ḥasan Muḥammad (d.1575), and a Naqshbandī lineage under Kalīmu'llāh.[17] Once any of these masters took on an outside initiation, they transmitted it to their successors, and so Niẓām al-Dīn received all four initiations. (Kalīmu'llāh also had a Shaṭṭārī initiation, but did not put as much emphasis on this connection). These were additions to the central repertoire of the order rather than competing techniques. It would be easy to read the attitude of Kalīmu'llāh and Niẓām al-Dīn as a purely political struggle between Sufi orders, but that would be a drastic over-simplification of the issues of religious practice and the master–disciple relationship.[18]

Niẓām al-Dīn Awrangābādī later composed a comprehensive account of Chishtī meditation techniques in a treatise called 'The Order of Hearts'. Composed in twenty-one chapters, it emphasizes vocal *dhikr*, and it includes detailed descriptions of many individual practices. The circumstances of its composition are described as follows:

> The reason for composing this treatise was that, on many prior occasions, certain spiritually sincere ones (in particular, that indubitable lover, Muḥammad 'Alī the calligrapher) repeatedly and passionately demanded that the author (may God forgive him) should compose an explanation of the benefits of *dhikr*s, joining these precious pearls into a single string, which would be the order of hearts (*niẓām-i qulūb*) for the religiously sincere and the people of conviction.[19]

Although the benefits of this text are many, it is strongly suggested that it should not be used without the permission of a qualified guide, and that it should be concealed from the eyes of the unworthy. While many of the chapters of 'The Order of Hearts' are brief accounts of specialized practices, the longest chapters treat of breath control (chapter 3) or provide classifications and groupings of the most commonly used *dhikr* formulas (chapters 7 and 14). 'The Order of Hearts' may be said to illustrate the Chishtī approach to *dhikr* in four ways. First, it contains detailed prescriptions of meditations that are widely found wherever Sufism is practised. Second, beyond these generic practices it provides a series of particular exercises associated with masters of the Chishtī lineage. Third, the text delineates practices associated with other orders, which nevertheless form part of the

---

[16] K.A. Nizami, "Aḥmadpūrī, Gol Moḥammad," *EIr*, I, p. 666.

[17] Aḥmadpūrī, fols 24a, 45a, 76a. The Naqshbandī lineage goes via Khwāja Kalān, a son of Muḥammad Bāqī Billāh, thus bypassing Aḥmad Sirhindī.

[18] The thesis of political rivalry between Chishtīs and Naqshbandīs is maintained by S.A.A. Rizvi, *Shah Wali Allah and his Times: A Study of Eighteenth Century Islam, Politics, and Society in India* (Canberra: Ma'rifat Publishing 1980), esp. pp. 360, 372.

[19] Niẓām al-Dīn Awrangābādī, *Niẓām al-qulūb* (Delhī: Maṭba'-i Mujtabā'ī, 1309 A.Hsh./ 1891–2), p. 2.

Chishtī repertoire. Fourth, there are a number of explicit references to the Indic background and to yogic practices, which have been accepted and included in Chishtī practice, much like the exercises of other Sufi orders. Comparison with the way that some of the same topics are handled by a Naqshbandī Sufi, Shah Walī Allāh, highlights the distinctive characteristics of Chishtī practice.

Regarding the general practice of *dhikr*, Niẓām al-Dīn begins (in chapter 2) by emphasising the role of *dhikr* in initiation (*bay'at*), and he describes a three-day fast with numerous prayers in preparation for this event. After promising to uphold the *sharī'a* and to love God, the disciple shakes hands with the master and receives instruction in the *dhikr* formulas that are appropriate for his or her spiritual state. The disciple repeats each formula three times in order to memorize it. This is a tradition that is traced back all the way to the initiation of 'Alī by Muḥammad. The basic elements of *dhikr* include the recitation of the name Allāh, the first half of the Muslim profession of faith ('There is no god but God'), or the Arabic divine names; breath control; concentration on 'moving' a name or formula from one portion of the body (frequently from the navel to the throat or to the brain); and occasional visualizations of letters, words, or complicated visions. An example is the 'recollection of astonishment' (*dhikr-i ḥayrān*): "It has no fixed position. While holding the breath, seven times gradually raise the visualization of Allāh from beneath the navel in the seat up to the throat, where it becomes *hū* [He]. Then gradually release the breath and repeat. The effects will be obvious."[20] There are many such prescriptions. One of the only obvious ways of grouping these exercises is in terms of the numbers of 'beats' (*ḍarb*) contained in a single repetition, that is, the number of times one sharply focuses the attention on a part of the body with an effort equivalent to a physical blow; these may range from one up to twelve beats in any exercise.

Breath control (*pās-i anfās*) is a constant theme throughout this manual, repeatedly mentioned in many different exercises. Some of the longer descriptions are especially interesting for the effects they describe:

> By holding the breath, as soon as the breath becomes engaged, and one begins to breathe, one brings the breath up to the brain. When breath becomes short, one gradually exhales until the breath is no longer perceived. This is called peace and tranquillity. It is best to remain occupied in the *dhikr* of "Allāh, Allāh" by contemplation while holding the breath (*ḥabs-i dam*).[21]

The effects of these techniques lift one to the higher reaches of spiritual attainment.

---

[20] *Niẓām al-qulūb*, p. 6.

[21] *Ibid.*, p. 7.

> When the upper and lower breaths join the breath of life, they become one; "the meeting-place of the two oceans" (*majma 'al-baḥrayn*; Koran XVIII:60) is an allusion to this. That is the station of the water of life. One becomes a spiritual and enters the world of flight and journeying. Knowledge of the divine presence (*'ilm-i ladunnī*) – "by which we taught him a knowledge from us" (Koran XVIII:65) – appears. One has long life and meets Khiḍr (peace be upon him), becoming the Sufi of the age. Celibacy, asceticism, and isolation are prerequisites.[22]

Assiduous practice of breath control is essential. "My dear, one should so hold the breath in one breath of recitation that one runs out of breath and becomes unconscious. One should try so that a thousand breaths a day, and a thousand breaths a night, become easy. One is absorbed both night and day."[23]

Breath control in the Chishtī tradition is linked to the repetition of selected divine names in given sequences. These complex exercises have no obvious precedent in the early Arabic manuals of meditation like Ibn 'Aṭā' Allāh's 'Key to Salvation'. In particular, three divine names from the Koran (often joined with the 'essential name', Allāh) appear prominently in these Chishtī invocations: Hearing (*Samī'*), Seeing (*Baṣīr*), Knowing (*'Alīm*). Niẓām al-Dīn describes this as a three-stage process:

> Say Allāh in the heart, cleave the tongue to the palate, and hold it still. Start with the 'A' [of Allāh] from beneath the navel so that the *dhikr* recitation with all the breath has [no] defect. Prolong it in order to complete awareness and centering, repeating three times. This is 'descent'. Contemplate one [divine] attribute in each name. Some contemplate all three attribute names in the essential name, and so prolong it. Some contemplate nine attribute names by descent and ascent in one name. Some prolong the essential name until a constriction (*qabḍ*) of breath takes place, contemplating as many names as enter during this constriction. Force (*shadd*), prolonging (*madd*), above, and below mean that you grasp the *dhikr* 'Allāh' from below the navel, forcefully begin and prolong the breath, calling upon the beauty of the beloved until *dhikr* becomes the habit of worship. Through the effort of recollection of the heart, insinuating thought goes away. One grasps all the breath to the upper part of the chest, holding the breath for up to three or more *dhikr* recitations, until heat appears internally, and a spiritual state is born.[24]

Thus it is apparent how strongly these exercises are linked with worship of God as expressed in the scriptural legacy of the Koran.

Beyond these basic and general exercises, the Chishtī tradition contains a number of specific prescriptions associated with the great Chishtī masters of the past. These are incidentally not the most prominent practices in the book, although they only begin to be mentioned by chapter 5. Thus, Naṣīr al-Dīn Chirāgh-i Dihlī is said to have written that his master Niẓām al-Dīn Awliyā'

---

[22] *Ibid.*, pp. 7–8.
[23] *Ibid.*
[24] *Ibid.*, pp. 8–9.

recommended and taught the exercise of visualizing ʻAbd al-Qādir Jīlānī, "which up to today they do in Chisht and in the Qādiriyya Order."[25] The Chishtī masters are also said to have relied on proofs from the Koran and *ḥadīth* to justify the vocal recitation of *dhikr*.[26] Gīsū Darāz is quoted as reporting from Naṣīr al-Dīn a method of causing spirits to be unveiled by *dhikr*.[27] Specific *dhikr* formulas ascribed to Farīd al-Dīn Ganj-i Shakkar, including some in Indian languages (discussed below), are given.[28] A threefold division of these practices into meditation (*murāqaba*), witnessing (*mushāhada*), and vision (*muʻāyana*) is ascribed to Niẓām al-Dīn Awliyā', Chirāgh-i Dihlī, and Gīsū Darāz.[29] A few descriptions are remarkably detailed, in contrast to the laconic style that predominates in this treatise:

> In our order, most of the lovers who participate in the *dhikr* circle perform vocal *dhikr*. Always they sit from the end of the night until morning, and after dawn prayer they always recite the vocal Chishtī *dhikr* 7,000 times. Likewise from noon to mid-afternoon prayer, from mid-afternoon prayer to sunset prayer, and from sunset prayer to evening prayer, the lovers are bound to the circle of *dhikr*. After the master of longings, most pass the entire night in *dhikr*, most reaching 30,000 *dhikr*; 20,000 *dhikr* or 18,000 *dhikr* is their usual custom.[30]

These discussions make it clear that, as announced at the beginning of the book, the purpose is to demonstrate the Chishtī attachment to the vocal or spoken *dhikr*, in contrast to other Sufi groups (such as the Naqshbandīs) who practised a silent *dhikr*. It is also clear from this account that serious Sufi practice precluded having a regular job. Elsewhere, Niẓām al-Dīn Awrangābādī emphasizes that another characteristic of the Chishtīs ('our teaching') is the choice and arrangement of the divine names used in their invocations. There is a basic threefold arrangement of names. The first level consists of the fundamental names Hearing, Seeing, and Knowing. After calling upon those names, one can proceed to the second level, containing the five names Lasting, Standing, Present, Looking, and Witnessing, making a total of eight. The third level adds twelve more names: Holy, Loving, Living, Subsistent, Outer, Inner, Forgiving, Mild, Light, Guide, Renewer, Eternal. After mastering these three levels, one can go on to a fourth level and learn others of the ninety-nine names of God or isolated phrases from the discourses of the master. On the fifth level, additional names beyond the ninety-nine include superlative forms (e.g., 'Most Merciful of the Merciful Ones'). A lengthy prayer is given that

---

[25] *Ibid.*, p. 12.
[26] *Ibid.*, p. 14.
[27] *Ibid.*, p. 24.
[28] *Ibid.*, p. 30.
[29] *Ibid.*, p. 35.
[30] *Ibid.*, p. 22.

demonstrates all of the five levels.[31] These examples appear to be exclusive to the Chishtī tradition.

The emphasis on Chishtī practices does not preclude, however, the use of exercises specifically associated with other Sufi orders. The visualization of ʻAbd al-Qādir Jīlānī, founder of the Qādirī order, has already been mentioned. The Qādirīs too have their own choice and sequence of divine names: 'God is Hearing, God is Speaking, God is Seeing, God is Powerful, God is Desiring, God is Existent, God is Knowing'.[32] The Qādirīs employ variations on standard recitations (such as 'Allāh' and 'There is no god but God') of from one to twelve beats.[33] One also finds an extensive description of a Qalandarī *dhikr*, with variations:

> Recite in beats "Yā Ḥasan" between the knees, "Yā Ḥusayn" at the navel, "Yā ʻAlī" at the left shoulder, "Yā Muḥammad," saying it to oneself and pulling it from the head. Some ascetic masters say "Yā Muḥammad" thus: [they say] "Yā" to heaven and "Muḥammad" to the breast. In the Qalandarī order they say "Allāh Huwa Ḥaqq" in one breath. Interior exercises are of different types. Some gaze upon their own forms as seen in a mirror, some gaze upon a spiritual form, some gaze continuously at the master's face in a mirror, some gaze at the form of "Allāh," imagining the unimaginable form of God.[34]

A brief description is also given of the Shaṭṭārī method of reciting "Allāh."[35] Of all non-Chishtī Orders, the most extensive attention is paid to the methods of the Naqshbandī Order. Niẓām al-Dīn quotes a lengthy passage in Arabic on how to instruct disciples in *dhikr*, taken from the Naqshbandī master Saʻd al-Dīn al-Kāshgharī.[36] More extensively, in an appendix to an account of forty forms of meditation (*murāqaba*) in the lengthy chapter 18, Niẓām al-Dīn gives a four-page description of Naqshbandī techniques of instruction. He focuses on describing a series of 'unveilings' (*kashf*) peculiar to Naqshbandī teaching, as well as the triple method of concentration (*tawajjuh*) on the ineffability of God without words, concentration on the relationship (*rābiṭa*) with the master, and the silent *dhikr*.[37] We shall return to this striking emphasis on Naqshbandī practice. There are also several references to spiritual techniques associated with particular individuals such as Ibn ʻArabī and Rūmī.[38]

The last major topic that appears in Niẓām al-Dīn's treatment of meditation is the Indic background and the ascetic practices of yoga. This is extremely

---

[31] *Ibid.*, p. 25.
[32] *Ibid.*, p. 25.
[33] *Ibid.*, p. 10.
[34] *Ibid.*, p. 10.
[35] *Ibid.*, p. 11.
[36] *Ibid.*, pp. 13–14.
[37] *Ibid.*, pp. 46–50.
[38] A *dhikr* from Ibn ʻArabi is quoted in *ibid.*, p. 24 (cf. also p. 37), and one from Rūmī is given on p. 50.

prominent, as there is a lengthy discussion of the 'unstruck sound' (*anāhita*) experienced in certain yogic practices, and yogic breath control techniques, in chapter 3. Niẓām al-Dīn gives this an Islamic context by pointing out that this sound occurs when one recites the ninety-nine names of God while holding the fingers in the ears. He calls this (in Persian) the "endless cry" (*ṣawt-i lā yuzālī*), "which in yoga is called *anāhid* [Hindi for Sanskrit *anāhita*]." After enumerating the benefits of this technique, he observes:

> Among the Indian monotheists, although there are different types, the best of these practices is that which continuously comes forth from them in waking and in sleep, and is involuntary and unintentional. The Koranic verse "There is nothing that does not praise him, but they do not understand their praise" (XVII:44) alludes to this. That is expressed by two words. The breath that ascends, they call *hūn* and the breath that goes out, they call *hīn*, that is, "I am not he." Sufis understand that the practice of the two phrases *huwa Allāh* [he is God] and *allāh hū* [God is he], that is, inhaling *hū* and exhaling Aallāh, and inhaling *Allāh* and exhaling *hū*, is what occurs. The best breath control is just what has been said.[39]

Niẓām al-Dīn, like many Sufi commentators, fits yogic techniques into an Islamic framework that supplies the intentions and ultimate meaning that yogis may have been unaware of.

Along with this matter-of-fact description of yogic breath control, Niẓām al-Dīn makes frequent reference to the use of non-Arabic *dhikr* formulas, which in his view are perfectly valid for non-Arabs in particular. "It is right if one instructs the non-Arab (*'ajamī*) disciple with expressions in Hindi or Persian or whatever he understands."[40] Niẓām al-Dīn also quotes a line of Hindi poetry to comment on a Koranic verse.[41] But it is especially noteworthy that he also cites *dhikr* formulas in Punjabi and Hindi, such as the following, attributed to the famous Chishtī saint Farīd al-Dīn: "Say *wuhī hē* upwards, *hī hī* to the left side of the breast, *hīn hī* toward the heart."[42] Variations on this Hindi *dhikr* of Farīd al-Dīn are well known in a number of Indian Sufi texts, particularly among Chishtī and Shaṭṭārī masters. These phrases belong to a long tradition of adapting hatha yoga mantras to Islamic themes and Sufi practices, as illustrated in the many translations of the curious yogic text known as 'The Pool of Nectar'.[43]

The Chishtī approach to meditation by Niẓām al-Dīn Awrangābādī can be seen more clearly when compared to a discussion of *dhikr* techniques

---

[39] *Ibid.*, pp. 6–7.

[40] *Ibid.*, p. 19.

[41] *Ibid.*, p. 22.

[42] *Ibid.*, p. 30. Cf. p. 32, where a longer version is linked with the lotus position, the chief of the eighty-four yogic postures.

[43] For a detailed study of yoga and Sufism, see my forthcoming *Islam and Yoga: The Limits of Interpretation, with a Translation of* The Pool of Nectar.

presented by a contemporary Naqshbandī figure, Shāh Walī Allāh (see Marcia K. Hermansen's chapter in this volume). In his "Information on the Orders of the Friends of God and the Transmissions of the Heirs of the Messenger of God," Walī Allāh sets forth an account of all the spiritual practices to which he has been exposed, not only from the Naqshbandī but also from other Sufi orders, including Qādirī, Chishtī, Suhrawardī, Kubrawī, Shaṭṭārī, Shādhilī, Madyanī and 'Aydarūsī initiations. His purpose was "to describe the famous orders that I have been trained in for both external and internal knowledge, and in which I have participated."[44] His treatise may be compared to the synthetic works on Sufi practice that began to emerge in the seventeenth century by scholars located in Arabia, who, like the Indian Shaṭṭārī master Aḥmad Qushshāshī, were veritable collectors of *dhikr* techniques. Another example of this kind of collection is "The Clear Fountain on the Forty Paths," written by the North African scholar Muḥammad al-Sanūsī al-Idrīsī (d. 1859); as its name implies, it contains examples of *dhikr* practices from forty different Sufi orders from many Muslim countries.[45]

What are the differences between Chishtī and Naqshbandī approaches to *dhikr*, as expressed in these two texts? It may first of all be observed that the Chishtī author shows the overwhelming emphasis on vocal *dhikr* as the standard form of mystical exercise. The Naqshbandīs are insistent on performing the silent *dhikr*.[46] Walī Allāh shows not the slightest interest in Hindi, nor does he mention yoga at all.

As far as the practices discussed in both texts are concerned, to what extent does Niẓām al-Dīn Awrangābādī's account of Naqshbandī practices resemble that of Shāh Walī Allāh? Comparison indicates that Niẓām al-Dīn's description of meditation (*murāqaba*) is not very close to that of Walī Allāh. Niẓām al-Dīn's lengthy chapter on this topic, which was central to Naqshbandī observance, consists of six meditations containing elaborate visualizations, followed by fifty Koranic passages with mystical explanations for the meditator.[47] This differs substantially from Walī Allāh's precise description of *murāqaba* as an intensive concentration on 'Allāh' in the place of the pineal heart until it becomes a habit.[48] It is only in a short passage at the end of the chapter on *murāqaba* that Niẓām al-Dīn gives a succinct account of a threefold Naqshbandī method of concentration (described above) that roughly corresponds to practices described by Walī Allāh.[49] Other major themes of Naqshbandī practice and doctrine, such as the subtle centres (*laṭā'if*) and the

---

[44] Shāh Walī Allāh, *Intibāh fī salāsil awliyā' allāh*, Persian text ed. with Urdu trans. Muḥammad Isḥāq Ṣiddīqī (Deoband: Kutub Khāna Raḥīmiyya n.d.), p. 10.
[45] See *Guide*, pp. 110, 123, 205, and figure 9.
[46] *Intibāh*, p. 10.
[47] *Niẓām al-qulūb*, pp. 33–50.
[48] *Intibāh*, pp. 40–1.
[49] *Niẓām al-qulūb*, p. 49, to be compared with *Intibāh*, pp. 40–1.

debate over existential or testimonial unity (*tawḥīd-i wujūdī*, *tawḥīd-i shuhūdī*), are mentioned by Niẓām al-Dīn only in passing.[50] It may be worth pointing out that there are several overlapping discussions that are found in both these texts in nearly identical forms, suggesting either reliance on a common source or perhaps use of Niẓām al-Dīn's text by Walī Allāh.

To qualify Niẓām al-Dīn Awrangābādī as a Chishtī author is to point to a primary allegiance, not an exclusive one. His concern in providing a broad description of *dhikr* techniques is to note with interest a number of relevant aspects of other Sufi orders alongside the Chishtiyya, not with a view to completing a tradition that is deficient, nor as a borrowing from competitors, but rather as a comprehensive and practically useful overview of a common Sufi heritage. The yogic practices of non-Muslim ascetics are simply one more set of parallel techniques that can be added to the mix. Continuities in meditative practice help inform the structure of a Sufi order, but they do not constitute fixed boundaries. Indeed, *dhikr* is so fundamental that it underlies the basic fact of breathing, and perhaps life itself. As Niẓām al-Dīn observes, "The realizers of truth say that the recollection '*hū*' [he] occurs involuntarily, whether one knows it or not. Thus, everything always is in the recollection of God, but only the perfect one is aware and comprehends his own recollection."[51]

---

[50] *Niẓām al-qulūb*, pp. 47, 48.
[51] *Ibid.*, p. 6.

Plate 11: Persian Male Attire. From Chardin, *Voyages*, Pl. 22.

VI
PERSIANATE SUFISM IN INDIA, CENTRAL ASIA & CHINA

هو العزیز

عاقل به قوانین خرد راه تو پوید

دیوانه برون از همه آیین تو جوید

تا غنچه بشکفته این باغ که بوید

هر کس بزبانی صفت حمد تو گوید

بلبل به غزلخوانی و قمری به ترانه

The sages and the men of analytic intellect
Use postulations of their reason in the quest
For you; one mad with love, the wandering fool
Seeks you beyond tradition and religion too,
And yet, this garden's heady blossom who
Can scent? For each the tongue of praise is different:
The dove croons country tunes, the nightingale serenades.

The Role of the Sufis in the Changing Society of the Deccan, 1500–1750

M.Z.A. SHAKEB

I

To trace in any detail the beginnings of Sufism in the Deccan would be out of place in this essay, but it should be mentioned that Sufis existed there for centuries before the period covered by this volume, and also before the establishment of Muslim political rule in the Deccan in the middle of the fourteenth century.[1] During the early medieval period Sufism held a dominant cultural position in India in general and in the Deccan in particular, where almost all the major Sufi orders were busy in shaping the structure of Indian society, particularly its Muslim section.[2] The role of the Sufis in Deccani society was reinforced by the heavy influx of Muslim population when Muḥammad Tughluq (*reg.* 1325–51) shifted his capital from Delhi to Dawlatābād in 1327. ʻAlā' al-Dīn Ḥasan Bahman Shāh (*reg.* 1347–58), the founder of the first Muslim state in the Deccan, was himself an ardent disciple of the Sufi Shaykh Sirāj al-Dīn Junaydī, and there are a number of anecdotes suggesting that ʻAlā' al-Dīn had become a ruler with the blessings of the shaykh.[3] As a matter of fact, not only did ʻAlā' al-Dīn remain loyal to Junaydī throughout his life, but his descendants also followed the tradition set up by him and always sought the guidance and blessings of the shaykh, until the Sufi saint died in 782/1380.[4] At the coronation of Muḥammad Shāh I (*reg.* 1356–

---

[1] For an account of the Sufis in the Deccan see Muḥammad Sulaymān Siddīqī, *The Bahmani Sufis* (Delhi: Idarah-i Adabiyat-i Delhi 1989); Carl W. Ernst, *Eternal Garden* (Albany: SUNY Press 1992) and Annemarie Schimmel, *Islam in the Indian Subcontinent* (Leiden: Brill 1980).

[2] For the role of Sufis in India see K.A. Nizami, *Some Aspects of Religion and Politics in India During the Thirteenth Century* (Aligarh: S. Nural Hasan 1961); *idem*, *Studies in Medieval Indian History and Culture* (Allahabad: Kitab Mahal 1966) and A. Schimmel, *Mystical Dimensions of Islam* (Chapel Hill: University of North Carolina Press 1983).

[3] H.K. Sherwani, *The Bahmanis of the Deccan* (Hyderabad: n.p. 1953) pp. 36–7.

[4] *Ibid.*, pp. 100–1.

75), the shaykh "ordered some coarse cloth, a shirt, a turban and a girdle made from it, and it was this garb which became the coronation robe of the Bahmanī monarchs for a long time to come." Even after the death of Shaykh Sirāj al-Dīn Junaydī in 781/1380, the predominant influence of Sufis on the state and society of the Deccan remained unchanged. Although there were a number of other Sufis carrying on their respective missions during this period, none of them quite equalled the stature of this great shaykh, and both state and society were in need of someone to fill the spiritual vacuum left after his death.[5]

About sixteen years after the death of Shaykh Junaydī, there arrived from Delhi the great Chishtī saint Sayyid Muḥammad Gīsūdirāz (721/1321–825/1422) who was in his early eighties and settled in the then Bahmanī capital Aḥsanābād (Gulbarga) at the request of Fīrūz Shāh Bahmanī (800/1397–825/1422). Sayyid Muḥammad Gīsūdirāz was not only a Sufi of very high spiritual attainment but also a scholar of great accomplishment who is supposed to have written about 105 books on different aspects of Sufism and Islam. About 36 of the extant works attributed to him reflect his extensive knowledge and great insight into various aspects of Sufism.[6] His was a period during which the cultural tradition of Persianate Sufism could be seen flourishing both in the Deccan and in Iran in all its glory and magnificence.

II

Although the influence of Gīsūdirāz over Deccan society was unprecedented, the early fifteenth century was an age in which a new phase in the relation of politics to religion was emerging in the Deccan. The first indication of this change was the withdrawal of favour from Gīsūdirāz on the part of the monarch Fīrūz Shāh Bahmanī (1397–1422), a change which took place under the influence of Mīr Faḍlu'llāh Injū who had entered the scene quite dramatically, first as the teacher, then as the father-in-law of Sulṭān Fīrūz Shāh and, finally, as the prime minister of the state and the chief advisor of the Sulṭān. Faḍlu'llāh Injū was perhaps the first Shī'ite figure of a noticeable calibre in the history of the Deccan.[7] The differences between the monarch and the Sufi saint continued to grow for the rest of their lives. The saint lived, however, to see Fīrūz Shāh surrender his throne to his brother Aḥmad Shāh on 5 Shawwal 825/ 22 September 1422. Sayyid Muḥammad Gīsūdirāz died on 1 November 1422 (16 Dhu'l-qa'da 825) and Fīrūz Shāh a week later.[8]

---

[5] *Ibid.*, p. 118.
[6] For an excellent study of his life and work see Syed Shah Khusro Hussaini, *Sayyid Muḥammmad al-Husaynī Gīsūdirāz: On Sufism* (Delhi: Idarah-i Adabiyat-i Delhi 1983).
[7] Sherwani, *The Bahmanis*, pp. 143–61.
[8] *Ibid.*, pp. 164–6.

The new monarch Aḥmad Shāh (*reg.* 825/1422–839/1436) owed his blessings not only to Gīsūdirāz, but also to one Khalaf Ḥasan Baṣrī, for his military and political advice.[9] Baṣrī was a Shī'ite talent at whose suggestion Aḥmad Shāh ignored all the other great Sufis of the Deccan and invited instead an Iranian Sufi: Shāh Ni'maṭu'llāh of Kirmān[10] to grace his court, who in turn responded by sending two of his grandsons, Ḥabīb al-Dīn Muḥibu'llāh and Muḥib al-Dīn Ḥabību'llāh. Shāh Ni'maṭu'llāh also bestowed upon Aḥmad Shāh the title of 'Valī' (Saint, Friend of God), so that the monarch subsequently became known to posterity as 'Aḥmad Shāh Valī'. When the two young Persian Sufis married Indian Bahmanī princesses,[11] their aura of spiritual authority and sanctity was sucked in for the benefit of the Deccani state. These Ni'matu'llāhī Deccani Sufis were for some time seen at coronations and important state functions, but gradually they disappeared from the political scene. The more exoteric authorities representing the Shī'ite faith took the ruling family in their grip and the influx of Shī'ites into the Deccan increased. This led to serious conflicts between the Shī'ites and the Sunnis and to the unfortunate massacre of hundreds of Shī'ites in the valley of Chakana.[12]

The third important Shī'ite figure in the history of the late fifteenth-century Deccan was Maḥmūd Gāwān (assassinated 886/1481), who tried to restore balance to the new religious situation but himself fell victim to dirty court politics.[13] Following Maḥmūd Gāwān's death, day by day the Bahmanī rulers became weaker as their provincial governors gradually mustered more power within the regions under their control by winning the favour of the local people, mainly the Dakhanīs. In this process, most of the Shī'ite elite disappeared: they probably went back to Iran, since they called themselves 'universalists' (*āfāqī*s), professing themselves unattached to any particular clime or land.[14] Despite these changes, the Sufis remained in the Deccan, maintaining their usual traditions and customs in their *khānaqāh*s and carrying on their missions in peace and tranquillity.

---

[9] Muḥammad Qāsim Firishta, *Gulshan-i Ibrāhīmī* (*Tārīkh-i Firishta*) (Bombay: n.p. 1832), I, pp. 633–4; Sayyid 'Alī Ṭabāṭabā, *Burhān-i ma'āsir*, ed. Sayyid Hāshimī Farīdābādī (Hyderabad: n.p. 1936), pp. 54, 65.

[10] See the essay by Terry Graham in this present volume (EDS).

[11] Muḥammad Mufīd Mustawfī, *Jāmi'-i Mufīḍī*, ed. Īraj Afshār (Tehran: Asadī 1340 A.Hsh./ 1961) p. 46; E.G. Browne, *Literary History of Persia* (Cambridge: Cambridge University Press 1956), III, pp. 463–4; J. Briggs, *History of the Rise of the Muḥammadan Power in India* (Calcutta: 1958; repr. Lahore: Sang-e Meel Publications 1977), II, p. 420.

[12] Sherwani, *The Bahmanis*, pp. 40, 243.

[13] *Ibid.*, pp. 333–6.

[14] M.Z.A. Shakeb, *Religion and Politics in Golconda: A Chapter in Religion and Politics in South India* (Hyderabad: The Institute of Asian Studies 1978).

III

The beginning of the sixteenth century, however, marked a big change in the political and socio-cultural history of the Deccan. The Bahmanī empire disintegrated, to be succeeded by the five new sultanates of Berer, Aḥmadnagar, Bijapur, Golconda and Bidar, while the old Vijāyanagar empire became another important neighbour affecting the social and political life of these sultanates. The absence of a strong and unifying government in Delhi led the newly created native kingdoms of the Deccan to dream of attaining the status of world states. The recent Safavid revolution, based partially on a new-fangled, fanatically politicized version of Shī'ism of a totalitarian character, had not only shaken the whole fabric of Persian society with surprising success, but was also affecting the course of international politics, especially kingdoms and rulers in the regions of Transoxiana, Turkey and the Indian subcontinent. The Safavid revolution encouraged and substantially supported the Deccan sultanates' efforts to realize their dream of attaining the status of world states. The alliance of the Deccan sultanates with Persia had far-reaching consequences affecting Deccani society in many ways.[15]

The first major change which occurred in the Deccan was the adoption of Shī'ism as state religion and the inclusion of the names of the twelve Imāms, as well as those of the Safavid rulers, in the Friday ritual sermon (*khuṭba*): first, by the 'Ādil Shāhs of Bijapur, who claimed descent from the Turcoman 'White Sheep tribe'; second, by the Quṭb Shāhs of Golconda who were originally from the 'Black Sheep tribe'; while the third to convert to the Shī'ite faith were the Niẓām Shāhs of Aḥmadnagar, who had sprung from a Hindu family and whose progenitor had taken a leading part in a conspiracy against Maḥmūd Gāwān, becoming prime minister after Gāwān's assassination. In the space of about fifty years these three dynasties did away with the two Sunni sultanates of Berar and Bidar and annexed their territories. Thus, from the middle of the sixteenth century onwards, the Deccan became politically recognized as comprising the three Shī'ite sultanates of Aḥmadnagar, Bijapur and Golconda, all of which were closely affiliated with Safavid Persia.[16]

The second important change was the renewed influx of Persians into the Deccan, whose local rulers feted them with a respect and honour astounding to the minds of native Indian elites. The newcomers slowly began to replace the native Sunnis who had previously held all the higher levels of posts in the

---

[15] For an exhaustive study of this situation, see M.Z.A. Shakeb, "Relations of Golconda with Iran: 1518–1687," unpublished Ph.D thesis (University of Pune 1976); also Riazul Islam, *Indo-Persian Relations: A Study of the Political and Diplomatic Relations between the Mughal Empire and Iran* (Tehran: Iranian Culture Foundation 1970).

[16] Sherwani, *The Bahmanis*, pp. 165–70, 173; Schimmel, *Islam in the Indian Subcontinent*, p. 55; *Tārīkh-i Sulṭān Muḥammad Quṭb Shāh* (Hyderabad, Andhra Pradesh: State Archives), MS no. 23, fos 25, 26; Firishta, *Gulshan-i Ibrāhīmī*, II, pp. 329–30.

political and administrative hierarchy. Most Deccanis were associated with one or other of the Sunni Sufi orders flourishing in the Deccan. One glaring example of this ethnic change can be seen in Golconda which, as a Bahmanī province, was headed by a noble called Quṭb al-Mulk Dakkanī,[17] who was succeeded by Sulṭān Qulī Quṭb Shāh at the turn of the fifteenth century. By the middle of the seventeenth century the ethnic composition of the nobility in Golconda had been so radically altered that the top seven levels at the court of Sulṭān ʻAbdu'llāh Quṭb Shāh (1626–72) were all occupied by Persians. The Deccanis and the Arabs, who were obviously Sunnis, had been relegated to the peripheral eighth level along with the Hindus.[18] One writer compared the large crowd of Persians who frequented the fort of Golconda, with the royal palace at its centre, to the huge flocks of pigeons which clogged the harem of the Kaʻba.

Amongst all these elegantly attired Iranians at the Golgonda court, with their aristocratic airs, there appeared one Mullā Wajhī, a senior Deccani poet of the Sufi tradition. Although he occupied – quite unusually, given his ethnic background – the position of poet laureate at the Golconda court, he appeared quite out of place in these surroundings. One of his beautiful Persian couplets expresses his sense of alienation in this situation very well:

> I don't care, Wajīh, or anybody, whosoever they might be!
> I take pride in looking uneducated, yet self-fulfilled.[19]

Such sentiments would seem to demonstrate that the native elite kept away from the higher levels of the political and administrative hierarchy, finding virtually no resort elsewhere – except to their Sufi masters, to whom they gave vent to their feelings.

The third important change which occurred in the sixteenth-century Deccan relates to the missionary devices that the new Shīʻite elites adopted in order to bring about an overall change of faith in the society. Shīʻite missionaries from Iran started visiting the Deccan from the beginning of the sixteenth century. Perhaps the first of such missionaries was Shāh Ṭāhir, who emigrated to the Deccan in 1520. A descendant of the Ismāʻīlī sulṭāns of Egypt, he possessed a charming personality, being an accomplished scholar, skilful missionary and veteran teacher, as well as a good diplomat. Though he was not sent officially by Shāh Ṭahmāsp to gain further ground for the Safavid cause in the realm of Indo-Iranian politics, Shāh Ṭāhir volunteered to take up the mission of propagating the Shīʻite faith in the Deccan. He made

---

17 Ṭabāṭabā, *Burhān*, p. 150; *Tārīkh-i Sulṭān Muḥammad Quṭb Shāh*, fo. 41.

18 Niẓām al-Dīn Aḥmad Shīrāzī, *Ḥadīqat al-salāṭīn* (Hyderabad: Idara-i Siqāfat wa Tamaddun-i Dakkhan, Aywān-i Urdu 1961), p. 44.

19 Asadullāh Wajīh (also Wajhī): *Diwān-i Wajīh* no. 511; *Adab Naẓm* (Hyderabad: Salar Jang Museum n.d.)

Aḥmadnagar the centre of his activities developing large-scale contacts with both the nobility and the native Muslim masses. He started making eloquent public speeches and initiated open public debates with Sunni scholars. It was through his efforts that Burhān Niẓām Shāh, the Sulṭān of Aḥmadnagar, converted to Shī'ism in 943/1537. The conversion of Sunnis to Shī'ism under Shāh Ṭāhir's influence was so rapid that on occasions it reached the rate of three thousand per day. He carried his mission in the Deccan until his death in 956/1549.[20]

Another person who played an important role in the propagation and diffusion of Shī'ism in the Deccan was Mīr Muḥammad Mū'min, a nephew of the renowned scholar Amīr Fakhr al-Dīn Sammākī and a student of Sayyid Nūr al-Dīn al-Musavī al-Shushtarī. Formerly employed as a tutor of Shāh Ṭahmāsp's son Sulṭān Ḥaydar, Mīr Muḥammad Mū'min had come to the Deccan in 1581 and was soon appointed to the post of Prime Minister (*pīshwa*) of the sultanate. Due to Mū'min's royal patronage, other Shī'ite scholars soon flocked to the Deccan, and particularly to the Golconda/Hyderabad areas, in huge numbers. With a view to intensifying his Shī'itization campaign, Mīr Muḥammad Mū'min set up a *madrasa* in Golconda to produce Shī'ite scholars.[21]

During the same period, an enormous amount of Shī'ite literature, particularly theological books and treatises written by the Majlisī family, was imported to India from Iran. Mīr Mū'min himself wrote a few significant books on Shī'ite theology. Some books written against the doctrines of Sufism during this period can still be found on the shelves of Golconda libraries.[22]

The last important Shī'ite figure in the religious climate of the seventeenth-century Deccan is Shaykh Shams al-Dīn Abū Ma'ālī Muḥammad Ibn 'Alī Ibn Khātūn al-Amūlī, generally known as Ibn Khātūn. Born in Aynas, a village in Amūl, Ibn Khātūn received his education under the renowned Shī'ite scholar Shaykh Bahā' al-Dīn al-'Āmilī (953/1547–1030-1/1621). He reached Golconda in about 1600 and was appointed to the post of the Royal Epistolarian (*dabīr al-mamālik*). In 1616 he was sent as the Golconda envoy to Iran where he stayed for four years. On his return from Iran he was appointed Prime Minister (*pīshwā-yi salṭanat*) of Golconda by Sulṭān 'Abdu'llāh Quṭb Shāh. He died in 1059/1649 in Mocha on his way to Mecca for pilgrimage.[23]

---

[20] Ṭabāṭabā, *Burhān*, p. 254; Firishta, *Gulshan-i Ibrāhīmī*, II, pp. 22–3, 203; Ḥusayn Hidāyat "Shāh Ṭāhir of the Deccan" published in *Indian and Iranian Studies* (Bombay 1939).

[21] Muḥyī al-Dīn Qādirī, *Ḥayāt-i Mīr Mū'min* (Hyderabad: Idarah-i Adabiyat-i Urdu 1941); T.N. Devare, *A Short History of Persian Literature at the Bahmanī, 'Adīl Shāhī and Quṭb Shāhi Courts* (Poona 1961).

[22] See for instance: Majlisī's *Ḥaqq al-yaqīn*, MS no. 51; Faḍlullāh, *Risāla fī Ithbāt-i wājib al-wujūd*, MS no. 61, preserved under *'Aqayid wa kalām* (Hyderabad: Salar Jang Museum).

[23] *Kashkūl* MS no. 16 (Hyderabad: Salar Jang Museum). See also Dhu'l-faqār ibn Anṣār, *Dabistān* (Bombay 1262/A.Hsh./1846), p. 204.

An eminent scholar and skilful administrator as well as an able politician and diplomat, Ibn Khātūn played a balancing role in the external politics of the Golconda state. Most of the members of the Golconda *majlis* were appointed on his advice. Like Mīr Muḥammad Mū'min before him, he also set up a *madrasa* where he participated in teaching, holding learned discussions with scholars there almost every day. His scholarly efforts towards the spread of Shī'ism faith in the Deccan were similar to that of Mīr Muḥammad Baqir Majlisī of Iran. He invited a number of Shī'ite scholars from Iran to Golconda and wrote a few books on Shī'ism, some of which contained chapters hurling abuse at the first three caliphs.[24]

Under his direction, the redirection of popular piety along Shī'ite lines in Golgonda was intensified, with the first ten days of Muḥarram celebrated on a grand scale intended to involve as many people as possible. The explicitly Shī'ite phrase: *Alī Walī'ullāh* was added to the daily call to prayer and shouted along with the *adhān* throughout the whole Golconda kingdom. Special houses of mourning (*'āshūrā-khāna*) were set up in almost every village to lament the murder of Ḥusayn by Yazīd ibn Mu'āwiya and were generally used during the sacred month of Muḥarram.[25]

At the same time, a special new Shī'ite literature was also being produced in the vernacular Dakkanī language, intended to be read in popular assemblies to familiarize natives with the dogmas and tenets of Shī'ism.[26] By such devices Shī'ism was propagated and popularized throughout the entire Deccan.

IV

So it was against a background of clerical intimidation and Shī'ite fanaticism that the Sufis of the Deccan had to carry on their mission. Despite the many and varied challenges that they encountered at different levels of society, each of which supported a different warring sect or faction, they managed to preserve their tolerant and peaceful attitude. The Sufis generally kept aloof from the polemical debates raging in the Shī'ite literature of the period which,

---

[24] See *Tuḥfah-i majālis-i bihisht ā'in*, MS no. 10 Manaqib (Hyderabad: Salar Jang Museum).

[25] Hundreds of these *'āshūrā-khāna*s are still visible in different parts of the Deccan. A record of them is preserved in the State Archives, Hyderabad A.P. (= *Daftar-i ṣadārat al-'āliyya*) and also with the Muslim Waqf Board in Hyderabad. In some of these *'āshūrā-khāna*s, engravings and embroidered designs in cloth commemorating the martyrs of Karbalā are hung. Today, most of these houses are used as gathering places for Muslims who are both Shī'ite and Sunni. Although the *'āshūrā-khāna*s are still centres of great religious activity during the first ten days of Muḥarram, during my visits to a number of them between 1962 and 1977 I found that most of the persons in charge of them were Sunnis!

[26] Nāṣir al-Dīn Hāshimī, *Europe Mein Dakhanī Makhṭūṭāt* (Hyderabad 1932), pp. 318, 320; for later works of a popular nature in the Deccan, see, by the same author, *Kutub-khāna-i Salar Jang Museum kī Urdu qalamī Kitābon kī fihrist* (Hyderabad 1957), pp. 530–80.

whether it was produced in Iran or the Deccan, contained provocative theological discussions often filled with diatribes against the first three Sunni caliphs.

There were, however, some exceptions to this quietist attitude, among which could be mentioned Shāh Ṣibghatu'llāh (d. 1015/1606), who reacted very strongly to the Shī'ite movement. Born, educated and brought up in Gujarat, he had imbibed the anti-Shī'ite spirit prevalent among the Shaṭṭārī Sufis of Bijapur, as well as among some of the other Sufis in Bijapur who reacted against the increasing propagation of Shī'ism.[27] It may be noted that in contrast to Golconda where the regime of Shī'ite rulers was unbroken, Sunnis intermittently came to power in Bijapur.[28]

The Sufis, particularly of Golconda, but also generally elsewhere in the Deccan, maintained an attitude of passive resistance while persisting with their usual calm and constructive activities. Even viewed from the distant vantage point of history, it seems obvious that they intended to meet the challenges presented by the new religious climate by striving to deepen and intensify the spirituality of Indian society in different ways, and by preaching their message across diverse intellectual levels of society. In this fashion, Persianate Sufi teachings penetrated basically three areas of Indian culture, making use of (1) literary, (2) ritualistic, and (3) institutional forms.

Sufi literature in the Deccan assumed many different literary forms. On the one hand, Sufi writings included works of prose or verse written by a Sufi himself; on the other, one finds lectures or semi-biographical collections of aphoristic sayings (*malfūẓāt*) recorded in writing by a disciple. Sufi lectures and oral teachings were generally more accessible than prose compositions – the flow of expression being less hampered in speaking than in writing – and for this reason the *malfūẓāt* genre is often regarded as "the dominant literary form for the transmission of Sufi teaching" in India.[29]

The disciples of the great Deccani Sufi shaykhs of this period made a point of carefully recording the words uttered by their masters in various states of mind and social circumstances. Although the systematic recording of *malfūẓāt* can be seen in the Deccan from very early times, following the arrival of the Chishtī Sufis towards the close of the first quarter of the fourteenth century it seems to have became an almost indispensable part of the Indian Sufi literary tradition. *Malfūẓāt* continued to be composed through the following two centuries, so that the period with which this discussion is concerned is rich with collections of the warm, provocative and powerful utterances of such eminent Sufis as Shāh Mīrānjī Shams al-'Ushshāq (d. 905/1499); his son

---

[27] Richard Maxwell Eaton, *Sufis of Bijapur* (New Jersey: Princeton University Press 1978), pp. 114–16, 124.
[28] *Ibid.*, pp. 67, 71.
[29] Ernst, *Eternal Garden*, p. 64.

Burhān al-Dīn Jānam (d. 1006/1597); his *khalīfa* Shāh Maḥmūḍ Khush-dahān (d. 1026/1617);[30] Jānam's son Amīn al-Dīn 'Alā' (d. 1086/1675); Shāh Hāshim Pīr 'Alavī of Bijapur (1056/1646); Sayyid Abū'l Fayḍ Minu'llāh (d. early sixteenth century); Shāh Kalīmu'llāh Ḥusaynī (d. sixteenth century); Shāh Abū'l-Ḥasan Qādirī (d. 1635) of Bidar and Shāh Rājū Ḥusaīnī (d. 1096/1684) of Hyderabad.[31]

As far as literary activities were concerned, Islam was explained and taught by these Sufis in a style quite different from the teachings of professional mullās or theologians educated in religious seminaries. The Sufis endeavoured to transmit a truth by making use of the existing knowledge of their audiences, then adding their own personal insights and experiences to reveal the unseen secrets which lay behind local scenery and events. While this process of transmitting spiritual truth was at once lucid and appealing, it definitely made the listener feel slightly disturbed, in that he or she was not fully conscious of the real significance of the knowledge being thus received; yet, at the same time, when pondered more deeply, the full implications of the Sufi message usually led the listener to a renewed self-assessment. Thus, one fundamental aspect of the literature of late classical Persianate Sufism in India is the intensely personal nature of its expression, the personality and experiences of the author standing clearly present behind his words or sayings. Even though Persian was still the principal medium of their expression, often these soulfully recounted teachings sound more effective in the local Dakhanī Urdu idiom, suggesting that a considerable degree of concentration and effort must have been put into creating vernacular forms of expression.[32]

Examples of such teachings are particularly visible in the articulation of the Sufi concept of divine Unity (*tawḥīd*). The concept of *tawḥīd*, with its few nuances, is an oft-repeated theme in the Sufi literature of all times and places, and was especially prevalent in Sufi prose and poetry literature created in the Deccan; at the same time, monotony of expression seems to have been avoided, as the mystical manner of discourse always seems to sound fresh and original to the educated, discerning connoisseur. Their language was at once simple and academic; rational demonstrations were supported by stimulating quotations from the Koran, sayings of the Prophet and the great classical Sufi masters.

Among the interesting Sufi literature produced towards the end of the fifteenth century is a poem by Mīrānjī Shams al-'Ushshāq entitled *Waṣīyat un nūr*, written for the edification of girls. Composed in a simple regional

[30] See the essay by W.C. Chittick in this present volume (EDS).

[31] Ernst, *Eternal Garden*, *passim*; Sayyid Shah Khusro Hussaini, *Sayyid Muḥammad al-Husaynī Gīsūdirāz* p. 204; Schimmel, *Islam in the Indian Subcontinent*, pp. 59–61; Sayyid 'Alī Aṣghar Bilgramī, *Landmarks of The Deccan* (Hyderabad 1927), pp. 74–7.

[32] See also the essay by Annemarie Schimmel in this present volume (EDS).

Plate 12: Tomb of Muḥammad, son of ʻAdīl Shāh II. Bijapur, 12 December 1823. Drawing by Major-General John Briggs (1785–1875). From the Royal Asiatic Society's Briggs Collection 010.001. © Collection & Courtesy of the Royal Asiatic Society of Great Britain.

Dakhanī dialect, it instructs the reader how to have an experience with God; how to be enlightened with His light; how to discover the light of Muḥammad; how understand the essence of ritual prayer; what is the highest attainment of the human personality and how to discriminate between good and evil. The poem demonstrates how the literary forms of communication of Sufi teachings were adopted to meet the intellectual levels of the recipients. While perhaps of greater value for its practical appeal than its depth, its contents are identical to similar mystical works designed for the more mature, educated and discerning audience.[33]

This Sufi form of exposition of Islamic ritual practice is particularly evident in the *Zāḍ al-muwaḥḥidīn* composed in Persian by Shāh Rājū Ḥusaynī (d. 1096/1684) an outstanding Sufi of the Chishtī order in Golconda, who explained the meanings of ritual prayer (*ṣalāt*) as follows:

> *Ṣalāt* comprises four letters and involves four actions, the first of which is the praise of Allāh (*ḥamd*); the second is the laudation of Allāh (*takbīr*); the third is celebrating the praise of Allāh (*tasbīḥ*), and the fourth is offering salutation [to the angels and faithful believers] (*taḥiyyāt*). It also comprises four postures, the first of which is standing up (*qiyām*); the second is bowing (*rukū'*); and the third is sitting (*qu'ūd*) and the fourth is prostration (*sujūḍ*).
>
> Standing while praying is the proper behaviour to be maintained by a slave; bowing down is humbling oneself; sitting is the state of a fallen one; and prostration is an expression of total submission. This carries one through four stages. To perform *ṣalāt* thoroughly requires going through these stages in the presence of God. Best is the person who keeps trying.[34]

The practical training given in this passage was primarily based on the principle which was best summed up in the famous Persian Sufi adage of Abū Sa'īd ibn Abī al-Khayr: "[Keep your] heart with the beloved and [your] hands on the work" (*dil ba yār u dast ba kār*). Sufi devotees were thus instructed to be attentive towards God throughout various forms of meditation until their attention became habituated to being with Him constantly, not only during the appointed hours for ritual prayer, but at all other times as well. One should be mindful of Him during all one's daily activities, whether sitting or walking, looking at nature, frequenting human society, sleeping and so on. In this fashion, by referring to objects with immediate associations, popular Sufi teachers managed to boost morale and engage their readers' hearts and minds, realizing the objective of nearness to God.

Similarly, for working-class village women in the Deccan a special genre of simple poetry called *chakkī nāma* – sung or recited while grinding grain on

---

[33] Mīrānjī Shams al-'Ushshāq, *Waṣīyat un nūr*, ed Sabiha Nasrin (Hyderabad 1987).

[34] Shāh Rājū Ḥusaynī, *Zāḍ al muwaḥḥidīn*, collected and compiled by Husain Ibn Ḥasan (Hyderabad: Idarah-i Adabiyāt-i Urdu), MS no. 408, wrongly entered in the catalogue of vol. V as *Zāḍ al mū'minīn*.

Plate 13: Portrait of Sayyid Shāh Rājū. Mid-seventeenth-century drawing, Collection of the Archaeological Museum of Hyderabad, India.

the grindstone – and *charkha-nāma* – sung while spinning thread on the spinning wheel – or lullabies (*lorī nāmah*) were composed, providing them with a chance to sing in tune and keep their minds off the drudgery of daily chores while maintaining the moral and spiritual values of the Koran present in their minds. "The theology here," says R.M. Eaton, "is as simple as the language. ... These simple Islamic precepts were reinforced by parallels and metaphors drawn between them and various parts of the grindstone or spinning wheel at which the woman was working ...

See that our body is also a *chakkī*
And be careful in grinding.
The devil is my *saūkan* (one of the several wives)
Which prevents me from working and tires me.
  Yā bism Allāh, hū hū Allāh
The *chakkī*'s handle resembles alif, which means Allāh;
And the axle is Muḥammad, and is fixed there.
In this way the truth-seeker sees the relationship.
  Yā bism Allāh, hū hū Allāh.
We put the grains in the *chakkī*,
To which our hands are witnesses.
The *chakkī* of the body is in order
When you follow the *sharī'at*.
  Yā bism Allāh, hū hū Allāh
The name of Allāh comes from alif.
Know that *pīr*s and *murshid*s can lead our lives.
Grind the flour and then sift it –
  Yā bism Allāh, hū hū Allāh."[35]

Although the ideas, values, themes or even the forms may not have been original, such devices had their own charm and effectiveness and clearly demonstrated how the Sufis adapted Islamic rituals and literature to the needs of indigenous Indian traditions, thus reaching the minds of different levels of society.

So far as institutional activities were concerned, the Sufis' *khānaqāh*s were well established and well maintained. Sufis did not accept financial help from governments to run their *khānaqāhs*: these were maintained by the Sufis themselves with the support of their disciples. A *khānaqāh* was run with a very high degree of discipline. Sufis never liked leaving their *khānaqāh* except for communal prayers, which were performed in an adjacent mosque, or to attend a funeral, an *'urs* [36] or to visit another Sufi. They filled their time with the utmost care. The *khānaqāh* was a place where the disciples (*murīd*s)

[35] Eaton, *Sufis of Bijapur*, pp. 162–3; Hāshimī, *Europe Mein Dakhanī Makhṭūṭat*.
[36] Literally 'wedding', but in the context of Indo-Persian Sufism it refers to a large public celebration, often attended by thousands of ordinary believers and devotees, intended to mark the anniversary of a saint's death.

and other lay followers of the *ṭarīqa* could listen to short discourses of the master during the intervals between prayer times. Initiation into the order would take place generally in the presence of some close devotees. The procedure of initiating a *murīd* was traditional and meaningful. Generally, it consisted of promises given by the *murīd* to adhere to the *sharī'a*, to repent of his past sins, to renounce mundane attachments and to submit to and obey the orders of the *pīr*. For some Sufis this ceremony involved the candidate putting on a shroud, symbolic of his death to the world of secular attachments. The way a Sufi filled his time was exemplary to his followers. Thus, the *khānaqāh* and the way it was run were important factors in building up the religious and social attitude of their followers, for the *khānaqāh* was the real training house of the order.[37]

Although the annual celebration of *'urs* was not a part of normal *khānaqāh* activities, during the *'urs* special events could take place. As a major event attended by a large number of people, the *'urs* was an interesting public attraction, providing the best opportunity for the Sufis to exhibit their generosity, attract public goodwill for their cause and make their tenets beloved of the populace. Crossing religious boundaries, this celebration was attended by non-Muslims as much as Muslims, and participants often included Hindus, Jains, Shaivites, Harijans and aboriginal tribal folk, thus demonstrating the universalist nature of Islamic mysticism.

In contrast to the exclusivistic attitude of the formalist *'ulamā'* – whether Sunni or Shī'ite – the Sufis of the Deccan always maintained very good relations with the non-Muslim section of society which constituted the majority of the population. Hindu, Shivaite, Harijan and tribal devotees often played a role in organizing certain parts of a *khānaqāh*'s annual *'urs* celebration. Wherever they settled in the Deccan, the Sufis left no one in doubt that they belonged to the land of India. The masses always regarded them as their benefactors. They were greatly responsible for social stability of the society and furtherance of the spirit of Islam, together with respect for other faiths.

By the middle of the seventeenth century, the political powers are again seen waiting at the threshold of the Sufi *khānaqāh*s. 'Abdu'llāh Quṭb Shāh, whom we mentioned above, left the whole issue of royal succession to the throne in the hands of the Chishtī master Shāh Rājū Ḥusaynī, who in turn placed one of his lazy disciples, Abū'l-Ḥasan, on the throne of Golconda, forecasting his future success.[38] Then, in the early eighteenth century, the first Niẓām Nawāb Mīr Qamar al-Dīn (*reg.* 1724–48) paid a visit to Shaykh Niẓām al-Dīn of Awrangābād (1060/1650–1–1142/1730) to seek his blessings and

---

[37] Eaton, *Sufis of Bijapur*, pp. xxvii, 165–6, 203.

[38] Sherwani, *History of the Quṭb Shāhī Dynasty* (New Delhi: Munshiram Manoharlal Publishers, 1974), pp. 601–2.

was rewarded with a prophecy that his dynasty would remain in power for seven generations.[39]

For over two centuries, the Deccan had been the theatre in which Persianate Shī'ism tried to overpower Persianate Sufism, but without much success.

[39] The legend goes that when Niẓām al-Mulk Aṣaf Jāh I (d. 1748) was appointed as the head of the six provinces of the Deccan he went to pay his respects to a contemporary Sufi named Niẓām al-Dīn in Awrangābād. The Sufi treated him to a sort of bread called *kulchah* and kept urging the guest to eat as much as he could. Niẓām al-Mulk could eat about seven loaves of *kulchah* with much exertion. The saint then prophesied that his dynasty would remain in power for about seven generations. This legend has been related in slightly different versions. According to some, the Sufi in question was Shāh 'Ināyat; the seven loaves were picked up by Niẓām al-Mulk and given to him wrapped in a yellow piece of cloth. But the prophecy is common to both versions. The files concerning the renewal of the Niẓām's flag from ruler to ruler, with the seventh Niẓām's endorsement to continue to print *kulchah* on his state flag, are preserved in the Home Office records of the erstwhile state of Hyderabad. Also see Harriet Ronken Lynton and Mohini Rajan, *The Days of the Beloved* (Berkeley: University of California Press 1974), p. 24; Sayyid El-Edroos and L.R. Naik, *The Seven Loaves* (Hyderabad: Siasat Daily 1994).

Sufi Texts in Chinese

SACHIKO MURATA

The Prophet is reported to have said, "Seek knowledge, even unto China." However, Chinese Muslims, who were already in China, had to seek knowledge from Persia, or at least from Persian texts. Islam entered China early on in Islamic history, though clear historical records do not begin appearing until around the fourth/tenth century. No one knows to what extent the Islamic presence in China derives from immigrants or from Chinese converts to Islam. In any case, many of the immigrants gradually became indistinguishable from the native Chinese, and a large population of Muslims who considered themselves Chinese became established. Until the seventeenth century, however, it seems that Islamic learning was transmitted mainly in Persian and Arabic (and perhaps Turkic as well), since we have no Chinese texts on Islam written by Chinese Muslims before this time. Historians agree on two basic points – that Chinese Muslims began to write on Islam in Chinese in the seventeenth century,[1] and that Chinese Islam in general is heavily influenced by Persianate Sufism.

In order to grasp the full significance of this Chinese writing, we need to remember that China provides us with the only pre-modern case in which Muslims wrote in the language of a major, pre-existing intellectual tradition. Only the Indian, Buddhist, Greek, and a Judaeo-Christian traditions could compare with China in terms of richness and sophistication, but Muslims never had to express themselves in the languages of those traditions. This makes the Chinese example a sort of precursor of what some Muslims have been trying to accomplish today in Western languages, and the evidence seems to suggest that the Chinese Muslims were much more successful.[2]

---

[1] See Isaac Mason, "Notes on Chinese Mohammedan Literature," *Journal of the North China Branch of the Royal Asiatic Society*, 56 (1925), pp. 172–3; Donald Leslie, *Islam in Traditional China* (Canberra: Canberra College of Advanced Education 1986), pp. 136–8. The Japanese historian Kuwata Rokuro calls the seventeenth and eighteenth centuries the "renaissance" of Chinese Islam. See his "Minmatsu sinsho no kaiju," *Shiratori Festschrift* (Tokyo Tôyôshi Ronkô 1925), pp. 377–8.

[2] Of course, the Chinese Muslims were faced with a situation very different from that of the modern world, given that the principles that have moulded modern thought are largely

The Japanese historian Tazaka Kôdô analysed several book lists provided by Chinese, Japanese and European researchers in his monumental study of the history of Chinese Islam and came to the conclusion that the books used were mainly by Persian authors and mostly in Persian, though Arabic works also played an important role.[3] Saguchi Toru, another Japanese scholar, supported Tazaka's conclusions on the basis of fieldwork carried out in China in 1944. He visited seventeen mosques in Inner Mongolia and interviewed the local *'ulamā'*. He provides a list of books used in these mosques and their *madrasas* and concludes that most of the texts were written by Persians.[4] Altogether, he mentions twenty-one titles in Arabic and seventeen titles in Persian found in more than one mosque. The text found most commonly, in thirteen mosques, was *al-'Aqā'id*, the Islamic creed by the sixth/twelfth century theologian al-Nasafī (d. 537/1142-3).[5] According to Saguchi, though it certainly seems strange, only eleven mosques had copies of the Koran. Other commonly found works were on Arabic and Persian grammar, Ḥanafite jurisprudence, and *ḥadīth*. The most commonly found Sufi works were *Mirṣād al-'ibād*, the classic Persian compendium of Sufi lore by the seventh/thirteenth-century shaykh Najm al-Dīn Rāzī, in eight mosques; and the *Lama'āt* of his contemporary Fakhr al-Dīn 'Irāqī, one of the most important Persian Sufi texts on love in the perspective of the school of Ibn al-'Arabī, in seven mosques. In addition, Sa'dī's *Gulistān*, which can certainly be considered a book of Sufi moral teachings, was found in eight mosques.

This brings us to a second issue, which is the translation of Islamic works into Chinese. Few Islamic works are known to have been translated, and even the Koran was not fully translated until 1927. As far as I have been able to determine, only four Islamic books are known for certain to have been rendered into Chinese before the present century, and all are well-known Persian Sufi texts.[6] The earliest text to be translated was Rāzī's *Mirṣād al-*

hostile to religion, while no such hostility is found in the Chinese traditions. Although, one might argue that Far Eastern metaphysics and cosmology are impersonal and alien to the Islamic worldview, this was certainly not the view of the early Muslim authors of Chinese books.

[3] Tazaka Kôdô, *Chugoku ni okeru kaikyô no denrai to sono gutsû*, 2 vols (Tokyo: Tôyô Bunko 1924), pp. 1261–97.

[4] Saguchi Toru, "Chugoku isuramu no kyôten," *Toyôgakukô* 32 (1950), pp. 480–508.

[5] An English translation of the Arabic text, along with that of the commentary by Taftazānī, was done by E.E. Elder, *A Commentary on the Creed of Islam* (New York: Columbia University Press 1950).

[6] Other texts were certainly translated, but the present state of research makes their status difficult to determine. Most of the secondary literature has been written by scholars conversant with Chinese but unable to make use of the Islamic sources. Statements or suggestions by the Chinese authors that a work is a translation need to be tested against the original texts. Take, for example, Liu Chih's most famous book, to which he gave both a Persian and a Chinese title, *Tarjama-ye Muṣṭafā: T'ien-fang chih-sheng shih-lu* (The Translation of Muṣṭafā: The

'ibād, which was published by Wu Tzu-hsien in the year 1670.[7] The second was the *Lawā'iḥ* by 'Abd al-Raḥmān Jāmī, translated eighty years later, in 1751, by Liu Chih, perhaps the greatest Muslim scholar of China. The third book to be translated was the *Maqṣad-i aqṣā* by the well-known Sufi 'Azīz al-Dīn Nasafī (d. *c.* 700/1300). This was done in 1679 by She Yün-shan, who also went by the pen-name P'o Na-ch'ih. He was a disciple of Ch'ang Chih-me (d. 1683), who was author of a popular Persian grammar (which Saguchi found in eight mosques).[8] The fourth book, *Ashi"at al-lama'āt* – Jāmī's well-known commentary on 'Irāqī's *Lama'āt* – was also translated by She Yün-shan, though it is not known to have been published before 1930.[9] The fame of the first three of these books can be judged partly by the fact that they are among the small number of Sufi texts that have been translated into English.[10]

It should not be surprising that the Muslims of China translated Sufi texts rather than any other sort of Islamic text, given that the primary need of the Chinese Muslims, who were already practising their religion, was to be able to

Biography of the Ultimate Sage of Arabia). Leslie thinks that the main body of the text is in fact a translation of a fourteenth-century Persian work, *Tarjuma-yi mawlūd-i Muṣṭafā*, by 'Afīf ibn Muḥammad al-Kāzirūnī, which in turn is a translation from the Arabic original by 'Afīf's father (D. Leslie, *Islamic Literature in Chinese,* Canberra: Canberra College of Advanced Education 1981], p. 49). Another work, *Han i tao hsin chiu ching* (The Chinese Translation of the Final Investigation into the Progress of the Faith) by Ma Fu-chu, a prolific nineteenth-century scholar who was executed for his alleged involvement in a rebellion in Yunnan, is based on a Persian book by the same author (n.p.: 1870, p. 1). For present purposes, perhaps the most interesting of the works waiting to be carefully studied is *Ta hua tsung kuei* (The Great Transformation of All Returning), which is described as having been dictated and edited by Ma Fu-chu and written down by Ma Kai-ko. It is presented as a translation of the *Fuṣūs*, which must mean Ibn 'Arabī's *Fuṣūṣ al-ḥikam.* Nonetheless, Ma Kai-ko states in the introduction that the significance of the book is that, in contrast to the works of Wang Tai-yu and Liu Chih, it explains the nature of death and resurrection, but, as we know, the Arabic *Fuṣūṣ al-ḥikam* has little to say about this topic. It was compiled in 1865, when Fu-chus was 72 years old (Beijing 1922, p. 3; see also Chang-kuan Lin, "Three Eminent Chinese Ulama of Yunnan," *Journal of the Institute of Muslim Minority Affairs*, 11/1 [1990], pp. 103–8).

7 According to Leslie (*Islamic Literature in Chinese*, p. 29), a second translation of the *Mirṣād* was published in 1686–7, without the translator's name.

8 Leslie lists two translations of *Maqṣad-i aqṣā*, a dated one by She Yün-shan and an undated one with a different title by P'o Na-ch'ih (Leslie, *Islamic Literature in Chinese*, pp. 32–4). Yu Zhen-qui says that "P'o Na-ch'ih' is She's pen-name." (*Zhongguo yisinan wanxian zhuyi tiyao* [Ningshia] 1993), p. 111. This book does not seem to be extant, though an outline of its contents follows the Persian text closely (see R. Maerczak, "Littérature Sino-musulmane," *Revue du monde musulmane*, 28 [1914], pp. 147–9.

9 Leslie, *Islamic Literature in Chinese*, p. 43; Yu Zhen-qui, *Zhonggno yisinan wanxian zhuyi tiyao*, pp. 111–12; Saguchi, *Islam no kyôten*, p. 112.

10 *Mirṣād* has an excellent translation by H. Algar as *The Path of God's Bondsmen from Origin to Return* (Delmar, N.Y.: Caravan Books 1982), *Lawā'iḥ* an adequate translation by E. H. Whinfield and M.M. Kazwini as *Lawā'iḥ*: *A Treatise on Sufism* (London 1906), and *Maqṣad* a misleading and inadequate paraphrase by E.H. Palmer as *Oriental Mysticism: A Treatise on the Sufistic and Unitarian Theosophy of the Persians* (London 1867).

think about it adequately in their native language, which was by now Chinese. Of course, philosophy and *kalām* represent two other theoretical approaches to Islamic knowledge, but both were much more technical and assumed a broad acquaintance with the Islamic intellectual tradition. There is no book on philosophy or *kalām* that begins to approach *Mirṣād al-'ibād* in clarity, simplicity, and broad accessibility. In the Islamic languages themselves, only sophisticated scholars are able to read texts on philosophy and *kalām*, whereas various Sufi texts – especially Sufi poetry – are readily accessible to all Muslims.

Moreover, Sufism is well known for the broadness of its point of view, especially when compared with *kalām*. The earliest Muslim authors of books on Chinese demonstrate a great open-mindedness toward the three traditions of China – Confucianism, Taoism, and Buddhism – and they were well acquainted with Neoconfucian scholarship, which in certain respects brings the three Chinese traditions into harmony. They must have found the Sufi approach to metaphysical and cosmological teachings much more congenial than the polemical approach of *kalām*, and much easier to render into Chinese than the extremely technical discussions of the philosophers.

WANG TAIYU

The first Muslim author of Chinese books about Islam was Wang Taiyu, who seems to have died in 1657 or 1658. He was a member of a Muslim family that traced itself back to an astronomer who had come to China to serve the emperor three hundred years earlier. Despite the fact that his family had been in China for three centuries, he gained his Islamic learning in the Islamic languages. He did not begin a serious study of literary Chinese until the age of thirty when, he tells us, "I was so ashamed of my stupidity and smallness that I started to read books on metaphysics and history." Clearly, to be ashamed of his stupidity he must have been dealing mostly with learned Chinese-speakers, whether or not they were Muslims.

Wang provides a case study to demonstrate why Muslims should have undertaken to write in Chinese in the first place. One can conclude both from what he himself says explicitly and from the general content of his works that he was addressing two groups of people. One group consisted of the traditional Chinese intellectual classes, who would have been aware of Islam but had no idea about basic Islamic teachings other than the fact that Muslims did not eat pork (the truly outstanding Muslim characteristic in Chinese eyes). The other group was made up of Muslims who had become assimilated to the Chinese tradition to such a degree that they were unable to study Islamic literature in the Islamic languages, although they were familiar with the intellectual currents of China itself.

Wang has left us with one major work and four minor works. The major work, 'The True Commentary on the Real Teaching' (*Cheng-chiao chen ch'üan*), was first published in 1642 during his lifetime and has since been reprinted many times, most recently in 1987. This work has often been considered the foremost classic of Chinese Islam. In it, Wang summarizes Islamic teachings in two volumes, each of which is divided into twenty chapters. The first volume focuses on theological and metaphysical issues, such as the divine attributes, creation, predestination and the nature of the perfect human being. The second is more concerned with spiritual attitudes, ethics, and certain issues having to do with the *sharīʿa*. The book has little to say about Islamic practice, which was presumably being passed on in the social context. Rather, it focuses on why Islamic teachings make sense and why they should be accepted. In cases where practice is discussed, the issues are usually those that would go against traditional Chinese teachings, such as the prohibition of pork.

In explaining Islamic teachings, Wang makes skilful use of the terminology of the three Chinese traditions to prove his points. He depicts Islam in a way that agrees with basic Chinese ideas. He shows respect for the Chinese traditions and is happy to quote from the Chinese classics or to employ Buddhist and Taoist terminology to make his points. He is not uncritical of these traditions, but the degree of his criticisms probably does not transgress the degree of the mutual criticisms that were common among these traditions. Hence, his works do not suggest that Islam was alien to Chinese civilization. The Chinese reader would not feel that Islam is very different from the Chinese religions, and in fact, unless one has specific knowledge about Islam, it would be difficult to decide which religion much of the book is discussing. (When I showed this work to a Chinese colleague, opened randomly, and asked him about the topic, he read it for a few minutes and then said "Buddhism.")

Of course, I do not want to suggest that all Chinese Muslims were happy with the way in which Wang Taiyu was presenting Islam. He himself remarks that certain Muslim scholars had read his manuscript and criticized him for quoting too much from the Chinese classics and going too deeply into the metaphysics of Taoism and Buddhism. Wang says that his only concern was how the 'Principle' worked; he did not want to borrow any of the words. And why should his readers consider Buddhism or Taoism as strange? He agrees with his critics that everything can be found in the classical books of Islam, but he points out that Chinese speakers do not have access to these books. Hence, he has presented Islam in such a way that those unfamiliar with its teachings can understand it. In short, Wang followed the prophetic dictum, "Speak to listeners according to the level of their understanding."

Little is known about Wang's personal life or training, but it is obvious from his writings that he was thoroughly grounded in the Sufi intellectual tradition. It is well known that certain Sufi orders were active in China during this period, and there is no reason to suppose that the sophisticated theoretical doctrines of Sufism had not been brought along with more practically oriented teachings. The most obvious candidate for intellectual influence on Wang Taiyu was the school of Ibn 'Arabī, which was flourishing throughout the Islamic world at this time. However, Wang almost never cites Arabic words or mentions names of Muslim scholars in his writings, so it would be difficult to argue historically for such influence. Rather, I think we can assume the influence simply on the basis of the content of his works.

The influence of Sufi theoretical teachings is most obvious in one of Wang's shorter works, called 'The Great Learning of the Pure and the Real' (*Ch'ing-chen ta-hsüeh*), or, as one could also translate it, 'The Principles of Islam'. This book is a study of the concept of unity, and it employs a much more philosophical style than Wang's other books. Its basic topics are God, the Muḥammadan Reality, and the perfect human being, though these Arabic terms are not mentioned. Wang calls these realities 'The Real One' (*chenyi*), 'The Numerical One' (*shuyi*), and 'The Embodied One' (*tiyi*). He tells us that the Real One is the lord of heaven, earth, and the Ten Thousand Things; the Numerical One is the seed of heaven, earth, and the Ten Thousand Things; and the Embodied One is the fruit of heaven, earth, and the Ten Thousand Things. Throughout the text, Wang's goal is to explain the relationship between God and the perfect human being and to explicate the manner in which human beings can actualize their own true nature. Anyone familiar with the writings of the school of Ibn 'Arabī should find themselves quite at home in these discussions, despite the unfamiliar use of Chinese terminology.

LIU CHIH

A second important scholar, and a much more prolific author, is Liu Chih, who is ranked with Wang Taiyu as one of the two fathers of Chinese Islam.[11] He was born around 1670 and wrote the culminating work of his career in 1724, though it is not known when he died. Liu Chih tells us that he wrote several hundred manuscripts but only published ten per cent of them. His father was a scholar who felt deeply the lack of Islamic materials in Chinese. After a preliminary Islamic education, Liu Chih began studying the Chinese classics at the age of 15, then devoted six years to Arabic and Islamic literature, three years to Buddhism and a year to Taoism. He also tells us that he completed his education by studying 137 books from the West. Scholars have assumed that he means European books, and this is plausible, given the fact that the famous Jesuit Matteo Ricci had arrived in China more than a century earlier, in 1601, and he and his successors had written many Chinese tracts on Christianity and

---

[11] Several of the details about Liu Chih provided here are taken from the article by A.D.W. Forbes, *Encyclopaedia of Islam* (new edition), pp. 770–1.

Western knowledge in general. One Japanese scholar, however, thinks that this might simply mean Persian and Arabic books.[12]

From the age of 33, that is, around the year 1700, some forty years after the death of Wang Taiyu, Liu Chih turned his efforts towards making Islamic learning available in Chinese. Western scholars have remarked that he is more sympathetic toward Confucianism than any other Chinese Muslim author. Like Wang Taiyu, he saw no fundamental discrepancy between Islamic teachings on God and the world and the grand philosophical systems of Neoconfucianism, which by this period was the predominant philosophical and religious perspective of China. He wrote that the guiding principle of the Koran is similar to that which motivated Confucius and Mencius. Here he uses the term *li*, the basic Neoconfucian term for the 'principle of all things', and he writes that this "*li* is the same *li* that exists everywhere under heaven." He seems to be expressing in Chinese the Koranic view that God has sent prophets to teach *tawḥīd* to all peoples. In the preface to Liu Chih's first major work, 'The Philosophy of Arabia' (*Tien-fang hsing-li*), published in 1704, a non-Muslim mandarin, who was Vice-Minister of the Board of Ritual, wrote as follows: "The ancient Confucian doctrine has been undermined at different times by Buddhists and Taoists . . . Now, however, in this book of Liu Chih, we see once more the way of the ancient sages . . . Thus, although this book explains Islam, in truth it illuminates our Confucianism."

Liu Chih's 'Philosophy of Arabia' presents basic Islamic teachings on *tawḥīd* and cosmology. The six-volume edition that I have seen includes an introduction and five chapters. The introduction provides ten basic diagrams illustrating various relationships among macrocosmic, microcosmic, and metacosmic realities. The five chapters explain each of these diagrams in systematic detail, employing twelve more diagrams in each chapter. On the one hand the diagrams are reminiscent of those common in the Arabic and Persian works of the school of Ibn 'Arabī from about the eighth/fourteenth century onwards,[13] and on the other they appear to be traditional Chinese descriptions of the cosmos.

By 'Philosophy' Liu Chih does not mean *falsafa* in the technical Islamic sense, but rather 'wisdom' as formulated in Sufi texts. This becomes completely clear in the introduction, in which he quotes by name from seven different Persian and Arabic books. The titles of the books and the frequency of his mentioning them are highly significant. The most often cited is *Mirṣād al-'ibād* (twenty-nine times), then Jāmī's *Ashi"at al-lama'āt* (fifteen times), then Nasafī's *Maqṣad-i aqṣā* (twelve times), and then Jāmī's *Lawā'iḥ* (eleven

[12] Nohara Shiro, *Tempô tenrei taku yôkai no hôyaku ni saishite kaiyyôken*, IV, 2 (Tokyo 1940), p. 81.

[13] For a collection of twenty-eight such diagrams provided by the Sayyid Haydar Āmulī, see *Kitāb naṣṣ al-nuṣūṣ*, ed. by H. Corbin and O. Yahia (Tehran: Bibliothèque Iranienne 1975).

times). The next most frequently quoted book (nine times) is *Mawāqif*, the famous Arabic text on *kalām* by the eighth/fourteenth-century scholar al-Ījī (d. 756/1355). Liu Chih also quotes four times from what he calls *Tafsīr*, which is probably the well-known Persian commentary on the Koran by Ḥusayn Wāʿiẓ-i Kāshifī; and he quotes once from a book he calls *Aḥkām-i kawākib*, which is presumably a Persian work on astronomy.

In his 'Philosophy of Arabia' and in another well-known work called 'A Selection of Important Arabian Rules and Ceremonies' (*T'ien-fang tien-li che-yao-chiai*), Liu Chih provides lists of the titles that he has employed as his sources. Altogether, these consist of sixty-eight different works, of which eighteen are used in both books, and of which at least fifteen are on Sufism.[14] Although the identity of all these titles has yet to be established, there do not seem to be any significant works pertaining to the fields of *kalām* and *falsafa* other than the work of Ījī. In other words, most of the works that provide theoretical explanations of the nature of things – God, the cosmos, the soul – belong to the Sufi tradition. It is clearly the Sufi works, along with the Chinese intellectual tradition – Neoconfucianism in particular – that form the basis for Liu Chih's explanation of Islamic teachings.

Liu Chih's last major work, which he considered the climax of his career, was a biography of Muḥammad, completed in Nanking in 1137/1724. This work has been wholly or partly translated into Russian, French, English, and Japanese.[15] I have examined the English and Japanese translations, and both suffer from the translators' lack of knowledge of Islam, though they do provide a good idea of the contents of the work. Although the article on Liu Chih in the *Encyclopaedia of Islam* calls his life of the Prophet "undoubtedly Liu Chih's greatest work," we may be allowed to doubt this, given that 'greatness' should not necessarily be assumed on the basis of widespread appeal. I think that Liu Chih's efforts to harmonize Islamic metaphysical, cosmological, and spiritual teachings with the Chinese tradition may in fact have been a much more important contribution to the permanent establishment of Islam in China.

The Translation of the Lawāʾiḥ

One of the most interesting and significant of Liu Chih's works is his translation of the *Lawāʾiḥ* by ʿAbd al-Raḥmān Jāmī (d. 898/1492), which has already been mentioned. Jāmī, as is well known, was one of the most famous and influential of the later scholars in the eastern lands of Islam, and he was

[14] In his list of sources, he mentions several other Sufi works, including the *Kashf al-maḥjūb* of Hujwīrī, *Kashf al-asrār* of Maybudī, and *Tadhkirat al-awliāʾ* of ʿAṭṭār. Tazaka, *Chugoku*, gives twelve titles on Sufism, pp. 1286–89.

[15] The whole text was translated into Japanese, and about the first half of the book was rendered into English by Isaac Mason (Shanghai 1921).

widely read wherever Persian was known. Some of Jāmī's Persian works, including the *Lawā'iḥ*, are sophisticated presentations of the teachings of Ibn al-'Arabī and his followers, such as Ṣadr al-Dīn Qūnawī, Sa'īd al-Dīn Farghānī, and Dāwūd al-Qayṣarī.[16] In what follows, I would like to illustrate the way in which the Sufi texts were translated with an example of what Liu Chih does with the *Lawā'iḥ*. What I will say also holds more or less true for the translation of the *Mirṣād al-'ibād*, though, of course, the *Lawā'iḥ* is a much more difficult and technical book. It should not be surprising to anyone who has read both works that the *Mirṣād* should have become a standard text in the *madrasas*; the *Lawā'iḥ* was certainly reserved for a minority of philosophically and metaphysically minded scholars and students.

Like Wang Taiyu, the translators of these two works avoid mentioning Arabic or Persian words unless it is absolutely necessary. Thus, for example, in the translation of the *Lawā'iḥ*, Liu Chih mentions the words *Allāh* and *Raḥmān* only once. Neither translator makes any attempt to translate Islamic ideas in a literal way. The translations are really paraphrases, in which the translators are not concerned with finding exact equivalents for Arabic and Persian terms, but rather with presenting the general ideas in a manner that accords with the Chinese tradition. This is especially so when the ideas and concepts are alien to China. In such cases, the translators are likely to drop the passage. In short, they present the texts so that they will make sense not only to Chinese Muslims, but also to non-Muslim Chinese.

In the *Lawā'iḥ*, Jāmī alleviates the denseness of the philosophical discussion by interspersing his text with quatrains which summarize his points with the usual lightness of Persian poetry. If one has not quite understood what he is getting at in the prose sections, at least the poetry delights the ear and suggests in more straightforward language the point of the discussion. In his translation, Liu Chih is interested only in the prose text, and with two exceptions, he makes no attempt to translate the quatrains. Hence the Chinese text keeps the high philosophical level throughout, and readers have no opportunity to refresh themselves with poetical diversions.

Liu Chih not only drops the poetry, he also, on occasion, adds commentary to the text, and he does not tell the reader that the translator rather than the author is speaking. Some of his commentary helps us understand how he sees

[16] Jāmī's influence and fame, however, were far greater than these prose works would have warranted, because he was also a great poet. He was a master of the ghazal, and many of his ghazals are explicit in their use of the technical terminology of Ibn 'Arabī's school. No doubt his seven *mathnawī*s, however, were even more widely read, since they retell many of the classic stories of Islamic literature, such as "Yūsuf wa Zulaykhā," "Laylī wa Majnūn," and the "Iskandar Nāma." Like the *mathnawī*s of 'Aṭṭār or Rūmī, these stories are full of digressions in which the author explains points of Islamic doctrine, but in contrast to those works, the doctrines in these works are firmly grounded in the world view codified by Ibn 'Arabī and his followers.

this text in relation to traditional Chinese thinking. Thus, for example, at the end of the twelfth chapter, Liu Chih writes that the first twelve chapters have dealt with the virtues of seeking the path and walking upon it, while the remaining twenty-four chapters concern the meanings of the Principle that is both manifesting and non-manifesting. The Chinese term here is the already mentioned *li*, the key concept in Neoconfucian philosophy and cosmology, while the Persian/Arabic word that he has in mind is *ḥaqīqa*. In Neoconfucian thought, Tai Chi or the 'Great Ultimate' (also called the Tao) is considered the Principle of the universe. Then the movement and quietude of the Principle bring yang and yin into existence, and these are considered the *chi* – the 'energy' or the 'material force' of the Principle. Thus, the whole of creation is looked upon as a manifestation of the Principle by means of the Principle's two energies or forces. Liu Chih and other Chinese Muslim scholars saw this as completely in harmony with Islamic thinking.[17]

Jāmī calls each chapter of *Lawā'iḥ* simply a *lā'iḥa*, or 'flash', but Liu Chih provides a specific title for each. He calls chapter 18 'Gathering the Levels'. Before translating Jāmī's explanation of how everything goes back to the very reality of Being (*'ayn-i ḥaqīqat-i wujūd*), he provides his own commentary, employing the terms *li* and *chi*, Principle and Energy. I quote:

> When there is true Being, there is true knowledge. When there is true knowledge, there is true power. Knowledge and power are the functions of Being, and they act to create. After the action of creation, Principle and Energy become separate. After the separation of Principle and Energy, the things appear. After the things appear, the growing forms appear. After the growing forms appear, animate life is born. Then the kinds of the things become distinguished, and the classes of the things are divided in accordance with the names. Names and forms depend upon each other, but these are not real things. The real things are nothing but the True Being, which first manifests all its affairs on the level of knowledge, which is contained in the Principle. Then, on the level of power, the forms appear separately, which means that the things come into being outwardly. Existent things depend upon the demarcating names of the True Being. Life depends on growth; growth depends on the composition of the elements; the composition of the elements depends on Energy; Energy depends on Principle. Principle is the subtle storehouse of the True Being's knowledge and power.

Liu Chih now proceeds to paraphrase Jāmī's chapter. Jāmī is reviewing a well-known philosophical method of reducing all multiplicity to the One and showing that everything perceived in the universe manifests the Absolute

---

[17] Long before I was familiar with these Chinese books, I myself felt, on the basis of my Far Eastern background, that Islamic thought was basically in harmony with that of traditional China, and I tried to show this in my *Tao of Islam* (Albany: SUNY Press 1993). I have been delighted over the past three years to discover that I have been following in the footsteps of these Chinese teachers.

Being. He begins with the individuals, and then he shows how all the individuals go back to the species, the species back to the genera, the genera back to body, the body back to substance, substance back to possible existence, and possible existence back to the Necessary Being . Then he explains that the 'immutable entities' (*a'yān-i thābita*) – a term made famous by Ibn 'Arabī's writings – pertain to God's knowledge. These entities are the things as known by God, and hence they are the things 'before' their entrance into existence. God creates the universe by giving existence to these objects of his own knowledge. Hence God is at once the source of all multiplicity, because of his knowledge of all things, and of unity, because of his own one Being. As Ibn 'Arabī sometimes expresses this idea, God is *al-wāḥid al-kathīr*, 'the One/the Many'.

In order to give a flavour of the changes that occur in the Chinese, I will translate Jāmī's text from the Persian, passage by passage, then Liu Chih's text from the Chinese. Notice that Jāmī, in typical Persian style, employs a good deal of technical terminology, often using two different but basically synonymous words, in order to bring together various well-known ways of saying the same thing. In contrast, Liu Chih is not concerned to preserve the technical terminology, but rather to express the idea in a straightforward manner.

> Jāmī: "Once you remove the individuations and the entitifications that are subsumed under the individuals and species of the animals, then the individuals of every species come together under *species*. When you remove the distinctions of the species, which are the specific differences and the characteristics, then all come together under the reality of *growing body*."

Liu Chih summarizes this paragraph very briefly: "If you remove the distinctions of the names that demarcate the 'animate things' all of them become growing bodies."

> Jāmī: "When you remove the distinctions of the growing body and everything subsumed along with it under the body, then everything comes together in the reality of *body*. When you remove the distinctions of the body and everything subsumed along with it under substance – I mean the intellects and the souls – then everything comes together under the reality of *substance*. When you remove that through which substance and accident become distinct, everything comes together under the reality of the *possible thing*."

Here Jāmī has taken three steps to move from the concept of growing *body* to the concept of *possibility*. Possibility is contrasted with Necessity. Possibility is the characteristic of creation, while Necessity is the exclusive property of God or Being. Liu Chih does not bother trying to explain these three steps or to enter into a discussion of possibility and Necessity. Instead, he expresses a parallel idea in Neoconfucian terms. Thus he jumps from *growing body* to the matter in which Energy displays itself. Energy, of course, is *chi*, which is contrasted with *li* or Principle. *Chi* and *li* together play a role in Neoconfucianism analogous with possibility and Necessity in Islamic thought. Thus Liu Chih writes: "If you remove the distinctions of the names that demarcate the growing bodies, all of them become the matter of Energy."

Next Jāmī writes, "If you remove that through which the Necessary and the possible become distinct, both come together under the reality of the Absolute Existent [*mawjūd-i muṭlaq*]." Liu Chih renders this as, "If you remove the distinctions that demarcate the names of the matter of Energy, everything makes up one Principle."

Now Jāmī explains that the Absolute Existent is nothing but pure Being, which has the attribute of necessity. In contrast, possible existence is rooted in the immutable entities. These entities are also called the divine 'tasks' (*shu'ūn*), one of Ibn 'Arabī's technical terms, taken from the Koranic verse, "Each day He is upon some task" (LV:29). Thus each entity is a 'task' of God, or a concomitant of His very reality, which is nothing but Being. Hence all multiplicity goes back to the One Essence.

> Jāmī: "This [Absolute Existent] is nothing but the reality of Being. It exists through its own Essence, not through an existence that is superadded to its Essence. Necessity is the manifest attribute of Being, while possibility is Its nonmanifest attribute. [By possibility] I mean the immutable entities that are actualized when He discloses Himself to Himself as clothed in His own tasks. Thus all the mentioned distinctions – whether the specific differences, the characteristics, the entifications, or the individuations – are the divine 'tasks'' that are subsumed and contained under the Oneness of the Essence."

In his translation of this passage, Liu Chih once again ignores the discussion of Necessity and possibility; nor does he pay any attention to the issue of the immutable entities and the term divine 'task', a word which, after all, is used in Arabic and Persian mainly because it supports the argument with a Koranic context. The Koranic context is obvious in the Persian, but it is unknown to most Chinese readers and would take too much time to explain. Instead of going into the discussion of immutable entities and God's self-disclosure to Himself in the entities, Liu Chih presents the distinction between the entities and God's self-disclosure as the complementary attributes of Knowledge and Power, which can easily be assimilated with yin and yang, though he does not do so here. He writes:

> If you remove the distinctions of the names that demarcate the Principle of the things, all of them become the knowledge and the power of the One True Being. If you remove the distinctions that demarcate the names of Knowledge and Power, all of them become the Absolute Being.

In the next two sentences, Jāmī tells us that all the distinctions mentioned in reducing multiplicity to unity are already present in the immutable entities, and they become manifest when God bestows existence on the immutable entities, thus making manifest the existent entities. He writes:

> The distinctions come forth first at the level of knowledge in the form of the immutable entities. Second, they take to themselves the form of external entities at the level of actual existence. They do so by becoming clothed in the properties and the traces of the tasks through the manifest domain of Being, which is the locus of disclosure and the mirror for the non-manifest domain of Being.

In rendering this passage, Liu Chih pays no attention to the technical terminology, but instead represents the idea in straightforward terms. "True Being is one, but the manifesting demarcations of the names are not one." Then he provides his own commentary by summarizing the significance of the point: "Those who have a narrow vision do not reach the Origin, and thus they think that the Lord is outside the things. The fact is that the Lord delimits Himself through the Ten Thousand Things."

The Yasavī Order and Persian Hagiography in Seventeenth-Century Central Asia

'Ālim Shaykh of 'Alīyābād and his Lamaḥāt min nafaḥāt al-quds*

DEVIN DEWEESE

The well-defined historical eras that lend their names to the present volume – Safavid and Mughul – have a counterpart that is equally well defined, in chronological terms, but unfortunately inaptly named, for another centre of Persianate culture from the sixteenth to eighteenth centuries. I refer, of course, to Central Asia during what is usually called, for want of a better term, the 'Uzbek' era, so named after the Turkic tribes of the Dasht-i Qïpchāq that established themselves in Central Asia at the beginning of the sixteenth century, at the expense of both Safavid and Timurid (that is, 'Mughul') claims and ambitions. This era, which came to an end with the Russian conquest of Central Asia, was dominated politically by the interplay of the Chingisid 'royal' clans of the Shïbānid (or 'Shaybānid') and later Ashtarkhānid (or 'Tuqāy-Timurid') dynasties, on the one hand, and the chieftains – *amīr*s or *bek*s – of the leading Uzbek tribal groups, on the other; culturally, however, the 'Uzbek' era is marked by the emergence of a Central Asian synthesis of Islamic and Inner Asian civilization expressed primarily, if not exclusively, through Persianate literary and artistic conventions. The essentially Inner Asian polity represented by these Chingisids and Uzbek tribal chieftains, together with the specifically Central Asian cultural synthesis over which they presided, constituted, in effect, a third force in the eastern Islamic world, one that not only limited and hence defined the political and cultural spheres of influence of both Mughul and Safavid civilizations, but also maintained a circulation of commercial and cultural 'goods', and of political, intellectual, and spiritual 'talent', with the Mughul and Safavid worlds.

---

* Preparation of this chapter was made possible in part through the financial assistance of the Indiana University Russian and East European Institute and through the Andrew W. Mellon Foundation Endowment.

Sufism, or more properly its representatives and expressions, played a central role in the political, cultural, intellectual, economic, social, and spiritual life of this era, as other contributions in this volume make clear for the Safavid and Mughul contexts; but the remarkable vitality and dynamism of Central Asian Sufism during the Uzbek era, dominated by the political, economic, and social vigour of the Naqshbandī order, also clearly belong to the realm of 'Persianate Sufism' in this period, and its distinctively Central Asian features only underscore – as do the distinctively Indian features of Indian Sufism, for example – the broad range of cultural, social, political, and religious environments in which Persianate Sufism flourished. The serious study of Sufism in Uzbek-era Central Asia has barely begun, however, and it may be more helpful to offer a brief but focused glimpse of one example, distinctively Central Asian yet Persian in its expression, rather than attempt an overview or synthesis of what, for the scholarly world, remains – and will remain until more detailed studies are undertaken – quite unfamiliar territory. My focus, indeed, will not be the remarkably successful Naqshbandiyya; rather, I would like to highlight one of the less successful manifestations of Central Asian Sufism during the Uzbek era, one which died out as a Sufi order, but which nevertheless may illustrate even more clearly than the Naqshbandiyya – which is typically *expected* to have an Iranian cast in its literary expression and in its constituency – the dominance of Persianate cultural forms in late Central Asian Sufism.

My focus, that is, is on the Yasavī Sufi tradition, a tradition customarily referred to not only as the 'Yasaviyya', but also by two other designations (one rooted in spiritual practice, the other in an ethnic and linguistic consciousness that would seem incongruous with the thrust of this volume): the Yasaviyya is the Jahriyya, so-called after the vocal *dhikr* whose legitimacy the Yasavī shaykhs staunchly defended against (primarily) Naqshbandī attacks; and it is, in an expression traceable to the early thirteenth century, at least, "the Turkic shaykhs" (*mashā'ikh-i turk*). Broadly speaking, then, my task is thus to explain the relevance of these Turkic shaykhs to the phenomenon of late classical Persianate Sufism.

THE YASAVĪ TRADITION AND ITS LITERARY LEGACY IN PERSIAN

The Yasavī Sufi tradition, by way of orientation, takes its name from Khwāja Aḥmad Yasavī, whose centre of activity was the town of Yasï, now called Turkistan, in what is now southern Kazakhstan. Aḥmad Yasavī is ordinarily assigned a death-date of 562/1166–7, but this is clearly wrong, and it is likely that he lived into the early thirteenth century. He is perhaps best known not for his Sufi career, but for the magnificent mausoleum erected at his grave by order of Timur at the end of the fourteenth century; the mausoleum reminds us that our evaluation of the Shaykh's reputation and impact cannot be based entirely on the sparse and conflicting information recorded about him in written sources.

We cannot take up here the extensive early history of the Yasavī Sufi tradition;[1] suffice it to say that this tradition exhibited all the complexities of Central Asian Sufism from the thirteenth to the fifteenth centuries, reflecting various forms of communal organization and legitimation, linked with diverse principles of succession and authority, before one community in central Mawarannahr emerged during the fifteenth century with the markings of a *bona fide* Sufi order. This community was not the only part of the Yasavī tradition to survive this early phase; other Sufi communities traced back to Aḥmad Yasavī, based especially upon hereditary succession, continued to exist into the sixteenth century and beyond, but only one Yasavī *silsila* line produced the 'Order' that adopted principles of non-hereditary succession, competed for patronage and disciples with the Naqshbandī, Kubravī, 'Ishqī, and Zaynī Orders, and left a discursive legacy of its spiritual venture in the form of primarily hagiographical compilations that now define (or should define) the Yasavī tradition for us. We will return shortly to that discursive legacy.

The history of the Yasavī tradition has been seriously neglected through most of this century, leaving a host of misconceptions and wrong-headed assumptions about this most Central Asian of all Central Asian Sufi traditions. The tendency to view the Yasaviyya as a phenomenon of an entirely Turkic cultural world – and even as one to be studied primarily from the standpoint of its echoes, which are in fact quite faint, in Anatolian Turkish religious history – has played a central role in the misunderstanding of the Yasavī tradition; that misunderstanding is especially acute in the period of concern here, during which one *silsila* line traced to Aḥmad Yasavī served as the conceptual and organizational focus of an actual Sufi order of the type we find prevalent in the Islamic world during the sixteenth and seventeenth centuries. The Yasavī Order of this period, which must be distinguished from the broader range of manifestations of the Yasavī tradition known from the thirteenth to the twentieth centuries, was not only centred in traditionally Persophone regions of Central Asia (especially in the urban and agricultural regions of central Mawarannahr from Samarqand to Bukhārā, and also in Balkh), but left its most substantial literary legacy almost entirely in Persian; indeed, the only Turkic-language product of the Yasavī tradition during the sixteenth and seventeenth centuries is, in all likelihood, the famous *Dīvān-i Ḥikmat*, the collection of mystical verse typically ascribed to Aḥmad Yasavī himself, but unquestionably the work of later times, and most likely the work of sixteenth-century affiliates of the Yasavī Order.

---

[1] See my preliminary remarks in "The *Mashā'ikh-i Turk* and the *Khojagān*: Rethinking the Links between the Yasavī and Naqshbandī Sufi Traditions," *Journal of Islamic Studies*, 7 (1996), pp. 180–207; a fuller study of the Yasavī tradition is in preparation.

The Persian literary legacy of the Yasavī Order begins with the *Taʿlīm al-dhākirīn*, a defence of the vocal *dhikr* written by a disciple of the Yasavī shaykh Khudāydād (d. 939/1532) in 947/1541.[2] It includes two Persian works by 'Ḥazīnī', a native of Ḥiṣār in Mawarannahr (in present-day Tajikistan) transplanted to Istanbul late in the sixteenth century with the aim of establishing the Yasavī order in the Ottoman world, whose Ottoman Turkic *Javāhir al-abrār* shaped our image of the Yasavī tradition (not always helpfully) by serving as the chief and often only source utilized by Mehmed Fuad Köprülü in his classic study (noted below).[3] It also includes the *Manāqib al-akhyār*, by Sayyid Muḥammad Qāsim 'Riḍvān', written in 1036/1626 about the hereditary Sayyid Atā'ī Sufi lineage traced through the author's father,[4] and it continued into the second half of the seventeenth century in the doctrinal and hagiographical *Ḥujjat al-dhākirīn*, begun in

---

[2] MS St Petersburg Branch of the Institute of Oriental Studies of the Russian Academy of Sciences (hereafter "POIVRAN"), C1563, fos. 45b–120a; the work is not described in a published catalogue, but is listed and identified in *Persidskie i tadzhikskie rukopisi Instituta narodov Azii AN SSSR* (*Kratkii alfavitnyi katalog*), ed. O.F. Akimushkin, V.V. Kushev, *et al.* (Moscow: Nauka 1964), I (hereafter *Kr. alf. kat*), p. 125, no. 808.

[3] One of Hazīnī's Persian works (whose title is not known because the beginning of the text has been lost) is preserved in the same manuscript, at Istanbul University Library (TY 3893), in which the Turkic *Javāhir al-abrār* survives; the manuscript has now been published, partly in transcription (for the Turkic section) and partly in facsimile combined with modern Turkish translation (for the Persian section), by Cihan Okuyucu (Hazini, *Cevâhiru'l-ebrâr min emvâc-ı bihâr* (*Yesevî Menâkıbnamesi*) [Kayseri: Erciyes Üniversitesi 1995]). The editor assumes (as did Köprülü) that the work contains only one work, in which the author switches from Turkic to Persian, but the abruptness of the change (between folios) and the distinct contents (not to mention language) of each section make it more likely that two separate works were included in the manuscript; undoubtedly several folios were lost from the middle of the manuscript, containing the end of the Turkic *Javāhir al-abrār* (which is clearly drawing to a close as the text breaks off) and a somewhat more substantial part of the Persian work's beginning. Okuyucu was also unaware of Ḥazīnī's other Persian work on the Yasaviyya, written entirely in verse, the *Ḥujjat al-abrār*, known from a single manuscript preserved in Paris. (MS Pers. A.F. 263, fos 103b–173b, described in *Catalogue des manuscrits persans de la Bibliothèque Nationale* ed. E. Blochet, [Paris 1928], III, pp. 122–3, no. 1377; Blochet wrongly identified the author as 'Sayyid Murshid', which is merely an epithet assigned by the author to his shaykh.) Evidently Marijan Molé was the first to point out that the *Ḥujjat al-abrār*'s author was the same as that of the *Javāhir al-abrār* ("Autour du Daré Mansour: l'apprentissage mystique de Bahā' al-Dīn Naqshband," *Revue des études islamiques*, 27 [1959], pp. 35–66 [p. 41, n. 35]); the *Ḥujjat al-abrār* was also cited in Hamid Algar, "Silent and Vocal *dhikr* in the Naqshbandī Order," in *Akten des VII. Kongresses für Arabistik und Islamwissenschaft* (Göttingen, 15. bis 22. August 1974), ed. Albert Dietrich (Göttingen: Vandenhoeck & Ruprecht 1976), p. 44).

[4] I have briefly outlined the contents of this work, based on two known copies, in "A Neglected Source on Central Asian History: The Seventeenth-Century Yasavī Hagiography *Manāqib al-akhyār*," in *Essays on Uzbek History, Culture, and Language*, ed. Denis Sinor and Bakhtiyar A. Nazarov (Uralic and Altaic Series, 156 Bloomington: RIFIAS 1993), pp. 38–50.

1077/1666–7 by the Bukharan Yasavī Shaykh Mawlānā Muḥammad Sharīf al-Ḥusaynī al-'Alavī.[5]

Without any question, however, the most important Persian-language work produced in Yasavī circles, and our richest source on the Yasavī order in Central Asia, is the *Lamaḥāt min nafaḥāt al-quds*, a hagiography compiled in 1035/1626 and dedicated to the Ashtarkhānid ruler Imām Qulī Khān. Its author was himself a pivotal shaykh in the Yasavī *silsila*, Muḥammad al-'Ālim al-Ṣiddīqī al-'Alavī, known customarily as 'Ālim Shaykh 'Azīzān (d. 1041/1632); the *Lamaḥāt* survives in at least fifteen manuscripts,[6] and was lithographed in Tashkent in 1327/1909. The work is important both because it assembled much material on the early phases of the Yasavī tradition that had not been written down before its time (at least as far as we can judge by extant sources), and because it traced the history of the lineage that produced the actual Yasavī 'order' of the sixteenth and seventeenth centuries; it also came to define the later Yasavī *silsila* for many compilers of general hagiographical compendia in subsequent centuries.

Neither the history nor the literary and hagiographical legacy of the Yasavī order in the sixteenth and seventeenth centuries has received much scholarly attention, however. The classic, but now badly outdated, work on Yasavī

---

[5] I have used MS POIVRAN B3787 (*Kr. alf. kat.*, p. 152, No. 1027), fos. 110b–205b; other copies are preserved in St Petersburg, Tashkent, and Istanbul, and the author, Mawlānā Muḥammad Sharif, left other Persian works as well.

[6] I have used MS POIVRAN C1602, fos. 1b-124b, copied in 1036/1626–27 by one Ḥāmid b. Shāh Ayyūb al-Ḥusaynī, described in N.D. Miklukho-Maklai, *Opisanie tadzhikskikh i persidskikh rukopisei Instituta narodov Azii*, vyp. 2, Biograficheskie sochineniia (Moscow: Izdatel'stvo Vostochnoi Literatury 1961), pp. 133–5, no. 187; cf. *Kr. alf. kat.*, p. 478, no. 3659; the description notes the work's importance, but is misleading in referring to 'Ālim Shaykh as a member of "a special branch of the Naqshbandī order, bearing the designation Jahriyya-i Sulṭāniyya, of which the famous Aḥmad Yasavī was considered the founder." The St Petersburg collection includes one other copy (POIVRAN C1492, fos. 14b–163b, defective at the end; *Kr. alf. kat.*, no. 3658). Only one copy preserved in the Institute of Oriental Studies of the Academy of Sciences of Uzbekistan (hereafter IVANUz) is mentioned in a published catalogue: MS IVANUz 638 (a nineteenth-century copy), described in *Sobranie vostochnykh rukopisei Akademii nauk Uzbekskoi SSR*, ed. A.A. Semenov (hereafter 'SVR'), III (Tashkent: Fan, 1955), p. 354, no. 2671; the institute's card catalogue lists eight other uncatalogued copies of the work (MSS IVANUz 5587 [223 fos., copied in 1199/1784–5], as well as 495, 1483, 3408, 6168, 8081, 8813, and 10567, all copies from the nineteenth or twentieth centuries or undated). The Institute of Manuscripts in Tashkent holds two copies of the *Lamaḥāt* (Inventory nos. 1360 and 2604, both uncatalogued and late); one copy is preserved in Dushanbe (Firdousi State Public Library, Inv. no. 571, 200 fos., copied 1084/1673, described in A. Iunusov, *Fehrasti dastnavishoi tojiki-forsi*, I [Dushanbe 1971], pp. 177–8, no. 121); and one copy, poorly preserved, is kept in the Saulat Public Library in Rampur (on the latter see Abid Raza Bedar, *Catalogue of Persian and Arabic Manuscripts of Saulat Public Library* [Rampur 1966], pp. 186–7, Tasawwuf no. 420). The *Lamaḥāt* is mentioned briefly in C.A. Storey, *Persian Literature: A Bio-Bibliographical Survey*, I/2 (London: Luzac & Co. 1972, rprt), p. 983, no. 1308.

history by Mehmed Fuad Köprülü, *Türk edebiyatında ilk mutasavvıflar*,[7] first published in 1918, dispensed with the Yasavī order of the sixteenth and seventeenth centuries in about half a page; for his treatment even of earlier phases of the Yasavī tradition, moreover, Köprülü relied almost entirely upon a single source written in Istanbul in the late sixteenth century (Ḥazīnī's *Javāhir al-abrār*, noted above), and was unaware of the Central Asian hagiographical corpus, including ʿĀlim Shaykh's *Lamaḥāt* (it is largely this neglect of the Central Asian sources that now leaves Köprülü's work so inadequate). In the 1920s, the Uzbek scholar (and victim of Stalin's purges) ʿAbd ar-Raʾūf Fiṭrat utilized the *Lamaḥāt* and other Central Asian hagiographies in a brief discussion of the Yasavī tradition's literary legacy,[8] and his use of these sources was slightly expanded in a fuller philological study, published in 1948 by a Russian scholar, of the *Dīvān-i ḥikmat*.[9] Zeki Velidi Togan published, in 1953, a brief but very important article highlighting the significance of the *Lamaḥāt* and the *Ḥujjat al-dhākirīn*;[10] more recently the *Lamaḥāt* was mentioned as a potentially useful source on the history of the Qazaqs in the late sixteenth and early seventeenth centuries,[11] while in the last few years a new generation of scholars in Uzbekistan and Kazakhstan has begun to pay some attention to the *Lamaḥāt* and other Central Asian hagiographical sources.[12] Otherwise, however, both the *Lamaḥāt* and the history of the Yasavī Order in the sixteenth and seventeenth centuries have been essentially ignored.

---

[7] *Türk edebiyatında ilk mutasavvıflar* (Istanbul: Maṭbaʿah-i ʿĀmirah 1918; Latin-script edition, 5th printing, Ankara: Arısan Matbaacılık 1984), p. 97.

[8] Fiṭrat's articles appeared in the journal *Mäarif vä oqituvchi* in 1927; they have been reprinted in modern Cyrillic Uzbek transcription in *Yässäviy kim èdi? (Mäqalälär vä "Hikmätlär" dän pärchälär)*, ed. Baybota Dostqaräev (Tashkent: Äbdullä Qadiriy namidägi Khälq Merasi Näshriyati 1994), pp. 18–28.

[9] A.K. Borovkov, "Ocherki po istorii uzbekskogo iazyka (opredelenie iazyka khikmatov Akhmada Iasevi)," *Sovetskoe vostokovedenie*, 5 (1948), pp. 229–50.

[10] Zeki Velidi Togan, "Yesevîliğe dair bazı yeni malûmat," in *[60 doğum yılı munasebetiyle] Fuad Köprülü Armağanı* (Istanbul: Osman Yalçın Matbaası 1953), pp. 523–9.

[11] M.Kh. Abuseitova and Zh.M. Zhapbasbaeva, "Znachenie arkheograficheskikh èkspeditsii dlia istochnikovedeniia istorii Kazakhstana XVI–XIX vv.," in *Voprosy istoriografii i istochnikovedeniia Kazakhstana* (*Dorevoliutsionnyi period*) (Alma-Ata 1988), pp. 254–5 [pp. 244–63]; the authors repeat the characterization of ʿĀlim Shaykh, from the Miklukho-Maklai catalogue, as belonging to a 'branch' of the Naqshbandiyya.

[12] The *Lamaḥāt* is cited in connection with Ahmad Yasavī's genealogy in Äshurbek Mominov, 'Yässäviyä: ildiz vä mänbälär', *Fän vä turmush*, (1993), 9–10 pp. 18–19, 21, and in an expanded and better annotated version of this article in Russian, A.K. Muminov, "O proiskhozhdenii bratstva iasaviia," *Islam i problemy mezhtsivilizatsionnykh vzaimodeistvii* (Moscow: Obshchestvo 'Nur' 1994), pp. 219–31. Preliminary steps toward utilizing the *Lamaḥāt* for Yasavī history appear in B. Babadzhanov, "Iasaviia i Nakshbandiia v Maverannakhre: iz istorii vzaimootnoshenii (ser. XV–XVI vv.)," *Yäsaui Taghïlïmï* (Turkistan: "Mura" baspagerlik shaghïn kasipornï/Qoja Akhmet Yäsaui atïndaghï Khalïqaralïq Qazaq-Türik Universiteti 1996), pp. 75–96.

‘ĀLIM SHAYKH AND HIS PLACE IN THE YASAVĪ *SILSILA*

The Yasavī *silsila* line to which ‘Ālim Shaykh belonged was traced back to Aḥmad Yasavī through a series of mostly quite obscure shaykhs of the thirteenth, fourteenth, and fifteenth centuries. The historicity of the early relationships, if not of the shaykhs themselves, is subject to doubt, but this need not concern us here; the *silsila* was accepted as genuine not only within the Yasaviyya, but within other traditions as well, by the late fifteenth century, and while Naqshbandī and Kubravī polemics against the Yasaviyya often targeted the latter tradition's penchant for hereditary Sufi succession, always vulnerable to the charge of being purely formal, the *silsila* itself was not typically attacked or dismissed.

The *silsila* of the Yasavī order runs from Aḥmad Yasavī, through one of his disciples known as Ḥakīm Ata (*‘ata’* is the Turkic word for ‘father’), to the latter's disciple, a saint of Tashkent called Zangī Ata; four disciples are typically ascribed to the latter, including the figure of Sayyid Ata, from whom stem the Sayyid Atā'ī *sayyid*s. The latter hereditary group included prominent political and military figures of the Uzbek era,[13] but one lineage, at least, claimed a spiritual transmission as well, and formed the basis for a separate Sufi community that produced the *Manāqib al-akhyār* mentioned earlier. Another of Zangi Ata's disciples was Ṣadr Ata, from whom the lineage proceeds thus: Ṣadr Ata > Almīn Bābā > Shaykh ‘Alī Shaykh > Mawdūd Shaykh; the latter marks another significant ‘branching’, but already we know of these branches almost entirely from the *Lamaḥāt*. The two chief disciples of Mawdūd Shaykh from whom substantial lineages descend are Kamāl Shaykh Īqānī and Khādim Shaykh (both of these were contemporaries of Khwāja Aḥrār and thus lived in the middle part of the fifteenth century). The principal lineage, leading to ‘Ālim Shaykh, is that of Khādim Shaykh: his disciples included his sons and son-in-law, as well-as Sulaymān Ghaznavī, whose chief successor, Sayyid Manṣūr, was the master of Ḥazīnī (the latter's acephalous Persian work devotes considerable attention to Sayyid Manṣūr).

For our purposes, however, the chief disciple of Khādim Shaykh was Jamāl ad-Dīn Kāshgharī Bukhārī, who died *c.* 1500 in Herāt; Jamāl ad-Dīn's disciple, in turn, was the pivotal Yasavī shaykh of the early sixteenth century, Khudāydād (d. 939/1532). Fully one quarter of the *Lamaḥāt* is devoted to Khudāydād himself, a shaykh celebrated as much for his partisan zeal as for his extreme poverty and austerity, with another sixth of the work covering several of his disciples, who are said to number in all around fifty, or by another tradition seventy-two. Two of these, Khwāja Mawlānā-yi Nūrī and Mawlānā Valī Kūh-i Zarī, were regarded as instrumental in the spiritual

---

[13] I have explored these in my “The Descendants of Sayyid Ata and the Rank of *Naqīb* in Central Asia,” *Journal of the American Oriental Society*, 115 (1995), pp. 612–34.

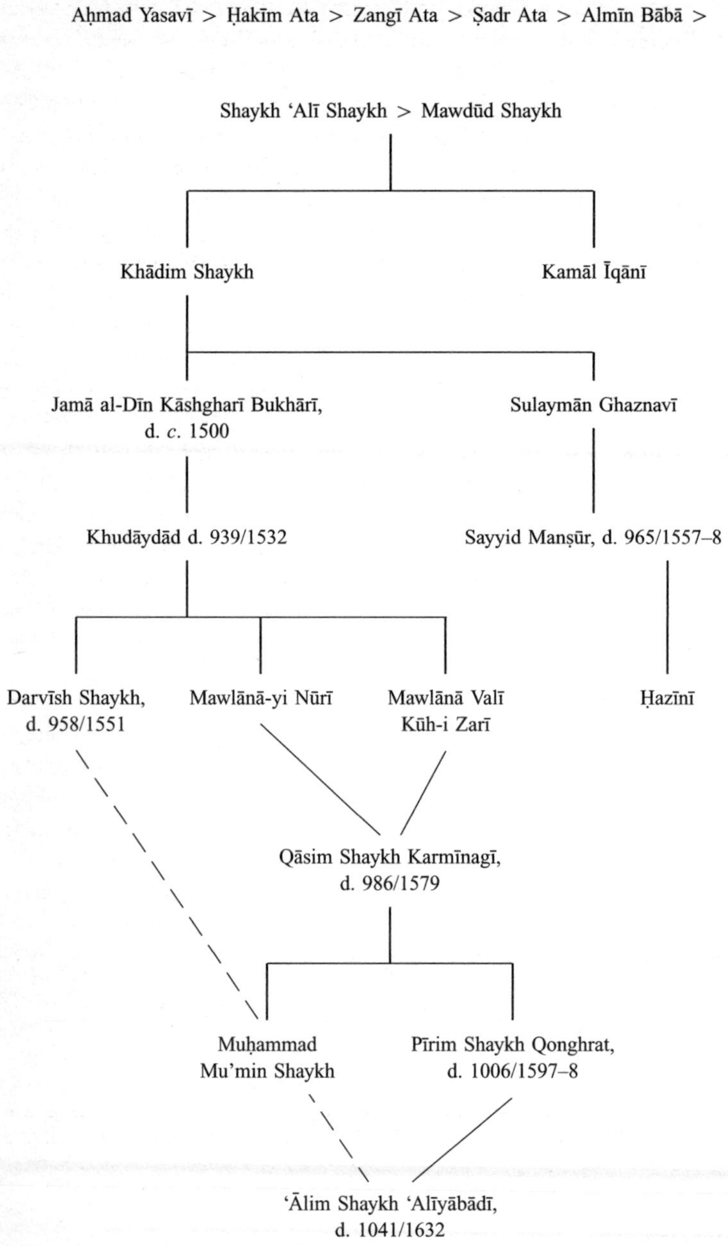

Figure 4: The Yasavī *Silsila* of ʻĀlim Shaykh ʻAlīyābād

training of the most important Yasavī shaykh of the *second* half of the sixteenth century, Qāsim Shaykh of Karmīna (d. 986/1579). Qāsim Shaykh's career coincided with the rise of 'Abdu'llāh Khān b. Iskandar, who consolidated all the Shïbānid domains of Central Asia under his control in the second half of the sixteenth century; Qāsim Shaykh was perhaps best known, however, not for his early support of 'Abdu'llāh (relations between the shaykh and the *khān* appear to have soured considerably), but for his 'sacrificial' death during a plague that ravaged the region of Samarqand.[14]

With Khudāydād and Qāsim Shaykh we find the Yasavī Order at its height, and 'Ālim Shaykh was intimately connected with both of these figures. The senior successor of Khudāydād, by most accounts, was 'Azīzān Darvīsh Shaykh (d. 958/1551),[15] who was 'Ālim Shaykh's paternal grandfather; Darvīsh Shaykh's son, Muḥammad Mu'min, was trained by his father, by other disciples of Khudāydād, and finally by Qāsim Shaykh; 'Ālim Shaykh himself married two great-granddaughters of Khudāydād; and 'Ālim Shaykh, while a boy, met Qāsim Shaykh (as discussed below), and became a disciple of the latter's senior successor, Pīrīm Shaykh. The latter figure had in fact associated with several direct disciples of Khudāydād before becoming a trusted follower of Qāsim Shaykh;[16] according to the *Baḥr al-asrār*, an encyclopaedic historical work compiled in Balkh around 1640, Pīrīm Shaykh – who is further identified as belonging to the Qonghrāt tribe – inherited his master's disciples when Qāsim Shaykh died in the plague.[17] Pīrīm Shaykh died, at the age of 87, in 1006/1597–8,[18] leaving several known successors, 'Ālim Shaykh clearly the most prominent among them.

Although subsequent hagiographies and *silsila* charts show 'Ālim Shaykh simply as a disciple of Pīrīm Shaykh, his familial connections within the Yasavī tradition are significant in view of the importance of hereditary succession within that tradition; hereditary succession was not only a fixture of several

---

[14] Qāsim Shaykh's death, when he resolved to take the plague upon himself and thereby sacrifice his life in order to relieve the rest of the people of the illness, is noted in many sources of the sixteenth and seventeenth centuries; the fullest account appears in the court history of the Shïbānid ruler 'Abdu'llāh Khān b. Iskandar, the *Sharaf-nāma-i shāhī* of Ḥāfiẓ Tanïsh Bukhārī (see the Russian translation in Khafiz-i Tanysh ibn Mir Mukhammad Bukhari, *Sharaf-nama-ii Shakhi* (*Kniga shakshkoi slavy*), facsimile. ed. and trans. M.A. Salakhetdinova [Moscow: Nauka, GRVL 1989], chap. 2, pp. 237–9 [fos. 234b–236a]).

[15] *Lamaḥāt*, ff. 87a–97b.

[16] Pīrīm Shaykh also had hereditary ties to the Yasavī order; his father Qanbar Shaykh was a disciple of Khudāydād (*Lamaḥāt*, fo. 97; cf. fo. 64b, where Qanbar Shaykh is also referred to as having been formerly an *amīr* in the service of the Shïbānid ruler Abū Sa'īd Khān).

[17] Maḥmud b. Amīr Valī, *Baḥr al-asrār fī manāqib al-akhyār*, MS India Office Ethé 575, fo. 145b.

[18] Pīrīm Shaykh's is the last biographical notice in the *Lamaḥāt*, fos. 120a–123a; his death date is given in the the *Tārīkh-i Sayyid Rāqim* from the late seventeenth century (MS Edinburgh University Library, no. 246, fos. 161b–162b).

Yasavī Sufi lineages (e.g. Sayyid Atā'ī, Ismā'īl Atā'ī lineages), but was an important focus of attack by rival groups, especially Naqshbandī shaykhs, for whom hereditary succession implied little more than a natural descent of purely formal shaykhs. In more practical terms, Yasavī history during the sixteenth and, especially, the seventeenth century is one of gradual erosion and a failure to compete effectively with the Naqshbandiyya, as even hereditary affiliates of the Yasaviyya abandoned their natural legacy and enter the Naqshbandī order; we will note 'Ālim Shaykh's own flirtation with that path shortly.

'Ālim Shaykh's grandfather, Darvīsh Shaykh (d. 958/1551), was a descendant of Abū Bakr, and of Shihāb al-Dīn 'Umar Suhravardī; he dwelled in the village of 'Alīyābād, not far from Samarqand. Darvīsh Shaykh is already mentioned in sixteenth-century biographical and historical works as the Sufi master of several Chingisid princes and *khāns* of the Shībānid 'Uzbek' dynasty of Mawarannahr.[19] 'Ālim Shaykh's father, meanwhile, Muḥammad Mu'min Shaykh, served Darvīsh Shaykh and later became a disciple of Qāsim Shaykh. He evidently maintained important contacts among the Uzbek tribal chieftains whose political stature rose steadily, at the expense of the *khāns*' power, during the seventeenth century; an eighteenth century source, indeed, credits Muḥammad Mu'min with engineering the death and replacement of the ineffectual Bāqī Muḥammad Khān in 1014/1605.[20] 'Ālim Shaykh's hereditary ties to the Yasavī tradition came not only through his father and grandfather, but also through his mother's side, through which he was a natural descendant of Ṣūfī Muḥammad Dānishmand; the latter figure was a quite important, but hitherto relatively obscure, disciple of Aḥmad Yasavī (a work ascribed to him is discussed below).

Outside the hagiographical sources we will review shortly, 'Ālim Shaykh is mentioned in the *Baḥr al-asrār* from around 1640; there 'Ālim Shaykh is praised as both a juridical scholar and a master of the Yasaviyya, and is named among the disciples of Qāsim Shaykh 'inherited' by Pīrīm Shaykh.[21] The *Baḥr al-asrār* elsewhere notes 'Ālim Shaykh's political prominence as well: at the elevation of Imām Qulī Khān as *khān* in 1019/1611–by which time four Sufi shaykhs had replaced the four tribal chieftains traditionally charged with raising the new Chingisid *khān* on a felt rug – 'Ālim Shaykh is said to have represented the Yasavī Order.[22] Neither the *Lamaḥāt* nor any of the

---

[19] Ḥāfiẓ Tanīsh, *Sharaf-nāma-i shāhī*, trans. M.A. Salakhetdinova, (Moscow: Nauka 1983), chap. 1, p. 137 (fo. 59b); *Mudhakkir-i-Aḥbāb ('Remembrancer of Friends') of Khwāja Bahā al-Dīn Ḥasan Nithārī Bukhārī*, ed. Syed Muḥammad Fazlullah (Hyderabad: Osmania University, Da'iratu'l-Ma'arif Press 1969), pp. 85–7.

[20] The account appears in the *Tadhkira-i Muqīm-khānī* of Muḥammad Yūsuf Munshī (see the Russian translation: Mukhammed Iusuf Munshi, *Mukim-khanskaia istoriia*, trans. A.A. Semenov [Tashkent: Izdatel'stvo AN UzSSR 1956], pp. 78–9.

[21] *Baḥr al-asrār*, MS India Office Ethe 575, fo. 145b.

[22] *Ibid.*, fo. 91a.

hagiographical sources dealing with ʻĀlim Shaykh mention this event, though several do note his prominence in the reign of Imām Qulī Khān.

To follow ʻĀlim Shaykh's own spiritual career, we have not only his own comments in the *Lamaḥāt*, but a series of later sources produced within primarily Naqshbandī circles from the later seventeenth to the mid-nineteenth centuries.[23] We also have a very important untitled biographical work about ʻĀlim Shaykh, preserved in a single manuscript that contains also the earliest copy of the *Lamaḥāt;*[24] the brief work was written by a direct disciple of ʻĀlim Shaykh, Fatḥu'llāh b. Khwāja ʻAbd al-Bāsiṭ al- Ṣiddīqī (the *nisba* may suggest a familial connection to ʻĀlim Shaykh, likewise a descendant of Abū Bakr, but Fatḥullāh is identified only as a descendant, in the female line, of Khudāydād). This is clearly the same Fatḥu'llāh mentioned in several sources as the senior disciple of ʻĀlim Shaykh, and his work, written near Samarqand apparently in 1045/1635–6, was intended as an account of 'recent' shaykhs of the *silsila-i jahrīya-i faqrīya-i sulṭānīya.*

ʻĀlim Shaykh was born, the account begins, in Tashkent in 972/1564–5; his name, Muḥammad ʻĀlim, was selected by his maternal grandfather, Ḥāfiẓ Kūhaki, a descendant of Ṣūfī Muḥammad Dānishmand, and the same maternal grandfather served as ʻĀlim Shaykh's first teacher. Evidently, while ʻĀlim Shaykh was still a boy, his father, Mu'min Shaykh, left Tashkent because of unspecified "turmoil" there (undoubtedly referring to Qazaq raids), and settled in his "ancestral homeland" of ʻAlīyābād, near Samarqand; soon thereafter ʻĀlim Shaykh was sent to Samarqand to study under Mawlānā ʻIṣmatu'llāh (a figure linked to Qāsim Shaykh, who is often cited in the *Lamaḥāt* as a transmitter of sayings and anecdotes about various Yasavī shaykhs). ʻĀlim Shaykh's studies in the exoteric sciences were continued in Kābul, where he spent six years; then, after a dream in which Shaykh

---

[23] The *Ḥujjat al-dhākirīn*, noted above as the last major Persian work produced in Yasavī circles, includes important material, but other information is found in a series of non-Yasavī sources. The most important of these are (1) the *Thamarāt al-mashā'ikh* by Sayyid Zinda-ʻAlī al-Muftī b. ʻAzīzān Khwāja Mīr al-Ḥusaynī al-Qāsimī al-Bukhārī, a voluminous compendium of *silsila*s and hagiographical lore devoted to Yasavī, Kubravī, and Naqshbandī shaykhs, compiled in the 1680s (MS IVANUz 2619/II, fos. 38b–598b; SVR III, p. 353, no. 2669); (2) the *Ashjār al-khuld*, by a certain Muḥammad Aʻzam, completed in Kashmir in 1139/1726 (MS IVANUz 498/II, fos. 39a–211a; *SVR*, III, p. 363, no. 2689); (3) the *Tadhkira-i Ṭāhir Īshān*, completed in 1157/1744 (MS IVANUz 855; *SVR* III, no. 2694); and (4) a massive hagiographical compendium assembled between 1256/1840–1 and 1263/1846–47 by a certain Mīr Musayyab Bukhārī (MS St Petersburg University Library, no. 854 [fos. 438b-546b on the Yasaviyya], described in A.T. Tagirdzhanov, *Opisanie tadzhikskikh i persidskikh rukopisei Vostochnogo otdela Biblioteki LGU*, t. I, Istoriia, biografii, geografiia [Leningrad: Izd-vo Leningradskogo Universiteta 1962, pp. 362–8, no. 150]).

[24] MS POIVRAN C1602/II, fos. 125a–138a (Miklukho-Maklai, II, pp. 136–7, no. 189); the manuscript was completed in 1045/1635–6, in the *khānaqāh* of Khudāydād in the village of Ghazīrah in 'Sughd-i Kalān of Samarqand'.

Khudāydād appeared and summoned him, 'Ālim Shaykh returned to Samarqand, but first considered entering the *silsila* of the Khwājagān (i.e. the Naqshbandiyya). He was dissuaded from this plan by a dream in which the eminent shaykhs of the Jahrī *silsila*, led by Aḥmad Yasavī, approached him; Shaykh Khudāydād cried out among them, "Bring him and hang him!" but 'Ālim Shaykh's grandfather, Darvīsh Shaykh, came forth and interceded for him. As a result of his grandfather's appeal, the account concludes, 'Ālim Shaykh's 'sin' (*gunāh*) was excused and he escaped punishment; when he awoke, he said (according to one version), "The zeal of the eminent shaykhs (*buzurgān*) of this *silsila* will not allow us to enter another *ṭarīqa*", and at once entered the service of the Yasavī master Pīrīm Shaykh.[25] This dream offers some idea of the competitive atmosphere of sixteenth-century Central Asian Sufism, and it is fitting that Khudāydād, perhaps the most zealous partisan the Yasaviyya produced, is cast as the guardian of the order's integrity and solidarity.

'Ālim Shaykh's own allusions, in the *Lamaḥāt*, to his training and early life are somewhat difficult to reconcile with the version in Fatḥu'llāh's work. In the *Lamaḥāt*, we hear nothing of 'Ālim Shaykh's studies in Kābul (though his connection with Mawlānā 'Iṣmatu'llāh is repeatedly affirmed), and the sequence of his training (not to mention its actual chronology) as reflected in the two accounts is also somewhat unclear. Most remarkably, Fatḥu'llāh's work does not discuss any direct connection between 'Ālim Shaykh and Qāsim Shaykh, a relationship noted already in the *Baḥr al-asrār*; in the *Lamaḥāt*,[26] by contrast, 'Ālim Shaykh himself describes his encounter with Qāsim Shaykh, when, at the age of 13, he was present at one of the Shaykh's *majlis*es, together with his uncle, Ṭāhir Shaykh. Qāsim Shaykh spoke to him on that occasion, saying three times, *oghlum, mullā bolup-sän* ('My son, you have become a *mullā"*): From then on, the young 'Ālim Shaykh's affection for Qāsim Shaykh and his devotees grew stronger and stronger, and he began to hope to be included among them. He was then just learning the Koran by heart, and because of his own weakness, he says, that process was prolonged until he was 21. Then one night, 'Ālim Shaykh had a dream in which the Prophet and the caliphs Abū Bakr and 'Umar appeared together; Abū Bakr (claimed as an ancestor by 'Ālim Shaykh) took his hand and placed it in the hand of the Prophet: when he awoke, he was able to master the Koran in only eighteen days. 'Ālim Shaykh notes further that forty years had passed between that time and the time he was writing (1035/1626), placing his dream around 995 and his birth in approximately 973 or 974; Fatḥu'llāh dated his master's birth to 972 and dating 'Ālim Shaykh's birth to either 972 or 973 would allow

[25] The account appears in Fatḥūllah's work, MS POIVRAN C1602/II, fo. 128b; the comment on the Yasavī shaykhs' zeal appears only in the *Ḥujjat al-dhākirīn*, fos. 175b–176a.
[26] *Lamaḥāt*, fos. 114a–b.

for his encounter, at age 13, with Qāsim Shaykh before the latter's death in late 986.[27]

We must assume that the association with Qāsim Shaykh described in the *Lamaḥāt* occurred during 'Ālim Shaykh's days as a student of Mawlānā 'Iṣmatu'llāh in Samarqand, and that his six years in Kābul came after Qāsim Shaykh's death; nevertheless, it is remarkable that such a prominent figure as Qāsim Shaykh plays no role, to judge from Fatḥu'llāh's account, in the dreams that led 'Ālim Shaykh to return from Kābul and enter the Yasavī order. It is also not clear whether his relationship with Qāsim Shaykh was ever formalized to make him a *murīd*, at least in name, of his master's shaykh; the *Baḥr al-asrār*'s account would suggest that it was, but that work's author may have been less attuned to the technicalities of Sufi relationships than was 'Ālim Shaykh (who in the *Lamaḥāt* seems pointedly to refrain from claiming formal discipleship under Qāsim Shaykh). Fatḥu'llāh's silence on the matter is more difficult to explain; perhaps his aim was to stress the formal succession of his own master in the lineage through Pīrīm Shaykh, or perhaps he simply saw no reason to repeat what 'Ālim Shaykh himself had already written.

Fatḥu'llāh's work provides rich material on 'Ālim Shaykh's activity as a shaykh in 'Alīyābād, including information about his relations with Chingisid princes and tribal *amīr*s during the reign of Imām Qulī Khān. One story relates how he prevented a certain Tilāq Bahādur Qūngrāt (a former servant of Keldī Muḥammad Khān who, through service to Imām Qulī Khān, had been given control of 'Alīyābād) from establishing a tavern in the district;[28] another credits the shaykh with the destruction of Tursūn Sulṭān Qażāq [*sic*], whom 'Ālim Shaykh, calling him "this despotic Qażāq sulṭān," blamed for repeatedly spoiling his attempts to make the pilgrimage to Aḥmad Yasavī's shrine in Turkistan (according to the account, an *amīr* of the Keneges tribe cut off Tursūn Sulṭān's head and sent it to 'Ālim Shaykh in Samarqand).[29] Still another narrative notes the unexpected death of a Qazaq *amīr*, formerly in the service of 'Ishim Khān Qażāq' but then a retainer (*nöker*) of Imām Qulī Khān, who had inadvertently committed an offence against 'Ālim Shaykh.[30] Such stories, of course, are intended to explain the real, spiritual causes of these Qazaqs'

---

[27] Ālim Shaykh notes further, shortly after the account of his first meeting with Qāsim Shaykh and his subsequent dream, that he was with Qāsim Shaykh when the latter heard a report about the course of a siege of Samarqand conducted by 'Abdu'llāh Khān, but that he left the shaykh and went to 'Alīyābād, before Qāsim Shaykh's unsuccessful attempt to mediate between 'Abdullah and the ruler of Samarqand, Javānmard-'Alī Khān (*Lamaḥāt*, fos. 114b–115a); the siege in question took place in the spring of 986/1578 (see Tanïsh, *Sharaf-nāma-i shāhī*, trans II, pp. 187–207), little more than half a year before Qāsim Shaykh's death.

[28] MS POIVRAN C1602, fo. 131b–132a.

[29] *Ibid.*, fos. 132a–b.

[30] *Ibid.*, fo. 133b.

demise, but they convey a clear sense of the Shaykh's hostility toward the Qazaqs as a people outside the governance of Islam (as represented by Imām Qulī Khān); the first account, especially, applauds the extermination of one group of this 'rabble' (*awbāsh*) and the transformation of another group of Qazaqs into servants of the *khān*. Such accounts are naturally more revealing about 'Ālim Shaykh's own attitudes than about the virtues or vices of the Qazaqs (or about the quality of Qazaq Islam in this era), but they are worth noting in view of the supposed affinity, so often evoked even in scholarly literature, between the Yasavī Order and the nomadic Turks of the Central Asian steppe.

'Ālim Shaykh's death is dated in Fatḥullāh's work to the last decade of Dhū'l-Ḥijja 1041/July 1632;[31] he was, the account says, 72 years old, a figure not quite in accord with the date of his birth (972) given in the same work, or with the date of 973 suggested by the data from the *Lamaḥāt* cited above. In the *Ḥujjat al-dhākirīn*, moreover, Mawlānā Muḥammad Sharīf writes that "at present," in the year AH 1080, thirty-seven years had passed since 'Ālim Shaykh's death,[32] placing that event in 1043, and another hagiographical source from the early eighteenth century affirms that 'Ālim Shaykh was born in 970/1562–3 and died in 1043/1633–4 at the age of 72;[33] the discrepancies remain unresolved, but most likely Fatḥu'llāh's dating should be accepted as the most authoritative.

The familial legacy of 'Ālim Shaykh leads away from Central Asia, and away from Sufism, but deserves comment in view of his descendants' renown in India. 'Ālim Shaykh himself refers in the *Lamaḥāt* to two of his sons, born from great-granddaughters of Khudāydād, namely Khwāja 'Abd al-Rashīd and Amīr Bahā' al-Dīn;[34] only the former is mentioned by Fatḥu'llāh,[35] but the *Ḥujjat al-dhākirīn* mentions, in addition, not only Amīr Bahā' al-Dīn and a daughter of 'Ālim Shaykh, but another son, Khwāja Muḥammad 'Ābid, known as 'Ābid Khān. Little is known of 'Abd al-Rashīd, but other sources tell us much more about Amīr Bahā' al-Dīn and Khwāja Muḥammad'Ābid, whose descendants found success under the Mughul rulers Shāh Jahān (*reg.* 1037/1628–1068/1657) and Awrangzīb (*reg.* 1068/1658–1118/1707). Amīr Bahā' al-Dīn is perhaps the most prominent son of 'Ālim Shaykh in Central Asian hagiographical sources. He reportedly "served the successors" of his father and "kept the lamp lit at his father's shrine," but evidently ran afoul of 'Abd al-'Aziz Khān, ruler of Bukhārā. When the Khorezmian ruler Anūsha Khān

[31] *Ibid.*, fo. 136b.
[32] *Ḥujjat al-dhākirīn*, MS POIVRAN B3787, fo. 181a.
[33] *Ashjār al-khuld*, MS IVANUz 498, fos. 121a–122a; 1043 is also given as his death date in the *Tārīkh-i Sayyid Rāqim* (MS Edinburgh, fo. 185a).
[34] *Lamaḥāt*, fos 52b, 68b.
[35] MS POIVRAN C1602, fos 137b–138a.

tried to seize Bukhārā, agents of ʿAbd al-ʿAzīz Khān accused Amīr Bahāʾ al-Dīn of collaborating with the Khorezmian ruler and killed him;[36] after Bahāʾ al-Dīn's execution, the hagiographical sources affirm, his sons departed for India and lived under ʿĀlamgīr (i.e. Awrangzīb), under whom one of them, Mīr Muḥammad Amīn, became a high official.[37] This "Mīr Muḥammad Amīn Khān" is the subject of a brief notice in an important biographical compendium of Mughul officials compiled in the late eighteenth century, the *Maʾāthir al-umarā*;[38] the account confirms the circumstances of his father's death, and notes that Mīr Muḥammad Amīn served at Awrangzīb's court and received the title "Chīn Bahādur."

According to the Central Asian hagiographical sources, the other son of ʿĀlim Shaykh, Khwāja Muḥammad ʿĀbid, travelled to India on the way to perform the *ḥajj* during the reign of Shāh Jahān, and met the latter's son ʿĀlamgīr; upon his return from the pilgrimage, he settled in India, first at the court of ʿĀlamgīr, where he was known as Navvāb ʿĀbid Khan. These accounts affirm that Muḥammad ʿĀbid was of a saintly character, but "chose intimacy with rulers" despite his Sufi training; his son, Amīr Shihāb al-Dīn, identified as a commander in ʿĀlamgīr's army, is mentioned in the same accounts.[39] Both figures have a much larger profile, however, in the *Maʾāthir al-umarā*, which makes clear the important historical role of these descendants of ʿĀlim Shaykh of ʿAlīyābād: in this work "Khwāja ʿĀbid," the son of "ʿĀlim Shaykh of Samarqand," is identified as the grandfather (and Mīr Shihāb al-Dīn as the father) of the famous Niẓām al-Mulk Āṣaf Jāh (d. 1161/1748), founder of the dynasty of Niẓāms of Hyderabad, which survived until 1948, after Indian independence.[40] Khwāja ʿĀbid himself, according to this work (which affirms his descent from Shihāb al-Dīn Suhravardī), had served as *qāḍī* and *Shaykh al-islām* in Bukhārā before travelling through India on the way to

---

[36] *Ashjār al-khuld*, MS IVANUz 498, fos 122a–b.

[37] Mīr Musayyab Bukhārī (MS St Petersburg University, fos no. 854, fo. 542b) says that he became *Ṣadr-i ṣudūr* of all Hind for forty years.

[38] See *The Maāthir al-umarā; Being Biographies of the Muḥammadan and Hindu Officers of the Timurid Sovereigns of India from 1500 to about 1780 A.D., by Nawwāb Ṣamṣām-ud-Daula Shāh Nawāz Khān and his son ʿAbdul Ḥayy*, 2nd edn, trans H. Beveridge, rev. Baini Prashad (repr. Patna: Janaki Prakashan 1979), II/1, pp. 114–17. A son of Amīr Bahāʾ al-Dīn's sister who served under ʿĀlamgīr is mentioned elsewhere in the same work (I, pp. 308–11).

[39] These figures are discussed in the *Ḥujjat al-dhākirīn* from the latter seventeenth century (MS POIVRAN B3787, fos 181a–b, on Muḥammad ʿĀbid alone), in the *Ashjār al-khuld* from the early eighteenth century (MS IVANUz 498, fo. 122b), and in the work of Mīr Musayyab Bukhārī from the mid-nineteenth century (MS St Petersburg University, no. 854, fo. 543a).

[40] *Maāthir-ul-umarā*, II/1, pp. 539–41 (the notice on "Khwāja ʿĀbid"), pp. 409–59 (on Āṣaf Jāh); I, pp. 587–92 (on Shihāb al-Dīn, accorded the title "Fīrūz-jang"). Shihāb al-Dīn, incidentally, is said to have been accompanied on one of his campaigns by Muḥammad Amīn b. Amīr Bahāʾ al-Dīn, his first cousin (II/1, pp. 114–15).

perform the ḥajj; he met both Shāh Jahān and Awrangzīb then, and remained in India upon his return, serving Awrangzīb in various posts before being killed by cannon shot during the siege of Golconda, near Hyderabad, in 1098/1687.

These sons and grandsons of ‘Ālim Shaykh may have retained some connection with their Sufi heritage, but it is no doubt significant that the Indian sources, while noting the prestige of their natural descent from Shihāb al-Dīn Suhravardī, make no mention of the Yasavī Order; in any case, neither of his sons is listed in Central Asian accounts of ‘Ālim Shaykh's Sufi successors. The fullest list we have of ‘Ālim Shaykh's disciples is found in the *Thamarāt al-mashā'ikh*,[41] where he is ascribed seven followers: (1) Khwāja Fatḥu'llāh Ghazīragī, author of the brief biography of ‘Ālim Shaykh; (2) Ṣāliḥ Khoja Urganjī, a native of Khorezm, called Muḥammad Ṣāliḥ Khoja Ṣiddīqī in the nineteenth-century hagiography of Mīr Musayyab Bukhārī; (3) Ākhūnd Ḥājjī Ismā‘īl, otherwise unidentified; (4) Mawlānā ‘Uthmān (whose lineage is traced to the famous Bukhāran saint Mawlānā Imlā [d. 1162/1749], who claimed multiple affiliations but belonged principally to the Naqshbandiyya); (5) Mawlānā Muḥammad Sharīf, discussed below; (6) Mawlānā Amīr Ḥusayn Farākhīnī, otherwise unidentified; and (7) Ḥusayn Shaykh ‘Azīzān. The latter figure appears to be linked with lineages presented in quite contradictory ways in a number of seventeenth- and eighteenth-century sources; one of these also names, as another direct disciple of ‘Ālim Shaykh, Mawlānā Ibrāhīm Turkistānī Qawghānī,[42] who was further associated with a number of other shaykhs from the middle Syr Darya valley (that region is typically regarded as a stronghold of the Yasavī Order, but in fact our sources name almost no Yasavī shaykhs active in that area between the fourteenth and seventeenth centuries, and very few in the seventeenth century). Neither the *Thamarāt*'s list, finally, nor other sources from the latter seventeenth and eighteenth centuries, mentions the "Muḥammad Amīn Shaykh Urā-tīpagī" (whose *nisba* identifies him as a native of a town south-west of Khujand) named in the work of Fatḥu'llāh as a disciple of ‘Ālim Shaykh,[43] suggesting that still other followers may have continued Yasavī lineages stemming through him; these will most likely remain unknown, however, since further lineages stemming even from those listed in the *Thamarāt* are relatively few.

The most prominent among these figures was Mawlānā Muḥammad Sharīf, author of the last major Yasavī source, the *Ḥujjat al-dhākirīn*; he served not only ‘Ālim Shaykh, but two of the latter's disciples, Mawlānā Ismā‘īl and Khwāja Fatḥullāh, as well, and spent considerable time in the service of a Naqshbandī shaykh, Kamāl al-Dīn Faghānzavī Bukhārī

---

[41] *Thamarāt*, MS IVANUz 2619, fo. 67a.
[42] *Tadhkirah-i Tāhir Īshān*, MS IVANUz 855, fo. 75a.
[43] MS POIVRAN, C1602, fo. 133a.

(d. 1063/1652).[44] Muḥammad Sharīf clearly regarded himself as a Yasavī shaykh, and defended the Yasavī style of vocal *dhikr* in his *Ḥujjat al-dhākirīn*, but his association with Naqshbandī circles typifies the gradual process whereby the Yasaviyya was sapped of its vitality and communal integrity; within at most three spiritual generations after 'Ālim Shaykh, we can no longer trace separate Yasavī *silsila*-lines – that is, lines found outside the 'bundled' *silsila*s collectively transmitted by shaykhs claiming the multiple affiliations that become the rule by the late seventeenth and early eighteenth centuries – or distinctive Yasavī Sufi communities, anywhere in Central Asia.

All the Yasavī Sufi lineages traced through these disciples of 'Ālim Shaykh disappear from our sources after little more than a century following his death; while it is difficult to argue from the silence of such sources as we have, the weight of evidence would suggest that the Yasaviyya had ceased to function as a distinct Sufi community by the middle of the eighteenth century at the latest, however much its practices may have shaped both specific Naqshbandī circles in Central Asia and more general communal rites among nomadic and sedentary communities, and however much its *silsila* may have been preserved, in fossilized form, in later 'bundled' transmission lines of Central Asian Sufi communities. For us, then, 'Ālim Shaykh's most enduring legacy is the *Lamaḥāt* he compiled, to which we may now turn.

RESPONSE TO THE NAQSHBANDIYYA: THE *LAMAḤĀT MIN NAFAḤĀT AL-QUDS*

'Ālim Shaykh's *Lamaḥāt*, as noted, is unquestionably the most important hagiographical work produced in the Yasavī tradition, and the most important source on the Yasaviyya; we cannot fully explore its riches here, but it may be worthwhile briefly to take note of its style and sources, by way of understanding the likely motivation that underlay the composition of this remarkable repository of Yasavī lore.

To begin with, the *Lamaḥāt* is not marked by any distinctive organizational structure. In the introduction (fos. 1b–3a), after noting the circumstances of the work's composition, its dedication to Imām Qulī Khān, and its title, 'Ālim Shaykh promises two sections (*maqṣad*s), the first on Koranic verses, *ḥadīth*s and stories confirming "the lawful and customary and meritorious character of *dhikr* in the vocal fashion," and the second on "the wonders and experiences and inspirations of the worthy shaykhs of this noble *silsila* of the Jahriyya." The first *maqṣad* is quite brief (fos 3a–12a), however, while the second, forming the bulk of the work, has no internal structure, consisting simply of a long series of hagiographical entries. The first of these, naturally, is an account of the tradition's eponym, Khwāja Aḥmad Yasavī, whose Sufi training is

---

[44] *Thamarāt*, MS IVANUz 2619, fos. 123a–b, 508a–b.

discussed in a way quite different from the usual presentation offered by Naqshbandī sources, and on the basis of important sources now lost (see below). After the account of Aḥmad Yasavī, the work presents notices of subsequent Yasavī shaykhs, most consisting only of one or more brief anecdotes; these notices focus primarily, but not exclusively, on shaykhs belonging to ʻĀlim Shaykh's lineage, with some collateral lines followed as well. This last section is by far the largest, comprising over two-thirds of the work; together the work amounts to a history – not comprehensive, but the best we have – of the Yasavī Order from the thirteenth to the early seventeenth century.

The simplicity of the *Lamaḥāt*'s structure is matched in its literary style; the work is distinctive above all for its simple, direct, unadorned – even spare – language, typically free of the florid literary adornment that characterizes much Central Asian Persian prose of this era (in this regard the *Lamaḥāt* offers a sharp contrast, for example, with the nearly contemporary *Baḥr al-asrār*, cited earlier). To account for the simplicity of the *Lamaḥāt*'s style and diction, we might resort to the standard caricatures of the Yasavī tradition often encountered in general and even specialized scholarly literature: the Yasaviyya is typically represented as less 'civilized', less Islamic, and less literate than other Sufi traditions of Central Asia, and this portrayal is often linked with the supposed prevalence of the Yasaviyya in nomadic and Turkic milieus. Such a representation, however, rests more on shopworn images of nomads (and of Turks), and on baseless assumptions about Aḥmad Yasavī's historical and cultural milieu, than on a serious appraisal of Yasavī history; yet it remains quite widespread, and is often invoked to justify sweeping generalizations about the cultural legacy of the Yasaviyya. It has been used, for instance, to 'explain' the simplicity of the *Dīvān-i ḥikmat*, whose language and content, we are told, were in effect 'dumbed-down' in order to appeal to its presumed audience of nomadic Turks[45]. We can easily imagine such a characterization being carried over, with minor adjustments, to 'explain' the *Lamaḥāt*'s simple language in terms of its audience, which, although presumably familiar with Persian, might still, because of its Yasavī provenance and resulting 'marginality', be labelled as too 'simple' to understand or appreciate a more refined

[45] Such notions have been advanced most recently (together with many other misrepresentations of the Yasavī tradition) in a series of articles based on the *Dīvān-i ḥikmat*, by A.J.E. Bodrogligeti: "The Impact of Aḥmad Yasavī's Teaching on the Cultural and Political Life of the Turks of Central Asia," *Türk Dili Araştırmaları Yıllığı Belleten 1987* (Ankara: Türk Tarih Kurumu Basımevi 1992), pp. 35–41; "Aḥmad Yasavī's Concept of 'Daftar-î Sanî'" [*sic*], *Milletlerarası Ahmed Yesevî Sempozyumu Bildirileri 26–27 Eylül 1991* (Ankara: Feryal Matbaası 1992), pp. 1–11; "Yasavī Ideology in Muḥammad Shāybānī [*sic*] Khān's Vision of an Uzbek Islamic Empire," *Journal of Turkish Studies*, 18 (1994; = *Annemarie Schimmel Festschrift: Essays Presented to Annemarie Schimmel on the Occasion of her Retirement from Harvard University by her Colleagues, Students and Friends*), pp. 41–57.

and complex literary style. In all likelihood, however, the *Lamaḥāt*'s simple style has less to do with the work's intended audience than with the types of sources utilized in writing the work (and with 'Ālim Shaykh's decision to let those sources speak for themselves), and these in turn bear also on the question of 'Ālim Shaykh's purpose in compiling the *Lamaḥāt*.

For substantial bodies of material included in his work, 'Ālim Shaykh explicitly cites only three written sources,[46] none of which survives independently in its original form. One of these was a collection of sayings by Khudāydād, compiled by one of his disciples (and hence produced in the middle of the sixteenth century), from which the *Lamaḥāt* includes almost twenty folios of excerpts; the other two, however, go back, if authentic, to the earliest phase of Yasavī history. One is the *Manāqib* of Aḥmad Yasavī, ascribed to his disciple Ṣūfī Muḥammad Dānishmand, and the other is a treatise on Aḥmad Yasavī's spiritual career by 'Imām Sïghnāqī' (referring to the prominent Ḥanafi jurist of the late thirteenth and early fourteenth centuries, Ḥusām al-Dīn al-Ḥusayn b. 'Alī b. Ḥajjāj al-Sïghnāqī).[47] Excerpts from the latter work are relatively brief, but over twenty folios in the oldest copy of the *Lamaḥāt* purport to be excerpts – in Persian – from the work of Ṣūfī Muḥammad Dānishmand;[48] these passages, assuming that the attribution may be trusted, would clearly bring us closer to the teaching of the 'historical' Aḥmad Yasavī than any other extant source.

Far more important among the *Lamaḥāt*'s sources, however, is the extensive body of orally transmitted anecdotal material collected by 'Ālim

---

[46] A fourth written source he cites is the *Maqāmāt* of Shaykh Nūr al-Dīn Baṣīr, a fifteenth-century work about a thirteenth-century saint of Samarqand, from which 'Ālim Shaykh says he drew a brief anecdote (*Lamaḥāt*, fos 94a–b); this work has survived in independent copies, and was incorporated, with substantial abbreviation and alteration, and under the heading *Risāla-i quṭb-i chahārdahum*, into the Persian 'sacred history' of Samarqand known as the *Qandīya* (see *Qandīya va Samarīya*, ed. Īraj Afshār [Tehran: Mu'assasa-i Farhangī-i Jahāngīrī 1367 A.Hsh./1988], pp. 84–128; on the *Qandīya*, see most recently Jürgen Paul, "The Histories of Samarqand," *Studia Iranica*, 22 [1993], pp. 69–92 [pp. 75–81]). A fifth is the famous *Nafaḥāt al-uns* of Jāmī, but it is cited quite sparingly. As noted below, it is clear that 'Ālim Shaykh used material from the *Rashaḥāt-i 'ayn al-ḥayāt*, the important Naqshbandī hagiography focused on the career of Khwāja Aḥrār, compiled at the beginning of the sixteenth century, but he does not explicitly cite this work. Finally, 'Ālim Shaykh also identifies one of Qāsim Shaykh's disciples as the compiler of that saint's sayings; he does not explicitly identify any material in the *Lamaḥāt* as having been drawn from such a work, however, and cites the compiler only as a source of orally transmitted narratives about Qāsim Shaykh.

[47] On this Sïghnāqī, best known as author of the *Nihāyah*, a 'supercommentary' on the famous *Hidāyah* of Burhān al-Dīn Marghīnānī, see *GAL* I, 376, *GALS* I, 644, II, 142; for further references, see W. Madelung, "The Spread of Maturidism and the Turks," *Actas de IV Congresso de Estudos Arabes e Islâmicos, Coimbra–Lisboa* (Leiden: Brill 1971), p. 155, n. 125.

[48] *Lamaḥāt*, fos. 15a-37a; however, after fo. 30b, there are occasional references to Khudāydād as well, indicating that 'Ālim Shaykh has edited or reshaped at least the last portion of these excerpts.

Shaykh. Within this material we find not only stories of more recent shaykhs of the Yasavī Order, usually with scrupulous attention to attribution and to the identification of transmitters, but also a considerable amount of oral tradition about earlier figures, from the thirteenth to the fifteenth centuries, written down for the first time, we must surmise, in the *Lamaḥāt*. Some of this material is unique to the *Lamaḥāt* (or is otherwise found only in subsequent sources dependent upon it), appearing in no other extant source (or, for that matter, in any ethnographic recordings of oral tradition), making 'Ālim Shaykh's work an important source for internal accounts, preserved within a Yasavī Sufi lineage, about the earliest phases of the Yasavī tradition. We find, for instance, a story about Ḥakīm Ata miraculously widening the cave-*khānaqāh* of Aḥmad Yasavī in order to accommodate his master's 99,000 disciples,[49] and another remarkable narrative about Ḥakīm Ata's dealings with the *'ulamā'* of Khorezm (possibly echoing Sufi–Mu'tazilī confrontations there), which is attested nowhere else.[50] Similarly, a story of Bābā Māchin, a little-known disciple of Aḥmad Yasavī, resurrecting a flock of sheep eaten by Mongol invaders[51] appears not to be found in other hagiographical sources. The same holds true for a story about Zangī Ata, in which he received a prayer rug and staff sent by Najm al-Dīn Kubra, only to tear up the former and break the latter (the story may echo communal rivalries no longer relevant in the time of 'Ālim Shaykh, who explains the story as demonstrating Zangī Ata's high mystical attainment).[52] The *Lamaḥāt* even includes tales about Ismā'īl Ata, spiritual and natural ancestor of primarily hereditary Yasavī lineages, which are not found in the sources produced within those lineages.[53]

More revealing, however, are the many instances in which the *Lamaḥāt* presents versions of anecdotes that are also reflected in other written sources or in more recent ethnographic recordings of oral tradition; these offer insight into 'Ālim Shaykh's use of the material available to him, and allow us a better understanding of even those narratives for which we have no such 'control'. For example, the *Lamaḥāt* includes a brief allusion to the story, otherwise known primarily from Naqshbandī sources, in which Aḥmad Yasavī is portrayed riding a lion and holding a serpent;[54] it includes a

---

[49] *Ibid.*, fo. 14a.

[50] *Ibid.*, fos 38a–b.

[51] *Ibid.*, fos. 39a–b.

[52] *Ibid.*, fo. 39b.

[53] *Ibid.*, fo. 42a, a story in which another Yasavī saint, Uzun Ḥasan Ata, miraculously suckles the infant Isma'il Ata.

[54] *Ibid.*, fo. 14a; for illuminating discussions of this hagiographical motif, though without reference to the Yasavī examples, see Martin van Bruinessen, "Haji Bektash, Sultan Sahak, Shah Mina Sahib and Various Avatars of a Running Wall," *Turcica*, 21–3 (1991), pp. 55–69 (+ 3 plates), and Simon Digby, "To Ride a Tiger or a Wall? Strategies of Prestige in Indian Sufi Legend," in *According to Tradition: Hagiographical Writing in India*, ed. Winand M. Callewaert and Rupert Snell (Wiesbaden: Harrassowitz Verlag 1994), pp. 99–129.

similarly brief version of two stories about Aḥmad Yasavī's relationship with the *'ulamā'* known in fuller forms from other Yasavī sources;[55] it presents a version of the story about the murder of Yasavī's son, reflected in other Yasavī sources and in oral tradition;[56] and it presents an explanation of the origins of the *khum-i 'ishq*, the 'vat of mystical ardour,' a fixture at Yasavī's cave-*khānaqāh* and later at his shrine, that differs markedly from that found in the *Javāhir al-abrār*.[57]

In all these (and other) cases in which we are able to compare the *Lamaḥāt*'s narrative material with other versions of the same anecdotes, it is clear that 'Ālim Shaykh, or his source, has telescoped and heavily abbreviated the stories; whether this reflects the compiler's inability to make sense of traditions he had received in an already essentially synopsized 'outline' form, or rather his assumption that the tales were widely known and could thus be elaborated by reciters on the basis of the *Lamaḥāt*'s quite condensed 'prompts', is difficult to judge. In some of the instances in which he transmits a bare narrative outline rather than a fully elaborated story, to be sure, 'Ālim Shaykh appears not to have fully understood accounts drawn from earlier Yasavī oral tradition. On the one hand this means that the *Lamaḥāt*'s hagiographical material, particularly for the earliest generations of the Yasavī tradition, often appears fragmentary or disjointed; on the other hand, it also means that 'Ālim Shaykh usually refrained from adding yet another layer of interpretative recasting (apart from his occasional doctrinal 'explanations') on top of the archaic narratives, and what the *Lamaḥāt*'s material lacks in narrative coherence it makes up, we may assume, in the faithful transmission of allusive, if spare, narrative 'cues'. In addition, we may note, the *Lamaḥāt* gives versions of several tales about Ḥakīm Ata that are also preserved in much more extensive versions in a Turkic collection of popular hagiographical narratives known as the *Ḥakīm Atā kitābï*;[58] the *Lamaḥāt*'s versions reveal, in addition to considerable abbreviation, a pattern of reidentifying the personages assigned particular roles in the stories, and of emphasizing the

---

[55] One of these, a version of the 'cotton and fire' story sanctioning (or disavowing) Yasavī's supposed penchant for allowing men and women to participate together in his *dhikr* circles (*Lamaḥāt*, fo. 14b), is known also from the *Manāqib al-akhyār* and the *Javāhir al-abrār*; the other, about a scholar who came to challenge Yasavī but whose books, and mind, were miraculously erased on Yasavī's command (*Lamaḥāt*, fo. 39a), is reflected in the *Javāhir al-abrār* and in oral tradition.

[56] *Lamaḥāt*, fo. 14b; a version appears in the *Javāhir al-abrār*, and in Ismā'īl Atā'ī tradition, as well as in oral material recorded in this century.

[57] *Ibid.*, fo. 14a.

[58] *Ibid.*, fos 37b–38a; the *Ḥakīm Atā kitābï*, probably compiled no earlier than the later seventeenth century but preserving narratives known to have been in circulation as early as the later fifteenth century, survives in several manuscript versions and was published in K.G. Zaleman, "Legenda pro Khakim-Ata," *Izvestiia Akademii nauk* (SPb.), 9/2 (1898), pp. 105–50.

terminology and concerns (i.e. specific practice, succession, authority) of a Sufi community (as opposed to the more general interests evident in the popular hagiography).

'Ālim Shaykh's use, in the *Lamaḥāt*, of material drawn from oral tradition naturally raises important questions about the interplay of literary hagiographies and oral material (the latter category covering both 'internal' oral tradition passed down within a Sufi lineage, and a 'popular' oral tradition reflecting the broader reputation of a saint in his society). Does popular oral tradition borrow tales from written venues, or from Sufi lore transmitted within a narrower community, and distort or 'degrade' them, or do literary hagiographies such as the *Lamaḥāt* assemble, and often imperfectly transmit (or purposefully 'domesticate') narratives circulated for decades or centuries in oral venues ranging from the public to the familial? Both extremes, no doubt, may be argued in certain cases, and the path of exchange is in most cases considerably more complex than is implied by the alternatives posed here, but the example of the *Lamaḥāt* might suggest that the orally transmitted material was both richer and, arguably, more 'authentic' than whatever material might have been available in written form.

More to the point, however, the *Lamaḥāt*'s use of oral material may have served a broader purpose, which was also met in other ways that together may help us understand 'Ālim Shaykh's essential aim in compiling the work. Of his motives for writing the *Lamaḥāt* 'Ālim Shaykh actually says very little, but what he does say is revealing. In his brief introduction, he notes that he had often considered recording "the lives and deeds of the guides and devotees of this exalted and noble *silsila*" (i.e. the Yasaviyya), in accord with the *ḥādīth* according to which "God's mercy descends where the pious are mentioned;" he had not begun the task, however, until he received what he interpreted as 'a welcome sign' from the *Sulṭān al-ṭarīqa*, "Khwāja Aḥmad al-'Alavī al-Yasavī." The sign was a vision he saw one evening:

> I saw that I was sitting on the blessed back (*pusht*) of the holy *Sulṭān al-ṭarīqa*, discoursing on divine wisdom (*ma'ārif-i ilāhī*), when all of a sudden the *quṭb* of the age appeared and cried out, "Hey, you ill-mannered wretch!" The holy *Sulṭān al-ṭarīqa* said, "I am content for him to sit upon my back and speak on my behalf!" That sign was the reason I began the assemblage and composition of the wonders and experiences of his holiness and of his disciples and companions.[59]

The implication of this brief comment seems to be that 'Ālim Shaykh sought not only to 'speak about' the Yasavī Sufi tradition, but to 'speak for' it, and in the context of 'Ālim Shaykh's own life and times, such an aim was clearly shaped by the ongoing rivalry between Yasavī and Naqshbandī Sufi

---

[59] *Lamaḥāt*, fos. 1b–2a.

communities during the sixteenth and early seventeenth centuries:[60] the *Lamaḥāt*, we may suppose, was intended to counter the virtual Naqshbandī monopoly on the presentation of Yasavī history and identity.

'Ālim Shaykh's own life, as we have seen, reflected the tension between the two rival Sufi communities; the *Lamaḥāt* as a whole may be regarded as his affirmation of his choice of the Yasavī path, and the work's contents and even style come into clearer focus as part of a discursive response to the Naqshbandiyya. The defence of the vocal *dhikr* that begins the work naturally assumes the polemic against the *dhikr-i jahr* that in the fifteenth and sixteenth centuries was maintained primarily by Naqshbandī shaykhs. In the hagiographical anecdotes that comprise the bulk of the *Lamaḥāt*, moreover, two processes are at work. On the one hand, there is simply a record of the many more recent Yasavī shaykhs (that is, from the early sixteenth century onwards) who were ignored, or defamed, in Naqshbandī hagiographies of that era; through the anecdotes about these more recent figures, given with careful attribution (often to renowned scholars and jurists of Mawarannahr) and attention to hagiographical detail, the Yasavī shaykhs are given a voice, to be sure, but are also given something much more basic: names. Naqshbandī hagiographical polemics of the sixteenth century often ignore even the identities of shaykhs from the Yasavī tradition, directing their disparaging stories against unnamed 'Jahrī' shaykhs, or merely using them indiscriminately as foils to illustrate Naqshbandī superiority. The *Lamaḥāt*, almost alone among extant hagiographical sources from this era, allows us to fill in, and balance, the Naqshbandī representation of the Yasaviyya, and to understand more clearly who represented the Yasavī tradition during the sixteenth century.

On the other hand, the hagiographical anecdotes recounted by 'Ālim Shaykh with regard to earlier Yasavī saints in effect reclaims them for the Yasaviyya. Their legacy had already been discursively appropriated by the Naqshbandiyya at the beginning of the sixteenth century, in a work 'Ālim Shaykh clearly used, but did not cite, namely the pivotal Naqshbandī hagiography compiled then, devoted to Khwāja Aḥrār, the *Rashaḥāt-i 'ayn al-ḥayāt*; that appropriation had gone essentially unchallenged until the *Lamaḥāt*. The *Rashaḥāt*, as I have discussed elsewhere,[61] firmly situated the Yasavī tradition within a Naqshbandī framework, at once appropriating the charisma of Aḥmad Yasavī for the Naqshbandiyya and subordinating the subsequent Yasavī *silsila* as, in effect, a 'branch' of the Naqshbandiyya; the fact that its portrayal of Yasavī history has been uncritically accepted in much current scholarship should not obscure the partisan and tendentious character of the *Rashaḥāt*'s portrayal, nor should the fact that the *Lamaḥāt* – the earliest

[60] I have briefly discussed some aspects of this rivalry during this period in "The *Mashā"ikh-i Turk* and the *Khojagān*', pp. 199–205.

[61] "The *Mashā'ikh-i Turk* and the *Khojagān*," pp. 187–92.

surviving discursive response produced in Yasavī circles to the Naqshbandī version – was compiled over a century after the *Rashaḥāt*.

The *Lamaḥāt* in effect subverts the *Rashaḥāt*'s appropriation of the Yasavī legacy by adding other voices to establish the independence and authority of the Yasaviyya. This is clear above all in the basic issue of the order's *silsila*, for the *Lamaḥāt*, after citing two 'alternative' sources affirming that Aḥmad Yasavī's master was Shihāb al-Dīn 'Umar Suhravardī, first repeats the *Rashaḥāt*'s well-known account making Yasavī a disciple of Yūsuf Hamadānī (here we should stress that the *Rashaḥāt* was so popular in Central Asia, and was considered so authoritative, that 'Ālim Shaykh could hardly have ignored its account of Yasavī history) but then reaffirms the Suhravardi connection, neither expressly rejecting the Hamadānī link nor allowing it to overshadow the Suhravardī connection (as was implicitly the case in Naqshbandī tradition). The *Lamaḥāt*, in addition, ignores entirely the *Rashaḥāt*'s contrived presentation of the Yasavī *silsila* after Aḥmad Yasavī, beginning with the Naqshbandi-style ascription of four *khalīfas* to Aḥmad Yasavī.[62] 'Ālim Shaykh here simply gives what must be regarded as an internal Yasavī version of the succession to the order's 'founder', identifying three saints as Yasavī's disciples – Ḥakīm Ata, Ṣūfī Muḥammad Dānishmand, and Bābā Māchīn – but tracing subsequent spiritual generations through only the first of these.

In addition to its alternative vision of the Yasavī *silsila*, the *Lamaḥāt* may also subvert the Naqshbandī presentation of the Yasavī tradition through its heavy dependence upon, and treatment of, oral material. The simplicity of the *Lamaḥāt*'s language, diction and structure, to be sure, together with the rather earthy anecdotes for which 'Ālim Shaykh often shows a noticeable taste, may simply reflect either the popular oral form in which much Yasavī lore had been circulated down to his time, or the pragmatic religious (rather than artistic) aims of the author. At the same time, however, it may also reflect the author's conscious decision to present that orally transmitted material 'raw', without embellishment or elaboration, both in order to enhance the spiritual impact of the implied dialectic invoked by ignoring the conventions of florid hagiography or abstruse doctrinal formulations, and, above all, in order to give voice to an alternative vision of Yasavī history and identity, one distinguished by both style and content from the earlier tradition of literary hagiography in which Yasavī circles had little or no part.

---

[62] Two of the successors ascribed to Aḥmad Yasavī in the *Rashaḥāt* – Manṣūr Ata and Sa'īd Ata – are little more than names (the first is at least described as a son of Arslān Bābā and a great-grandfather of Zangī Ata, a familial link that itself no doubt provided the motive for calling Manṣūr Ata a disciple of Yasavī, while no identification is offered at all, in any source, for the second). The *Rashaḥāt* also appears to garble the positions in the Yasavī lineage held by Ismā'īl Ata and his son Isḥāq Khwāja, and in general seems to have provided a rationalized *silsila* structure that in many cases obscures the original traditions of the Yasavī communities themselves.

The reliance upon oral tradition of this sort may thus be understood as a subtle response to the treatment of Yasavī history, and of the Yasaviyya's current status in 'Ālim Shaykh's time, in the literary sources produced in rival Naqshbandī circles. Another aspect of this response, of course, was the *Lamaḥāt*'s composition in Persian. 'Ālim Shaykh's choice of language (he clearly knew Turkic, and frequently cites Turkic sayings, often without translation) no doubt reflects his intention to compete with Naqshbandī circles, and Naqshbandī writings, on their own ground. The other Persian works produced in Yasavī circles, noted earlier, represent a similar development in presenting the lore of the 'Turkic shaykhs' in Persian, and for the most part they did so independently of one another (among them, only the *Ḥujjat al-dhākirīn* is clearly linked to the *Lamaḥāt* or to any of the other Persian Yasavī works), with the clear focus upon countering the Naqshbandī vision of the Yasaviyya that is also evident in other features of its style and content. However, 'Ālim Shaykh's *Lamaḥāt* is perhaps the most vivid product of this process whereby the heirs of the *mashā'ikh-i turk* resorted to Persian in order, we may suggest, to compete with the Naqshbandiyya.

The *Lamaḥāt* illuminates, then, both the historical circumstances of Yasavī–Naqshbandī rivalry in the sixteenth and early seventeenth centuries (the particulars of which must naturally be balanced with accounts drawn from partisan Naqshbandī sources, a task that need not detain us here), and especially the discursive response of the Yasavī tradition (or at least of one prominent Yasavī shaykh) to that rivalry. The *Lamaḥāt*, to be sure, is hardly an ideal source on the Yasaviyya: it concentrates almost exclusively on Mawarannahr, slights Yasavī lineages known to have been active in Balkh, all but ignores Sayyid Atā'ī and Ismā'il Atā'ī lineages dominated by hereditary succession, and fails to note still other natural descent lines linked, whether actually or retrospectively, to other early Yasavī saints such as Uzun Ḥasan Atā, known from later, non-Yasavī sources, and so on. Without the *Lamaḥāt*, however, we would lack not only a vital source on the Yasavī tradition, but also an internal product of that tradition that should go far to overturn many of the standard assumptions about Yasavī history, and about the Yasavī phenomenon in general, including the habit of relegating the Yasaviyya to a purely Turkic, or even nomadic Turkic, environment.

Yet abandoning the customary relegation of the Yasavī tradition to a wholly Turkic cultural environment does not mean that we should situate the Yasavī Order in a purely Persian context. Rather, the literary legacy of the Yasaviyya during the sixteenth and seventeenth centuries is replete with a deep familiarity not only with the Turkic language of Central Asia, but with the practices and mystical 'style' that were associated with the Turkic adaptation of Islam in Central Asia precisely *because* they were preserved among the *mashā'ikh-i turk*. It is this interweaving of Turkic and Persian, of Inner Asian and Iranian, of Islamizing and long-Islamized, that gives Central Asia its distinctive cultural, political, and religious heritage – and the role of the Yasavī tradition in effecting this synthesis is perhaps its most long-lasting contribution to Central Asian civilization.

Other Sufi traditions of Central Asia, to be sure, demonstrate a similar involvement in both sets of worlds; the Kubravī and Naqshbandī traditions reached out from their Persianate cultural environments to embrace Turkic (and other) worlds, and in the case of the Naqshbandiyya quickly proved intellectually and organizationally dominant over all other Sufi groups in Central Asia, the Yasaviyya included. But the Yasavī tradition reflects a different process, it would seem, and does so precisely in the period with which we are concerned here. The Yasavī Order of the sixteenth and seventeenth centuries, which had originated in and was still associated with the Turkic world, turned to Persian for its religious expression, and did so precisely during a period that saw the reinvigorated domination of Inner Asian steppe traditions in Central Asia, in political and social terms.

If modern politics and various nationalisms have divided up the unique and integral religious heritage of Islamic Central Asia along linguistic or 'ethnic' lines, and if the Yasavī legacy has more recently become a target for even narrower national appropriations (e.g. of Qazaqs vs. Uzbeks), the lesson learned from a closer study of the Yasavī tradition during the sixteenth and seventeenth centuries is precisely the indivisible coherence of Central Asian civilization as a religiously ordered world conceived not in ethnic or even ethno-cultural terms, but in spiritual terms that could evoke and rely on a wide array of idioms (even including elements of sacred imagery rooted in pre-Islamic tradition) for authority, duty, and communal cohesion – for example, spiritual transmission and inspiration, standard *silsila*-based initiatic lineages, or kinship and genealogy – without in any way dimming the essentially Islamic vision that shaped it.

VII

PERSIANATE SUFI POETRY IN IRAN & INDIA

هو العزیز

بیچاره بهائی که دلش زار غم توست

هرچند که عاصی است ز خیل خدم توست

امید وی از عاطفت دمبدم توست

تقصیر «خیالی» به امید کرم توست

یعنی که گنه را به از این نیست بهانه

Though racked and rent by grief for you, Baha'i's heart
May be distressed, in dire straits oppressed and worn
By sin and wickedness, but still he is your slave,
A lackey in your company; he pins his hopes
In every breath on your benevolence. Presuming on
Your charity: his 'sins' are thus the fault of fantasy...
I mean – no better pretext does exist for sin than this.

*The Vernacular Tradition in Persianate Sufi Poetry in Mughal India**

ANNEMARIE SCHIMMEL

To the common people leave
Grammar and syntax –
I am contemplating the Beloved.

Qaḍī Qādan

Unlike many of the learned contributors to this volume who have discussed the political implications of Sufism and Sufi literature in the Safavid and Mughal period, in this chapter I shall focus on Sufi poetry and the poetical tradition, both within and without the Sufi Orders, in India during the Mughal period. Elsewhere in this volume David Morgan presented an interesting and original thesis concerning the theological persuasion of Shāh Ismā'īl I, but an equally important literary dimension of Ismā'īl's character should not be overlooked: the fact that he wrote all his poetry in Turkish rather than classical Persian, such that his *Dīvān* represents one of the best examples of a regional language being used for the purpose of propagation of faith (despite the fact that Turkish poetry existed in Anatolia long before him). The topic of Sufi poetry composed in the vernacular languages in India during the Mughal period is thus a somewhat neglected field of inquiry which I shall endeavour to elucidate below.

As is well known, Persian was first introduced into India by Maḥmūd of Ghazna who, in 1026, made the city of Lahore his Indian capital. As a consequence of his invasion, a kind of Persianate culture began to flourish in the Subcontinent. In the context of Persian Sufism, 'Alī ibn 'Uthmān al-Hujwīrī, the author of the first theoretical treatise in Persian on Sufism, *Kashf al-maḥjūb*, who settled in Lahore in the eleventh Christian century, was perhaps the most famous contributor to the early formation of this culture.

* This chapter is based on a recording of Professor Schimmel's lecture given extempore at the School of Oriental and African Studies, University of London, on 21 May 1997, which under her direction was later edited, revised and annotated by the editors.

Even after the Ghaznavids' empire collapsed and succumbed to conquering dynasties, Persian remained the language of polite culture in India, generating a literature which has flourished over the centuries down to the present day, when, with Muḥammad Iqbāl, we have seen perhaps the last great writer in Persian.

But it was not only by the medium of the Persian tongue that Sufi teachings spread throughout India. One of the most effective means by which Sufi teachings were disseminated was through the local and indigenous languages. Beginning with Hujwīrī and the onset of the penetration of the Persian language into India, records remain of numerous Sufi saints and poets such as Farīd Ganj-i Shakar (d. 1265) and Niẓām al-Dīn Awliyā' (1242–1325), as well as many others who composed small songs and ballads in local dialects – rather than in the high Persian of the literati or the Arabic of the theologians – in order to convey the beauty of their mystical doctrines to some of their less literate followers. One witnesses, in fact, a steady and progressive development of indigenous languages – to which the essay by Simon Weightman on Shaykh Manjhan's *Madhumalti* in the present volume bears eloquent witness. *Lor Chanda* by Mawlānā Da'ud (*c.* 1370) and other mystical poems – or poems that could be mystically interpreted – belong to such a category. Finally, with the great Sindī mystical poet Qaḍī Qādan (d. 1551 in Sehwan Sharīf; he was, incidentally, the maternal great-grandfather of Prince Dārā Shikūh's *pīr* Miyān Mīr, d. 1635), whose verse was cited at the beginning of this essay, a new trend towards use of the vernacular in the Sufi poetry and mystical teachings of the Indus Valley, and to a certain extent, the Punjab, was inaugurated.

Yet it was only at a certain point in history, when the political situation in the Punjab, Sind and the Deccan changed, that we find the regional languages coming into use among the Sufis. In this respect, I would highly recommend the famous study by Baba-yi Urdu Maulvi 'Abd al-Ḥaqq entitled *Urdu kī nashw u namā mēn ṣūfiyya-yi kirām kā kām*[1] on the role of Sufis in the development of Urdu literature. The point made in that study is equally valid for other languages of the Subcontinent – and in a strange way is also true in regard to the development of mystical poetry in medieval Europe. For instance, what would German literature have amounted to without the daring examples set by Meister Eckhart (1260–1327) in addressing his nuns and monks in German rather than Latin, or of Mechthild von Magdeburg (d. 1283) who composed her glowing mystical poetry in German at exactly the same time as Rūmī? Both authors were mystics and both contributed significantly to the development of modern spoken and written German. Coincidentally, owing to the activities of the Sufis, exactly the same phenomenon occurred in the Subcontinent.

---

[1] Published Karachi: Anjumar-i taraqqī-yi Urdū 1953 (2nd edn).

Although many of the Sufis of the Mughal period in India composed important works and expounded the theoretical teachings of *taṣawwuf* in classical Arabic or Persian in order to convey the secrets of the love of God, the Prophet and humankind, they often reverted to their own vernacular languages which everyone, including even simple women, could understand. Everywhere in the Subcontinent, Sufis can be found whose written teachings are addressed to the ordinary masses. Since they had to give spiritual instruction through examples drawn from daily life – spinning, grinding grain and other simple daily chores – new genres of literature were spawned as an indirect consequence of their popular spirituality.

One lovely example of this occurs in the Dakhni folk poetry of the Deccan, specifically in the *charkha-nāma* or 'spinning poem' genre. In this genre, the mundane activity of spinning is integrated into the spiritual practice of the constant repetition of the name of God, the *dhikr*, illustrating how the Sufis used everyday language in their poetry so that even the simplest housewife could understand it. As with cotton, the more it is spun, the thinner, and more refined the thread becomes, so with the spiritual heart: the more engaged it is in the discipline of remembrance, the more conscious it becomes of the divine, and the more refined. Such poems tell us how at the end of the mystic housewife's life, God will buy her finely spun yarn at a very high price. One recalls, in the same context, the Koranic verse "God has bought from the believers their selves and their possessions against the gift of paradise" (IX:111), which testifies that the righteous soul, having performed many meritorious deeds, "will be decorated and adorned with the beautiful garment which she has herself spun and woven."[2] However, when the marriage day (i.e. death: the divine Spouse's embrace) of the lazy soul who did not devote herself to spinning (that is, did not remember God by *dhikr* in the heart) approaches, she will find herself naked and with no dowry. Such simple poetic genres, making use of common imagery drawn from the activities of rural life, flourished all over India wherever cotton was grown, not just in the Deccan, but in Sind and the Punjab as well.[3]

A similar concentration on local colour and imagery is quite evident in Qaḍī Qādan, the poet cited at the beginning of this essay. All that was known to be extant of his work until recently were a mere seven *doha*, until a few decades ago a scholar discovered a hitherto unknown manuscript in Hariyana containing 110 more examples of his poetry. Although his style is extremely dense and his meaning often difficult to decipher, constant references to nature

---

[2] The same idea of course occurs in Hinduism, where the every soul is said to weave his or her own destiny, construct his or her own karma by actions performed during the course of life.

[3] Cf. esp. Richard Maxwell Eaton, *Sufis of Bijapur* (New Jersey: Princeton University Press 1978).

and the rural landscape of India feature strongly in his work. On the other hand, Sufis such as Qaḍī Qādan were far from being 'naturalist' or 'pastoral' poets as defined according to the criteria of Western literary criticism. Rather, in accordance with a well-known Koranic doctrine,[4] these poets interpreted everything in nature as constituting 'signs' pointing to God. Thus, the banyan tree, with its branches that send out shoots which grow down to the soil and root to form secondary branches, giving it the appearance of a vast forest, becomes in the poetry of Qaḍī Qādan a symbol of the Divine disguised in multiplicity by its manifold forms, but in Essence a single tree.

The influence of Ibn 'Arabī's thought, that is to say, the impact of his ideas of *waḥdat al-wujūd* or the 'Oneness of Being' on Indian Sufism in general, and on this metaphysical vision of nature in particular, was very profound. M.Z.A. Shakeb, William Chittick and several others in this volume have underlined the central role played by Sufis such as Gīsūdarāz (d. 825/1422) in Indian Sufism and observed how the teachings of Ibn 'Arabī became more and more popular in India during the fourteenth and, especially, the fifteenth century. The correspondence carried on by Gīsūdarāz, who was not a supporter of Ibn 'Arabī, for instance, with some of his colleagues, like Ashraf Jahāngīr (d. *c.* 1415), shows that there were wide divergencies of opinion about Ibn 'Arabī's thought among the different Sufi orders.

These orders had penetrated into the subcontinent in the earliest days. The first of them was the Chishtiyya, famous for their practice of musical audition (*samā'*) and love of poetry, whose founder Mu'īn al-Dīn Chishtī (d. 634/1236) having gone first to Delhi, then immediately settled in Ajmer, where the order presently has its centre. In Delhi resided his famous follower Quṭb al-Dīn Bakhtiyār Kākī (d. 634/1236). Almost at the same time (the late twelfth, early thirteenth century), members of the Suhrawardiyya settled in the southern Punjab. In Multan one of their centres can still be found. Another important Order was the Qādiriyya, whose members settled first in the Deccan in the late fifteenth century, and then in Ucch, north-east of Multan in the southern Punjab, where they came to play an important role in the history of Sufism in the Punjab and Sind. One of the most important Qādirī personalities in India was Dārā Shikūh, the heir-apparent of the Mughal Empire, and disciple of a Qādirī master named Miyān Mīr of Lahore and his successor Mullā Shāh Badakhshī. Although by the end of the sixteenth century the Qādiriyya had begun to play an important role in Indian society, with the advent of the seventeenth century and the age of Akbar, and especially following the execution of Dārā Shikūh in 1659, their influence vis-à-vis the more 'official' orders had considerably waned.

---

[4] Sūra XLI:53: "We shall show them Our signs in the horizons in their souls." Also cf. my *Deciphering the Signs of God: A Phenomenological Approach to Islam* (Albany: SUNY Press 1994).

Plate 14: Prince Dārā Shikūh as a Young Man. By Chitarman, *c*. 1640. No. 053.001. © Collection & Courtesy of the Royal Asiatic Society of Great Britain.

Contemporaneous with the rise of the orders, one finds the spread of ecstatic love-mysticism. One of the chief representatives of this trend was Lāl Shāhbāz (Royal Red Falcon) Qalandar of Sehwan in Sind. As the word 'Sehwan' (or Sivistan) indicates, the town where he lived was the site of a Shiva sanctuary on the lower Indus, the main centre of the cult of the Hindu god Shiva found in the western part of Sind and Baluchistan. Thus it is hardly surprising to learn that Shāhbāz's mysticism took on strange forms, and that his followers became known as the *bī-shar'*, or lawless, Sufis. When one reads in later Sufi poetry how Sufi seekers from this area climbed its sacred mountain Hinglaj and visited the sacred cave in Makran, one may deduce that the Sufis had close relations with the Shivaites and Yogis who trekked there on their annual pilgrimages. I myself have visited Hinglaj – definitely not the most attractive place on God's earth – and in its rugged landscape one can vividly sense how Sufis like Shāh 'Abd al-Laṭīf of Bhit had travelled through the mountains and the hills until they reached the pilgrimage site, the sacred cave and the well on the heights of one of those mountains in southern Baluchistan. Thus, one cannot exclude the possibility of Shivaite influences on Sindhi Sufi poetry. These influences seem to be especially visible in the rites practised at the sanctuary of Lāl Shāhbāz Qalandar, where even today the remains of a *lingam* can be found.

However, it is the age of Qaḍī Qādan – the sixteenth century – that is especially significant in the context of the subject of Persianate vernacular poetry. Writing in the year 1593 at the court of Akbar the Great (1542–1605), the historian Badāyūnī recorded in his *Muntakhab al-tawārikh* that a group of wandering Sindhi musicians had arrived in Lahore where they sang lovely tunes about divine love, moving some people in the royal audience. This anecdote demonstrates that as early as the sixteenth century Sindhi mystical music had developed into an important and powerful art form. This Sufi musical tradition remains to the present day the most attractive aspect of Sufism in Sind and in the Punjab. Interestingly enough, it was in the same year, 1593 that Mādhō Lāl Ḥusayn (1539–93), the first major Punjabi Sufi mystic to write in his mother tongue, Panjabi, passed away. The commemoration of the anniversary of his death held at his modest tomb in Lahore close to the Shalimar Garden on the last Saturday in March is still celebrated today as the 'Fair of Lamps' (Mēlā Chirāghān).

Qaḍī Qādan's Sindhi lyrics obviously typify a Sufi interpretation of love. Some resemblances can be found between his vernacular verse and the classical Persian tradition. Such vernacular verse in general and Rūmī's poetry in particular had been known in India since the beginning of the fourteenth century. It is related that in the early fourteenth century Bū 'Alī Qalandar of Panipat had visited Konya, where Sulṭān Valad, Rūmī's son and successor (d. 1312) was living. He remained there a while, probably studying the *Mathnawī* with him, before returning to his native India, bringing Rūmī's mystical lore back with him in the process. His own *mathnawīs*, though rather unimportant in their own right as works of poetry, do show the influence of Rūmī's *Mathnawī* very clearly. From his day onwards, the *Mathnawī* was read and reread and commented on in India – so much so that by the end of the fifteenth century, a Bengali historian observed that "The holy Brahmin recites Rūmī's *Mathnawī*."[5] Thus even the Hindu intellectual elite, many of whom studied Persian, were able to read the *Mathnawī* and find similarities between Muslim mystical concepts and their own Hindu spiritual doctrines. Specifically, Krishna's flute was compared to Rūmī's *ney*, and Vedantic monism became assimilated into Islamic unitarianism. From the middle of the fourteenth century, it becomes difficult to find a single poet writing in Persian in the Subcontinent who did not make at least a few allusions in his work to Rūmī's *Mathnawī*. It was natural that the Sufis writing in the province of Sind knew at least parts of the *Mathnawī*, if only the opening eighteen verses of the great epic describing the 'Lament of the Reed Pipe'.

Although one cannot detect the direct influence of the *Mathnawī* on Qaḍī Qādan's poetry, he probably knew as much of the book as any of his literate contemporaries and Sufi compatriots. One verse of his poetry, however, does directly indicate the extent of his understanding and awareness of the classical definitions of Sufi terminology. In this verse, he refers to the concept of the inspired ecstatic utterance: *shaṭḥ* – or "paradox" as Henry Corbin called it – which, according to the definition given to the idea by Abū Naṣr Sarrāj's *Kitāb al-luma'*, signifies an overflowing of water from a vessel too shallow to contain it. As a type of spiritual experience, these ecstatic utterances (*shaṭḥ*) are the outcome of divine grace which so suffuses the narrow vessel of the mystic's heart that he or she, so Sarrāj declares, gives utterance to matters normally beyond ordinary human ken and comprehension. Ḥallāj's famous utterance: "I am the Truth" (*anā 'l-Ḥaqq*) is a case in kind of this experience. Qaḍī Qādan's verse provides a beautiful poetical interpretation of Sarrāj's classical definition of *shaṭḥ*:

> When the Indus is in spate
> Canals are too tight to contain it;
> Thus the influx of Grace
> Forces me to speak.

It was with this same sense of being overwhelmed in heart with the divine presence that Qaḍī Qādan had beheld the Beloved beneath the Banyan tree as One in Essence but myriad in his multiple manifestations. Over the centuries following Qaḍī Qādan there came into being a whole series of poets writing in

---

[5] M. Enamul Haq, *Muslim Bengali Literature* (Karachi 1957), p. 42. For further discussion of this subject, see my *The Triumphal Sun: A Study of the Works of Jalāloddin Rumi* (London: Fine Books 1978), chap. 4.

Sindhi who used such Sufi ideas, images and technical terminology in their work.

Alongside the classical Persian Sufi poetic imagery, these poets also developed a type of mystical imagery based on Hindu mythology and imagery which is extremely important for our understanding of Islamic mystical thought and expression in the subcontinent. Thus, one finds in Sindhi poetry of the seventeenth century a constant reference to themes drawn from popular Indian folk tales, such as, for example, the topos of the *virahini*, 'the longing woman-soul', which deals with the theme of the 'love in separation' of the bride from the bridegroom. There are also allusions to the classical stories of Sohnī Mehanwal, Sassi Punhun and of Omar Marui in the early Sindhi poetry of the seventeenth century, of which the verse of Shāh 'Abd al-Karīm Bulrrīwārō (d. 1623) provides many good examples.

The supreme master of such popular Sufi poetry was Shāh 'Abd al-Laṭīf (1689–1752), whose tomb is still an object of pilgrimage in Bhit where the anniversary of his death, or *'urs*, is celebrated with great devotion. Shāh 'Abd al-Laṭīf left behind a book of poems in Sindhi entitled *Shāha jō risālō* (The Book of Shāh), containing thirty chapters named and arranged according to traditional Indian musical modes (*raga*s), many of which he composed himself, sometimes using classical Indian *ragas*, sometimes his own original compositions and sometimes improvised mixtures of various musical traditions: Persian, Sindhi and Indian.[6]

The *Risālō* soon became a poetic work equally sacred to Muslims and Hindus. In fact, the first commentaries on the work were published in the late nineteenth century by Hindu scholars who claimed that Shāh 'Abd al-Laṭīf's thought was nothing but an Islamicized form of Vedanta! While the native Hindu standpoint on the matter can obviously be appreciated, it is more regrettable that many European orientalists were unable to view Sufism as anything more than an Islamicized version of Vedanta. Neither the orientalists nor the Hindus had the least knowledge of the great veneration accorded to the Prophet Muḥammad in the Sufi mystical tradition in general and in the Indian folk tradition in particular – in which the 'Light of Muḥammad' and great love for the Prophet of Islam feature as one of the main distinguishing characteristics.[7]

The *Risālō* reflects the poet's varied moods. While some of his lyrics are undoubtably purely mystical in tenor, the majority of his poems are inspired

---

[6] It is interesting to note, in the context of the influence of Sufi literature on Europe analysed by Farhang Jahanpour in this volume, that his *Risālō* was printed in 1866 and published by the German missionary Ernest Trumpp who worked for the British Bible Society, and in 1963 nobody had yet cut open the pages of the copy in the British Library!

[7] See my *And Muhammad is His Messenger: The Veneration of the Prophet in Islamic Piety* (Chapel Hill: University of North Carolina Press 1985), chap. 7.

by the folk tales and legends of the Indus Valley and Punjab. However, in the context of comparative mysticism, what is of fundamental importance in his work is that all these stories have as their main hero – or rather, heroine – a woman. All his Sindhi and Punjabi stories revolve around the fate and fortunes of a woman, who serves as symbol of the soul longing for, and completely dedicated to regaining, union with her lost Beloved, in the course of searching for whom she undergoes many trials and tribulations. Shāh 'Abd al-Laṭīf's symbol of the 'woman-soul' exemplifies the *virahini* tradition in the Hinduism, and is probably related to the poetical genre of *bārahmāsa* as well.[8]

The story of the heroine Sassui illustrates this genre very well. Sassui, a Brahmin's daughter, was born with an unlucky horoscope foretelling she would marry a Muslim. This inauspicious fortune prompts her parents to place her in a basket in the river to rid themselves of this child. Retrieved from the river by a washerman, she soon grows to be such a beauty that suitors come from all over the land seeking her hand. Finally even Punhun, the prince of Kecch in Baluchistan, falls in love with her, and they live together for a short time. Punhun's relatives, who are, of course, distressed at the apparent impropriety of their liason – she is apparently a low-caste washerwoman whereas he is a nobleman – do what they can to ruin their marriage. Accordingly, they make the couple drunk and kidnap the prince. Waking up in the morning, Sassui finds her bed empty. She sets out to search for him, and finally achieves union with him – in death.

This typical folk tale can also easily be understood as an expression of classical Sufi teachings: Sassui's drunken slumber symbolizing the Sufi's *khwāb-i ghaflat*, 'sleep of heedlessness', which is a common theme in classical Persian Sufi texts; and her setting out in search of Punhun as symbolic of 'entering the Sufi Path', *ṭarīqa*, always beset with trials and difficulties. Although, unlike 'Aṭṭār, Shāh 'Abd al-Laṭīf does not specify the precise number of valleys of seeking (*ṭalab*) through which his heroine must pass, he does convey something of the terrors she endures while scaling mountains and traversing the dangerous hills and valleys on the way. Her sore and weary feet are described, and how she attends to and entreats the crows to bring her news of her beloved Punhun, offering to feed them with her own flesh, even the very eyes that once beheld the beloved. Perhaps the essence of this beautiful, passionate and tragic story is captured in one chapter in which Shāh 'Abd al-Laṭīf describes how the lover (Sassui) is completely transformed into Love:

---

[8] For further information on the symbol of the 'woman-soul' see my two works: *As Through A Veil: Mystical Poetry in Islam* (New York: Columbia University Press 1982), chap. 4, pp. 147–8, 152–5 and *My Soul is a Woman: The Feminine in Islam*, trans. Susan Ray (New York: Continuum 1997).

O voice in the desert, as though it were a wild goose:
A call from the water's depth –
  It is the Ah of Love!
O voice in the desert, like a fiddle's melody:
It is the song of Love – only common people thought it to be a woman's voice.[9]

Utilizing classical Persian Sufi themes derived from the works of Aḥmad Ghazālī and Rūzbihān Baqlī, the poet explains here that Love is a force which unites lover and beloved, both of whom are 'devoured' by love, leaving no separation between them. In this sense, Sassui's passion and transformation into 'Love' itself expresses the deepest secret of Sufism.

Another folk tale employed by Shāh 'Abd al-Laṭīf, also based on the theme of the 'woman-soul', features a kind of inversion of the classical Greek Hero and Leander legend, with a female swimmer instead of a man. In this tale the poet tells us how Sohnī, a potter's daughter, swam through the Indus river every night to meet her beloved, Mehanwal, a formerly wealthy man who had spent all his fortune on pottery to be close to her, and who then eked out a living as a buffalo-herder on a little island. One night, however, Sohnī's sister-in-law switches the baked pot that the heroine had been using as a lifebuoy for a simple unbaked earthenware jar, so that midway through the river the pot dissolves and the reckless lover loses her life to the waves. Here again, it is only in death that the heroine is united with her beloved. Of course, since this tale is essentially a romance glorifying love as adultery (Sohnī was married), it sometimes aroused the wrath of orthodox theologians, although the Sufis evidently saw the spiritual and allegorical dimension of the story.[10] In any case, such ballads and stories, whether they be of Sassui and Punhun, of Sohnī and Mehanwal, of Līlā and Chanesār or 'Umar and Maruī and their like, are all part and parcel of Sindhi folklore and the indigenous Indian Sufi tradition.

One story, which incidentally illustrates the strong influence of Rūmī on Shāh 'Abd al-Laṭīf, is that of Maruī, a lovely village girl from the Thar desert, who is kidnapped by King 'Umar of Omarkot, who intends to marry, or at least seduce, her. However she disdains his advances and does all she can to make herself unattractive, until finally she is sent back home. For the poet, Maruī is a symbol of a longing soul exiled in an alien land, separated from the beloved and yearning for her homeland. To convey this message, Shāh 'Abd al-Laṭīf deliberately inserts translations of certain Persian verses from the *Mathnawī*

---

[9] *Shāh jō risālō*, ed. Kalyān B. Adwānī (Bombay: Hindūstān Kitābghar 1958), Sur Ma'dhurī VII, vv. 21, 22.

[10] I personally saw the consequences of narrating the legend of Sohnī and Mehanwal when some years ago I told it to an audience at a Muslim conference in Karachi, after which a local mullā accused me of favouring immoral literature!

Plate 15: Awrangzīb holding a Koran, *c*. 1850. No. 054.001. © Collection & Courtesy of the Royal Asiatic Society of Great Britain.

into his Sindhi mystical poetry, comparing Maruī – using Rūmī's image – to the reed pipe (*nay*) shorn from the reedbed (*nayistān*). Her complaint, described in ever new poetical images, is that of the soul, that is, of the *nay* that longs for its pre-eternal home.

This influence of Rūmī is even more visible in the second chapter of his *Risālō*, where a whole series of verses (although their authenticity is disputed by scholars) end with the refrain: "Thus spoke Rūmī." Although many of his statements about the *via mystica* or Sufi *ṭarīqa* in such passages are not at all remarkable or even particularly profound, it is telling that he always refers to Rūmī as their source. In one of the most touching episodes of the Sassui and Punhun tale, the poet depicts Sassui wandering, thirsty and lonely, through the desert, in a hopeless mood, concluding with a translation of this verse from the *Mathnawī* in order to draw his moral from her plight:

> Not only the thirsty seek the water
> but the water seeks the thirsty as well.[11]

In this simple poetic image, using the symbol of the water and human thirst, and without recourse to complicated philosophical arguments, Rūmī expresses the longing of the Divine for the human. Shāh 'Abd al-Laṭīf's *Risālō* is permeated with many such verses which show, between the lines, the influence of Rūmī.

Very little is known of Shāh 'Abd al-Laṭīf's external life. Like most Sufi poets, his works are replete with Koranic and *ḥadīth* references, and the legend that he was illiterate, applied to so many other Sufi poets, was also told of him. In this context, it is interesting that almost every great writer in the Sufi tradition who used the vernacular instead of Persian or Arabic has been dubbed 'illiterate', whether they hailed from Persia, Anatolia, Arabia or anywhere else in the Islamic world. Yet, while all of Shāh 'Abd al-Laṭīf's poetry indicates that it must have been written by someone belonging to a spiritual tradition, it is somewhat strange that his *ṭarīqa* affiliation is not given by any source. There is a suspicion that he might have been a Qādirī, although throughout his entire oeuvre no reference to any specific *ṭarīqa* can be found.

His sectarian persuasion also remains uncertain. Whereas on the one hand he speaks in orthodox 'Sunnī' terms in one chapter of his *Risālō*, on the other, he relates the sufferings of the two Shī'ite Imāms Ḥasan and Ḥusayn at Karbalā, (in *Sur Kēdārō*). While obviously his reference to *two* brothers is historically inaccurate, the account does reflect a popular folkloric tradition which always portrayed the two brothers side by side at Karbalā and depicted them both as martyrs on the path of love. According to Shāh 'Abd al-Laṭīf's account, Ḥasan and Ḥusayn are no longer simple martyrs for the Faith, but

---

[11] *Mathnawī*, ed. R.A. Nicholson, 8 vols. (London: Luzac & Co. 1925–40), I: 1741.

rather lovers of God upon whom God bestowed martyrdom as a kind of special robe of honour, so that the angels shed roses and other flowers upon them. Here, Ḥasan and Ḥusayn feature as bridegrooms, a theme characteristic not only of Shāh ʿAbd al-Laṭīf's verse but of all Sindhi and Punjabī poetry in the vernacular.

This theme is also reflected in the *Bārahmāsa* (Twelve-months-poem) poetical genre, which belongs to the Indian literary tradition. It describes the seasons of the year through the eyes of a loving woman, and was adopted by many Muslim poets writing in the vernacular in Sind and the Punjab. Quite often, these poets replaced the Indian months by Muslim lunar months. Beginning with Muḥarram, the soul-bride suffers, pondering the fate of the martyrs Ḥasan and Ḥusayn, and lives through the festive seasons of the year until in the end she reaches, in the final month of Dhū'l-Ḥijja, the abode of the Beloved, which is either the Kaʿba, the House of God, or else Medina, the 'Garden of the Prophet'. In this context, it should be pointed out that among the Sufis of the Subcontinent – especially from the Mughal period onwards – the Prophet in his role as the archetypal *ḥaqīqa muḥammadiyya* becomes more and more the object of mystical love and devotion, and in this fashion the ancient Indian genre of the *Bārahmāsa* also became used to express the longing of the Muslim mystic's soul for God or His Prophet.

Another important theme which pervades the vocabulary of the vernacular poets in a very subtle and often covert manner was the idea of the 'Unity of Being' (*waḥdat al-wujūd*). As the main theoretician and author of this concept, Ibn ʿArabī was probably completely unknown among the writers in Sind and the Punjab, and hence his influence as a Sufi thinker can only be indirectly acknowledged. Nonetheless, certain theoretical works based on his doctrines, ascribed to mystics otherwise considered to be simple ecstatics, can be found. One such mystic was Sulṭān Bāhū (d. 1691), a poet who came from the district of Jhang in the southern Punjab and whose *Sīḥarfī* (Thirty-Letter Poem) is known to everyone who reads Panjabi, as it contains one of the finest treatments of the relationship between man and God.

For the first line of this poem, Sulṭān Bāhū, using a wonderful simile, compares God to a jasmine flower planted in his heart by his spiritual master. His master has nurtured the flower with the water of negation of other than God (*lā*) and affirmation of God (*illā*) – here referring to the profession of faith and inculcation of the *dhikr* by his *pīr* – until it grew into a mature plant, so that now its fragrance has permeated his whole being. By constant repetition of "There is no god but God" (an obvious reference to the *dhikr* of *Lā ilāha illā Allāh* favoured by the Qādirī order to which Sulṭān Bāhū belonged) the presence of God is nurtured into a fully-grown 'plant', imbuing the mystic's heart with the fragrance of the divine:

Allāh is a jasmine planted
By my master in my heart,
  Yā Hū!
By the water of negation and affirmation it abided
Beside the jugular vein,[12] and everywhere,
  Yā Hū!
It spread a fragrance inside
When it approached the time of blossoming,
  Yā Hū!
May the efficient preceptor live long
Says Bāhū, who planted this plant!
  Yā Hū!

While these unforgetable verses of Sulṭān Bāhū are still recited and sung today in the Punjab by men and women from every walk of life, very few realize that their author also wrote many theoretical treatises in Persian which treat the classical and traditional forms of Sufi mystical instruction.[13] This combination of ecstatic and theoretical mysticism was by no means typical of Sulṭān Bāhū alone; many poets whom we know only through their ecstatic verses have at the same time written theoretical treatises in Persian in order to satisfy the scholarly inclinations of a Sufi intellectual audience.

Here, it will not be amiss to return to the theme of the woman-soul which, in my opinion, played a most important role in vernacular poetry in Mughal India. Why did Shāh 'Abd al-Laṭīf and his successors in the Punjab such as Bullhē Shāh (d. 1754) and Wārith Shāh (late eighteenth century) always choose to relate stories in which a woman stars as the main character? Personally, I believe that their choice represented a different approach to some very basic ideas of Sufism. It is well known that the classical Sufi ascetics of Persia, Baghdad or Egypt loved to draw an analogy between 'woman' and man's base instincts or the 'lower soul' (the *nafs*, or the 'flesh' in Christian terms) – and the fact that the word *nafs* is a feminine noun in Arabic made this comparison both easy and apt. The term 'soul-which-incites-to-evil' (*al-nafs al-ammāra bi'l-sū'*) mentioned in the Koran (Sūra XII:53) furnished these mystics with an appropriate expression and a doctrinal basis for their theories, and the same scripture also gave them the possibility of attaining two higher degrees of soul-development: 'the blaming soul' (*al-nafs al-lawwāma;* Sūra LXXV:2) and 'the soul at peace' (*al-nafs al-muṭma'inna;* Sūra LXXXIX:27). Although all these references to the *nafs* in the Koran are unrelated to each other, for the Sufi seers they provided the perfect image of the soul's development through various stages: from self-indulgence in passions and

[12] Cf. Koran, L:16.

[13] Recently, two of his theoretical works devoted to the secret of the Spirit (*rūḥ*) and the Soul (*nafs*) after the fashion of classical Persian Sufi works have been translated into English by a Pakistani scholar, Syed A. Hamadani.

lusts, to the awakening to a sense of penitence and conscience, and finally, to becoming 'recollected-in-peace'.

In the same way that the *nafs* was equated with the female, who in early Sufism was considered to be very dangerous to the poor ascetic who was always prone to fall into her snares, it was also natural that the image of woman became used in a different cultural context, namely that of the woman-soul personified in heroines such as Sassui, Sohnī, Maruī and so on. Such personifications were, in fact, not without precedent in Persian literature, as Christopher Shackle elsewhere in this volume points out in regard to the development of the classical Yūsuf and Zulaykhā story in Jāmī's poetry, in which the female, Zulaykhā (Potiphar's wife, mentioned in Sūra XII), is portrayed as the supreme symbol of the soul in her longing for the divine beloved. The basic contours of the tale of Zulaykhā were elaborated by numerous Sufi poets who wrote in Persian, Sindhi and Urdu. In their verse the woman is initially depicted as the 'lower soul' or *al-nafs al-ammāra* attempting to seduce Yūsuf; then, after becoming purified by suffering, traversing the valleys of love and poverty, the woman-soul, desiring nothing but to contemplate the Eternal Beauty which manifests itself in Yūsuf, finally becomes united with him. With such a classical precedent for the manifestation of the soul through the figure of a woman, it was very easy for the Sindhi and Panjabi poets, whose recourse was also to the poetry of their Hindu neighbours with a similar indigenous *virahini* tradition in the *bhaktī* movement, to apply such images to the women in their native stories. In fact, that is one reason why the stories strike so close to the bone and sound so close to life, and why, despite their usage of an age-old imagery and mythology, they still remain contemporary and relevant to everyday life.

As mentioned above, there was very little theoretical treatment of the topos of *waḥdat al-wujūd* on the part of Persianate Sufi poets writing in the vernacular languages in Mughal India. These folk poets very much endorsed the idea that *hama ūst*, 'everything is Him', i.e., that everything is God, who manifests Himself both through the famous Sufi martyr Manṣūr Ḥallāj (d. 309/922) and also through the judge who gave the infamous *fatwā* for his execution. One finds lengthy poems both in Sindhi and Panjabi in which the simple, undifferentiated unity of everything, the divine immanence which embraces all beings, is expressed. However, in studying such poetry it should always be kept in mind that it is meant to be sung and audited by the ear of the heart, rather than theologically dissected for the purposes of uncovering doctrinal truths couched in the orthodox language of dogmatic theology.

If Shāh 'Abd al-Laṭīf exhibited a certain reticence about disclosing the deepest mysteries of love and always spoke in allusions, hiding behind the oblique language of symbolism and strange words, no such inhibitions were shown by his younger contemporary Sachal Sarmast (1739–1826). In his Sindhi poetry, Sarmast (the intoxicated one) openly declared the all-embracing unity-of-being, announcing everything that exists to be a revelation of One Existence:

> Now, he's the judge;
> Now, he's Ḥallāj.
> Now, he is Pharaoh;
> Now, Moses.
> Now, he's Hanuman;
> Now, Abū Ḥanīfa[14]

Even if Sarmast's identification of Abū Ḥanīfa (d. 767) with the sacred Monkey, Hanuman, would probably not have been appreciated by the great orthodox legalist and founder of a major school of Islamic law, the ecstatic tenor of his lyrics is typical of most of the vernacular poets of the Indo-Muslim Sufi tradition. Much of the Panjabi and Sindhi Sufi poetry written in the Mughal period dwells with infinite and inexhaustible detail and variation on this theme of the all-embracing of presence and unity of God within the world.

The combination of the theme of the unity-of-being with the spiritualized interpretation of medieval Hindu folk tales is especially evident in the poetry of Bullhē Shāh (1680–1752), considered to be the greatest Sufi poet writing in Panjabi. Relating the story of the love of Rānjhā, son of a wealthy landlord, for Hīr, daughter of the king of Jhang, with whom he is finally spiritually united (only in death of course), in the following verse Hīr appears as a symbol of the woman-soul longing for the divine beloved, Rānjhā:

> *Rānjhā, Rānjhā kar dī niñh meñ*
> *apē Rānjhā huī –*
>
> Repeating Rānjhā, Rānjhā in my mind,
> I myself have become Rānjhā .[15]

A good example of the extremely rich symbolism utilized by the Indo-Muslim Sufi poets to express their feelings for the unity-of-being can be found in the lovely short poem by Bullhē Shāh with the refrain: "All flakes of cotton are equally white." Using what is one of the finest images of the unity-of-being ever employed by an Indo-Muslim Sufi poet, he explains that the differentiation of the oneness of cotton (= being) into a multiplicity of garments (= phenomena) occurs only when cotton is spun and woven into various types of fabrics. In another image (in the last verse of this poem), he notes that although silver (= Reality-of-Being) is but a single metal, the silversmith makes of it various types of ornaments (= multiplicity) such as nose-rings, earrings, necklaces, anklets and bracelets, yet leaving the reality of the basic silver ore unaltered.

---

[14] Sachal Sarmast, *Risālō Sindhī*, ed. 'Uthmān 'Alī Anṣārī (Karachi 1958).
[15] Bulhē Shāh, *Qānūn-i 'ishq*, Kafi no. 109, p. 240.

However, one should not imagine that all the late medieval Sindhi and Panjabi poets were ecstatics. While Qaḍī Qādan, Shāh 'Abd al-Laṭīf, Sachal Sarmast and others were, of course, the supreme masters of such Sufi poetry in the vernaculars, their literary endeavours also paved the way for a more sober and orthodox type of poetry. At the same time that Shāh 'Abd al-Laṭīf was writing his ecstatic lyrics under the influence of Rūmī (the Sindhi poet was even given a fine copy of the *Mathnawī* by Nūr Muḥammad Kalhora, ruler of Sind[16]), some of the more formalist Naqshbandī Sufi shaykhs under the influence of the highly orthodox mystical theologian Aḥmad Sirhindī (1564–1624) were in the process of migrating from major urban centres such as Delhi and Agra to the provinces. On settling in Sind, some of these shaykhs translated portions of the Koran into Sindhi, and also composed a number of important theoretical treatises in Sindhi, thus effecting the prose development of this vernacular language.

As in the case of Sindhi, Panjabi and Urdu, mystics also contributed to the development of other neo-Indian languages. The first to use Pashto as a language of religious instruction was Bāyazīd Anṣāri, known as the Pīr-i Rawshan (Radiant Master), who was killed in battle in north-western India in 1575 at the time when his religious movement in the Pathan areas between what is now Pakistan and Afghanistan seemed to threaten the stability of the Mughal Empire.[17] The theories about Pīr-i Rawshan's religious attitude are widely divergent, but there is no doubt that he was a mystic who emphasized meditation and asceticism and who may also have been influenced by some Ismā'īlī currents in the area of his activities (Badakhshān, Hunza). Yet, whatever his actual affiliation, he was the first mystic to use his native Pashto to create a major religious work, the *Khayr al-bayān*. Among his descendants is to be found Mirzā Anṣārī, a Sufi known for his ecstatic verse in Pashto in which the feeling of *waḥdat al-wujūd*, unity-of-being, looms large – a mystical tendency that had grown strong from the late fifteenth century onwards. Pashto religious poetry reached its zenith with the Chishtī Sufi Raḥmān Bābā (d. *c.* 1709), whose great hymns in praise of the Creator figure are among the most impressive expressions of deep piety in world literature but seem to be closer to the classical Persian poetry of Sanā'ī and his followers than to the overflowing lyrical ecstasy prevalent in the plains of the Indus and the Punjab. Even the great warrior Khūshḥāl Khān (1022/1613–1100/1689) at times wrote religious poetry in Pashto, a language which by his time had become most pliable. His writings betray the author's interest in the Persian Sufi tradition and wisdom literature.

Religious writers also served the development of poetry in other indigenous Indian languages. Awadi owes its first and most important work,

---

16 For further discussion, see my *The Triumphal Sun*, p. 380.

17 See the essay by Sergei Andreyev on the Rawshaniyya movement in this volume (Eds).

Padmavati, to Mālik Muḥammad Jāisī (d. after 1570); he was a disciple of the Mahdawī leader Burhān al-Dīn of Kalpi.

In Kashmiri as in Bengali, the time-honoured topic of Yūsuf and Zulaykhā inspired poets to compose epical versions of the well-known Koranic tale – apparently even before Jāmī's famous epic poem was written on this theme, – for a Bengali version of *Yusuf Jalikha* by one Muḥammad Ṣaghīr dates back to the early fifteenth century. On the whole, Bengali mystical poetry shows itself in small lyrical songs, *marifati*, in which the bards took their imagery from their environment (as they did in other parts of India as well). Whether they sang of the little water-hyacinths or the mirror-like water, they often blended the Hindu stories of Lord Krishna and his flute with the Song of the Reed at the beginning of Rūmī's *Mathnawī*. For, as mentioned above, Mawlānā Rūmī's work was known to and appreciated by the Bengalis – even the Brahmins – from the late fifteenth century onwards.

The poets who sang of divine love or their love of the Prophet in the vernaculars often claimed to be illiterate, thus following the example of the *nabī ummī*, 'the unlettered Prophet' (Koran VII:157–8), yet the influence of the great mystics who wrote in the Persian language and their sophisticated poetry always remains palpable in their writings. While Rūmī's role in Indo-Muslim poetry is firmly established, it would be worthwhile to study 'Aṭṭār's influence. 'Aṭṭār, who is praised in Sindhi poetry as one of the martyrs of love, seems to have been much more influential than was hitherto realized and his role would deserve a special study.

Yet, the mystics probably did not ponder too intensely this or that influence from Persian, Arabic, or Indian sources; they would have probably agreed with Pīr-i Rawshan, who said:

> God speaks in every language, be it Arabic, Persian, Hindi or Afghani: He speaks in the language which the human heart can understand.

Persian Poetry and Qādirī Sufism in Later Mughal India

Ghanīmat Kunjāhī and his Mathnawī-yi Nayrang-i 'ishq

CHRISTOPHER SHACKLE

Ghanīmat, whose Persian poem of 1685 entitled *Nayrang-i 'ishq*, 'The Charm of Love' forms the subject of this chapter,[1] had by the 1940s come to maintain a dim afterlife in popular local memory only as a miracle worker with some notable but minor specialist powers of the kind attributed to the lesser sort of departed Sufi saint all over the Muslim world. Various beliefs involving enhancement of the mental faculties were associated by both Muslims and non-Muslims with his tomb which is situated in his native town of Kunjah, some seven miles east of the historic city of Gujarat in the north-western Punjab. Besides the tomb being thought to be a good place for the curing of the insane, it was believed that chewing the leaves of the tree growing on its northern side improved students' performance in examinations, while a forty days' vigil would help those aspiring to become poets to realize their ambition.[2]

Although it is possible that these beliefs and practices may survive in some reduced form today, the many changes which have taken place since that report was compiled seem likely to have seriously diminished the appeal of Ghanīmat and his tomb. With the creation of Pakistan in 1947, the non-Muslim inhabitants of the region were forced across the new frontier into India, while the remaining Muslims were to be exposed to several different kinds of cultural and religious reconstruction in the ensuing decades. The abolition in the 1950s of Persian as a compulsory part of the curriculum was effectively to cut off ensuing generations of even the highly educated from the

[1] Access to a variety of source materials was facilitated by the following, to all of whom I extend my thanks: Mike Hutt, Javed Majeed, Zawahir Moir, Rosemary Seton and Ahsan Wagha.

[2] See Ṣadiq 'Alī Dilāwarī, "Ghanīmat Kunjāhī," *Oriental College Magazine*, 69 (May 1942), (pp. 36–7).

long association of the region with an active cultivation of Persian literature, which had persisted since Ghaznavid times. The parallel momentum of religious changes, with powerful currents towards secularization on the one hand and the increasing spread of reformist or fundamentalist interpretations of Islam on the other, was similarly calculated to weaken the appeal of a local saint-poet whose reputation derived from his former standing in a world which had given such special and overlapping importance to both Sufi values and Persian letters.

The present study takes as its broader context that grand double narrative, memorably traced in the writings of Annemarie Schimmel and others, of the parallel evolution of Sufism as a spiritual discipline on the one hand, with an esoteric core of teachings, rituals and devotional practices designed to lead to inner transformations ultimately impermeable to academic investigation, and of Sufi-inspired poetry on the other, as the public art chiefly responsible for the wider diffusion of Sufi values, whose own long-fashionable diffusion always implied a whole series of gradations in its closeness to systematic teachings. Within this context, one purpose of this chapter is to explore this relationship between Sufism and Sufi poetry, and to suggest that understandings of any one-to-one congruence between the two are not always well founded. Part of the problem here may be terminological, and while too many neologisms can have a stifling effect, it is tempting at this point to indicate the often imperfect reflection of systematic mystical teachings in much Sufi-related verse by adding the term 'Suficate' to the semi-naturalized 'Islamicate' and 'Persianate' – those useful adjectives coined by Marshall Hodgson to embrace the broader cultural traditions associated with the Islamic religion and the Persian language.[3] While doubtless too inelegant for repeated use, the term may at least serve to foreground the area of Persianate Sufi studies around which this study circles, namely the problematic of disentangling the relationships between Sufism and Sufi poetry and poetry which uses Sufism.[4]

Focused upon the Punjab, the essay also emphasizes the Indian context in which the distinction between 'Persian' and 'Persianate' is always worth attention, given the special circumstances of the cultivation of Persian as a literary language in South Asia by speakers of the local Indo-Aryan languages. The opening part of the study begins with a sketch of the establishment of the Qādiriyya in the Punjab in Mughal times before first touching on the role of some affiliates of the order in the contemporary local development of Sufi poetry written in Persian, then describing the part played by others in the

---

[3] M.G.S. Hodgson, *The Venture of Islam* (Chicago and London: University of Chicago Press 1974), I, pp. 58–9; III, p. 49.

[4] For the first distinction, cf. e.g. the remarks in Seyyed Hossein Nasr, "Persian Sufi Literature," in *The Heritage of Sufism*, II: *The Legacy of Medieval Persian Sufism*, ed. L. Lewisohn (Oxford: Oneworld, 1999), pp. 8–9; and for second, those in E.J.W. Gibb, *A History of Ottoman Poetry* (London: Gibb Memorial Trust 1900), I, pp. 24–32.

creation of Sufi poetry composed in Panjabi, which lives on in Pakistan as a still vital cultural offshoot of the Persianate Sufi past, while Persian itself is almost entirely forgotten. Against this background, the central part of this chapter is devoted to a study of Ghanīmat as a Sufi-affiliated poet writing in a once flourishing provincial South Asian tradition of Persian literature, and to an assessment in 'Suficate' terms of his *Nayrang-i 'ishq* as a literary work not without its puzzles and ambiguities. The final part of the study explores the later history of this once very popular poem, and suggests how the versions of Ghanīmat's poem subsequently produced in South Asian languages can contribute to an understanding of the later cultural history of Persianate Sufism in South Asia.

THE QĀDIRIYYA AND SUFI POETRY IN MUGHAL PANJAB

Most general accounts of the development of Sufism in the Punjab[5] rightly emphasize the importance of a few great figures, whose historic status is matched by the continuing veneration of their tombs. These include 'Alī al-Hujwīrī (d. 463/1071), the author of the *Kashf al-maḥjūb* from the pre-*ṭarīqa* period, followed by the great Chishtī founding father Farīd al-Dīn Ganj-i Shakar (d. 664/1265) and his Suhrawardī contemporary Bahā' al-Dīn Zakariyā Multānī (d. 667/1267), who under their popular titles Dātā Ganj Bakhsh, Bābā Farīd and Bahāwal Ḥaq continue to be revered at their shrines in Lahore, Pakpattan and Multan. These figures are also those which have come chiefly to figure in the nation-building ideology promulgated by official sources in Pakistan and to receive the particular attention of the Awqāf Department now responsible for the administration of their great resources.

From the perspective of later spirituality, however, an even wider significance attaches to the Qādiriyya. This order was introduced with increasing success into India by descendants of Shaykh 'Abd al-Qādir Gīlānī (d. 561/1166) and their disciples from the fifteenth century onwards.[6]

[5] E.g. Annemarie Schimmel, *Mystical Dimensions of Islam* (Chapel Hill: University of North Carolina Press 1975), pp. 344ff.

[6] In English, besides such older official sources as the summary account in H.A. Rose, *A Glossary of the Tribes and Castes of the Punjab and North-West Frontier Province* (repr. Patiala: Languages Department 1970), I, pp. 528–44, fairly convenient and reliable outline guides to the main lines of development of the Qādiriyya in the Panjab may be found in J.A Subhan, *Sufism: Its Saints and Shrines* (Lucknow: Lucknow Publishing House 1960), pp. 264–85, and Sayyid Athar Abbas Rizvi, *A History of Sufism in India* (New Delhi: Munshiram Manoharlal 1983), II, pp. 57–70. Much of their data derives from the mass of information on the Qādiriyya placed by Muḥammad Ghulām Sarwar, in keeping with his own Qādirī affiliation, at the beginning of the first volume of his *Khazīnat al-aṣfiyā'* (Kanpur: Nawal Kishar 1894), 2 vols, itself a historical monument, as the last of the great *tadhkira* collections of Indian Sufis to have been compiled in Persian. Ghulām Sarwar himself catered for a local public more familiar with Urdu in the summary *Ḥadīqat al-awliyā'*

Doctrinally notable for its emphasis on the teaching of *waḥdat al-wujūd*,[7] the Qādiriyya is generally acknowledged to have been introduced into the Punjab from his seat at Uch in the south-west by Sayyid Muḥammad al-Ḥusaynī, called Muḥammad Ghawth (d. 923/1517), a linear descendant of Shaykh 'Abd al-Qādir in the tenth generation.[8] Although internationally less well-known than the great early Sufis listed above, by the seventeenth century the descendants of Sayyid Muḥammad Ghawth and their disciples had, in conjunction with numerous other lines of spiritual descent, established the Qādiriyya as the major Sufi presence in the Punjab.

Some indication of the order's spread and influence through the Mughal period may be gained from a brief enumeration of major figures and the still venerated shrines associated with them. Disciples of later generations of the Uch-based family of Sayyid Muḥammad Ghawth's eldest son Sayyid 'Abd al-Qādir II (d. 940/1533), which itself attracted imperial attention, included the well-known Sufi and scholar Shaykh 'Abd al-Haqq Muḥaddith Dihlawī (d. 1052/1642), author of the *Akhbār al-akhyār*.[9] Sayyid Muḥammad Ghawth's second son Sayyid Mubārak Haqqānī (d. 957/1550) attracted the allegiance of Shāh Ma'rūf (d. 987/1579), a descendant of Bābā Farīd. This mixed Chishtī–Qādirī line had as its most famous disciple Shāh Ḥājī Muḥammad (d. 1065/1654), given the title 'Nawshāh Ganj Bakhsh', whose shrine at Naushahra in District Gujranwala is one of the most important in the region.[10] Other Qādirī lines in this widespread network of spiritual authority are associated with one of those mysterious and long-lived figures who are so frequently encountered at the start of spiritual genealogies, Ḥayāt al-Mīr, called 'Zinda Pīr', who is said to have been a direct disciple of Shaykh 'Abd al-Qādir himself. Besides the powerful Sufi dynasty established by Sayyid Muqīm Muḥkam al-Dīn

---

(Lahore: Islamic Book Foundation 1906), which deals with Sufis of the Panjab, with the Qādiriyya being described on pp. 27–71 of the modern edition by Muḥammad Iqbāl Mujaddidī (Lahore 1976), whose useful notes clear up some of the chronological and other confusion to which Ghulām Sarwar was notoriously prone. Much further useful information is to be derived from another prime Urdu source, Nūr Aḥmad Chishtī, *Tahqīqāt-i Chishtī*, ed. Sayyid Iḥsān 'Alī (Lahore: Punjabi Adabi Board 1964).

[7] Rizvi, *History of Sufism* II, pp. 54–5, underlines the importance here of the Qādirī initiation of Ibn 'Arabī.

[8] The relationship at this period between the transmission from Iran to India of Qādirī and of Ismā'īlī affiliations certainly deserves further attention. The occurrence in both contexts of the name of Shāh Ni'matullāh Walī (d. 1431), in e.g. Rizvi, *History of Sufism* II, pp. 55–7, and Farhad Daftary, *The Isma'ilis: Their History and Doctrines* (Cambridge: Cambridge University Press 1990), pp. 462–7, is certainly suggestive, as is the historic prominence of Uch as a centre of the Ismā'īlī *da'wa* in north-western India, cf. C. Shackle and Z. Moir, *Ismaili Hymns from South Asia: An Introduction to the Ginans* (London: SOAS 1992), p. 204. The Qādirī dynasty of Uch is usefully described in M.H. Shihāb, *Awliyā'-i Bahawalpūr* (Bahawalpur: Urdu Academy 1976), pp. 225–36.

[9] Cf. Rizvi, *History of Sufism* II, pp. 80ff.

[10] Cf. *Taḥqīqāt-i Chishtī*, pp. 244–52.

(d. 1055/1645) at Hujra Muqim Shah in District Sahiwal in the central Punjab, where his descendants were able to establish themselves as virtually independent chieftains in the eighteenth century,[11] these also include Shāh Laṭīf Barrī (d. 1117/1705),[12] whose shrine in the northern Panjab at Nurpur Shahan has gained prominence in recent years from its incorporation into the federal territory of Islamabad.

Subsequent processes, including the interlocking ties of *bay'at* between one lineage and another as well as simultaneous initiation into orders besides the Qādiriyya, in addition to regular pilgrimage from one shrine to another or mutual participation at *'urs* ceremonies, have tended to emphasize the growing later similarities rather than any initial differences between these many lines. Particular mention must however be made here of the most famous of all Qādirī lines in the seventeenth century Panjab, that associated with Miyān Mīr (957/1550–1045/1635) whose obscure origins in Sind preceded a long residence outside Lahore, where he came to attract the favour of the imperial family. It was of course his disciple Mullā Shāh (d. 1072/1661) who attracted the passionate spiritual allegiance of the Mughal prince Dārā Shikūh, whose fate ever since his execution in 1070/1659 on the orders of his brother Awrangzīb has been to figure as symbolic chief spokesman for the possibilities of maximal toleration of Hinduism by Islam in the name of some higher theosophical union between Vedantic and Sufi ideas.[13]

Much more might of course be said on this well-worn topic on the basis of Dārā Shikūh's writings, the best-known examples of the considerable literature produced in Persian prose by Indian Qādirīs. But the emphasis of the present study is on poetry rather than theology, which makes it more relevant to draw attention here to Qādiriyya involvement with Persian poetry. Sayyid Muḥammad Ghawth himself is said to have composed poetry under the pen-name 'Qādirī',[14] while Shaikh Abū'l-Ma'ālī (d. 1615), the nephew of one his great-grandson's disciples, achieved some poetic reputation under the pen-name 'Ghurbatī'.[15] Underlining his allegiance with the appropriation of the pen-name 'Qādirī', Dārā himself produced a slim Persian *Dīwān*, composed in the simple style said also to characterize the Persian verse of his guide Mullā

[11] An account of Shāh Muqīm is given in *Taḥqīqāt-i Chishtī*, pp. 357–63. The later history of Hujra is alluded to in Veena Sachdeva, *Polity and Economy of the Punjab during the late Eighteenth Century* (New Delhi: Manohar 1993), pp. 55, 62, 149.

[12] Cf. Manẓūr al-Ḥaqq Ṣiddīqī, *Shāh Laṭīf Barrī* (Lahore: Meri Library 1972), especially pp. 58ff.

[13] As attempted, if hardly achieved, in his well-known treatise *Majma' al-baḥrayn*, ed. Mahfūẓ al-Ḥaq (Calcutta 1929).

[14] Rizvi, *History of Sufism* II, p. 58.

[15] *Ibid.*, pp. 62–3, including some verses in translation, cited from the *Muntakhab al-tawārīkh*. A few verses are quoted in the original in Maqbūl Beg Badakhshānī (ed.), *Tārīkh-i Adabiyyāt-i Musalmānān-i Pāk u Hind*, IV: *Fārsī Adab 2 (1526–1707)* (Lahore: University of the Punjab 1971), pp. 420–1. There is a fuller account in *Taḥqīqāt-i Chishtī*, pp. 273–8.

Shāh.[16] So far as its content is concerned, two aspects of Dārā's verse may be emphasized here. The first is the extreme devotion to the Ghawth-i A'ẓam Shaykh 'Abd al-Qādir himself, around whose cult the varieties of practice and thought embraced by the Qādiriyya have always found their single most important unifying focus, as in the ghazal beginning:

> O holy Mīrān, Lord of all the world.
> O Ghawth of men and jinn, and King of saints.[17]

The other is Dārā's reiteration of the essential unity of religions:

> Should you revile the followers of God
> Then unbelief outdoes all your Islam.
>
> Since all that lives is God's creation
> All your objections are nonsensical.[18]

It has also to be said that Dārā's stilted verses are stylistically rather unremarkable, and in poetic quality they are far surpassed by those of his *munshi* Chandarbhān Brahman (d. 1074/1662). The latter is often reckoned to have been the best of all Hindu Persian poets, a dual status to which many of his verses pay elegant allusion:

> I'm bound by fondness to the thread
> I bear as Brahmin souvenir.[19]

A similar elegance characterizes Chandarbhān's handling of the theme of the unity of all Being, a favourite theme of his poetry too, which receives memorable expression in such verses as:

> The Builder of houses and temples and taverns is one.
> The buildings are many, the Master of each though is one.[20]

On the one hand, then, it might be said that the direct style associated with this strand of Persian Sufi poetry in Mughal India attains its artistic apogee with Chandarbhān. But the transcendence of religious boundaries involved in this triumph of Persianate Sufi art was seen also to imply a threat to the very

---

[16] Cf. Badakhshānī, *Tārīkh-i Adabiyyāt*, pp. 423–4.

[17] *Dīwān-i Dārā Shikūh*, ed. Aḥmad Nabī Khān (Lahore: University of the Punjab 1969), p. 96: *Ḥaḍrat-i Mīrān khudāvand-i jahān, ghawth-i jinn ū uns, shāh-i 'ārifān.*

[18] *Dīwān*, p. 116: *ahl-i Ḥaq-rā ki bad tu mīkhwānī, kufr bihtar az-īn musalmānī ... āfarīnanda-yi hama ḥaq ast, mīkuni i'tiraḍ hazyānī.*

[19] Quoted in Sayyid 'Abdu'llāh, *Adabiyyāt-i fārsī men Hindu'on kā Ḥiṣṣa* (Lahore: University of the Punjab 1967), p. 82, corresponding to the Persian translation by Muḥammad Aslam Khān, *Adabiyyāt-i fārsī dar miyān-i Hinduvān* (Tehran 1371 A.Hsh./ 1992), p. 84: *marā ba rishta-yi zunnār ulfatī khaṣṣ-ast, ba yādgār man az barhaman hamīn dāram.*

[20] Ẓuhūr al-Dīn Aḥmad in Badakhshānī, *Tārīkh-i Adabiyyāt*, pp. 367–72. This well-known verse is also quoted in Sayyid 'Abdu'llāh, *Adabiyyāt-i fārsī*, p. 81 (Persian translation, p. 84): *bānī-yi khāna u but-khāna u may-khāna yakīst, khāna bisyār walī ṣaḥib-i har khāna yakīst.*

Islamic values which this art had been created and developed to adorn. The awareness of this tension is well captured in the anecdote of how the emperor Shahjahan was said to have been moved to extreme displeasure by this teasing verse of Chandarbhān:

> My heart's so prone to unbelief that every time
> It's taken to the Ka'ba, back it comes a Brahmin.[21]

Somewhat paradoxically, therefore, it might be argued that the equivocation of such conceits in the Indian context was more fruitful in allowing those non-Muslims – typically drawn from the service classes – who chose to participate in the elite Persianate culture, to maintain an authentically non-Muslim voice in their adopted idiom[22] than it proved suitable to sustain Persian lyric poetry as a locally authentic vehicle of Sufi expression.

From the viewpoint of subsequent cultural and spiritual history, the truly significant achievement of the Qādiriyya in Mughal Punjab was to have fostered the development of the Sufi lyric not in Persian, but in Panjabi. While there had been an earlier tradition of writing Sufi poetry in the local languages of the Indus Valley, little has been preserved besides the verses attributed to Bābā Farīd which are included in the Sikh *Adi Granth* (1604).[23] During the Mughal period, this meagre corpus was considerably extended by the Panjabi compositions attributed to several outstanding poets, all having a strong Qādirī affiliation, though none with the major lineages described above.[24] The earliest name is that of Shāh Ḥusayn (d. 1008/1599) of Lahore,[25] the disciple of Bahlūl Shāh Daryā'ī (d. 983/1575) of Chiniot, another of those local Qādirī saints

[21] Quoted with predictable approbation of the emperor's displeasure in Badakhshānī, *Tārīkh-i Adabiyyāt*, p. 191; with appropriate scepticism as to its historicity in Dhabīḥ Allāh Ṣafā, *Tārīkh-i Adabiyyāt dar Īrān* (Tehran: Chāpkhāna-yi Rāmīn 1373 A.Hsh./1994), V/ 2, p. 1237.

[22] Another notable example is that of Nand Lāl Goyā (1633-1712), a Khatri fully conversant with Persianate culture who became a disciple of the last Sikh Guru Gobind Singh, and whose numerous Persian poetic compositions have a canonical, if nowadays rather marginal status in Sikhism: cf. L. Fenech, "Persian Sikh Scripture: The Ghazals of Bhā'ī Nand La'l Goyā," *International Journal of Punjab Studies*, 1/1 (1994), pp. 49–70.

[23] Cf. C. Shackle, "Early Vernacular Poetry in the Indus Valley: its Contexts and its Character," in *Islam and Indian Regions*, ed. A.L. Dallapiccola and S. Zingel-Ave Lallemant (Stuttgart: Franz Steiner 1993), I, pp. 259–89.

[24] Cf. L. Rama Krishna, *Pañjābī Ṣūfī Poets* (Calcutta: Oxford University Press 1938), pp. 12–71.

[25] Notorious for his association with the Brahmin boy Mādho, subsequently his spiritual successor, cf. C. Shackle, "Beyond Turk and Hindu: Crossing the Boundaries in Indo-Muslim Romance," to be published in the proceedings of a conference on Indo-Muslim Cultural Identity, Duke University, April 1995, ed. J. Richards and B. Lawrence. An English translation of the compositions attributed to Shāh Ḥusayn is available as Ghulam Yaqoob Anwar (trans.), *The Paths Unknown* (*Kafian Shāh Hussain*) (Lahore: Majlis Shah Hussain 1966).

whose lineage is associated with the mysterious Ḥayāt al-Mīr Zinda Pīr. More authentically preserved are the acrostically arranged Panjabi quatrains (*sī-ḥarfī*) of Sulṭān Bāhū (d. 1103/1691) of Jhang, the originator of an important local Sufi dynasty, but himself the disciple of an otherwise obscure Qādirī teacher called Ḥabīb Allāh. The greatest of all these poets, with the most substantial corpus of preserved lyrics (*kāfī*) comes at the end of the period. This is Sayyid 'Abdullāh called 'Bullhe Shāh' (1091/1680—1172/1758) of Kasur, the proudly self-proclaimed disciple of Shāh 'Ināyat (d. 1141/1728) of Lahore, himself the disciple of the Qādirī-Shaṭṭārī Shāh Raḍā Lāhawrī (d. 1119/1707).

Given what has been said about the rather etiolated vitality generally characteristic of the Persian poetry of Dārā Shikūh and his school,[26] what is most striking about the Panjabi Sufi lyrics of the period is the extraordinary degree to which they represent a new and vital synthesis of a fresh variety of artistic elements.[27] The mixture may be analysed as comprising a triple association of features drawn from different sources. The most obvious and the most attractive to contemporary Pakistani critics are the local 'folk' elements, including both images drawn directly from Panjabi rural life and those taken from 'the matter of Panjab', whether folk songs or local romances, notably the allusions to the Hīr–Rānjhā romance which figure so importantly in Bullhe Shāh as symbols of the Sufi lover and the Divine Beloved:

Repeating 'Rānjhā, Rānjhā'
I too am Rānjhā now.
O call me Dhīdo Rānjhā
Let no one call me Hīr.[28]

Especially in Bullhe Shāh, a very prominent role is also played by Hindu references, whether to yogis or the Krishna cult, naturally less attractive to Pakistani critics than to others seeking to explain the poet's appeal across religious frontiers.[29] The mixture of these two elements is, of course, entirely characteristic of much local non-Muslim devotional and spiritual poetry of the

---

[26] To which judgement, however, the *Rubā'īyāt* of Sarmad constitute at least one memorable exception.

[27] Belonging to the category of literature made most widely familiar through the sympathetic studies of Annemarie Schimmel, notably in the chapter "The Voice of Love: Mystical Poetry in the Vernaculars" in her *As through a Veil: Mystical Poetry in Islam* (New York: Columbia University Press 1982), pp. 137–69. See also her chapter in this volume.

[28] Faqīr Muḥammad Faqīr (ed.), *Kulliyyāt-i Bullhe Shāh* (Lahore: Panjabi Adabi Board 1964), p. 123.

[29] Among recent examples of the latter approach, cf. the detailed analysis in Denis Matringe, "Kṛṣṇaite and Nāth Elements in the Poetry of the Eighteenth-Century Panjabi Sūfī Bullhe Śāh," in *Devotional Literature in South Asia: Current Research, 1985–1988*, ed. R.S. McGregor (Cambridge: Cambridge University Press 1992), pp. 190-206, also the more general approach in Robin Rineheart, "Interpretations of the Poetry of Bullhe Shah," *International Journal of Punjab Studies*, 3/1 (1996), pp. 44–63.

period, notably including the hymns of the Sikh scriptures. Finally, however, what differentiates the Panjabi Sufi lyric is the expressly Islamic element, which remains very firmly rooted in the core Arabic terminology of Koran, *ḥadīth* and Sufi teaching.

The long and wide diffusion of Persianate culture which had occurred in north-western India by this time would lead one to suppose that there would also be a notable prominence of Persian elements in this Panjabi poetry. Contrary to this expectation, however, Persian poetic vocabulary and imagery appear only very rarely in the Panjabi Sufi lyric of this period.[30] For whatever reason, there are in fact more such elements in the first Panjabi narrative poems (*qiṣṣa*) in which a Sufi element may be distinguished, like the early eighteenth-century version of the full story of Hīr by the Qādirī poet Muqbil Shāh,[31] where the structural influence of the *mathnawī* is greater than that of the ghazal on the sung strophic lyric.

GHANĪMAT AND HIS *NAYRANG-I 'ISHQ*

This phenomenon is, of course, entirely in keeping with the extraordinarily prolonged separate existence of Persian literature in India. This may be contrasted with the otherwise comparable situation in the Ottoman realms, where the sophisticated language of Ottoman poetry evolved from the same language base as the simple Turkish of popular literature, first to parallel, then largely to supplant Persian as the preferred poetic language of the elite.[32] The process by which Urdu came to occupy a similar position in Indo-Muslim culture was, by comparison, much delayed, and it is perhaps in part due to this

---

[30] This Indianization of Persianate Sufism can hardly have been other than the result of a deliberate strategy, also manifested in the recasting of Sufi romance as Awadhi *premākhyān*, discussed in the paper by Simon Weightman in this volume. But in the post-Mughal period Persianate elements assume increasing significance in local Panjabi and Sindhi lyrics, which come to show a corresponding lesser prominence of Hindu elements: cf. C. Shackle, "Styles and Themes in the Siraiki Mystical Poetry of Sind," in *Sind through the Centuries*, ed. H. Khuhro (Karachi: Oxford University Press 1981), pp. 252–69. The still greater prominence of Persian vocabulary at a yet later period is a noteworthy feature of the Siraiki lyrics of Khwāja Ghulām Farīd (d. 1901), himself also notable as a member of an important dynasty stemming from the late eighteenth century Chishtī revival in south-western Panjab, and thus an important exception to the general rule of Qādirī primacy in this field.

[31] Discussed in J. Deol, "Acceptable Poetry: Muqbil's Mystical *Qiṣṣah Hīr Rānjhā*," *International Journal of Punjab Studies*, 3/2 (1996), pp. 181–212. Muqbil's poem is considered as a forerunner to the classic treatment by Wārith Shāh (1766) in C. Shackle, "Transition and Transformation in Vāris Shāh's *Hīr*," in *The Indian Narrative: Perspectives and Patterns*, ed. C. Shackle and R. Snell, (Wiesbaden: Harrassowitz 1992), pp. 241–63, which includes an annotated bibliography.

[32] Cf. however the interesting observations on the survival of "Mevlevi Persian" in V.R. Holbrook, "Diverse Tastes in the Spiritual Life: Textual Play in the Diffusion of Rumi's Order," in Lewisohn, *Heritage of Sufism*, II, p. 101.

cultural diglossia that, while Persianate Sufism became indigenized in India, at least in such long-settled regions as the Panjab, Persian literature – including a great deal of Persian Sufi literature – did not. For most, this literature instead remained an endlessly demanding subject of the school curriculum, as is hinted at by the local Sufi poetry's frequent use of the topos of 'useless learning', as, for example, in the following lines by Bullhe Shāh:

> Why make up all these stories?
> Why quote Būstān and Gulistān?
> Why quarrel so for nothing?
> Who taught you Veda backwards?[33]

Beyond the narrow confines of courtly and aristocratic circles, with their associates in the clerical and Sufi establishment, the cultivation of Persian literature in India was actively pursued chiefly by professionals involved in administration and education. Indeed, the sheer quantity of its production has so far proved greatly to exceed the capacity of the much diminished number of modern scholars able and willing to pursue its study. The broad outlines of its development are, however, relatively familiar, particularly in relation to the apex of its production, the poetry executed at the Mughal court itself under the patronage of the emperors or the connoisseur grandees in their entourage.[34] For various reasons, most overviews of the period tend to give particular emphasis to the artistic supremacy over such Indian Persian poets as Fayḍī (d. 1004/1595) or Bīdil (d. 1134/1721) of the many Persian-born poets attracted from the time of 'Urfī (d. 1000/1591) at least down to that of Ṣā'ib (d. 1088/1677) by the lavish prospects of Indian patronage:

> Lead lives of endless pleasure; India's land of delight
> Makes enjoyment's finest means available.[35]

---

[33] Cf. the translation in J.R. Puri and T.R. Shangari, *Bulleh Shāh: The Love-Intoxicated Iconoclast* (Dera Baba Jaimal Singh: Radha Soami Satsang Beas 1986), p. 360, of Faqīr, *Kulliyyāt*, p. 88: *enven qiṣṣe kāhnūn gharnā'en, te Gulistān Bostān paṟhnā'en, enven be-mūjab kyūn laṟnā'en, kis ulṭa ved paṟhāyā ai.*

[34] Besides the fairly detailed survey in Urdu in Badakhshānī, *Tārikh-i Adabiyyāt*, general accounts in English are provided in J. Marek, "The Golden Age of Indo-Persian Literature," in J. Rypka (ed.) *History of Iranian Literature* (Dordrecht: D. Riedel Publishing Co. 1968), Annemarie Schimmel, *Islamic Literatures of India* (Wiesbaden: Harrassowitz 1973), and her "Persian Poetry in the Indo-Pakistan Subcontinent," in *Persian Literature*, ed. E. Yarshater (New York: Persian Heritage Foundation 1988), pp. 405–21. There are handy biographical sketches in Nabi Hadi, *Dictionary of Indo-Persian Literature* (New Delhi: Abhinar Publications 1995). The literary context is sketched as the background to a detailed analysis of a *qaṣīda* produced for a Mughal patron by the emigré Persian poet 'Urfī (d. 1591) in S. Sperl and C. Shackle *Qasida Poetry in Islamic Asia and Africa* (Leiden: Brill 1996), I, pp. 205–12; II, pp. 182–91, 436–8.

[35] *Qasida*, II, p. 190: *'Aysh mīrān jāvidān k-andar zirangistān-i hind, dārī asbāb-i tana' 'um bar lubb-i lubāb.*

The talents of all these stars were chiefly engaged in the competitive extension of the fresh artistic possibilities opened up by the newly fashionable baroque style of Persian poetry called the 'Indian style' (*sabk-i hindī*),[36] and the genre in which most chose to work, when not required by the demands of courtly life to produce *qaṣīda*s, was the ghazal.

Alongside this high literature of the imperial court, a corresponding level of literary activity in Persian was actively pursued in the provinces, with the courtly models providing inspiration to the more ambitious local poets, who in the Panjab might be further encouraged by the area's geographical closeness to the imperial capitals and the special status of Lahore under the Mughals. It is to this intermediate level of provincial Persian literature that Ghanīmat belonged: as a poet, he apparently neither achieved the eminence that might have brought him to imperial favour, nor languished in the complete obscurity to which the level of the talents of many poets of the period was rightly to consign them.[37]

One of the few certain facts about Ghanīmat's life – apart from his association with Kunjah and his given name of Muḥammad Akram – is that he was a disciple of Sayyid Muḥammad Ṣāliḥ of the village of Sada near Gujrat, himself one of the two favourite disciples of the most prominent local Qādirī saint, the already-mentioned Ḥājī Muḥammad Nawshāh.[38] Later pious annalists of the Nawshāhī dynasty and its disciples added elaborate details

---

[36] The salient features of the Indian style are variously described in Rypka, *History of Iranian Literature*, pp. 290–5; W. Heinz, *Der Indische Stil in der Persischen Literatur* (Wiesbaden: Franz Steiner 1972); Shāfi'ī Kādkānī, "The Safavid Period (Indian Style)," in *History of Persian Literature from the Beginning of the Islamic Period to the Present Day*, ed. G. Morrison (Leiden: Brill 1981), pp. 145–65; E. Yarshater, "The Indian Style: Progress or Decline?," in *idem*, *Persian Literature*, pp. 249–88; and J.T.P. de Bruijn, "Sabk-i hindī," *EI*².

[37] Citations from the older Persian *tadhkira* writers are usefully collected in Khwāja 'Abd al-Rashīd (ed.), *Tadhkira-yi Shu'arā-yi Panjāb* (Karachi: Iqbal Academy 1967), pp. 364–7. Modern scholarly investigation in Urdu was apparently initiated by Dilāwarī, "Ghanīmat Kunjāhī," further defended in *ibid*., "Ghanīmat kā Waṭan," *Oriental College Magazine*, 75 (November 1943), pp. 26–32, against the questions raised in Muḥammad 'Abdullāh Chughatā'ī, "Nayrang-i 'ishq kā ek Qalamī Nuskha," *Oriental College Magazine*, 74 (August 1943), pp. 54–6. The biographical account in the introduction to, *Dīwān-i Ghanīmat* ed. Ghulām Rabbānī 'Azīz, (Lahore 1958), pp. alif-yā, is largely based on Dilāwarī, though without acknowledgement. The publication of Ghanīmat's letters (see note 42 below) stimulated further questioning of some received wisdom in Sharīf Kunjāhī, "Ruq'āt-i Ghanīmat Kunjāhī par ek Naẓar," *Funūn*, 18/5–6 (1974), pp. 33–42. A judicious summary of all this material is presented in the key entry in Ẓuhūr al-Dīn Aḥmad, *Pākistān men Fārsī Adab* (Lahore: University of the Punjab 1977), III, pp. 10–32. Notices in other literary histories, including Ṣafā, *Tarikh-i Adabiyyāt dar Irān*, V/2, pp. 1411–4, derive from this Pakistani scholarly tradition, to which the entry in Nūr al-Ḥasan Anṣārī, *Fārsī Adab ba'ahd-i Awrangzīb* (Delhi: Indo-Persian Society 1969), pp. 53–62, is an interesting addition by an Indian scholar.

[38] Cf. the brief notice in *Khazīnat al-aṣfiyā'*, I, p. 189, giving the date of his death as AH 1118 (= 1706–7).

to the poet's own expressions of his personal devotion to Shaykh 'Abd al-Qādir and his own *pir*, and his loyalty to the reigning monarch Awrangzīb made at the beginning of his *Nayrang-i 'ishq* of 1685, which are described further below. One highly embroidered story depicts the poet going in search of fame to Delhi, where his rustic attire attracts much mirth until he is taken before the leading contemporary poet and man of letters Mīrzā Afḍal Sarkhush (d. 1128/1715), whom he vastly impresses with a display of extempore composition. Another emphasizes the extreme nature of his devotion to Shaykh 'Abd al-Qādir, at the mere mention of whose name he would go into ecstasy, and tells how he was once at court before Awrangzīb. When the emperor sternly condemned as un-Islamic the practice of excessive devotion to 'Abd al-Qādir, Ghanīmat was found to have prostrated himself, so impressing Awrangzīb that he was excused the general proscription.[39] Sadly unsupported by any reliable evidence, this hagiographic tradition is nevertheless a telling indication of how notable figures of the past with some spiritual connection are remembered as 'saints', overlaying many aspects of what may in their own time have been much more diverse personalities with strongly developed 'secular' sides.

Literary history is of little help here either, since the evidence which can be gleaned from the Persian *tadhkira* writers is either scant or unreliable. The earliest of these is Sarkhush himself in his well-known *Kalimāt al-shu'arā'*, whose notice of Ghanīmat is so brief that it serves only to demonstrate that the apocryphal story of their association must surely be false.[40] As will be shown below, readings of the *Nayrang-i 'ishq* supply the often contradictory details added by later writers.[41] Only with the fairly recent publication of some letters by Ghanīmat[42] has some fleshing out of this meagre portrait become possible. Lacking details of addresses and dates, and unfortunately quite silent as to the spiritual side of Ghanīmat's life, these letters do cast some interesting light on his period of service to some unnamed nobleman, on his travels, notably a trip across the Indus at Attock to Kabul, which also receives a passing reference in his *Dīwān*, and on his literary activity, notably as a copyist of Persian poetry, as an expert asked to undertake the emendation of faulty texts and as a bibliophile exasperated by the repeated failure of a

[39] These stories are transmitted in Dilāwarī, "Ghanīmat Kunjāhī," pp. 16ff. with acknowledgement of his sources, and are repeated without further comment by 'Azīz at the beginning of his introduction to the *Dīwān-i Ghanīmat*.

[40] Quoted in 'Abd al-Rashīd, *Tadhkira*, p. 296: *Az khākiyān-i hind Ghanīmat būda. Ṭab'ī durust dāsht, wa dīwānī mukhtaṣar dārad. Mathnawī nīz fikr karda*.

[41] Cf. 'Abd al-Rashīd, *Tadhkira*, pp. 265–7. Further references are supplied in E. Sachau, *Catalogue of the Persian, Turkish, Hindûstânî and Pushtû Manuscripts in the Bodleian Library*, ed. H. Ethé (Oxford : Clarendon Press, 1889), columns 241, 299, 357.

[42] Sayyid Sharafat Nawshāhī, "Ruq'āt-i Ghanīmat Kunjāhī," *Ṣaḥīfa*, 63 (January 1973), pp. 1–13, containing the text of thirteen letters discovered in an MS in the Panjab University Library. Anṣārī, *Fārsī Adab*, p. 56, mentions the existence of a further letter (*ek fuḥsh khaṭ*) addressed to a courtesan called Dardāna Bā'ī, in another MS.

friend to respond to requests for the return of a manuscript lent two years before. Composed in the complicated rhyming style of formal *inshā*,[43] Ghanīmat's letters have that urbanely tolerant tone so characteristic of correspondence evidently prepared with at least half an eye to eventual publication, whether in his delight at the prospect of one friend's imminent visit to the Panjab, in his despatch of a homeopathic concoction (*ma'jūn*) to another, in his request for *bhang* so as to be able to entertain another friend addicted to it, or in his description of the only hawk he had been able to locate for the fowler of a wealthy acquaintance.

As is true of most Persian poets of the period, quantitatively the greatest part of Ghanīmat's recorded output is contained in his *Dīwān*, consisting mostly of some 250 ghazals.[44] Only a dubious tradition makes him the pupil of the then quite prominent poet Mīr Muḥammad Zamān Rāsikh of Sirhind (d. 1107/1695–6).[45] Explicit references in his ghazals are only to lesser figures like his Kabul friend the poet Fā'iz, and his letters mention only poets of similar rank like the Nadīm Gīlānī, Ṣaydī Iṣfahānī and Barahman Gurjistānī, whose *Dīwān*s he copied out with his own hand. It has also, however, been shown that his work reflects a familiarity with a wide range of earlier and modern poets, including – besides Ḥāfiẓ – a good range of Persian poets of the Indian style such as Fighānī, Abū Ṭālib Kalīm, Ṣā'ib and Jalāl Asīr. This list[46] also includes the name of Nāṣir 'Alī Sirhindī (d. 1108/1696), whose subsequent fame has been largely eclipsed by that of his younger rival Mīrzā

---

[43] Whether or not Ghanīmat himself was a professional *munshī* remains unprovable. An interesting local cross-communal connection is suggested by the notice in 'Abd al-Rashīd, *Tadhkira*, p. 147, of one Dabīr Lachhmī Narā'in Gujrātī, described as a Khatri of Kunjah who was a pupil of Ghanīmat's nephew Shaykh Muḥammad Ṣadāqat, who later became a pupil of Khān-i Ārzū. Although also an occasional poet, he was mainly known for his letters, which were later published, and which continued the strong tradition of Panjabi Hindu contributions to Persian *inshā* that is particularly associated with Harkaran, a Kamboh of Multan, whose collection of model letters was completed as *Inshā-yi Harkaran* in 1622 and continued in official use until after 1800 in the British period: cf. F. Balfour (ed.), *The Forms of Herkern* (London 1804).

[44] References here are to the standard modern text of Ghulām Rabbānī 'Azīz (ed.), *Dīwān-i Ghanīmat* (Lahore: Panjabi Adabi Board 1958), whose editorial procedure is explained in the introduction, pp. m–mw. For unpublished material additional to this text, cf. also Sayyid Nūr Muḥammad Qādirī, "Dīwān-i Ghanīmat Kunjāhī ke ek makhṭūṭe kā ta'āruf," *Funūn*, 20/5–6 (1965), pp. 48–51. A nineteenth-century MS (Or. 301) is listed in C. Rieu, *Catalogue of the Persian Manuscripts in the British Museum* (London: British Museum 1881), II, p. 700.

[45] Cited from Bindrāban Dās Khushgū (d. 1756), *Safīna-yi Khushgū*, in 'Abd al-Rashīd, *Tadhkira*, p. 205; this tradition is rejected by most modern scholars, e.g. Anṣārī, *Fārsī Adab*, p. 57, Sharīf Kunjāhī, p. 36, Ẓuhūr al-Dīn Aḥmad, *Pākistān men Fārsī Adab*, p. 21, citing the absence of any reference to Rāsikh by Ghanīmat.

[46] Cf. the critical comparisons of specimen ghazals by all these poets – also by the above-mentioned Ṣaydī Iṣfahānī–and the parallel versions (*naẓīra*) by Ghanīmat in the introduction to the *Dīwān*, ed. 'Azīz, pp. yā–m.

'Abd al-Qādir Bīdil, but who was in his lifetime regarded as the leading Indian practitioner of the *sabk-i hindī*.[47]

Ghanīmat's *Dīwān* contains some poems of straightforwardly devotional Sufi content, notably the long *qaṣīda* of eighty-three verses in honour of Shaykh 'Abd al-Qādir whose often contorted search for superlatives perfectly matches the hagiographic tradition's celebration of the extreme nature (*ghuluww*) of Ghanīmat's Qādirī devotionalism, as in this Indian style *tamthīl*:

> Gabriel's wing is marked with shame, unbidden
> To become his peacock-feather flywhisk.[48]

The character of the *Dīwān* as a whole is, much as might be expected from a poet who was very much of his time without always possessing a fully individual voice within it, a blend of such *sabk-i hindī* features – not always impeccably executed – with more straightforward, if unremarkable, lyrical expression. At his best, however, Ghanīmat is capable of verses which finely reflect the eternally pervasive central concerns of the Sufi mode of Persian poetry. Some are beautifully straightforward in language and tone, as in this verse on the theme of *waḥdat al-wujūd* from a ghazal composed in imitation of Ṣā'ib:

> Every spot you pass on earth stands as a gate to Him
> So why ask where that incognizant Beloved lives?[49]

Other verses give effective emotional expression to concepts of Sufi love by using the intellectual devices of the *sabk-i hindī*, as in this exploitation of the style's fondness for the pluralization of abstracts:

> Racings along the highway of Love are never short cuts
> This is a way which grows like a vine's shoots from cuttings.[50]

While much fuller quotation would be needed to do justice to his interesting *Dīwān*, Ghanīmat is principally remembered for his *Nayrang-i 'ishq*, or 'The

---

[47] As a disciple of the Naqshbandī dynasty of the Mujaddid of Sirhind, Nāṣir 'Alī was one of the few prominent literary figures of the time not affiliated with the Qādiriyya. He is given appropriately full coverage in Idrīs Aḥmad, *Sirhind men Fārsī Adab* (Delhi 1988), pp. 37–87, preceding a shorter notice of Rāsikh on pp. 87–99. His rivalry with Bīdil is described in Abdul Ghani, *Life and Works of Abdul Qadir Bedil* (Lahore: Publishers United 1960), pp. 76–9. Even if lacking firm contemporary evidence, an association of later literary reputation between Ghanīmat and Nāṣir 'Alī is suggested by the presence of the *Nayrang-i 'ishq* along with poems by Nāṣir 'Alī and others in the eighteenth-century SOAS MS 47653.

[48] *Dīwān*, p. 303: *Bāl-i Jibrīl shawad dāgh ki ṭā'us-ṣifat, ba-magas-rānī-yi ū nīst parash-rā farmān*.

[49] *Dīwān*, p. 267: *Ba-har jā mīgudhārī bar zamīn sar āsitān-i ūst, maqām u manzil-i ma'shūq-i ghāfil chi mīpursī*. The *maqṭa'* ends with a hemistich by Ṣā'ib.

[50] *Dīwān*, p. 3: *nagardard qaṭ' hargiz jāda-yi 'ishq az davīdanhā, ki mībālad ba-khud īn rāh chūn tāk az burīdanhā*. The contrived rhyme is quite as characteristic of the *sabk-i hindī* Persian ghazal as the apparently simple rhymes favoured by Bullhe Shāh are such pronounced features of the Panjabi *kāfī*.

Charm of Love'. Like almost all the rest of Indo-Persian literature, it nowadays sadly finds few readers, although this poem was once one of the most popular of Persian *mathnawī*s in India, as is attested by the abundant manuscript tradition.[51] Its attraction, however, has also been seen as embracing both mysterious and controversial qualities. These ambiguities are best explored after a survey of its content.

About one-seventh of the poem is occupied by the eight sections of the prologue. Deservedly famous, if barely translatable, the stunning beginning to the opening *ḥamd* (1.1) boldly combines invocation with direct reference to the characters of the poem:

ba-nām-i shāhid-i nāzuk-khayālān
'azīz-i khāṭir-i āshufta-ḥālān

In the name of the Shāhid, adored by the sensitive
The 'Azīz, who is dear to the hearts of the passionate ...

A supplicatory invocation (*munājāt*, 1.23), equally notable for its bold use of anaphora,[52] is followed by a panegryric addressed to the Prophet (*na't*, 2.24) describing his noctural ascent or *mi'rāj*. This leads naturally to a eulogy (*manqibat*) addressed to Shaykh 'Abd al-Qādir (4.1), followed by a slightly more extended one to Ghanīmat's own *pir* Shāh Ṣāliḥ Muḥammad (4.24). The final eulogy is a *madḥ* of the emperor Awrangzīb (6.1). Next comes the introduction proper with an important section on love and the play between unreal or figurative love (*majāz*) and the Real or divine Love (*ḥaqīqat*) (7.1), and its exemplification in the story of the gazelle hunted by Majnūn (7.21).

The story then opens with formal praise of the land of Punjab and its beauties (8.12), in a passage very appealing to modern Pakistani taste, and the birth there of the lovely Shāhid, orphaned in childhood and sold to a troupe of

[51] References here are to page and verse of the standard modern edition of Ghulām Rabbānī 'Azīz (ed.), *Nayrang-i 'ishq: Mathnawī-yi Ghanīmat* (Lahore: Panjabi Adabi Board 1962), a bare text without introduction or explanation of editorial procedure. Use has also been made of a representative of the main nineteenth-century printed text, which differs significantly in minor particulars from the 'Azīz edition, the Nawal Kishor *Nayrang-i 'ishq ma'rūf ba Mathnawī- yi Ghanīmat* (Kanpur 1878), with the usual marginal commentary. This is abundantly represented in the British Library collections: cf. the notice in A. Sprenger, *A Catalogue of the Arabic, Persian and Hindústány Manuscripts of the Libraries of the King of Oudh* (Calcutta: Baptist Mission Press 1854), p. 410. For the tellingly large numbers of MSS in British collections, cf. H. Ethé, *Catalogue of Persian Manuscripts in the Library of the India Office* (Oxford: Horace Hart 1903), I, (pp. 898–9, listing 3 MSS (nos. 1649–51), including one of 1152/1739–40, another of 1160/1747, with another three listed in Sachau, *Catalogue*, part I, nos. 1153–5, besides the abstract "written for Sir H. Elliot by Nayyir i Rakhshān in November and December 1851" in MS Or. 1904, listed in Rieu, *Catalogue*, II, p. 1034. The SOAS library has a version dated 1145/1732–3 in MS 47653, fos 63b–108a.
[52] Especially the lines (2.2–11) beginning *dil-ī*. . . (also 7.4–10, where the device is repeated): cf. Schimmel in Yarshater, *Persian Literature*, p. 418.

performers. Shāhid's fame as a dancer (10.3) reaches 'Azīz, the son of the governor of the city (*ḥākim-i shahr*). He comes with his friends to watch a performance and falls in love with Shāhid's beauty. Fearful of the damage to public morality (12.22), the local police officer (*muḥtasib*) intends to order Shāhid's expulsion, but when he is himself enraptured it falls to the judge (*qāḍī*) to pronounce banishment, upon which 'Azīz intervenes to have this order too rescinded. Shāhid's performances resume (16.1), causing 'Azīz completely to lose his heart. He is quite unswayed by the reports on Shāhid's behaviour prompted by his rivals (18.24). Eventually he removes Shāhid from his troupe and installs him in his own house (20.9). He spares no expense in the lavish furnishing of his beloved's new apartment (22.8).

Their happiness is ended when the matter is brought to the attention of 'Azīz's father, the governor (23.16), who orders Shāhid's expulsion, but 'Azīz follows his beloved. Much distressed, the father sends a messenger to beg 'Azīz to return (26.1). When his first overtures prove ineffectual, he sends a written undertaking not to interfere (28.2), and the lovers return. Concerned about his education, 'Azīz sends Shāhid to school (30.13), where all are devastated by Shāhid's beauty. In a remarkable passage which will be discussed later in this essay, Ghanīmat himself then pays a visit to Shāhid's school (33.15).

Shāhid begs leave of 'Azīz for a home visit (34.4). In the guise of a messenger, 'Azīz follows him (36.11), and when he is recognized by lamplight they spend the night together. 'Azīz then remains behind while Shāhid proceeds into open country (38.18). In pursuit of a stag (40.7), Shāhid comes upon a village and is struck by the sight of the village maidens at the well. He is particularly smitten by the lovely Wafā, daughter of the village headman, but that night the village is attacked by Afghan raiders who capture Shāhid and Wafā. Coming in search of Shāhid, 'Azīz discovers traces of the raid (44.1) and gets Shāhid freed. Shāhid then sends an old woman to Wafā to declare his love for her and set in motion arrangements for their marriage (47.21). The old woman reports how she has lured Wafā to a safe house (50.17). Shāhid and Wafā are united (52.5), and 'Azīz finds relief from his distress at losing his lover in adoration of the divine Beloved.

In a brief conclusion (54.9–5.12), the poet proclaims his art, announcing that his poem has 1,500 verses, a figure that is the same as the *abjad* total of his name,[53] and celebrating the date of its composition with the chronogram *gulzār-i bahār-i fikr-i rangīn* (55.1) 'the spring-filled garden of colourful fancy', which yields the figure 1096 (= AD 1685).

Most critical assessment of the poem has been chiefly preoccupied with the extent to which it is to be understood as the description of an actual

---

[53] I.e., 1000 + 50 + 10 + 40 + 400. In fact there appear to be 1497 verses in the 'Azīz edition, with two additional verses but one verse omitted in the Nawal Kishor text.

homosexual affair. The background is filled in quite early in the *tadhkira* tradition, which is otherwise so disappointingly short of reliable biographical details, with the information that Ghanīmat was a friend of a Mīrzā 'Abd al-'Azīz, the son of Mīrzā Artaq Beg the magistrate (*fawjdār*) of Sialkot, and was asked by him to tell the story of his love of the dancer Shāhid.[54] Later accounts transfer Ghanīmat into the service of Nawwab Mukarram Khān, governor of Lahore, and make 'Azīz out to have been his son.[55] The only peg that the poem itself provides is a verse in the poet's conclusion:

> I uttered this poem with an eye to discernment
> I threaded this pearl at the charge of a dear one.[56]

Relying on the interpretation here of the final word *'azīzī*, 'a dear one', as a proper name, the long-influential commentator in the margins of the printed Nawal Kishor edition incorporates the *tadhkira* tradition:

> That is, I have composed the poem in the hope that someone may appreciate it, and the meaning of 'one '*azīz*' is the son of Nawwab Mukarram Khān who was the lover of Shāhid and who was very close to Mawlānā Ghanīmat and believed in him. After Shāhid had gone and 'Azīz had turned from *majāz* to *ḥaqīqat*, he said to the Mawlānā, "If this story, which actually happened to me (*ki ba-chashm būda ast*), were recorded by you in writing, it would certainly cause us both to be remembered." It is to this that the Mawlānā refers.[57]

As has been observed by more recent scholars,[58] however, this whole construction rests on a base hardly less flimsy than that provided by another verse from the poet's prayer to the Prophet (3.18), which was inscribed upon his tomb:

> *asīram kard kāfir mājarā'ī*
> *rihā'ī ya nabī allāh rihā'ī*

It is reported that the existence of a village near Kunjah called Majra caused the general sense clearly intended in the first hemistich, i.e. 'I have been made captive by wretched circumstance',[59] to have become misunderstood locally as 'I have been captivated by a cruel beauty from Majra', as if Ghanīmat were speaking of his own infatuation with Shāhid.[60]

---

[54] *Safīna-yi Khushgū* (1724) by Bindrāban Dās Khushgū (d. 1756), a disciple of both Sarkhush and Bīdil, quoted in 'Abd al-Rashīd, *Tadhkira*, p. 265. Cf. *Gul-i ra'nā* by Shafīq Awrangābādī, quoted in Ẓuhūr al-Dīn Aḥmad, *Pākistān men Fārsī Adab*, pp. 26–7.

[55] Cf. the extracts in 'Abd al-Rashīd, *Tadhkira*; pp. 265 and 267, from *Tadhkira-yi Ḥusaynī* by Mīr Ḥusayn Dūst Sunbul, and from *Sham'-i Anjuman*.

[56] *Nayrang-i 'ishq*, 54.15: *Sukhan guftam ba-ummīd-i tamīzī, guhar suftam ba-taklīf-i 'azīzī.*

[57] *Nayrang-i 'ishq*, Nawal Kishor ed., p. 91.

[58] Notably by Sharīf Kunjāhī and Ẓuhūr al-Dīn Aḥmad, *Pākistān men Fārsī Adab*, pp. 26–9, pointing out that although Mukarram Khān (unlike Artaq Beg) is an attested historical figure, but he had no son.

[59] Cf. 43.21: *Chi jawr ast īn chi kāfir mājarā'ī-st.*

[60] Cf. Dilāwarī, "Ghanīmat Kunjāhī," pp. 30–1, Anṣārī, *Fārsī Adab*, p. 58.

Whatever their respective levels of sophistication, what such approaches share is an emphasis upon factualization as a sufficient explanation. The implicit rejection of the idea that the poem may be a fiction entirely or largely created by the poet is an interesting indication of the natural emphases both of traditional Islamicate literary criticism and of the modern literary scholarship modelled on what were originally Western techniques, which in South Asia has largely replaced the former.[61] A fictional hypothesis for the origins of the plot of the *Nayrang-i 'ishq* would certainly ease the great unease felt by modern Pakistani and Indian critics in dealing with its manifestly homosexual content. Some puzzlement has been caused by both the creation of apparently the first romantic *mathnawī* with a homosexual theme[62] in India and its great popularity at just the time when the regime introduced by Awrangzīb is supposed to have inculcated a new Puritanism in cultural values.

While the poem's theme of same-sex love is certainly to be associated with a quite prominent feature of the former Persianate culture of Muslim India subsequently suppressed by Victorian norms of sexual conduct,[63] it has equally certainly been influential in its later disappearance from the canon. In terms of literary history, however, its origins may also be associated with the whole emphasis on novelty (*tāza-gū'ī*) which is so important a feature of the Indian style. The choice of the clearly signalled local setting of the Panjab for the romance,[64] whether it was elaborated fact or concretized fiction, may perhaps also be associated with the contemporary fashion for composing *mathnawī* treatments in Persian of local Panjabi legends.[65]

---

[61] Cf. Earl Miner, *Comparative Poetics* (Princeton: Princeton University Press 1990), pp. 106ff., for a relevant and suggestive discussion of the roles of the factual, the fictional and the allegorical in understandings of East Asian lyric poetry. Comparative reflections of a different kind are stirred by the questioning in E.J. Kenney (ed.), *Cupid and Psyche* (Cambridge: Cambridge University Press 1990), p. 26, of the conventional scholarly explanation of the famous story as derived from an – inevitably and conveniently – unattested 'folklore tradition' rather than Apuleius' formidable imagination.

[62] Cf. Gyān Chand Jain, *Urdū Mathnawī Shimālī Hindmen* (Aligarh: Anjuman-i Taraqqi-yi Urdin 1969), p. 106.

[63] Highly pertinent here is the discussion of homosexual themes in the classical Urdu poetry of the later eighteenth and early nineteenth-centuries. which was pioneered in C.M. Naim, "The Theme of Homosexual (Pederastic) Love in Pre-Modern Urdu Poetry," in *Studies in the Urdu Ġazal and Prose Fiction*, ed. M. Umar Memon (Wisconsin: Dept. of S. Asia Studies, University of Wisconsin 1979), pp. 120–42, and developed in Tariq Rahman, "Boy-Love in the Urdu Ghazal,"*Annual of Urdu Studies*, 7 (1990), pp. 1–20, including a reference to Ghanīmat on p. 6.

[64] Ghanīmat's occasional use of Indian ('Hindī') words may also be noted in this context, e.g. the *bhagat-bāz* whose troupe Shāhid joins. But these are not unusually prominent for an Indo-Persian literary text of this type.

[65] It is not so much the Indianness of their setting (and certainly not the usually humble level of their rhetorical pretensions) so much as the novelty of theme which perhaps aligns

Ghanīmat himself is conspicuously less interested in signalling his poem as fact or fiction than as an allegory in the tradition, as well as in the *hazaj* metre (*mafāʿīlun mafāʿīlun mafāʿīl*), of Jāmī's *Yūsuf Zulaykhā*, a poem which for long enjoyed far greater popularity in India than the romantic *mathnawī*s of Niẓāmī or Khusraw.[66] Certain passages in Ghanīmat seem designed to recall well-known episodes in Jāmī's poem, like the evocation, in substance if not in precise verbal detail, of Jāmī's description of Yūsuf's prison in the description of the prison to which Shāhid and Wafā are consigned by the Afghan raiders.[67] Even more explicitly, the entire story of the *Nayrang-i ʿishq* is framed in two key passages which establish the poem's literary and spiritual placement by underlining definitions of love with quotations from Jāmī. Early in the poem, the closing passage of the poet's introductory section on the varieties of love includes the following verses:

> Let no heart lack its play with love
> Whether this be real or illusion.
>
> Illusion mirrors meaning's form
> It too can lead to meaning's lane.
>
> In seeming's cup the Saqi poured
> A wine of everlasting name.
>
> Hear Jāmī's words which sweetly rouse
> The rapture of reality:

---

these often humdrum poems with the *Nayrang-i ʿishq* as examples of provincial poetry in the age of *sabk-i hindī*. Persian treatments of the Hīr–Rānjhā story are described in Muḥammad Bāqir (ed.), *Pānjābi Qiṣṣe Fārsī Zabān men*, 2 vols. (Lahore: Panjabi Adabi Board 1957, 1960), including a discussion with examples of *Mathnawī-yi Hīr u Rānjhā* (*c.* 1575) by Ḥayāt Jān Bāqī Kūlābī, in vol. II, pp. 36–55, a composition chronologically followed by the several treatments discussed in vol. I, pp. 81–192, including among others *Afsāna-yi Dilpadhīr* (*c.* 1640) by Sāʿīd Saʿīdi, and *Mathnawī-yi Hīr u Rānjhā* (1685) by Mīr Muḥammad Murād Lāʾiq Jawnpūrī, exactly contemporary with Ghanīmat's poem. Also relevant are such local *mathnawī*s as Indarjīt Munshī, *Nāma-yi ʿishq*, ed. Waḥīd Qurayshī (Lahore: Panjabi Adabi Board 1959), a version of the Sassī–Punnūn legend of 1140/1727. The connection between this literary activity in the local Persian *mathnawī* and the roughly contemporary beginnings of the narrative treatments in Panjabi called *qiṣṣa* (for which cf. J.S. Deol, "Love and Mysticism in the Punjabi Qissas of the Seventeenth and Eighteenth Centuries," [University of London M.Phil. thesis 1996]) seems too striking to be coincidental, but it has yet to be properly explored, as have the links between the Sufi Persian ghazal and the Panjabi *kāfī*.

[66] Jāmī's reputation amongst modern critics is not very high: cf. e.g. Shāfiʿī Kadkānī, "The Safavid Period," pp. 139–140, or Bürgel in Yarshater, *Persian Literature*, pp. 175–6. But he was very highly regarded in India until well into the nineteenth century: cf. C. Shackle, "Between Scripture and Romance: The Yūsuf–Zulaikhā Story in Panjabi," *South Asian Research* 15 (1995), pp. 154–88, esp. pp. 157–61.

[67] Dilāwarī, "Ghanīmat Kunjāhī," pp. 35–6.

"First drain the wine from seeming's cup
Then taste the meaning at the bottom."[68]

This note is precisely echoed, with a brevity suitable to the smaller scale of the poet's conclusion, with the following pair of verses towards the end of the poem:

From beauty's face I heard this rule
Recalled in two lines by the Master:

"Turn not from even unreal love
For it sets up reality."[69]

Whatever view is taken of the homosexual aspect of the poem – and it is worth observing here that the poet's art is such that Shāhid's sex only becomes unambiguously apparent in the final section[70] – it is clear that the reader is being invited to follow classical Sufi literary precedent and take all as allegory. And only allegory can account for Ghanīmat's own intrusion of himself into the poem in the remarkable episode describing his visit to Shāhid's school (33.15-34.3, headed 'Our Master Ghanīmat's Trip to Visit Shāhid's School', *raftan-i mawlānā Ghanīmat barāy-i sayr-i maktabkhāna-yi Shāhid*). Although this passage also appears to have been sometimes sadly misunderstood as a description of fact, the allegory here can hardly be based on anything but a fiction. In terms of the poem's structure, the episode provides an ingenious bridge passage at the major turning point in the story, when the passing of adolescence is to take Shāhid away from 'Azīz and to unmask the true identity of the protagonists. In terms of style, too, it provides an excellent example of the skill of Ghanīmat's narrative technique within a poetic register closer to the smooth polish of Jāmī than to the laboured intricacies of the *sabk-i hindī*. It begins with a gracefully handled introductory formula:

Last night I heard that on love's way
There is no better place than school.

Especially love-making's school,
That place as fair as lovely Shāhid.[71]

---

[68] *Nayrang-i 'ishq*, 7.14–19: *Mabādā hīch dil bī-'ishqbāzī, agar bāshad ḥaqīqī yā majāzī. majāz ā'īna-dār-i rūy-i ma'nī-st, sar-i īn jāda ham dar kūy-i ma'nī-st. marā dar jām-i ṣūrat rīkht sāqī, sharābī-rā ki nāmash būd bāqī. ḥaqīqat nasha-yi mast-i fayḍ-i Jāmī, chunīn dādast dād-i khush-kalāmī. "ki bī jām-i may-i sūrat kashīdan, nayārī jur'a-yi ma'nī chashīdan."*

[69] *Ibid.*, 54.5–6: *Marā āmad zi rūy-i ḥusn irshād, du miṣra' az kalām-i mawlawī yād. "matāb az 'ishq rū garchi majāzī-st, ki ān bahr-i ḥaqīqat kārsāzī-st."*

[70] My own confusion, on a first reading of the story in the Urdu version by Rāḥat discussed below, is confirmed as a common experience by Ẓuhūr al-Dīn Aḥmad, *Pākistān men Fārsī Adab*, p. 29.

[71] *Nayrang-i 'ishq*, 33.15–16: *Shanīdam dūsh az ṭarz-i āshnā'ī, ki az maktab nikūtar nīst jā'ī, khuṣūṣan maktab-i 'ishq-āfirīnī, maqām-i hamchu Shāhid nāznīnī.*

In the ensuing verses, the handling of rapid dialogue (*sawāl u jawāb*) is – as in other passages in the poem – particularly noteworthy, as the episode moves to embrace within its short compass more than one of the universal themes of the Sufi message:

> I hoped to see that loveliness
> And made my way towards that school.
>
> I reached its door and there I cried,
> "Buy primers of the heart from me ..."

A voice is then heard from within:

> He said, "Come in," so disregarding
> Ceremony in I went ...
>
> He kindly brushed the dust off it
> Then read the Sūra of Ikhlāṣ.
>
> He liked it and he said, "I'll buy"
> "If you are lucky," I replied.
>
> He asked, "How much?" "A look," I said.
> "That's all?" he asked. "It's yours," I said.
>
> He said, "It's mine, but do not shout
> In case the silent master hears ..."[72]

The flickering of allegorical themes through this short episode mirrors on its small scale the larger allegory of whole poem. Like most romances with an allegorical dimension, whether of Sufi inspiration or affiliated to other traditions,[73] the narrative is not totally bound to the meta-narrative, in spite of the abstract nomenclature of its characters. In this respect, unlike those Sufi *mathnawī*s which are exactly constructed for the explanation and illustration of spiritual schemes,[74] the *Nayrang-i 'ishq* is closer to the generality of Sufi – or 'Suficate' – Persian romances in offering a story which may be understood allegorically, rather than a completely strict and consistent allegory.[75] Beyond

---

[72] *Ibid.*, 33.18–19, 23, 25–34.1: *Ba-ummīd-i tamāshā-yi nigārī, numūdam jānib-i maktab gudhārī. bar āmad bar dar-i maktab khurūsham, ki man sīpāra-yi dil mīfurūsham ... biguftā pīshtar ā pīsh raftam, takalluf bar ṭaraf az khwīsh raftam ... ba mihr awwal ghubārash-rā bar afshānd, pas āngah sūra-yi ikhlāṣ bar khwānd. pasandash kard u guftā man kharīdār, baguftam ar shawad ṭāli' madadgār. biguftā qīmatash guftam nigāhī, biguftā kamtarak guftam ki gāhī. biguftā yāftam z-īn bīsh makhrūsh, mabādā bishnawad ākhūnd-i khāmūsh.*

[73] Cf., e.g. Northrop Frye, *The Secular Scripture: A Study of the Structure of Romance* (Cambridge, Mass.–London: Harvard University Press 1976).

[74] As is the case with, for instance, the late Ottoman example of Shaykh Ghālib's *Ḥüsn ü Aşk* (1782), admirably described and analysed in Victoria Holbrook, *The Unreadable Shores of Love* (Austin: University of Texas Press 1994).

[75] The relevant context of Persian literature after Jāmī is briefly sketched by J. Bürgel in Yarshater, *Persian Literature*, pp. 176–7.

the exploration of the core relationship of 'Azīz and Shāhid, symbolizing the eternal dynamic between lover and beloved with its passage through cycles of closeness and distance bridged by suffering and sacrifice, Ghanīmat does not seem to have aimed for any complete consistency of the kind which would demand a complete allegoresis. In the third part of the poem, in particular, when female characters[76] first make their appearance, the momentum of the story is only awkwardly to be accommodated in any tidy allegorical scheme. While Beauty is fittingly matched with Fidelity, as Shāhid the erstwhile ephebe finds married bliss, the old woman he uses as his instrument to win Wafā, and who is, perhaps tellingly, not only one of the few female characters in the story but also its only villainous one, assumes a symbolic identity as the crafty crone who represents the world, an image which seems well worn rather than appropriate to this story. And 'Azīz, who has played so crucial a role throughout, is at the end left with little more than a madness which is far more marginal than is, say, that of Majnūn to his story. Just like the long-delayed definitive revelation of Shāhid's male identity, not to speak of other aspects of the poem and the poet, the *Nayrang-i 'ishq* reveals itself in its allegorical aspect also to be something of a tease. And as a Suficate confection, it perhaps stands revealed in its provincial Indian setting as eminently true to its Persianate cultural orientation.

LATER VERSIONS OF THE *NAYRANG-I 'ISHQ*

When it is regarded from another perspective, not the least interesting of the several questions raised by Ghanīmat's poem are those relating to issues of originality, never very straightforward in the cultural context of Islamicate literature, with its careful consciousness of the limits of human creativity as opposed to the divine inimitability (*i'jāz*) of Scripture. Nor is this all, for the popularity of the *Nayrang-i 'ishq*, quickly established and subsequently maintained until well into the nineteenth century in South Asia, is amply attested not only by the abundance of manuscripts and early printed editions, but also by the production of versified translations in other South Asian languages. The latter themselves raise numerous interesting questions. When so much work has yet to be done on the primary texts, it is hardly surprising that the whole process of literary translation in Islamicate literature has yet to receive the detailed attention it deserves.[77] But even apart from the details of their form and style which are interesting in their own right, these versions of the *Nayrang-i 'ishq* deserve description as markers of broader cultural trends. They are particularly noteworthy for showing how an Indian poem which had

[76] Disregarding the brief mention of Shāhid's mother at the beginning.

[77] Cf. Shackle, "Between Scripture and Romance" for a preliminary study of one relevant tradition.

won for itself a place in the canon of minor Persian classics, however unsuitable its content might have appeared to make it as an item for inclusion in a literary syllabus, was transferred from Persian into other languages in keeping with the general socio-linguistic shift in eighteenth- and nineteenth-century South Asian Islamic cultural tradition. In keeping with the emphasis of modern translation studies on the generative power of new versions of a literary work rather than on judging them exclusively by the retrospective yardstick of 'fidelity' to an original,[78] the implied changes to its character as well as its language involved in this process may usefully be described with an eye as much on the target languages as on Ghanīmat's Persian text. Regarding the *Nayrang-i 'ishq* as a Sufi poem from a Sufi studies viewpoint, this emphasis might be seen as a step in the quest for understanding of the ongoing need in all spiritually informed cultures for the unceasing practice of that *scientia litterarum, quae ornat animam*.[79]

The first recorded version must have been produced within a generation of the original. This is a translation into Pashto verse by 'Abd al-Ḥamīd Mohmand (fl. *c.* 1700), the details of whose life remain as obscure as Ghanīmat's,[80] but who is recognized along with Khushḥal Khān Khāṯak (d. 1101/1689) and 'Abd al-Raḥmān Bābā (d. *c.* 1122/1710) as one of the key figures responsible for the creation of a written Pashto literature – on largely Persianate lines – in and around the Peshawar region in later Mughal times. The evidence cited earlier in this study for Ghanīmat's own connections with literary circles in the region provides a reasonable basis for speculation as to why 'Abd al-Ḥamīd might have been inspired to undertake a translation of this particular poem, while, on the other hand, what is known of this Persianizing Pashto literature shows how a translation may transform the character of an original.

Perhaps the most striking feature of the Pashto art poets of the period is the way in which they add to the usual Sufi-amatory mode a particular emphasis on moralistic statement which, while famously characteristic of Raḥmān Bābā, is also a very noticeable feature of many of the ghazals in the *Dīwān* for which 'Abd al-Ḥamīd Mohmand is best known.[81] His Pashto version of the *Nayrang-i 'ishq* deserves a description in English by a scholar linguistically more competent than the present writer. It keeps the *mathnawī* format of rhyming hemistichs and the marking of sections by invocations to the Saqi, although the

---

[78] Cf. E. Gentzler, *Contemporary Translation Theories* (London–New York: Routledge 1993), especially on the Czech and Israeli schools associated respectively with Jiri Levy and Itamar Even-Zohar.

[79] St Bernard, *Sup. Cant.* 37.2, quoted in J. Leclercq, *The Love of Learning and the Desire for God: A Study of Monastic Culture* (New York: Fordham University Press 1982), p. 259.

[80] All later accounts appear largely to rely upon the brief notice supplied in H.G. Raverty, *Selections from the Poetry of the Afghans* (London: Williams & Norgate 1862), pp. 85–6.

[81] Sixty ghazals are translated in Raverty, *Selections*, pp. 87–141.

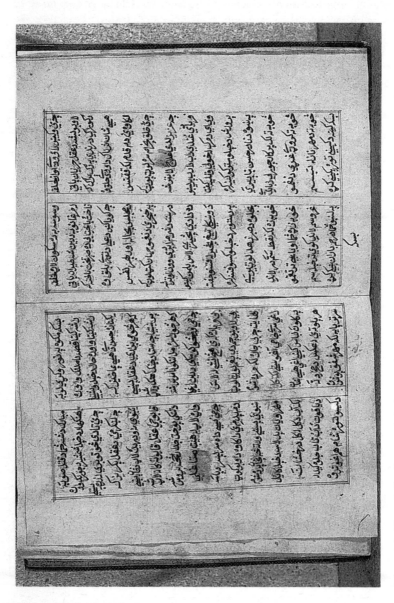

Plate 16: First Folio from ‘Abd al-Ḥamīd’s Pashto Translation of the *Mathnawī-yi Nayrang-i ‘ishq* AD 1845. Courtesy of SOAS Library, London.

metre is of the usual Pashto accented type.[82] While considerably longer overall, at some 1,800 verses, the introduction is notably abbreviated. Ḥamīd makes no attempt to match the splendid ingenuity of Ghanīmat's *ḥamd* or to reproduce his statements of devotion to Qādirī saints. Instead, he chooses to follow a very brief formal opening with a statement of his own desire to produce a Pashto version of 'the tale in Persian by Muḥammad Akram of Kunjah' as an exemplar of the figuring of *ḥaqīqat* by *majāz*. It is this aspect of the poem which deserves attention here, rather than the homosexual theme or the Afghan intrusion later in the narrative, which might be presumed to have been additional attractions to an Pashto audience. A similar motive presumably prompted Ḥamīd to choose also to translate the Persian Sufi mathnawī *Shāh u gadā* by Hilālī (d. 936/1529), a poem of comparable length to the *Nayrang-i 'ishq*.[83] All in all, it may be speculated that Ḥamīd's Pashto version, whose speedy appearance may be linked to Ghanīmat's known ties to the Peshawar region, represents the desire to enhance the Persianate heritage of Pashto with a romance whose homosexual content was safely embraced by its palpably Sufi tone, a purpose for which it was made very suitable by the generalizing tone of the poem and the abstract nomenclature of its characters.

Over the greatest part of northern India, however, the great linguistic shift away from Persian in the Islamicate culture of South Asia was that towards Urdu, which was chiefly effected in the hundred years from 1760 to 1860. One very significant part of this process was the large-scale production of Urdu translations of all sorts of Persian literary and non-literary texts. In the all-too-typical fashion of most studies of nineteenth-century India, however, these have yet to receive a fraction of the attention devoted to the culturally far more peripheral production around 1800 of simple vernacular prose texts under British patronage at Fort William College in Calcutta. As a small part of that wider translation process, numerous versions of Ghanīmat's poem are said to have been produced, but only one appears to have achieved the popularity indicated by publication. This is by Bhagwant Rā'e Rāḥat, whose name indicates that he belonged to one of those Hindu groups culturally oriented towards the Persianate cultural world, which might be almost as legitimately described as essential 'service castes' in the context of Indo-Persian literature as they were for the requirements of imperial administration. Born a

[82] The metre is described in *Qasida*, II, p. 59 (as C1). A modern edition has been published by the Pushto Academy as Siddīq Allāh Rishtīn (ed.), *Da Ḥamīd Nayrang-i 'ishq* [Hamid's *Nairang-i-Eshq* (The Ecstasy of Love)] (Kabul 1970). There is an earlier printed edition, *Nayrang-i 'ishq ba-zabān-i afghānī* (Peshawar: Ghulam Mursalin and Ghulam Hamadani 1882). Three nineteenth-century MSS are listed in J.F. Blumhardt and D.N. MacKenzie, *Catalogue of Pashto Manuscripts in the Libraries of the British Isles* (London: British Museum 1965), pp. 102–4 (nos. 129–31), the oldest being the SOAS MS 41377 of 1261/1847.

[83] Cf. Yarshater, *Persian Literature*, pp. 176–7.

Kayasth[84] in Kakori, a small town in Awadh known for its traditions of learning and literature, and also the site of an important Sufi shrine,[85] Rāḥat (d. *c.*1293/1876) was active during the final decades of the 'kingdom' of Lucknow before its annexation in 1856, years that were so important in the evolution of Urdu literary culture in northern India. A pupil of the quintessentially Lucknow poet Amānat (d. 1275/1858), Rāḥat is known only as a *mathnawī* writer.[86] He is best remembered for his Urdu *Nal u Dāman*, taken from the Persian version produced by Akbar's laureate Fayḍī of the famous romance from the Sanskrit epic.[87] Rāḥat was, therefore, one of the many journeyman poets of the period responsible for transmitting the Persian literary heritage of the past into the new poetic medium of Urdu – in the somewhat peculiar cultural hothouse of the Lucknow kingdom which existed as a protected Muslim statelet surrounded by territories under British rule. In the present context, it may be noted that this kingdom was moreover one in which ostentatiously fostered patterns of Ithnā 'Asharī observance rather than Sufi practice provided the main counterbalance to powerfully 'secular' cultural trends.[88]

Dating from 1852, Rāḥat's version of Ghanīmat's poem is called *Nigāristān-i Rāḥat*.[89] It appears to have remained quite popular, at least while the cultural values associated with the Lucknow kingdom retained a certain vitality, but is now forgotten like so much of literature produced in that period. Superficially, this Urdu version preserves a certain formal similarity with the original, although it too is slightly longer at some 1,600 verses, and the metre is now the *hazaj* of Niẓāmī's *Laylā Majnūn* (*maf'ūlu mafā'īlun mafā'īl*). The transformed emphasis of the treatment is both explicitly and implicitly conveyed by the introductory sections, which move from brief *ḥamd* and *na't* to the praise of the ruler Wājid 'Alī Shāh (*reg.* 1847–56) and the amenities of Lucknow, his delightful capital. The new cultural age then makes a telling appearance with a section praising Rāḥat's publishers, the Gulzār-i Awadh

---

84 Cf. Karen I. Leonard, *Social History of an Indian Caste: The Kayasths of Hyderabad* (Berkeley: University of California Press 1978).

85 Belonging to the Qādirī-affiliated Shāh Muḥammad Kāẓim (1745–1806), which is studied in C. Liebeskind, "Sufism, Sufi Leadership and 'Modernization' in South Asia since c. 1800" (University of London Ph.D. thesis 1995). The most prominent scion of Kakori in Urdu literature was the poet Muḥsin (1827–1905), for whom cf. *Qasida*, II, pp. 452–53.

86 Rāḥat's *oeuvre* is assessed in Jain, *Urdū Mathnawī Shimālī Hind men*, pp. 470–3, and in Farmān Fatḥpurī, *Urdū kī Manẓūm Dāstānen* (Karachi: Anjuman-i Taraqqi-yi Urdu 1971), pp. 420–32.

87 Cf. the plot summary of the original appended to J.D. Smith, "The Hero as Gifted Man: Nala in the Mahābhārata," in Shackle and Snell, *The Indian Narrative*, pp. 14–31.

88 Classically described in Abdul Halim Sharar, *Lucknow: The Last Phase of an Oriental Culture*, trans. and ed. E.S. Harcourt and Fakhir Hussain (London: Paul Elek 1975).

89 Bhagwant Rā'e Rāḥat, *Nigāristān-i Rāḥat: tarjuma-yi Mathnawī-yi Ghanīmat* (Lucknow 1899).

Press and its capable staff. The Sufi dimension is all at second hand, however, since it is the *pīr* of this firm's director who is briefly praised before the poet introduces himself as Bhagwant Rā'e of Kakori and praises Shāh Kāẓim as the town's patron saint. Rāḥat's own inspiration is purely literary, as he tells of how he was prompted to follow up the success of his *Nal u Dāman* by listening to Dayā Shankar Nasīm's *Gulzār-i Nasīm*, published in 1844, the most successful romantic Urdu *mathnawī* by a Hindu writer.

If his final boast of having completed his poem in a couple of months is to be believed, Rāḥat's treatment of the story – to which, it may not be unfair to speculate, he was perhaps attracted by the *risqué* piquancy of its principal theme – reflects the speed with which it was composed. It is a straightforward telling, often speeding through the narrative,[90] and omitting apparently incidental episodes like Ghanīmat's visit to Shāhid's school in favour of dwelling on lengthy set pieces in the form of interposed *sarāpā* descriptions of the beloved's appearance or of ghazals introduced into the *mathnawī* text, thus bringing the treatment closer in tone to that of Amānat's *Indar Sabhā*. While successfully achieving in its presentation of Shāhid's act a vivid evocation of the atmosphere of a dancer's performance, which was so prominently cultivated a feature of Lucknow culture, there is little room for *ḥaqīqat* in this version. Its relentless elegance trivializes even the *majāz* of suffering, as in the early description of the orphaned Shāhid's hunger as a child:

> To find each day a bread crust's rim
> Was like a daily moon of Eid for him.[91]

But although the Lucknow style is rightly seen as a key feature of much nineteenth-century Urdu poetry, a broader perspective quickly shows that it was representative of only one strand of Indo-Muslim culture. Nearly contemporary with Rāḥat's, another version of the *Nayrang-i 'ishq* appeared, which better preserves Ghanīmat's seriousness, if not his elegance. Produced not far from Kunjah, this is the Panjabi translation by Miyān Muḥammad Bakhsh (1830–1907), who was in the ensuing period to achieve an immense and still enduring fame as the premier vernacular Sufi poet of the entire northern Punjabi region. This fame is chiefly associated with his vast version in some ten thousand verses of the story of *Sayf al-Mulūk wa Badī' al-Jamāl* (1863) based on that in the *Thousand and One Nights*, which is unquestionably one of the outstanding nineteenth-century masterpieces of the Panjabi verse romance tradition primarily exemplified in Wārith Shāh's earlier *Hīr* (1766).[92]

---

[90] When compared with Ghanīmat, the greater carelessness of Rāḥat's technique emerges in the excessive use of such devices as his over-frequent recourse to the metrical possibility of beginning verses with *al-qiṣṣa*, 'anyway' as a loose narrative link.

[91] *Nigāristān-i Rāḥat*, p. 6: *Milnā lab-i nān-i khushk kā roz, us mah ko hilāl-i 'īd thā roz.*

[92] Salient features of the nineteenth-century Panjabi *qiṣṣa* are outlined in Shackle, "Between Scripture and Romance," pp. 164–88.

Miyān Muḥammad was born in the Panjabi-speaking Mirpur region, which British interests were content to let form part of the domains of the Maharaja of Kashmir, into the family of the Qādirī *pīr*s of Khari who were associated with the great dynasty of Muqīm Shāh.[93] Not only passionate in his devotion to Shaykh 'Abd al-Qādir and a close associate of the numerous Qādirī dynasties of the region, but also possessed of a remarkable poetic fluency, Miyān Muḥammad undertook as a young man the ambitious project of recasting a vast range of local and Islamic materials as Panjabi verse narratives. A profoundly Sufi treatment of the local romance of *Sohnī Mahīnwāl* (1273/1857)[94] was rapidly followed by *Tuḥfa Mīrān*, describing the miracles of 'Abd al-Qādir, and *Shaykh Ṣan'ān*, based on 'Aṭṭār (both 1274/1857–8), before his treatment of the *Nayrang-i 'ishq* (1275/1858-59).[95]

Panjabi poetry typically follows South Asian models[96] in its metres rather than traditional Persian metrical '*arūḍ* types, so Miyān Muḥammad's decision to preserve the *hazaj* of the original in his version is a notable stylistic innovation, perhaps inspired by its also being the metre of Jāmī's *Yūsuf Zulaykhā*, which is known to have been his favourite Persian romance. It is rather shorter overall than the original, at some 1300 verses, but it does include all the original episodes, including, for instance, Ghanīmat's visit to Shāhid's school, although this is treated with rather little of the original's flair. Unlike the other two versions considered here, however, Miyān Muḥammad's does have a notably full introductory section which naturally preserves not only *ḥamd* and *na't* but also a full laudatory address to 'Abd al-Qādir. The days of Muslim political authority in the region having ended, there is no praise of the ruler, only of his own *pīr*, Ghulām Muḥammad of the nearby shrine of Palir – now submerged under the vast Mangla reservoir – and of a local *sayyid* who had encouraged him to write the poem. This leads to a version of Ghanīmat's introductory treatment of *ḥaqīqat* and *majāz*. At the end of the poem, a conclusion again refers at length to the inspiration of 'Abd al-Qādir.

The treatment is therefore overtly Islamic and unambiguously Sufi in tone. Miyān Muḥammad's version begins with Islamic formulae, first in Arabic, then in Urdu, before his first Panjabi verse, which makes no attempt to match Ghanīmat's startling exordium:

---

[93] Besides his large corpus of Panjabi poetry, Miyān Muḥammad also contributed in Persian prose a substantial supplement to the *Tadhkira-yi Muqīmī*, available only in MS but which was subsequently translated into Urdu as *Bostān-i Qalandarī* (Jhelum 1920) by his disciple Malik Muḥammad, the author of the primary hagiography of Miyān Muḥammad, the *Sawāniḥ-'umrī* which is attached to many editions of *Sayf al-Mulūk*.

[94] Described in Shackle, "Beyond Turk and Hindu."

[95] Muḥammad Bakhsh, *Mathnawī Nayrang-i 'ishq pānjābi* (Jhelum: Malik Ghulam Nur 1964).

[96] Cf. *Qasida*, II, p. 60.

My book starts with the name of God
Remembering which excels all verse.[97]

A similarly remarkable macaronic technique, not practised to anything like this degree by Miyān Muḥammad in his other compositions, surfaces at many other points in the poem. In the section on *ḥaqīqat* and *majāz*, for instance, the Panjabi veers into Urdu as it introduces first a quotation from Ghanīmat, then another from Jāmī.[98] The kaleidoscopic impression thus produced of a constructed cultural and linguistic palimpsest is at times disconcerting, but we are left in no doubt as to the depth of the cultural tradition to which Miyān Muḥammad's version of the *Nayrang-i 'ishq* belongs, nor as to the centrality of Sufism to it.

But let us end as we began, with disciples rather than the masters. Miyān Muḥammad's version ends with the mention of a faithful attendant who had always hoped to get into a poem:

I have an old and faithful friend,
A carpenter called Muḥkam Dīn,

Most able in his craft and skilled,
And with some taste for poetry . . .

He asked me but a while ago,
"Please put me in a story, sir."

So here his name is written down,
In answer to my friend's appeal.[99]

We know no more of the humble Muhkam Dīn, but it would be appropriate to end by observing that he was through Miyān Muḥammad doubtless able to gain a better understanding of Ghanīmat's Sufi tale of love than was vouchsafed to the custodians of the latter's shrine at Kunjah who – apparently without benefit of the faculty-enhancing powers of that miraculous tree – preserved only the garbled memory that it housed the remains of a holy man who had written a book called something like '*Ishq nawrang*.[100]

---

[97] Miyān Muḥammad, *Nayrang*, p. 3: (Arabic) *Rabb yassirū lā ta'sirū tammim bi'l-khayr.* (Urdu) *Ba-nām-i khudā ibtidā-yi sukhan, huā jis se paydā liwā-yi zaman.* (Panjabi) *Karān nāma shurū' allāh de nāmon, je os dā yād bihtar har kalāmon.*

[98] *Ibid.*, p. 13.

[99] *Ibid.*, p. 76.

[100] Dilāwarī, "Ghanīmat Kunjāhī," p. 26.

Symbolism and Symmetry

Shaykh Manjhan's Madhumālatī *Revisited*

SIMON WEIGHTMAN

This study returns to a subject I first addressed as long as twelve years ago in a seminar on narrative styles in Indian literature.[1] Twelve seems to be a significant number for Manjhan, so it is at an appropriate interval, in addition to being within a particularly appropriate context, that I return to a work which, even more than before, I hold to be among the finest of all Sufi mystical romances, as well as being one of the most powerful invocations of Love in any of the world's mystical traditions. In this interval, I found a kindred spirit in the person of Dr Aditya Behl of the University of California at Berkeley, who completed a doctoral thesis at Chicago with *Madhumālatī* as the centrepiece.[2] Not only have we had many fruitful exchanges but we have also together translated the entire poem into English for publication in the very near future. Indeed, so close has been our collaboration, that it is now almost impossible to identify the origins of any given insight, save one which will be discussed below, so I here gladly acknowledge his overall contribution to this subject and this essay, even if I cannot necessarily identify every instance owed to him within the text. The outcome of the passing of the years, the further work and this fruitful collaboration, is certainly a deeper understanding of the poem itself and of the context which gave it birth, and it is this new understanding that constitutes the justification for contributing this study to the present volume, even though *Madhumālatī* is not strictly a work of the Mughal dynasty but of the brief Afghan interregnum between the defeat of Humayun by Sher Shāh Sār in 1540 and 1557, when all pretensions of the Sār dynasty were brought to an end by Akbar.

[1] S.C.R.Weightman, "Symmetry and Symbolism in Shaykh Manjhan's *Madhumālatī*," in *The Indian Narrative: Perspectives and Patterns*, ed. C. Shackle and R. Snell (Wiesbaden: Harrassowitz 1992), pp. 195–226

[2] The dissertation is entitled "Rasa and Romance: The *Madhumālatī* of Shaykh Manjhan Shaṭṭāri," and was accepted by the University of Chicago in June 1995.

THE AUTHOR OF *MADHUMĀLATĪ*, MĪR SAYYID MANJHAN RĀJGĪRĪ

The natural hostility of the Mughal historians towards these upstart Afghans perhaps explains the paucity of information available on the subject of Manjhan, the author of *Madhumālatī*. The only independent reference to him occurs in the *Afsān-e Shāhān* of Muḥammad Kabīr, in the section dealing with Islām Shāh, the son of Sher Shāh. He writes: "Wherever he [Islām Shāh] happened to be, he kept himself surrounded by accomplished scholars and poets, and villas *(khūshak)* provided with perfume and betel leaves were set up. Men like Mīr Sayyid Manjhan, the author of *Madhumālatī*; Shāh Farmālī and his younger brother Māsan Sūrdās and many other learned scholars and poets assembled there and poems in Arabic, Persian and Hindi were recited."[3] While not the most historically reliable informant, Muḥammad Kabīr would have been on surer ground here as his maternal grandfather, Shaykh Khalīl Ḥaqqānī, of whom he gives a detailed account, was the spiritual disciple of Mīr Sayyid Manjhan in Rajgir,[4] and Manjhan himself devotes four verses to Islām Shāh in his prologue.[5]

From Hasan Askari's work on Bihar Sufism,[6] it is possible to establish that Manjhan's mother was Bībī Khunja Dawlat, the daughter of the renowned Shaykh Muḥammad Qāzin 'Alā, who, while originally a Chishtī, later was one of the principal proponents of Shaṭṭārī Sufism in Bihar. Manjhan's father was Sayyid Muḥammad 'Alī Manjhan Dānishmand, son of Sayyid Muḥammad Chakkan of Jawnpur, who compiled his father-in-law's *malfāzāt*, the *Ma'dan al-asrār*. Manjhan's own grandson, Imām ad-dīn Rājgīrī, was the author of *Manāhij al-Shaṭṭār*, a compendium of Shaṭṭārī practices, and the *malfāzāt* of Rukn ad-dīn Aḥmad Shaṭṭārī.

Manjhan was, then, brought up at the very centre of Shaṭṭārī Sufism in Bihar during one of its most influential periods. He was clearly a respected teaching shaykh of the Shaṭṭārī order, with both impressive family and spiritual pedigrees. His own teacher was the renowned Shaykh Muḥammad Ghawth, to whom he dedicates eight verses in the prologue to his poem. He frequented court circles as a poet, if not as a courtier, and was presumably competent in

---

[3] Translated by S.H. Askari, "Historical Value of Afsana-i Badshahan or Tarikh Afghani," *Journal of Indian History*, 43 (1965), p. 194.

[4] *Ibid*.

[5] The text of *Madhumālatī* used throughout is that of Mataprasad Gupta (ed.) *Madhumālatī* (Allahabad: 1961).

[6] See for example "A Fifteenth century Shuttari Sufi Saint in North Bihar," *Journal of the Bihar Research Society*, 37 (1951), pp. 66–82, and "Gleaning From Malfuz of the Seventeenth Century Shuttari Saint of Jandaha," *Current Studies* (Patna 1963), pp. 1–26. Unfortunately A.A. Rizvi in his *History of Sufism in India* (2 vols; New Delhi: Munshiram Manoharlal 1983) has confused Manjhan with the Shāh Manjhan mentioned in the *Gulzār-i abrār*. The reasons for rejecting this identification are given in Weightman *Summetry and Symbolism*, p. 196.

Persian and Arabic, in addition to the Awadhi dialect of Eastern Hindi, of which he was an outstanding exponent.[7] It could not have been easy for him at Islām Shāh's court since both his teacher and his teacher's brother, Shaykh Phūl, were at one time especially close to the Mughal emperors Bābur and Humāyūn. After the defeat of the Mughals by the Afghan Sūrs, Shaykh Muḥammad fled to Gujarāt, although he was to be reconciled with Islām Shāh after the death of Sher Shāh in 1545. The very presence of Shaykh Manjhan at the court, and possibly even one of the motivations for the production of his poem, could well have been an attempt by the Shaṭṭāri Order to establish similarly close relations and influence with the Sūr court as they had enjoyed with the Mughals; while, from the monarch's side, it would have provided a legitimization of the ruler from the Shaykh's supernatural authority. They were not to know that the Afghan dynasty was to be so short lived.

THE SHAṬṬĀRIYYA SUFI ORDER

If the Sufi orders provided spiritual sustenance and legitimization for kings, they sought in return patronage and prestige. In this, as in spiritual matters, they were in competition one with another. As others have shown regarding non-Muslims in this period of Muslim hegemony, they practised a form of cultural colonialism which some have, almost certainly wrongly, interpreted as syncretism. The Shaṭṭāriyya, for example, practised a form of yogic breath control so openly that in two verses Manjhan invites the reader of *Madhumālatī* to try it, giving clear instructions as to what should be done and what was to be expected. Further, in the manuscript form of the Shaṭṭārī *Gulzār-i abrār*, as Carl Ernst has pointed out, Muḥammad Ghawth's translation of yogic practice is described in terms of being a militant assertion of dominance.[8] It may become necessary to consider the writing of Sufi romances in Awadhi in a similar light to breath control, that is, useful, beneficial, even beautiful, when once rendered Islamic. Apart from the appropriation of certain Hindu practices,[9] the Shaṭṭāriyya proclaimed their method as swifter than that of other orders in effecting the transformation of their disciples' inner natures. Rizvi, in his account of the order, translates from the *Gulzār-i Abrār*:

---

[7] This triple competence is a valuable corrective to the tendency to treat Sufi and other literature in each of these languages as separable and sometimes completely isolated traditions, when often they were interconnected in the persons of the poets themselves.

[8] Behl "Rasa and Romance," p. 175, in which he refers to Carl W. Ernst, "Sufism and Yoga According to Muḥammad Ghawth," (Paper presented to the American Academy of Religion Conference, Anaheim, 1989), p. 6; later published in *Sufi*, 29 (1996), pp. 9–13.

[9] Shaykh Bahā'al-Dīn, the author of the *Risāla-i Shaṭṭārī*, in addition to regarding breath control as essential also advocates the use of Hindi words in *zikr* and the use of yogic postures for sitting, after first purifying the chosen place (Rizvi, *History of Sufism II*, p 156).

> According to the Shattariyya technique, the neophyte at the very beginning of his training is required to consider himself at the '*ayn* (essence) of Being and then descend step by step from the realm of self-manifestation of the Absolute to the phenomenal world. Then step by step he re-ascends and reaches the Divine sphere, effacing all traces of the stages of ascent. In contrast to this method, the other Sufis direct their disciples to ascend step by step from the realm of humanity to *Wahdat al-Wujud*.[10]

When summarizing Muḥammad Ghawth's influential work, the *Jawāhir-i khamsa*, Rizvi writes:

> The Shattars however adopted the role of lovers of Allah and reached their goal through *jazba* (ecstasy); therefore they were able to achieve in the initial stages of their mystical progression what others obtained at the final stage. The Shattariyya technique, observed Shaikh Muḥammad Ghaus, could only be acquired after obtaining perfection in the mystic practice of *abrar* and *akhyar*, and after mastering the secrets of exorcism by a mysterious invocation of the names of Allah. The Shattars did not have to pass through the stage of *fana'* (evanescence) or the final stage of *fana' al-fana'* (extinction in evanescence). Their mystical progression was designed to efface everything from the heart other than Allah. ... Their intuitive perception of Allah in their own beings was permanent. This state was described as *baqa' al-baqa'*, the everlasting reintegration of the spirit with Allah. Mystics of other *silsila*s were either conscious of their love for God or experienced ecstasy while the Shattars transcended these two states as separate conditions producing a new combination of their own.[11]

The ontological, metaphysical and cosmological framework of the Shaṭṭāriyya derived ultimately from Ibn 'Arabī, as it did for a number of orders, so there is no need to describe here what has been excellently handled elsewhere.[12] Shaykh Muḥammad Ghawth was a considerable systematizer of this material, and there were intermediary texts such as, for example, the prose work of Maghribī, the *Jām-i jahān namā*, which was the subject of at least three Shaṭṭārī commentaries. For present purposes it will be useful simply to mention that one of the most frequently used visual symbols in the exposition of this tradition was the circle. There are circles with a line across representing the *barzakh*, there are circles split into fifty-six divisions round the circumference, twenty-eight of which are filled with the Names of God, and the other twenty-eight filled with various aspects or elements of the created world, and there are circles divided into twelve parts giving the signs of the

[10] Rizvi, *ibid*., pp. 151–2.

[11] *Ibid*, p. 160.

[12] See in particular the two magisterial studies of W.C. Chittick: *The Sufi Path of Knowledge: Ibn al-'Arabī's Metaphysics of Imagination* (Albany: SUNY Press 1989) and *The Self-Disclosure of God: Principles of Ibn al-'Arabī's Cosmology* (Albany: SUNY Press1998). Both contain further bibliographies. From these works it is clear that there is often a wide divergence between what was understood as being the position of Ibn 'Arabī by medieval Sufi orders in India and that which is to be found in his actual works.

zodiac. However, the commonest symbol is that of a number of concentric circles, usually six, each designated as a world or level of manifestation. In the *Jawāhir-i khamsa* these are given as follows:

1.	*Martaba al-aḥadiyya*	*Lā ta'ayyun*	
2.	*Martaba al-waḥda*	*Ta'ayyun awwal*	Divine names and attributes
3.	*Martaba al-waḥdāniyya*	*Ta'ayyun thāni*	Names and Immutable entities
4.	*Martaba al-arwāḥ*	*Ta'ayyun thālis*	
5.	*Martaba al-mithāl*	*Ta'ayyun al-rābi'*	
6.	*Martaba al-ḥiss*	*Ta'ayyun al-khāmis*	

Sometimes the inner circle is the world of bodies, sometimes the outer circle, depending on the emphasis. The poet, Shaykh Manjhan, would have been familiar with all of this, which was incorporated into a body of practice which also included *dhikr*, the invocation of the Names, forty day periods of seclusion, visualization, fasts and dietary restrictions, to name some of the essential features of the Shaṭṭārī path.

THE GENRE OF THE SUFI *PREMĀKHYĀN* IN AWADHI (EASTERN HINDI)

There are four surviving works that stand as the main exemplars of the early tradition of writing Sufi romances in Awadhi. The first of these is *Candāyan* (1379) by Mawlānā Dā'ūd, a member of the Chishtī *silsila*, based on the folk tale of Lorik and Candā which still survives as an oral epic in north-east India today. This work is the first complete work to survive in Hindi, and is extremely early for this literature. McGregor writes of it: "With Dāūd the tradition of the Sufi literary romance, as illustrated by the Persian *mathnavī*s of Khusraw, becomes fully Indianized." Although we know the names of two other romances by Sufi poets, the next extant work is *Mrgāvatī* (1504) by Shaykh Quṭban, a disciple of the Suhrawardī Shaykh Burhān. The basis of the story is traditionally Indian, with the heroine able to transform herself into a hind with which the hero falls in love. The third work is the *Padmāvatī* of Muḥammad Jāyasī, as far as we know a Chishtī, written from about 1540, but reputed to have taken twenty years, so not completed until after the fourth work, the *Madhumālatī*, which was begun in 1545.

All four works are written in the same metre and form, alternating five lines of *chapais* with a *doha*. They all have an introductory prologue beginning with praise of God and Muḥammad and the four caliphs, praise of the king of the time and their immediate patron, and praise of their shaykh, followed by a disclaimer of their own poetic abilities. The stories are set in an ambience of the court, with princes, princesses, retainers and handmaidens, and wonderful gardens with picture galleries in them. Fairies, fabulous beings and magical events add to the imaginal nature of these works. Divine beauty is introduced early, the beloved being described in twenty verses, from the top of her head to at least her thighs, in what is termed a *nakh-śikh varnan*, a traditional Indian literary form parallel with the Persian *sarāpā*, and used with the same symbolism and usually alternating *jamālī* with *jalālī* verses. After this initial contact with Divine beauty, which is then taken away, the hero suffers the agony of love in separation, *viraha*, a traditional Indian literary concept. Disguising himself as a yogi, he sets out in search of the beloved. He undergoes all sorts of trials and tribulations, shipwrecks and demons, until finally he achieves union with the beloved through his achievements. Apart from the *Madhumālatī*, which will be examined in detail, all the other works have the hero already married to a queen or somebody else suggestive of the worldly side of life, or of the *nafs* rather than the *rūḥ*, who is then deserted when the hero sets off on his quest. He then sings a traditional *bārahmāsā* describing the sufferings of her love in each of the twelve months, which is sent to the hero. He brings the heroine back, but the two co-wives become jealous and quarrel and have to be reconciled. At the end, the hero is killed, suggestive of *fanā'*, and the two wives commit *sati* on the hero's funeral pyre.

Not only are these four works masterpieces but, I believe, they were designed to be masterpieces, constructed so as to make statements at a number of levels. With regard to the assertion of cultural dominance, they appropriated to themselves the poetics of *rasa* and *vyanjana*. *Rasa* is taste, juice, essence, and was used in Sanskrit poetics for the property in a poem that evoked the emotive response in the reader or hearer. *Rasa* is also the liquid essence produced by yogic practice that leads to the highest state, and *rasa* is also love. Since the fundamental motif in these works is the circulation of desire and love between the human and divine worlds, these poets found in place a poetics ideally suited to their purposes, and they exploited it to the full, appealing to their hearers as *rasik*s, people of taste, sensibility and discernment. *Vyajñana*, suggestion, was the means of arousing *rasa*, and this was ideally suited to their Sufi imagery and symbolism, since we have here not allegories, but works which, at every point, are suggestive of different orders of meaning and interpretation. They share one message in common, the assertion that their works have different levels of meaning; that they are deliberately polysemic and multivalent. This is not done through the one-to-one fixed analogies of allegory, but subtly, through the powers of *vyanjana*, suggestion. Although all of them are impressive at this symbolic level, the most spectacular in terms of poetics is *Padmavatī* by Muḥammad Jāyasī, truly the poets' poet, which must rate, in Sanskrit terms, as a *mahākāvya*.

THE STORY OF *MADHUMĀLATĪ*

The story itself begins at verse 44, following the prologue. It tells of the king of Kanaigiri, Sūrajbhānu, who had no son but was filled with longing for one.

He honours and serves a *muni* (ascetic) for several years and eventually the *muni* gives his queen a morsel of special food which results in her giving birth to a son. Astrologers give him the name Manohar and predict that in his fourteenth year he will meet his beloved and love will be born, but they will become separated so that he will have to wander as a *yogi* for a year. Thereafter he would be king in all his births. He is brought up and made king-designate at the age of 12. When he reaches the age of 14 some passing fairies, greatly taken by his good looks, resolve to find a princess of matching beauty for him and decide on Madhumālatī, the daughter of King Vikram Ray of Mahāras ('the place of the great *Rasa*': love). To compare them side by side, they transport Manohar on his bed and put it next to Madhumālatī's. Amazed by the resulting beauty they decide that the pair are a perfect match, after which they go off to play. Manohar wakes up and is overcome by Madhumālatī's beauty, which is then described in a *nakh-śikh-varnan* or *sarāpā*. When Madhumālatī wakes up and sees this unknown prince she is highly alarmed, but as they talk, love from a previous birth is born and they pledge eternal fidelity, make love (but not fully) and then fall asleep. The fairies return and, horrified by what they see, transport Manohar back to his palace. When Manohar wakes up he is consumed by the fire of love in separation (*viraha*). He tells his nurse Sahajā what had happened and various kinds of doctors try unsuccessfully to cure his condition. Finally Manohar decides, against his parents' wishes, to set off to find Madhumālatī and Mahāras. Disguised as a yogi he sets out with a large retinue but is shipwrecked by a storm at sea and all his party is lost. Manohar is washed up on an unknown shore, alone except for the name of Madhumālatī and the mercy of God.

He sets off into the forest and finds a hut in which there is a young, innocent princess called Pemā (Love) who is the daughter of King Citrasen of Citbisarāu (forgetfulness or peace of mind). She tells him how she had been out playing with her girlfriends and they had had to shelter in the picture gallery from a swarm of bees. When they came out a demon had seized her and was holding her here. Manohar in turn tells her about himself and Madhumālatī. She says she has known Madhumālatī since childhood and that he should stop worrying because she comes with her mother once a month to Citbisarāu to visit her. Hearing this, Manohar resolves to confront the demon and save Pemā. The demon returns and Manohar wounds it but it miraculously recovers. Pemā tells Manohar that the miraculous recovery is due to a tree whose fruits both cure and grant immortality. Having cut down the tree Manohar again confronts the demon, which he now succeeds in killing. He then takes Pemā to Citbisarāu where her parents are so grateful that they offer him everything, including Pemā in marriage. He declines, since his soul is pledged to Madhumālatī. He is becoming increasingly impatient to set off on his search when Pemā announces that Madhumālatī and her mother are arriving the next day. Next day, Manohar waits in the picture gallery:

Pemā brings Madhumālatī to him and then waits outside at the door. Manohar keeps fluctuating between consciousness and unconsciousness and Madhumālatī is angry with him at first for his cruelty in deserting her until their former love reasserts itself. They respect their vow not to make love fully until they are married and fall asleep in one another's arms. Meanwhile, Madhumālatī's mother, who had become worried wondering what had happened to her daughter, comes to the picture gallery and finds them asleep together. Beside herself with rage, she has Madhumālatī taken back to Mahāras and there, overwhelmed with shame, she puts a spell on Madhumālatī, who is turned into a bird. When Manohar wakes up in the picture gallery he finds Madhumālatī gone and sets off again in search, disguised as a yogi.

Madhumālatī, flies round most of the world in the form of a bird, in search of Manohar, suffering the pain of love in separation. Finally, she sees a prince called Tārāchand, who resembles Manohar and allows herself to be caught by him. He puts her in a cage and learns from her who she really is and what has happened to her. He leaves his kingdom to serve her, taking her to Mahāras, where her mother turns her back into a human being and offers her in marriage to Tārāchand. He declines, knowing she will only be happy with Manohar. Madhumālatī's parents write to Pemā telling her what has happened and Madhumālatī includes in a *bārahamāsā* an account of her suffering from separation in each of the twelve months. As the letter arrives, so does Manohar, still in the guise of a yogi. Further letters are exchanged and Madhumālatī and Manohar get married and enjoy their first full union. Tārāchand stays with them at Citbisarāu, until one day he sees Pemā and falls in love. Madhumālatī realizes that it is Pemā who has affected him and tells Manohar, who says that since Pemā had been offered to him it would be easy to arrange her marriage to Tārāchand. The marriage of Tārāchand and Pemā takes place and after a while they decide to return to their respective kingdoms. Goodbyes are said and eventually Manohar and Madhumālatī arrive in their kingdom where there is great celebration. Those who take refuge in the path of love will overcome death in this life and attain immortality.

The story's origin is not known but most probably it was created by Manjhan himself. It is characteristically Indian and utilizes only Indian themes and motifs. Within the story not only are there no references that could be called Islamic, but there are also no words of either Arabic or Persian origin within the text. What is particularly satisfying is the way two pairs of lovers are used to bring the story to a beautifully balanced and happy conclusion. The *nakh-shikh-varnan* and the *bārahamāsā* are the only two formal elements in the poem, which is told with a lightness and sensitivity throughout. It fully justifies Manjhan's claim to be pervaded by *prema-rasa*, the tone evocative of love, which is the *rājārasa*, the greatest of all the *rasa*s.

THE PROLOGUE OF *MADHUMĀLATĪ* AND THE TREATMENT OF LOVE

Prior to the beginning of the actual story at verse 44, in common with the other three extant works in this genre, there is a prologue, which in the case of *Madhumālatī* is longer and fuller than that of the others. It begins with six verses in praise of God which stress the Oneness of God in contrast to the multiplicity of forms in creation behind which God hides. These verses are essentially apophatic, in that they constantly emphasize the indescribability of God and the impossibility of expressing adequate praise. There then follow two verses, in praise of Muḥammad, from which it is clear where Manjhan stands:

> Listen now while I tell of him by whose very act of separation the Creator Himself became manifest. Taking bodily form, He Himself came to His creation, and the whole universe is of His essence. Then did the Lamp of Creation, whose name was Muḥammad, shine forth in glory everywhere. For him was creation fashioned and for him was the trumpet of Love sounded in the three worlds. The name of the king of the three worlds is Muḥammad, who was himself the inspiration of creation. At the pointing of his finger the moon was split in two and the universe took firm and final form when touched by the dust of his feet.
>
> Muḥammad is the root; the entire universe the branches. On his head the Creator placed a priceless crown. Equal to him no other is. He is the substance, all this is mere shadow. Everyone knows the Creator though He is hidden but no one knows Muḥammad although he is manifest. The Unseen One, He whom the senses cannot reach, He it was who assumed the form of Muḥammad and to this form he gave the name Muḥammad. This has no meaning other than the Unity of the One. I cry aloud and let the whole world hear: "Know that it is he who is manifest and bears the name Muḥammad who is the hidden Lord."[13]

These two verses are followed by a verse in praise of the four caliphs, which is in turn followed by four verses in praise of Islām Shāh, who is praised in the most extravagant terms for his might, his mercy and his bounty – which are not the qualities most people would have attributed to him. Eight verses then follow in fulsome praise of Shaykh Muḥammad Ghawth, who was Manjhan's own teacher. Two verses then are given in praise of Khizr Khān, who was a regional governor in Bengal for a short period and must have been Manjhan's sponsor. Next come three verses in praise of Speech which is described as a gift directly sent from God. "In the beginning, even before creation," writes Manjhan:

> Speech, was incarnate in the mouth of Hari. There was then but the one word OUM, in aspect both malevolent and benign, pervading totally this universe. God gave to Speech a high place in creation, for through Speech is man distinguished from the beasts. All know of Speech, and, through it, God Himself is manifest.

---

[13] *Madhumālatī*, vv. 7–8.

> No one has seen His form nor knows of His abode, yet, through Speech, God, Lord of the Three Worlds, became manifest in creation.[14]

Now come the four verses in praise of love which will be given in full since love is the true theme of the entire poem: indeed, the word for love begins the poem and a couplet on love ends it:

> Before all else was Love born, then began the process of creation. From Love creation sprang and Love resides in each created form. He alone within whose heart is born the pain of Love obtains the full rewards of life upon this earth. But he whose heart contains no Love can never know the mysteries of Sahaj. King of the three worlds is he to whom God gives the pain of Love in separation. Let no one think the pain of Love in separation to be grief, for it is through this alone that joy comes to the world. Blessed indeed is he whose life is given to suffering the pain of Love in separation.
>
> Love is the world's most precious jewel. Blessed is he in whose heart Love abides. It was for Love that God fashioned creation, and it is through Love that God Himself is manifest. The whole of creation is radiant with the glory of Love and nothing can there be to equal it. But few, alas, are those upon whom destiny bestows the boon of Love. This clarion call resounds down through the ages: "The King is he who in the path of Love gave up his head. Love is a market open to all, O people, come and buy. Those seeking benefits and bargains both should not allow this chance to slip away."
>
> The pain of Love came at that first moment of creation, but to feel this pain is only given to those who earned it in a former life. Love is the world's most treasured possession, of this you may be certain. From all that I have seen or heard this much I know: nothing is excluded from Love. All is light from birth to death for him in whose heart the torch of Love is burning. He whose heart contains the pangs of Love will be immortal and will never die. The pain of Love, wisdom and perfection, treasures such as these were never won by study but were given only to those on whom the Grace of God was pleased to fall.
>
> Wherever that man looks whose heart is marked by Love he sees the One who is unseeable. If within his soul enlightenment is born, then everywhere he looks he sees only himself. Further, if the tree of knowledge then bears fruit he will abandon all and partake of nothing else. For him within the world duality has ceased to be and everywhere he looks reveals eternal joy. It is you who are the lamp in the house of creation; never mistake the body for the soul. The joys and sorrows of this world are as many as it pleases but Love comes to you and colours everything and there can be nothing else.[15]

Love then is a divine energy, a cosmic force, the instrument of God's purpose and the means of God's manifestation. For humanity, Love is inseparable from suffering but this is a suffering which yields great blessing because it is the means by which the soul becomes self-conscious. This theme is developed in the following two verses, which are put into the mouth of Manohar:

---

[14] *Ibid.*, v. 25.
[15] *Ibid.*, vv. 27–30.

> Suffering overwhelmed mankind at the very beginning of creation. The lotus of Brahmā was the dwelling place of grief. The day pain entered creation the soul learnt of its own existence. The pain I feel for you was not born in me today but has been my companion from the start. Now I go on carrying the burden of this grief, sacrificing all the pleasures of the two worlds. I have given up my own self and accepted suffering for you. By dying I have tasted the nectar of immortality. O Madhumālatī, the pain of Love for you brings happiness to the world. Blessed is the life of the man in whose heart is born the pain of Love for you.
>
> On the day I heard creation had been born I released the bird of Love. It searched the three worlds but could not find a suitable abode so it returned to me and, entering my heart, found it to be so agreeable there that it never wished to fly away again. The three worlds asked it then: "Why are you so enamoured of the heart of man ?" "The pain of Love," it answered, "is the sole hope of mankind. Where there is pain I dwell." Where there is pain in the world Love has its dwelling. What can a poor man know of Love whose heart does not know pain ?[16]

Love then is the sole means of salvation for humanity. Through it the soul becomes self-conscious and attains immortality. The oft-quoted tradition attributed to the Prophet, "Die before you die" is reinforced by the indigenous Indian concept of the *jīvan-mukta*, somebody who has attained salvation while still alive. This first death, to self, is brought about through the sufferings of Love, and thus immortality is attained before the intervention of physical death. In the final couplet of the poem Manjhan again emphasizes that Love is the sole means available to humanity to attain salvation and immortality.

Following the verses on Love, Manjhan next addresses the soul, telling it that it is an ocean of treasures and wondering why it has filled itself up with pride. He then gives two verses of spiritual advice which must be unique in any Sufi romance:

> Come now and hear some practical advice. Sit down and meditate upon that formless Form which is devoid of attributes. Draw up the breath within your body and retain it so that the air may flow towards the fire which is in your heart. If then the air flows freely that fire begins to blaze consuming all the defects of your being. As long as you can stand to hold your breath throughout your body there will vibrate a mystic sound. Be there within that sound, for in this flame is heaven itself. Out of millions there are few indeed who can enjoy that heaven. It is to live in bliss and free from care within the Absolute Void.
>
> Abandon consciousness, take leave of reason and knowledge. With total bodily detachment give yourself to meditation. Then you will reach that state of union wherein your own true self is to be found. In that place wherein resides the Pure, the Void, the Absolute devoid of qualities, there will your self become detached from selfhood. Beyond knowledge lies unknowing in which your self will lose all knowledge of itself. There, in the mystic union of Sahaj, your own true self will be revealed. Within that impenetrable retreat remain motionless as if in sleep, in pure spontaneous communion, where 'you' does not exist nor any other, and there is no activity.[17]

---

[16] *Ibid.*, vv. 116–7.
[17] *Ibid.*, vv. 32–3.

The use of appropriate Hindu techniques and an interest in yoga were hallmarks of the Shaṭṭāriyya order and the above verses are in full accord with Manjhan's apparent intention to keep his text as Indian as possible. After two verses in praise of the fortress town of Cunar, Manjhan then gives a warning about the dangers of being deceived by Kali, who is an enchantress bent on leading the whole world astray. It would have been possible for Manjhan to have expressed his warning in terms of the dangerous prompting of the lower self, or *nafs*, or of the deviousness of Iblīs, but he sticks to the more Indian notion of the deceptiveness of the eponymous sponsor of the present degenerate age, the *kali yuga*. Finally, he addresses five verses to the reader asking that any poetic mistakes might be overlooked since he has made enjoyment his sole aim. This disclaimer of poetic expertise and the pre-empting of any criticism was very much a feature of the time. He makes full play of the wide range of meanings of the word *rasa*, treating the reader as a *rasik*, a connoisseur of fine taste and discernment as well as a 'lover'. He ends the prologue with the words: "and now I sing upon the theme of Love which is the very crown of all enjoyment."[18]

THE SYMBOLISM OF *MADHUMĀLATĪ*

Manjhan wrote against a background of presuppositions and expectations that went far beyond those of the genre of the Sufi *premākhyān* in Awadhi. Intertextuality was certainly important, in that the poets acknowledged their predecessors in the genre, typically citing earlier authors' heroes and heroines as examples of true lovers, and largely following the conventions that had become established, but at the same time always with the intention of somehow going one better. The larger background was provided, on the one hand, by the poetics of symbolism found in Sufi poetry – particularly Persian – and, on the other hand, by the poetics of *rasa* and suggestion found in Indian literature. Particularly relevant in this case were the *Gītagovinda* of Jayadeva and the poetry of Cadīdāsa and Vidyāpati, which were widely known in Bengal and Bihar and which were pervaded by an interplay between profane and divine love similar to that found in Sufi poetry. It was expected that the beloved, the lover, beauty, demons and various types of difficulties would all have at least a double reference. Symbolism is not allegory, and it was not expected that a crude one-to-one correspondence should be maintained consistently throughout a poem, and certainly not in ones as long as these Sufi romances. The approach was altogether more subtle, using suggestion and allusion to hint at symbolic levels which were co-present with the literal so that in any one context, in any particular verse or passage, one level might be applicable, or two or several. The richness of a symbol lies in its multivalence;

---

[18] *Ibid.*, v. 43.

the number of its levels being determined by the various levels of understanding and response it evokes in the reader. Underhill in describing mystical symbolism writes:

> The greater the suggestive quality of the symbol used, the more answering emotion it evokes in those to whom it is addressed, the more truth it will convey. A good symbolism, therefore, will be more than a mere diagram, or mere allegory: it will use to its utmost the resources of beauty and passion, will bring with it hints of mystery and wonder, bewitch with dreamy periods the mind to which it is addressed. Its appeal will not be to the clever brain, but to the desirous heart, the intuitive sense, of man.[19]

Such a person is precisely the *rasik* to whom Manjhan addresses his poem.

Within *Madhumālatī* Manjhan has intertwined three classic types of symbol: that of the traveller on the way, the *sālik*; that of the lover seeking the beloved, the *'āshiq;* and that of the seeker of inner transformation, the *sādhak*. By the sixteenth century it had become a well-established convention in this genre that the lover separated from the beloved should set out on his search disguised as a yogi, and in particular as a Nāth-panthī, an order of yogis who claimed Gorakhnāth as their eponymous founder. Although the yogic symbolism is not so fully elaborated in *Madhumālatī* as in *Padmāvatī*, nevertheless Manjhan uses a number of key concepts and terms. The highest mystical state is often termed *sahaj*, a kind of spontaneous emptiness, in which is experienced *mahārasa*, the great *rasa* – which significantly, is the name of Madhumālatī's city. Manohar has a nurse called Sahajā, and the name of Tārāchand's city is Paunerī, which is perhaps to be taken as indicative of *pavana* or breath, which is controlled in yogic disciplines. Citbisarāu can mean either 'peacefulness of mind' or 'forgetfulness of mind', and it is the home of Pemā, Love. Throughout the poem there are numerous images drawn from yogic usage, as for instance when Manohar tells Madhumālatī that he is the sun and she is the moon, which clearly refers to the *iḍā* and *pingalā nādīs* or psychic veins which are so important for reaching the highest state of *sahaj*.

The convention of the genre is that the yogic imagery and symbolism are a disguise, and, in fact, Manohar has always shed his yogic guise by the time he meets Madhumālatī. Underneath the yogic disguise is the *'āshiq* and the *sālik*, the lover and the traveller or Sufi, with which we move to the more usual symbolic conventions of Sufi poetry. Manohar here would be the soul of man, which is either granted a foretaste of Divine Beauty, Madhumālatī, or else recalls the Love and Beauty of God from the time before the spirit entered existence, which would explain how the love between Manohar and Madhumālatī pre-existed in a former life and was simply reawakened. Whichever the case, Manohar is seriously affected by the pain of love in

---

[19] E. Underhill, *Mysticism* (London: Image Books, Doubleday 1990), p. 126.

separation, *viraha*, and becomes ill. Doctors, often symbolic of *'aql*, intelligence, in the sense here of the rational mind and learning, are unable to understand the illness or effect a cure, because it is caused by Love. Eventually Manohar sets out on his search, encountering many difficulties, including being shipwrecked. He then meets Pemā, Love, who has to be set free from a demon, but it is Love that then becomes his guide or *murshid* and leads him to Madhumālatī, whom he then encounters for a short time again. If all the difficulties and struggles that Manohar endures and undergoes are taken as symbolizing Underhill's second stage of the mystical path, the *via purgativa* – the first being the stage of Awakening represented by Manohar's first encounter with Madhumālatī – then the meeting in the picture gallery arranged by Pemā must be considered to be the third stage, the *via illuminativa*, or, as some Sufi schemes have it, *ma'rifa*, Illumination. It is in the short meeting in the picture gallery that Madhumālatī for the first and only time indicates, on Manohar's requesting her to draw back the veil of her locks, that her beauty is something more than human beauty and cannot be seen with one's ordinary eyes.

Between the stage of illumination and the fourth and final stage of Union, the *via unitiva*, lies the 'dark night of the soul'. This is beautifully represented by Madhumālatī, the image and experience of God, being turned into a bird which, after a year flying around in search of Manohar, finally allows itself to be caught by Tārāchand, a prince who resembles Manohar. If on the level of yogic symbolism Tārāchand is representative of breath, on the Sufi level of symbolism he is representative of selflessness, of devoted selfless service to Madhumālatī, for whom he deserts his own kingdom and for which he neither expects nor is willing to accept anything in return. If it is through Pemā, Love, that Manohar is able to meet Madhumālatī, it is through the selfless service of Tārāchand that Madhumālatī is able to reach Manohar. It is at this point that there is an interesting departure from the conventions of the genre. In the three other works the *bārahmāsā*, which is addressed to the lover and tells of the different sufferings of the beloved in each of the twelve months of the year, is put into the mouth of a deserted wife who, in the symbolism, is taken to be either the lower self, the *nafs*, or else the world, or both. Manjhan goes deliberately against this convention. He gives the *bārahmāsā* to Madhumālatī, who expresses it in a letter she writes to Manohar when she has been restored to human form by her repentant mother. In doing this Manjhan is able to express, in a strong and, in terms of the genre, surprising way, the love and yearning that God has for the human soul.

The final state of the mystical path, Union, is handled in two stages by Manjhan, within the tradition of Indian marriage. Certainly in the case of child marriages, after the actual marriage ceremony the child bride remained with her parents until she reached the appropriate age, when there was a second ceremony, the *gavana*, at which all the goodbyes were said and she set out for her husband's home. It is not uncommon in mystical literature to represent

Union as a marriage of the soul to God. Nor is it uncommon to represent some aspect of Union in sexual terms. Saint Teresa of Avila, who was coincidentally Manjhan's contemporary, did both. Manjhan has a grand marriage ceremony followed by the first night of full Union and then there is a period which allows Tārāchand to fall in love with Pemā and for the pair to get married, so that all four form an integrated foursome who live together in pleasurable harmony. After a while, the time comes for the second ceremony, the leave-taking and goodbyes and the final setting off. Here Manjhan not only deals with the leave-taking from parents, relatives, friends and retainers but also has a wonderful passage in which Madhumālatī takes her leave of the material world, saying good-bye to the walls, the doors, the ramparts, her bed, her clothes and her toys. The four then leave the conditioned world and set out. After a while Tārāchand and Pemā have to say their goodbyes as the paths diverge. Manohar and Madhumālatī travel on into the unconditioned world from which Manahar originally came, until he reaches his former kingdom where the couple are received with great rejoicing. In Manjhan's treatment of the unitive state there is the initial act of Union, then the unification of human love with selfless service and their integration within the human soul united with God. Then there is the separation and detachment from the conditioned world, that of materiality and relationships, and finally the separation from human love and selfless service, before the human soul in Union moves off into the unconditioned world from whence it came. This is the way Manjhan treats the *via unitiva* which in some Sufi schemes is termed *ḥaqīqat*, Reality.

Beneath this Sufi symbolic level, which accords so well with Underhill's account of the stages in the spiritual path, it is possible to identify a further level of specifically Shaṭṭāriyya symbolism which encompasses the general Sufi symbolism but adds a further particularity. Here the two passages from Rizvi on the Shaṭṭārī spiritual path, quoted earlier, will be helpful. It will be recalled that the neophyte, here Manohar, is required at the very beginning of his spiritual journey to place himself at the very essence of Being, which would mean fixing in his awareness the image of God and Divine Beauty, here Madhumālatī. The whole of the episode of the fairies and the first meeting in which love is reawakened between the two coming from a former birth, which Manjhan describes as both real and unreal at the same time, could be taken as precisely this process. Then the neophyte is required to descend one step after another from this realm of the Self-Manifestation of the Absolute to the phenomenal world. This Manohar does from the moment he wakes up to discover that Madhumālatī is gone and that he is suffering the burning pains of Love in separation, *viraha*. His journey, culminating in the shipwreck, is clearly representative of precisely such a descent, whose final result is that he is cast up on the unknown shore of what is presumably the phenomenal world, alone except for the name of Madhumālatī and the mercy of God. It is the name of Madhumālatī that is to prove his eventual salvation because, when he encounters Pemā, human Love, who is imprisoned by the demon, it is Madhumālatī's name that Pemā recognizes and which gives Manohar the courage to confront the demon. The battle with the demon is interesting too because it clearly refers to a major transformation in the disciple's nature, through destroying the lower inhibiting forces that constrain the freedom of Love, Pemā, portrayed as young, innocent and unawakened. The turning point comes when Manohar hears about the tree whose fruit restores the demon, for he then knows "that God had given him victory," thereby acknowledging his second companion, the Mercy of God. The demon killed, he is then guided by Pemā to her home, Citbisarāu. The word *cita* means either 'mind' or 'consciousness' but *-bisarāu* could either derive from *viṭrāma*, rest, calm, tranquillity, or from the verb meaning 'to forget' or 'be forgotten', so that it can mean both tranquillity of mind and forgetfulness of everyday consciousness. It is to this place that Madhumālatī comes once a month and from which Manohar, the disciple, begins his ascent back to the divine sphere. But the nature of Manohar's problems change. Hitherto he has encountered the difficulties of being separated from God and descending to the phenomenal world and also the confrontation with the lower inhibiting forces in his own nature: now, he confronts temptations. He is offered everything by Pemā's parents in their gratitude: the kingdom of Citbisarāu, tranquillity of mind and Pemā, Love, as his bride. So great is his commitment to Madhumālatī that he is able to decline. When he is with Madhumālatī again there is the further temptation to act as if they were married, that is, as if this state were permanent – in Sufi terminology as if the *ḥāl*, state, were *maqām*, a permanent station – but they both remember their former vow to wait until they are properly married. Further difficulties are now caused by the queen of Mahāras, Madhumālatī's mother, who not only brings to an end their transient and partial reunion but turns Madhumālatī into a bird. The implication here is that the image of God and the awareness of Divine Beauty is somehow flying around longing to reach Manohar but unable to do so. Help comes in the form of Tārāchand, representative of service and selflessness, who lures Madhumālatī down with pearls, which in Shaṭṭārī symbolism are representative of *ḥaqīqat*, or Reality. Through Tārāchand, marriage and final union are finally accomplished and, after the integration of Tārāchand and Pemā and their eventual return to their own respective places, the couple return to the unconditioned realm from which they came in the very beginning. The Shaṭṭārī disciple has reached the state of *baqā' al-baqā'*, everlastingly reintegrated with God. In the other poems of this genre the heroes all die and their wives commit *satī* on their husbands' funeral pyres. This is symbolic of *fanā'*, or the annihilation of the self, but in the Shaṭṭārī path there is no *fanā'*, but rather the aim to reach beyond this still further to *baqā'*, everlasting Union. In *Madhumālatī* then there are no deaths and in this sense the Shaṭṭārī poem may be said to go one better than the other poems in the genre.

While it is hoped that this analysis of the three possible levels of symbolism has been helpful, it has to be emphasized that this is not how the symbolism works. All three levels are fully intertwined, perfectly blended with the underlying literal story into a fully integrated whole. In fact, they are not levels of the story at all, they are levels of interpretation. The richness of a symbol derives from the various levels of interpretation it can evoke. Its power lies in its form and shape and its potentiality for analogy. Sufi writers considered that form, shape and analogy had the power to settle within the reader or hearer and transform the understanding, which is why there are so many Sufi teaching stories and anecdotes. The great Sufi poet and storyteller Rūmī describes this as the process by which blood is able to turn into milk. It will be apparent from all that has been said so far that Manjhan produced a beautifully balanced and delightful poem, rich in its potentiality for mystical interpretation. This, it might be thought, was enough – but closer examination of the form and shape and structure of the work indicate that there is much more to it than that.

THE SYMMETRY AND STRUCTURE OF *MADHUMĀLATĪ*

In my previous essay on *Madhumālatī* I was, I believe, far too tentative in suggesting not only that the plot of *Madhumālatī* is symmetrical but that the actual structure of narration of the poem is as well. After reading the entire poem several times a number of questions had arisen which demanded answers. These were as follows. Why does the point referred to above, when Manohar learns of the restorative tree and says that he knows that God had given him victory over the demon, which constitutes the true turning point in the story, come exactly halfway through the story in terms of verses? Why does his shipwreck and the introduction of Pemā come exactly one third of the way through, and the introduction of Tārāchand and his capture of the bird Madhumālatī come exactly two-thirds of the way through? Why does the episode with the fairies occupy precisely the second eighth of the poem ? Why is the ultimate union of Manohar and Madhumālatī at exactly five-sixths of the way through the poem, and why do the leave-takings begin at exactly eleven-twelfths? To these initial questions there are more that could be added. Why is the end of the first meeting of the couple at verse 135 exactly 180 verses, a third of the text, from their second meeting at verse 315? Why is the final union at verse 450 exactly 270 verses, half of the total, from Manohar's shipwreck and total solitude at verse 180? And why is Pemā's story to Manohar in the forest exactly 270 verses from the story of Tārāchand falling in love with her and marrying her, and spread over the same number of verses? Such proportionality and precision cannot possibly have arisen accidentally: it must have been deliberate. These are clear indications to readers that they are to probe further and uncover the structure of the text and the fullness of

Manjhan's purpose. Before doing this, however, there are some general considerations that need to be noted, if for no other reason than to provide reassurance that what is being proposed is soundly based and not the outcome of whimsy.

Traditional scholarship, founded on the principles of textual and literary criticism, has tended to approach pre-modern texts from all over the world as if they were modern and Western. This means that scholars have had regard to the meaning of sentences which built up sequentially to produce the 'content' of a work, which was then amenable to some form of hermeneutics. It is now increasingly becoming apparent that such an approach, which could be called micro-compositional, while necessary, is no longer sufficient. Many works from the ancient and medieval worlds additionally have macro-compositional features such as ring-composition, chiasmus and thematic parallelism, which place segments of text and content in a non-sequential juxtapositioning by means of thematic parallelism according to well-known macro-compositional conventions. This can produce a higher order of significance from which it is often possible to see not so much what a text means but what it is seeking to do. Thus, a recent analysis of a thirteenth-century Sanskrit text written in praise of the greatness of Banaras has shown that it was written in the form of a *maṇḍala*, with the eight directions clearly marked when the text was plotted around a circle. This was particularly appropriate, in that the content of the text sought to establish the cosmologization of Banaras, and the role and function of a *maṇḍala* is to connect the microcosm with the macrocosm.[20] There are many other examples of texts that have been structured on well-established macro-compositional principles, from Homer, Herodotus and Virgil through various books of the Old Testament to *The Confessions of St Augustine* and many mystical works of ultimately Neoplatonic inspiration in both Christianity and Islam. *The Third Spiritual Alphabet* of Francisco de Osuna is one such work. The production of a work in the ancient and medieval worlds was a highly professional and deliberate undertaking, and there are always intelligent reasons why one thing comes before another and is in the place that it is. The notion that a work should be structured by nothing more than the accidental sequentiality of an author's stream of consciousness would be astonishing to the pre-modern mind, as would be the idea that inspiration is of necessity chaotic and unconventional as opposed to being intelligent and ordered. The growing body of studies uncovering the macro-compositional structures of pre-modern texts and showing how these structures accomplished different kinds of purposes should give some confidence that the approach here is no longer to be thought of as being in some way eccentric. The failure of the modern mind to detect these structures in texts before is probably due to

[20] I. Bermijn, "An Investigation into the Fifty-six Vināyakas in Banaras and their Origin," 1998, an unpublished doctoral dissertation submitted to the University of London.

nothing more than the fact that we have lost the conventions and the genres which would tell us how to read the works.[21]

Returning to *Madhumālatī*, it is necessary to answer the questions posed by Manjhan's proportionality and precision. One of the Shaṭṭārīs' most persistent symbols is the circle, in which they follow Ibn 'Arabī, as has already been indicated. The story of Madhumālatī and Manohar is unquestionably circular. Their love comes from a former birth and they will be king and queen together in all their births. Accordingly, the poem was plotted round a circle, at which it became clear what was going on. The poem has 539 verses in the critical text which has substantial support from the various manuscript traditions. When the poem is plotted in this way, verse 1 in praise of God and beginning with the word Love also becomes verse 540, which is taken to be the total number of verses. Verse 270, the turning point, occurs exactly at the bottom of the circle and divides it into two halves. The other proportionalities raised in the questions above, when plotted around the circle, show that Manjhan in fact marks nine points around the circle, as shown in figure 5. Since the intervals between succeeding points is forty-five verses, it is clear that Manjhan's complete design has twelve terms.[22] The full symmetry is shown in figure 6.

What then is the standing of this diagram? On one hand, it is apparent that Manjhan constructed it as the design of his poem, the overall plan to which he wrote. It would, incidentally, have been at least as difficult to write with such a plan as without, since it creates its own constraints and problems for an author, even if he does know exactly where he is going. But the issue must be: why this design? And what purpose does it fulfil? The answer is surely that this design would most effectively highlight and underline the various levels of symbolism, on the one hand, and, on the other hand, would produce a beautifully proportioned and symmetrical story. The clues to the symmetrical design are given by the proportionality, as has been demonstrated, and these

[21] The Romantic movement, to which we are still heirs in some sense, did not help in this regard, and one must be sympathetic to the dilemma of the postmodernist anxious not to privilege any one passage over another when that is precisely what a text is telling the reader to do.

[22] A preliminary analysis of the macro-compositional structure of the two other complete works of the genre, *Mrgāvatī* and *Padmāvatī*, suggests that they too are similarly organized but not necessarily as twelve-term symbols. For example, in *Padmāvatī* it is highly suggestive that union is first achieved exactly halfway through the poem, and the description of the Beloved begins at verse 99, which must surely be connected with the ninety-nine Names and Attributes of God. In *Mrgāvatī* the description of the Beloved occupies a similarly precise proportion and position to that in *Madhumālatī*. Further analysis would be needed to uncover the precise structures of these other works but it is enough for present purposes to know that this feature is not unique to Manjhan and constituted a hitherto unsuspected convention of the genre. In the case of *Candāyan* the text is incomplete, but if the structure is identified from the existing portions it should easily be possible to establish at least the total number of verses in the original complete text.

Figure 5: Manjhan's Clues

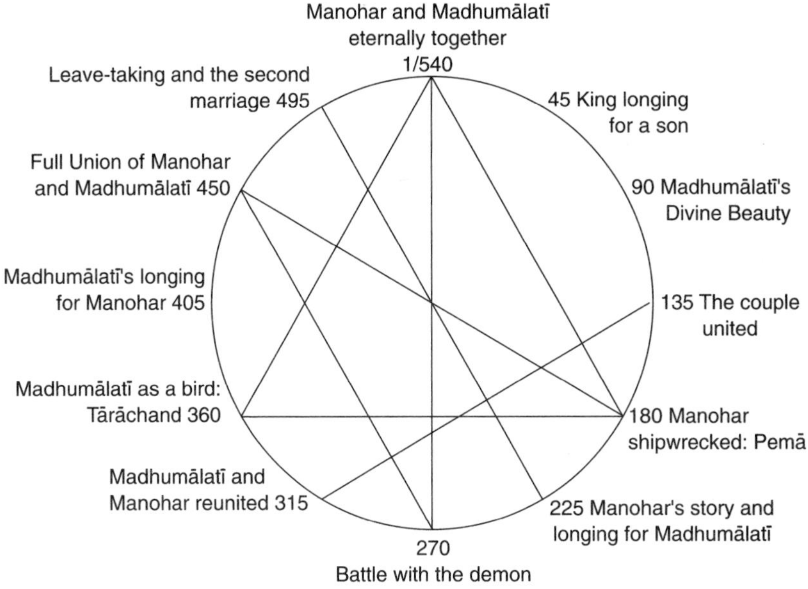

Figure 6: The Full Symmetry

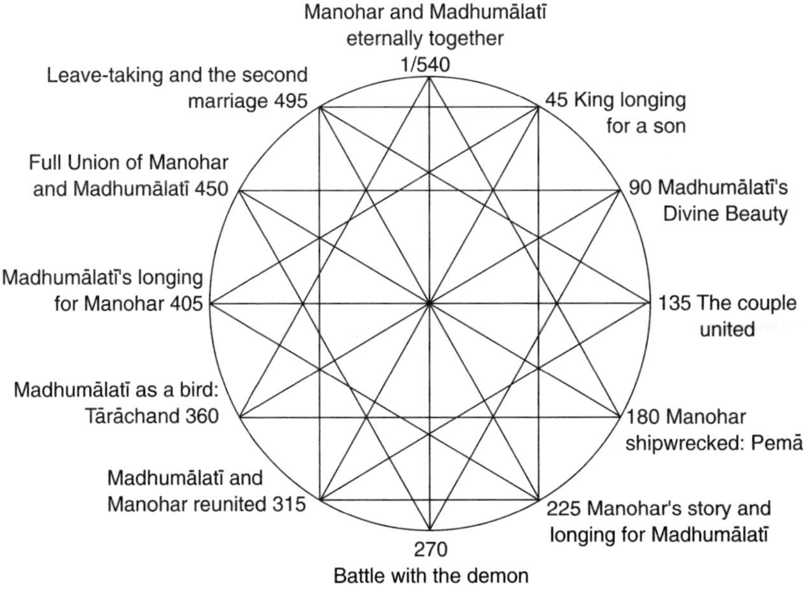

clues are to the symmetry as suggestion is to the symbolism. Symbolism ultimately depends on the form and shape of situations that will permit by analogy as many interpretations as there are contexts of understanding. Further, these levels of interpretation are co-present, in that they stack up all at the same time and one does not exclude another. The symmetry and the various systems that go together to make the total design are closely integrated with the symbolism but are able to take it even deeper and make it even richer. Before looking at the various systems, though, it is interesting to look at the three points that were not initially apparent as clues to the symmetry.

Verse 45 is the first of these points. The prologue consists of forty-three verses and the story seems to begin at verse 44, which introduces King Sūrajbhānu, the Glory of the Sun, who reigns in Kanaigiri, the Mountain of Gold. This verse is rather like setting up the pieces in chess, it does not itself start the game. The story really begins in verse 45, which gives the motivation for the whole story: the king had everything except a son, for whom he yearned to complete his happiness and to continue his line. Without this desire, nothing else would have happened. Placing it at this highlighted position in the design causes one to reflect, and various symbolic possibilities open up. The shape of the situation is suggestive of the Creator who prior to creation loved that He be known, as the tradition has it. Manjhan in his prologue puts this Love prior to creation, just as he suggests that Muḥammad was the real reason for creation. In the description of Manohar's education particular care is taken over his learning all words and their various meanings, just as Adam was taught the names of everything. So this king, whose very name and the name of whose kingdom are so suggestive, fits into the shape of the situation of creation as the Creator, whose Love is like the king's longing, and whose offspring is at once creation, Muḥammad and Adam, just as the king's offspring is Manohar. Such rich symbolism would perhaps have gone unnoticed had the symmetrical design of the work not given this verse a special emphasis.

The other two points that require attention are verses 90 and 405. Both occur in the midst of longer sequences. Verse 90 is part of the *nakh-śikh-varnan* or *sarāpā*, which runs from verse 77 to verse 97; verse 405 is part of the *bārahmāsā*, which runs from around 401 to 417. The actual verses, being part of longer rhetorical set-pieces, are not able to highlight the points in the symmetry but in these two cases it is the geometry of the points themselves that underline the great importance of the two set-pieces. Here are two excellent examples of the mutual reinforcement of the symmetry and the symbolism. The *nakh-śikh-varnan*, which describes Madhumālatī from the top of her head to her thighs as she sleeps, is symbolic of the Divine Names and Attributes. It alternates verses treating Divine Beauty and Grace, *asmā-i jamālī*, with those treating of God's might and majesty, *asmā-i jalālī*. Although this convention with its imagery and allusions was very well established, and indeed had been the subject of a near contemporary work in Hindi giving a Sufi interpretation along the same lines for some genres of sensuous Hindi religious poetry,[23] this in a way diminishes the importance attached to this sequence of verses treating of Divine Beauty and Majesty which, as has been shown, the Shaṭṭārī neophyte had to reach and plant deep within his being at the very beginning of the spiritual journey. The *bārahmāsā* too is conventional, although the way that Manjhan uses it in this poem is not, as has already been discussed. Again, it is the geometry of the design which places particular emphasis here on the Love that God has for humanity, by placing the *bārahmāsā* in its precise position three-quarters of the way through the text.

Perhaps one of the most unexpected uses of Manjhan's design is the way it reinforces and develops the yogic level of symbolism. When the circle is bisected vertically by the line 1/540–270, it draws attention to the fact that the right-hand side of the circle is told mainly from the point of view of Manohar, while the left-hand side is told mainly from the point of view of Madhumālatī. It will be recalled that Manohar at one point said to Madhumālatī that he was the sun and she was the moon, which would be interpreted yogically as the *iḍā* and *piñgala nāḍīs*, the two main psychic veins which run up either side of the spine and connect with the central psychic channel, the *suṣumnā*, which runs up from the base of the spine to the top of the head. It is possible to locate the *iḍā nāḍī* on the right of the circle as the line 45–225, and the *piñgala nāḍī* on the left as the line 495–315. This would make the *suṣumnā nāḍī* the line 1/540–270. Then it becomes quite clear what is implied. The battle with the demon to release Pemā, Love, is precisely the battle undertaken by every yogi who seeks to set free the force of *kunḍalinī* so that the *śakti*, or energy, can travel up the *suṣumnā*, awakening the various *cakra*s it passes through until it reaches the topmost *cakra*, the *sahasrāra cakra*, where it effects the final integration, represented as the union of Śiva and Śakti, and brings about the highest state of Sahaj. The yogic symbol is identified in figure 7 by emboldening the relevant lines. It is also apparent from the diagram that the symbol locates the seven *cakra*s; the *mūlādhāra cakra*, wherein the *śakti* is detained, is at the base of the *suṣumnā nāḍī* represented by 270; the *svādhiṣṭhāna cakra*, which is more or less the sex centre, is represented as the intersection of the *suṣumnā* line by the line 315–225; the *manipūra cakra*, the navel, is represented as the intersection of line 360–180; the *anāhata cakra*, the heart *cakra*, as the intersection of the line 405–135; the *viśuddha* or throat *cakra* as the intersection of line 450–90; the *ajña cakra*, situated between the eyebrows, is at the intersection of line 495–45 and 540 is the *sahasrāra cakra*. In this way Manjhan has included a full model of the Tantric psycho-spiritual process within his design, astonishing well integrated with the symbolism and the story. The story, however, makes Manohar only disguise himself as a yogi,

---

[23] The *Ḥaqā'iq-i Hindī* of Mīr 'Abdul Wāḥid Bilgrāmī, which was written in 1566.

Figure 7: The Yogic Symbol

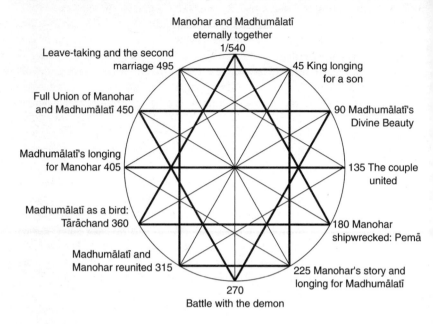

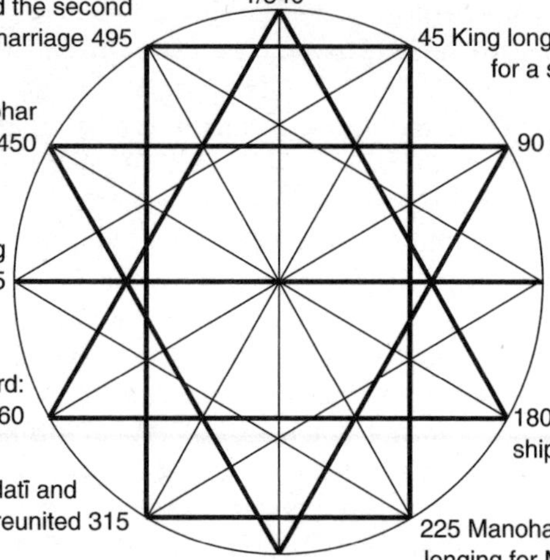

not actually become one, so how does Manjhan somehow indicate this in his visual model? In fact, the two interpenetrating triangles 540–180–360 and 450–90–270 within the circle are the recognized symbol for the *anāhata cakra*, the heart *cakra*, and it is as if Manjhan, in situating his yogic model within the heart *cakra*, is indicating that the main purpose he sees in setting Pemā free and letting the energy flow is to awaken the heart to love.

It can now be noted, before examining the four triangles within the circle, that the six lines across the circle that act as spokes in a wheel, are all arranged so that if Manohar and Madhumālatī are together at one end of the spoke, they are separate at the other. This may be an accidental outcome of the narration but there is very little that has been detected so far that is not fully deliberate, so it is worth considering what this could imply. Since they all intersect at the very centre of the circle it could be indicating that, from the highest standpoint, Love in union and Love in separation are simply two different aspects of the same power of Love which, at the centre, is the one Love. This representation of the *coincidentia oppositorum* of Love at the very centre of his design is yet another facet of the architecture of Manjhan's text.

Turning now to figure 8, it is possible to identify specific characteristics in each of the four triangles. Again, the relevant lines are emboldened. The triangle 1/540–180–360 is *the triangle of outer narration*. At 1/540 there are the two main characters, Manohar and Madhumālatī, eternally together,

Figure 8: The Four Triangles

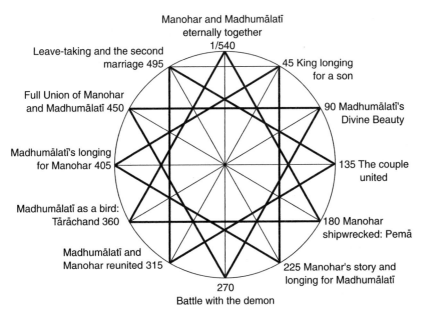

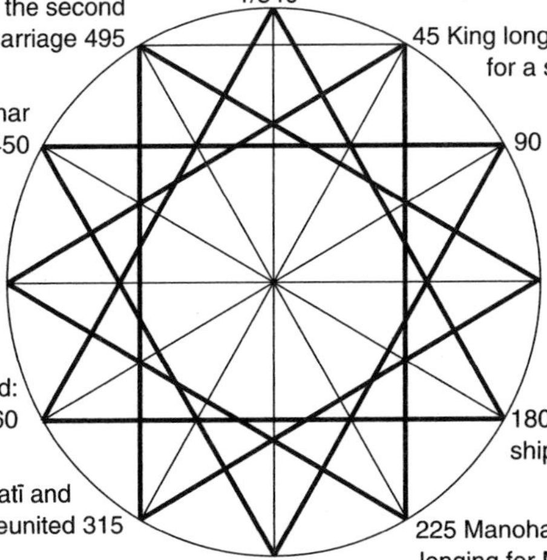

waiting to begin the story. At 180 Manohar is totally alone and just about to meet Pemā, while, at 360, Madhumālatī in the form of a bird, suffering from *viraha*, is about to allow herself to be caught by Tārāchand. Statically, the three points identify the four central characters in the poem; dynamically, however, they represent the different starting points for three separate processes which work together to produce the final successful outcome. The first process is the story of Manohar and Madhumālatī which starts at 1 and goes right round the circle until it reaches 540 again. The second process, beginning at 180, is the story of Pemā, which could only begin when Manohar was shipwrecked and washed up on the shore near to where she was detained. While this is an independent process and story, it is mutually dependent on the first process or story of Manohar and Madhumālatī. Pemā's story continues very nearly to the end of the poem. The third process or story, beginning at 360, is that of Tārāchand, which again is an independent story but is mutually dependent on both the first and the second processes or stories. Thus this triangle shows the main characters and the three separate but mutually dependent stories working together in harmony to produce the final harmonious ending.

The next triangle to be considered is the inverted triangle 90–270–450 which interpenetrates the triangle of outer narration. This triangle is *the triangle of inner narration*; it is the inner meaning of the first triangle. It shows Manohar establishing his contact with Divine Beauty, then the descent to the phenomenal world and the struggle with the lower forces of that world and finally the ascent and the attainment of Union. It is, at once, Shaṭṭārī symbolism, Sufi symbolism, Neoplatonic symbolism and universal mystical symbolism. The two triangles taken together show the outer narration interpenetrated by the inner; the *bāṭin* within the *zāhir* in Sufi terminology.

The triangle 45–225–405 can be called the *triangle of Love and yearning*. Point 45 has already been discussed: it was found that the king's yearning for a son to continue his line, which is the primary motivation for the whole story, is analogous to and symbolic of the longing of God to be known and the Love of God which inspires and permeates creation. Point 225 is Manohar longing for Madhumālatī, both human Love and yearning and also the Love and yearning of humanity for God. Point 405 is again both the human Love and longing of Madhumālatī for Manohar, and also the Love and longing of God for humanity. Finally, the triangle 135–315–495 is *the triangle of Union and unification*. The first union is at point 135, the second at 315 and the third is at 495, the culmination of the final union prior to the return to the unconditioned world.

It is possible to see how these four triangles relate together to form a tetrad almost along the lines of Aristotle's *aitiae*. The literal story and the characters provide the ground, the actual material in need of transformation, which would be Aristotle's material cause. The goal or ideal is the descent to the phenomenal world and the ascent back to God, which would be the formal cause. The instrumental term is Love and yearning, which is Aristotle's efficient cause, and the intentional term, the aim of humanity, Union, would be Aristotle's final cause. This tetrad of triads is clearly deliberate and one of the primary systems or facets of Manjhan's twelve-term structure. Before moving to what is in many ways the most remarkable aspect of Manjhan's symmetrical structural symbolism, it can be noted that there is another tetrad formed by the line 1/540–270 crossing the line 405–135, which effectively divides the circle into four quarters. These, interestingly, correspond to Underhill's four stages in the mystical path. The first quarter is the awakening, the second quarter the *via purgativa*, the third quarter the *via illuminativa* and the fourth quarter the *via unitiva*. In Manjhan's terms they would more appropriately be identified as Union, Descent, Ascent and Reunion along classic Neoplatonic lines.

Finally, there remains to be examined perhaps the most fundamental aspect or facet of Manjhan's structure and design, which informs the storytelling, imagery and symbolism at every level. This is the way in which Manjhan has made his cosmology fundamental to his design, a cosmology which derived ultimately from the Greatest Shaykh, Ibn 'Arabī, but which reached Manjhan through a number of interpreters and intermediaries as the received Shaṭṭārī cosmology. In the second section of this study the six worlds or levels of manifestation were given as they are arranged by Shaykh Muḥammad Ghawth in his work the *Jawāhir-i khamsa*. These are represented by Manjhan as a hierarchy of six levels into which he divides the circle, as shown in figure 9.

Figure 9: Manjhan's Cosmology

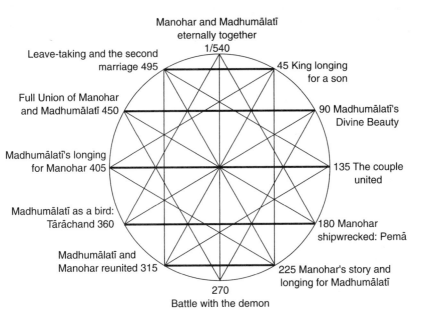

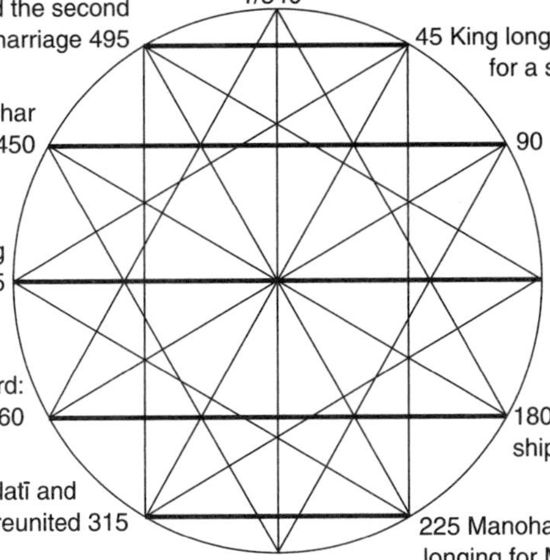

The first level is that segment of the circle above the line 495–45 which is the *Martaba al-aḥadiyya*, or the degree of Oneness, which is entirely beyond attribution and determination. The second level is the *Martaba al-waḥda*, or the degree of Unity, which is the first determination or manifestation. This occupies the segment of the circle between the line 495–45 and the line 450–90. To this level belong the Divine Names and Attributes which exist in the Divine Presence and are identical with it. The third level is that of the *Martaba al-waḥdāniyya*, which occupies that segment of the circle which lies between the lines 450–90 and 405–135. Here Divine Unity is found in the *a'yān al-thābita*, the immutable entities or prototypes by which the multiple forms of creation are differentiated. They never enter existence themselves and only their shadows are manifested at lower levels. The fourth level is that of the *Martaba al-arwāḥ*, which occupies the segment between the lines 405–135 and 360–180. This is the level of spirits or souls, the *'ālam al-Arwāḥ*, who can recognize one another and who acknowledge their prototypes as their masters. The fifth level is the *Martaba al-mithāl*, which lies between the lines 360-180 and 315–225. This is the level of the determination of subtle and imaginal forms which are as shadows of the prototypes, and have a type of subtle materiality. Finally, below line 315–225 is *Martaba al-ḥiss*, the sensible world of bodies, *'ālam al-ajsām*.

When Manjhan's narration and symbolism are examined with regard to these six levels of manifestation, or six worlds as they are sometimes termed, it is apparent that he has respected the characteristics of each world as far as he was able, given the constraints of telling the story. In level one, the world of Oneness, on the right-hand side the first forty-three verses constitute the prologue, that is, they are prior to the opening of the story. Verse 44, which has already been discussed, introduces King Sārajbhānu. The fact that he is just in this first world suggests it is correct to assume he has a major symbolic role. On the left-hand side of this world it is to the king that Manohar finally returns, to great rejoicing. The rest of the left-hand side is taken up with leave-taking and the journey away from the conditioned world. Coming to the next level of manifestation, the world of Unity, it is here that Manohar is born and taught the names of everything, as was Adam, and, above all, it is here that the greater part of the description of Madhumālatī is given in the *sarāpā*, indicative of the Divine Names and Attributes. On the left-hand side there is the first full union of Manohar and Madhumālatī on the one hand and the marriage and union of Pemā and Tārāchand on the other. The harmony and unity of the four is constantly stressed. In the next level, which is associated with *a'yān al-thābita*, the fixed entities referred to as prototypes above, there is greater diversity and plurality. It is also the world in which Love features more prominently, or in a somewhat more concrete way. On the right-hand side, after the completion of the *sarāpā*, Manohar and Madhumālatī come to know one another and Love is born between them, but as a pre-existent Love reawakened from a former birth. They swear an oath of eternal fidelity and after some innocent love-making fall asleep together. The central part of this exchange is conversation between the two in which they tell one another their names and fully identify themselves. On the left-hand side, the section begins with Madhumālatī's *bārahmāsā* in which she tells of her Love and suffering in separation from Manohar throughout each of the twelve months of the year. Most of the characters occurring in the story appear in this section: Madhumālatī and her parents, Pemā and her parents, Manohar and Tārāchand. They converse and exchange letters and the final outcome of it all is the arrangement and the performance of the marriage between Madhumālatī and Manohar, although full Union takes place in the world above.

This world then is marked by plurality, identities, relationships and interaction. It is also the place of the covenants made between God and humanity, and of the arising of Love between them and its culmination in marriage.

The next level down is the world of souls or spirits, the *'ālam al-Arwāḥ*, which is a world in which the human soul and God are aware of their separation and suffer the pain of Love in separation. On the right, Manohar begins the section by waking up alone suffering from the pain of Love, realizing that he has fallen out of paradise. This is treated as a malaise for which reason, arguments and doctoring are unable to effect a cure. He ends the section cast up alone on the unknown shore of the world below. On the left, Madhumālatī, in the form of a bird, has resolved to allow herself to be caught by Tārāchand. He puts her in a cage. This image of the bird in the cage is one of the most persistent symbols of the soul in Sufi literature – there are many examples in Rūmī, to name but one author. The restoration of Madhumālatī is brought about through the selfless service and love of Tārāchand (perhaps this is to be taken as *'ubūdiyya*, servanthood?) and the tears and repentance of her mother who, having first turned her into a bird to protect the family's reputation, is now overcome with grief, remorse and love to the point that she restores Madhumālatī to her former beauty. Tears, as Rūmī often says, are the certain way of unlocking the mercy of God, provided they are not the tears of the professional mourner! But the primary characteristic of this world is the human soul's awareness of its separation from God and the *viraha* that this produces which, it will be recalled, Manjhan considers the sole means of salvation for humanity, because it is the way the human soul becomes conscious of itself.

The next world down, the world of subtle and imaginal forms, is symbolized by the picture gallery, mango groves and gardens reminiscent of paradise and young and beautiful unawakened maidens.[24] It was when she emerged from the picture gallery that Pemā was captured and it is in the picture gallery that Manohar and Madhumālatī meet for the second time and that Madhumālatī tells Manohar her beauty cannot be seen with his ordinary eyes. Pemā is Love, but the shadowy metaphorical love of this imaginal world, *'ishq-i majāzī*, as opposed to the Love of the higher worlds to which this human love can lead. It is in this imaginal world that Madhumālatī is transformed into a bird flying everywhere in search of Manohar.

Finally there is the world of bodies, which is where Pemā is detained and where Manohar has to fight the demon to set her free. This is the world to which the Shaṭṭārī neophyte has to descend before beginning his ascent. The symbolism of Pemā detained in the world of bodies, incarnate, is clear enough. It is interesting, in conclusion, that Manjhan and Madhumālatī never meet in this world.

Manjhan has, then, fully respected the character of each of the worlds of his cosmological diagram and utilized it in further developing the symbolism. There are other symbolic interpretations that could be applied to the six levels, such as Manjhan's teacher, Muḥammad Ghawth's, integration of the six days

[24] This section of the text has been excellently and fully handled by Behl in his thesis, in which he shows how the world of imaginal forms is beautifully represented by the allegorical and symbolic treatment of the gardens and the picture gallery ("Rasa and Romance," pp. 230–40).

of creation with the six worlds just discussed in the *Kalīd-i makhāzin*.[25] Behl writes:

> He [Muḥammad Ghawth] describes the manifestation of God's hidden essence in a scheme approximating the six days of creation, beginning with the stage of pre-manifest Being. Then primal matter is infused with the divine breath. Next, angels are created in the stage of light and the stars. The next circle is the circle of fire, where love (*'ishq*) comes into existence. The fourth stage is the circle of wind and the realm of the soul. The fifth day sees the creation of water and the world of subtle forms and images. The sixth circle is the circle of earth, which is the station of corporeal forms and human beings.

This is yet another level of possible interpretation, and one is aware that major questions like that of the *barzakh*s remain undiscussed. Sufficient has been shown, however, to illustrate how Manjhan has used the macro-compositional design of his poem to add deeper and richer levels of symbolism.

CONCLUSION

Not too long after Manjhan completed his poem, two versions were produced in Persian. They are not very good in themselves, being somewhat inelegant summaries, and they completely failed to observe the symmetry and proportionality of Manjhan's poem. A very renowned version of the story in Dakkhanī Urdu, the *Gulshan-i 'ishq* by Nusratī also failed to maintain contact with Manjhan's symmetry. It has not yet been possible to examine the Bengali rendering to see whether it too departed from Manjhan's proportionality. It seems that one of the important and interesting features of this genre was lost not long after the two last representatives, *Madhumālatī* and *Padmāvatī*, were completed. One may be forgiven therefore for not having detected it before. Now, however, that this type of analysis is increasingly being applied to Biblical and other texts, under the name of rhetorical analysis, there is no longer any justification for ignoring the macro-compositional structures of Sufi works.

Manjhan did not innovate in the matter of his structure; he followed the genre. But what he did do was to produce a delightful and well-balanced love story, rich in symbolism, deepened further by his symmetry, which produces one of the finest evocations of Love in any of the world's mystical traditions. It is time that *Madhumālatī* and the other works in this genre were better known and enjoyed. It is therefore fortuitous that *Madhumālatī* falls within the time span of interest to this volume. I am grateful for this opportunity to bring *Madhumālatī* to the attention of a wider audience so that its very considerable merits may be the better known.

---

[25] *Ibid.*, pp. 232–3.

The Imagery of Annihilation (Fanā') *in the Poetry of Ṣā'ib Tabrīzī*

HEIDEH GHOMI

PRELUDE

The present study examines the imagery of annihilation or *fanā'* in relation to the concept of the 'four elements' in the verse of Ṣā'ib Tabrīzī. It comprises four sections. First, the biography of the poet is examined in order to clarify the effect his education, surroundings and historical circumstances had upon his religious outlook. Since very little in English has been written on Ṣā'ib,[1] this section is longer than the rest of the chapter. In the second section, the concept of annihilation in Ṣā'ib's verses is discussed. Section three analyses his poetic style in relation to the imagery of annihilation, discussing the notion of the 'four elements' in relation to the concept of annihilation – a relationship crucial to understanding Ṣā'ib's expression of this idea. Lastly, the reason behind Ṣā'ib's particular presentation of the concept of annihilation is discussed, followed by a brief conclusion.

I. ṢĀ'IB: THE MAN, POET AND SUFI

The Man

Ṣā'ib Tabrīzī, or Mīrzā Muḥammed 'Alī Iṣfahānī. as his full name is given in the *Ātash-kada* of Luṭf 'Alī Beg,[2] was born in 'Abbāsābād, a village near Iṣfahān to which Shāh 'Abbās had transferred his father's family from Tabrīz.

[1] Aside from the classic treatments by E.G. Browne and, more recently, E. Yarshater ("The Indian or Safavid Style: Progress or Decline," in *Persian Literature*, ed. E. Yarshater [Albany: SUNY Press 1988], pp. 249–88), too few studies exist in English on Ṣā'ib's poetry. One notable exception to the prevailing scholarly neglect of the poet is Paul Losensky's "The Allusive Field of Drunkenness: Three Safavid-Moghul Responses to a Lyric by Bābā Fighānī," in *Reorientations: Arabic and Persian Poetry*, ed. S.P. Stetkevych (Bloomington: Indiana University Press 1994), pp. 227–62, where Ṣā'ib's poetry is discussed on pp. 232–8.
[2] (Bombay 1277/1860-1), pp. 30–1.

Although the exact date of his birth remains uncertain, it is almost sure to have been before 1039/1629–30;[3] according to Professor Browne[4] it was in 1035/1625–6. Others have speculated that since Ṣā'ib travelled to India at a young age, his approximate date of birth was 1010/1601.[5] Regarding the date of Ṣā'ib's death in Iṣfahān more certainty exists: from the chronogram devised for it, *Ṣā'ib vafāt yāft* (Ṣā'ib passed away), the date 1081/1669–70 may be computed.[6]

Ṣā'ib's early education in Iṣfahān consisted in the study of theology, *belles-lettres* and the common philosophical sciences of his time. Among his teachers during this period, he speaks highly of Ḥakīm Ruknā Masīḥ Kāshānī (d. 1070/1659–60) and Sharaf al-Dīn Shafā'ī (d. 1037/1628). In his *Shi'r al-'ajam*,[7] the Indian scholar and critic Shiblī Nu'mānī mentions Ṣā'ib as coming from a respected merchant family, indicating that Ṣā'ib must have experienced a comfortable childhood and adolescence. It is certain that he had a caring father who, at the age of 70, following two years of separation, went all the way to India out of love for Ṣā'ib in order to see his son and persuade him to return home.[8]

Despite his deeply religious mind, Ṣā'ib's personal faith transcended the limitations of popular orthodoxy which, he believed, betrayed the wider aspirations of the human soul. The heartless asceticism and dry rhetoric of the mullās only evoked his strong disdain. Advocating the religion of the heart instead, he espoused, like Ḥāfiẓ, the superiority of Love (*'ishq*) to Reason (*'aql*), describing Love as the only real guide to Truth, as the following verses from two different ghazals illustrate:

> *Zāhid kay buvad khushktar az dāna-yi tasbīḥ*
> *ḥaqq-i namak-i girya-yi mastāna nadānand.*
>
> The ascetic who is dryer than the beads of a rosary
> Cannot understand the worth of drunkards' tears.[9]
>
> *Tā sālikān bih 'ishq nagardand āshinā*
> *Ṣā'ib, bih nūr-i 'aql bi-jā'ī nimīrasand.*
>
> Unless the spiritual travellers are acquainted with Love
> By the light of Reason, Ṣā'ib, they'll get nowhere.[10]

---

[3] Shiblī Nu'mānī Hindī, *Shi'r al-'ajam*, translated into Persian by D. Gīlānī (Tehran: Dunyā-yi Kitāb 1363 A.Hsh./1984), III, p. 161.
[4] E.G. Browne, *A Literary History of Persia* (Cambridge: Cambridge University Press 1956), IV, p. 267.
[5] Munibur Rahman, "Ṣā'ib, Mīrzā Muḥammad 'Alī," *EI*^{2}, VIII, p. 852.
[6] *Kulliyyāt-i Ṣā'ib Tabrīzī*, ed. Amīrī Firūzkūhī (Tehran: Khayyām 1373 A.Hsh./1994), introduction, p. 41.
[7] *Shi'r al-'ajam*, III, p. 160.
[8] *Ibid.*, p. 162.
[9] *Kulliyyāt-i Ṣā'ib Tabrīzī*, p. 463, no. 1288.
[10] *Ibid.*, p. 375, no. 1032.

Ṣā'ib lived what seems to have been an uneven life, experiencing rejection as well as fame and popularity at the courts of Persian and Indian rulers. He enjoyed his greatest recognition when he was appointed poet laureate to Shāh 'Abbās II at the Safavid court although, sadly enough, Shāh Sulaymān, who succeeded 'Abbās, was annoyed by a poem Ṣā'ib had offered him on accession to the throne and, as Shibli indicates,[11] thereafter ceased to favour the poet with his royal attentions.

His popularity at the court of the great Mughals of India and, in particular, the mutual love and respect between himself and the Mughal administrator Ẓafar Khān encouraged Ṣā'ib, in spite of certain religious differences between the two men, to praise him in a long *qaṣīda*. Ẓafar Khān was also Ṣā'ib's patron and paid tribute to him for being his teacher in poetry.[12] As Ṣā'ib wrote:

Kulāh gūsha bih khūrshīd u māh mīkasham
bih īn ghurūr kay madḥatgar-i Ẓafar-khānām.

I boast to the sun and the moon
With the pride of having praised Ẓafar Khān[13]

Although quite early in his life Ṣā'ib had made pilgrimages to Mecca and the holy city of Mashhad, he soon felt inclined to follow in the footsteps of some of his fellow poets and journey to India. He felt very excited about this journey, writing:

Ṭalā'ī shud chaman, Sāqī bigardān jām-i zarīn rā
bikish bar rū-yi awrāq-i khazān dast-i nigārīn rā
bi-jā-yi la'l u gawhar az zamīn-i Iṣfahān Ṣā'ib,
bih mulk-i hind khwāhad burd īn ash'ār-i rangīn rā.

The grass has gone golden, Oh Sāqī, take the golden cup round,
Lay your hands on the autumn leaves
Instead of rubies and pearls from Iṣfahān,
Ṣā'ib is taking these colourful verses to India.[14]

In order to avoid compromising his own Sunni religious beliefs and risking the wrath of the puritan Shī'ite clerics, Ṣā'ib seems to have decided to adopt a metaphoric style of expression which enabled him to speak his heart relatively safely. Although he sometimes voiced his dissatisfaction with his worldly situation, indicating this to be the chief cause of his journey to India (as seen in the line below), the tone of his verse is generally mild and conservative.

Dāshtam shakvih zay Īrān bih talāfī gardūn
dar farāmūshkada-yi Hind rahā kard marā.

---

[11] *Shi'r al-'ajam*, III, p. 163.
[12] *Ibid.*, p. 161.
[13] *Kulliyyāt-i Ṣā'ib Tabrīzī*, p. 818, v. 1.
[14] *Ibid.*, p. 99, no. 270.

> I complained of Persia, so in retaliation, Fate
> Left me deserted in the oblivious land of India.[15]

Among the many reasons for Ṣā'ib's departure from Iran and journey to India, socio-political circumstances within seventeenth-century Safavid Persia have been adduced,[16] specifically caused by the harassment he had suffered at the hands of the Qizilbāsh. It has also been indicated[17] that another cause for his journey to the East was his opposition to the predominant literary taste in Iran that emphasized strict Shī'ite piety at the expense of Persian language and literature which was under-appreciated and under-supported.[18] The fact that Persian language and literature was highly valued by the Great Mughuls of India, whose court language was mainly Persian, indicates the probable accuracy of the latter view. In contrast to Persia under the Turkish-speaking rulers of the Safavid dynasty, the Mughals warmly welcomed and honoured Persian poets. On a number of occasions, Ṣā'ib alludes to the popularity and appreciation of verse in India, as in these lines:

> *Hind rā chūn nasatāyam kay darīn khāk-i siyāh*
> *shu'lih-i shuhrat-i man jāmah-yi ra'nā'ī yāft.*
>
> Why shouldn't I admire India, when in this dark soil
> The flame of my fame is given such an elegant dress?[19]

The withdrawal of state patronage from poets in Persia and the generosity of the Great Mughals of India towards Persian poets was a distinctive feature of the Safavid and Mughal period, underlying the attraction which many of Ṣā'ib's contemporaries felt for the Subcontinent.[20] However, unlike most of the other Persian poets who migrated to India, Ṣā'ib did not use his position as a poet in India to make a fortune. Coming from a respected merchant family, he travelled as a businessman and found success independently at the court of the Great Moguls of India in both business pursuits and his poetic career.

From the frequent references to the beauty of the Indian landscape in his verses,[21] another reason underlying his voyage to India may have been Ṣā'ib's fascination with nature and its beauties. But whatever his motive, his poetic talent was warmly welcomed in India by Shāh Jahān and Ẓafar Khān,

---

[15] *Ibid.*, p. 39.
[16] See 'Isā Ṣadīq, *Tārīkh-i Farhang-i Īrān* (Tehran: The Teachers College Press 1342 A.Hsh./ 1963), pp. 237–55.
[17] *Ibid.*, p. 251.
[18] Browne, *Literary History of Persia*, IV, p. 165.
[19] *Kulliyyāt-i Ṣā'ib Tabrīzī*, p. 275, no. 752.
[20] Sa'ib was rewarded several times by the Mughal kings and administors of India. According to Shiblī (*Shi'r al-'ajam*, III, pp. 160–3), Sa'ib was awarded 12,000 rupees by Shāh Jahān and 5,000 rupees or gold coins by Ja'far Khān, the prime minister.
[21] *Kulliyyāt-i Ṣā'ib Tabrīzī*, p. 811, vv. 4–20.

amongst others, with whom he remained close friends even after his return to Persia.[22]

Although Ṣā'ib was generally appreciative of the generous reception accorded him in India, homesickness for Persia occasionally did overshadow his mind, leading him to make some unkind remarks, as the following verses indicate:

Khūshā 'ishrat-sarā-yi Kābul u dāmān-i kuhsārish
kat nākhun bar dil-i gul mīzanad muzhgān har khārish.

How sweet is the pleasure land of Kabul and its mountains laps
As the lashes of each of its bushes scratch the flower's heart.[23]

Ay khāk-i surma-khīz bih faryād-i man biras
shud surma ustakhwān-i man az khāk-i māl-i Hind.

O you, whose earth is the source of all antimony, rescue me
For my bones have turned to antimony in this dusty land of India.[24]

As E.G. Browne pointed out, Ṣā'ib ended his stay in India – which began in 1035/1625–6 – after his father visited him in 1042/1632–3 and encouraged him to return home.[25] Obtaining permission[26] from his patron, Ẓafar Khān, he accompanied his father back to Isfahan where he was welcomed as a native son and soon became appointed poet laureate to Shāh 'Abbās II.

Ṣā'ib's education and travel had an impact on his religious insight in general, and on his concept of annihilation in particular. While his traditional education had given him a religious bent, his exposure to other traditions had provided him with a worldliness and open-mindedness he had hitherto not possessed. This cosmopolitan frame of mind in turn affected Ṣā'ib's expression of the concept of annihilation. Although he shared this concept with many other Sufi poets, in his verse the conventional connotation of death and isolation was less emphasized than its relation to live phenomena of nature, such as the four elements, thus underlining its real and eternal dimension.

The Poet

Ṣā'ib is perhaps the most notable of the group of poets who composed their verse in what was known as the 'Indian style' (*sabk-i hindī*). Despite his position as poet laureate to Shāh 'Abbās II and his popularity at the court of

---

[22] *Shi'r al-'ajam*, III, p. 163.
[23] *Kulliyyāt-i Ṣā'ib Tabrīzī*, p. 811.
[24] *Ibid.*, p. 1493.
[25] Browne, *Literary History of Persia*, IV, p. 267.
[26] *Shi'r al-'ajam*, III, p. 162.

the Great Mughals of India, Ṣā'ib was not a panegyric poet. The relative lack of panegyric verse in his *Dīvān* is perhaps attributable to the contemporary Persian political milieu in which the favoured form of poetry was religious eulogy and praise of the Prophet and the Shī'ite Imāms. Among his few *qaṣīdas* with religious themes is found an ode to 'Alī, in which he praises him as supreme among the saints following the Prophet. Ṣā'ib's panegyrical poetry was quite scarce: he composed only one *qaṣīda* in honour of Shāh 'Abbās II, in which he praised the monarch's justice, his efforts at peace and reconciliation, his aptitude as a ruler, and piously expressed the wish that the whole world be subject to him until the advent of the Twelfth Imām. The following verses are from his *qaṣīda* on 'Alī and Shāh 'Abbās respectively:

> *Bihtarīn-i khalq ba'd az bihtarīn-i anbiyā'*
> *īn 'amm-i Muṣṭafā dāmād-i khayr al-mursalīn.*
>
> [He is] ...The best of men, after the best of the Prophets
> This cousin of Muṣṭafā, the good Prophet's son-in-law.[27]
>
> *Bād dar zīr-i nigīn-i ū rā jahān chūn afitāb*
> *tā shavad nūr-i ẓuhūr-i ṣāḥib al-amr ashikār.*
>
> May the whole world be under his ring, like the sun
> Until the light of the Owner of affairs is revealed.[28]

Although Ṣā'ib tried his hand at all kinds of poetry, it is in the ghazal genre that he is most celebrated. He was without a doubt one of the greatest composers of the ghazal in the seventeenth century, although describing him as "the last great Persian poet and superior to Qā'ānī in originality,"[29] or "the most capable poet of the Indian style,"[30] seems rather exaggerated, and is certainly unfair to some of the great other 'Indian style' poets contemporary with him, such as Kalīm Kāshānī (d. 1061/1650) or Bīdil (Bedil; d. 1133/1721).

If Ṣā'ib's original use of the Indian style of poetry made a crucial contribution to Persian *belles lettres*, his innovation in this genre might best be characterized as the creation of a 'novelty in content' while remaining within the framework of the great Persian classics regarding style and expression. As an 'Indian-style' poet and a Sufi thinker, Ṣā'ib's particular talent may be examined under eight basic rubrics: textual originality, innovative usage of slang, artful use of grammatical faults, density of metaphor, personification of nature, fantastical exaggeration, and distance from socio-political events.

---

[27] *Kulliyyāt-i Ṣā'ib Tabrīzī*, p. 804, v. 20.
[28] *Ibid.*, p. 808, v. 7.
[29] *Shi'r al-'ajam*, III, p. 158.
[30] *Kulliyyāt-i Ṣā'ib Tabrīzī*, introduction, p. 14.

TEXTUAL ORIGINALITY

Amongst Ṣā'ib's merits is the originality of the content and texture of his poetry as well as in its expression, a feature acknowledged by the poet himself in the following verse:

> *Chū shākh-i gul az shikastan chigūna dar pīcham*
> *hizār ma'nā-yi rangīn dar āsitīn dāram.*
>
> From breaking like a flower why should I twitch and turn
> When I have a thousand colourful ideas up my sleeve.[31]

INNOVATIVE USAGE OF SLANG

The use of such slang expressions as 'stitch' (*bakhiyya*), 'unsettled' (*khāna bar dūsh;* literally, 'carrying my house on my back'), 'single shirt to wear' (*yiktā pirahān*) are regular features in Ṣā'ib's verse. He had a talent for placing such familiar expressions in normal Sufi settings and creating novel images out of them. This can be seen in the following verse in which Ṣā'ib contrasts the caustic image of *khāna bar dūsh* with the solemn gravity of a mountain to convey the pain that is borne on the shoulders of the Lover:

> *Khāna bar dūshtar az abr-i bahārān būdam*
> *langar-i dard-i tu chūn kūh-i girān kard marā.*
>
> I was more unsettled than the Spring clouds
> The anchor of your pain made me like a heavy mountain.[32]

ARTFUL USE OF GRAMMATICAL FAULTS

Ṣā'ib's verses sometimes retain phrases or expressions that do not accord with the standards of normal Persian grammar or fit the quality of high literary language. In the following verse, for instance, he uses a slang expression *chiqadr* (how much?) which is seldom found in poetry:

> *'Aql az ān ḥusn-i jahāngīr chih idrāk kunad*
> *dar ḥubābī chiqadr jilva kunad daryā'ī?*
>
> What does the Reason comprehend of that world-conquering beauty?
> How much of itself can the sea show in a bubble?[33]

In this context, the Iranian literary critic 'Alī Dashti[34] accuses Ṣā'ib of being careless in making grammatical mistakes which, he believes, only lower the level of his poetry. Before passing any such value judgements, however, one should remember Ṣā'ib's inexhaustible efforts to create novelty in his poems. The use of slang (such as *chiqadr*) as a poetic device in the above verse is

---

[31] *Ibid.*, p. 718, no. 2008.
[32] 'Alī Dashtī, *Nigāhī bih Ṣā'ib* (Tehran: Asāṭīr 1364 A.Hsh./1985), p. 111.
[33] *Ibid.*, p. 70.
[34] *Ibid.*, pp. 65–74.

probably meant to create sufficient poetic shock to rescue his verse from banality and focus the reader's attention on the topos of the 'Unity of Being' which is the poem's central theme.

DENSITY OF METAPHOR

A general feature of the poets of all the Indian style poets, including Ṣā'ib, is that their verse is often heavily loaded with complicated similes, symbols and multi-dimensional metaphors. This sometimes creates obscurity in the given image and connotations which are not always easily decodable. This facet appears in the following verse where Ṣā'ib presents a single word (*dida*) as a *double entendre* meaning both 'the eyes of those who are scorched (in love),' and 'the sight of those who are scorched (in love),' and also as a description of the antimony which improves the sight. These meanings, presented in the second hemistich below, are not easily distinguishable:

> *Lālih rawshangar-i chishm u dil-i sūdā'ī-ye mā-st,*
> *dīda-yi sūkhtagān surma-yi bīnā'ī-yi mā-st.*
>
> The tulip illuminates our melancholic eyes and heart;
> The eyes/vision of those who are scorched is our enlightening antimony.[35]

PERSONIFICATION OF NATURE

While Ṣā'ib remains very close to nature in his verses, he does not describe it in the same way which more 'imagist' poets such as Manūchihrī portrayed it. Rather, he utilizes it in order to express his own subjective emotions, as can be seen from the following verse in which the falling of an autumn leaf makes him sense the proximity of his own death:

> *Ṣubḥ az jānhā-yi rawshan yād mī-āyad marā,*
> *shām az tārīkī-yi tan yād mī-āyad marā,*
> *az dam-i sard-i khazān bargī kay mī-aftad bih khāk,*
> *az jahān-i bī-barg raftan yād mī-āyad marā.*
>
> Dawn reminds me of the enlightened souls;
> Dusk reminds me of the darkness of the body.
> The leaf which the cold breath of Autumn casts to upon the earth
> Reminds me of passing away from this world, withered, empty-handed.[36]

FANTASTICAL EXAGGERATION

Although *mubālagha* or hyperbole has long been a familiar device in Persian poetry, it is more pronounced in the poetry of the Indian-style poets. However, in Ṣā'ib's poetry the lack of realism in such exaggeration sometimes makes the

---

[35] *Kulliyyāt-i Ṣā'ib Tabrīzī*, p. 230, no. 629.
[36] *Ibid.*, p. 122, no. 332.

poetic image less impressive, as is seen in the following verse, where drinking one's blood and biting one's liver, which symbolize suffering and being patient, are pictured as the ointment for one's negligence. Ṣā'ib's stressed application of the /q/ and /kh/ phonemes here has an impact on this image, rendering it more emphatic:

Marham-i tīgh-i taghafful khūn-i khud rā khwurdan ast;
bakhiyya-yi īn zakhm dandān bar jigar afshurdan ast.

The (sole) salve for the sword of forgetfulness is drinking one's own blood;
The (sole) stitch for such a cut is to gnash one's teeth on one's liver.[37]

DISTANCE FROM SOCIO-POLITICAL EVENTS

Although formally attached to the court, Ṣā'ib rarely wrote panegyrical poems in praise of temporal rulers or royalty. Socio-political realities and events relating to his own time, place and fellow men are not familiar issues in his poetry, at least not to the extent and depth that one finds in Rūmī, Sa'dī or Ḥāfiẓ.[38] The distance between Ṣā'ib and his audience consequently prevents him from speaking as a voice of the masses. Occasionally, however, he does mention the hardships of contemporary society and hints at diffficulties he experienced in resisting the tide of events, as in the following lines:

Dast u tīgh-i 'ālam-i khūn-rīz rā
shīsha u paymāna mīdānīm mā
istiqāmat rā darīn waḥshat-sarā
laghzish-i mastāna mīdānīm mā.

The hand and sword of this blood-shedding world
We understand to be the wine-glass and cup;
Resistance in this house of terror
We understand to be like drunken slipping.[39]

The Sufi

The age of Ṣā'ib was one of the least fortunate periods in the history of Sufism, which had already experienced many ups and downs in Persia. Sufi doctrines, which emphasized the unity of existence, perceiving all phenomena in the light of the immanence of the Divine, with Love as the central motivation of the devotional life, and asceticism, which aimed to rise above the limitations of the flesh, were all notions that stood in utter contrast to the puritanical approach of orthodox Islamic clericalism characteristic of the Safavid

[37] *Ibid.*, p. 290, no. 795.
[38] See Qāsim Ghanī, *Tārīkh-i taṣawwuf dar Islām* (Tehran: Zavvār 1340 A.Hsh./1961), pp. 169–93.
[39] *Kulliyyāt-i Ṣā'ib Tabrīzī*, p. 128, no. 346.

theocracy. Feeling insecure in openly expressing such ideas, Sufis resorted to the use of symbolism and occult poetic allusions, stylistic features which Ṣā'ib's verse also shares. He often refers to the precautions he felt necessary to take in regard to concealing his meaning from the vulgar:

> *Pās-i guftār nigahbān-i ḥiyāt-i abadī-st;*
> *sham' az tīz-zabānī kay sar mībāzad.*
>
> To be careful of one's words is a guard of eternal life
> The candle due to its sharp tongue loses its life[40]

During the reign of Shāh 'Abbās II, as with most of his predecessors, religion and politics were bound together despite the fact that religion was at an all-time low in terms of morality. Since during the young Shāh's reign the clergy regarded science, philosophy and *belles-lettres* as relatively insignificant compared with the study of Shī'ite theology and religious texts, poetry was consequently denigrated as a vehicle of expression for Sufism. Religious fanaticism, encouraged by the Islamic extremists who predominated in the Safavid court,[41] had cast its dark shadow over Persian intellectual life.

Compared to previous centuries, this era showed less tolerance – sometimes none at all – for freedom of thought and speech. The ideological impositions of the Safavid state were tremendous, although this situation improved slightly during the reign of Shāh 'Abbās II, a more moderate king who showed more tolerance towards other traditions than Shāh Ismā'īl I (1501–24), who had first introduced Shi'ism into Iran as state religion and established the ritual cursing of the three other caliphs besides 'Alī (Abū Bakr, 'Uthmān and 'Umar), or Shāh Ismā'īl II (1576–7), who systematically killed or blinded all members of his father's power elite.[42] However, it is obvious that institutional Sufism could neither flourish nor be manifested openly in such conditions, although both its spirit and indeed letter continued to live on among certain members of the intellectual elite.

Sufi doctrines, ideas and symbolism appear in the poetry of Ṣā'ib in two basic ways: (1) in paying homage to celebrated Sufi poets who preceded him, and (2) by preservation and continuation of Sufi poetic imagery and symbolism in his own verse.

HOMAGE TO SUFI POETS

Although there are no direct indications in Ṣā'ib's *Dīvān* regarding which Sufi order he belonged to, or which spiritual master (*pīr*) he followed, it is evident,

---

[40] *Ibid.*, p. 462, no. 1285.
[41] See Ṣadīq, *Tārīkh-i Farhang-i Īrān*, pp. 128–30.
[42] Roger Savory, *Iran Under the Safavids* (Cambridge: Cambridge University Press 1980), p. 69; and Browne, *Literary History of Persia*, IV, s.v. Ismā'īl II.

if only from the following verse, that he was steeped in, and perhaps secretly adhered to, the Sufi tradition:

> *Gar chih az mardum-i dunyā-st ba-ẓāhir Ṣā'ib*
> *ṭīnat-i khākī-yi ū az gil-i darvīshān-ast.*
>
> Although superficially Ṣā'ib appears a man of the world,
> the natural composition of his flesh is formed of dervish dust.[43]
>
> *Khirqa-yi darvīshī-yi mā chūn zira zīr-i qabā-st*
> *pīsh chishm-i khalq-i ẓāhirbīn qabā-pūshīm mā*
>
> Under the mullā's robe like a coat of mail I wear a dervish mantle
> which to men of superficial sight seems but the common cleric's garb.[44]

Ṣā'ib frequently paid tribute to Rūmī and Ḥāfiẓ and some of the other great Sufi Persian poets, admiring their power of poetical expression and recognizing that it was their way of life as Sufis that caused them to be celebrated:

> *Fatād tā bih rah- ṭarz-i Mawlawī Ṣā'ib*
> *Sapand-i shu'la-yi fikrish shuda-ast kūkabhā.*
>
> As soon as Ṣā'ib encountered the style of Rūmī
> The flaming incense of his thoughts became like stars.[45]
>
> *Bi-fikr-i Ṣā'ib az ān mīkunad righbat khalq*
> *kay yād mīdahad az ṭarz-i Ḥāfiẓ-i Shīrāzī.*
>
> People are attracted to Ṣā'ib's type of thinking
> since it reminds them of the style of Ḥāfiẓ of Shīrāz.[46]

Insofar as the socio-political situation did not favour any strong public commitment to the ideals of Sufism, perhaps it was only in verses such as these, penned by way of indirect allusion, that Ṣā'ib could safely allow himself to express his inclination for Sufism.

PRESERVATION AND CONTINUATION OF THE SUFI TRADITION

In his use of religious imagery, Ṣā'ib's verse substantially resembles that of many Sufi poets of Persia. Four characteristics found in his verse – Sufi mystical themes, amorous diction, strict hierarchial distinctions among mystics, and Sufi tolerance – that are common to both Ṣā'ib and the classical Persian Sufi poets, seem to suggest that he himself was a Sufi.

Sufi Mystical Themes. Despite his favourable rapport with the Safavid court, his ties of royal patronage and the inhibiting religious milieu in which he lived,

---

[43] *Kulliyyāt-i Ṣā'ib Tabrīzī*, p. 255, no. 697.
[44] *Ibid.*, p. 6, no. 14.
[45] *Ibid.*, p. 2, no. 5.
[46] *Ibid.*, p. 602, no. 1678.

Ṣā'ib did not shirk from expressing himself in the poetic imagery of Sufism. Many of his ghazals are built upon the themes of the Unity of Existence, love and love-making, the Lover and Beloved, the unreliability of reason and annihilation – the same themes which lie at the heart of Sufi theosophy. The Sufis' 'mystical states' (*aḥwāl*) and 'spiritual stations' (*maqāmāt*) are also themes raised frequently in Ṣā'ib's *Dīvān*.

These metaphysical themes, as well as Sufi moral teachings, which also interested Ṣā'ib, are sometimes preserved and reproduced by the poet according to the dictates of the classical Sufi tradition; and at other times illustrated with original settings following his whim for novelty. In the first of the following verses, the theme of the Unity of Existence is expressed by Ṣā'ib after the fashion of the great Sufi poets of Persia;[47] in the second example, Ṣā'ib expresses the stock topos of 'spiritual poverty' (*faqr*), but demonstrates his originality by employing the image of the barren thorn as a novel and shocking element personifying detachment from the world.

Parda-yi pindār sadd-i rāh-i waḥdat gashta-ast
chūn ḥubāb az khud kunad qālib tuhī, daryā shavad.

The veil of thinking has become an obstacle on the path to Unity
When the bubble shatters its shell, it becomes the sea.[48]

Panāhī nīst dar rū-yizamīn bihtar zay bībargī,
kujā khār-i sar-i dīvār parvā-ī khazān darād?

On earth no better refuge exists than poor withered leaflessness;
Since when do barren thorns atop a wall fear the autumn?[49]

Amorous Diction (zabān-i 'āshiqāna). Like most Persian Sufis, Ṣā'ib employs a special 'language of love' or 'amorous diction' when referring to certain expressions used of God, man, or the unity of being. Most often, he uses similes, metaphors and poetic figures to express the mysterious allusions between lover and beloved and their love relationship. In this respect, Ṣā'ib's ghazals function as nostalgic love songs of the 'Lover' sung to and for his 'Beloved', infused with a Sufi ambiance:

Nay takht-i jām nay mulk-i Sulaymānam ārizū-st;
rāhī ba khalvat-i dil-i jānānam ārizū-st.

Neither Jamshīd's throne nor Solomon's kingdom I desire;
The way into the cloistered shrine of my heart's Beloved is what I desire.[50]

In the following lines the melancholic tone indicates the depth of love in the Lover's heart and the pain of his being separated from the Beloved:

---

[47] See Ghanī, *Tārīkh-i taṣawwuf dar Islām*, pp. 212–7.
[48] *Kulliyyāt-i Ṣā'ib Tabrīzī*, p. 371, no. 1023.
[49] 'Alī Dashti, *Nigāhī bih Ṣā'ib*, p. 199.
[50] *Kulliyyāt-i Ṣā'ib Tabrīzī*, p. 238, no. 652.

Yād ayyāmī kay bā ham āshinā būdīm mā,
ham khiyāl u ham ṣafīr u ham navā būdīm mā.
Ma'nā-yi yak bayt būdīm az ṭarīq-i ittiḥād
chūn dū miṣra' gar chih dar ẓāhir judā būdīm mā.

Recall that time when there was intimacy between us,
Dreaming one dream, speaking one voice, singing one song;
By way of unity with one meaning like a distich of verse
Although outwardly we were separate like two hemistiches.[51]

Hierarchial Distinctions among Mystics. Persian Sufi poets tend to make a distinction between true and false Sufis, between those who are genuinely and those who are superficially religious in their verse, a distinction generally expressed by terms such as 'visionary adepts' (*ahl-i naẓar*), 'people of the heart' (*ahl-i dil*), contrasted with their various antonyms, such as 'exotericists' (*ẓāhir-bīn*) or 'formalists' (*ahl-i ẓāhir*), 'the preacher' (*vā'iẓ*), 'the ascetic' (*zāhid*) and similar compounds.[52] Such hierarchial distinctions amongst members of the religious classes of society, in which the Sufi is defined in contradistinction to the non-mystic, are very much a feature of Ṣā'ib's verses. In the following verse, for instance, Ṣā'ib magnifies this distinction by referring to himself as a traveller on the path of Love, heading for the supreme goal of annihilation. However, the meaning of the second hemistich is quite subtle, indicating both that his companions on the path of love in the world of nature are as infinite as the desert sands and that the image of the forlorn desert landscape alludes to the actual dearth of such companions:

Tanhā na-īm dar rah-i dūr u darāz-i 'ishq
Āvārgī chūn rīg-i ravān ham 'anān-i mā-st.

We are not alone on this long, far-flung path of love
Vagrancy like the flowing sands, is our companion.[53]

In another verse, Ṣā'ib illustrates the isolation of true Sufis vis-à-vis the common herd of humanity, noting that, to the discerning mystic, the public's intolerance of and opposition to his vision is, in fact, a blessing:

Khvārī-ye bīkhiradān 'uzlat-i ahl-i khirad-ast
ṣīqal-i sīna-yi rawshan-gawharān dast radd-ast.

To hold fools in contempt: that's how the sage makes his solitary retreat;
What burnishes bright the ore within the chests of enlightened hearts
is the hand of their [the fools'] scornful rejection.[54]

---

[51] *Ibid.*, p. 107, no. 291.
[52] See Ghanī, *Tārīkh-i taṣawwuf dar Islām*, pp. 241–3.
[53] *Kulliyyāt-i Ṣā'ib Tabrīzī*, p. 243, no. 664.
[54] *Ibid.*, p. 202, no. 546.

Sufi Tolerance. Two virtues which Ṣā'ib shared in common with the Persian Sufi poets were his tolerance of religious diversity and his sincere respect for the genius of fellow artists. He generally maintained a respectful attitude towards both his contemporaries and his predecessors. Among poets contemporary to him, Ṣā'ib paid particular tribute to Fayḍī (d. 1595–6), Ṭālib, 'Urfī (d. 1590–1) and Mīrshawqī, with verses entirely free from jealousy or rivalry.[55] Ṣā'ib's admiration of his predecessors, especially the great classical Persian Sufi poets such as Rūmī, Awḥadī, Sa'dī and Ḥāfiẓ, whom he looked upon as guides, clearly distinguishes him from Muslim formalists and fundamentalists, and places him amongst the true Sufis. In the following verse he pays tribute to Ḥāfiẓ:

Halāk-i husn-i khudā-dād-i ū shavam kay sarāpā
chū shi'r-i Ḥāfiẓ-i Shīrāz intikhāb nadārad.

May I be obliterated before her God-given beauty
Since from top to toe, one cannot choose [what part is best]
Like the verses of Ḥāfiẓ of Shīrāz.[56]

Ṣā'ib maintained a tolerant attitude towards all disciplines and fields of inquiry, perceiving the Truth both within and beyond every single tradition. In the following verses he pays his respects to Christianity, expresses an antipathy towards religious bigotry, and recommends, in the second hemistich, 'compromise' as the key to peace and harmony amongst various religious traditions. Although such liberal views were common among Sufi poets, they clearly demonstrate the Sufi ambiance of Ṣā'ib's poetry:

Munkarān chūn dīda-yi sharm u ḥiyā bar-ham nahand
tuhmat-i ālūdigī bar dāman-i Maryam nahand
kīmiyā-yi sāzgarī khār rā gul mīkunad
gham chih sāzad bā ḥarīfānī kay dil bar gham nahand?

When the unbelievers close their eyes to all shame and honour
They accuse Mary of impurity;
The alchemy of compromise turns thorns to flowers
How can grief afflict those whose hearts are dedicated to grief?[57]

The notion that Truth can be apprehended above and beyond all religious traditions, an idea frequently encountered in Sufi poetry, is illustrated by Ṣā'ib's contrast of the image of the Muslim Ka'ba with the pagan pagoda in the following verse. The 'madness' of divine love which absorbs the poet, however, is beyond such religious distinctions:

---

[55] *Shi'r al-'ajam*, III, p. 165.
[56] *Kulliyyāt-i Ṣā'ib Tabrīzī*, p. 366, no. 1005.
[57] *Ibid.*, p. 364, no. 1002.

Dar Ka'ba'ām u 'yā ṣanam!' āyad bih zabānam;
sar garm-i junūn, Ka'ba u butkhāna nadānad!

I am in the Ka'ba, and yet
the expression 'oh idol!' falls from my tongue –
One empassioned in love-madness, cannot distinguish
Pagoda from Ka'ba.[58]

A similar expression of the same idea appears in the following verses, which distinguish the Sufi mystical vision from puritanical Islam:

Vā'iẓ turā pāya-yi guftār buland-ast
āvāz-i tū az gunbad-i dastār buland-ast.
Dar Ka'ba zay asrār-i ḥaqīqat khabarī nīst;
īn zamzama-yi az khāna-yi khammār buland-ast.

O preacher, although the pedestal of your sermon indeed is high
it is the turban's dome which raises your voice's volume
In the Ka'ba, no report is found of Reality's mysteries
Any evidence for that is raised in the Vintner's house.[59]

In conclusion, *as a man*, Ṣā'ib integrated the learning and intellectual theory he had obtained through his traditional education in Iṣfahān with practical experience gained through travel to India and pilgrimage to Muslim holy places, utilizing both, as will be seen below, to expound his Sufi doctrine of annihilation.

As a poet, Ṣā'ib was one of the most talented writers of his generation. Although he generously utilized and followed the traditional spiritual themes and poetic topoi of classical Persian Sufi poets, these he moulded into original literary forms, creating his own unconventional compositions and settings for them. Producing over 80,000 verses,[60] his creative understanding of annihilation and conception of the four elements remains one of the most novel aspects of his genius.

Lastly, *as a Sufi*, despite the puritanical social and fundamentalist political climate of Iran during Ṣā'ib's lifetime and the Safavids' generally intolerant attitude to mysticism, he managed not only to preserve, but also to revive many of the doctrines and ideas of the Persian Sufi tradition, successfully passing on this wisdom to future generations through the medium of his poetry. His Sufi vision of annihilation, involving detachment from the temporal world of phenomena vis-à-vis the Eternal Beloved on the one hand, and his expression of this doctrine in tangible terms and natural imagery involving the 'four elements' on the other, was a major contribution to the exposition of Persianate Sufism in the Safavid period.

---

[58] *Ibid.*, p. 463, no. 1288.
[59] *Ibid.*, p. 287, no. 784.
[60] *Ibid.*, introduction, p. 29.

II. THE CONCEPT OF ANNIHILATION IN THE POETRY OF ṢĀ'IB

Central to Ṣā'ib's religious imagery is the concept of annihilation, which in his lexicon generally signifies flight from the superficiality and vanity of worldly desires and realization of the Unity of Existence. In this regard, it brings to mind Bāyazīd Bisṭāmī's reply to someone who asked him the way to Truth. "Get yourself out the way," he said, "and then you will then have reached the Truth."[61]

Amongst the many images that Ṣā'ib uses to discuss and define the concept of annihilation is the concrete idea of the destruction of corporeal existence:

Mīrasad zūd bih mi'rāj-i fanā' dast bih dast
har kay rā khāna-barāndakhtagān mi'mār-and.

Whoever employs demolition experts for an architect
Will readily attain to the *mi'rāj* of annihilation.[62]

In another verse, he provides a slightly different image of the same idea, describing the absolute detachment and freedom from bondage that 'annihilation' demands:

Dar manzil-i nakhust fanā' mīshavad tamām
har chand zād-i rāh muhayyā kunad kasī.
Az dār pā bih kursī-yi aflāk mīnahad
khwud rā agar sabuk chū Masīḥā kunad kasī.

In the first Stage, annihilation is completed
Even though one prepares provision for the whole journey.
From the gallows one would step on the throne of firmament
If one makes oneself light and free like the Messiah.[63]

Many Sufis have drawn attention to the elimination of worldly encumbrances and ties as the most crucial aspect of the process of annihilation. Rūmī, for example, expressed this idea as follows:

Chūn Muḥammad pāk shud zīn nār u dūd
har kujā rū kard wajh Allāh būd.

When Muḥammad purged himself of this fire and smoke
Wherever he turned, there was the visage of God.[64]

Another expressive image of annihilation, denoting detachment from the bonds of selfhood and corporeality, is that of the dissolution of the bubble in

---

[61] Farīd al-Dīn 'Aṭṭār, *Tadhkirat al-awliyā'*, ed. Muḥammad Isti'lāmī (Tehran: Gulshan 1372 A.Hsh./1993; 7th printing), p. 198.
[62] *Kulliyyāt-i Ṣā'ib Tabrīzī* p. 362, no. 994.
[63] *Ibid.*, p. 774, no. 2168.
[64] Jalāl al-Dīn Rūmī, *Mathnawī*, ed. R.A. Nicholson, (Tehran: Amīr Kabīr 1357 A.Hsh./1978), I: 1397.

the sea, the former symbolizing the body, and the latter, Existence and Eternity in God.

Dil zay qayd-i jism chūn āzād gardad vā shavad
chun ḥubāb az khwud kunad qālib tuhī daryā shavad.

Once the heart from the bonds of the flesh is freed
like a bubble it breaks the mold of Selfhood,
then becomes itself the sea.[65]

As this verse states, one who would find eternal life must first find life in the Beloved through dissolution of his temporal self. This is, of course, the traditional doctrine of annihilation from self (*fanā'*) and subsistence in God (*baqā' bi'llāh*), which Ṣā'ib adopted from Sufi poets such as 'Aṭṭār whose poetry is replete with such expressions:

Nīst shū tā hastīyat az vay rasad
tā tū hastī hast dar tū kay rasad
Tā nagardī maḥv-i khwārī u fanā'
kay rasad ithbāt az 'izz u baqā'?

Become nothing so that your being may come from him;
As long as 'you' exist, how can [real] existence come to you?
As long as you are not obliterated (*mahv*) and abased in annihilation,
how can affirmation (*ithbāt*) [of existence] ever be granted you
by the Almighty and Eternal?[66]

As can be seen from the selection of verses cited above, the definition and imagery of annihilation in Ṣā'ib's poetry lays stress on the transcendence of corporeal desires and worldly attachments, in becoming absorbed in God who is the beloved 'Oversoul' (*jān-i jānān*), and ultimately, in attaining dissolution in the Unity of Existence. Following Sufi tradition, Ṣā'ib's definition of annihilation adhered to two basic stages: (1) absorption in God and passing away of individual consciousness (*fanā' fi'llāh*) and (2) subsistence in the divine attributes (*baqā' bi'llāh*).[67] At the second stage, the Sufi who rediscovers his true Self in God may be prompted, like Ḥallāj, to say 'I am God' (*Anā al-Ḥaqq*), or else like Rūmī, may contemplate his annihilation throughout all the various manifestations of nature:

Az kanār-i khvīsh yābam har damī man bū-yi yār,
chūn nagīram khvīsh rā man har shabī andar kanār?
Har darakht u har giyāhī dar chaman raqṣān shuda
līk andar chishm-i 'āma basta būd u bar qarār.

In every breath I feel the fragrance of the Beloved beside myself,
Why should I not embrace myself every night?

---

[65] *Kulliyyāt-i Ṣā'ib Tabrīzī*, p. 488, no. 1360.
[66] Farīd al-Dīn 'Aṭṭār, *Manṭiq al-tayr*, ed. M.J. Mashkūr (Tehran: 1374 A.Hsh./1995), p. 278.
[67] See F. Rahman, "Baḳā' wa-Fanā," EI^2, I, p. 951.

Every tree and every plant is dancing in the fields in ecstasy
But to the eyes of commoners they are solemn and solid.[68]

Albeit, in the poetry of Ṣā'ib, the notion of *baqā' bi'llāh* and the exclamation of *Anā al-Ḥaqq* are expressed rather conservatively. Images such as the dissolution of the drop in the ocean and obliteration of the dew in sunlight abound and only occasionally does one find direct allusions to Ḥallāj. The following lines are typical examples:

Shabnam bih āfitāb rasīd az fatādigī
bingar kay az kujā bi-kujā mītavān shudan.

The dew reached the sun out of humbleness;
Look! how far, from here to there, one can reach.[69]

Har dharrah-i kay dīdīm hamīn zamzama rā dāsht
īn naghma-i nay az pardih-yi manṣūr bar-āmad.

Every minute particle that I saw sang this same song:
This melody is not just played to the tune of Manṣūr.[70]

III. ANNIHILATION AND THE IMAGERY OF THE FOUR ELEMENTS IN ṢĀ'IB'S POETRY

Relating the idea of the four elements to the concept of annihilation was not an entirely new invention on Ṣā'ib's part, but was rather a continuation of the Sufi tradition to which he belonged.[71] However, in his imagery of annihilation these elements assume a dual role. On the one hand, the elements relate to Nature, emphasizing and manifesting the transitory mortality of phenomena, offering Ṣā'ib substantial space to exercise his talent as a poet through use of imagery drawn from Nature, and thus introduce freshness and novelty into his poetry. On the other, the four elements figure as fragments of the concept and imagery of annihilation, lending them a new metaphysical value. Thus, from a stylistic point of view, the four elements in Ṣā'ib's imagery serve to broaden his repertoire of poetic devices with which to express the idea of annihilation, while from a metaphysical and doctrinal standpoint, the four elements themselves are lent a deeper Sufi connotation, so ceasing merely to be familiar phenomena of everyday life.

In the following verse, Ṣā'ib uses the elements of earth and air to signify the perishable nature of mortal life, juxtaposing an unusual metaphor such as

---

[68] Jalāl al-Dīn Rūmī, *Dīvān-i Shams-i Tabrīzī*, ed. Badī' al-Zamān Furūzānfar (Tehran: Jāvīdān 1341 A.Hsh./1962), no. 1082.
[69] *Kulliyyāt-i Ṣā'ib Tabrīzī*, p. 723, no. 2025.
[70] Cited by Dashtī, *Nigāhī bih Ṣā'ib*, p. 165.
[71] See for instance, 'Aṭṭār, *Manṭiq al-tayr*, "Dar bayān-i vādī-yi haftum kay Faqr va Fanā'st," p. 38.

"the breeze of an alibi" with a stock simile, "writing by fingertip," in order to emphasize the evanescent nature of existence before non-existence:

> *Fanā'-yi man bih nasīm-i bihāna-ī band-āst*
> *bih khāk bā sar angusht nivishta-ānd marā.*
>
> My annihilation is bound and tied to the breeze of an alibi
> I have been etched and writ upon the earth by a fingertip.[72]

While on the one hand, the element of 'air' – "the breeze" – in this couplet sheds light on the process of annihilation, the element of earth indicates the instability of the corporeal existence. Both elements thus serve to glorify the (paradoxical) Sufi idea of annihilation as constituting the ground of real Existence or Eternal life, whilst themselves receiving more sense and significance than they would usually possess.

In the following couplet, the poet adopts the imagery of the element of (flooding) 'water' to illustrate the difficulties encountered by the lover on the path to the Beloved – which is the voyage from the temporal to the Eternal, from the vanity of worldly existence to the life of the spirit, the latter being symbolized here by non-existence or annihilation:

> *'Āshiqān rā bā fanā' az shādī u gham chāra-yi nīst*
> *sayl rā past u bulandī hast tā daryā shudan.*
>
> On the road to annihilation, lovers cannot escape from joy and woe
> As the flood must course through hill and vale to reach the sea.[73]

Ṣā'ib's conception of annihilation in this couplet is to be read in the context of the mystical doctrine of the 'mystical states and spiritual stations' (*aḥwāl va maqāmāt*) which the seeker must traverse on the Sufi path. According to Abū Naṣr al-Sarrāj's (d. 378/988) celebrated classification of these states and stations in his *Kitāb al-luma' fī 'l-taṣawwuf*,[74] there are ten basic states and seven stations through which every aspirant must pass. The seven stations are repentence (*tawba*) → abstinence (*wara'*) → renunciation (*zuhd*) → spiritual poverty (*faqr*) → patience (*ṣabr*) → trust (*tawakkul*) → contentment (*riḍā'*). The ten states are contemplative vigilance (*murāqaba*) → closeness (*qurb*) → love (*'ishq*) → fear (*khawf*) → hope (*rajā'*) → yearning (*shawq*) → intimacy (*uns*) → confidence in God (*iṭmīnān*) → witnessing (*mushāhida*) → certainty (*yaqīn*). Realization of these states and stations involves a gradual lifting of veils, a discarding of attachments and vices and the acquisition of good character traits and virtues, until final illumination (*ishrāq*) is obtained. At the final stage, through unconditional Love for the Beloved which sweetens all the

---

[72] *Kulliyyāt-i Ṣā'ib Tabrīzī* p. 128, no. 347.
[73] *Ibid.*, p. 747, no. 2095.
[74] R.A. Nicholson (ed), *Kitāb al-luma' fi'l-taṣawwuf* (E.J.W. Gibb Memorial Series vol. 22; London: Luzac & Co. 1914).

hardships of this journey, and with the annihilation of his temporal selfhood, the lover rediscovers his real existence in the Oversoul, hence realizing the Unity of Existence.

In the verse above, the image of the flood and its various connotations give us a clear picture of this process. The flood's wildness represents the Lover's passionate yearning, enthusiasm and determination to attain union with the Beloved. Its harsh ups and downs are to be endured as well as its moments of joy. Once the flood is in spate, however, it cannot control its course, illustrating the lover's acquiescence to all that befalls him of good and ill upon his path. Finally, the flood's reaching the sea represents annnihilation in the Unity of Existence wherein the seeker finds peace and relief after his exhausting journey.

Illustrating the fourth and fifth of Sarrāj's ten mystical states, which are respectively 'fear' and 'hope', Ṣā'ib again resorts to using the element of water and flood imagery. In the following verse, the poet portrays himself as the lover whose states oscillate between 'hope', of reaching the sea of annihilation in unity, and 'fear', of being halted in his course:

> *Khūshā saylī kay mīdānad bih daryā mīrasad ākhar,*
> *ma-āl īn takāpū nimīdānam nimīdānam.*
>
> How happy the flood that knows it will attain the sea at last
> Alas, I know nothing – nothing, of what
> shall be the end of this restless quest.[75]

In the following verse, where the element of water is used again to illustrate *fanā'*, Ṣā'ib notes that the lover will not really be effaced by "the flood of annihilation," but that the transformation and destruction which it indeed wreaks are followed by the restoration of 'eternity in the heart' (*baqā'*):

> *Zay saylāb-i fanā' bar khūd nalarzad*
> *banā'-yi muḥkam-i kāshāna-yi dil.*
>
> The firm structure of the house of the heart
> Does not tremble before the flood of annihilation.[76]

In another verse, "the flood of annihilation" is said to bear the body away, leaving nothing behind:

> *Bas-ast pīrahan-i tan muḥīṭ-i waḥdat rā*
> *kay pīsh-i sayl-i fanā' kūh u kāh har dū yakīst.*
>
> This garment of body and flesh suffices to cover the sea of Unity
> for before the flood of annihilation
> flimsy straw and mighty mountain are one.[77]

---

[75] *Kulliyyāt-i Ṣā'ib Tabrīzī*, p. 852, v. 1.
[76] *Ibid.*, p. 653, no. 1830.
[77] *Ibid.*, p. 169, no. 454

The element of fire also plays a – perhaps the – fundamental role in Ṣā'ib's, imagery of annihilation. Fire functions to purify the lover of veils; it dissolves the dross of the flesh and corporeal existence, leaving behind the gold of eternal being. Paradoxically, while fire is a symbol of the process of annihilation *par excellence*, it also can illustrate the constrictions of physical life and egocentric existence. In a ghazal whose rhyme-word is *khwīshtanam* (myself), Ṣā'ib thus confesses:

> *Bih tang hamchū sharar az baqā'-yi khwīshtanam*
> *tamām-i chishm zay shawq-i fanā'-yi khwīshtanam.*
>
> Like dancing fire I'm bound and gagged since my 'self' still subsists
> My eye are fixed in longing, riveted upon annihilation from my 'self'.[78]

In the following line, Ṣā'ib adopts the element of fire as a symbol of annihilation. Using the stock Sufi metaphor of the immolation of the moth (lover) in the candle (Beloved), he describes the moth as possessing a heart of fire, painting a realistic picture of the state of contemplative vision (*mushāhada*) or perception, depicting the moment when the lover perceives the Beloved with his heart and is dissolved in Her, thus stepping into annihilation of self and finding eternal life. In Ṣā'ib's image here, the butterfly is so absorbed by its Love that it turns into flame, and at some point it becomes impossible to distinguish butterfly from candle:

> *Zān shu'lahā kay az dil-i parvāna sar kishīd*
> *rawshan nashud kay sham' dar īn anjuman kujāst.*
>
> From all those flames which jump up from the butterfly's heart
> Just where the candle lies in this gathering is unclear.[79]

In two other verses the poet focuses on both the destructive and constructive activity of the element of fire, underlining the creative side of the fire of annihilation. The lover must denude himself of 'self', detach himself from his private identity to find an identity grounded in Universal Being. He must dwell in the fire of annihilation, gaining his divine 'wings' but burning his physical powers of flight, thus attaining *baqā' bi'llāh*:

> *'Ārifānī kay azīn rishta sarī yāfta-ānd*
> *bīkhabar gashta zay khwud tā khabarī yāfta-ānd.*
> *Hamchū parvāna dar īn bazm zay sūz-i dil-i khwīsh*
> *bārhā sūkhta tā bāl u parī yāfta-ānd.*
>
> Those adepts who've found something of this mystery,
> only in selflessness found themselves with any consciousness.
> Over and over again, through their own heart's burning in this soirée,
> they've scorched themselves until they found wing and pinion.[80]

---

[78] *Ibid.*, p. 689, no. 1936.
[79] *Ibid.*, p. 855, v. 6.
[80] *Ibid.*, pp. 548–9, no. 1536.

In the following couplets, in which Ṣā'ib exhorts his reader to pass beyond phenomena (*'ālam-i ṣūrat*) and attain to the Tavern – a Sufi symbol for divine unity – he uses imagery relating to the element of fire to illustrate the lover's ascent to the zenith of annihilation, whereupon he regains his origin:

Khīz tā zay 'ālam-i ṣūrat safar kunīm
tā rawshan-āst rāh-i kharābāt sar kunīm.
Az dūdmān-i shu'la bigīrīm himmatī
parvāna tā bih awj-i fanā' chūn sharar kunīm.

Get up and let us travel from the world without,
Let us take the road to the tavern before it gets dark.
From fire's own ancestry let us take our inspiration,
Like sparks, we'll fly to the heights of annihilation.[81]

Considering the imagery of the element of 'earth' in relation to annihilation, the connection between 'earth' and the 'dust of the flesh' with physical 'death' and 'annihilation' (*fanā'*) is quite clear. Biologically, this connotation makes sense as well, since the body turns to dust after death. This familiar connotation is sometimes used by Ṣā'ib to illustrate that beyond death and destruction lies eternal life:

namurda 'umr-i kasī jāvidān nimīgardad
khurāb tā nashavad īn dukkān nimīgardad.

Unless dead none gain eternal life
Unless ruined no building was ever built.[82]

In the following couplets, pastoral imagery is used to illustrate the enthusiastic rising up of the lover from captivity in the earth of annihilation, his abandonment of corporeal existence and his longing for the Beloved:

Zay jām-i bīkhwudī chū lālih mast az khāk bar-khīzam,
zay mahd-i ghunchih chūn gul bā dil-i ṣad chāk bar-khīzam,
chūn shabnam karda-ām girdāvarī-yi khwud rā dar bun-i gulshan
bih andak-i jadhba az hastī-yi khud pāk bar-khīzam.

From the cup of selflessness, like the drunken tulip, from earth I'll rise;
From the bud's cradle, like a flower with a heart rent hundredfold, I'll rise
Like the dew, I've curled up myself deep in the garden's bed
So by the slightest attraction, from self-existence, I'll wholly rise.[83]

The element of 'earth' may also represent the lover's enthusiasm and longing (*shawq*), as in the following verse where the "desert of annihilation" is contrasted to a cloud of dust which heralds an approaching desert caravan:

---

[81] *Ibid.*, p. 656, no. 1837.
[82] *Ibid.*, p. 510, no. 1419.
[83] *Ibid.*, p. 695, no. 1956.

Dar biyābān-i fanā' qāfila-yi shawq-i man-āst
kārvānī kay ghubārish zay khabar mīgudharad.

In the desert of annihilation, it is the train of my longing –
like a cloud of dust cast aloft – which heralds the caravan coming.[84]

The blithe lightness of the element of air makes it a good symbol for the lover's spirit. In the following lines, this element is portrayed as a tornado, a whirlwind of love which cleanses the lover of his temporal selfhood, conveying him by force from one stage to another on his journey to annihilation:

Tā pīch u tāb-i 'ishq napīchad turā bih ham
chūn girdbād marḥalah-paymā nimīshavī
Ṣā'ib bih gird-i khwud nakunī tā safar chū charkh
sar tā bih pā-y dīda bīnā nimīshavī.

Not until the twists and turns of love turn you inside out
shall you traverse, tornado-like, the stages of the Way.
Unless you whirl away from self like a wheel, Ṣā'ib,
from top to toe your eye will never be all one light.[85]

In another verse, the tornado portrays the lover's frenzy and yearning, mentioned above as one of the stages of the journey to annihilation:

Īn girdbād nīst kay bālā girifta-āst
az khwud ramīda-īst kay bālā girifta-āst.

This is not the tornado raising its tail aloft
It is one in flight from self, and thus raised aloft.[86]

Sometimes all four elements appear arranged together as fragments of a single tableau. In the following verses, the poet piously exhorts his reader to practise asceticism (the third of annihilation's seven stations), levelling his fences, humbling himself in dust. Although the three elements of water, air and fire recognize the original centre of their being, man is an alien on earth, unaware of his spiritual centre:

Khvāhī kay āsimānhā dar bar rukhat nabandand
bā khāk kun barābar awwal ḥiṣār-i khvīsh rā
āb u havā u ātash markaz shinās gashtand
tū bī-khabar nadānī rāh-i diyār-i khūd rā.

If you wish the Heavens never slam its door in your face,
on earth level to dust all your fences first.
Water, air and fire all comprehend their mutual centre
But, to an ignoramus like you, the way to your homeland is unknown.[87]

---

[84] *Ibid.*, p. 363, no. 999.
[85] *Ibid.*, p. 787, no. 2202.
[86] *Ibid.*, p. 281, no. 770.
[87] *Ibid.*, pp. 127-28, no. 345.

As can be seen from the above examples, each of the four elements, and sometimes all of them in unison, figure as constant and crucial features in Ṣā'ib Tabrīzī's imagery of annihilation. Used as poetic images not only do they illustrate the mystical processes and modes of annihilation in Ṣā'ib's eyes, they also provide a comprehensive description of this notion by illustrating it with simple settings comprehensible to the common man. However, the question remains: why did Ṣā'ib decide to utilize such elemental imagery to depict the concept of annihilation? The answers to this question are varied.

Although the examples cited above represent no more than a fraction of verses from his *Dīwān*, it should be noted that in Ṣā'ib's religious imagery most of the references to annihilation and its processes are usually linked with one or more of the four elements. As an Indian-style poet, his adoption of such natural imagery is partly derived from his curiosity for, and pursuit of, novelty both in the content and the form of his poetry. It is also partly an attempt to describe the concept of annihilation with more clarity, by relating it to such concrete natural phenomena as the four elements.

The juxtaposition of the four elements in relation to the concept of annihilation is also influenced by his knowledge of the Persian poetic tradition. Steeped as he was in the classics as well as his contemporary masters, according to Shibli[88] Ṣā'ib had carefully studied the works of his ancient and modern predecessors and had compiled an anthology of their best verses. Of course, Ṣā'ib's imagery of the elements is also influenced by his fascination with nature, where the predominant influence on him in adopting this form of expression seems to have been the Sufi implications of the elements.

Perhaps the main reason why four elements had such a crucial impact on Ṣā'ib's Sufi perspective is that they are all phenomena drawn from the outer world whilst, at the same time, being sources of physical life. As each is in a cycle of constant transition, they reflect the Sufi journey within the soul, and beyond, to God. When used as imagery of annihilation, they make quite expressive symbols. The transition of water, fire, earth and air in the cycle of life corresponds well to the mystical notion of 'annihilation of annihilation' (*fanā' al-fanā'*), denoting the lover's absolute selflessness during his journey within, his total absorption by the Beloved and alienation from all else. Similarly, the apparently inexhaustible motions of the four elements reveal the lover's efforts to strip himself of all false personae and masks in order to be worthy of the perception of the absolute beauty of the Beloved and experience the degree of 'witnessing' (*mushāhada*) following *fanā' al-fanā'*.

The four elements therefore explicitly assist Ṣā'ib in describing Sufi doctrines. Representing the world without, the four elements also help him to put man in the perspective of the whole universe, in his journey from his physical origins back to his spiritual Origin, which is indeed the Sufi path to annihilation.

---

[88] *Shi'r al-'ajam*, III, p. 168.

AFTERGLOW

As the above discussion has shown, Ṣā'ib's considerable poetic talents and deep mystical insight were the product of both the religious *madrasa* and the university of life. He combined experience and academic learning to produce over 80,000 verses, some of which rank among the most exquisite masterpieces in all Persian literature.

While religious imagery obviously occupies an outstanding place in Ṣā'ib's poetry, in expressing the concept of annihilation his primary emphasis, exactly like that of many other Persian Sufis, is on the transcendence of corporeal existence. Detachment from corporeality is a prelude to annihilation, to the dissolution of the self in the Beloved and realization of 'absolute eternity' (*baqā-yi moṭlaq*).

In expressing this idea, Ṣā'ib utilized and combined various poetic techniques and devices, the imagery of the four elements making a substantial contribution to his style of expression. The elements appear as sources of life without frontier, bridging the realms of psyche and nature, soul and world, all of which are in motion and constant transition from one state to another. When combined, the elements provide a vivid display of the circle of life and its never-ending turnings, creating a bridge stretching from pre-eternity to post-eternity. This is the essence of Ṣā'ib's conception of annihilation, which he describes in the delicate image of the life and death of a dewdrop transfixed by the sudden glare of the sun:

> *Mībarad chishish kay khūrshīd az kujā paydā shud*
> *shabnam-i mā dar fanā'-yi khwud baqā'-yi khwud dīda-ast.*
>
> Though bereft of its sight, wondering from whence has come the sun,
> Our dewdrop has seen eternal life in self-annihilation.[89]

---

[89] *Kulliyyāt-i Ṣā'ib Tabrīzī*, p. 210, no. 572.

Bibliography

A Chronicle of the Carmelites in Persia and the Papal Mission of the XVIIth and XVIIIth Centuries. London: Eyre Spottiswoode 1939.

Abisaab, Rula. "The Ulama of Jabal 'Amil in Safavid Iran, 1501–1736: Marginality, Migration and Social Change." *Iranian Studies*. 28/1–4 (1994): 103–22.

Abuseitova, M. Kh. and Zh. M. Zhapbasbaeva. "Znachenie arkheograficheskikh èkspeditsii dlia istochnikovedeniia istorii Kazakhstana XVI–XIX vv." In *Voprosy istoriografii i istochnikovedeniia Kazakhstana* (*Dorevoliutsionnyi period*). Alma-Ata 1988: 244–63.

Abū al-Fazl. *The Ain-i-Akbari by Abul-Fazli-Allami*. Ed. in the original Persian by H. Blochmann, XII: Bibliotheca Indica no. 58. Calcutta 1872–7.

Adas, M. *Prophets of Rebellion: Millenarian Protest Movements against European Colonial Order*. Chapel Hill: University of North Carolina Press 1979.

Afandī, Mīrzā 'Abdu'llāh. *Riyāḍ al-'ulamā'*. Qum 1980.

Afnan, S.M. *A Philosophical Lexicon in Persian and Arabic*. Beirut: Dār al-Mashriq 1969.

Afẓal Khān. "Tarikh-i Muraṣṣa." In *The Gulshan-i-Roh: Being Selections, Prose and Poetical, in the Pus'hto, or Afghan Language*. Ed. Captain H.G. Raverty. London: Williams & Norgate 1860.

Aḥmad, Idrīs. *Sirhind men Fārsī Adab*. Delhi 1988.

Ahmad, Aziz. "Ṣafavid Poets and India." *Iran*. 14 (1976): 117–32.

Ahmed, Akbar S. "Religious presence and Symbolism in Pushtun Society." In *Islam in Tribal Societies: From the Atlas to the Indus*. Ed. Akbar S. Ahmed and David Hart. London: Routledge & Kegan Paul 1984.

Akhūnd Darwīzah. *Tadhkira al-abrār wa'l-ashrār*. Delhi 1892.

—— *Makhzan al-Islām*. Peshawar 1969.

Akimushkin, O.F., V.V. Kushev *et al.* (eds.). *Persidskie i tadzhikskie rukopisi Instituta narodov Azii AN SSSR* (*Kratkii alfavitnyi katalog*). Moscow: Nauka 1964.

Alam, Muzaffar. *The Crisis of Empire in North India: Awadh and the Punjab 1707–1748*. Delhi: Oxford University Press 1986.

Algar, Hamid. "Ni'mat-Allāhiyya." In *EI²*, VIII: 44–8.

—— "Some Observations on Religion in Safavid Persia." *Iranian Studies*. 7 (1974): 287–93.

—— "Silent and Vocal *Dhikr* in the Naqshbandī Order." In *Akten des VII. Kongresses für Arabistik und Islamwissenschaft*. Ed. A. Dietrich. Göttingen: Vandenhoeck & Ruprecht 1974.

—— (trans.). Najm al-Dīn Rāzī, *Mirṣād al-'ibād* as *The Path of God's Bondsmen from Origin to Return*. Delmar, N.Y.: Caravan Books 1982.

Allāh, Shāh Walī. *Intibāh fi salāsil awliyā' Allāh*. Trans. Muḥammad Isḥāq Ṣiddīq. Deoband: Kutub Khāna Raḥmiyya, n.d.

Amanat, Abbas. "The Nuqṭawī Movement of Maḥmūd Piskhān and his Persian Cycle of Mystical-Materialism." In *Mediaeval Isma'ili History and Thought*. Ed. F. Daftary. Cambridge: Cambridge University Press 1996.

'Āmilī, Muḥammad b. Ḥasan Ḥurr-i. *Amal al-āmil*. Baghdad 1385/1965–6.

'Āmilī, 'Alī b. Muḥammad b. al-Ḥasan b. Zayn al-Dīn al-. *Al-Durr al-manthūr*. Qum 1398/1977.

'Āmilī, Bahā' al-Dīn Muḥammad al-. *Kulliyāt-i ash'ār va āthār-i fārsī Shaykh Bahā' al-Dīn Muḥammad al-'Āmilī*. Ed. Ghulām Ḥusayn Jawāhirī. Tehran: n.d.

—— *Kulliyāt-i Ash'ār-i Farsī u Mūsh u Gurba-yi Shaykh Bahā'ī*. Ed. Mihdī Tawḥīdīpūr. Tehran: Intishārāt-i Kitābfurūshī-yi Maḥmūdī 1336 A.Hsh./1957.

Andreyev, Sergei. "Notes on the Ormur people." *Peterburgskoe Vostokovedenie*. 4 (1993): 230–8.

—— "British Indian Views (Nineteenth and Early Twentieth Centuries) of the Later Followers of the Rauxaniyya Sect in Afghanistan and Northern India." *Iran*. 32 (1994): 135–8.

—— *Sufi Illuminati: The Rawshani Movement in Muslim Mysticism, Society and Politics*. London: Curzon Press 2000.

Ansari, A.S. Bazmee. "Al-Dāmād." EI^2, II: 103.

'Anṣārī, 'Abdullāh. *Ṭabaqāt al-sūfiyya*. Ed. 'Abd al-Ḥayy Habībi. Kabul 1961.

—— *Ṭabaqāt al-sūfiyya*. Ed. Muḥammad Sarvar Mawlāyī. Tehran: Sahāmī 'ām 1362 A.Hsh./1983.

'Anṣārī, Bāyazīd. *Maqṣūd al-mu'minīn*. Islamabad 1976.

—— *Ṣirāt al-tawḥīd*. Peshawar 1952.

—— *Khayr al-bayān*. Peshawar 1967.

—— *Khayr al-bayān*. Facsimile edition of the Berlin manuscript of *Khayr al-Bayān*, Kabul 1975.

Anṣārī, Nūr al-Ḥasan. *Fārsī Adab ba'ahd-i Awrangzīb*. Delhi: Indo-Persian Society 1969.

Arberry, A. J. *The Koran Interpreted*. London: Allen & Unwin/New York: Macmillan 1971.

Ardabīlī, Muqaddas-i. *Ḥadīqat al-Shī'a*. Tehran: Intishārāt-i 'Ilmiyya-yi Islāmiyya 1343 A.Hsh./1964.

Arjomand, S.A. "Religious Extremism (*Ghuluww*), Sufism and Sunnism in Safavid Iran (1501–1722)." *Journal of Asian Studies*. 15/1 (1981).

—— *The Shadow of God and the Hidden Imam*. Chicago: University of Chicago Press 1984.

—— *The Turban for the Crown: The Islamic Revolution in Iran*. Oxford: Oxford University Press 1988.

—— (ed.) *Authority and Political Culture in Shī'ism*. Albany: SUNY Press 1988.

Arlinghaus, J.T. "The Transformation of Afghan Tribal Society: Tribal Expansion, Mughal Imperialism and the Roshaniyya Insurrection, 1450–1600." Duke University Ph.D. thesis 1988.

Arnaldez, Roger. "Insān al-Kāmil, al-." In EI^2, III: 1239–41.

Arberry, A.J. *Classical Persian Literature*. London: George Allen & Unwin 1958.

Ashtiyānī, S.J. and H. Corbin (eds). *Anthologie des Philosophes Iraniens* [Introduction Analytique par Henry Corbin]. *Muntakhabātī az āthār-i ḥukamā'ī ilāhī-yi Īrān az 'aṣr-i Mīr Dāmād u Mīr Findariskī tā zamān-i ḥāḍir*, edited, introduced and annotated by Sayyid Jalāl al-Dīn Ashtiyānī. 2 vols. Tehran: Departement d'Iranologie de l'Institut Franco-Iranien de Recherche/Paris: Adrien-Maisonneuve 1971.

Ashtiyānī, S.J. *Hastī az naẓar-i falsafah va 'irfān*. Mashhad: Intishārāt-i Zavvār 1996.

Aslanov, M.G. "Narodnoe dvizhenie roshani i ego otrazhenie v afganskoi literature XVIXVII vv." *Sovetskoe Vostokovedenie*, 5 (1955).

'Aṭṭār, Farīd al-Din. *The Tadhkiratu'l-awliya (Memoirs of the Saints) of Muhammad ibn Ibrahim Faridu'ddin 'Attar*. Ed. R.A. Nicholson. 2 vols. London–Leiden: Luzac & Co. 1905–7.

—— *Tadhkirat al-awliyā'*. Ed. M. Isti'lāmī. (3rd edn). Tehran: Zawwār: 1365/1986.

—— *Manṭiq al-tayr*. Ed. M.J. Mashkūr. Tehran 1374 A.Hsh./1995.

Aubin, Jean "Études Safavides, I: Shah Ismā'īl et les notables de l'Iraq Persan." *Journal of Economic and Social History of the Orient* II. (1959): 37–81.

—— "La Propriété Foncière en Azerbayjan sous les Mongols." *Le Monde iranien et l'Islam*. 4 (1976–7): 79–132.

—— "Révolution chiite et conservatisme: les Soufis de Lāhejān, 1500–1514 (Études Safavides II)," *Moyen Orient & Océan Indien* (1984): 1–40.

—— "L'avènement des Safavides reconsidéré (Études Safavides III)." *Moyen Orient et Océan Indien*, V (1988): 1–130.

Augustine, Saint. *Confessions*. Trans. Frank Sheed. Indianapolis, Ind. – Cambridge, Mass.: Hackett Publishing Co. 1993.

Avery, P. "Fitzgerald's Persian Teacher and Hafez." *Sufi: A Journal of Sufism*. 6 (1990): 10–15.

Awn, Peter. "Sufism." In *The Encylopedia of Religion*. Ed. M. Eliade. New York: Macmillan 1993.

Awrangābādī, Niẓām al-Dīn. *Niẓām al-qulūb*. Delhi: Maṭba'-i Mujtabā' 1891.

Babadzhanov, B. "Iasaviia i Nakshbandiia v Maverannakhre: iz istorii vzaimootnoshe-nii (ser. XV–XVI vv.)," *Yäsaui Taghïlïmï* (Turkistan: 'Mura' baspagerlik shaghïn kasipornï/Qoja Akhmet Yäsaui atïndaghï Khalïqaralïq Qazaq-Türik Universiteti 1996): 75–96.

Babayan, Kathryn. "The Waning of the Qizilbash: The Temporal and the Spiritual in Seventeenth Century Iran." Princeton University Ph.D. thesis 1993.

—— 'The Safavid Synthesis: From Qizilbash Islām to Imāmite Shī'ism'. *Iranian Studies*, 27/1–4 (1994): 135–61.

—— "Sufis, Dervishes and Mullas: The Controversy over Spiritual and Temporal Domination in Seventeenth-Century Iran." In *Safavid Persia*. Ed. Charles Melville. London: I.B. Tauris 1996.

Babadzhanov, B. 'Iasaviia i Nakshbandiia v Maverannakhre: iz istorii vzaimootnoshenii (ser. XV–XVI vv.)'. In *Yäsaui Taghïlïmï*. Turkistan: 'Mura' baspagerlik shaghïn kasipornï/Qoja Akhmet Yäsaui atïndaghï Khalïqaralïq Qazaq-Türik Universiteti, 1996: 75–96.

Bābur, Ẓāhir al-Dīn Muḥammad (Pādshāh Ghāzī). *Bābur-nāmah*. Trans. A.S. Beveridge. London 1969.

Badakhshānī, Maqbūl Beg (ed.). *Tārīkh-i Adabiyyāt-i Musalmānān-i Pāk u Hind*. IV: *Fārsī Adab 2 (1526–1707)*. Lahore: University of the Punjab 1971.

Bahār, M.T. *Sabk-shināsī*. 3 vols. Tehran: Chāp-i tābān 1337 A.Hsh./1958.

Bahari, Ebadollah. *Bihzad: Master of Persian Painting*. London: I.B. Tauris 1996.

Bakhsh, Muḥammad. *Mathnawī Nayrang-i 'ishq pānjābi*. Jhelum: Malik Ghulam Nur 1964.

Baldwin, M.W. (ed.) *A History of the Crusades*. I: *The First Hundred Years*. Madison, Milwaukee–London: University of Wisconsin Press 1969.

Baljon, J.M.S. *Religion and Thought of Shah Wali Allah al-Dihlavī*. Leiden: Brill 1986.

Banuazizi, Ali. *Iranian Nationality and the Persian Language 900–1900: The Roles of Court, Religion and Sufism in Persian Prose Writing*. Trans. J. Hillmann. Washington: Mage 1992.

Banuazizi, Ali and Myron Weiner (eds). *The State, Religion, and Ethnic Politics: Pakistan, Iran and Afghanistan*. Lahore: Vanguard Books 1987.

Bāqir, Muḥammad *Pānjābi Qiṣṣe Fārsī Zabān men*. 2 vols. Lahore: Panjabi Adabi Board 1957, 1960.

Barkātī, Maḥmūd Aḥmad. *Shāh Walī Allāh aur unkā Khāndān*. Delhi: Maktaba Jāmi'a 1992.

Bausani, A. *The Persians: From the Earliest Days to the Twentieth Century*. London: Elek 1971.

Bayat, Mangol. *Mysticism and Dissent: Socioreligious Thought in Qajar Iran*. Syracuse: Syracuse University Press 1982.

Bertels, Y.E. *Taṣawwuf wa adabiyāt-i taṣawwuf*. Persian trans. by Sīrūs Īzādī. Tehran: Amīr Kabīr 1976.

Bījan. *Jahān'gushā'ī-yi Khāqān (tārīkh-i Shāh Ismā'īl)*. Ed. Allāh Datā Muḍtarr Islamabad: Markaz-i taḥqīqāt-i fārsī-i Īrān va Pākistān 1984.

Bodrogligeti, A.J.E. "Aḥmad Yasavī's Concept of 'Daftar-î Sanî' [*sic*]," *Milletlerarası Ahmed Yesevî Sempozyumu Bildirileri 26–27 Eylül 1991*. Ankara: Feryal Matbaası 1992: 1–11.

—— "The Impact of Aḥmad Yasavī's Teaching on the Cultural and Political Life of the Turks of Central Asia." In *Türk Dili Ara¤tırmaları Yıllığı Belleten 1987*. Ankara: Türk Tarih Kurumu Basımevi 1992: 35–41.

—— "Yasavī Ideology in Muḥammad Shāybānī [*sic*] Khān's Vision of an Uzbek Islamic Empire." In *Annemarie Schimmel Festschrift: Essays Presented to Annemarie Schimmel on the Occasion of her Retirement from Harvard University by her Colleagues, Students and Friends*. Ed. M.E. Subtelny. *Journal of Turkish Studies*. 18 (1994): 41–57.

Borovkov, A.K. "Ocherki po istorii uzbekskogo iazyka (opredelenie iazyka khikmatov Akhmada Iasevi)." *Sovetskoe vostokovedenie*, 5 (1948): 229–50.

Bosworth, Edmund. *Bahā' al-Dīn al-'Amilī and His Literary Anthologies*. Journal of Semitic Studies Monograph, no. 10. Manchester: Manchester University Press 1989.

Böwering, G. (1994). "Ideas of Time in Persian Sufism." In *The Heritage of Sufism*, I: *Classical Persian Sufism From its Origins to Rumi*. Ed. L. Lewisohn. Oxford: Oneworld 1999: 199–233.

Briggs, J. *History of the Rise of the Muḥammadan Power in India*. Calcutta 1958.

Browne, E.G. *A Literary History of Persia*, 4 vols. Cambridge, Cambridge University Press 1956 rpt.

Bruijn, J.T.P. de "Nizārī Ḳuhistānī." *EI*[2], VIII: 83–4.

—— "Sabk-i hindī." *EI*[2], VIII: 683–5.

Bruinessen, Martin van. "Haji Bektash, Sultan Sahak, Shah Mina Sahib and Various Avatars of a Running Wall." *Turcica*, 21–3 (1991): 55–69.

Buehler, Arthur R. *Sufi Heirs of the Prophet: The Indian Naqsbandiyya and the Rise of the Mediating Sufi Shaykh*. Columbia: University of South Carolina Press 1998.

Bukhārī, Ḥasan Nithārī. *Mudhakkir-i-Aḥbāb of Khwāja Bahā al-Dīn Ḥasan Nithārī Bukhārī*. Ed. Syed Muḥammad Fazlullah. Hyderabad: Osmania University, Da'iratu'l-Ma'arif Press 1969.

Bukhārā'ī, Aḥmad 'Alī Rajā'ī. *Farhang-i ash'ār-i Ḥāfiẓ*. Tehran: Intishārāt-i 'Ilmī, n.d.

Bullhe Shāh. *Kulliyyāt-i Bullhe Shāh*. Lahore: Panjabi Adabi Board 1964.

Calder, N. "Legitimacy and Accommodation in Safavid Iran: The Juristic Theory of Muḥammad Bāqir al-Sabziwārī (d. 1090/1679)." *Iran* (1987): 91–105.

Canfield, Robert. (ed.). *Turko-Persia in Historical Perspective*. Cambridge: Cambridge University Press 1991.

Canfield, Robert L. and Nazif Shahrani (eds). *Revolutions and Rebellions in Afghanistan: Anthropological Perspectives*. Institute of International Studies, Research Series no. 57. Berkeley: University of California Press 1984.

Caroe, Sir Olaf. *The Pathans 550 B.C.–A.D. 1957*. London: MacMillan/New York: St Martin's Press 1964.

Chardin, John. *The Travels of Sir John Chardin into Persia and the East Indies, the First Volume, Containing the Author's Voyage from Paris to Ispahan to which is added the Coronation of this Present King of Persia, Solyman the Third*. London: Printed for Moses Pitt in Duke Street, Westminster 1686.

—— *Voyages du Chevalier Chardin, en Perse et Autres Lieux de l-Orient*. Ed. L. Langlès. 10 vols. Octavo, plus atlas, folio. Paris: Le Normant 1811.

—— *Travels in Persia 1673–1677*, with a preface by N.M. Penzer and an introduction by Sir Percy Sykes London: Dover Publications 1927.

Chishtī, N.A. *Tahqīqāt-i Chishtī*. Lahore: Punjabi Adabi Board 1964.

Chittick, W.C. "Notes on Ibn al-'Arabī"s Influence in India'. *Muslim World*. 82 (1992): 218–41.

—— 'Rūmī and *Waḥdat al-wujūd*'. In *Poetry and Mysticism in Islam: The Heritage of Rūmī*. Ed. A. Banani and G. Sabagh. Cambridge: Cambridge University Press 1994.

—— "The School of Ibn al-'Arabī." In *History of Islamic Philosophy*, I. Ed. Oliver Leaman and S.H. Nasr. London: Routledge 1996: 510–23.

Chodkiewicz, M. *Seal of the Saints: Prophethood and Sainthood in the Doctrine of Ibn 'Arabī*. Trans. L. Sherrard. Cambridge: ITS 1993.

Chughatā'ī, Muḥammad 'Abdullāh. "Nayrang-i 'ishq kā ek Qalamī Nuskha." *Oriental College Magazine*, 74 (August 1943): 54–6.

Clarke, C.J.S. *Reality Through the Looking-Glass: Science and Awareness in the Postmodern World*. London: Floris Books 1996.

Corbin, Henry. "Confessions extatiques de Mīr Dāmād, Maître de Théologie à Ispahan (Ob. 1041/1631–1632)." In *Mélanges Louis Massignon*. Vol.I: Damascus: L'Institut Français de Damas/L'Institut d'Études Islamiques de l'Université de Paris 1956.

—— *Histoire de la philosophie islamique*. Paris: Éditions Gallimard 1964.

—— *En Islam iranien: aspects spirituels et philosophiques*. 4 vols. Paris: Éditions Gallimard 1972.

—— *La Philosophie iranienne islamique aux XVII et XVIII siècles*. Paris: Buchet Chastel 1981.

—— *History of Islamic Philosophy*. Trans. L. Sherrard. London–New York: KPI in assoc. with Islamic Publications for the Institute of Ismaili Studies 1993.

—— (ed.). *Trilogie ismaélienne*. Tehran: Institut Français de Téhéran/Paris: Adrien Maisonneuve 1961.

Cowell, E.B. *Life and Letters of Edward Byles Cowell*. London: Macmillan 1904.

Dabashi, Hamid. *Theology of Discontent: The Ideological Foundation of the Islamic Revolution in Iran*. New York: New York University Press 1993.

—— "Mīr Dāmād and the Founding of the 'School of Iṣfahān'." In *History of Islamic Philosophy*, I. Ed. Oliver Leaman and S.H. Nasr. London: Routledge 1996: 597–634.

Daftary, Farhad. *The Ismā'īlīs: Their History and Doctrines*. Cambridge: Cambridge University Press 1990.

—— (ed.) *Mediæval Isma'ili History and Thought*. Cambridge: Cambridge University Press 1996.

Dārā Shikūh. *Majma' al-baḥrayn*. Calcutta. 1929.

—— *Dīwān-i Dārā Shikūh*. Ed. Aḥmad Nabī Khān. Lahore: University of the Punjab 1969.

Darwīzah, Khānd. *Tadhkirah al-Abrār wa'l-ashrār*. Delhi 1892.

—— *Makhzan al-Islām*. Peshawar 1969.

Dashtī, 'Alī. *Nigāhī bih Ṣā'ib*. Tehran: Asāṭīr 1364 A.Hsh./1985.

Dihqāhī-Taftī, B.H.B. *Christ and Christianity among the Iranians [Masīḥ va masīḥiyyat nazd-i Īrāniyān*). 3 vols. London: Sohrab Books 1992.

Deol, J.S. "Acceptable Poetry: Muqbil's Mystical *Qiṣṣah Hīr Rānjhā*'." *International Journal of Punjab Studies*, 3/2 (1996): 181–212.

—— "Love and Mysticism in the Punjabi Qissas of the Seventeenth and Eighteenth Centuries." University of London M.Phil. thesis 1996.

Devare, T.N. *A Short History of Persian Literature at the Bahmanī, 'Adīl Shāhī and Quṭb Shāhi Courts*. Deccan: Poona: 1961.

DeWeese, Devin. "A Neglected Source on Central Asian History: The 17th-Century Yasavī Hagiography *Manāqib al-akhyār*." In *Essays on Uzbek History, Culture, and Language*. Ed. Denis Sinor and Bakhtiyar A. Nazarov. Uralic and Altaic Series, vol. 156. Bloomington: RIFIAS 1993: 38–50.

—— "The Descendants of Sayyid Ata and the Rank of *Naqīb* in Central Asia." *Journal of the American Oriental Society*, 115 (1995): 612–34.

—— "The *Mashā'ikh-i Turk* and the *Khojagān*: Rethinking the Links between the Yasavī and Naqshbandī Sufi Traditions." *Journal of Islamic Studies*, 7 (1996): 180–207.

Digby, Simon. "To Ride a Tiger or a Wall? Strategies of Prestige in Indian Sufi Legend." In *According to Tradition: Hagiographical Writing in India*. Ed. Winand M. Callewaert and Rupert Snell. Wiesbaden: Harrassowitz 1994: 99–129.

Dilāwarī, Ṣādiq 'Alī. "Ghanīmat Kunjāhī." *Oriental College Magazine*, 69 (May 1942): 14–27.

—— "Ghanīmat kā Waṭan." In *Oriental College Magazine*, 75 (November 1943): 26–32.

Dīnānī, G.E. *Falsafah-i Suhrawardī*. Tehran: Intishārāt-i Ḥikmat 1985.

Dvornik, F. *The Ecumenical Councils*. New York: Hawthorn Books 1961.

Eaton, Richard M. *Sufis of Bijapur, 1300–1700: Social Roles of Sufis in Medieval India*. Princeton: Princeton University Press 1978.

Edmundson, Phillip. "The Persians of Concord." *Sufi: A Journal of Sufism*. 3 (Spring 1989): 14–18.

—— "Hawthorne Turns to the East: Persian Influences in the *Blithedale Romance*." *English Language Notes*. 28/2 (1990): 25–38.

Elder, E.E. *A Commentary on the Creed of Islam*. New York: Columbia University Press 1950.

Elphinstone, Mountstuart. *An Account of the Kingdom of Caubul and its dependencies in Persia, Tartary and India*. London 1839.

Emerson, John. *Chardin, Sir John*. *EIr*. V: 369–77.

Emerson, Ralph Waldo. *Complete Works*. Boston: Riverside Press, centenary edition 1903–4.

—— *Letters of Ralph Waldo Emerson*. Ed. Ralph L. Rusk. 6 vols. New York: Columbia University Press 1939.

—— *Collected Poems and Translations*. Ed. Harold Bloom. New York: Library of America 1994.

Ernst, Carl. *Eternal Garden: Mysticism, History, and Politics at a South Asian Sufi Center*. Albany, SUNY Press 1992.

—— *The Shambhala Guide to Sufism*. Boston–London: Shambhala 1997.

Ethé, H. (ed.) *Catalogue of the Persian, Turkish, Hindustani and Pushtu Manuscripts in the Bodleian Library*. Oxford: Clarendon Press 1889.

Falsafī, Naṣru'llāh. *Zindagī-yi Shāh 'Abbās awwal*. Tehran: 1332 A.Hsh./1953.

Fannārī, Ḥamza. *Miṣbāḥ al-uns*. Persian trans. M. Khajavī. Tehran: Intishārāt-i Mullā 1994.

Fārābī, al-.*Risāla fī 'l-'Aql*. Beirut: Imprimerie Catholique 1938.

Faruqi, Isma'il R. al- and Lois Lamya al-Faruqi. *The Cultural Atlas of Islam*. New York: Macmillan 1986.

Farzan, Massud. "Whitman and Sufism: Towards 'A Persian Lesson'." *American Literature*. 40/4 (1976): 572–82.

Fenech, L. "Persian Sikh Scripture: The Ghazals of Bhā'ī Nand La'l Goyā." *International Journal of Punjab Studies* 1/1 (1994): 49–70.

Ferrier, Ronald. *A Journey to Persia: Jean Chardin's Portrait of a Seventeenth-Century Empire*. London: I.B. Tauris 1996.

Fischel, Walter. "The Jews in Mediæval Iran from the Sixteenth to the Eighteenth Centuries: Political, Economic, and Communal aspects." *Irano-Judaica* (1982): 265–96.

Fleischer, C. "Alqās Mīrzā." *EIr*. I: 907–9.

Floor, W. "The Rise and Fall of Mirza Taqi, the Eunuch Grand Vizier (1043–55/1633–45), Makhdum al-Omara va Khadem al-Foqara." *Studia Iranica* 26/2 (1997): 237–66.

Friedman, Y. *Prophecy Continuous: Aspects of Aḥmad Religious Thought and Its Medieval Background*. Berkeley: University of California Press 1986.

Frye, N. *The Secular Scripture: A Study of the Structure of Romance*. Cambridge Mass.–London: Harvard University Press 1976.

Fryer, John. *A New Account of East India and Persia, being Nine Years' Travels 1672–1681*. Ed. William Crooke. 5 vols. London: Hakluyt Society 1909–15.

Fusfeld, Warren. "The Shaping of Sufi Leadership in Delhi: The Naqshbandiyya-Mujaddidiyya, 1750–1920." University of Pennsylvania Ph. D. dissertation 1981.

Ghani, Abdul. *Life and Works of Abdul Qadir Bedil*. Lahore: Publishers United 1960.

Ghanī, Qāsim. *Tārīkh-i taṣawwuf dar Islām*. Tehran: Zavvār 1340 A.H.sh./1961.

Ghanīmat Kunjāhī. *Dīwān-i Ghanīmat*. Ed. G.R. 'Azīz. Lahore: 1958.

—— *Nayrang-i 'ishq: Mathnawī-yi Ghanīmat*. Ed. G.R. 'Azīz. Lahore: Panjabi Adabi Board 1962.

Ghazālī, Abū Ḥāmid al-. *Tahāfut al-falāsifa*. Beirut: Imprimerie Catholique 1962.

Gibb, E.J.W. *A History of Ottoman Poetry*. 6 vols. London: E.J.W. Gibb Memorial Trust 1900, rpt. 1984.

Goodman, L.E. "Time in Islam." *Asian Philosophy*, 2/1 (1992): 3–6.

—— "Time, Creation and the Mirror Of Narcissus." In *Divine Intervention and Miracles in Jewish Theology*. Ed. Dan Cohn-Sherbok. Jewish Studies, vol.16, Lewiston–Queenston–Lampeter: The Edwin Mellen Press 1996: 99–151.

Gosling, J.C.B. *Plato*. The Arguments of the Philosophers, London: Routledge & Kegan Paul 1973.

Graham, Terry. "Abū Sa'īd ibn Abī'l-Khayr and the School of Khurāsān." In *The Heritage of Sufism*, I: *Classical Persian Sufism From its Origins to Rumi*. Ed. L. Lewisohn. Oxford: Oneworld 1999: 83–135.

—— "Shāh Ni'matullāh Walī: Founder of the Ni'matullāhī Sufi Order." In *The Heritage of Sufism*, II: *The Legacy of Medieval Persian Sufism*. Oxford: Oneworld 1999: 173–90.

Gran, Peter. *The Islamic Roots of Capitalism: Egypt 1760–1840*. Austin: University of Texas Press 1979.

Grunebaum, Gustave E. von (ed.). *Klassizismus und Kulturverfall: Vorträge*. Frankfurt am Main: V. Klostermanns 1960.

Gyān Chand Jain, U. *Mathnawī Shimālī Hind men*. Aligarh: Anjuman-i Taraqqi-yi Urdu 1969.

Haar, J. ter. "The Importance of the Spiritual Guide in the Naqshbandī Order." In *The Heritage of Sufism*, II: *The Legacy of Medieval Persian Sufism*. Ed. L. Lewisohn. Oxford: Oneworld 1999: 311–21.

Hadi, N. *Dictionary of Indo-Persian Literature*. New Delhi: Abhinar Publications 1995.

Hādī, Akbar. *Sharḥ-i ḥāl-i Mīr Dāmād va Mīr Findariskī*. Iṣfahān: Intishārāt-i Mītham Tamār 1363 A.Hsh./1984.

Ḥāfiẓ. *Dīwān-i Ḥāfiẓ*. Ed. P.N. Khānlarī. 2 vols. Tehran: Sahām 'ām 1983.

Haq, M.E. *Muslim Bengali Literature*. Karachi 1957.

Hāshimī, Nāṣir al-Dīn. *Europe Mein Dakhanī Makhṭūṭāt*. Hyderabad 1932.

—— *Kutub-khāna-i Salar Jang Museum kī Urdu qalamī Kitābon kī fihrist*. Hyderabad 1957.

Hazini. *Cevâhiru'l-ebrâr min emvâc-ı bihâr* (*Yesevî Menâkıbnamesi*). Ed. Cihan Okuyucu. Kayseri: Erciyes Üniversitesi 1995.

Heinz, W. *Der Indische Stil in der Persischen Literatur*. Wiesbaden: Franz Steiner 1972.

Helfgott, L.M. "Tribalism as a Socioeconomic Formation in Iranian History." *Iranian Studies*. 10 (1977): 36–61.

Herbert, Thomas. *Travels in Persia, 1627–29*. Abridged and edited by Sir William Foster, with an Introduction and Notes. The Broadway Travellers Series, London: George Routledge & Sons 1928.

Hermansen, Marcia. "Mystical Paths and Authoritative Knowledge: A Semiotic Approach to Sufi Cosmological Diagrams." *Journal of Religious Studies and Theology*. 12/1 (1992): 52–77.

Hewitt, R.M. *Essays and Studies by Members of the English Association*. Ed. R.W. Chapman. Oxford: Clarendon Press 1943.

Hidāyat, Ḥusayn. "Shāh Ṭāhir of the Deccan." In *Indian and Iranian Studies*. Bombay: 1939.

Hindī, S.N. *Shi'r al-'ajam*. Tehran: Dunyā-yi Kitāb 1984.

Hodgson, Marshall G.S. *The Venture of Islam: Conscience and History in a World Civilization*. 3 vols. Chicago: University of Chicago Press 1974.

Holbrook, Victoria. *The Unreadable Shores of Love*. Austin: University of Texas Press 1994.

—— "Diverse Tastes in the Spiritual Life: Textual Play in the Diffusion of Rumi's Order." In *The Heritage of Sufism*, II: *The Legacy of Medieval Persian Sufism*. Ed. L. Lewisohn. Oxford: Oneworld 1999: 99–120.

Hujwīrī, 'Alī al-. *The* Kashf al-maḥjūb: *The Oldest Persian Treatise on Sufism*. Trans. R.A. Nicholson. London: Luzac & Co. 1911 rpt. 1976.

—— *Kashf al-maḥjūb*. Ed. Zhūkūfskī, Tehran: Ẓuhūr 1375 A.Hsh./1996.

Humā'ī, Jalāl al-Dīn. *Mawlavī chih mīguyad*. 2 vols. Tehran: High Council of Culture and Art 1976.

Ḥusayn, Shāh. *The Paths Unknown* (*Kafian Shāh Hussain*). Trans. Ghulam Yaqoob Anwar. Lahore: Majlis Shah Hussain 1966.

Hussaini, S.S.K. *Sayyid Muḥammad al-Husaynī-i Gīsūdirāz* (*721/1321–825/1422*)*: On Sufism*. Delhi: Idarah-i Adabiyat-i Delhi 1983.

Ibn 'Arabī. *Kitāb al-futūḥāt al-makkiyya*. Cairo: 1329.

—— *Sufis of Andalusia: The* Rūḥ al-quds *and* al-Durrat al-fākhirah. Trans. by R.W.J. Austin. London: Allen & Unwin 1971.

—— *Futūḥāt al-Makkiyya*. Cairo: Al-Hay'at al-Miṣriyyat al-'Āmma li'l-Kitāb 1972.

—— *Bezels of Wisdom*. Trans. by R.J.W. Austin. New York: Paulist Press, 1980.

Ibn Bābawayh, Abū Ja'far Muhammad b. 'Alī al-Qummī. *Ma'āni al-akhbār*. Qum: Intishārāt-i Islāmī 1361 A.Hsh./1982.

Ibn Karbalā'ī, Ḥāfiẓ Ḥusayn. *Rawḍāt al-janān wa jannāt al-jinān*. Ed. Ja'far Sulṭān al-Qurrā'ī. 2 vols. Tabriz: B.T.N.K. 1344 A.Hsh./1965.

Ibn Khātūn (Shaykh Shams al-Dīn Abū Ma'ālī Muḥammad Ibn 'Alī Ibn Khātūn al-Amūlī). *Tuḥfah-i majālis-i bihisht ā'in*. MS. no. 10 Manaqib. Hyderabad: Salar Jang Museum.

Ibn Ma'ṣūm. *Salāfat al-'Aṣr*. Cairo 1906.

'Irāqī, Fakhr al-Dīn. *Risāla-yi lamā'at wa risāla-yi iṣṭilāḥāt*. Ed. J. Nūrbakhsh. Tehran: Intishārāt-i Khānaqāh-i Ni'matu'llāhī 1353 A.Hsh./1974.

Iṣfahānī, M.Y.V. *Khuld-i Barīn: Īrān dar rūzgār-i Ṣafaviyān*. Tehran: Bunyād-i Mawqūfāt-Duktur Maḥmūd Afshār 1372 A.Hsh./1993.

Isfandiyar, M.K. *Dabistān-i-madhāhib*. 2 vols. Tehran Ed. Riḍāzāda Malik. 1362 A.Hsh./1983.

Iskandari, Ibn 'Aṭā Allāh al-. *The Key to Salvation: A Sufi Manual of Invocation*. Trans. Mary Ann Koury-Danner. Cambridge: Islamic Texts Society 1996.

Istakhrī, Iḥsānu'llāh 'Alī. *Uṣūl-i taṣawwuf*. Tehran: Kānūn-i Ma'rifat 1338 A.Hsh./1959.

Ivanow, W. "An Ismā'īlī Interpretation of the Gulshani Raz." *Journal of the Bombay Branch of the Royal Asiatic Society*. New Series, 8 (1932): 69–78.

—— "A Forgotten Branch of the Ismā'īlīs." *Journal of the Royal Asiatic Society* (1938): 57–79.

—— "Tombs of Some Persian Ismā'īlī Imams." *Journal of the Bombay Branch of the Royal Asiatic Society*. New Series, 14 (1938): 49–62.

—— *Brief Survey of the Evolution of Ismā'īlism*. Leiden: Brill, for the Islamic Society 1952.

—— *Ismā'īlī Literature: A Bibliographical Survey*. Tehran: Ismaili Society, 1963.

Ja'fariyān, Rasūl. *Dīn va siyāsat dar dūra-yi Ṣafavī*. Qum: Intishārāt-i Anṣāriyān 1370 A.Hsh./1991.

—— (ed.) *Mīrāth-i Islāmī-yi Irān*. Qum: Mar'ashī Najafī Public Library 1374 A.Hsh./ 1995.

Jahānābādī, Kalīm Allāh. *Maktbūbāt-i Kalīmī*. Delhī: Maṭba'-i Mujtabā'ī 1315/1897.

Jain, Gyān Chand. *Urdū Mathnawī Shimālī Hind men*. Aligarh: Anjuman-i Taraqqi-yi Urdu 1969.

Jambet, Christian. *La Grande résurrection d'Alamūt*. Lagrasse: Verdier 1990.

Jāmī, 'Abd al-Raḥmān. *Nafaḥāt al-uns*. Ed. Maḥmūd 'Ābidī. Tehran: Intishārāt-i Iṭilā'āt 1370 A.Hsh./1991.

Johnson, Rosemary Stanfield. "Sunni Survival in Safavid Iran: Anti-Sunni Activities during the Reign of Tahmasp I." *Iranian Studies*, 27/1–4 (1994): 123–33.

Juwaynī, ʻAṭā' Malik. *Genghis Khan: The History of the World Conqueror*. Trans. & Ed. J.A. Boyle, with an introduction by David Morgan. Manchester: Manchester University Press 1997.

—— *Ta'rīkh-i jahān-gushāy*. Ed. M. Qazvīnī. Leiden: Brill/London: E.J.W. Gibb Memorial Series 1912–37.

Kākā'ī, Qāsim. "Shīrāz, mahd-i ḥikmat." In *Khiradnāma-yi Ṣadrā*. 1/2 (August 1995): 63–9.

—— "Āshnā'ī bā maktab-i Shīrāz." *Khiradnāma-yi Ṣadrā*. 1/3 (March 1996): 82–9.

—— "Āshnā'ī bā maktab-i Shīrāz-i Amīr Ghiyāth al-Dīn Manṣūr Dashtakī." *Khiradnāma-yi Ṣadrā*. 2/5–6 (Autumn–Winter 1997): 83–90.

Kāshānī, Muḥsin Fayḍ-i. *Risāla-yi mishwāq*. Ed. Muṣṭafā'ī Fayḍī Kāshānī. Tehran: 1348 A.Hsh./1969.

—— *Kulliyāt-i ash'ār-i Mawlānā Fayḍ-i Kāshānī*. Ed. Muḥammad Paymān. Tehran: n.p. 1354 A.Hsh./1975.

—— *'Ilm al-yaqīn*. 2 vols. Qum: Intishārāt-i Bīdār 1358 A.Hsh./ 1979.

—— *Dah risālah-yi Muḥaqqiq-i Buzurg-i Fayḍ-i Kāshānī*. Ed. R. Ja'fariyān. Iṣfahān: Markaz-i taḥqīqāt-i 'ilmī va dīnī Imām Amīr al-Mū'minīn 'Alī 1371 A.Hsh./1992.

Kāshānī, Qāḍī Aḥmad Ghaffārī Qazvīnī. *Tārīkh-i jahān-ārā*. Ed. Ḥasan Narāqī. Tehran: Kitāb-furūshī-i Ḥāfiẓ 1342 A.Hsh./1963.

Kasravī, Aḥmad. "Tabār va kīsh Ṣafaviyān." *Iran Nameh*. 13/3 (1995): 377–86.

Keddie, Nikki and Juan Cole (eds). *Shi'ism and Social Protest*. New Haven: Yale University Press 1986.

Kenney, E.J. (ed.). *Cupid and Psyche*. Cambridge: Cambridge University Press 1990.

Keyvani, Mehdi. *Artisans and Guild Life in the Later Safavid Period*. Berlin: Klaus Schwarz 1982.

Khattak, Afzal Khān. *Tārīkh-i-Muraṣṣa'*. In *The Gulshan-i-Roh: Being Selections, Prose and Poetical, in the Pus'hto, or Afghan Language*. Ed. Captain H.G. Raverty. London: Williams & Norgate 1860.

Khātūnābādī, 'Abd al-Ḥusayn. *Waqā'i al-Sinīn*. Tehran 1352 A.Hsh./1973.

Khwāndamīr. *Tārīkh-i ḥabīb al-siyar*. Tehran: Kitābkhāna-yi Khayyām 1945.

—— s.v. "Thackston."

Khān, M.A. *Adabiyyāt-i fārsī dar miyān-i Hinduvān*. Tehran 1371 A.Hsh./1992.

Khunjī-Iṣfahānī, Faḍlullāh b. Rūzbihān. *Tārīkh-i 'ālam-ārā-yi Amīnī*. Ed. John Woods. London: Royal Asiatic Society 1992.

Khwāndamīr, Ghīyāth al-Dīn. *Ḥabīb al-sīyar*. 4 vols. Ed. J. Humā'ī. Tehran: Khayyām 1333 A.Hsh./1954.

Khwānsarī, Muḥammad Bāqir al-. *Rawḍāt al-Jannāt*. Ed. M.T. al-Kashfī and A. Ismā'īlīyān. Tehran/Qum: 1390–2.

Kieffer, Ch. M. "La maintenance de l'identité ethnique chez les Arabes arabophones, les Ormur et les Parācī en Afghanistan." In Erwin Orywalī, ed., *Die ethnischen Gruppen Afghanistans*. Wiesbaden: Dr Ludwig Reichert Verlag 1986: 13031.

Kieffer, Ch. M. "Afrīdī." *EIr*. I: 79.

King, L. White. *The Orakzai Country and Clans*. Lahore 1984: being a reprint of L. White King, *Monograph on the Orakzai Country and Clans: A Government Report*. Lahore: Vanguard Books 1900.

Kiyānī, M. *Tārīkh-i khānaqāh dar Irān*. Tehran: Ṭahūrī 1369 A.Hsh./1990.

Knysh, Alexander. "Ibrāhīm al-Kūrānī (d. 1101/1690), an Apologist for *waḥdat al-wujūd*." *Journal of the Royal Asiatic Society*. 5/1 (1995): 39–47.

Kohlberg, E. "Bahā' al-Dīn 'Amelī," *EIr* III: 429–30.

Köprülü, Mehmed Fuad *Türk edebıyatinda ilk mutasavvıflar*. Istanbul: Maṭba'ah-i 'Āmirah 1918. Latin script edition, 5th printing. Ankara: Arısan Matbaacılık 1984.

Krishna, L.R. *Pañjābī Ṣūfī Poets*. Calcutta: Oxford University Press 1938.

Lāhījī, 'Abd al-Razzāq. *Dīvān-i Fayyāḍ Lāhījī*. Ed. Jalīl Misgarnizhād. Tehran: Dānishgāh-i 'Allāma Ṭabāṭabā'ī 1373 A.Hsh./1994.

—— *Dīvān-i Fayyāḍ Lāhījī*. Ed. Amīr Bānū'ī Karīmī. Tehran: Dānishgāh-i Tihrān 1372 A.Hsh./1993.

—— *Gawhar-i murād*. Ed. Z. Qurbānī Lāhījī. Tehran: 1372 A.Hsh./1993.

Lāhījī, Muḥammad. *Mafātīḥ al-i'jāz fī sharḥ-i Gulshan-i rāz*. Ed. R. Khāliqī and 'I. Karbāsī. Tehran: Zawwār 1371 A.Hsh./1992.

Lambton, A.K.S. "Quis custodient custodes?" *Studia Islamica*. 6 (1956).

Landolt. Hermann. "Walāyah." In *The Encyclopedia of Religion*. Ed. M. Eliade. 15 vols. New York: Macmillan 1995, XV: 316–22.

Lapidus, Ira. *A History of Muslim Societies*. New York: Cambridge University Press 1988.

Lawrence, Bruce. "Biography and the Seventeenth-century Qadariyya of North India." In *Islam and Indian Regions*. Ed. Anna Libera Dallapiccola and Stephanie Zengel-Ave Lallemant. Stuttgart: Franz Steiner 1993.

Leaman, Oliver and Nasr, S.H. (eds). *History of Islamic Philosophy*. 2 vols. London: Routledge 1996.

Leclercq, J. *The Love of Learning and the Desire for God: A Study of Monastic Culture*. New York: Fordham University Press 1982.

Leonard, K.I. *Social History of an Indian Caste: The Kayasths of Hyderabad*. Berkeley, University of California Press 1978.

Leslie, D. *Islamic Literature in Chinese*. Canberra: Canberra College of Advanced Education 1981.

—— *Islam in Traditional China*. Canberra: Canberra College of Advanced Education 1986.

Levtzion, Nehemia and John Voll. *Eighteenth-Century Reform and Renewal in Islam*. Syracuse: Syracuse University Press 1987.

Lewisohn, Leonard. "Sulūk." *EI*², IX: 861–3.

—— *Beyond Faith and Infidelity: The Sufi Poetry and Spiritual Teachings of Maḥmūd Shabistarī*. London: Curzon 1995.

—— (ed.). *Divān-i Muḥammad Shīrīn Maghribī*. Persian text edited with notes, introduction, and indices. Wisdom of Persia Series. Tehran: McGill Institute of Islamic Studies, Tehran Branch/London: SOAS 1994.

—— (ed.). *The Heritage of Sufism*, I *Classical Persian Sufism From its Origins to Rumi*. Oxford: Oneworld 1991.

—— (ed.). *The Heritage of Sufism*, II *The Legacy of Medieval Persian Sufism*. Oxford: Oneworld 1991.

Liebeskind, C. "*Sufism, Sufi Leadership and 'Modernization' in South Asia Since c.1800*". University of London Ph.D. thesis 1995.

Lin, C.-K. "Three Eminent Chinese Ulama of Yunnan." *Journal of the Institute of Muslim Minority Affairs*, 9/1 (1990): 103–8.

Lockhart, Laurence. 'European Contacts with Persia, 1350–1736'. In *The Cambridge History of Iran, The Timurid and Safavid Periods*. Ed. P. Jackson and L. Lockhart. Cambridge: Cambridge University Preess 1968: 373–409.

Loloi, Parvin. "Islamic Influences on Peter Russell's Poetry." International Conference on British and Irish Poetry in the Making. University of Salzburg 1996.

Losensky, Paul. "The Allusive Field of Drunkenness: Three Safavid-Moghul Responses to a Lyric by Bābā Fighānī." In *Reorientations/ Arabic and Persian Poetry*. Ed. S.P. Stetkevych. Bloomington: Indiana University Press 1994: 227–62.

Lynton, Harriet Ronken and Mohini Rajan. *The Days of the Beloved*. Berkeley–Los Angeles London: University of California Press 1974.

Macbeath, Murray and Robin Le Poidevin (eds). *The Philosophy of Time*. Oxford Readings in Philosophy. Oxford: Oxford University Press 1995.

Maerczak, R. "Littérature Sino-musulmane." *Revue du monde musulmane*, 28 (Sept. 1914): 147–9.

Majlisī, Muḥammad Bāqir. *Jawāhir al-'uqūl*. Tehran: lithograph edition, n.p. 1303/ 1885.

Makkī, Abū Ṭālib. *Qūt al-qulūb*. Beirut: Dār Ṣādir, n.d.

Mans, Rafael Du. *Estat de la Perse en 1660*. Ed. Ch. Schefer. Paris 1890.

Marek, J. "The Golden Age of Indo-Persian Literature." In *History of Iranian Literature*. Ed. J. Rypka. Dordrecht, D. Riedel Publishing Co. 1968.

Mason, I. "Notes on Chinese Mohammedan Literature." *Journal of the North China Branch of the Royal Asiatic Society*. 56 (1925): 172–3.

Ma'ṣūm 'Alī Shāh Shīrāzī. *Ṭarā'iq al-ḥaqā'iq*. Ed. M.J Maḥjūb. 3 vols. Tehran: Kitābkhāna-i Bārānī 1345 A.Hsh./1966.

Matringe, D. "Kr̥ṣnaite and Nāth Elements in the Poetry of the Eighteenth-Century Panjabi Sūfī Bullhe Śāh." In *Devotional Literature in South Asia: Current Research 1985–1988*. Ed. R.S. McGregor. Cambridge: Cambridge University Press 1992: 190–206.

Matthee, Rudi. "The Career of Muhammad Beg, Grand Vizier of Shah Abbas II (r. 1642–1666)." *Iranian Studies*. 241 (1991): 17–36.

—— "Politics and Trade in Late Safavid Iran." Unpublished Ph.D. thesis, University of California, Los Angeles 1991.

—— "Administrative Change and Stability in Late Seventeenth-Century Iran: The Case of Shaykh Ali Khan Zanganah (1669–89)." *International Journal of Middle East Studies*. 26 (1994): 77–98.

Mazzaoui, M. *The Origins of the Safawids: Šī'ism, Ṣūfism, and the Ǧulāt*. Freiburger Islamistudien. Wiesbaden: Franz Steiner 1972.

McChesney, Robert. "Ālamārā-ye Šāh Esmā'īl." *EIr*. I: 796–7.

—— "Comments on the 'Qajar Uymaq in the Safavid Period." *Iranian Studies*. 14 (1981): 87–105.

Meier, Fritz "Soufisme et déclin culturel." In *Classicisme et déclin culturel dans l'histoire de l'Islam*. Actes du Symposium Internationale d'Histoire de la Civilisation Musulmane. Ed. R. Brunschvig and G.E. Von Grunebaum. Paris: Chantemerle 1957: 217–45.

—— *Meister und Schuler im Orden der Naqshbandiyya*. Heidelberg: C. Winter 1995.

Membré, M. *Mission to the Lord Sophy of Persia (1539–1542)*. Trans. A.H. Morton. London: SOAS Publications 1993.

Miklukho-Maklai, N.D. *Opisanie tadzhikskikh i persidskikh rukopisei Instituta narodov Azii*. Vyp. 2, Biograficheskie sochineniia. Moscow: Izdatel'stvo Vostochnoi Literatury 1961.

Minorsky, V. "The Poetry of Shāh Ismā'īl I." *BSOAS*. 10 (1942): 10–9.

Mīr Dāmād. *Jadhawāt*. Lithographed edn., Bombay 1302/1884.

—— *Kitāb al-Qabasāt*. Ed. M. Mohaghegh, T.Izutsu, A. Mūsavī Bihbahānī and I. Dībājī, with English introduction by T. Izutsu. Wisdom of Persia Series no. 7 Tehran: McGill University Institute of Islamic Studies, Tehran Branch with Tehran University 1977.

Mīr Findiriskī. *Risāla-yi ṣanā'iyya*. In *Muntakhabātī az āthār-i ḥukamā'ī ilāhī-yi Īrān*. Ed. S.J. Ashtiyānī. Tehran: Departement d'Iranologie de l'Institut Franco-Iranien de Recherche 1971: I: 59–80.

—— *Tuḥfa al-murād: sharḥ-i qaṣīda-yi Mīr Findiriskī*. Ed. Muḥammad Akbarī Sāvī. Tehran: n.p., 1372 A.Hsh./1993.

Mīr Lawḥī. *Salvat al-Shī'a*. In *Mīrāth-i Islāmī-yi Irān*. II. Ed. Rasūl Ja'fariyān. Qum: Mar'ashī Najafī Public Library 1374 A.Hsh./1995.

Mirjafari, Hossein. "The Ḥaydarī–Ni'matī Conflicts in Iran." Trans. and adapted by J.R. Perry. *Iranian Studies* 15 (1979): 135–62.

Moir, S. *Ismaili Hymns from South Asia: An Introduction to the Ginans*. London: SOAS Publications 1992.

Molé, M. "Autour du Daré Mansour: l'apprentissage mystique de Bahā' al-Dīn Naqshband." *Revue des études islamiques*, 27 (1959): 35–66.

—— "Les Kubrawiya entre sunnisme et shiisme aux huitième et neuvième siècles de l'hégire." *Revue des études islamiques*. 29 (1961).

Mominov, Äshurbek K. "Yässäviyä: ildiz vä mänbälär." *Fän vä turmush*, 9–10 (1993).

—— "O proiskhozhdenii bratstva iasaviia." *Islam i problemy mezhtsivilizatsionnykh vzaimodeistvii*. Moscow: Obshchestvo 'Nur' (1994): 219–31.

Monserrate, Father. *The Commentary of Father Monserrate, S.J., on his Journey to the Court of Akbar*. Oxford: Oxford University Press 1922.

Morgenstierne, Georg. *Indo-Iranian Frontier Languages*, I: *Parachi and Ormuri*. Oslo 1929.

Morton, A.H. "The Date and Attribution of the Ross Anonymous. Notes on a Persian History of Shāh Ismā'īl I." In *Pembroke Papers I*. Ed. C. Melville. Cambridge, University of Cambridge Centre of Middle Eastern Studies 1990: 179–212.

—— "The *chūb-ṭarīq* and Qizilbāsh ritual in Safavid Persia." In *Etudes Safavides*. Ed. Jean Aubin Paris/Tehran: Institut Français de recherche en Iran–Louvain. Editions Peeters 1993.

Morris, James Winston.*The Wisdom of the Throne: An Introduction to the Philosophy of Mullā Ṣadrā*. Princeton, NJ: Princeton University Press 1981.

Mossadegh, 'Ali Asghar. "La Famille Monajjem Yazdi." In "Notes Sur Des Historiographes de l'époque Safavide." Ed. Jean Calmard, 'Ali Asghar Mossadegh and M. Bastani Parizi. *Studia Iranica* 16 (1987): 125–6.

Mūbad Kiykhusraw Isfandiyar. *Dabistān-i-Madhāhib*. Tehran 1983.

Mufīd Yazdī, Muḥammad. *Jāmi' Mufīdī*. 3 vols. Ed. I. Afshār. Tehran: Asadī 1340 A.Hsh./1961.

Muḥammadī, Kāẓim. *Mawlānā wa difā' az 'aql*. Tehran: Mahdi Press 1994.

Mukhliṣ, 'Alī Muḥammad *Ḥālnāma-i-Bāyazīd Rawshān*. Kabul 1986.

Mullā Ṣadrā, Ṣadr al-Dīn Muḥammad ibn Ibrāhīm Qawāmī Shīrāzī.

—— *Majmū'ah-i maqālāt*. Qum: Intishārāt-i Muṣṭafavī, n.d.

—— *Risāla-yi Sih aṣl*. Ed. S.H. Nasr. Tehran: Tehran University Press 1340 A.Hsh./ 1961.

—— *'Arshiyya*. Edited with a Persian translation by Ghulām Ḥusayn Āhanī. Iṣfahān: Kitābfurūshī-yi Shahriyār 1341 A.Hsh./1962.

—— *Kasr aṣnām al-jāhiliyya fī al-radd 'alā Mutasawwafa*. Ed. Muḥammad Taqī Dānish-pazhūh. Tehran: Dānishkadih-i 'ulūm-i ma'qūl va manqūl 1340 A.Hsh./ 1962.

—— *Al-Ḥikmat al-muta'āliyya fī 'l-Asfār al-arba'a al-'aqliyya*. Qum: Intishārāt-i Muṣṭafavī 1344 A.Hsh./ 1965.

—— *Al-Shawāhid al-rubūbiyya fī al-manāhij al-sulūkiyya*. Mashhad: Mashhad University Press 1346 A.Hsh./1967.

—— *Le Livre des pénétrations métaphysiques* (*Kitāb al-mashā'ir*). Arabic text edited with a Persian version and French translation and annotation by Henry Corbin. 2nd edn. Tehran: Ṭahūrī 1363 A.Hsh./1984.

Munshi, Mukhammed Iusuf. *Mukim-khanskaia istoriia*. Trans. A.A. Semenov. Tashkent: Izdatel'stvo AN UzSSR 1956.

Munshī, Indarjīt. *Nāma-yi 'ishq*. Ed. Waḥīd Qurayshī. Lahore: Panjabi Adabi Board 1959.

Munshī, Iskandar Beg. *Tārīkh-i 'ālam-ārā-yi 'Abbāsī*. Ed. Iraj Afshār. 2nd edn. 2 vols. Tehran: Amīr Kabīr 1350 A.Hsh./1971.

—— *History of Shah 'Abbas the Great*. Trans. Roger Savory. 2 vols. Persian Heritage Series 28. Boulder, Colorado: Westview Press 1978.

Murata, Sachiko. *The Tao of Islam: A Sourcebook on Gender Relationships in Islamic Thought*. Albany: SUNY Press 1992.

Musavī, Aḥmad Kāẓimī. "Jāyigāh-i 'ulamā' dar ḥukūmat-i Qājār." *Iran Nameh*, 15/2 (1997): 199–227.

Muṣliḥ, Javād. *Falsafa-yi Ṣadr al-muta'allihīn*. Tehran: Tehran University Press 1974.

Naim, C.M. "The Theme of Homosexual (Pederastic) Love in Pre-Modern Urdu Poetry." In *Studies in the Urdu Ġazal and Prose Fiction*. Ed. M. Umar Memon. Wisconsin: Dept. of S. Asia Studies, University of Wisconsin 1979: 120–42.

Nasr, S.H. "Spiritual Movements, Philosophy and Theology in the Safavid Period." In *The Cambridge History of Iran. The Timurid and Safavid Periods*. Ed. P. Jackson and L. Lockhart. Cambridge: Cambridge University Press 1968: 656–97.

—— *Three Muslim Sages*. Cambridge, Mass.: Harvard University Press 1969.

—— "Religion in Safavid Persia." *Iranian Studies*. 7 (1974): 271–86.

—— *Ṣadr al-Dīn Shīrāzī and His Transcendent Philosophy*. Tehran: Iranian Academy of Philosophy 1978.

—— "Oral Transmission and the Book in Islamic Education: the Spoken and the Written Word." *Journal of Islamic Studies* 3 (1992).

—— *The Islamic Intellectual Tradition in Persia*. Ed. M. A. Razavi. London: Curzon Press 1997.

—— "The School of Iṣfahān." In *A History of Muslim Philosophy*. Ed. M.M. Sharif. Wiesbaden: Harrassowitz 1996: vol. II, 904–61.

—— *The Transcendent Theosophy of Ṣadr al-Dīn Shīrāzī*. Tehran: Institute for Humanities and Cultural Studies, reprt. 1997.

—— *A Narrative of Italian Travels in Persia in the Fifteenth and Sixteenth Centuries*. Hakluyt Society, XLIX, pt. 2. London 1873.

Naṣrābādī, Mīrzā Muḥammad Ṭāhir. *Tadhkira-yi Naṣrābādī*. Ed. V. Dastgirdī. Tehran: Furūghī 1352 A.Hsh./1973.

Naṭanzī, Maḥmūd Afūshteh-ī. *Nuqāwat al-āthār fī dhikr al-akhyār*. Ed. Ishrāqī. Tehran 1350 A.Hsh. 1971.

Nawshāhī, Sayyid Sharafat. "Ruq'āt-i Ghanīmat Kunjāhī." *Ṣaḥīfa*, 63 (January 1973): 1–13.

Netton, I. R. *Allāh Transcendent: Studies in the Structure and Semiotics of Islamic Philosophy, Theology and Cosmology*. Richmond: Curzon Press 1994.

—— *Text and Trauma: An East-West Primer*. Richmond: Curzon Press 1996.

Newman, A. "Dāmād, Mīr." *EIr*, VI: 623–6.

—— "Towards a Reconsideration of the 'Isfahan School of Philosophy': Shaykh Bahā'ī and the Role of the Safawid 'Ulamā." *Studia Iranica* 15/2 (1986).

—— "The Nature of the Akhbārī/Uṣūlī Dispute in Late-Safawid Iran." *Bulletin of the School of Oriental and African Studies*. 55/1 (1992): 22–51; 55/2 (1992): 250–61.

—— "The Myth of Clerical Migration to Safawid Iran." *Die Welt des Islams*, 33 (1993): 66–112.

—— "Anti-Sufi Polemics in Safavid Iran: *Ḥadīqat al-Shī'a*." Forthcoming.

Nicholson, R.A. "A Historical Enquiry Concerning the Origin and Development of Sufiism, With a List of Definitions of the Terms 'ṣūf' and 'ṭaṣawwuf,' Arranged Chronologically." *Journal of the Royal Asiatic Society*, 1 (1906).

—— *Studies in Islamic Mysticism*. Cambridge, Cambridge University Press 1921.

Nizami, Khaliq Ahmad. "Čishtiyya." *EI*² I: 50–6.

—— "Shah Wali Ullah Dehlavi and Indian Politics in the Eighteenth Century." *Islamic Culture*. 25 (1951): 133–45.

—— "Naqshbandi Influence on Mughal Rulers and Politics." *Islamic Culture*, 39 (January 1965): 41–62.

—— *Some Aspects of Religion and Politics in India during the thirteenth Century*. Aligarh 1961.

Nurbakhsh, Javad. *Ma'ārif-i Ṣūfiyya. London: Intishārāt-i Khāniqāh-i Ni'matullāhī 1983–4. 4 vols.*

—— *Sufism*, I: *Meaning, Knowledge and Unity*. Trans. W.C. Chittick and P.L. Wilson. New York: Khaniqahi Nimatullahi Publications 1992.

Obeidat, Marwan M. "Ralph Waldo Emerson and the Muslim Orient." *The Muslim World*. 78/2 (1988): 132–45.

Olearius, Adam. *The Voyages and Travels of the Ambassador Sent by Frederick Duke of Holstein, to the Great Duke of Muscovy and the King of Persia*. London: Starkey & Basset 1662.

Palmer, E.H. *Oriental Mysticism: A Treatise on the Sufistic and Unitarian Theosophy of the Persians*. London 1867.

Perry, J.R. *Karim Khan Zand: A History of Iran 1747–1779*. Chicago: University of Chicago Press 1979.

Piscatori, James (ed.). *Islam in the Political Process*. Cambridge: Cambridge University Press 1983.

Poonawala, I.K. *Biobibliography of Ismā'īlī Literature*. Malibu, Calif.: Undena Publications 1977.

Qādirī, Sayyid Nūr Muḥammad. "Dīwān-i Ghanīmat Kunjāhī ke ek makhṭūṭe kā ta'āruf." *Funūn*, 20/ 5–6 (1965): 48–51.

Qādirī, Muḥyī al-Dīn. *Ḥayāt-i Mīr Mū'min*. Hyderabad: Idarah-i Adabiyat-i Urdu 1941.

Qazwīnī, Mīrzā Muḥammad Ṭāhir Vaḥīd. *'Abbās-nāma*. Ed. I. Dihgān. Tehran 1329 A.Hsh./1951.

Quinn, Sholeh. "Historical Writing during the Reign of Shāh 'Abbās I." University of Chicago Ph.D. thesis 1993.

Qumī, Qaḍī Aḥmad Munshī. *Khulāṣat al-tawārīkh*. Ed. Iḥsān Ishrāqī. 2 vols. Tehran: Dānishgāh-i Tihrān 1363 A.Hsh./1984.

Radke, B. and R.S. O'Fahey. "Neo-Sufism Reconsidered." *Islam: Zeitschrift fur Geschichte und Kultur des Orients*, 70/1 (1993): 52–87.

Rāḥat, Bhagwant Rā'e. *Nigāristān-i Rāḥat: tarjuma-yi Mathnawī-yi Ghanīmat*. Lucknow 1899.

Rahman, Fazlur. "Baḳā' wa-Fanā." *EI*², I: 951.

—— *The Philosophy of Mullā Ṣadrā*. Albany: SUNY Press 1975.

Rahman, Munibur. "Ṣā'ib, Mīrzā Muḥammad 'Alī." *EI*², VIII: 852.

Rahman, Tariq. "Boy-Love in the Urdu Ghazal." *Annual of Urdu Studies*, 7 (1990): 1–20.
Raverty, H. G. *Selections from the Poetry of the Afghans*. London: Williams & Norgate 1862.
Rehder, R. "Review Article: Persian Poets and Modern Critics." *Edebiyat* 2/1 (1977).
Reid, James J. *Tribalism and Society in Islamic Iran: 1500–1609*. Malibu, Calif.: Undena Publications 1983.
Richards, John F. *The Mughal Empire: New Cambridge History of India*. I/5. New York: Cambridge University Press 1993.
Rineheart, Robin. "Interpretations of the Poetry of Bullhe Shah." *International Journal of Punjab Studies*, 3/ 1 (1996): 44–63.
Rizvi, S.A.A. *Shah Wali Allah and his Times: A Study of Eighteenth Century Islam, Politics, and Society in India*. Canberra: Ma'rifat Publishing 1980.
—— *A History of Sufism in India*. 2 vols. New Delhi, Munshiram Manoharlal 1983.
Robinson, Francis. "Technology and Religious Change: Islam and the Impact of Print." *Modern Asian Studies*. 27/1 (1993): 229–51
Roemer, H.R. "The Safavid Period." In *The Cambridge History of Iran*, VI: *The Timurid and Safavid Periods*. Ed. Peter Jackson and Laurence Lockhart. Cambridge: Cambridge University Press 1986: 189–350.
—— "The Qizilbash Turcomans: Founders and Victims of the Safavid Theocracy." In *Intellectual Studies on Islam*. Ed. M. Mazzaoui and Vera Moreen. Salt Lake City: University of Utah Press: 1990: 27–39.
Rokuro, Kuwata. "Minmatsu sinsho no kaiju." *Shiratori Festschrift*. Tokyo: Tôyôshi Ronkô 1925: 377–8.
Romodin, V.A. *Istoriia Afganistana*. Moscow: Nauka 1965.
Rose, H.A. *A Glossary of the Tribes and Castes of the Punjab and North-West Frontier Province*. Lahore 1914.
Rosenthal, F. *Sweeter than Hope*: *Complaint and Hope in Medieval Islam*. Leiden: Brill 1983.
Roy, Olivier. *L'Afghanistan: Islam et modernité politique*. Paris: Éditions du Seuil 1985.
—— "Groupes de solidarité au Moyen-orient et en Asie centrale: états, territoires et réseaux." *Les Cahiers du CERI*. 15 (1996).
Rūmlū, Ḥasan. *Aḥsan al-tawārīkh*. Ed. C.N. Seddon. Baroda: Oriental Institute 1931. *Aḥsan al-tawārīkh*. Tehran: Bābak 1978.
Rūmī, Jalāl al-Dīn. *Dīvān-i Shams-i Tabrīzī*. Ed. Badī' al-Zamān Furūzānfar. Tehran: Jāvīdān 1341 A.Hsh./1962.
—— *Mathnawī*. Ed. R.A. Nicholson. Tehran: Amīr Kabīr, 1357 A.Hsh./1978
Sachdeva, V. *Polity and Economy of the Punjab during the late Eighteenth Century*. New Delhi: Manohar 1993.
Sa'dī. *The Gulistan or Rose Garden by Musle-Huddeen Sheik Saadi*. Translated from the original by Francis Gladwin with ... a Preface by R.W. Emerson. Boston: Ticknor & Fields 1865.
Ṣadīq, 'Isā. *Tārīkh-i Farhang-i Īrān*. Tehran: The Teachers College Press 1342 A.Hsh./ 1963.
Ṣafā, Dhabīḥu'llāh. *Tārīkh-i adabiyāt-i Īrān*. 8 vols. 13th edn. Tehran: Intishārāt-i Firdaws 1373 A.Hsh./1994.
Ṣafavī, Mīrzā Muḥmmad Khalīl Mar'ashī. *Majma' al-tawārīkh*. Ed. 'A. Iqbāl. Tehran: 1949.
Saguchi Toru. "Chugoku isuramu no kyôten." *Toyôgakukô*, 32 (1950): 480–508.
Sahīm, Hāyida. "Khāṭirāt-i Yahūdiyān-i Īrān." *Iran Nameh*, 15/1 (Winter 1997): 51–76.

Ṣā'ib Tabrīzī. *Kulliyyāt-i Ṣā'ib Tabrīzī*. Ed. Amīrī Firūzkūhī. Tehran: Khayyām 1373 A.Hsh./1994.

Said, E.W. *Orientalism*. Harmondsworth: Penguin Books 1995.

Sarmast, Sachal. *Risālō Sindhī*. Ed. 'Uthmān 'Alī Anṣārī. Karachi 1958.

Sarwar, Muḥammad Ghulām. *Khazīnat al-aṣfiyā'*. 2 vols. Kanpur: Nawal Kishar 1894.

——. *Ḥadīqat al-awliyā'*. Lahore: Islamic Book Foundation 1906.

Savory, Roger. "The Principal Officers of the Safawid State during the Reign of Isma'il I (907–30/1501–24." *BSOAS*. 23 (1960): 91–105.

—— "The Consolidation of Power in Safavid Persia." *Der Islam* (1976).

—— "Some Reflections on Totalitarian Tendencies in the Safavid State." *Der Islam*. 52, (1976): 226–41.

—— *Iran Under the Safavids*. Cambridge: Cambridge University Press 1980.

—— *Studies on the History of Ṣafawid Iran*. London: T. Variorum 1987.

Sayyid 'Abdu'llāh. *Adabiyyāt-i fārsī men Hindu'on kā Ḥiṣṣa*. Lahore: University of the Punjab 1967.

Schimmel, Annemarie. *Mystical Dimensions of Islam*. Chapel Hill, University of North Carolina Press 1975.

—— *Pain and Grace: A Study of Two Mystical Writers of Eighteenth Century Muslim India*. Leiden: Brill 1976.

—— *The Triumphal Sun: A Study of the Works of Jalāloddin Rumi*. London: Fine Books 1978.

—— *Islam in the Indian Subcontinent*. Leiden-Koln, E.J. Brill 1980.

—— *As Through A Veil: Mystical Poetry in Islam*. New York: Columbia University Press 1982.

—— *And Muhammad is His Messenger: The Veneration of the Prophet in Islamic Piety*. Chapel Hill, University of North Carolina Press 1985.

—— *The Mystery of Numbers*. Oxford: Oxford University Press 1993.

—— *Deciphering the Signs of God: A Phenomenological Approach to Islam*. Albany, SUNY Press 1994.

—— *My Soul is a Woman: The Feminine in Islam*. New York: Continuum 1997.

Semenov, A.A. (ed.). *Sobranie vostochnykh rukopisei Akademii nauk Uzbekskoi SSR*. Tashkent: Fan 1955.

Shackle, C. "Styles and Themes in the Siraiki Mystical Poetry of Sind." In *Sind through the Centuries*. Ed. H. Khuhro. Karachi: Oxford University Press 1981: 252–69.

—— "Early Vernacular Poetry in the Indus Valley: Its Contexts and its Character." In *Islam and Indian Regions*. Ed. A.L. Dallapiccola and S. Zingel. Stuttgart: Franz Steiner 1993, I: 259–89.

—— "Between Scripture and Romance: The Yūsuf–Zulaikhā Story in Panjabi." *South Asian Research*. (1995): 154–88.

—— "Beyond Turk and Hindu: Crossing the Boundaries in Indo- Muslim Romance." Proceedings of a Conference on Indo-Muslim Cultural Identity, Duke University, April 1995. Ed. J. Richards and B. Lawrence. Forthcoming.

—— "Transition and Transformation in Vāris Shāh's 'Hīr'." In *The Indian Narrative: Perspectives and Patterns*. Ed. C. Shackle and R. Snell. Wiesbaden: Harrassowitz 1992: 241–63.

Shackle, C. and Z. Moir. *Ismaili Hymns from South Asia: An Introduction to the Ginans*. London: SOAS 1992.

Shackle, C. and S. Sperl (eds). *Qasida Poetry in Islamic Asia and Africa*. 2 vols. Leiden: Brill 1996.

Shāfi'ī-Kadkānī, M.R. "The Safavid Period (Indian Style)." In *History of Persian Literature from the Beginning of the Islamic Period to the Present Day.* Ed. G. Morrison. Leiden: Brill 1981: 145–65.

Shāh 'Abd al-Laṭīf. *Shāh jō risālō.* Ed. Kalyān B. Adwānī. Bombay: Hindustān Kitābghar 1958.

Shāh Walī Allāh. *Lamaḥāt.* Hyderabad. Sindh: Shāh Walī Allāh Academy, n. d. Reissued and re-edited by D.B. Fry as *Sufism and the Islamic Tradition*: *Lamahat and Sata'at of Shah Waliullah of Delhi*. London: Octagon Press 1986; and *Saṭa'āt.* Hyderabad, Sindh: Shāh Walī Allāh Academy 1964. English translation by G.H. Jalbani Hyderabad. Sindh 1970. Urdu translation with commentary by Muḥammad Matīn Hāshimī: Lahore: Idāra Thaqāfiyya Islāmiyya 1986.

Shaibi, Kamil Mustafa al-. *Sufism and Shī'ism*. London: LAAM 1991.

Shakeb, M.Z.A. "Relations of Golconda with Iran: 1518–1687." University of Pune Ph.D thesis 1976.

—— *Religion and Politics in Golconda: A Chapter in Religion and Politics in South India*. Hyderabad: The Institute of Asian Studies 1978.

Shaked, Shaul. "Two Judeo-Iranian Contributions, 1: Iranian Function in the Book of Esther." In *Irano-Judaica: Studies Relating to Jewish Contacts with Persian Culture Throughout the Ages*. Ed. Shaul Shaked. Jerusalem: Ben-Zvi Institute for the Study of Jewish Communities in the East 1982: 292–303.

Shangari, T.R. and J.R. Puri. *Bulleh Shāh: The Love-Intoxicated Iconoclast*. Dera Baba Jaimal Singh, Radha Soami Satsang Beas 1986.

Sharafuddin, M. *Islam and Romantic Orientalism*. London: I.B. Tauris 1994.

Sharar, A.H. *Lucknow: The Last Phase of an Oriental Culture*. London: Paul Elek 1975.

Sharif, M.M. (ed.). *A History of Muslim Philosophy.* 2 vols. Wiesbaden, Harrassowitz 1966.

Sherwani, H.K. *The Bahmanīs of the Deccan*. India, Hyderabad: n.p. 1953.

—— *History of the Quṭb Shāhī Dynasty.* New Delhi: Munshiram Manoharlal Publishers 1974.

Shiblī Nu'mānī Hindī. *Shi'r al-'ajam*. Translated into Persian by D. Gīlānī. 5 vols. Tehran: Dunyā-yi Kitāb 1363 A.Hsh./1984.

Shihāb, M.H. *Awliyā'-i Bahawalpūr.* Bahawalpur: Urdu Academy 1976.

Shikūh, D. *Dīwān-i Dārā Shikūh*. Lahore: University of the Punjab 1969.

Shīrāzī, Niẓām al-Dīn Aḥmad. *Ḥadīqat al-salāṭīn*. Hyderabad: Idara-i siqāfat wa tamaddun-i Dakkhan, Aywān-i Urdu 1961.

Shīrāzī, Zayn al-'Ābidīn 'Alī Abdī Beg. *Takmilat al-akhbār*. Ed. 'Abd al-Ḥusayn Navā'ī. Tehran: Nashr-i Nay 1369 A.Hsh./1990.

Shiro, Nohara. *Tempô tenrei taku yôkai no hôyaku ni saishite kaiyyôken*, IV/2. Tokyo 1940.

Shūshtarī, Qāḍī Nūrullāh. *Majālis al-mu'minīn*. 2 vols. Tehran: Islāmiyya 1354 A.Hsh./ 1975–6.

Siddiqi, Muhammad Suleman. *The Bahmanī Sufis*. Dehli, India: Idarah-i Adabiyat-i Delhi 1989.

Ṣiddīqī, M.H. *Shāh Laṭīf Barrī*. Lahore: Meri Library 1972.

Simsār, Muḥammad Ḥasan. "Farmān nivīsī dar dawra-yi Ṣafaviyya." *Barrasīhā-yi tārīkhī*. 2 (1967): 127–52.

Soucek, P.P. "'Abd-al-Bāqī Yazdī" *EIr*, I: 105–6.

Southern, R.W. *Western Views of Islam in the Middle Ages*. Cambridge, Mass., Harvard University Press 1962.

Spellberg, Denise A. *Politics, Gender, and the Islamic Past: The Legacy of 'Ai'sha bint Abi Bakr*. New York: Columbia University Press 1994.

Stevens, S.R. *The Land of the Great Sophy*. London: Methuen & Co. 1965.

Stewart, Devin J. "A Biographical Notice on Bahā' al-Dīn al-'Āmilī (d. 1030/1621)." *Journal of the American Oriental Society*. (July–Sept. 1991): 563–71.

—— "Notes on the Migration of 'Āmilī Scholars to Safavid Iran." *Journal of Near Eastern Studies*. 55/2 (1996): 81–103.

Storey, C.A. *Persian Literature: A Bio-Bibliographical Survey*. 4 vols. London: Luzac & Co. 1972. Vols. V-VII are being continued and updated by Francois de Blois. London: Royal Asiatic Society 1992–.

Subhan, John A. *Sufism: Its Saints and Shrines*. Lucknow: Lucknow Publishing House 1960.

Suhrawardī (Shaykh al-Ishrāq). *Opera Metaphysica et Mystica*. Ed. by Henry Corbin. 3 vols. Académie Impériale Iranienne de Philosophie, Publication no. 13, Bibliothèque Iranienne, N.S. Tehran: Académie Impériale de Philosophie/Paris: Librairie Adrien-Maisonneuve 1977.

Suratgar, L. "Traces of Persian Influence upon English Literature During the Fifteenth and Sixteenth Centuries." University of London Ph.D. thesis 1939.

Surūsh, 'Abd al-Karīm. *Qiṣṣa-yi arbāb-i ma'rifat*. Tehran: Mi'raj 1373 A.Hsh./1994.

Szuppe, M. *Entre Timourides, Uzbeks et Safavides: Questions d'histoire politique et sociale de Hérat dans la première moitié du XVIe Siècle*. Paris: Association pour l'Avancement des Études iraniennes 1992.

—— "La Participation des Femmes de la Famille royale à l'Exercice du Pouvoir en Iran safavide au XVIe Siècle." *Studia Iranica*, 23 (1994).

Tabrīzī, Muḥammad 'Alī. *Rayhānat al-adab*. 10 vols. Tehran 1331 A.Hsh./1952.

Tabataba'ī, 'Alī. *Burhān-i ma'āthir*. Ed. G. Yazdani. Hyderabad 1936.

Ṭabāṭabā'ī, 'Allāmah. *Shi'ite Islam*. Trans. S.H. Nasr. Albany: SUNY Press 1977.

Tadhkirat al-mulūk. Trans. V. Minorsky. London: E.J.W. Gibb Memorial Series 1943.

Taftazānī. *A Commentary on the Creed of Islam*. New York: Columbia University Press 1950.

Tagirdzhanov, A.T. *Opisanie tadzhikskikh i persidskikh rukopisei Vostochnogo otdela Biblioteki LGU*, t. I, Istoriia, biografii, geografiia. Leningrad: Izd-vo Leningradskogo Universiteta 1962.

Takeshita, M. *Ibn 'Arabī's Theory of the Perfect Man and its Place in the History of Islamic Thought*. Tokyo Institute for the Study of Languages and Cultures of Asia and Africa 1987.

Tanish (Bukhārī), Ḥafiẓ. *Sharaf-nāma-i shāhī*. Trans. Salakhetdinova. Moscow: Nauka 1983.

—— *Sharaf-nāma-i shāhī*. The Russian translation in Khafiz-i Tanysh ibn Mir Mukhammad Bukhari, *Sharaf-nama-ii Shakhi* (*Kniga shakshkoi slavy*). Facsimile ed. and trans. M.A. Salakhetdinova. Moscow: Nauka, GRVL 1989.

Tapper, Richard. "Holier than Thou: Islam in Three Tribal Societies." In *Islam in Tribal Societies: From the Atlas to the Indus*. Ed. Akbar S. Ahmed and David Hart. London: Routledge & Kegan Paul 1984.

Tārīkh-i Sulṭān Muḥammad Quṭb Shāh. Hyderabad: Andhra Pradesh State Archives, n.d.

Tavernier, J.B. *Travels through Turkey, Persia and the East Indies*. London: 1684.

Taylor, John. "Ja'far al-Sadīq, Spiritual Forbear of the Sūfīs." *Islamic Culture*. 40/1 (1966): 97–113.

Tazaka, Kôdô: Tazaka. *Chugoku ni okeru kaikyô no denrai to sono gutsû*. 2 vols. (Tokyo: Tôyô Bunko 1924.

Thackston, W.M., (ed.) *Habīb al-siyar*. Sources of Oriental Languages and Literatures, 24. Cambridge, Mass.: Harvard University Department of Near Eastern Languages and Civilizations 1994. See also, s.v. "Khwāndamīr."

Tholuck, F.R. *Sufismus sive Theologia Persica Pantheistica*. Berlin 1821.

—— *Bluthensammlung aus der Morgenlaendischen Mystik*. Berlin 1825.

Ṭihrānī, Āghā Buzurg Muḥammad. *Al-Dharī'a ilā Taṣānīf al-Shī'a*. Tehran/ Najaf, 1353–98.

Togan, Zeki Velidi. "Yesevîliğe dair bazı yeni malûmat." In *[60 doğum yılı munasebetiyle] Fuad Köprülü Armağanı*. Istanbul: Osman Yalçın Matbaası 1953: 523–29.

Trimingham, J. Spencer. *The Sufi Orders in Islam*. Oxford: Oxford University Press 1971.

Tunikābunī, Muḥammad. *Qiṣaṣ al-'ulamā'*. Tehran: 'Ilmiyya Islāmiyya n.d.

Wajīh (also Wajhī), Asadu'llāh. *Dīwān-i Wajīh*. no. 511; *Adab Naẓm*. Hyderabad: Salar Jang Museum, n.d.

Watt, W.M. *The Faith and Practice of al-Ghazálí*. Oxford: Oneworld 1994.

Wilson, P.L. and N. Pourjavady. "Ismā'īlīs and Ni'matullāhīs." *Studia Islamica*. 41 (1975): 113–35.

Woods, John E. "The Rise of Timurid Historiography." *Journal of Near Eastern Studies* 46 (1987): 81–107.

Yarshater, Ehsan. "Persian Poetry in the Timurid and Safavid Periods." In Yarshater. *The Cambridge History of Iran. The Timurid and Safavid Periods*. Ed. P. Jackson and L. Lockhart. Cambridge: Cambridge University Press 1968: 965–94.

—— "The Indian or Safavid Style: Progress or Decline." In *Persian Literature*. Ed. E. Yarshater. Persian Heritage Foundation, New York: SUNY Press 1988.

—— "Persian Poetry in the Indo-Pakistan Subcontinent." In *Persian Literature*. Ed. E. Yarshater. Persian Heritage Foundation, New York: SUNY Press 1988.

Yazdī, Muḥammad Mufīd Mustawfī. *Jāmi'-i mufīdī*. Ed. Iraj Afshār. Tehran: Asadī 1961.

Yazdī, Mullā Jalāl al-Dīn Munajjim. *Tārīkh-i 'Abbāsī yā rūznama-yi Mullā Jalāl*. Ed. Sayf Allāh Vaḥīd Nīyā. Tehran: Intishārāt-i Vaḥīd 1366 A.Hsh./1987.

Yeroushalmi, David (ed.). *The Judeo-Persian Poet 'Emrānī & his Book of Treasure: Emrānī's* Ganj-nāme, *a versified Commentary on the Mishnaic Tractate Abot*. Leiden: Brill 1995.

Yohannan, J.D. *Persian Poetry in England and America: A 200-Year History*. New York: Caravan Books 1977.

Zaleman, K.G. "Legenda pro Khakim-Ata." *Izvestiia Akademii nauk* (SPb.), 9/2 (1898): 105–50.

Zarrīnkūb, 'Abd al-Ḥusayn. *Dunbāla-yi Justujū dar tasawwuf-i Īrān*. Tehran: Amīr Kabīr 1983.

Zhen-qui, Yu. *Zhonggno yisinan wanxian zhuyi tiyao*. Ningshia 1993.

Ziai, Hossein. "The Source and Nature of Authority: A Study of al-Suhrawardī's Illuminationist Political Doctrine." In *The Political Aspects of Islamic Philosophy*. Ed. Charles Butterworth. Cambridge: Harvard University Press 1992: 304–44.

—— "Shihāb al-Dīn Suhrawardī: Founder of the Illuminationist School." In *History of Islamic Philosophy*. Ed. Seyyed Hossein Nasr and Oliver Leaman. 2 vols. London: Routledge 1996, I: 434–64.

Zāhidī, Ḥusayn ibn Shaykh Abdāl. *Silsilat al-nasab-i Ṣafaviyya*. Berlin: Orientalischer Zeitschriftenverlag iranschahr 1924.

Index

OCT 0 6 2000

BIBL. UNIV. DE / OF SUDBURY LIBR.
3 0007 00728 5330